D0147062

A REVIEW OF
Economic Doctrines
1870-1929

A REVIEW OF
Economic Doctrines
1870-1929

BY

T. W. HUTCHISON

READER IN ECONOMICS IN THE
UNIVERSITY OF LONDON

GREENWOOD PRESS, PUBLISHERS
WESTPORT, CONNECTICUT

Library of Congress Cataloging in Publication Data

Hutchison, Terence Wilmot.
    A review of economic doctrines, 1870-1929.

    Reprint of the 1953 ed. published by Clarendon
Press, Oxford.
    Bibliography: p.
    Includes index.
    1. Economics--History--19th century. I. Title.
HB85.H85 1975   330.1   74-9273
ISBN 0-8371-7637-9

*To trace the affiliation of ideas in the progress of science
is calculated to correct one's estimates of authority. . . .
The history of theory is particularly instructive in
political economy.*

F. Y. EDGEWORTH

*A study of the history of opinion is a necessary
preliminary to the emancipation of the mind.*

LORD KEYNES

Originally published in 1953 by the Clarendon Press, Oxford.

This reprint has been authorized by the Clarendon Press,
Oxford.

Reprinted in 1975 by Greenwood Press,
A division of Congressional Information Service, Inc.
88 Post Road West, Westport, Connecticut 06881

Library of Congress catalog card number 74-9273
ISBN 0-8371-7637-9

Printed in the United States of America

10 9 8 7 6 5 4 3 2

PREFACE

THE composition of this book has posed rather severe problems of selection and arrangement. The table of contents gives in outline my attempted solution, but there are one or two explanations I should like to add. First, as to the different principles of arrangement adopted in Part I (by individual economists and schools) as compared with Part II (by the different main branches of economic theory). In Part I the work has been taken separately of each of the leading economists at the close of the nineteenth century. The majority and the most important of these economists constructed unified comprehensive systems of economic principles, which, in many cases, they elaborated through a number of writings and over long lives of intellectual achievement. There are clearly great advantages in considering each of these systems of thought, with its origins and subsequent developments, separately and as a whole. It is possible to put the close of this part of our survey as lying in the decade before the First World War. The fifth edition (approximately the final version) of Marshall's *Principles* appeared in 1907; Wicksteed's *Common Sense of Political Economy* in 1910; Pareto's *Manuale* and *Manuel* in 1907 and 1909; Wieser's *Theorie des Gesellschaftlichen Wirtschaft* in 1913; and various editions of Wicksell's *Lectures* throughout this decade. I expect that a number of readers will wish to study this period without going through all of the seventeen chapters which I devote to it. Though I hope that each will make his own selection, I would suggest that the following nine chapters will cover the most important and representative parts of the ground: Ch. 1 on Political Economy in England; Ch. 2 on Jevons; Ch. 4 on Marshall; Ch. 8 on German Political Economy; Ch. 9 on Menger; and Chs. 13–16 on Walras, Pareto, Wicksell, and J. B. Clark.

In the second part of the book, covering a period when the comprehensive treatise was no longer the main vehicle of progress in the subject, which had tended to break up and undergo its development in specialized branches, we have taken one by one the main divisions of economic theory and have attempted a severely selective survey of some of the leading writings, with the intention of tracing the main thread of internal logical development in each branch. We have called this part, which is more compressed and unified than Part I, 'From Static to Dynamic Analysis', not because there was some steady trend from the cultivation of purely 'static' analysis in 1870 to a mainly, or much more, 'dynamic' analysis at the end of the period. There was, of course, no such simple regular development. But the working out after 1870 of micro-economic maximization analysis, often mathematically formulated, and of the self-equilibrating dynamics that went with it, was accompanied by a more deliberate and rigorous process of abstraction on static and stationary assumptions. As the full rigour of these assumptions was gradually realized, or more or less deliberately imposed, it became more obvious how many problems of the real world would require a systematic 'dynamic' analysis to replace the simplifying assumptions of general and partial self-equilibration, which had been employed to supplement the static maximization formulae. A very great deal of the controversy of the period, in all branches, centred around this difficult process of clarifying the significance of 'static' and 'dynamic' analysis, and the transition from the one to the other.

Part III on the 'Economics of Instability and Disturbance' is about theories of crises and cycles. This subject could not be treated like the subjects in Part II, because the story of trade cycle theories could not consist of a summary of the main doctrines of the leading neo-classical authors, continued by an account of the more important later writings on the subject. The majority of the leading economists discussed in Part I either hardly wrote at all on crises and cycles (e.g. Sidgwick, Wicksteed, Edgeworth, Menger, Wieser, Böhm-Bawerk, Walras, and J. B. Clark) or else only contributed chapters of comparatively minor scope (e.g. Marshall and Pareto). Even Wicksell's *Interest and Prices* is not primarily concerned with cyclical fluctuations. Jevons here is a leading exception, and Hobson an exception the treatment of whose ideas proves the rule. Fisher's and Cassel's works on the trade cycle came in the second half of our period. Many, or most, of the important earlier contributors, before about 1910, to the problems of crises and cycles, were outside the main group of the architects of neo-classical 'marginal' economics: for example, Juglar, Tugan-Baranovsky, Spiethoff, Aftalion, Johannsen, and Mitchell. However, from the start of the century, and especially after 1919, this subject gradually absorbed more and more attention by economists of all schools of thought. In Britain in the 1920's it was inevitably examined in close connexion with the new problem of chronic unemployment. It is with the state of British economic opinion in 1929 on this problem of the causes and cure of unemployment that we end our survey.

As regards the branches of the subject to be included or omitted, the main problem has been how far to accommodate theories of money and credit. We have included theories of money in so far as they have been closely integrated parts of the general theory of a monetary economy, but more specialized doctrines of money, credit, and banking have been omitted, as have theories of international trade and the foreign exchanges. We have especially tried to review the thought and doctrines of the leading economists on the principles of economic policy and on the role of the State in economic life. But discussion of the particular problems of applied economics which arose in our period (for example, bimetallism, tariff reform, the capital levy, and reparations) has been left out. An exception has been made in the last chapter on the problem of unemployment in Britain, a special problem which eventually had such profound effects on general theory.

We are not attempting in this book, and certainly not relying on, any comprehensive generalizations about the economic thought of our period, or the construction of any general interpretation of it in terms of contemporary economic events, or in other terms. This is not out of any great confidence in the common liberal-professional assumption that intellectual progress in a particular subject arises simply out of professional intellectual ingenuity working purely on its own particular subject-matter as though in a vacuum. Over the later part of our period there may be wide scope for the economic, or other, interpretation of economists in respect especially of theories of money, monetary economics, and unemployment. But particularly in the earlier part of our period the development of economics as an academic specialism coincided with a period of *comparatively* stable politico-economic development in the Western world, during which economic reality did not force itself *too* brusquely or strikingly on the more detached student. At the same time there had been discovered in 1871 a principle capable of much precise and abstract mathematical elaboration, and of a considerable range of applications. This principle was, of course, that of the maximizing individual acting in the conditions in which succinct formulae for compatible maximization by a number of parties can be deduced, that is, conditions of perfect competition or isolated monopoly. Therefore, over several of the decades with which we are here concerned, the 'internal' logical requirements of economic theory exercised—for better or for worse—a predominant directing influence comparatively more immediate than the problems of the contemporary economic world. This was the case to a much greater extent than in much of the previous history of the subject. At any rate, the development of 'marginal' economics consisted mainly in the logical elaboration and application to successive branches of the subject, of one or two fundamental concepts or assumptions. On the other hand, the subsequent development of the theory of crises, trade cycles, and aggregate employment and unemployment, had a certain broad and obvious relation to world economic events.

In so far as we attempt any interpretation 'external' to, or in addition to, the 'internal' logical development of the central problems themselves, we do so individually (or 'micro-historically') in terms of the particular intellectual biographies of the leading great economists. In this way we have tried, on the one hand, to capture, for its own sake, something of what Edgeworth referred to as 'the interest which attaches to the working of great minds', and also to show, where possible, some of the particular external influences of contemporary thought and philosophy, and of topical economic problems, which helped to shape and direct economic ideas at particular points.

We would, however, mention here one very broad generalization about the background of economic history which is implied in the transition from the 'equilibrium' economics of our first part to the economics of instability and disturbance discussed in Part III. Today any priority given to static and 'stationary-dynamic' analysis is usually defended heuristically or propaedeutically. Analysis of the stationary state is pursued as a highly simplified exercise, useful perhaps as what is described as 'a first approximation'. This was also to some extent the contention of the neo-classical equilibrium economists, and in any case their loose, normal quasi-stationary models were not understood or employed with the same extreme mathematical precision as subsequent more rigorous analysis imparted to them. This meant that though they were vested with a certain degree of ambiguity, they were not necessarily so thoroughly stripped of realistic content. But our point is that these static or 'stationary' self-adjusting models had a far greater realistic justification when compared with the economic life of the last quarter of the nineteenth century than they can have today.

The world which economists were then living in, and which they set out to explain, was one in which the dangerous adjective 'normal' still had some considerable immediate significance in economic life. The economic life which they set out to explain was, in fact, by no means so impossibly remote from their looser quasi-stationary models, which were in some genuine sense recognizable as 'first approximations' to it. As A. C. Pigou said in 1939:

Economists had then grown up in, and their whole experience was confined to, a world which as regards politics and economics alike was reasonably stable. There were of course local political disturbances. There were the ups and downs of the so-called trade cycle, fairly moderate in amplitude. There were also large basic changes going on due to the impact of American and later Antipodean agriculture upon the structure of our economy. But the basic changes were gradual and slow-working. There were no catastrophes. How different is the experience of economists today! (*Economic Journal*, 1939, p. 217.)

Marshall, writing in 1898, had held that there had been a 'perceptible change' towards a lessening in the realism and relevance of the analysis of stationary State since J. S. Mill's day. 'Perceptible' may be the right description for the change from 1848 to 1898, but we can only guess at the adjective Marshall would have applied to the change from 1898 to 1948.

The adequacy of the static and stationary analysis built up by our authors must be judged in the first place by the contemporary conditions it was devised as a 'first approximation' to explain. At the same time we are, of course, today entitled, or rather obliged, to examine its relevance for a world where it is reasonably certain, or can 'normally' be expected, once or twice per decade, that the economic systems of most countries will be going through either acute inflation, open or suppressed, or acute deflation, either wholesale conversion to war, or wholesale reconversion to peace, monetary collapse or monetary reconstruction, prolonged mass unemployment or prolonged over-full employment, extensive rationing or drastic de-rationing, a New Deal or a New Economic Policy, 'Democratic Planning' or a Four-Year or Five-Year Plan.

Having enjoyed or endured so expensive an education in the Economics of Disturbance, Instability, and Insecurity, it would surely be stupid to exploit it in captious criticism of the achievements of those who missed its advantages, or its lessons. On the other hand, conservatively to deny or obscure the great limitations of doctrines formulated for a different sort of world might be even more disastrous practically. In this book we are trying, primarily, simply to expound the economic doctrines of our period with fair accuracy, in the way and often in the words of their originators. But in trying to expound a doctrine we must indicate some of its implicit as well as its explicit assumptions, and therefore, to some extent, we define its applicability and suggest a judgement on its significance. Applicability and significance, however, also depend on the economic world for which the doctrine is being formulated and applied. Therefore, some effort of the imagination must constantly be made not to forget that much of what may today seem to betray a lack of realism in what economists in, say, 1890 took as their 'normal' model, is due simply to the immense differences in the economic world with which they were confronted, as contrasted with that of our own day.

My debts to other writers are very numerous though in the main very widely scattered. I must especially acknowledge the very valuable help in a number of chapters in Part I which I have had from Professor G. J. Stigler's distinguished work, *Production and Distribution Theories, the Formative Period.* I must also mention here my indebtedness to the essays of Schumpeter (now collected in the volume *Ten Great Economists*), and to some of Keynes's *Essays in Biography.* Professor Marget's book, *The Theory of Prices,* is a vast mine of learning on which I have drawn particularly in Chapter 21. Finally, I am most grateful to Professor L. C. Robbins and Professor R. S. Sayers. Professor Robbins read an earlier draft of a considerable part of the book and made many valuable comments and suggestions. Professor Sayers gave valuable aid and encouragement with regard to publication. Of course the usual formula holds good in this case that the author alone is responsible for the contents and shortcomings of the book as it finally stands.

T. W. H.

LONDON
August 1952

ERRATA

p. v   line 19: For *des* read *der*
p. 83   line 30: *For* his objection *read* this objection
p. 153 10 lines from bottom: For *Theory of Social Value* read *Theory of Social Economy*
p. 181 footnote: For *de* read *der*
p. 188 16 lines from bottom: For *Wahrungsfrage* read *Währungsfrage*
p. 189 1st line of footnote: For *gesamte* read *gesamten*
p. 222 line 4 of footnote: *For* 1923 *read* 1932
p. 251 line 4: For *Value and Price* read *Value and Prices*
p. 325 line 17: *For* Rosenstein Rodan, on Grenznützen, *read* Rosenstein-Rodan, on Grenznutzen
p. 336 line 5: *For* Stewart *read* Steuart
p. 444 1914: For *Theorie des ges. Wertes* read *Theorie der ges. Wirtschaft*

CONTENTS

Part I

THE ARCHITECTS OF EQUILIBRIUM ECONOMICS AND THEIR MAIN CRITICS

Contents   xiii

xiv *Contents*

PART III

THE ECONOMICS OF INSTABILITY AND
DISTURBANCE

Part I
THE ARCHITECTS OF EQUILIBRIUM
ECONOMICS AND THEIR MAIN CRITICS

1
Political Economy in England after 1870

1. *Prelude: The Centenary of the 'Wealth of Nations'*

ON 31 May 1876 the Political Economy Club of London held 'a grand dinner and a special discussion' (as Jevons described it), in honour of the 100th anniversary of the publication of *The Wealth of Nations*. Mr. Gladstone was in the chair. The company was representative, in the most distinguished way, of politics, learning, the city, the civil service, and the aristocracy (a duke, two earls, &c.), and comprised a social and intellectual blend remarkable even in the England of that period. The eight Cabinet Ministers, or ex-Ministers, were headed by the Chairman, Forster, Goschen, and Lowe. The regular members included Chadwick, Newmarch, Bagehot, and Morley, and the comparatively small company of university professors was represented by Fawcett, Thorold Rogers, Cliffe Leslie, and Jevons. Among the visitors were Cardwell, Acton, Froude, and M. Léon Say, the French Minister of Finance and grandson of J. B. Say.[1]

After dinner Mr. Lowe,[2] ex-Chancellor in the greatest of Gladstone's administrations, opened the discussion of the following question: 'What are the more important results which have followed from the publication of *The Wealth of Nations* just one hundred years ago and in what principal directions do the doctrines of that book still remain to be applied?' Rather than a commemoratory anthology of after-

---

[1] v. Political Economy Club: *Revised Report of the Proceedings at the Dinner of 31st May 1876*, London, 1876.

[2] Robert Lowe, Viscount Sherbrooke, Chancellor 1868–73: claimed to have taken £12 millions off taxation. On his leaving office the income tax was at about the lowest level it has ever attained—2d. in the pound. Author of the phrase, 'We must educate our masters' (or, more accurately, 'induce our future masters to learn their letters'). First Member of Parliament for the University of London.

dinner oratory, the subsequent discussion reads more like a forthright politico-economic debate with something of a *Methodenstreit* being waged in the background.

This rather high temperature was not simply due to the fact that it was the political heavyweights, rather than the academic economists, who dominated the occasion. In any case, in those days there were not the same gulfs in understanding, terminology, and approach, between these two categories, that were to open up in subsequent decades.[1] On the one hand, economics had hardly begun to develop as an academic specialism, and, on the other, public men and officials still had plenty of time to read and reflect. Professor, banker, and Cabinet Minister still approached the subject with, to a large extent, a common language and not too widely diverging intellectual standards. In spite of their differences of view, they contributed together to a body of informed opinion, already in 1876 severely rent by disagreement, which in the next half-century was gradually and partially to dissolve, or, at any rate, totally to change its composition. This wide acceptance of the classical system of political economy, though the source of its great practical strength, was at the same time the source of one of its most vulnerable weaknesses and ambiguities, that is its failure adequately to distinguish, and keep separate, scientific doctrines from practical maxims and political principles.

The ex-Chancellor, a keen representative of Ricardian orthodoxy, opened with a methodological challenge. He claimed: 'The test of science is prevision or prediction, and Adam Smith appears to me in the main to satisfy that condition. He was able to foresee what would happen, and to build upon that foresight the conclusions of his science. ...I think that Adam Smith is entitled to the merit... of having founded a deductive and demonstrative science of human actions and conduct.' Lowe did 'not pretend to account for the fact how it should be that Political Economy may boast of this precision or prediction, which has been denied to the cognate arts or sciences'. (p. 7.)

He had no difficulty in epitomizing the good that had been derived from Adam Smith in the demonstration that 'any proceeding on the part of a government which attracts capital to a course in which it otherwise would not go, or repels capital from a course in which it

---

[1] That the gulf was opening up by 1885 may be deduced from Sidgwick's remark about a meeting of the Club: 'The bankers came to the front. It is an exaggeration to say that they know *no* political economy; I think they read Mill some time ago, and look at him from time to time on Sundays'. (*A Memorial*, p. 408.) Such comments would hardly have been possible while the figure or spirit of Ricardo still dominated the Club.

would go, must be injurious, because every man is the best judge of his own interest, and in doing the best for himself he is doing the best for the state.' (p. 13).

After noting that there is 'nothing more lamentable in these times than to see the errors and follies' of 'Unionism', Mr. Lowe concluded with some rather bleak and restricted views about the future of political economy:

I do not myself feel very sanguine that there is a very large field—at least according to the present state of mental and commercial knowledge—for Political Economy . . . [but] should other sciences relating to mankind, which it is the barbarous jargon of the day to call Sociology, take a spring and get forward in any degree towards the certainty attained by Political Economy, I do not doubt that their development would help in the development of this science; but at present, so far as my own humble opinion goes, I am not sanguine as to any very large or any very startling development of Political Economy. I observe that the triumphs which have been gained have been rather in demolishing that which has been found to be undoubtedly bad and erroneous, than in establishing new truth; and imagine that before we can attain new results, we must be furnished from without with new truths to which our principles may be applied. The controversies which we now have in Political Economy, although they offer a capital exercise for the logical faculties, are not of the same thrilling importance as those of earlier days; the great work has been done.' (p. 21.)

In due course the oldest member (and sole surviving foundation member) of the Club, Mr. G. W. Norman,[1] described how 55 years previously 'by being a member of this club I became the companion of Mr. Ricardo, of the two Mills, of Col. Torrens, of Mr. Malthus, and of Mr. Tooke'. He added: 'It seems to me that the real doctrines of Political Economy as they were first taught by Adam Smith, and as they were subsequently explained by the persons whose names I have ventured to quote, remain unimpeached, . . . that they are in fact unattackable; they are true now and will be true to all time.' (p. 26.)

M. de Laveleye then brought word from foreign parts of new developments and new schisms, particularly in Germany:

Some, the old school, whom for want of a better name I will call the Orthodox School, believe that everything regulates itself by the effect of natural laws. The other school, which its adversaries have named the Socialists of the Chair, the Katheder-Sozialisten, but which we ought rather

---

[1] Author of *Remarks upon some Prevalent Errors with respect to Currency and Banking &c.*, 1833, an early contribution to the monetary analysis of economic crises. Grandfather of Governor Montague Norman.

to call the Historical School . . . holds that distribution is governed in part doubtless by free contract; but also and still more, by civil and political institutions, by custom and historical tradition. This is the path pursued by nearly all German economists. (p. 31.)

The next speaker was the economic historian, Thorold Rogers, who took up Mr. Lowe's methodological challenge, expressing surprise at having heard Adam Smith spoken of

as a writer who possessed an eminently deductive mind. . . . There is to my mind nothing more significant than the difference of the process by which Adam Smith collected his inferences, and that by which his followers or commentators have arrived at theirs. Of this I am sure, that if they had adopted the principles on which he reasoned, we should have been saved a vast number of those fallacies which discredit our science. (p. 32.)

Then came the Treasurer of the Club, William Newmarch, F.R.S., later described by a distinguished fellow-member as possessing 'the downright rigour and vigour of an old style hard-headed economist'.[1] Though Newmarch's views about the future of the subject were in some ways similar to those of Lowe he remained hopeful:

I am sanguine enough to think that there will be what may be called a large negative development of Political Economy tending to produce an important and beneficial effect; and that is, such a development of Political Economy as will reduce the functions of government within a smaller and smaller compass. The full development of the principles of Adam Smith has been in no small danger for some time past; and one of the great dangers which now hangs over this country is that the wholesome spontaneous operation of human interests and human desires seems to be in course of rapid supersession by the erection of one Government department after another, by the setting up of one set of inspectors after another, and by the whole time of Parliament being taken up in attempting to do for the nation those very things which, if the teaching of the man whose name we are celebrating today is to bear any fruit at all, the nation can do much better for itself. I am speaking with as much severity as I may assume on this occasion. . . . (p. 38.)

Newmarch was especially anxious about the growth of State action in the field of education.

The Chairman then rose to put his finger on one problem of economic policy which seemed to remain for solution, and which certainly has given economists much to think about since 1876: 'I do not mean to say that there is a great deal remaining to be done here in the way of direct legislation, yet there is something. It appears at least to me, that

[1] H. Higgs in *Proceedings of Political Economy Club, 1821–1920*, p. 350.

perhaps the question of the currency is one in which we are still, I think, in a backward condition.' Apart from this there only, or mainly, remained for economists 'the duty of propagating opinions which shall have the effect of confining government within its proper province and preventing it from all manner of aggressions and intrusions upon the province of the free agency of the individual.' (p. 46.)

The last speakers of the evening were two Liberals, W. E. Forster and L. Courtney.[1] The former had been mainly responsible for carrying through the great pioneer Education Act of 1870. He answered Newmarch and Gladstone as follows:

I gather from Mr. Newmarch's remarks that he is an advocate of the old laissez-faire principle. Well, if we were all Mr. Newmarches, if we had nothing to deal with in the country but men like ourselves, we might do this. But we have to deal with weak people; we have to deal with people who have themselves to deal with strong people, who are borne down, who are tempted, who are unfortunate in the circumstances of life, and who will say to us, and say to us with great truth: 'What is your use as a parliament if you cannot help us in our weakness, and against those who are too strong for us?' ... I think that our President ... rather considered that we were interfering a little too much with the freedom of individuals. The question is, are we doing so? Are we doing it a whit more than the country is expecting us to? (p. 50.)

Mr. Leonard Courtney concluded the discussion by insisting, against Newmarch, that the relations between landlord and tenant, and land policy generally, were within the proper sphere of government action. He was 'strongly impressed by the faith' that by the next centenary, in 1976, 'the opinion of that day will have advanced beyond us in declaring that to be a proper part of the sphere of Government, and I do not wish it to be understood that this Club are now unanimous in thinking that it is not so.'

2. *Unsettled Questions in the Seventies: Policy-Theory-Method*

There may be certain passages in the above discussion evocative now of Herbert Spencer's remark about 'the way in which a system of thought may be seen going about in high spirits after having committed suicide'. Nevertheless from the point of view of a sympathetic hindsight the 1870's appear today as one of the three or four out-

---

[1] Brother-in-law of Beatrice Webb and uncle of Sir Stafford Cripps. Financial Secretary to the Treasury under Gladstone, 1882. Later Deputy Speaker of the House of Commons. First Baron Courtney.

standing decades of creative debate in the history of English political economy. That is certainly not how it seemed on a close-up view at the time. As the *Pall Mall Gazette* said the following day, the centenary dinner did not seem 'to coincide with an auspicious moment in the history of the science which Adam Smith founded'. Already a short while previously Cairnes had discerned 'signs of a belief that Political Economy has ceased to be a fruitful speculation' (Cairnes, *Essays in Political Economy*, p. 238). Jevons, in the same year as the centenary, held that 'there have been for some years premonitory signs of disruption, . . . we find the state of the science to be almost chaotic'. A year or two later there was even an attempt to exclude economic science and statistics from the British Association.[1] Bagehot, also, referring soon after to the state of the subject said: 'It lies rather dead in the public mind. Not only . . . it does not excite the same interest as formerly but there is not exactly the same confidence in it.' He contrasted the present disillusionment with the 'optimism' of earlier decades: 'Political Economy was indeed the favourite subject in England from about 1810 to 1840. . . . From a short series of axioms and definitions it believed that a large part of human things, far more than is really possible, could be deduced. . . . At that time economists indulged in happy visions, they thought the attainment of truth far easier than we have since found it to be.' (Bagehot, *Economic Studies*, New ed., 1895, pp. 201–3–5.)

What were to be some of the key elements in the reconstruction of theoretical economics had already been discovered in the seventies. But the process of reconstruction was for some time to make slow progress. In fact, 'marginal' or neo-classical economics only really came into its own in the nineties. Meanwhile, what was far more striking was the melting away of comfortable mid-century certainties, and the reopening of issues long proclaimed as finally settled.

The controversies of this lively transitional period may conveniently be considered under the three heads of policy, theory, and method.

(*a*) First, there was the public debate about the principles of the State's economic activity, and in particular about the *laissez-faire* maxim. Behind this again was a much wider movement of thought which was both bringing about, and brought about by, a heightened

---

[1] See J. K. Ingram's presidential address to Section F of the British Association, 1878, on 'The Present Position and Prospects of Political Economy'. Also, Sir F. Galton, 'Considerations Adverse to the Maintenance of Section F', *Journal of the Royal Statistical Society*, Sept. 1877, p. 468.

public attention to 'the social problem', and an increased confidence in scientific study as an aid in its solution and control.

(*b*) There was specialized criticism, coming to a head around 1870, of a number of the particular theoretical doctrines of the classical economists.

(*c*) The methodological controversy, dormant in Britain since the isolated protests of Richard Jones in the 1830's, was reopened by Bagehot's and Toynbee's critical examinations of the postulates of the classical economists, and by the more extreme historical challenge of Cliffe Leslie and Ingram (to whom might well be added the Australian David Syme).[1]

(*a*) ECONOMIC POLICY, PUBLIC OPINION, AND THE SOCIAL QUESTION

The story is well known of how the growth of urban industrialism in the 1850's and 1860's, in spite of the unparalleled prosperity of the times, brought increasingly pressing problems of hours and conditions of work, of child and female labour, of trade unions, of public health, and of the ownership and management of the rapidly growing public utilities, all resulting in a steady piecemeal encroachment of State action in social and economic life. In fact, the 'new intervention' (factory acts, &c.) had got under way long before the 'old intervention' (Corn Laws, &c.) had been removed. The acknowledged exceptions to the *laissez-faire* maxim, or to the individualist minimum of State action, steadily and inevitably increased in number and importance. Later, after the onset of the great depression in 1873, they were to increase still more rapidly. As Bagehot put it, an age of great cities requires strong government.

Urbanization, and increased communications of every kind, had created not, of course, poverty, but the social problem of poverty, 'the social question', and had brought on the dawning of a much more sensitive social conscience, and of a much wider social self-consciousness. As André Gide has observed: 'Real poverty is that of cities, because it is there such a close neighbour to the excesses.'

An irrevocable step was being taken in the transition from the 'closed', unselfconscious, spontaneously functioning society of tradition and inheritance, into the 'open' selfconscious society of choice, plan, and design. As in the life of individuals, a growing new con-

---

[1] David Syme, known as 'the Father of Protection in Australia', was the author of *Outlines of Industrial Science* (1876), *v.* La Nauze, *Political Economy in Australia*, Ch. IV.

sciousness of alternatives cut off retreat into the habitual and natural, and made deliberate choice about the economic form of society increasingly inevitable. There was, in fact, being taken an important step towards 'this modern age' with its 'fanaticised consciousness' and all the bewildering burdens and instability which heightened self-consciousness or 'sophistication' is apt to bring. Matthew Arnold, for example, wrote in *Culture and Anarchy* (1869):

> And is not the close and bounded intellectual horizon within which we have long lived and moved now lifting up, and are not new lights finding free passage to shine in upon us? For a long time there was no passage for them to make their way in upon us, and then it was no use to think of adapting the world's action to them. . . . But now the iron force of adhesion to the old routine,—social, political, religious,—has wonderfully yielded; the iron force of exclusion of all that is new has wonderfully yielded. The danger now is, not that people should obstinately refuse to allow anything but their old routine to pass for reason and the will of God, but either that they should allow some novelty or other to pass for these too easily, or else that they should underrate the importance of them altogether, and think it enough to follow action for its own sake, without troubling themselves to make reason and the will of God prevail therein. (*Culture and Anarchy*, popular edition, 1894, p. 7.)

Moreover, with the steady expansion of the franchise, and the growth of trade unions, the less short-sighted observers recognized that in the urban masses industrialism had created a vast new force, as yet largely inarticulate and unorganized, and about which very little was known at all, though it was clearly a force with which the political classes would eventually have to come to terms, and one whose betterment it was both far-sighted, as well as philanthropic, to study. As it seemed to Arnold in 1869:

> A new power has suddenly appeared, a power which it is impossible yet to judge fully, but which is certainly a wholly different force from middle-class liberalism; different in its cardinal points of belief, different in its tendencies in every sphere. It loves and admires neither the legislation of middle-class Parliaments, nor the local self-government of middle-class vestries, nor the unrestricted competition of middle-class industrialists. . . . It has its main tendencies still to form. (Op. cit., pp. 24–25.)

At this juncture, too, important sections of the English intellectual classes were losing their belief in Christian doctrine, while, with the triumph of Darwinism, the belief in science and the scientific method as the key to the rapid solution of all mundane problems reached its most naively hubristic heights (in Britain, at any rate). It was these factors which made up what Beatrice Webb described as 'the mid-Victorian time-spirit', the union of faith in the scientific method with the 'transference of the emotion of self-sacrificing service from God to man'. (*My Apprenticeship*, Penguin edition, p. 153.) Of 'the new influx of ideas, and the activity of thought and discussion' in the sixties stirred by the later Mill, by Comte, Spencer, Strauss, Arnold, Darwin, and others, Sidgwick wrote: 'What we aimed at from a social point of view was a complete revision of human relations, political, moral and economic, in the light of science directed by comprehensive and impartial sympathy; and an unsparing reform of whatever, in the judgement of science, was pronounced to be not conducive to the general happiness.' (H. Sidgwick, *A Memoir*, p. 39.)

The various modern political religions might be traced as distant stunted descendants of this movement of thought, but in England in the sixties and seventies what it was bound to lead to was a heightened interest in political economy and social investigation, and a confident belief in their potentialities for social policy and social control. Social knowledge must mean social power. The later phases of J. S. Mill's thought, the political philosophy of T. H. Green, the Comteist movement, the rise of various new socialist sects, the Henry George crusade, the pioneer studies of Booth, university settlements in the East End of London, and a steady literary output of new kinds of social and scientific Utopias from Winwood Reade, Morris, and Edward Bellamy, to Wilde and Wells; all these were waves of varying date and importance in this long sweeping tide. It was on this tide that Alfred Marshall, for example, in the late sixties came to abandon his undergraduate ambitions of becoming a Christian missionary, and with the same objectives of serving his fellow men, turned to the scientific study of political economy, thinking 'that man's own possibilities were the most important subject for his study'. (Quoted by J. M. Keynes from a manuscript, *Memorials*, p. 166.)[1] Ten years before, the 22-year-old Jevons—on so many issues so far ahead of his time—had written to his sister from Australia: 'You may feel assured that to extend and perfect the abstract or the detailed knowledge of man and society is perhaps the most

---

[1] 'The 'seventies and 'eighties were years in which the prevailing political ethos, the system of duties and privileges on which institutions were built, and the economic structure, were all being criticised by the younger school of liberals, by the Fabians and the imperialists. Alfred Marshall did not abandon the moral sciences for economics by accident; economics became for him the study which bore most obviously on moral problems.' (N. Annan, *Leslie Stephen*, p. 243.)

useful and necessary work in which anyone can now engage.' (*Letters and Journals*, p. 101.) While later, towards the end of the seventies, Wicksteed was to come, via Comte and Henry George, to the enthusiastic study of Jevons's *Theory of Political Economy*.

Inevitably this wide movement of opinion brought with it a sharp and often hostile scrutiny of what was commonly regarded as the ruling orthodox principle of economic policy, and of the assumptions on which it was based. In a timely lecture in 1870 on 'Political Economy and Laissez-Faire' Cairnes complained that political economy had become 'known to the general public as a scientific development of *laissez-faire*', or 'very generally regarded as a sort of scientific rendering of this maxim—a vindication of freedom of enterprise and of contract as the one sufficient solution of all industrial problems'. (*Essays in Political Economy*, 1873, pp. 182 and 241.) Jevons and Bagehot in the seventies and Sidgwick later on, all felt it necessary very explicitly to dissociate political economy from what Jevons called the 'metaphysical incubus' of the *a priori laissez-faire* prejudice. We have already seen that such leaders as Gladstone, Lowe, and Newmarch took the view of the teachings of political economy which Cairnes had complained of.[1] We cannot examine here the complex development by which this state of opinion had come about, or whose had been the main responsibility, direct or indirect, or what had been the role, active or passive, of leading classical economists. J. S. Mill, it is true (in 1868—rather late in the day), sternly rebuked Lowe in Parliament for exalting *laissez-faire* into a universal and established principle of political economy,[2] and there are certainly enough proposals outlined in Mill's *Principles* to make up a thorough-going programme of socialistic reform. But Mill still continued to leave in the People's edition of his *Principles* a section headed 'Laissez Faire—the General Rule' (Bk. V, Ch. 11, sect. 7), and he left it very much to his popular readers to discern how far this was simply a political rule of thumb and how far an established conclusion of the science.

---

[1] Sir Leslie Stephen, the distinguished critic, and editor of the *Dictionary of National Biography*, might be cited as another leading intellectual case in point. In his views on political economy he was strongly under the influence of his friend Fawcett—Marshall's predecessor in the chair at Cambridge. Of Fawcett Stephen's biographer writes: 'Uninterested in science, theology, or the arts, he was the kind of utilitarian who gloried in using the felicific calculus like a sickle. . . . Fawcett confirmed him (Stephen) in many of the prejudices of his class. . . . Stephen lacked the courage to probe beneath the fatty degeneration of classical economics and philosophic radicalism'. (N. Annan, *Leslie Stephen*, pp. 42 and 244.)

[2] Cf. D. H. Macgregor, *Economic Thought and Policy*, p. 86.

What was above all called for was a sharp intellectually disciplined distinction between *laissez-faire* as a practical political rule of thumb, and as a scientifically established and authorized conclusion of the science of political economy. J. Viner has said of Adam Smith (and the judgement may be more widely applied), that he

made many exceptions to his general argument for laissez faire. But his interest as a reformer and a propagandist was not in these exceptions. He nowhere gathered together in orderly fashion the exceptions which he would have made to his general restriction of government activity to protection, justice, and the maintenance of a few types of public works and public institutions. When considering in general terms the proper functions of government, he forgot all about these exceptions.[1]

It was not that there occurred in the seventies any very marked or sudden change in the political attitude of leading economists. But gradually, instead of the free market being held innocent or beneficent until it was proved guilty, while State action was held guilty until proved innocent, the two came to be weighed up on rather more equal terms. In particular, a more systematic attempt came to be made 'to gather together in orderly fashion', and to concentrate more attention on, the cases for State intervention. As Toynbee wrote:

Competition we now recognize to be a thing neither good nor bad; we look upon it as resembling a great physical force which cannot be destroyed, but may be controlled and modified. As the cultivator embanks a stream and distributes its waters to irrigate his fields, so we control competition by positive laws and institutions. . . . The old economists thought competition good in itself. The socialists think it an evil in itself. We think it neither good nor evil, but seek to analyse it, and ascertain when it produces good and when it produces bad results. (*Lectures on the Industrial Revolution*, 1923 ed., p. 157.)[2]

[1] Cf. *Adam Smith 1776–1926* (ed. J. M. Clark), p. 139.

[2] Of Toynbee's remarkable influence at Oxford in the 1870's Lord Milner wrote (Introduction to Toynbee's *Lectures*, p. xxv): 'Now the years which I spent at Oxford [1872–6] and those immediately succeeding them, were marked by a very striking change in the social and political philosophy of the place, a change which has subsequently reproduced itself on the larger stage of the world. When I went up, the Laisser-faire theory still held the field. All the recognized authorities were "orthodox" economists of the old school. But within ten years the few men who still held the old doctrines in their extreme rigidity had come to be regarded as curiosities.

'In this remarkable change of opinion, which restored freedom of thought to economic speculation and gave a new impulse to philanthropy, Toynbee took, as far as his own University was concerned, a leading part.' On his death in 1883 Marshall succeeded Toynbee at Balliol as tutor to the Indian Civil Service candidates. On the 'Toynbee period', as it might be called, cf. Sidgwick's comment (1884): 'The impression produced

The 'bad results of competition', which were being especially challenged, were mainly those on the side of distribution. Just as the reaction in economic theory to the classical economists' concentration on productive efficiency was a new emphasis on individual consumer's demand, so in 'social economics', or in the discussion of economic policy, the shift in emphasis was from production to distribution. 'The problem of distribution', said Toynbee, 'is the true problem of Political Economy at the present time.' (Op. cit., p. 168.) The 'iron force' of the classical distribution theory (or of the common interpretation of it), was lifting, and its theoretical justification (such as it ever had been), in the earlier versions of Malthus's doctrine, had dissolved. For the social reformer this came as a great release. The very narrowing limits set to the manipulation or redistribution of the social income seemed largely to have disappeared, and it was to be two decades before the new marginal productivity analysis could be taken, by some of its interpreters at any rate, as imposing new restrictions. Meanwhile, there was much greater scope both for the sober consideration of problems of distribution and redistribution, and also for the Utopian heralds of 'the Age of Plenty'.[1]

(b) THEORETICAL CRITICISM OF THE CLASSICAL SYSTEM

As contrasted with the mainly monetary *macro*-economic analysis of much of eighteenth-century economics, and with the *micro*-economic theories of value and distribution which followed after 1870, the classical theoretical system represented a blend of the two approaches. It was certainly much more loosely knit than the micro-economic maximization analysis of individual consumers and producers which to a large extent superseded it between 1870 and 1900 and later. The classical account of distribution, especially in Ricardo, was mainly in aggregative 'class' terms. Malthus, Ricardo, and to some extent J. S. Mill, linked up this macro-economic distribution analysis with a sort of historical 'macro-dynamics' which had much in common with what is now known as the 'stagnation' thesis. Combined with these theories went an analysis of production which started rather from the maximizing individual entrepreneur or farmer. The whole

upon me is that the world is in a rather sternly philanthropic frame of mind, rather socialistic, rather inclined to find culture frivolous and to busy itself with the poverty in the East End of London. However research must go on, though a third of the families in London do live in one room.' (*A Memorial*, p. 380.)

[1] Cf. G. B. Shaw in *Fabian Essays*, pp. 26–7; also G. O'Brien's essay on Utopian economic theories, *The Phantom of Plenty* (1948).

system rested on four main pillars: (1) the Malthusian population doctrine; (2) the Wages Fund theory; (3) the theory of rent; (4) the labour (and subsequently cost of production) theory of value.

The 1850's and 1860's saw such a great increase in population accompanied by such a palpable rise in living standards that the classical population theory, and its law of 'natural' subsistence-wages, could only in some degree be saved by putting the main emphasis on those qualifications (already rather vaguely introduced by Malthus and Ricardo) which robbed the doctrine of almost all its sting and content. Senior, Richard Jones, Hearn, and Bagehot were among those highly critical of the Malthusian generalization (though Cairnes remained pessimistically faithful). In any case, soon after the opening of our period the turn in the rate of increase of the population was to set in. Once a permanent rise in working-class standards became accepted as an accomplished fact, the entire notion of a 'subsistence' level became extremely nebulous, and what might have been regarded as the one fairly firm anchor for the classical account of distribution was removed. As Professor Knight has described the Ricardian distribution theory, apart from the theory of rent, 'the only sense in which the treatment gets beyond the circle of each claimant getting what the other does not get lies in the idea that labour gets what it "has to have".'[1] As it gradually became more obvious that the notion of what labour 'had to have' was losing all trace of any content it might once have possessed, the classical distribution theory was adrift. The void left by the decline in prestige of the classical 'natural' laws of distribution was not filled until the nineties, and then hardly with a doctrine of equal inexorability.

The Wages Fund doctrine was one of those aggregative macro-economic generalizations, or definitional equations, first propounded as explaining how a key element in the economic system is 'determined' (as Edgeworth once said, there is a certain indeterminacy in economists' use of the verb 'determine'), but which later emerges, if it is retained at all, either as a definition, or as a *non-sequitur*, or, at best, as a platitude. J. S. Mill's spectacular abandonment of the doctrine in 1869 as a 'shadow which will vanish if we go boldly up to it', was one of the more overt signs of the crumbling of the classical system. There is little to regret in the fairly abrupt demise of the doctrine itself. But much was lost when the very problem of macro-economic distribution which it sought to answer was almost completely dropped, particularly because, in the debates immediately preceding, a number of

[1] See his article in the *Canadian Journal of Economics and Political Science, 1935*, pp. 3 ff.

valuable ideas had been broached. There had been Longe's fleeting rediscovery, not followed up at all, of Malthus's concept of 'the general demand for labour', Thornton's emphasis on the 'prospectiveness' of supply and demand schedules, along with Cairnes's distinction between realized (*ex post*), and estimated (*ex ante*), supply and demand, as well as his analysis of aggregate general demand and supply, as contrasted with demand and supply for a particular commodity. These were all ideas arising out of the Wages Fund controversies, which hardly received any of the development and emphasis they deserved in the following decades.

The third of the classical pillars, the theory of rent, with its basis of individual maximizing and marginal productivity analysis, was to survive, especially in Marshall's version, in an outwardly only slightly altered form in the new edifice of production and distribution theory built up in the nineties, like some Anglo-Saxon masonry left in a Norman cathedral.

It is Jevons's *Theory of Political Economy* (1871), with his marginal utility theory of value, and his incisive attack on the labour and cost-of-production theories, which is generally taken today as the decisive moment in the transition from the classical system. Every doctrine has its anticipation, and before Jevons's there had been the works of lesser-known writers like Lloyd, Banfield, and Jennings, passages in Senior, and Mill's emphasis on the demand side in his analysis of International Values, to mention English sources only.[1] But the obvious intellectual ancestor of Jevons's marginal utility analysis is Bentham. He is the first great English originator of individual maximization analysis, and the great propounder of the idea that something of profound clarificatory significance, normative or positive, is being said about human actions, or some aspect of them, when they are described as 'maximizing' actions. Bentham also explored the principle of the diminishing utility of wealth, essential for distinguishing between the significance of physically similar units, and (following from that) for the marginal concept and the equi-marginal allocation formula of

---

[1] T. E. Banfield (who was indebted to German writers, including Hermann) and Richard Jennings are both cited by Jevons. But the Oxford utility school of Whately, Senior, and Lloyd (*flor. c.* 1830) got nearest to a systematic account of the relation of utility to value, and to a correspondingly sound criticism of cost-of-production theories. Richard Whately (author of the famous phrase 'Pearls are not valuable because men have dived for them, but men dive for them because they are valuable'), may also be said to have been partly responsible for founding a marginal productivity school of thought when he went to Dublin, since he endowed the chair occupied by Longfield and Isaac Butt.

Jevons. What is remarkable is that there was so long an interval between Bentham and Jevons, and how significant Bentham's hedonism
still seemed for Jevons and Edgeworth. It is strange that it had been
left to the unknown German H. Gossen to develop first (1854) an
economic calculus on Benthamite principles.

The playing up or playing down of the revolutionary newness of a
writer's contribution is, of course, often largely a matter of temperament and intellectual vested interest. Jevons's new doctrine, certainly
at first, ran into considerable conservative resistance and made, for
some time, slow progress. Not only Marshall in reviewing the *Theory*,
but Bagehot, Sidgwick, and Cairnes were all markedly unenthusiastic.
Bagehot complained that the new theory of Jevons and Walras was
'much worse' than the old, in looking 'too unlike life and business'.
(*Economic Studies*, p. 20.) Later Sidgwick, like Marshall, deplored the
'revolutionary' claims of Jevons and his taking up 'in reference to the
received mode of treating the subject an attitude almost similar to that
which each new metaphysical system has hitherto adopted towards its
predecessors'. (*Principles*, p. 5.) Cairnes analysed the new theory as
simply stating: 'Value depends upon utility and that utility is whatever
affects value. In other words, the name "utility" is given to the aggregate
of unknown conditions which determine the phenomenon, and then
the phenomenon is stated to depend upon what this name stands for.'
(*Some Leading Principles*, p. 21.) Today, in view of the very tenuous
empirical content (or 'operational significance') of the theory of consumers' behaviour, Cairnes's negative criticism seems to be by no
means without point.

At the time the new analysis did straighten out some tiresome
terminological tangles and resolve certain long-standing paradoxes
(with regard, for example, to the values of diamonds and water) which
were involved in the classical definitions of 'value'. Further, the new
analysis got demand and supply broadly and logically the right way
round. Roscher complained that when one read some of the followers
of Adam Smith one got the impression that goods were not produced
for man, but man was there for the sake of the goods. This is almost
certainly a gross exaggeration, but not an absolutely unfounded
exaggeration. Marshall in his *Principles* was logically to put the demand
for goods first (Book III) and their production second (Book IV).

More definitely than this, Jevons's marginal utility analysis posed
the allocation problem for the individual consumer, and formulated
the maximizing solution. The form of the solution had much in

common with the Ricardian principle of how entrepreneurs, in general, so distribute their investments and activities that the rate of profit is (*cet. par.*) equalized in each direction. But the marginal utility formula related to the individual and, through the marginal concept, had much more precision. As Marshall pointed out, the allocation problems of the consumer are of small interest compared with those of the producer, and it was to be some time before the firm's allocation problems were generally solved on parallel lines to those of the household. But the marginal utility theory of value provided the archetype of a 'micro-economic' maximizing allocation problem, capable of a pure and simple mathematical formulation, and using the concept of the marginal unit to formulate a precise maximizing solution. Except in so far as the notion of consumers' utility implied also an approach fundamentally different from that of the classics to the problem of distribution, or the pricing of the factors of production—which was not clearly brought out by Jevons—what was important in marginal utility was the adjective rather than the noun. Marginal utility analysis introduced the marginal concept as an instrument of maximization analysis. 'Utility' was only for a brief period to have any substantial or unchallenged role in economic theory. By the nineties Wicksteed, Fisher, Pareto, and others were wearing it away to a shadow.

We may perhaps briefly digress at this point to explore why the marginal concept had hardly appeared in classical political economy. The need for the marginal concept emerges where similar successive units (of goods or factors) have a different (rising or falling) significance (in utility to the consumer, or physical or monetary return to the producer). The classical system had no important place for utility, and therefore none for diminishing and marginal utility. It analysed mainly competitive markets, where there is, therefore, no divergence between average and marginal revenue to the firm. In manufacture constant costs were generally assumed, where there is no divergence between marginal and average costs. At the one point—agricultural production—where the differing significance of successive similar units was assumed, i.e. diminishing returns to successive 'doses' of capital and labour, the beginnings of marginal analysis appear. There was, therefore, little scope for the marginal concept, or the distinction between marginal and average, in the main classical models. The pioneers of marginal analysis are naturally in many cases those who had to deal with problems of monopoly, with obviously and sharply increasing returns, with heavy fixed and low variable costs, and where the utility of the consumers may be an inescapable part of the problem. The case of public utilities, and above all of railways and transport systems, contains all these elements, and their practical pricing problems were rapidly increasing in importance in the middle decades of the nineteenth century. Cournot was not directly concerned with any practical problem, though his case of the mineral spring from which he starts strongly resembles a public utility. But Dupuit, the Director-General of French 'Ponts et Chaussées' conspicuously bears out our argument. So does the American railway engineer Charles Ellet[1] (whom Professor Viner has ranked with Cournot and Dupuit). Lardner's analysis of the pricing problems of railways, closely resembling Cournot's discussion of monopoly, is another example. And Lardner's book (*Railway Economy*, 1850) in turn interested and influenced the youthful Jevons when he was writing his first economic essays on the railway problems of New South Wales. (In this episode of the problems of public utilities and the emergence of marginal analysis—*as also throughout the nineteenth century*—it is remarkable how much of the most original and enduring work was due to complete outsiders unknown in orthodox circles, or at any rate to thinkers who met with very little recognition from other economists in their own day, e.g. Lloyd, Longfield, Cournot, Dupuit, Ellet, John Rae, Auguste (and to some extent Léon) Walras, Thünen, Mangoldt, J. A. Hobson, and Johannsen.)

One might have thought that the new emphasis after 1871 on the consumer and on the demand side in economic theory, and on distribution in economic policy, might have led to at least some questionings of Say's, Ricardo's, and the Mill's doctrines on aggregate consumer's demand, or total consumption or 'effective demand'. But here, in orthodox circles in Britain at any rate, there was hardly as much as a ripple on the surface. Jevons, almost pathologically ready to attack any doctrine of J. S. Mill, and vigorously assaulting, in particular, Mill's famous four propositions on capital, never questioned or raised the subject of Mill's analysis of 'general over-production', which suc-

---

[1] C. Ellet (1810–62) wrote *An Essay on the Laws of Trade in Reference to the Internal Works of Improvement in the United States* (1839), 'a work that was written in almost every tavern on the line between Richmond and Ohio'. *v.* C. D. Calsoyas, *Journal of Political Economy*, 1950, p. 162, and J. Viner, *Journal of Political Economy*, 1928, p. 411. Jevons mentions the book in his list of works on mathematical political economy, but had never seen it. In several respects Ellet's work hardly seems to compare with those of Cournot and Dupuit, having more affinities with Thünen's analysis of the theory of location.

ceeded in combining dogmatism and ambiguity to a quite remarkable degree. For all Jevons had to say, the last words on this question might have been what seems now to be the highly problematic and ambivalent, even schizophrenic, treatment given in various sections of J. S. Mill's *Principles*. And what is true here of Jevons is also true, by and large, of Sidgwick, Marshall, Edgeworth, and Wicksteed. (See below, Part III, Ch. 22.)

(c) METHODOLOGICAL CRITICISM AND THE HISTORICAL APPROACH

The criticism of what had come to be regarded as the main conclusion for policy of classical economics, along with the weakening of its main theoretical pillars, was combined with an examination of its method, previously challenged by Richard Jones in the 1830's. The orthodox account of the scope and method of classical political economy had been given, with only comparatively minor divergencies, by J. S. Mill in his early essay (1829), published in *Unsettled Questions*, by Senior in his *Lectures* (1826 and 1852), and by Cairnes (*Character and Logical Method of Political Economy*, 1857 and 1875).

Thorold Rogers was justified in claiming that the method developed by these writers differed considerably in emphasis from that of Adam Smith. There had subsequently entered into classical political economy a strong rationalist and *a-priorist* infusion, partly from French sources, and partly via the unselfconscious deductive procedure of Ricardo, 'who had', according to Marshall, 'very little in common with the English tone of thought'. (*Memorials*, p. 153.) When Cairnes, for example, claims that 'the economist starts with a knowledge of ultimate causes', he is describing very closely the rationalist Cartesian approach of the Physiocrats. But neither Mill, Senior, nor Cairnes would have gone so far as to diverge fundamentally from the empirical tradition of Locke and Hume, nor would they have agreed that the procedure and criteria of the social sciences, and of political economy, differed crucially from those of the natural sciences, a view which became, of course, to a large extent the orthodox German teaching. On the contrary, they held that it was essential to try to uphold the criteria of the natural sciences in the study of the social world, and Cairnes specifically complained that: 'Unfortunately, many who perfectly understand what science means when the word is employed with reference to physical nature, allow themselves to slide into a totally different sense of it, or rather into acquiescence in an absence of all distinct meaning in its use, when they employ it with reference to social existence.' (*Essays*, p. 252.) Mill, also, opened Book VI of his *Logic* (*On the Logic of the Moral Sciences*) by insisting that the way forward to more agreed conclusions in the moral sciences must be 'by generalising the methods successfully followed in the natural sciences'.

The methodological criticism in England in the seventies of classical political economy seems to have been reinforced, rather than to have directly followed, or to have been inspired, by continental influences. These were notably that of Comte, who probably acquired his greatest influence in England in the later sixties, and that of the German historical school, when after 1870 a strong tide of German thought flowed in. Only the Comteist and historicist Ingram, but not Bagehot, Toynbee, or even Cliffe Leslie, seems to have derived much from these two sources. A further extremely important native influence towards a more institutional or historical approach was that of Darwinism, evident in Hearn's *Plutology* and later in the biological analogies of Marshall.

The more moderate criticism of Ricardian procedure came from Bagehot, in his *Postulates of Political Economy* (1877) (of which Marshall later introduced a special edition for Cambridge students), and in the posthumously published lectures of Toynbee. They both attacked not the use of deduction as such, but the lack of explicitness in the assumptions on which the whole deductive structure was built. Bagehot's object was 'not to examine the edifice of our English Political Economy, but to define its basis. Nothing but unreality can come of it till we know when and how far its first assertions are true in matter of fact, and when and how far they are not.' (*Economic Studies*, 2nd ed., p. 94.)

Toynbee criticized the more extreme historical attacks:

Advocates of the Historical Method, like Mr. Cliffe Leslie, therefore go too far when they condemn the Deductive Method as radically false. There is no real opposition between the two. The apparent opposition is due to a wrong use of deduction; to a neglect on the part of those employing it to examine closely their assumptions and to bring their conclusions to the test of fact. (*Lectures*, p. 3.)

He specifically warned against the dangers of historicist generalizations:

By the historical method we mean the actual observation of the course of economic history, and the deduction from it of laws of economic progress; and this method, while most useful in checking the results of deduction, is, by itself, full of danger from its tendency to set up imperfect generalisations. (p. 111.)

The most able exponent of the thorough-going historical approach, comparable with that of the German School, was Cliffe Leslie, though his criticism is of the kind often referred to as 'unconstructive'. Leslie had listened to the lectures of Sir Henry Maine at Lincoln's Inn, who had said of the 'natural law' theory of jurisprudence: 'It gave birth or intense stimulus to vices of mental habit all but universal, disdain of positive law, impatience of experience, and the preference of a priori to all other reasoning.' Leslie sought to apply the same line of criticism to the natural laws of the classical political economy: 'Political Economy is not a body of natural laws in the true sense, or of universal and immutable truths, but an assemblage of speculations and doctrines which are the result of a particular history and coloured even by the history and character of its chief writers.' He argued for 'the deletion of the deductive method of Ricardo: that is to say, of deduction from unverified assumptions respecting "natural values, natural wages, and natural profits." But we are not against deduction in the sense of inference from true generalisations and principles, though we regard the urgent work of the present as induction, and view long trains of deduction with suspicion.' (*Essays in Political Economy*, 2nd ed., p. 72.)

In a series of essays, of which an early one was an attack on the Wages Fund (1868), he fastened particularly on the vagueness of 'the desire for wealth' as the basic assumption of political economy, complaining that a great variety of different and heterogeneous motives have been mistaken for a single homogeneous force. This is a criticism that can fairly easily be answered, but not in terms which leave much content in a system of theory built on any such postulate. Moreover, Leslie went on to point out, in a notable paper, 'The Known and the Unknown in the Economic World', how extensively in economic theorizing it was assumed that much was certainly known to economic individuals which could not possibly be known in an uncertain changing world, and how far this immense simplification vitiated many of the practical conclusions being drawn:

The orthodox, a priori, or deductive system thus postulates much more than a general desire of wealth. It postulates, also . . . full knowledge of the gains in different employments. . . . The deductive economist . . . assumes that the choice of occupations and investments, and the movements of labour and capital, are determined by knowledge so accurate that the result is the same percentage of profit on capital all round. (pp. 228–9.) . . . Instead of the world of light, order, equality and perfect organisation, which orthodox political economy postulates, the commercial world is thus one of obscurity, confusion, haphazard, in which, amid much destruction and waste, there is by no means always a survival of the fittest, even though cunning be counted among the conditions of fitness. . . . The part of chance in the matter is really so great, the venture so often chiefly at other people's risk, and the ramifications of commercial relations and credit, the sudden changes in the activity of business and in demand, the fluctuations of prices, make the trader's future dependent on so many other conditions than his own skill and care, that not a few hardly try to exercise judgment or foresight. (p. 235.)

The main upshot of the methodological debate was in accordance with the moderate point of view of Bagehot and Toynbee and the anti-exclusivist approach of Jevons. History and analysis in the main went their separate ways (though not entirely so in Marshall's works), each more or less tacitly acknowledging, or at least tolerating, the role of the other, a practically admirable compromise, which, however, did lead to the evasion of some of the very relevant questions that Bagehot, Toynbee, and Leslie had raised. The eighties saw the consolidation of economic history in the pioneer works of Rogers (*Six Centuries of Work and Wages*, 1884), Cunningham (*The Growth of English Industry and Commerce*, 1882), and later on Ashley (1892–3). The emphasis in economic history in England was much more strongly on the 'history' and less on the 'economics', than in the work of Schmoller and his followers.[1] Whether some more constructive and positive relation between history and analysis was, or is, possible cannot be discussed here, but at any rate in England there was none of the absurd intolerance and waste of spirit that accompanied for so long the *Methodenstreit* in central Europe, though a certain amount of sporadic sniping continued on and off, notably from Ashley, a thorough-going follower of Schmoller; and at one stage Sir John Clapham put some interesting questions ('Empty Economic Boxes', *Economic Journal*, 1922). The weightiest consequence of the historical movement on English political economy was Marshall's synthesis of history and analysis. But whether or not his great attempt at a synthesis fully succeeded, it certainly was not an aspect of his work which received anything like the minute examination and devoted defence which the detailed theoretical concepts of his *Principles* attracted.

Methodological principles were summarized for the ensuing decades

[1] *v.* Sir F. Rees, *History*, vol. xxxiv, 1949.

in J. N. Keynes's *Scope and Method of Political Economy* (1890), which Marshall had wanted to make 'more favourable to Schmoller'. As time went on the emphasis of Bagehot and Toynbee on the importance of clarity and precision in the basic postulates of economic theory wore off and was forgotten. A point of view, which has been well described by Professor Robertson, became dominant about 'the topic of what sort of a study economics is and what it is about':

> This is a topic which, when I started to read economics at Cambridge in 1910, it was not, I think, fashionable among us to think much about—less fashionable, I dare say, than it may have been a few years previously, when the separate course in economics had not yet been extracted like Eve from the ribs of the Moral Sciences Tripos. To us, I think, it seemed a topic more suitable for discussion by Germans than by Englishmen. There was on our reading list what I have since come to regard as a good, if dry, book about it, J. N. Keynes's *Scope and Method of Political Economy*,[1] but to be quite honest I doubt if many of us read it. We thought we knew pretty well what sort of things we wanted to know about. . . . (*Manchester School*, May 1951, p. 111.)

Toynbee had noted 'the most curious contrast between the looseness and unreality of the premisses', of classical political economy, and 'the closeness and rigour of the argument'. Fifty or sixty years later J. M. Keynes was to contrast 'the lack of clearness and of generality in the premisses' of orthodox economics, with 'the great care for logical consistency', of 'the superstructure'. (*General Theory*, p. v.)

3. *The 'Leading Principles' of J. E. Cairnes*

At the outset of our period there was published what is often regarded as the last statement of the classical system of ideas, J. E. Cairnes's *Leading Principles of Political Economy* (1874). The work never had anything like the wide influence of Mill's *Principles*, but it presents in a more clear-cut way most of the main doctrines of classical political economy. Cairnes's trenchant attack in his lecture of 1870 on what was widely accepted as being the very close relations between 'Political Economy and Laissez-faire', makes him, in this particular respect,

[1] This book seems not when it appeared (1890) to have been very closely representative of Marshall's views. He wrote: 'Most of the suggestions which I made on the proofs of Keynes' *Scope and Method* were aimed at bringing it more into harmony with the views of Schmoller. Some were accepted.' (*v.* J. M. Keynes on H. S. Foxwell, *Economic Journal*, 1936, p. 597.)

something of a transitional figure. But its cost-of-production theory of value, its reformulation of the Wages Fund doctrine, and, above all, its unqualified acceptance of what is called 'the great Malthusian difficulty', stamp his *Leading Principles* as broadly representative, as far as any single work can be, of classical political economy.

The framework of Cairnes's system consists of (1) his analysis of Normal and Market Values, (2) his analysis of Supply and Demand, and (3) his theory of the Wages Fund or of 'average aggregate wages'.

(1) *Normal and Market Values*. Part I studies Value, 'the ratio in which commodities in open market are exchanged against each other' (1874 ed., p. 3). 'Normal' values (which are 'average' or 'permanent' values) are given under competitive conditions by cost of production, 'undoubtedly the principal and most important of the conditions on which normal value depends' (p. 47). When competition does not hold, in the case described as that of 'non-competing groups' (which Cairnes seems to regard as applying simply or mainly to labour), the principle of 'Reciprocal Demand' is invoked, which had been developed by Mill in his analysis of International Values, and which is described by Cairnes as 'Supply and Demand in relation to a particular commodity, or even to a considerable number of commodities'. (p. 103.) For the explanation of market value, or 'actual market prices', 'Supply and Demand' provide the principle of analysis.

The general family resemblance, in outline, to Marshall's 'pair of scissors', and long and short period analysis, is apparent.

(2) *Supply and Demand*. Cairnes's very significant analysis of Supply and Demand is developed at various points in the book. First, great emphasis is laid on the distinction between *aggregate* supply and demand, and supply and demand *for a particular commodity*. In seeking to employ the Supply and Demand for particular commodities to explain their market values, Cairnes argued, perhaps unfairly to Mill, but with considerable wider significance, that on Mill's definitions (which seemed to him to amount to *ex-post* 'realised' definitions)

the doctrine of the equality of Demand and Supply as the condition of market price becomes a mere identical proposition. The quantity demanded and the quantity supplied at the market price are necessarily equal when the quantity demanded is only another name for the quantity bought, and the quantity supplied another name for the quantity sold. They are necessarily equal, since they are one and the same quantity. (p. 117.)

On these definitions 'supply and demand' can explain nothing. Cairnes decides that 'we must give to the words "supply" and "demand" a much more extended signification than is given to them in the formulas either of Adam Smith or of Mill. By "supply" as affecting market price, I would understand, not merely the quantity of a commodity sold, offered for sale, or present in a given market, but the quantity intended for sale wherever it exists which the dealers in the particular market know or believe to be available, to meet, within certain limits of time, the demand which falls within the range of their dealing, and by "demand" a strictly analogous conception.' (p. 118.)

Whether or not he is fully justified in his correction of Mill, Cairnes obviously deserves the highest credit for making and seeing the significance of this fundamental distinction, one which was still disregarded in important works many decades later. Unfortunately, what is catastrophic for his system is that he throughout denies, absolutely rigidly and consistently, that any such distinction is applicable to Aggregate Supply and Demand. For those who seek for a classical 'Aunt Sally' (in the Keynesian sense of 'classical'), Cairnes's *Leading Principles*, unlike J. S. Mill's, provides all the purest components and materials without flaw or stint.

Demand, as an aggregate, cannot increase without supply, nor supply without demand. This is fundamental: 'The notion that the demand for commodities may increase independently of the supply'. . . is 'at the bottom of nearly all the confusion of thought that prevails in this subject'. (p. 233.) 'Neither can increase or diminish without necessitating and implying a corresponding increase or diminution of the other.' (p. 18.)

After demonstrating that this identity must hold in a barter economy, Cairnes insists:

Now the essential character of exchange is not altered by the employment of a circulating medium, however the increased complexity of the facts may tend to conceal its true nature. The process is facilitated but what happens is in effect the same. It is still an exchange of commodities and services against commodities and services and the relation between Demand and Supply remains what it was in the simpler case. (p. 27.)

All assumptions to the contrary must be regarded as 'baseless and absurd'. (p. 28.)

Consistently with this analysis Cairnes takes for granted Adam Smith's analysis of saving: 'The act creative of capital (is) saving, parsimony, abstinence' (p. 93). Cairnes on all these fundamental issues was far more unqualified than J. S. Mill (especially than Mill's early essay on the *Influence of Consumption upon Production*).

(3) *The Wages Fund and Average General Wages*. Cairnes's Part II is concerned with aggregate 'macro-economic' analysis. He claims that the 'laws of value' discussed in Part I solve also the problems of relative wages and profits, which follow the same laws that govern the exchange value of commodities:

> What the doctrine of value reveals to us on this subject is the causes which determine the *relative* remuneration of labourers as amongst themselves, and that of capitalists among themselves. It tells us why some classes of workmen and some classes of capitalists receive the same or equivalent remuneration, while in other cases inequality in various degrees prevails; but it tells us nothing as to what determines the positive remuneration which any class of capitalists or of labourers receives, nor as to the causes on which depend the average well-being of all classes. (p. 174.)

The principle of Supply and Demand is bound to be useless in explaining average aggregate wages. For, as we have seen, according to Cairnes, aggregate Supply and Demand are always necessarily equal. Attempts, therefore, to replace the Wages Fund analysis by an explanation in terms of the Demand for Labour are completely misconceived. Longe, an important critic of the Wages Fund doctrine had, somewhat inconsistently with his general attack on aggregate macro-economic concepts, found the size of total wages to depend on 'the demand for labour'. This is one of the very few occasions in nineteenth-century English writings where the concept Malthus sought to discuss in the first meetings of the Political Economy Club in the early 1820's, emerged again for a moment to the surface: 'The demand for commodities', Longe wrote, 'certainly does not directly determine the quantity of labour or number of labourers in a country, nor the quantity of corn or other things available for the maintenance of labourers, but it does determine the quantity of labour employed, and the quantity of wealth spent in the wages of labourers.' (F. D. Longe, *A Refutation of the Wages-Fund Theory, &c.*, 1866, p. 46.)

Cairnes sought to crush this argument with all the sweeping certainty with which the Mills had attacked Malthus, Sismondi, Chalmers, and eighteenth-century writers generally: 'It is in truth about the most popular of all popular fallacies. . . . From this root has sprung a whole cluster of maxims such as that "the extravagance of the rich is the gain of the poor", &c.' (p. 190.) For, 'as has been explained in a former chapter . . . the aggregate demand for commodities depends on the aggregate production of commodities' (p. 193): or rather not 'depends on' but 'is' necessarily at all times both in a barter and in a monetary economy, aggregate Supply and Demand being 'reciprocals of each other, and in effect the opposite faces of the same facts'. (p. 229.)

Having shown that aggregate Supply and Demand can explain nothing, Cairnes passes to his exposition of the Wages Fund doctrine. As Marshall noted (*Principles*, p. 825), Cairnes explained away so much which is characteristic of the doctrine, that there is very little left in it to justify its title. In the main it is an analysis of what determines the level of investment and of the different kinds of investment, in particular the hiring of labour:

A capitalist engages and pays a workman from precisely the same motives which lead him to purchase raw material, a factory, or a machine. In searching, therefore, for the causes which govern the amount of wealth spent in the hiring of labour, we must advert to the considerations which weigh with men in devoting their means to productive investment. Why, for example, does A. B. employ his wealth in productive operations? . . .
We find the amount of A. B.'s investment determined by the following circumstances: Firstly, the amount of his total means; secondly, his character and disposition as affected by the temptation to immediate enjoyment on the one hand, and by the prospect of future aggrandisement on the other; thirdly, the opportunities of making profit. Alter any of these and the effect will be an alteration in the amount of his investment. (p. 197.)

But investment may be either in 'Fixed Capital', 'Raw Material', or 'Wages Fund'. What determines the proportion in which these are combined? (p. 199.)

Here Cairnes is far from satisfactory. On the one hand he recurs to a notion of fixed proportions given, it would seem from some passages, technically, 'by the nature of the national industries', which is the main circumstance governing the proportion which the Wages Fund shall bear to the general capital of a nation (p. 200). (The notion of a naturally or technically fixed level of employment for labour given by the industrial fixed capital of the country recurs, paradoxically, in J. A. Hobson's under-consumption analysis of unemployment.) But Cairnes mentions also the 'Ricardo effect' notion of changes in the level of wages changing the proportions of fixed capital and Wages Fund. The reconciliation of these two notions is not very clearly worked out.

Cairnes, however, notes in passing in the brief two pages he devotes to the subject, that crises bring a contraction in the Wages Fund since they are the result of a conversion of circulating capital into fixed. (p. 209.)

Cairnes summarizes his theory of investment as follows:

I believe that, in the existing state of the national wealth, the character of Englishmen being what it is, a certain prospect of profit will 'determine' a certain proportion of this wealth to productive investment, that the amount thus 'determined' will increase as the field for investment is extended, and that it will not increase beyond what this field can find employment for at that rate of profit which satisfies English commercial expectation. Further, I believe that, investment thus taking place, the form which it shall assume will be 'determined' by the nature of the national industries—'determined', not under acts of Parliament, or in virtue of any physical law, but through the influence of the investor's interests, while this, the form of the investment, will again 'determine' the proportion of the whole capital which shall be paid as wages to labourers. It is in this sense I say that I understand the 'predetermination' implied in the Wages Fund doctrine. (pp. 217–18.)

Cairnes's following chapters on the long-run dynamics of the Wages Fund and the historical course of the relative shares of wages, profits, and rent, is imbued with the deepest Ricardian and Marxian pessimism. As things are, 'the rich will be growing richer; and the poor, at least relatively, poorer. It seems to me . . . that these are not conditions which furnish a solid basis for a progressive state'. (p. 340.) What he refers to as 'the great Malthusian difficulty' overhangs everything. Nearly all forms of trade-union and governmental action are likely, either only to benefit a section of the workers at the expense of the rest, or to strike at that private accumulation which is the indispensable condition of economic progress. Cairnes only sees hope in the gradual growth of producers' co-operation whereby the workers will gradually become small profit-makers, cutting down their expenditure on drink (pp. 343–5) and practising and receiving the rewards of 'abstinence'.

Cairnes's *Leading Principles*, in a sense the last statement of the classical system, is equally divided between the study of relative values in Part I, and of the size and distribution of the aggregate national income in Part II. His analysis in Part I was to be replaced by Jevons, and built upon or supplemented by Marshall. But nothing replaced or supplemented the analysis of the Wages Fund doctrine, or that of its critics. Not merely did the doctrine itself die away, but the whole problem it sought to deal with was in the main shelved or abandoned. The marginal productivity analysis of distribution which emerged a quarter of a century later, was an explanation of relative wages, which Cairnes regarded as dealt with, along with the problem of the relative values of commodities, in Part I of his book. This loss was all the greater because on either side of the debate, as well as the misconceptions, valuable and fundamental insights had been developed, in Longe's fleeting rediscovery of the 'Demand for Labour', and Cairnes's analysis of the determinants of aggregate investment.

4. *Jevons on the Future of Political Economy: Economics as an Academic Discipline*

The centenary debate brought out the main background of practical problems which were to engage English political economists in the coming decades: the problems of poverty, the claims of labour, the distribution of wealth, the role of the State, and the difficulties of a conscious monetary policy (or 'our backward condition' in respect of 'the currency'). The problems of Britain's industrial and financial position in the world, and whether or how this should be defended by an abandonment of free trade, was not to come to the forefront of discussion for another two or three decades, though Jevons had foreseen Britain's twentieth-century problem some time previously in *The Coal Question* (1865), and it was later coming to worry the far-sighted Sidgwick.[1] But the centenary debate brought out no agreed or constructive ideas about the development of the theoretical system of political economy. There was simply the backward-looking bleakness of Lowe, and the historical enthusiasm of Thorold Rogers. The deficiency was shortly after to be filled by Jevons.

Jevons was one of the comparatively very few professors present at the Adam Smith centenary. He did not, of course, speak on that occasion, but, a few months later, on taking over the chair at University College, London, he devoted his introductory lecture entitled 'The Future of Political Economy' to a review of the centenary debate.[2] Though it anticipates the next chapter, it is convenient to consider at this point Jevons's review and the constructive suggestions he made about the future.

Jevons saw no shortage of tasks and clearly outlined the three main fields for economic studies. Only what he called 'the fallacy of exclusiveness' could keep alive debates about methods of approach. He ac-

---

[1] 'Reading the growth of England's commercial greatness rouses a mixture of curiosity and patriotic anxiety; it seems clear that we are past all culmination, relatively speaking, and it would be contrary to all historic precedents that we should not go down hill; but will it be by destructive, disastrous shocks, or gradual painless decline?' (1885.) *v. A Memoir*, p. 399.

[2] Reprinted in the *Principles of Economics*, edited by H. Higgs, p. 187.

knowledged that historical treatment was valuable and necessary, but insisted on the role of theoretical formulae. The principle of scarcity provided a basis for a central structure of analysis of wide generality, which it was essential to work out:

Now the laws of political economy treat of the relations between human wants and the available natural objects and human labour by which they may be satisfied. These laws are so simple in their foundation that they would apply more or less completely to all human beings of whom we have any knowledge. . . . The most fundamental of its laws is that of Senior and Banfield—namely that human wants are limited in extent.

But Jevons certainly did not hold that the inevitably rather platitudinous elaboration of the scarcity concept comprised by itself the whole, or even the pre-eminent, task of political economy, which for Jevons was a house of many mansions.

Secondly, there must be a systematic analysis of the principles of economic policy to replace the single over-simplified maxim of the politicians, the publicists, and the popularizers:

While population grows more numerous and dense, while industry becomes more complex and interdependent, as we travel faster and make use of more intense forces, we shall necessarily need more legislative supervision. If such a thing is possible we need a new branch of political and statistical science which shall carefully investigate the limits to the *laissez-faire* principle and show where we want greater freedom and where less. . . . Instead of one dictum '*laissez-faire laissez-passer*' we must have at least one science, one new branch of the old political economy.

Thirdly, continued Jevons: 'We need a science of the money market and of commercial fluctuations which shall inquire why the world is all activity for a few years and then all inactivity, why in short there are such tides in the affairs of men.'

These three branches of political economy for which Jevons saw the need, were eventually to receive the attention he called for. But for some decades the two latter were to have a more subsidiary role than Jevons had seemed to envisage. Indeed his third branch, that of the aggregate fluctuations of economic activity, in spite of Jevons's own example, was not really to come in for much systematic attention, especially in England, for another thirty or forty years. Between 1880 and 1910—the main formative period of 'micro-economic' marginal analysis—the writings in English on aggregate fluctuations, and on 'macro-economic' problems generally, were fairly few and unrecognized as compared with previous and subsequent decades. Jevons had insisted that, 'it will no longer be possible to treat political economy as if it were a single undivided and indivisible science'. He did not foresee how much, in the next three decades, of the constructive effort of economists was to be devoted to a central theoretical system considerably more tightly and exclusively organized around a single postulate of rather uncertain content—that of the maximizing individual unit—than ever the classical system had been. The rough pioneer macro-economic analyses of the classics, were to a large extent to disappear, along even with the questions they had set out to ask.

Jevons himself was not to have much longer in which to follow up the plans he had sketched out, and in the next few years nearly all the stalwarts of the Adam Smith centenary were removed. It was Marshall whose work was to give the answer to the problems of the seventies. In 1885 when he gave his inaugural lecture as professor at Cambridge he recorded: 'Twelve years ago England possessed perhaps the ablest set of economists that there have ever been in a country at one time. But one after another they have been taken from us, Mill, Cairnes, Bagehot, Cliffe Leslie, Jevons, Newmarch, and Fawcett.' All these except Mill and Newmarch failed to live beyond their early fifties.

The turmoil of the seventies did not seem to have led to any commensurate constructive developments. For over a decade in English political economy there had been something of a vacuum. There had seemed to be 'no single volume paramount, no code, no master spirit, no determined road', all of which in due course were to arrive in full measure. But meanwhile there supervened in the eighties, mainly it seems for reasons of personnel, a period of stagnancy which was in marked contrast with the great activity of the Austrian School in what was probably its greatest decade.

Economic theory was to be rebuilt mainly by university economists, by men who specialized much more thoroughly than their mainly non-academic predecessors—financiers, journalists, and civil servants. But what might be called the first generation of *universitaires* began their specialization in economics mainly at a much later age than their successors. Marshall first turned to political economy in his 26th year, but hardly began to specialize before he was about 30 (1871–4), and then was lecturing on moral and political philosophy, economic history, and the history of economic thought. Edgeworth was over 30, and Wicksteed nearer 40, before turning systematically to theoretical economics, Sidgwick and Hobson never 'specialized' at all. Most had lectured for some time in subjects other than economics, often on logic and scientific method (but not on law which was the most closely related discipline in Germany).

In 1870 Cairnes put the number of students of political economy in the whole of London at well under 100. But towards the turn of the century an immense development of the subject as an academic specialism was to begin, marked by the founding of the Royal Economic Society and its specialist journal (1890-1), of the London School of Economics (1895), and of the Cambridge Economics Tripos (1903).

Standards of rigour and precision in the formulation of pure theory, or rather in the superstructure thereof (hardly in the foundations) were to be higher, beyond all recognition, than ever before, and progress in this respect was to be unprecedentedly rapid. A heightened detachment of view and also a closer professional spirit are discernible. But such progress, along with the more intense specialization, naturally has a reverse side or opportunity cost, and this sort of cost notoriously often tends to be underestimated. Economics had been, on the one side, the product of the topical writings of bankers, merchants, and administrators, about their own pressing practical problems, and, on the other side, of the thinking of philosophers, and particularly of political and 'moral' philosophers, who connected up their ideas about man 'in the everyday business of life', with their ideas about the rest of man's nature and activities. The development of economics as an academic specialism tended to result, in some degree at any rate, in less close and direct relationships with both these original sources of inspiration. We are not here attempting to weigh these costs of specialization against the immense and spectacular gains. We are, of course, only dealing with a small particular example of a universal development pervading all branches of knowledge and all human activities:

> No one, not even Cambridge was to blame;
> —Blame if you like the human situation—

Cf. G. M. Young, writing of the close of the Victorian age:

The common residual intelligence is becoming impoverished for the benefit of the specialist, the technician, and the aesthete: we leave behind us the world of historical iron-masters and banker historians, geological divines and scholar tobacconists, with its genial watchword: to know something of everything and everything of something: and through the gateway of the Competitive Examination we go out into the Waste Land of Experts, each knowing so much about so little that he can neither be contradicted nor is worth contradicting. (*Victorian England, Portrait of an Age*, p. 160).

2

W. S. Jevons

1. The 'Letters and Journal'

WILLIAM STANLEY JEVONS was born in Liverpool in 1835, a
year after the death of Malthus, and died in 1882, a year before
the birth of Keynes. At the age of 15 he was sent to London
to University College School, and a year later to University College
itself. It was at this time, as a rather unhappy boarder in lodgings in
London, that his interests first turned to the study of the urban society
around him. With a very serious sense of mission he pondered deeply
how he should best make use of his intellectual gifts: 'I began to think
that I could and ought to do more than others. A vague desire and
determination grew upon me . . .': a determination he was to describe
later from Australia to be 'powerfully good, that is to be good not
towards one, or a dozen, or a hundred, but towards a nation or the
world'.[1] Jevons's *Letters and Journal* is not only a book unique among
the published writings of economists, but a Victorian document, not
as representative as Mill's *Autobiography*, but with as many intensely
interesting and sympathetic passages. It makes it particularly tempting
and profitable to follow his intellectual growth, particularly in his
Australian years.[2]

Jevons was studying chemistry and botany at University College.
But his first inclinations towards the study of society are traceable to
these opening years of the 1850's. 'It was in 1851 that I first began, at
the age of sixteen, to study the industrial mechanism of society.'[3] As
Marshall was to do in industrial cities some fifteen years later, Jevons

---

[1] *Letters and Journal* (edited by his wife), 1886, pp. 12 and 96.
[2] Keynes discovered Jevons's *Letters and Journal* during his first readings on economics. See his letter to Lytton Strachey of 8.7.1905 (*Life of J. M. Keynes*, by R. F.
Harrod, p. 107): 'I am convinced that he was one of *the* minds of the century. He has the
curiously exciting style of writing which one gets if one is good enough—particularly
in his Investigations into Currency and Finance, a most thrilling volume. Moreover his
letters and journal prove that he was probably apostolic.' 'Apostolic' seems to have been
about the highest adjective Keynes could have bestowed at this time. Nevertheless we may
doubt whether Jevons was in fact 'apostolic' in the sense this seems to have had for
Lytton Strachey and Keynes. For one thing, Sidgwick was held to be emphatically *not*—
'apostolic'.
[3] *Principles of Economics* (edited by H. Higgs), p. vii.

used to go for long walks through the poorest parts of the Dickensian London of the early fifties looking at 'the condition of the people'. He writes (*aet.* 17) that the book he wants most to obtain is that wonderful pioneer social survey, Mayhew's *London Labour and London Poor*, 'the only book I know of to learn a little about the real condition of the poor in London'. (*Letters and Journal*, p. 29.) Among his early projects was *Notes and Researches on Social Statistics or the Science of Towns, especially as regards London and Sydney*. Some chapters on Sydney were completed and have been published in Australia, including one with the title 'Social Cesspools of Sydney', written in 1858, from which we may quote a few passages:

> To a person of humane feelings, . . . the sight and acquaintance of social ills, has the same lively, although painful, interest that a rare and terrible bodily disease has to the devoted physician. . . . A great city is to him a thing worthy of deep research and reflection. . . . That man who can witness all the phases of a city unmoved, and uninterested, is himself a criminal, a slave of pride and evil feelings. . . . It seems to me that he who bears a right feeling towards his fellowmen, should feel a very lively and exciting interest in many subjects social and sanitary.[1]

Jevons is sometimes held up as a pioneer of the cool detached approach to social and economic problems, supposedly characteristic of the natural scientist. This is to a large extent true, but in his original interest and impetus he was warm and *engagé* enough, as his Australian sociological work clearly witnesses.

Jevons never followed up later his *Science of Towns* or social surveys, the idea of which seems to have been entirely his own, stimulated possibly by Mayhew. But as the footnotes to his unfinished *Principles* show, he always retained a very healthy appetite—not invariably enjoyed by contributors to theoretical economics—for the detailed facts about mankind 'in the everyday business of life'.

The economic crisis of 1847–8 had brought a sudden Victorian bankruptcy on the family firm, a Liverpool engineering business, which had lasting effects on Jevons's life, and seems to have made a deep impression on him. When in 1853 a chance occurred of a very well-paid post as assayer at the Sydney mint his father pressed him to cut short his studies without a degree and sail for Australia, where he spent his 19th to his 24th years. From the first he regarded his Australian

---

[1] *v.* La Nauze, *Political Economy in Australia*, pp. 33 ff. Professor La Nauze mentions also a further unpublished paper called 'Sydney by Night' which is apparently not quite as interesting as its title might suggest.

sojourn as a temporary financial necessity and family duty. He used it to amass a small financial capital for his future studies and, infinitely more important, profiting by his long periods of solitary thought, to build up a capital of embryo ideas, which much of the rest of his life work as an economist was devoted to developing. The family misfortune had led Jevons to the ideal conditions for independent and original thought: solitude, much free time, and the important books but not too many of them.[1]

It was in the middle of his period at Sydney that the social sciences and political economy came more and more to be Jevons's main— though never by any means his exclusive—scientific interest, and it is easy to trace back to their Australian origin the seeds of what were to be his three main contributions to economics.

1. His most important spare-time activity in Sydney was meteorology, and he soon established himself as the leading authority on Australian climate. His later expertise in the recording and charting of vast quantities of numerical data, his diagrammatic presentation of statistics, and, furthermore, his meteorological way of looking at the economic 'weather', all deployed so superbly in his '*Investigations* in *Currency and Finance*', clearly derive from this early self-training. Obviously, also, his post as assayer, though in itself that of a chemist or metallurgist, prompted his interest in problems of gold supply and currency.

2. The origin of Jevons's theory of capital is also clearly traceable in the *Letters and Journal* to his Australian years. Those who emphasize the role of introspection in the construction of economic and other theories have a model example for their case, such as it is, in Jevons's theory of capital or capitalization. His ideas about capital, time, and productivity grew steadily and directly out of his introspective ponderings about how best to 'lay out' his own life and abilities, and how to justify his decision at a critical turning-point in his life. In Sydney he had 'an income of £700, a light and not uninteresting business, a pretty country and cheerful town, a few not unpleasant acquaintances, plenty of employments, scientific, musical or otherwise, and finally a

---

[1] John Morley's dictum apropos of Burke may well be cited here: 'Few men, if any, have ever acquired a settled mental habit of surveying human affairs broadly, of watching the play of passion, interest, circumstance, in all its comprehensiveness, and of applying the instruments of general conceptions and wide principles to its interpretation with respectable constancy, unless they have, at some early period of their manhood, resolved the greater problems of society in independence and isolation.' (*Encyclopaedia Britannica*, 11th ed.)

house of one's own'. (Letter 1.10.1856.) His decision was to sacrifice all this in the present, to increase his intellectual capital and his future abilities and usefulness: 'I have always worked and thought of the future instead of enjoying the present.' (Ibid.) 'It is perfectly right to lay out one's life before one, to invest a large capital in it, as it were, even with the hope of very distant and uncertain returns; this indeed is the only way of using life with true economy and effect.' (11.1.1858.) Finally, he counsels his sister (30.1.1859):

I think you do not duly appreciate the comparative importance of *preparation and performance*; or perhaps, as I may illustrate it, of capital and labour. You desire to begin and hammer away at once, instead of spending years in acquiring strength and skill, and then striking a few blows of immensely greater effect than your unskilled ones, however numerous, could be. We enter here into one of those deeply-laid and simple propositions of economy which I hope some day to work out in a symmetrical and extensive manner, hitherto unattempted even by Mill or Adam Smith. It comprehends the whole question of education and the employment of capital and industry, and will define the proper relation of *preparation and performance*.[1] (*v. Letters and Journal*, pp. 103, 114–15, and 226.)

3. There are not the same overt traces in Jevons's journal of the origins of his marginal utility theory of value. But it was only nine months after his return to England that he announced to his brother, at about the same time as his theory of capital, his discovery of 'the true theory of economy' . . . ('so thoroughgoing and consistent that I cannot now read other books on the subject without indignation', *Letters and Journal*, p. 151). Some of the first steps towards this discovery can be found in the later Australian pages of the *Letters and Journal* and in Jevons's first writings on political economy in Sydney newspapers.

It was 1857 that was the crucial year in Jevons's development as an economist. It was then that he wrote that 'the subject I have been most of all concerned in for the last six months is political economy'. (*Letters and Journal*, p. 89.) In the same year, too, he read Lardner's *Railway Economy*, and wrote his first articles on economic subjects in criticism of the land and railway policy of the New South Wales Government.[2] From his earliest studies Jevons saw pure economic

---

[1] Quoted by L. Robbins, 'The Place of Jevons in the History of Economic Thought', *Manchester School*, 1936. See also a letter of Jevons for 9.7.1858, in the *Letters and Journal*.

[2] Dionysius Lardner (1793–1859) is one of a number of curious characters who have their niche in the history of nineteenth-century economic thought. After holding the chair of Natural Philosophy at University College, London, he eloped with an Army

problems as optimum-allocation problems: 'Economy, scientifically speaking,' he noted in 1858, 'is a very contracted science; it is in fact a sort of mathematics which calculates the causes and effects of man's industry, and shows how it may best be applied.' (*Letters and Journals*, p. 101.)

Jevons's approach to theoretical economics was thus by way of practical controversies over railway-rate fixing and railway development. The problems of public utilities, and of their costing and pricing policies, were growing very rapidly in importance in the middle decades of the nineteenth century, and the labour and cost-of-production theories of value as then formulated, had little to contribute to their elucidation. The cost-of-production theory was at least a part of an explanation of competitive pricing, but the pricing policies of public monopolies, often with obviously heavy fixed costs and low variable costs, were a challenge to fresh thinking which, as we noted in the previous chapter, was clearly at work on some of the main pioneers of marginal analysis.

So much for Jevons's route to the more important half of 'marginal utility', the 'marginal' half. The 'utility' half was at hand in a number of earlier English 'utility' theorists, notably in Bentham. The challenging opening statement of his 1862 paper (para. 2) to the British Association is obviously of Benthamite inspiration: 'A true theory of economy can only be attained by going back to the great springs of human action—*the feelings of pleasure and pain.*'

Jevons arrived back in England in September 1859, and after an interruption of a similar length, and at a similar age, to those that were to be experienced by many in the twentieth century, set to work again

officer's wife and spent much of the rest of his life in Paris compiling encyclopaedic works on popular science. As J. R. Hicks discovered, Cournot translated some of these works into French. In the middle of his compendious book *Railway Economy* (1850), in a chapter on 'Receipts, Tariffs, Profits', there is a diagram plotting total receipts and total costs against price. It is pointed out that the point of maximum profit is not that of maximum total receipts, but occurs where the curve of gross receipts is parallel to that of 'the expenses of conveyance'. Jevons acknowledged his debt to Lardner's method of presentation of this piece of analysis, which so closely resembles Cournot's treatment of monopoly. But Jevons could hardly have extricated this from a work like Lardner's, if his own thoughts had not been moving in the same direction. Lardner's is a very miscellaneous book. The next chapter is entitled 'Accidents on the Railways' and is followed by 'Plain Rules for Railway Travellers' ('Rule I: Never Attempt to Get Out of a Railway Carriage while it is moving—no matter how slowly'). Lardner's book apparently also has some importance in the history of accounting ideas for providing an early case of the distinction between fixed and variable costs, the concept of variable costs coming very near, of course, to that of marginal costs. See also Hicks, *Econometrica*, 1934, p. 339.

at University College, London, for his B.A. and M.A. The next five or six years, when Jevons was an unknown student in London, show a marvellous record of arduous and original intellectual achievement in the face, often, of much discouragement. His pioneer works on financial statistics were published at his own expense and met with little recognition, and his paper to the British Association summarizing, albeit not too lucidly, his theories of value and capital, attracted no attention.

It was with the publication of *The Coal Question* in 1865 that Jevons's work first began to receive attention. It was his first full-length book, written with great speed and ardour, with the intention of shocking and attracting public opinion. The thesis of the book was modelled somewhat on Malthus's population theory, with British industry in the role of the consuming population, and limited coal stocks in the place of limited corn supplies and agricultural land. Just as Malthus did not allow for the vast granaries of the New World, so Jevons did not allow sufficiently for the development of alternative sources of power. In 1936 Keynes found the book 'overstrained and exaggerated' tracing it to 'a certain hoarding instinct' . . . 'a readiness to be alarmed and excited by the idea of the exhaustion of resources', an element in his make-up linked, perhaps, with the family bankruptcy in his boyhood.[1]

After another world war, however, *The Coal Question* undoubtedly makes much more impressive reading. It clearly foresaw the gradual rise in the cost of coal, and the embarrassment this would probably bring to Britain's industrial position. For 1865 it shows a clairvoyant understanding of the fleeting temporary nature of British industry's supremacy as the workshop of the world, and called (though rather vaguely) for social action while there was yet time: 'As a nation we have too much put off for the hour what we ought to have done at once. We are now in the full morning of our national prosperity—and are approaching noon. Yet we have hardly begun to pay the moral and the social debts to millions of our countrymen which we must pay before the evening.' (Introduction to 2nd ed., 1866, p. l.)

Jevons foresaw, too, the rise to industrial supremacy and the incalculable economic potential of the United States, and in particular that 'at last a sound system of metallurgical industry will grow up on the banks of the Ohio, capable of almost indefinite expansion'. (p. 428.)

The Coal Question established Jevons's name and position among

[1] *Journal of the Royal Statistical Society*, 1936, p. 519.

political economists. His intellectual biography subsequently becomes rather less interesting, and we may turn now to his main work under the three heads of 'Investigations in Currency and Finance', 'The Theory of Political Economy', and 'Political Economy and the Economic Role of the State'.

2. *Investigations in Currency and Finance*

The first of Jevons's 'Investigations' was a brief paper written in 1862 on seasonal fluctuations. He explains his approach by stating that 'all commercial fluctuations should be investigated according to the same scientific methods with which we are familiar in other complicated sciences, such especially as meteorology and terrestial magnetism'. (*Investigations*, 1st ed., 1884, p. 4.) The paper was accompanied by some of the charts (modelled of course on meteorological charts), of the kind which Jevons was among the pioneers in employing for the portrayal of economic statistics. But Jevons's outstanding work in this field, and perhaps the greatest of all his many and varied achievements, is his second paper in this volume, a study of secular movements, 'On a Serious Fall in the Value of Gold' (1863). In the ten or fifteen years following the gold discoveries in California and Australia at the middle of the century there had been considerable speculation about the effect of the increased gold supply on the price-level. For some time such authorities as Newmarch and McCulloch had doubted whether any appreciable fall in the value of gold had taken place. Jevons in his paper: (1) gave what proved to be a remarkably accurate measure of the depreciation of gold (9% between 1848–50 and 1860–2); (2) solved virtually all the basic problems in the technique of calculating price index-numbers (the problems of weighting, of 'representative' commodities, &c.); (3) gave a penetrating analysis of the effects on the different types of income of changes in the value of money, and a prescient hint or two about the trade cycle. He concluded that the fall in the value of gold had, on balance, a beneficial stimulating effect.

Here is Keynes's verdict on this work:

In the subject of index numbers Jevons made as much progress in this brief pamphlet as has been made by all succeeding authors put together. . . . For unceasing fertility and originality of mind applied, with a sure touch and unfailing control of the material, to a mass of statistics, involving immense labour for an unaided individual ploughing his way through with no precedents and labour-saving devices to relieve his task, this pamphlet stands unrivalled in the history of our subject. (Op. cit., p. 525.)

In the course of this essay Jevons had referred in passing to the subject of economic crises, suggesting that

the remote cause of these commercial tides ... seem(s) to lie in the *varying proportion which the capital devoted to permanent and remote investment bears to that which is but temporarily invested soon to reproduce itself.* [Jevons's italics.] ... Permanent investments in houses, ships, improvements of land, manufactures, mines, railways, foreign loans or undertakings ... are the great means by which the wealth of the country is increased. ... It is the peculiarity of these great and permanent works to be multiplied at particular periods ... when any new discovery or fresh employment is eagerly taken up. During such a mania, industry is thrown into extraordinary activity and also into unusual channels. (p. 28.)

Jevons never found time to follow up these ideas, which may have been suggested to him by James Wilson's essays, and certainly by those of fellow members of the Manchester Statistical Society in the 1860's.[1] After some further papers on the history of prices since 1782, and on the autumnal pressure in the money market, he made no further investigations in currency or finance for about ten years. When he eventually did so, he was concerned partly with bimetallism, but mainly with his theory that sun-spots cause bad harvests and in turn economic depressions. He never succeeded in formulating his theory, in particular the lengths of the periods involved, with his usual clarity, but it may well have contained a much more valuable contribution to the explanation of some of Britain's mid-nineteenth-century depressions than it seems to afford for the twentieth-century phenomena.

In statistical studies Jevons was a pioneer among theoretical economists of his period, of whom only Pareto attempted anything at all comparable in economic statistics. Some notes he had prepared for an introduction to his volume of *Investigations* state his purpose:

These papers are throughout an attempt to substitute exact inquiries, exact numerical calculations, for guess-work and groundless argument ... to investigate inductively the intricate phenomena of trade and industry. ... Perhaps one might say that theory is all-important, and yet fact is all-important also. ... It is natural, moreover, in approaching the difficulties of the moral sciences, to look for aid and example to the most nearly proximate sciences. (p. xxiv.)

Jevons's great Austrian contemporary, Carl Menger, also called for more *exakt* economic studies, but the 'exactness' which each of the two pioneers of marginal utility was urging differed completely. The

[1] See below Chapter XXII, Sections 4 and 5.

'exactness' which Jevons wanted to begin to aim at meant the replacing of impressionist *a-priori* guesswork by some attempt at relative
quantitative precision, where possible. The *exaktheit* which Menger
valued, was definitional exactness, or pure logical precision and the
inevitability of logical deduction. Secondly, the 'theory' which was for
Jevons 'all important', in investigating crises or any other phenomena,
was not to be obtained simply by setting out some extremely general
postulate and deducing conclusions from it, as one deduces allocation
formulae from a postulate about maximizing behaviour. 'Theory' for
Jevons meant rather the formulation of explanatory hypotheses, by
the testing of which inductive investigations could be directed and
controlled.

As to monetary policy Jevons was a *laissez-faire* agnostic, because
in his day the factual basis and the machinery for a policy simply did
not exist: 'The amount of money itself can be no more regulated than
the amounts of corn, iron, cotton, or other common commodities produced and consumed by a people.' (*Money*, 23rd ed., p. 340.)

Finally, we may note at this point that on the subject of effective
demand Jevons, in the odd sentence or two in which he approached
the problem, followed precisely the line of his *bête noire*, J. S. Mill, in
holding that no meaning other than an 'evidently absurd and self-
contradictory' one can be given to the concept of a general glut or
general over-production, 'so that industry would be stopped, employment fail, and all but the rich would be starved by the superfluity of
commodities'. In spite of his onslaught on Mill's four propositions on
Capital, Jevons never questioned Millian orthodoxy on general gluts
and effective demand, although shortly before the brief section on
'Overproduction', from which we have just quoted, he had referred to
a suggestive passage in Berkeley's *Querist*, one of the most notable of
the numerous eighteenth-century champions of the effective demand
principle. (*v.* Jevons's *Theory of Political Economy*, 4th ed., pp. 183
and 202–3 and the sections on Mill in the *Principles of Economics*.)

3. *The Theory of Political Economy*

As we have seen, Jevons had formulated the essentials of his theory
of value by 1860, and he presented them briefly in his paper to the
British Association (sent in 1862 and published 1866). The article
passed unnoticed, and for some years Jevons was devoting himself to
a wide range of other subjects. In 1868 the publication of Fleeming

Jenkin's *Graphic Representation of the Laws of Supply and Demand* apparently decided Jevons to hasten the completion of his own work on theoretical economics, his ideas on which he had previously been intending to let develop for some further years.[1] Here is the reason for that lack of finish and thoroughness for which the *Theory of Political Economy* has sometimes been criticized. But whatever signs of hastiness the *Theory* may show, Jevons, especially in the Preface to the Second Edition, always showed a painstaking and generous regard for the work both of his predecessors and for still-living contemporaries, with the single exception of his hyper-critical attitude to J. S. Mill, and a certain, perhaps excusable, impatience with Ricardo.

The book opens with a fanfare of incisive challenges to orthodoxy and to J. S. Mill's *Principles* in particular, which was now 23 years old though still the dominant authority. Jevons expresses high confidence in the 'substantial correctness' of his notions (notably that 'value depends entirely on utility'), but in the first edition he was somewhat uncertain about its significance: 'The usefulness of the theory is a different question from that of its truth, and is one upon which I am not quite so confident.' (p. 25.) This reservation did not appear in later editions, as perhaps it should. A part of Jevons's general challenge in his Introduction consisted in his enthusiastic claims for the mathematical method, by which Jevons meant the full econometric combination of the mathematical formulation of theory filled out with statistical content.

From the chapters on the Theory of Pleasure and Pain and the Theory of Utility, with their investigations of the seven Benthamite

[1] Fleeming Jenkin (1833–85) was Professor of Engineering at Edinburgh, and his economic studies started from the criticisms of the wage-fund doctrine which were being made at the end of the sixties by W. T. Thornton and others. This led him (like Thornton) to an analysis of supply and demand, in the first instance for labour, and he became a pioneer of the graphic treatment. His papers (first published 1868–72; see the London reprint, 1931) contain many valuable and fundamental, though brief, suggestions, including:

1. A very fair and able treatment of the economic power and possibilities of trade unions.

2. The clarification of the concepts of demand and supply as depending on subjective estimates of the future (p. 99).

3. The criticism of Jevons's concept of utility in that it 'admits of no practical measurement' (p. 109), and the basing of demand and supply analysis on the facts of the market.

4. The concept of consumers' surplus is suggested (though not named) in his paper on *The Incidence of Taxes*.

5. The importance of new demand and a high level of consumption is emphasized as necessary to maintain activity and wealth in a progressive society (see the admirable popular paper on *Is One Man's Gain Another Man's Loss?*).

'circumstances' of pleasure and pain and of the dimensions of utility, we may note simply: (1) that for Jevons the degree of utility of a commodity is a function of the quantity of that commodity only; (2) that he holds that for his purposes the 'utilities' of different people need not be compared, and that in any case they cannot be ('Every mind is thus inscrutable to every other mind, and no common denominator of feeling seems to be possible', 4th ed., p. 14); (3) His formulation of the Law of the Variation of Utility (p. 45) and of the 'final degree of utility' (p. 51), which is, in later terminology, marginal utility (or the utility of the marginal increment) divided by the size of the marginal increment (Jevons, of course, never used the word 'marginal'); (4) His statement of the consumer's allocation formula for a commodity capable of several uses, that the final degrees of utility in the different uses must be equal (pp. 59–60), a pattern for so much of theoretical economics in the coming decades.

It is interesting to speculate as to how Jevons would have met the powerful criticisms of hedonist and utilitarian psychologizing which two or three decades later were to be levelled at his form of marginal utility analysis. On the whole, it seems quite probable that Jevons might well have been ready to accept, or even to put himself at the head of, the sort of criticism of which Irving Fisher was the pioneer.[1] His 'solipsism', or his objection to the interpersonal comparison of utilities, marked him off as a much more cautious utilitarian than Edgeworth. The very high praise which Jevons has for Cournot's work which is concerned with 'the phenomenal laws of supply and demand', would also seem to support our speculation. And although Jevons recognized that Cournot 'did not frame any ultimate theory of the ground and nature of utility and value', his conception of and respect for the principles of scientific method might well have induced him to carry through a reformulation of his theory, even if this meant abandoning much of its original content.

Proceeding to the Theory of Exchange, Jevons gives a clear account of the conditions necessary for a competitive market, summarizing them in his Law of Indifference. But he defines a market as consisting of 'two or more persons' dealing in two or more commodities, without discussing at all how very differently the market mechanism will almost certainly work if there are only two parties and two commodities, or (very many) more. In fact his confusing concept of 'Trading Bodies' seems to be intended to make one model cover both

---

[1] See, for example, his posthumous *Principles of Economics*, p. 12.

two-party and two-commodity barter, and a competitive market in a monetary economy. As a result neither case gets clearly formulated.

The general result of exchange will be that 'a person procures such quantities of commodities that the final degrees of utility of any pair of commodities are inversely as the ratios of exchange of the commodities'. (p. 139.) From this it is concluded, with little or no qualification, that 'so far as is consistent with the inequality of wealth in every community, all commodities are distributed by exchange so as to produce the maximum of benefit' and 'a perfect freedom of exchange must be to the advantage of all'. (pp. 141–2.) Jevons did not draw much on this doubtful generalization in his discussion of economic policy.

Jevons had shown more caution in a discussion of statics and dynamics:

> We must carefully distinguish . . . between the Statics and Dynamics of this subject. The real condition of industry is one of perpetual motion and change. . . . If we wished to have a complete solution of the problem in all its natural complexity, we should have to treat it as a problem of motion— a problem of dynamics. But it would surely be absurd to attempt the more difficult question when the more easy one is yet so imperfectly within our power. It is only as a purely statical problem that I can venture to treat the action of exchange. Holders of commodities will be regarded not as continuously passing on these commodities in streams of trade, but as possessing certain fixed amounts which they exchange until they come to equilibrium. (p. 93.)

This is pressing towards a vital distinction, though it overestimates the range and content of his static formulae. Even under the simplifying assumption of fixed initial stocks the path to equilibrium cannot be described in purely static maximization formulae. Jevons makes no attempt at a dynamic model such as Walras's model of *tâtonnements*, or trial and error, by the 'crying' of prices.

Jevons's chapter on Exchange concludes with a deservedly celebrated passage attacking labour and cost of production theories of value: ·

> The fact is, that *labour once spent has no influence on the future value of any article*: it is gone and lost for ever. In commerce bygones are for ever bygones; and we are always starting clear at each moment, judging the values of things with a view to future utility. Industry is essentially prospective, not retrospective; and seldom does the result of any undertaking exactly coincide with the first intentions of its promoters.
>
> But though labour is never the cause of value, it is in a large proportion

of cases the determining circumstance, and in the following way:—*Value depends solely on the final degree of utility. How can we vary this degree of utility?—By having more or less of the commodity to consume. And how shall we get more or less of it?—By spending more or less labour in obtaining a supply.* According to this view, then, there are two steps between labour and value. Labour affects supply, and supply affects the degree of utility, which governs value, or the ratio of exchange. In order that there may be no possible mistake about this all-important series of relations, I will re-state it in a tabular form, as follows:—

> *Cost of production determines supply;*
> *Supply determines final degree of utility;*
> *Final degree of utility determines value.* (pp. 164–5.)

It is this passage that evoked Keynes's comment that Jevons chiselled in stone while Marshall knitted in wool.

Whether one is concerned to play up or to play down the 'revolutionary' significance of Jevons's *Theory of Political Economy*, it must be agreed that he only really completed one-half of the marginal 'revolution' or evolution. With the aid of the marginal concept he expounded the maximizing allocation formula for the consumer buying or exchanging (or, in isolation, using) consumers' goods and services. He did not work out the corresponding formula for the producer buying producers' goods or services from their owners. One of the most important contributions of Menger's contemporary work was that it straightway applied the same allocation analysis to producers' goods and services as it did to consumers' goods and services, thus laying the essential foundation for a marginal productivity analysis of distribution.

It is true that already in 1860 Jevons was claiming, in a letter to his brother, to have discovered 'a determining principle for *interest, profits of trade, wages*'; that 'the common law is that demand and supply of labour and capital determine the division between wages and profits'; and that 'the whole capital employed can only be paid for at the same rate as the last portion added; hence it is the increase of produce or advantage which this addition gives, that determines the interest of the whole'. (*Letters and Journal*, p. 155.) It is true, also, that in the course of three or four pages (pp. xlvi ff.) in the very valuable Preface to the Second Edition (1879), Jevons is again on the verge of formulating the distribution problem in terms of marginal productivity. He there gives a clear statement of the alternative cost doctrine, and then goes on to emphasize the 'parallelism' between the theories of rent and of wages, which might have been the beginnings of a 'co-ordination of the laws of distribution' according to the marginal productivity principle. But these brief suggestions in the new preface were not followed up in the text of the chapters on Rent and Labour, which were left as in the first edition. In his last treatment of wages, in *The State in Relation to Labour*, there are similar hints of a marginal productivity theory, not fully worked out or followed up.

Jevons's chapter on the Theory of Rent follows closely that of McCulloch and James Mill, being based on differences in the fertility of different pieces of land, and on the law of diminishing returns. His Theory of Labour is a theory of allocation according to a formula by which the marginal disutility of the labour is balanced against the utility of the produce. The production unit, the firm, and the entrepreneur appear very little in Jevons's *Theory of Political Economy*, and profits are hardly treated at all beyond resolving them into 'wages of superintendence, insurance against risk, and interest'. (p. 270.)

The most interesting of the later chapters is that on the Theory of Capital, or, rather, Capitalization: originating in his introspective ponderings in Australia of his own and his sister's personal educational problems, Jevons's marginal productivity theory of capital was first expounded in the letter to his brother of 1860 which we have just quoted above.

In his chapter in the *Theory of Political Economy* Jevons defines capital as consisting 'merely in the aggregate of those commodities which are required for sustaining labourers of any kind or class engaged in work'. (p. 223.) This includes food and clothing, but not housing, whether these goods are still held as stocks by producers or are already owned by the final consumer. (p. 261.) In fact 'capital' for Jevons is free capital, and he prefers to speak of a railway or a factory rather as representing so much capital 'fixed in it', than as 'fixed capital'.

The single and all-important function of capital [Jevons explains] is to enable the labourer to await the result of any long-lasting work,—to put an interval between the beginning and the end of an enterprise. . . . Capital enables us to make a great outlay in providing tools, machines, or other preliminary works, which have for their sole object the production of some important commodity, and which will greatly facilitate production when we enter upon it. (pp. 223–4.)

Jevons then proceeds to screw up this blend of definition, and rather loose and wide generalization, into a much tighter formula in which it is still more difficult to tell how much is definition and how much is empirical generalization, technical or economic:

> Whatever improvements in the supply of commodities lengthen the average interval between the moment when labour is exerted and its ultimate result or purpose accomplished, such improvements depend upon the use of capital. (p. 228.) . . . The function of capital is simply this, that labour which would produce a certain commodity M_1, if that commodity were needed immediately for the satisfaction of wants, is applied so as to produce M_2 after the lapse of time t. The reason for this deferment is that M_2 usually exceeds M_1 and the difference or interest M_2–M_1 is commodity having the same dimensions as M_1. (p. 249.)

There may be many interesting facts, economic and technical, about the relations between different methods of production and the periods of time involved, in one sense or another, in using them. It was certainly tempting to try to organize these facts into some concise and precise formula, and comprehend this formula in a wider generalization about production 'periods', productivity, the quantity of 'capital', and the rate of interest. No doubt the attempt had to be made, and it was Jevons, linking up his introspective ponderings with Ricardian analysis, who launched the tempting generalizations about 'capital', 'time', and 'productivity', which were to receive such profound and prolix development in the celebrated volumes of Böhm-Bawerk.

4. *Political Economy and the State*

By every circumstance of family or early environment, Jevons's social philosophy was likely to start from, if not to end with, a vigorous individualism, and this is expressed very strongly in some of his earlier papers on social reform. 'Freedom for all commercial transactions is the spirit of improved legislation' he had written in his very first published sentences on political economy.[1] In the sixties he saw as the greatest danger that 'our working classes, with their growing numbers and powers of combination, may be led by ignorance to arrest the true growth of our liberty, political and commercial'.[2] In raising their own wages trade unions were only making things dearer for their fellow workers, and 'even if all could combine with equal ease they would only make all things dear and hinder the production of the commodities upon which we live'.

---

[1] *Empire*, Sydney, Australia, 8/4/1857.
[2] Introductory Lecture at Manchester, 1866.

More striking, as Keynes pointed out, is a vigorous attack on 'medical charities including all free public infirmaries, dispensaries and hospitals, and a large part of the vast amount of private charity as nourishing the dependence of the poor on the rich'.[1] Jevons's vision of social progress here implied a diminution in the social services as self-reliance and independence increased, rather than a steady expansion of public provision.

During the seventies, with the onset of the great depression, Jevons's views as to the functions of the State may have developed somewhat. One sort of activity in which he constantly supported a big increase was public expenditure on the 'Amusements of the People' (the title of one of his Essays in Social Reform). These he wanted to provide for by a far greater expenditure on State and municipal museums, orchestras, parks, libraries, and public clocks.

We have seen how in his 1876 Lecture on 'The Future of Political Economy', he called for a complete new branch ('statistical and political') of political economy, which should analyse the economic policies open to the State. In various essays and articles Jevons discussed problems of the state and economic policy, in particular the problem of nationalization. He supported the nationalization of the telegraphs, but opposed that of the railways. But the main contribution Jevons had time to make to this new branch of political economy was in *The State in Relation to Labour*, which deals in a non-specialist way with a range of practical problems of State policy. It displays to the full Jevons's power to give a live and lucid treatment of a great and complicated subject in a brief volume, but is not concerned very far with that analysis of economic principles in relation to State action on which Sidgwick was to found modern English 'welfare' economics.

He still holds that trade unions can only benefit themselves in a beggar-my-neighbour way by raising prices at the expense of their fellow workers. But he joins the attack on the Wages Fund doctrine, and recognizes that: 'One result which clearly emerges from a calm review is that all classes of society are trades unionists at heart, and differ chiefly in the boldness, ability and secrecy with which they push their respective interests.' (p. vi.) He held that 'the supposed conflict of labour with capital is a delusion. The real conflict is between producers

---

[1] Keynes's comment in his Centenary Lecture may be of interest: 'Perhaps it would brace us and strengthen us if we could feel again those astringent sentiments and face that vigorous east wind, believing so firmly in the future as to make almost anything endurable in the present' (1936).

and consumers.' Certainly there is here a 'contradiction' not confined to 'capitalism', and therefore in a sense more profound than the 'contradictions' of capitalism. But the direction in which Jevons looked for progress—whatever else there is to be said for his ideas—would hardly help to resolve this basic clash of interest. He placed his hopes in industrial partnership, and 'in such a modification of the terms of partnership as shall bind the interests of the employer to workman more closely together'. (p. 146.)

The State in Relation to Labour contains many model statements of the English empirical approach, that of Jevons, Sidgwick, Marshall, and Edgeworth, to problems of law and policy: law is

a system of adjustments and compromises, founded upon experience and trial. (p. 7.) . . . As in philosophy the first step is to begin by doubting everything, so in social philosophy, or rather in practical legislation, the first step is to throw aside all supposed absolute rights or inflexible principles. (p. 9.) . . . In discussing these matters we need above all things *discrimination*. One hundred modes of Government interference might be mentioned of which fifty might be very desirable and fifty condemnable. (p. 40.) . . . This question involves the most delicate and complicated considerations, and the outcome of the inquiry is that we can lay down no hard-and-fast rules, but must treat every case in detail upon its merits. (p. vii.)

In his conclusion to this, his last completed work, Jevons is at his eloquent best:

It is clear that there can be no royal road to legislation in such matters. We cannot expect to agree in utilitarian estimates, at least without much debate. We must agree to differ, and though we are bound to argue fearlessly, it should be with the consciousness that there is room for wide and bona fide difference of opinion. We must consent to advance cautiously, step by step, feeling our way, adopting no foregone conclusions, trusting no single science, expecting no infallible guide. We must neither maximise the functions of Government at the beck of quasi-military officials, nor minimise them according to the theories of the very best philosophers. We must learn to judge each case upon its merits, interpreting with painful care all experience which can be brought to bear upon the matter.

Moreover, we must remember that, do what we will, we are not to expect approach to perfection in social affairs. We must recognise the fact clearly that we have to deal with complex aggregates of people and institutions, which we cannot usually dissect and treat piece-meal. Tolerance, therefore, is indispensable. We may be obliged to bear with evil for a time that we may avoid a worse evil, or that we may not extinguish the beginnings of good. In the end we shall not be disappointed if our efforts are really directed towards that good of the people which was long ago pronounced to be the highest law. (p. 166.)

Jevons was drowned at the age of 46, an age by which Marshall, Edgeworth, and Wicksteed, for example, had not completed a fraction of the works for which they were subsequently renowned. There were only 23 years before his death from the time when he restarted his studies as an undergraduate on returning from Australia. In that time, in addition to the wide range of works we have touched upon, Jevons completed his weightiest single book *The Principles of Science* (1874), constructed a logical machine, wrote several best-selling textbooks on logic and political economy, 'discovered' Cantillon, gave detailed advice to the Chancellor, Robert Lowe, on taxation, completed several pioneering bibliographies, investigated muscular fatigue by experiments on himself, and wrote many essays on public utilities and social policy. For a number of years he had (unlike Marshall) to publish rapidly with an eye to establishing his own position and academic future. Inevitably many of his ideas were left incompletely worked out at the time of his death. He left unfinished a treatise on religion and science, an edition of Adam Smith, and his *Principles of Economics*. Of this Foxwell wrote: 'He had planned and partly written a great Treatise on Economics, which was, as he hoped, to be *the* achievement of his life, and in which he would have worked up the immense store of classified materials which he had been accumulating for more than twenty years.' There can be little doubt that in this work he would, among much else, have carried through much more completely the marginal analysis in which he had been a pioneer. Perhaps also he would have contributed to that science of commercial fluctuations which he had called for in 1876, and to which previously he had made such contributions. Anyhow, English economists would have faced the twentieth century with two main guides to the principles of the subject instead of one.

3
H. Sidgwick

1. *Sidgwick, Philosopher and Economist*

KEYNES once wrote of the English philosophical tradition as that 'of Locke and Berkeley and Hume, of Mill and Sidgwick, who in spite of their divergences of doctrine are united in a preference for what is matter of fact, and have conceived their subject as a branch rather of science than of the creative imagination, prose writers, hoping to be understood'. (*Treatise on Probability*, p. v.) That is the company in which Sidgwick belongs, that of the great philosophers and democratic thinkers of the English tradition, who were also the main architects of political economy. Sidgwick is, in fact, the last major English moral philosopher who made a noteworthy contribution to political economy, and for that reason alone his work would have a special interest. Modern intellectual conditions seem to make it increasingly unlikely that a thinker combining his particular range and quality can emerge in the twentieth century.

At a critical period in the seventies and eighties Sidgwick in Cambridge revised and restated for his day the tradition of Hume and J. S. Mill, when elsewhere in Britain, and notably at Oxford, this tradition was being more thoroughly abandoned and attacked in its own country than at any previous time. If in England political economy has been able to progress on its way, and often exercise a more powerful and comparatively more united influence, for better or for worse, than in most other countries, it has been because of the wide basis of common agreement on political and philosophical principles which the great writers of the English empirical tradition created. For they conceived their task as belonging not in the realms of theology and metaphysics, but in clearing a site, and providing an agreed foundation, for 'scientific' inquiry, and here, incidentally, unlike the German tradition, they drew no specially significant or dramatic distinction between the two broad groups of sciences included under the very rough headings of the 'natural' and 'social' (or 'moral') sciences. To compare the relation of Sidgwick to Marshall with that of Hume to Adam Smith a century before, would be to invite misunderstanding. Later on, apparently over the formation of the new separate Economics Tripos, they had fundamental differences. Nevertheless, Sidgwick guided the young Marshall at an important moment in his career (1867), and Marshall said of Sidgwick: 'I was fashioned by him. He was so to speak my spiritual father and mother.'

But Sidgwick's place in the history of economic thought—he is not much mentioned in most of the standard histories—is not simply that of a great political philosopher who, as he himself said of J. S. Mill, 'brought a higher degree of philosophical reflection to bear upon the exposition of the common doctrines of the science'. Nor was his role simply the significant one of having been Marshall's spiritual father (and mother). As Dr. Myint[1] has shown, Sidgwick contributed some very important pioneering distinctions and clarifications for that systematic analysis of economic policies, of which Jevons had seen the need. In addition to its analytical contribution, rendered in highly untechnical language, 'the great third book', as Edgeworth called it, of Sidgwick's *Principles*, is a classic discussion of the perennial problem of the role of the State in economic life. For those who set themselves the task of framing a practicable contribution to economic policy which will not break completely with the politico-economic principles of nineteenth-century Britain, there can surely be no better starting-point than Sidgwick's writings.

A lecturer in Classics, and later in Moral Philosophy, it was only after much work in the latter subject, and towards the end of the seventies, that he began to write on political economy. Long before that he relates how under Mill's influence: 'I was also strongly led as a matter of duty to study political economy thoroughly', though his views about the nature of the subject for some time seem to have been somewhat incomplete: 'I have been reading all kinds of things lately. I find out that political economy is what I really enjoy as an intellectual exercise. It is just in the right stage of scientific progress, and there are not too many facts to be got up.' (1865, *A Memoir*, p. 131.)

2. *The Principles of Economic Policy*

The first two of the three books of Sidgwick's *Principles* are arranged in the traditional pattern of Production, Distribution, and Exchange. A blend of ancient and modern, they illustrate Sidgwick's effort, followed by Marshall, to develop the knowledge of the subject without breaking with the treatment and terminology of the classics—in

---

[1] See H. Myint, *Theories of Welfare Economics*, pp. 125 ff.

contrast with Jevons and Wicksteed. No such modern conveniences as the concepts of the marginal unit or of elasticity are available in Sidgwick's *Principles*. The work is primarily founded on J. S. Mill's *Principles* of thirty-five years previously. But Sidgwick concentrated much more than Mill on a full discussion of

the principles of governmental interference with industry: whether with a view to a better organised Production or a more satisfactory Distribution of Wealth: since I conform so far to the older and more popular view of my subject as to consider the discussion of these principles an integral part of the theory of Political Economy. (*Principles*, 3rd ed., 1901, p. 26.)

One way of estimating Sidgwick's achievement in the third of the three books of his *Principles*, is to compare this with Mill's final book (V), *On the Influence of Government*. The comparison would not be in respect of Sidgwick's greater apparent readiness to accept and recommend government intervention or consider far-reaching measures of equalization, a comparison it would be difficult to draw because of the ambivalence of Mill's treatment at critical points, in which sweeping proposals for reform are combined with stern warnings against the extension of State action. The significant contrast between the two books would be in the far greater detail and precision of Sidgwick's scheme of analysis, in itself neutral, rather than in its particular political estimates.

More than a half of Mill's Book V is about taxation and different particular taxes. Income tax, Mill argues, should be *proportionate* above a certain minimum subsistence income, and savings must be exempt. (In opposing 'progression' Sidgwick followed Mill—and, in fact, the rule of most nineteenth-century liberal utilitarians—fairly precisely.) The strongest objection to any direct taxes, Mill held, was 'the present low state of public morality' which made fair assessment impossible. In Sidgwick's book taxation is given very brief treatment.

Both Mill and Sidgwick emphasize how elastic are the interpretations that can very well be put on the 'individualist minimum' of State action (i.e. the protection of the person and of property, the prevention of fraud, and the enforcing of contracts), and that a great extension of State action *could* have been based simply on these principles. When he comes to divergencies between private and social interests, Mill mentions monopolies and public utilities as 'even more irresponsible and unapproachable by individual complaints than the government' (Bk. V, Ch. XI, sect. 11) and goes so far as to argue that the State might as well take over in all cases in which individuals can only manage the concern by delegated agency: 'Whatever, if left to spontaneous agency, can only be done by joint-stock associations will often be as well, and sometimes better done, as far as the actual work is concerned, by the State. Government management is proverbially jobbing, careless and ineffective, but so likewise has generally been joint-stock management.' (Bk. V, Ch. XI, sect. 11.) Previously Mill had laid down that any industry which tends towards oligopoly (where 'competitors are so few' that warfare or combination is the rule) should be treated at once as a public utility and come under a unified public control, if not direct public operation (Bk. I, Ch. IX, sect. 3).

In the nationalization of all joint-stock associations and oligopolistic industries, in an inheritance law limiting the amount any one person should be allowed to acquire by inheritance to 'the amount of a moderate independence' (Bk. V, Ch. IX, sect. 1), and in the guaranteeing by law of subsistence to the destitute able-bodied (Bk. V, Ch. XI, sect. 13), Mill provides a basis for a very far-reaching socialistic programme. But throughout his book Mill constantly insists, much more strongly even than Sidgwick, on the great political dangers in the growth of governmental power and activity, which must be watched 'with un-remitting jealousy', and that 'perhaps this watchfulness is even more important in a democracy than in any other form of political society'. (Bk. V, Ch. XI, sect. 3.) We have already noticed Mill's section entitled '*Laisser-faire the General Rule*': 'Letting alone, in short, should be the general practice: every departure from it, unless required by some great good, is a certain evil.'

Thirty-five years later, and after there had been important reforms in the civil service, Sidgwick, though much more coolly critical of Utopian designs than Mill, was, nevertheless, prepared to give much less prominence to 'General Rules' in favour of *laisser-faire* and get down to cases. Sidgwick seemed to regard the tide of socialist legisla-tion as inevitable, and realized there might be still greater dangers to peace and freedom in bigoted and indiscriminate resistance to it.

His approach to the principles and method of economic theory is that of an empirical utilitarian, profoundly mistrustful of what he once described as that 'eager receptivity for abstract theory which is often found in powerful but imperfectly trained intellects'. (*Essays*, p. 138.) When preparing his address to the British Association on the Scope and Method of Political Economy, he noted in his diary: 'Really, in this as in other departments, my tendency is to scepticism, but scepti-cism of a humble empirical and more or less hopeful kind. I do not argue, or even think, that nothing is known, still less that nothing can be known by the received methods, but that of what is most important to know, we, as yet, know much less than most people suppose.' (*A Memoir*, p. 417.)

Sidgwick was bound to oppose to the uttermost any *a priori*, all-or-none, rules of policy claimed to render superfluous the piecemeal empirical study of particular cases:

There is indeed a kind of political economy which flourishes in proud independence of facts; and undertakes to settle all practical problems of Governmental interference or private philanthropy by simple deduction from one or two general assumptions of which the chief is the assumption of the universally beneficent and harmonious operation of self-interest well let alone. This kind of political economy is sometimes called 'orthodox', though it has the characteristic unusual in orthodox doctrines of being repudiated by the majority of accredited teachers of the subject. But whether orthodox or not, I must be allowed to disclaim all connection with it; the more completely this survival of the a priori politics of the eighteenth century can be banished to the remotest available planet, the better it will be, in my opinion, for the progress of economic science. (*Essays*, p. 171.)

It was apparently still necessary to emphasize such principles to the British Association, at any rate in 1885. Sidgwick went on to outline his constructive task as follows:

There will always be considerable disagreement in details among competent persons as to the propriety of Governmental interference in particular cases; but, apart from questions on which economic considerations must yield to political, moral, or social reasons of greater importance, it is an anachronism not to recognise fully and frankly the existence of cases in which the industrial intervention of Government is desirable, even with a view to the most economical production of wealth. Hence, I conceive, the present business of economic theory in this department is to give a systematic and carefully reasoned exposition of these cases, which, until the constitution of human nature and society are fundamentally altered, must always be regarded as exceptions to a general rule of non-interference. The statesman's decision on any particular case it does not belong to abstract theory to give; this can only be rationally arrived at after a careful examination of the special conditions of each practical problem at the particular time and place at which it presents itself. But abstract reasoning may supply a systematic view of the general occasions for Governmental interference, the different possible modes of such interference and the general reasons for and against each of them, which may aid practical men both in finding and in estimating the decisive considerations in particular cases. (*Essays*, p. 176.)

Sidgwick opens his Book III by asking how one is to formulate the desirable result which Political Economy seeks to realize, 'economy' being 'the art or method of attaining the greatest possible amount of some desirable result for a given cost, or a given result for the least possible cost'. According to Sidgwick, Adam Smith and his immediate successors conceived it as the maximization of the national production of wealth; and,

hardly appear to have entertained the notion of aiming at the best possible Distribution.... The subject of Political Economy considered as an Art [must] include besides the theory of provision for governmental expenditures, (1) the Art of making the proportion of produce to population a maximum, taking generally as a measure the ordinary standard of exchange value, so far as it can be applied: and (2) the Art of rightly distributing produce among members of the community, whether on any principle of Equity or Justice, or on the economic principle of making the whole produce as useful as possible. (*Principles*, 3rd ed., 1901, p. 396.)

Many economists today might have serious qualms about this free and easy introduction of 'Equity', 'Justice', and the 'useful', and certainly it is not without dangers. But Sidgwick was not trying to insist that any single optimum distribution can be laid down by the economist—we have already quoted him to the contrary. He does freely indulge in adjectives like 'beneficial' and 'harmful', and presents the argument that, other things being the same, the more equal the distribution of the national wealth the greater the aggregate of satisfactions derived from that wealth. But he at once insists that other things never are the same, or anything like the same, so that the proposition has little significance. Sidgwick's ambiguities are trivial, and Sidgwickian senses have always a disciplined lucidity. The purport of his argument is clear throughout, and his terminology therefore is as he employs it, harmless and, at worst, outmoded. It is always readily translatable, if such translation is preferred, into strictly neutral terms. (What is not harmless in this field is obscurity for which no clarification is obtainable, because it is there for the purpose of wrapping up prejudices and propaganda in a pseudo-scientific argument and terminology.)

Indispensable for the analysis of economic policies is Sidgwick's (and also Walras's) separation of the different effects of a policy into production and distribution effects, and his attempt to assess these separately. He does not try to suggest any scale or common denominator, in terms of 'welfare' or anything else, by which the two kinds of effects can be weighed and a balance struck. Of course, in particular cases he does give his judgement that 'beneficial' distribution effects would be outweighed by 'harmful' production effects, but he does not claim or suggest that such judgements rest on anything more solid than 'those vague and uncertain balancings of different quantities of happiness with which the politician has to content himself' (*Principles*, p. 397). Nor does he find it in any way necessary to introduce the concept of 'welfare' or 'economic welfare'. In some of his other works these terms very occasionally occur, but they have no role in the third book of his *Principles*, which could only be impaired in its lucidity and precision by their introduction.

Sidgwick points out that previous discussions of the inadequacies of the *laissez-faire* maxim (e.g. Cairnes's) had been based on a questioning of the assumption that men are the best judges of their own interests. Sidgwick is concerned to show that even in a society of 'economic men', natural liberty would have no tendency to realize the beneficial results claimed for it. (*Principles*, p. 403.) He presents a number of now well-known cases where the individual is unable 'to obtain through free exchange adequate remuneration for the services which he is capable of rendering to society', for instance, 'a well-placed lighthouse', afforestation, and scientific discovery. (*Principles*, p. 406.) He then notices the problem of self-perpetuating low wages and the vicious circle of low wages breeding inefficiency, which it is not in the interest of any single private employer to raise, but which it would increase productivity and benefit society as a whole to raise,—that is, the economic case for Trade Boards.

Sidgwick turns next to monopoly and industrial combination. He argues that combinations desirable in the interests of social production (e.g. in combating floods and pests, or in regulating fisheries, &c.) will not be carried through without social intervention, and goes on to discuss the wastes of imperfect competition, which he describes as competition of the sort that increases the number of producers, 'without augmenting their aggregate produce owing to the increased difficulty that each has in finding customers'. This 'seems to occur most conspicuously in the case of services of which the purchasers are somewhat deficient in commercial keenness and activity; so that each producer thinks himself likely to gain more on the whole by keeping up the price of his services rather than by lowering it to attract custom'. (*Principles*, p. 411.) Sidgwick is careful to distinguish such waste from the case of 'rational' preferences, or 'the convenience of maintaining established good will and business connections', and 'the saving of time and trouble in maintaining fixed habits of dealing with certain persons'. Advertising and selling costs are a related source of waste which Sidgwick discusses at this point.

Having outlined these cases of waste of productive resources, Sidgwick emphasizes that 'it does not, of course, follow that wherever laissez-faire falls short governmental interference is expedient; since the inevitable drawbacks and disadvantages of the latter may in any particular case, be worse, than the shortcomings of private industry'. These disadvantages are political, and would vary with the level of political morality. They include the dangers of adding to the central state power and of overburdening a single central organization, as well as those of irksome taxation and legislation leading to evasion of the law, and finally the danger of 'wasteful expenditure under the influence of popular sentiment,—since the mass of a people, however impatient of taxation, are liable to be insufficiently conscious of the importance of thrift in all the details of national expenditure'. (*Principles*, pp. 414–15.)

Sidgwick later reviews critically the chief actual cases in which governments had taken into their management branches of industry or had regulated private activities, the currency, education, land tenure, forestry, &c. He suggests as desirable the State guardianship of small-savings and even a State pawnbroking system. He has, also, a brief discussion of the pricing policies of public undertakings:

> Indeed if this capital were not borrowed, and if we had not to consider the need of raising supplies for other branches of governmental expenditure, there would seem to be no reason why the condition of paying interest should be regarded at all, any more than it would be regarded in a community socialistically organised: it would be economically advantageous to extend the supply of the commodity by cheapening its price so long as it more than repaid the total cost of labour spent in furnishing it—including the labour required for keeping it in repair and duly improving the instruments used in the business. (*Principles*, p. 558.)

However, Sidgwick then alters what might seem to be the significance of this conclusion by adding that it will only be desirable to make such a reduction where it is important for the community that the commodity in question should be widely used, since the national income sacrificed by this reduction in price must be made up by some other tax. (*Principles*, p. 559.)

3. Distribution and the Functions of the State

Sidgwick opens his discussion of Distributive Justice by taking up the very difficult task of trying to clarify those common notions of what is 'just', 'fair', and 'equitable', so often applied in discussions of the distribution of wealth. It is necessary to make this attempt because 'the conclusions of economic science have always been supposed to relate ultimately—however qualified and supplemented—to actual human beings; and actual human beings will not permanently acquiesce in a social order that common moral opinion condemns as unjust'. He reviews the main sources of income, wages, rent, interest, salaries, and profits, to see how far contemporary inequalities are to be condemned or justified on the grounds of distributive justice.

He arrives at a definition of fair wages as 'market wages as they would be under the conditions of the least possible inequality'. He is impressed by what seems to him, 'the growing element of fluctuation and uncertainty in the relations of demand and supply in consequence of the more extensive organization of industry through international exchange'. As a result,

the complexity of the causes affecting any worker's remuneration tends to increase in far greater ratio than his intellectual resources for forecasting their effects; so that the element of 'desert' in his gains and losses of income tends to become continually less instead of greater. . . . And if any Government were to attempt the extensive interference that would be required to make the security against unmerited fluctuations approximately complete, it would, I conceive, find an insuperable difficulty in discriminating between losses really inevitable and those that could have been prevented or largely reduced by foresight, promptitude, and versatility in adapting action to changed circumstances, so that governmental interference, by checking this spontaneous adaptation of the industrial system to the conditions of its growth, could be liable to impair seriously its productive efficiency. (*Principles*, pp. 509–10.)

Like most nineteenth-century economists Sidgwick was thoroughly suspicious of incomes from land rent. Though he felt it would be manifestly unjust to mulct the particular property owners who keep their wealth in the form of land, he contemplated, though rather unenthusiastically, a scheme for the nationalization of land with compensation. He links together high profits and salaries as both being not simply due to differences in ability and effort, but to the scarcity of persons able to obtain capital either for industrial investment or for personal investment in expensive training and education. There is, therefore, a strong distributional argument in favour of governmental action to remove the scarcities of educational opportunity which cause these differences, in addition to the argument on grounds of production.

This brings Sidgwick to the problems of interest and of distribution and the social order. He defines interest as the payment to the capitalist for the delay he allows to intervene between the application of labour and the consumption of its product.

> The real question therefore is not whether instruments ought to be made but whether it is fair that this delay involved in making them should have to be paid for. . . . It must be admitted, I think, first, that the social accumulation of instruments might conceivably be carried on by the community, and without any payment of interest; and secondly that there is no principle of abstract equity which renders it morally obligatory to carry it on as at present, by first allowing individuals to divide up the whole produce of social industry, and then promising them future payments if they will allow a portion of their shares to take the form of fresh instruments. . . . Nor do I think, that the difficulties of transition from the one system to the other, or the inevitable disappointment of expectations involved in it, would necessarily be more intense—though of course they would be indefinitely greater in extent—than those which in the course of modern history have actually attended the abolition of slavery in our colonies, of serfdom in Russia, or of oppressive feudal privileges in other European states. I do not mean to imply that the transition to socialism is to be classed with the changes just mentioned, even if it be regarded merely as a distant stage of social progress; but I conceive that in urging the reasons for not so regarding it we have to pass—as in the case of the remedies for inequality of opportunity that we have before discussed—from the point of view of distribution to that of production. I object to Socialism not because it would divide the produce of industry badly but because it would have so much less to divide. (*Principles*, p. 516.)

Sidgwick was unable to dismiss or overlook the self-interest of the individual as a continuous powerful motive force: 'I am convinced that no adequate substitute for it either as an impulsive or as a regulating force has as yet been found by any socialistic reformer'. (*Essays*, p. 202.)

Meanwhile the socialistic legislation for which, with no warm starry-eyed enthusiasm, Sidgwick was making a case, was in the first instance only recommended as 'a supplementary and subordinate element in a system mainly individualistic'. (*Elements of Politics*, p. 146.) Nevertheless, 'it seems to me quite possible that a considerable extension of the industrial functions of government might be on the whole advantageous, without any Utopian degree of moral or political improvement in human society. But at any rate to be successful such extension must, I think, be gradual.' (*Principles*, p. 529.)

As contrasted with the loss of the motive force of self-interest, the difficulty under socialism of distributing the produce of joint labour so as to apportion remuneration to desert seems comparatively slight.

It is clear that in a completely socialistic community the remuneration of superior qualities of labour could not be determined by reference to the 'market price' of such labour, as there would be no market outside the service of government, by which its price could be fixed: the 'fair' wages of such superior labourers would have to depend entirely on a governmental estimate of the value of their work. I do not, however, see that the influence of competition need be excluded altogether; there might be competition between one locality and another for the best workers, or even, to some extent, between different departments of a central government: and through such competition a tolerable estimate of the amount necessary to stimulate adequately to the acquisition of the required qualifications, and to compensate for any special outlay or sacrifices involved in such acquisition, might be gradually determined on the basis of experience. And for remuneration of special services—e.g. useful inventions—special rewards, pecuniary or honorific, might be added. Still such a system, at its best, could hardly be as stimulating as the present open competition. (*Principles*, p. 530.)

We may leave a concluding impression of the insight, detachment, caution, and tolerant, if rather sceptical, good humour with which Sidgwick approached the perennial problem of the economic functions of the State, by quoting the following passage from his Journal:

I have a certain alarm in respect of the movement of modern society towards socialism, i.e. the more and more extensive intervention of Government with a view to palliate the inequalities in the distribution of wealth. At the same time I regard this movement as *on the whole* desirable and beneficent—the expectation of it belongs to the cheerful side of my forecast of the future; if duly moderated it *might*, I conceive, be purely beneficent, and bring improvement at every stage. But—judging from past experience—one must expect that so vast a change will not be realised without violent shocks and oscillations, great blunders followed by great disasters and consequent reactions; that the march of progress perturbed by the selfish ambitions of leaders and the blind appetites of followers, will suffer many spasmodic deviations into paths which it will have painfully to retrace. Perhaps—as in the movement of the last century towards liberty—one country will have to suffer the pains of experiment for the benefit of the whole system of states; and if so, it is on various grounds likely that this country may be England.

In this way I sometimes feel alarmed even for my own 'much goods laid up for many years'—but not, on the whole, seriously. Considering all the chances of misfortune that life offers, the chance of having one's railway shares confiscated is not prominent, though I should not be surprised at being mulcted of a part of my dividends.

My recent fear and depression has been rather of a different kind: has related rather to the structure of Government than the degree of its interference with property and contract. I have hitherto held unquestioningly the Liberal doctrine that in the modern industrial community government by elected and responsible representatives was and should remain the normal type. But no one has yet found out how to make this kind of government work, except on the system of alternating parties; and it is the force of resistance which this machine of party government presents to the influence of enlightened and rational opinion, at crises like this, which alarms. I find myself asking myself whether perhaps, after all, it is Caesarism which will win in the competition for existence, and guide modern industrial society successfully towards its socialistic goal. However, I do not yet think this; but it is a terrible problem what to do with party government. (*A Memoir*, p. 442, entry for 17 March 1886.)

4

A. Marshall

1. *Introductory*

CONCERNING the subjects of most of these chapters there exist usually only some two or three articles, perhaps an obituary or anniversary essay, or a critical account of some special aspect of their work. The discussion of Marshall's writings, or rather of his *Principles*, has, of course, been on an entirely different scale. All its leading analytical concepts and contributions have been exhaustively discussed, dissected, criticized, defended, interpreted, and reinterpreted. In fact, for some time, theoretical economics in England consisted very largely of the discussion and interpretation, often textual, of Marshall's *Principles*, as a glance through the *Economic Journal* of the 1920's will confirm. Either as the standard textbook, or as the authoritative starting-point for advanced analysis, it has probably had, and still has, ten or more times as many readers as any other of the works we are discussing.

The immense extent of the Marshallian literature is obviously in large part due to the unique standing and importance and the wealth of original and fertile ideas in Marshall's work. But this is not the only reason. Much of the discussion could hardly have continued so long were it not for the variety of interpretations, some times conflicting some times complementary, which can be put on Marshall's work at so many points, from detailed issues of the definitions of particular concepts (like consumers' surplus and the demand curve) to much wider issues of general methodological principle (like the role of economic history in the scheme of his life-work). It would be very difficult to tell, if one wanted to do so, to what extent the source of these difficulties of interpretation lay in an intellectual virtue or an intellectual defect: a constant recognition of the variety and complexity of the social universe: the steady refusal to sacrifice more of the variety of reality to rigid definition and logical precision than is absolutely necessary for the analysis in hand: a readiness to suspend judgement when the facts do not justify a judgement, or when any generalization of finite length can only result in distortion or over-simplification: all these are the well-known hall-marks of the great sage. Less uncriticizable, on the other hand, would be 'an excessive use of the context to interpret shifts of meaning',[1] or an ultimate hesitation or indecisiveness of choice as to the level of abstraction, or a refusal to decide which price to incur of the two prices, one or other of which all social scientists have to pay for the pronouncement of any non-platitudinous proposition: either the price of full realism and wide applicability, or that of compactness and precision. Of course, it is not necessary always to choose to pay the *same* price. But in each and every proposition one price or the other must be paid, and if it is not clear which is being paid nothing clear is being stated.

The 'internal' difficulties of interpretation are added to, rather than is with most authors the case, alleviated, by the 'external' biographical record. Less than with almost any other comparable writer does the chronological record of Marshall's publications give clues to the shifts of emphasis, interest, and approach, which certainly must have occurred in such a life-long intellectual development, pre-eminently single-minded though it was. With many or most writers, for example with Pareto, each main stage of his thought, or shift of interest, is recorded with rough chronological accuracy in one of his publications. What scope there is for deriving this kind of assistance in the interpretation of Marshall's writings lies mainly in the slight alterations, additions, subtractions, and substitutions, in the footnotes and appendices to the successive editions of the *Principles*, a source which has already been exploited perhaps more intensively than conclusively. We may, how-ever, begin by summarizing the biographical facts and dates of Marshall's work, beyond the limits of which speculation, if considered legitimate, has to take over.

2. *Biographical*

Marshall was at a number of points generous and explicit in his acknowledgements to his intellectual ancestors. The son of a Victorian paterfamilias 'a tough old character of great resolution and perception cast in the mould of the strictest Evangelicals... surviving despotically-minded into his 92nd year',[2] Marshall was himself to become for a generation the great father figure of English economics, firmly up-holding the virtue of respect for one's elders and betters in the family of economists. After the middle eighties there were in England patently

---

[1] *v.* Guillebaud, *Economic Journal*, 1937, p. 23.
[2] *Memorials*, edited by A. C. Pigou, p. 1.

no betters than Marshall himself, and, of course, fewer and fewer comparable elders. From his contemporaries, English and foreign, he seems to have derived little or nothing, as he was once or twice concerned to emphasize (see for example his early review of Jevons's *Theory*, and letters to J. B. Clark, *Memorials*, pp. 93 and 412).

When Marshall came to the subject in 1867 via mathematics, metaphysics, and ethics, his first essays, as might be expected of a second wrangler, were in pure mathematical theory. Between 1867 and 1870, regarding himself 'as a mere pupil in the hands of great masters, especially Cournot, von Thünen and Ricardo', he 'translated Mill's version of Ricardo's or Smith's doctrines into mathematics'. (*Memorials*, p. 417.) If, therefore, there is any significant sense in which Marshall's theory represents a synthesis, it is of Cournot and Thünen with the English classics, and not of the latter with Jevons and the Austrian school. The works of Cournot (read 1868) and Thünen (read 1869 or 1870) were certainly at that time very little known, and one may venture to admire the breadth of reading, and persistence in intellectual exploration, which must have been necessary at that date for finding one's way to such works, and for perceiving and extracting their significance. Hearn's *Plutology*, a well-written but not original work, may also have led to a number of valuable sources and to the approach to the subject from the side of human wants, then somewhat neglected by the more orthodox English writers.[1] It is not clear what Marshall owed to the essays of the celebrated and encyclopaedic Master of Trinity William Whewell, whose mathematical formulation of Ricardian doctrines, and other papers, are among the pioneer works of mathematical economic theory. They can hardly have been unknown to Marshall.[2]

[1] Hearn's *Plutology* was published at Melbourne in 1864, and its sub-title 'The Theory of the Efforts to Satisfy Human Wants', is echoed in the title of Marshall's Book III. Hearn's book is noteworthy for the primary emphasis it lays on the demand side, for its strenuously optimistic biological analogies (later indulged in by Marshall), and some very able chapters on Capital and Production. These latter are not, however, as original as has sometimes been thought. Hearn had read widely, including the valuable and original works of Longfield and John Rae, which were then largely neglected in Britain, and he summarized and quoted them extensively (particularly Rae), not always with fully adequate acknowledgement. See J. A. La Nauze, *Political Economy in Australia*, Chapter on 'Hearn and Economic Optimism'. Hearn's *Plutology* is mentioned by Mrs. Marshall (*What I Remember*, p. 20) as 'thought well of for beginners' on the Cambridge reading-lists of the early seventies.

[2] It is very surprising that no reference seems ever to have been made by Marshall to the pioneer essays in Mathematical Economics of William Whewell, Master of Trinity. Whewell attempted in them exactly what Marshall attempted when, in 1867, he 'translated

By about 1870 Marshall had worked out that comprehensive outline
of mathematical theory which later went into the mathematical appendix
of the *Principles*. He said later (1908): 'My whole life has been and will

Mill's version of Ricardo's or Smith's doctrines into mathematics'. Whewell attempts, in
fact, just that restatement of classical supply and demand doctrines in a mathematical form
which later came to be recognized as characteristically Marshallian, though of course his
treatment is only a brief outline. Whewell's three main papers were (1) 'A Mathematical
Exposition of some Doctrines of Political Economy' (1829), (2) 'A Mathematical Exposition of the Leading Doctrines of Mr. Ricardo's Principles of Political Economy and
Taxation' (1833), and (3) a paper with a similar title as (1) published in 1850. All appeared
in the *Transactions of the Cambridge Philosophical Society*. Here is Whewell's view of the
general relations of supply, demand, and value: 'Price is determined by the conflict of
supply and demand; price is also determined by cost of production, in which latter expression demand is not mentioned: how then do these agree? In answer to this it is to be
observed, that the former is the immediate, the latter the permanent, determination of
price: the price today is that which arises from the bargaining of today's buyers and
sellers, that is from the intensity of demand and the extent of the supply. But this price
cannot be long above or below the cost of production, for the reason already mentioned.
This cost is the permanent and ultimate regulator of price. And the demand will affect
the *extent* of supply; and if the cost of production varies with the extent of production,
as, for instance, in the case of land of different fertilities, the demand affects the cost, and
the two determinations ultimately run together.' (*Transactions*, vol. iii, p. 202.)

Whewell was especially interested in and gave a thorough mathematical analysis of the
concept Marshall was to christen 'elasticity of demand' (and/or of supply). Here is his
verbal summary of his analysis: 'It appears from what has been said, that we have four
classes of commodities, which differ according to different values of m, the susceptibility
in the price to change of supply, or the rate of change in the money demand for a change
of price. The classes occur as m is 1, is between 1 and 0, is 0, or is negative. So far as
these classes of commodities are exemplified by the instances above adduced, we may
call them Conventional Necessaries, General Necessaries, Articles of Fixed Expenditure,
and Popular Luxuries. For the first class the quantity sold is the same whatever be the
price. For the second class, when the price rises the quantity sold diminishes, but the
money demand increases. For the third class the money demand is always the same, and
therefore the quantity sold is inversely as the price. For the fourth class, when the price
falls the quantity sold is augmented, so that the money demand is augmented.

'I suppose that there are no commodities of which a greater quantity would be sold if
the price were increased and a less quantity sold if the price were diminished. It is conceivable that this might be, as a matter of caprice or fashion. For instance, we may conceive that diamonds might in some way (by the discovery of abundant mines or the like)
become so common as to grow out of use, so that a less quantity might be sold than at
present. If there should be such commodities, they would correspond to values of m
greater than 1.' (*Transactions*, vol. ix, pp. 133–4.)

Whewell pointed out that in the measurement of this concept 'large changes are not
proportionately the same above and below the starting point' (p. 133).

Like Marshall, Whewell, though a pioneer of the mathematical formulation of economic
theory, was highly cautious and critical about its limitations, and he inclined markedly to
historical economics, as his very able support of Richard Jones's strictures on the Ricardian
method testify (see his Introduction to Jones's works). Whewell's 1833 paper on Ricardo's
doctrines contains one of the best critical discussions of the postulates of equilibrium
analysis and of the precise sense in which it might be significant to describe such analysis
as 'a first approximation'. (pp. 165 ff.) Whewell's Six Lectures on Political Economy

be given to presenting in realistic form as much as I can of my Note XXI' (*Memorials*, p. 417) which he had worked out within two or three years of his turning to economics in 1867.

Simultaneously Marshall was exploring the historical approach: 'One of the first books on economics that I came across' was that of Richard Jones, the English pioneer of the historical method, whose works had been edited and published by Whewell in 1859. Jones 'gave a direction to a good deal of my subsequent thinking'. (*Economic Journal*, 1892, p. 510.)[1] 'In 1868' as he later wrote of himself 'when he was still in his metaphysical stage, a desire to read Kant in the original led him to Germany'. (*Memorials*, p. 10.) He continued his visits when he had passed to economics, in particular spending the winter of 1870–1 during the Franco-Prussian war in Berlin, and they mark the opening of the stage which he later described as that of 'the early seventies, when I was in my full fresh enthusiasm for the historical study of economics'. (*Memorials*, p. 378.) The German historical school, notably Roscher, but also Marx, Lassalle, and other socialists, 'attracted him', and as late as the early editions of his *Principles* he was to hold: 'The most important economic work . . . that has been done on the Continent in this century is that of Germany.' (2nd ed., p. 66.)

Mrs. Marshall has described his teaching at this time, when he was a lecturer for the Moral Sciences Tripos:

> Mixed up with the lectures on theory were some on the History of Economics, Hegel's Philosophy of History, and Economic History from 1350 onwards, on the lines of the Historical Appendices to the Principles. He would give half an hour to theory and half an hour to history. He was keenly interested in Economic History. . . . Mr. Marshall also gave a course on Moral and Political Philosophy scattered over the years 1873–4. This was chiefly on Bentham and Mill's Utilitarianism. (*What I Remember*, pp. 18 and 20.)

delivered in 1861 to the Prince of Wales at the direction of the Prince Consort are not of the interest today which perhaps they were to their original audience. Incidentally, Whewell stood no nonsense from 'Say's Law', referring to 'Say's extreme opinion, of which the fallacy appears so very obvious. . . . If I recollect, Malthus has well disposed of this fallacy.' See *Writings and Letters of William Whewell*, Todhunter, vol. ii, p. 341.

[1] Marshall said later (1896) that Jones's 'influence, though little heard of in the outer world, largely dominated the minds of those Englishmen who came to the serious study of economics after his work had been published by Dr. Whewell in 1859' (*Memorials*, p. 296). As J. A. La Nauze comments, 'If this is so, these Englishmen were slow to acknowledge such an important influence'. (*Political Economy in Australia*, p. 102 n.) But it remains true that the historical movement of the 1870's in England was largely indigenous and original, and not an importation from Germany.

Marshall justly resented his work being described as a compromise or reconciliation between divergent schools of thought: 'Such work seems to me trumpery. Truth is the only thing worth having, not peace.' But certainly Marshall saw truth as something many-sided, or, as a famous contemporary put it, as something 'seldom pure and never simple'. Bentham and Hegel, Ricardo and List, Historical Economics and Mathematical Economics, utility and cost of production, all had something to contribute to Marshallian truth.

Ricardo, Mill, Cournot, Thünen, Jones, and Roscher, representing the English classical system, mathematical analysis, and the historical approach, give the background from which Marshall started. Perhaps one other economist should be mentioned, 'one of the ablest, most broad minded and acute of British economists', and that is Walter Bagehot. (He edited a special edition of Bagehot's *Postulates of Political Economy* for Cambridge students.) To some extent (whether or not entirely suitably for his different task, and almost certainly with no success), Marshall seems to have tried to model his style of presentation on Bagehot's: 'Bagehot, a master of literary form, and a leader in affairs, urged economists "to write more as we do in common life where the context is a sort of unexpressed interpretation clause"; and warned them against attempts to "express various meanings on complex things with a scanty vocabulary of fastened senses" (*Postulates of Political Economy*, pp. 7, 8, 9): and an attempt is made here, as in my *Principles of Economics*, to conform to this precept.' (*Industry and Trade*, p. 680.)

After this opening phase we may summarize the rest of the facts and dates mainly from the *Memorials*. It is the mode of his early approach to the subject that is important and, in any case, after that there is little that is firm beyond the skeleton outline of dates and publications, for the brief autobiographical statements available relate simply to his early years as an economist.

1868–77: Lecturer at Cambridge, 'laying the foundations of his subject but publishing nothing' (*Memorials*, p. 13).

1875: American visit, 'with the purpose of studying the problem of Protection in a new country'.

1875–7: First draft of 'The Theory of Foreign Trade with some allied problems relating to the doctrine of laissez-faire' (unpublished).

1877–82: First Principal of University College, Bristol.

1877–9: Writing, with Mrs. Marshall, *The Economics of Industry*.

1879: Private printing of *The Pure Theory of Foreign Trade and the Pure*

68 *A. Marshall*

Theory of Domestic Values (originally intended for his unpublished work on the theory of foreign trade).

1879–81: Ill health: The *Principles* begun.

1881: At Palermo: 'Book III on Demand largely thought out and written on the roof at Palermo' (including his formulation of the concept of elasticity of demand).

1883–4: Succeeds Toynbee as lecturer at Balliol College, Oxford. 'His theory of distribution taking shape' (for the *Principles*).

1885: Professor at Cambridge: 'The volume began to assume its final form. The work done during this year was not very satisfactory, partly because I was gradually out-growing the older and narrower conception of my book, in which the abstract reasoning which forms the backbone of the science was to be made prominent, and had not yet mustered courage to commit myself straight off to a two-volume book which should be the chief product (as gradually improved) of my life's work.'

1886: 'I then put the contents of my book into something like their final form.' Answers on the subject of Currency and Prices to the Royal Commission on the Depression of Trade.

1887: Article on 'Remedies for Fluctuations of General Prices'. Evidence before the Gold and Silver Commission.

1888: 'Book V at the printers, Book IV being almost out of my hands.'

1889: Presidential Address on Cooperation to the Cooperative Congress: 'Behold the hero of this year's Congress; the distinguished man whom working-men cooperators have elected to give the inaugural address, Professor Marshall of Cambridge. He looks every inch a professor. A small slight man with bushy moustache and long hair, nervous movements, sensitive and unhealthily pallid complexion, and praeternaturally keen and apprehending eyes, the professor has the youthfulness of physical delicacy. In spite of the intellectuality of his face he seems to lack the human experience of everyday life.' (Beatrice Webb, *My Apprenticeship*, Pelican edition, vol. ii, p. 415.)

1890: *Principles*, vol. i published.

1891–4: Royal Commission on Labour.

1892: Reply to Cunningham's attack, 'The Perversion of Economic History', in the *Economic Journal*.

1894: 'In 1894 he began a historical treatment which he later on called a White Elephant because it was on such a large scale, that it would have taken many volumes to complete'.

1895: Third edition of *Principles*: New formulation of beginning of Book VI: Plans announced for three further volumes: I. Modern Conditions of Industry and Trade: II. Credit and Employment: III. The Economic Functions of Government.

1903: Founding of independent Economics Tripos at Cambridge.
1907: Fifth edition of *Principles*: Historical chapters of Book I moved to Appendix.
1908: Retires from chair at Cambridge.
1910: Sixth edition of *Principles*: Sub-title, 'Vol. I', becomes, 'an introductory volume'.
1919: *Industry and Trade.*
1923: *Money Credit and Commerce*: Still at work on a further volume on *Progress, its Economic Conditions.*

3. *History and Analysis in Marshall's Work*

(a) MARSHALL AND ECONOMIC HISTORY

By the early seventies Marshall had both worked out the mathematical framework of his theory and plunged into the historical study of economic life. A synthesis of analysis and history seems to have remained his objective, but as to how this was to be achieved, in particular as to the role of history in the scheme of his life-work, he seems to have had many hesitations, and made many shifts of emphasis, in what G. F. Shove called 'his restless quest after realism'. Some impression of the balance of history and analysis that he planned at this time may be derived from his first brief textbook which he wrote with Mrs. Marshall. This is the only complete survey he made of the whole field of economics. It was warmly applauded by Cliffe Leslie, and brief though it is, it treats most of its topics historically almost as much as analytically. After his decision not to proceed with a series of specialist monographs, Marshall was at work through much of the eighties formulating his first volume of analytical principles, and it was only after its completion in 1890 that the problem of the role of history in his work had to be fully faced.

According to Mrs. Marshall: 'He wasted a great deal of time because he changed his method of treatment so often', notably when he was working on his multi-volume historical 'white elephant' in the early nineties. It was just before this that Cunningham made his fierce and unjustified attack on the competence of the (then) opening historical chapters of the *Principles*. Cunningham's attack shows signs of that professional departmentalism, or trade unionism, that resents any treatment of its subjects by anyone other than a full-time specialist with no other interests. The attack of the Archdeacon and Fellow of Kings could hardly have been more calculated to offend one so professionally conscientious as Marshall and to touch what Keynes referred to as his 'extreme sensitiveness to criticism'. One can only speculate as to the part this incident played in Marshall's gradual abandonment, or whittling down, of the historical side of his work. When he formed his new independent Economics Tripos in 1903, it was commented at the time with some surprise how comparatively slight was the scope it gave to economic history,[1] and there is certainly a contrast with the proportions of his earlier teaching. Further, in 1907, in the fifth edition of the *Principles* (still 'Volume I'), the opening historical chapters were relegated to the appendices. Finally, in *Industry and Trade*, which took the place of what was to have been Volume II, and which seemed at one time to have been intended partly as a historical complement to his mainly analytical first volume, the more definitely historical sections are again shut off in appendices, and it is insisted, twice in the first few pages, that the work 'has no claim whatever to be' (p. vi), and 'is not in any sense a contribution to' (p. 11) economic history.

It would seem that the lecturer of the early seventies on economic history after 1350, in his 'full, fresh enthusiasm for the historical study of economics', had moved a long way by the time *Industry and Trade* was advancing to completion. But it is impossible to follow precisely the path by which he moved and the reasons moving him. It is impossible to say how far there was an important shift of methodological views, how far an acceptance of academic trade-union demarcations between analysis and history, then being strongly asserted (and with which at one point he experienced a sharp collision), and how far, finally, the historical work simply got crowded out from the scarce time of his old age, when what were to have been the later volumes of the *Principles* were being pushed to completion at the same time as constant minor adjustments were being made to the analysis of the first volume. This is not simply a problem of 'the interest which attaches to the working of great minds', ample though that pure interest may be. This particular great mind was mainly responsible for the shaping of economic science in England and elsewhere for a generation, formulating the approach and the questions to be asked, and also, by implication, the questions not to be asked. The path Marshall actually followed represented the *de facto* outcome of the methodological controversies of the 1870's.

[1] Gay, *Quarterly Journal of Economics*, May 1903, pp. 492 ff.

(*b*) MARSHALL AND PURE THEORY

From the same early date at which he was formulating mathematically the framework of his theory, Marshall came to hold and express
a severe distrust of the isolated pursuit of pure analysis. He declined
to publish his diagrammatic analyses when urged to do so, 'because
he feared that if separated from all concrete study of actual conditions
they might seem to claim a more direct bearing on real problems
than they in fact had'. (*Memorials*, p. 21.) Indeed, considering how
essentially his mathematical scaffolding must have helped him in
building his own original, comprehensive, and far superior theoretical
structure, the depreciation of pure analysis, and in particular of mathematical analysis, by so eminent a student of mathematics, seems to
have an aspect of exaggeration and excessive modesty. As time went
on he came to introduce even such terms as 'elasticity of demand' with
almost an air of apology as 'an academic term' (*Industry and Trade*,
p. 186). Some of his severest comments in this vein were addressed
to Edgeworth (1902). After illustrating from Cournot 'the *mischievous-
ness* of an academic education in *abstract* economics not continued into
real economics', he went on:

> You would perhaps take the kernel to be the essential part: I take it to be
> a small part; and, when taken alone, more likely to be misapplied than in the
> case of other sciences. In my view 'theory' is essential. No one gets any real
> grip of economic problems unless he will work at it. But I conceive no more
> calamitous notion than that abstract, or general, or 'theoretical' economics
> was economics 'proper'. It seems to me an essential but a very small part of
> economics proper: and by itself sometimes even—well, not a very good
> occupation of time. . . . Economic theory is, in my opinion, as mischievous
> an impostor when it claims to be economics *proper* as is mere crude un-
> analysed history. (*Memorials*, pp. 435–7.)

In fact, for Marshall, economics 'proper' is what came later sometimes to be called 'applied economics' and what came to be called
'principles' was, for Marshall, 'a very small part of economics proper'.

The great exponent of the one-at-a-time principle was not prepared
to take his pure analysis and history separately. What are, by many
theoretical economists, introduced and treated as mainly analytical
concepts, Marshall employed straightway as historical categories for
understanding current economic and industrial developments—for
example, his treatment of diminishing and increasing returns. Much
more than most economists, in spite of their frequent use of such

phrases as 'tools of thought', 'instruments of analysis', 'techniques of thinking', and so on, Marshall insisted on the purely instrumental character of abstract analysis. Each realistic economic problem was dominated by its particular characteristics of time and place, and the general tools had to be to a considerable extent made to measure for each case. Consequently, though it was essential for the student to understand the general nature and functions of his tools—his hammers, his saws, his mallets, nails, and screws—it was a waste of time to keep working on a vast array of finely adjusted tools (and still more to argue over slight differences as to their most suitable weight, size, and finish), since in any case each particular realistic task would demand its own particular modifications to measure. As he notes:

The remedy for such difficulties as these is to be sought in treating each important concrete case very much as an independent problem, under the guidance of staple general reasonings. Attempts so to enlarge the *direct* applications of general propositions as to enable them to supply adequate solutions of all difficulties, would make them so cumbrous as to be of little service for their main work. The principles of economics must aim at affording guidance to an entry on problems of life, without making claim to be a substitute for independent thought and study. (*Principles*, 8th ed., p. 459.)

Marshall's conception of the 'organon' of pure analysis seems to have been one of a body of propositions for which universality and a certain instrumental value, but no practical content, could be claimed: 'That part of economic doctrine, which alone can claim universality, has no dogmas. It is not a body of concrete truth, but an engine for the discovery of concrete truth.' (*Memorials*, p. 159.) To the classical 'natural' laws both universality and practical content had been ascribed, and Marshall, held, perhaps misleadingly, to the established terminology in his discussion of 'long-run economic laws'. It is true he adopted Cairnes's adjective 'normal' in place of the earlier classical adjective 'natural', but the extent of the significance of this change might easily seem to be fairly small, especially as when he first adopted the adjective 'normal' he took it to mean 'competitive', though later recognizing a 'normality' apart from free competition. One might imagine that if anything can embody 'concrete truth', it ought to be, in some way or another, 'long run natural or normal laws', though in fact the propositions stating these laws, surely in the main at any rate, are highly abstract analytical propositions, and therefore rather part of the purely instrumental organon not embodying 'concrete truth'.

This lack of clarity is rather increased by Marshall's use of the highly ambiguous word 'tendency'. The ambiguity apt to surround this word had been previously pointed out in economic controversy, during the later discussions of Malthus's population theory. Finding the blunt generalization that population increased faster than food too advanced a position to maintain, Malthus soon took up an ambiguous second line of defence to the effect that there was a *tendency* for population to increase faster than food, a tendency which, in face of subsequent argument, was agreed to be perfectly consistent with the *regular fact* of food increasing faster than population. This use of the word 'tendency' as a smoke-screen to cover a withdrawal of indefinite extent, and perhaps even the abandonment of all practical content, was attacked by Whateley and Senior.[1] But Marshall relied extensively on this word 'tendency' in his discussion, in Chapter 3 of Book I, perhaps the most ambiguous chapter in the volume. These difficulties again all ultimately seem to have their source in the diametrically diverging pulls of, on the one hand, Marshall's extreme intellectual caution and unique grasp of the complexity of the social universe, and, on the other hand, his strong ethical intent and desire to hand on some practical message in the accepted time-honoured terminology.

In his paper *The Old Generation of Economists and the New*, Marshall claimed that 'the nineteenth century has in great measure achieved qualitative analysis in economics'. But mere qualitative analysis 'will not show the resultant drift of economic forces. . . . The achievement of quantitative analysis stands over for the twentieth century.' (*Memorials*, p. 301.) That seems to imply that the pure qualitative analytical organon (the long chains of reasoning) had been carried as far as it usefully could be for the time at any rate. The comparatively more important task Marshall foresaw to be practical applied quantitative analysis. As R. F. Harrod has put it, Marshall's programme of work for his successors was 'to study the workings of the economic system in all their rich and varied detail, with the aid of principle; it was a programme for the development of applied economics'. (*The New Economics*, ed. S. Harris, p. 65.)

Those who wish to indulge a possibly pedantic taste for lucidity and precision in these fundamental matters will not always find Marshall's early chapters (*Principles*, Book I) easy to follow. At least they may care to agree with Cliffe Leslie in his very favourable review of Marshall's first book of 1879 when he suggested as a possible improvement, 'the total dismissal of the phrase "in the long run" from these

[1] *v.* Senior, *Outline of Political Economy*, p. 47.

pages', and 'a more sparing application of the term "laws" to provisional and hypothetical assumptions'. (*Essays*, 2nd ed., p. 82.)

4. '*Partial*' Analysis and the Competitive Industry

The forces to be dealt with are, however, so numerous, that it is best to take a few at a time; and to work out a number of partial solutions as auxiliaries to our main study. Thus we begin by isolating the primary relations of supply, demand and price in regard to a particular commodity. We reduce to inaction all other forces by the phrase 'other things being equal': we do not suppose that they are inert, but for the time we ignore their activity. (*Principles*, p. xiv.)[1]

This is Marshall's broad account of his partial analysis of the supply and demand of a particular commodity. It is a procedure which exacts a heavy price in return for any gain in realism which it may bring, *if* a high degree of logical precision and explicitness is being aimed at. The exponent of general Walrasian analysis is not faced with the problems of demarcating so precisely the sector for treatment, or of defining 'the other things' which are assumed to be equal. But in partial analysis, the producers and consumers of the particular commodity are all involved in the economy as a whole, having tastes for other goods, using their incomes to purchase them, and being confronted by other prices. It therefore has to be decided, if the analysis is to be clear and precise, just which of these 'other things' remain exactly equal. Marshall himself gave much higher priority to practical instrumental relevance, and serviceability for particular real problems, than to the drawing up of the precise and logical demarcations and definitions, logically needed by his partial methods. He was explicitly averse to 'a scanty vocabulary of fastened senses', particularly the 'fastened senses'. But logical precision has its claims, and in trying to make his book more easily comprehensible for one type of reader, he was posing a multitude of intricate problems and opportunities for another type. It has been said that 'the search for Marshall's hidden assumptions has occupied a whole generation'.[2] It is impossible to be sure in what light Marshall himself would have regarded such an immense effort of search. One may, however, venture two generalizations: First, that any great book imposes its demands on its readers, both to accept what it is aiming at, or at least to suspend rejection, and also to tolerate the terminology it is

---

[1] All references are to the 8th edition, unless otherwise stated.
[2] J. Robinson, *Economics is a Serious Subject*, p. 8.

adopting: a book can hardly be read successfully without such acceptance.[1] Secondly, what Marshall was aiming at, primarily at any rate, was not a construction of one, or a limited number, of precise logical self-consistent analytical models, described in a 'scanty vocabulary of fastened senses'. Hence, however important the question whether this *ought* to have been the primary aim of the *Principles*, a successful reading of the book demands acceptance by the reader of Marshall's different aim. It follows, also, that however helpful it may be to draw up the various precise logically self-consistent models, suggested by, or closely following various parts of Marshall's analysis, it is rather fruitless to attempt to insist that the precise definitions and assumptions of such models were, or ought to have been, Marshall's. In fact, as Professor Friedman has shown, various precise assumptions have been attributed to Marshall to which he nowhere unequivocally committed himself.[2] With his Pickwickian, almost Humpty-Dumptyish, attitude to his definitions and assumptions Marshall certainly did not always 'play the game' logically, as it is understood by those who above all value precise and logically self-consistent abstract models. That would have necessitated the 'fastened senses' which he rejected.

Let us now indicate the two key definitions and groups of assumptions where the difficulties for the precision-minded reader have proved particularly intricate and controversial: These are (i) the definition of the commodity, which on the demand side is involved with the precise assumptions on which the demand curve for it is drawn up, and on the supply side is involved with the definition of the 'industry' producing it: and (ii) the definition of 'competition' between the firms of the 'industry'.

(i) A precise, logically self-consistent, general model on Marshallian lines would seem to require, at a number of points, that the commodity is one which accounts only for a very small fraction of the individual buyer's total income, and on which the aggregate expenditure forms only a very small fraction of aggregate national income. There is at least one passage (*Principles*, p. 132) which suggests that Marshall accepts such a limitation. But there are other passages near by where he

---

[1] Cf. Bagehot on Adam Smith: 'Nothing could be more unjust to a great writer than to judge of him by a standard which he did not expect, and to blame his best book for not being what he never thought of making it, especially when, except for him, we should never have imagined the standard, or conceived the possibility of the book being that which we now blame it for not being.' *Economic Studies*, 1895 ed., p. 172.

[2] On Marshall's Demand Analysis, and on his general methodological approach, *v.* M. Friedman, *Journal of Political Economy*, 1950, p. 469 ff.

takes as examples such major commodities as wheat and houseroom (pp. 106–7) which suggest the reverse. Marshall does, however, give what may be taken to be a complete 'blanket' answer to the problem, however unsatisfactory it may seem to the vast majority of analytical economists who prefer to work with 'fastened senses': 'The question where the lines of division between different commodities should be drawn must be settled by convenience of the particular discussion. For some purposes it may be best to regard Chinese and Indian teas, . . . as different commodities. While for other purposes it may be best to group together . . . even . . . tea and coffee.' (p. 100.)

Marshall did not attempt to provide a single precise definition consistent with a single precise ready-made model. He held that each real problem to be investigated would require to some extent its own particular modifications of his purely instrumental general-purpose model, which would have to be adapted also to the probably meagre and unsatisfactory statistical material available. No practically serviceable model, could, therefore, be precisely cut in advance. Marshall held that his instrument, provided of course with the necessary *ad hoc* refinements, was generally adaptable to the vast majority of practical cases likely to be met with in the real world, a defence which has hardly been refuted.

(ii) *Competition*. Marshall regarded the term 'competition' as describing, rather unsuitably and inadequately, the broad characteristics of 'industrial life in the modern age', though he preferred for this purpose a term which he regarded as a more adequate equivalent, 'Freedom of Industry and Enterprise, or more shortly Economic Freedom' (*Principles*, pp. 9–10). 'Competition' is clearly, therefore, for Marshall the sort of term which neither seeks nor affords much precision in definition, and such qualifying adjectives as 'perfect' or 'pure' hardly occur in the *Principles* ('free' is sometimes added, but hardly seems to lend much fastened precision to the sense). In *Industry and Trade* the problems of industry are surveyed under the two broad headings of 'Competition' (Book II) and 'Monopoly' (Book III). But as soon as this division is made it is emphasized that there is no distinct line of division. This is later amplified:

Though monopoly and free competition are ideally wide apart, yet in practice they shade into one another by imperceptible degrees: there is an element of monopoly in nearly all competitive business: and nearly all the monopolies that are of any practical importance in the present age, hold much of their power by an uncertain tenure; so that they would lose it ere long, if they ignored possibilities of competition, direct and indirect. (*Industry and Trade*, p. 397.)

This 'interlacing', as Marshall calls it, of monopoly and competition is illustrated as follows:

Everyone buys, and nearly every producer sells, to some extent, in a 'general' market, in which he is on about the same footing with others around him. But nearly everyone has also some 'particular' markets; that is, some people or groups of people with whom he is in somewhat close touch: mutual knowledge and trust lead him to approach them, and them to approach him, in preference to strangers. A producer, a wholesale dealer, or a shopkeeper, who has built up a strong connexion among purchasers of his goods has a valuable property. (p. 182.)

Finally, generalizing at the end of Book II as to competitive markets, Marshall writes:

The general position is then: every manufacturer or other businessman, has a plant, an organisation, and a business connexion, which put him in a position of advantage for his special work. He has no sort of permanent monopoly, because others can easily equip themselves in like manner. (p. 196.)

These passages from *Industry and Trade* give Marshall's broad picture of 'competitive' markets in the economic world of his day. For purposes of analysis in the *Principles* he had to make some concessions, but hardly a complete surrender, to precision of definition. 'Competition' was taken as the general case (not that it was the 'normal' case, though Marshall had begun in his first book *The Economics of Industry* (1879) by equating 'normal' and 'competitive'):

The position then is this: we are investigating the equilibrium of normal demand and normal supply in their most general form; we are neglecting those features which are special to particular parts of economic science, and are confining our attention to those broad relations which are common to nearly the whole of it. Thus we assume that the forces of demand and supply have free play; that there is no close combination among dealers on either side, but each acts for himself, and there is much free competition; that is buyers generally compete freely with buyers, and sellers compete freely with sellers. . . . We have already inquired to some extent, and we shall have to inquire further, how far these assumptions are in accordance with the actual facts of life. But meanwhile this is the supposition on which we proceed; we assume that there is only one price in the market at one and the same time; it being understood that separate allowance is made, when necessary, for differences in the expense of delivering goods to dealers in different parts of the market; including allowance for the special expenses of retailing, if it is a retail market. (*Principles*, p. 342.)

Marshall is, therefore, not confining himself to 'perfect' competition in the sense of the extreme limiting case. His free competition meant 'atomistic' competition, that is that a large number of small units were involved. But this does not rule out a certain measure of imperfection. The type of market that Marshall did not deal with analytically, or not in any detail, was the oligopolistic market, or 'competition among the few'. Book III of *Industry and Trade* deals extensively with oligopolistic *practice*. Where he briefly approached problems of economic warfare at the end of his chapter in the *Principles* on monopoly, he notes that conflicts and alliances play a role of ever-increasing importance in modern economies, but that *abstract reasoning of a general character has little to say on the subject*. (*Principles*, p. 493: our italics.)

This is only a passing comment on a particular case, but taken with his actual practical treatment of oligopolistic conditions, and his omission of any analytical treatment, it may well have wider significance. He concludes his chapter on monopoly, with its brief discussion of certain problems of oligopoly, and notably that of complementary monopolies, by referring the reader to his realistic survey in *Industry and Trade*.

We have seen already how Marshall warned against 'attempts so to enlarge the *direct* applications of general propositions' . . . as 'would make them so cumbrous as to be of little service for their main work', and advised that 'each important concrete case' should be treated 'very much as an independent problem under the guidance of staple general reasonings'. The important concrete cases, to be selected out of the infinite variety Marshall saw in the real world, would obviously have to be representative cases, and in respect of firms, cases of representative firms. Though his concept of the representative firm may have no significant role in any purely abstract and precise model of the competitive industry, obviously a more realistic analysis of the multiformity of the real world must seek to reduce this multiformity to a manageable range of representative types or forms. This, surely, must be the essential notion behind Marshall's suggestion of the representative firm, both in the *Principles* and in *Industry and Trade*, though certainly the suggestion cannot be said either to be made very clearly, or followed out very far.

Concluding his critical examination of the developments in the

1930's of the pure analysis of imperfect and monopolistic competition R. Triffin wrote:

The way is now open for the building up of a different type of economics. Instead of drawing its substance from arbitrary assumptions, chosen for their simplicity and unduly extended to the whole field of economic activity, our theory may turn to more pedestrian, but more fruitful methods. It will recognise the richness and variety of all concrete cases, and tackle each problem with due respect for its individual aspects. More advantage will be taken of all relevant factual information, and less reliance will be placed on a mere resort to the pass key of general theoretical assumptions. (*Monopolistic Competition and General Equilibrium Theory*, 1940, p. 189.)

Perhaps we have shown that to turn to this 'different type of economics' is in fact very largely to *re* turn to Marshall's type. We have already quoted Marshall's note, at several points, in almost verbally the same terms as the foregoing modern quotation, urging that 'each important concrete case' must be treated 'very much as an independent problem under the guidance of staple general reasonings', and that 'attempts to enlarge the direct applications of general propositions' may be 'of little service'. (*v. above*, pp. 72 and 78 and *Principles*, p. 459 n.)

5. *Statics and Dynamics: Long and Short Periods*

The central structure of Marshall's analysis, around which the *Principles* is built, relates to the stationary state. C. W. Guillebaud has gone so far as to say:

At times he gives the impression that he has lived so long inside his imaginary state of 'the long period' that it has come to have for him the same sort of almost objective existence that the characters in his own novels have for Balzac. Thus, instead of saying that a given result 'tends' to occur in the long period, he says outright that it 'occurs' in the long period, thereby giving the unwary reader the impression that Marshall believes that this is what actually happens in the real world. (*Economic Journal*, 1937, p. 35.)

The stationary state has been authoritatively described by J. R. Hicks as follows:

The stationary state is that special case of a dynamic system where tastes, technique, and resources remain constant through time. We can reasonably assume that experience of these constant conditions will lead entrepreneurs to expect their continuance; so that it is not necessary to distinguish between price-expectations and current prices, for they are all the same. We can assume, too, that entrepreneurs did expect in the past that today's prices would be what they now turn out to be; so that the supplies of commodities are fully adjusted to their prices. Then it can be shown that the price system established in such a stationary state is substantially identical with that static price system whose properties we already know. (*Value and Capital*, 2nd ed., p. 117.)

Marshall was concerned to differentiate, perhaps unduly, his 'stationary' analysis from the more explicitly abstract 'static' analysis of J. B. Clark. But it is not entirely a verbal point to claim that Marshall's stationary state analysis is a limiting case of 'dynamics' and not strictly 'static', and moreover Marshall accompanied his stationary treatment —in spite of possible intervals of forgetfulness—with many more warnings of its limitations and many pioneering elements of a dynamic analysis.

Something of Marshall's distinction between short-period and long-period equilibrium is suggested, in embryo, in the classical distinction between 'normal' values and 'market' values, particularly as developed in Cairnes's *Leading Principles*, and it may even be traced back to Adam Smith. But Marshall built up the distinction into a powerful method of analysis. Book V, Chapter V, of the *Principles* is the key chapter: In the short period,

the supply of specialised skill and ability, of suitable machinery and other material capital, and of the appropriate industrial organisation, has not time to be fully adapted to demand; but the producers have to adjust their supply to the demand as best they can with the appliances already at their disposal.... In long periods on the other hand all investments of capital and effort in providing the material plant and the organisation of a business, and in acquiring trade knowledge and specialised ability, have time to be adjusted to the incomes which are expected to be earned by them: and the estimates of those incomes therefore directly govern supply, and are the true long-period normal supply price of the commodities produced.

In other words:

For short periods people take the stock of appliances for production as fixed; and they are governed by their expectations of demand in considering how actively they shall set themselves to work those appliances. In long periods they set themselves to adjust the flow of these appliances to their expectations of demand. (*Principles*, pp. 374-6-7.)

The essential contribution lies of course in the notion of different adjustments to change taking place through time, rather than in the particular classification or nomenclature. The long-period and short-period distinction marks off for isolated study particular reactions and adjustments, and is in the main simply an application of Marshall's one-at-a-time procedure. Indeed it is arguable that the terms 'short' and 'long period' are misleading if taken to refer to actual 'clock' time, the short-period adjustments being made first, and then subsequently, and in the end, the long-period adjustments.[1] The long-period adjustments might be under way before the short-period ones, depending on expectations about the permanence or transitoriness of the changes. Significant also is Marshall's explicit treatment of economic actions as being governed by expectations. But the introduction of expectations only really begins to be important when they are not implicitly or explicitly all assumed to be perfectly correct or in the main approximately correct.

As Marshall recognized 'in a stationary state the income earned by every appliance of production [is] truly anticipated beforehand', and further, that when precisely formulated, the notion of the theoretically perfect long period,

> will be found to involve the supposition of a stationary state of industry, in which the requirements of a future age can be anticipated an indefinite time beforehand. Some such assumption is indeed unconsciously implied in many renderings of Ricardo's theory of value, if not in his own versions of it; and it is to this cause more than any other that we must attribute that simplicity and sharpness of outline, from which the economic doctrines in fashion in the first half of this century derive some of their seductive charms as well as most of whatever tendency they may have to lead to false practical conclusions. (*Principles*, pp. 379 and 810.)

Of course, Marshall had little use for such a precise abstract model, but it remains logically implied in the background of his analysis. In fact to a large extent it is its backbone. J. R. Hicks has stated his 'firm belief that the stationary state is, in the end, nothing but an evasion',[2] —and many modern economists would agree. Marshall might well also have agreed, with qualifications, but he never finally cut loose from this evasion. But he analysed much more thoroughly and realistically than any of the other neo-classical theorists the main elements which any dynamic analysis of supplies, demanders, and markets, would have to comprehend, and there are many particular pieces of dynamic analysis throughout Book V, dealing specially with changing expectations and uncertainty. In his pioneering work on dynamic analysis in the 1920's

---

[1] *v.* R. Opie, 'Marshall's Time Analysis', *Economic Journal*, 1931, pp. 199 ff.
[2] *Value and Capital*, 2nd ed., p. 117.

Gunnar Myrdal gave 'generous recognition' to how Marshall had pointed the way.[1]

6. The Distribution of the National Income

We are not attempting any complete digest of Marshall's *Principles*, and several of his leading and most-discussed concepts, such as consumers' surplus, and quasi-rent, are not referred to here. But in the preceding sections something of the central problems and procedures of the *Principles* has been indicated in the sequence which they take in the book. First, there are the non-committal methodological generalizations in the opening chapters in Book I. The demand side or 'Wants and their Satisfaction' is taken first, a kind of tribute perhaps to the Jevonian 'revolution', and here are at once raised some of the main difficulties of the partial analysis of a sector of the economic cosmos separated off from the rest. The problems arise of defining this sector, the single 'commodity' which is being demanded and supplied in it, and of making clear what are the main 'other things' which have, or have not, to be assumed equal in the analysis: real incomes, money incomes, prices and tastes for other commodities. Much of Book IV 'On the Agents of Production' is historical and on the borderlines between the technical and the economic, the main analytical problems arising in connexion with the definitions of the factors of production. In Book V, the backbone of the book, entitled 'General Relations of Demand, Supply and Value', there are problems corresponding to those in Book III arising from the partial procedure, such as the definition of the 'industry', and of the commodity which the firms in it produce. There arise also the problems of 'competition', and of the equilibrium of the firms and the 'industry', and with equilibrium the problems of time analysis and economic periods. The preceding sections of this chapter have attempted to describe in order Marshall's treatment of some of the main features of these problems.

There remains Book VI on 'The Distribution of the National Income', which includes also the pure analysis of production, not undertaken in Book IV 'On the Agents of Production'. Professor D. H. Macgregor (*Economica*, 1942, p. 315) has pointed out the architectural logic of the *Principles*: 'The *Principles* is written in a logical order. Things are wanted (Book III), so they are produced (Book IV), and

[1] See A. W. Marget, *Theory of Prices*, vol. ii, p. 191 n., who also points out that Ohlin's description of Marshall as the *only* pre-depression writer who examined the question of how far economic activities are influenced by expectations is a very over-generous tribute.

are then exchanged (Book V), and the prices divided (Book VI). It is like the development of a plot.' This order does, however, involve a certain separation of the theory of production from the theory of distribution, and perhaps conceals somewhat the unity of the two theories as provided in the marginal productivity principle.

Marshall formulated the main principles of his treatment of distribution around 1870, building principally on Thünen's marginal productivity analysis. After a review of some previous distribution theories, and some brief preliminary analysis of completely abstract imaginary situations where everyone owns the capital he works with, Marshall starts with the maximizing individual employer taking on individual units of a factor, and substituting units to find the least-cost combination. This leads on to the celebrated example of the marginal shepherd, and to the marginal net productivity formula, which is stated only immediately to be severely qualified and even disparaged. There arises here the problem which according to G. J. Stigler, 'is clearly the problem calling for explanation', of Marshall's 'reluctance to accept unequivocally the marginal productivity theory'. Although through the successive editions he withdrew some of his qualifications as to the applicability of the marginal productivity doctrine, and although he comes to make what Stigler describes as 'an outright capitulation to the marginal productivity theory', Marshall left standing the well-known judgement which has been called by D. H. Robertson 'such a godsend to critics':[1]

> The doctrine has sometimes been put forward as a theory of wages. But there is no valid ground for any such pretension. The doctrine that the earnings of a worker tend to be equal to the net product of his work, has by itself no real meaning; since in order to estimate net product, we have to take for granted all the expenses of production of the commodity on which he works, other than his own wages. But though his objection is valid against the claim that it contains a theory of wages, it is not valid against a claim that the doctrine throws into clear light the action of one of the causes that govern wages. (*Principles*, p. 518.)

Whether or no it would be of assistance here, we cannot enter into the question of when a 'theory' is not a theory and when it is a maximization formula, or a corollary of a maximizing postulate. On the following page, after giving a standard illustration of the marginal productivity formula as applied to the employment of a piece of

---

[1] *v*. G. J. Stigler, *Production and Distribution Theories*, p. 354, and D. H. Robertson, 'Wage-Grumbles', *Readings in Income Distribution*, Blakiston, p. 227.

machinery, and to the rate of interest paid, Marshall again emphasizes that: 'Illustrations of this kind merely indicate part of the action of the great causes which govern value. They cannot be made into a theory of interest, any more than into a theory of wages, without reasoning in a circle.' (p. 519.)

Marshall's objections did not centre so much around the full applicability of the principle of variability of the proportions of factors used, which was often the issue at stake between critics and defenders of the marginal productivity doctrine. He was concerned rather with the difficulty he perceived in the measurement of a marginal net product, granted that it could be isolated. He may well, also, in persisting with his qualifications, have sensed that in any case very little applicable content remained in the doctrine when it had been formulated sufficiently strictly to be proof against the common objections. In one of his very illuminating letters to J. B. Clark (1900), he said of his theory of wages ('what by title of priority may be called the von Thünen doctrine'): 'I thought then and think still, that it covers only a very small part of the real difficulties of the wages problem: I cannot yet be sure whether you agree with this or not.' (*Memorials*, p. 413.) How far J. B. Clark and other exponents of the orthodox marginal productivity doctrine did or did not agree with Marshall it is unnecessary to attempt to generalize. But there must have remained some considerable difference of emphasis, or Marshall would hardly have left standing his 'godsend to critics'.

Nowhere than in his theory of wages does Marshall make a more strenuous effort to link up with the classical theory and treatment, though, in fact, the classical, mainly 'macro-economic' distribution theory is concerned with quite different questions of distribution than is, for the most part, a precisely and correctly formulated marginal productivity analysis. The two types of treatment and analysis, though not necessarily incompatible, cannot be said, when combined, to produce a very significant synthesis; they remain separate and, in some ways questionable, answers to separate questions. An interpretation of Marshall's denial that the marginal productivity doctrine provides a theory of wages may well be that, though regarding it as stating a formula for relative wages as a simple corollary of the postulate of the maximizing individual employer, he saw that it does not of itself bear on the problem of average absolute wages, or 'wages as a whole', as the doctrine of the Wages Fund, and the so-called Malthusian 'iron law', had tried to do. As D. H. Robertson wrote in commenting on the 'godsend' passage (*Readings in Income Distribution*, p. 227): 'Now so long as we are fixing our eyes on a single business or a single industry the assumption that all the other factors of production have clearly defined supply prices is perhaps sufficiently nearly valid to give no great trouble to anyone; but what we are in search of is the principle governing the level of wages *as a whole*.' Certainly that was what Marshall was in search of, for he proceeded in the following chapter to the classical problem of 'wages as a whole'. For the greater part of the world his answer is the Malthusian one: 'Over a great part of the world wages are governed, nearly after the so-called iron or brazen law, which ties them close to the cost of rearing and sustaining a rather inefficient class of labourers. As regards the modern western world the answer is materially different. . . .' Nevertheless: 'We conclude then that an increase of wages, unless earned under unwholesome conditions, almost always increases the strength, physical, mental, and even moral, of the coming generation; and that, other things being equal, an increase in the earnings that are to be got by labour increases its rate of growth; or, in other words, a rise in its demand price increases the supply of it.' (*Principles*, pp. 531–2.) Of this generalization, or at any rate of that part of it relating to 'the modern western world', one can only say that today its content seems both indefinite and questionable, and to relate to a very long period in which the 'other things' will certainly not remain equal as postulated.

Marshall then goes on to combine the two doctrines (as Mangoldt had done) of the marginal productivity doctrine of relative wages and of the quasi-Malthusian doctrine of the level of average aggregate wages:

Thus again we see that demand and supply exert coordinate influences on wages; neither has a claim to predominance; any more than has either blade of a pair of scissors, or either pier of an arch. Wages tend to equal the net product of labour; its marginal productivity rules the demand price for it; and on the other side, wages tend to retain a close though indirect and intricate relation with the cost of rearing, training, and sustaining the energy of efficient labour. (*Principles*, p. 532.)

The clarity of this passage might perhaps have been enhanced, along with that of Marshall's whole treatment of distribution, if Cairnes's clear-cut and rigidly maintained distinction between the problems and analysis of *aggregate* supply and demand, and those of the supply and demand *for a particular good or service*, as also the distinction between the relative and absolute levels of the values of goods and services, had been kept more explicitly before the reader throughout.

When he came to summarize his 'General View of Distribution', Marshall explained that his account 'falls far short of a complete solution of the problem before us: for that involves questions relating to foreign trade, to fluctuations of credit and employment, and to the influences of associated and collective action in its many forms'. (p. 660.) But he claims that it does provide 'a continuous thread' of explanation in terms of supply and demand.

'The influence of associated and collective action' had been dealt with by Marshall in what was for decades the outstanding treatment of trade unions and wage bargaining, in his *Economics of Industry* (Book VI, Chapter 13).[1] This is not repeated in the *Principles*, which, however, goes on to a historical review of the broad influences on the supply sides of the general factor markets, and of the effects on the levels of the main groups of incomes. One point in the discussion we would pick out, is Marshall's treatment of the problem of 'the inconstancy of employment' (the term 'unemployment' was only just beginning to come in in the nineties and if one looks up that term in the index to the *Principles* one is referred to 'inconstancy of employment').

Marshall's brief discussion in the *Principles* is based on his evidence to the Gold and Silver Commission (1887). He had there emphasized the difficulty of generalizing about the extent of unemployment with the statistics then available:

I have very little to go by except general impressions, and general impressions on a matter of this sort are not worth much; but, on the other hand, I do not know that anybody else has anything else but general impressions, and I have been studying for many years the question whether the tendency of our modern forms of industry is not to increase the irregularity of employment. I believe that it is not, and I believe that the statistical evidence brought forward to prove that it is, is invalid. (*Official Papers*, p. 92.)

Under the heading 'Employment is Not Becoming More Inconstant', Marshall writes in the *Principles*:

When a large factory goes on half time, rumour bruits the news over the whole neighbourhood, and perhaps the newspapers spread it all over the country. But few people know when an independent workman, or even a small employer, gets only a few days' work in a month; and in consequence, whatever suspensions of industry there are in modern times are apt to seem more important than they are relatively to those of earlier times. (*Principles*, p. 687.)

[1] The book of 1892 and subsequent editions, not the now much scarcer work written with Mrs. Marshall in 1879.

This generalization seems to suggest that any apparent increase in the importance of the unemployment problem at the end of the nineteenth century was largely illusory. It may afford some indication as to why, rightly or wrongly, Marshall gave that problem less priority in his life work, than many economists were to do two or three decades later when it had obviously taken on quite a different magnitude.

7. *'General Overproduction', Fluctuations, and Money*

Marshall's ideas on 'general overproduction', and on the theory of money, and also as to the place these subjects were to take, both analytically and in the chronological order of his works, were formulated very early, and seem to have undergone little further development. The treatment of many of the most important subjects in *Money Credit and Commerce*, published a year before his death, goes back forty or fifty years: that of the Quantity Theory to the earliest extant manuscript of Marshall's dating from 1871, and that of overproduction and crises to the *Economics of Industry* of 1879. The analysis of his paper on the *Pure Theory of Domestic Values* (published in 1879—the original nucleus of Book V of the *Principles*) is based on the assumption 'that the period analysed should not include any great change in the prosperity and purchasing power of the community'. (p. 15.)

On 'General Overproduction' the treatment follows J. S. Mill, and to some extent Cairnes, fairly closely. There is the same verbal insistance on the impossibility of general overproduction, and on 'the monstrous fallacy that there can be too much produced of everything', while a line or two farther down the business man is regarded as correct in grasping 'that when a long period of peace and invention has increased production in every trade, the volume of goods rises relatively to that of money, prices fall, and borrowers, that is men of business, generally lose'. There are, also, in Marshall's earlier writings, as in Mill, approving references to Adam Smith's concept of saving, or of the automatic investment of all savings, for example, in the well-known passage in the *Pure Theory of Domestic Values* (p. 34), referring to the *'familiar economic axiom'* (our italics) 'that a man purchases labour and commodities with that portion of his income which he saves just as much as he does with that he is said to spend'. On the other hand, it is recognized when commenting on one of Mill's more clear-cut assertions of the proposition known as Say's Law, that 'though men have the power to purchase they may not choose to use it. For when confidence has been shaken by failures, capital cannot be got to start new companies or extend old ones.' These remarks were repeated in the *Principles* from Marshall's *Economics of Industry* of 1879, with the additional comment:

> They indicate the attitude which most of those, who follow in the traditions of the classical economists, hold as to the relation between consumption and production. It is true that in times of depression the disorganisation of consumption is a contributory cause to the continuance of the disorganisation of credit and of production. But a remedy is not to be got by a study of consumption as has been alleged by some hasty writers. (*Principles*, p. 712 n.)

'Consumption' may perhaps be equated with 'effective demand', and it is reasonable to guess that one of the 'hasty writers' was J. A. Hobson.

Marshall never got round to developing, or clearing up, his views on this subject in a new full-scale treatment. As his life-work turned out he had no opportunity of doing so, though in 1895 his plans included a volume with the title *Credit and Employment*. Such indications as there are, suggest that he held to his previous views, which were broadly those of J. S. Mill.[1] His account of commercial crises, and of the cumulative spreading of booms and depressions through one industry after another, with his stress on fluctuations in business psychology, follows the main lines of Bagehot's chapter on 'Why Lombard Street is often Dull and Sometimes Excited'.

Marshall's abstraction, in the theory of domestic values, from 'any great change in prosperity and purchasing power', was clearly designed to rule out from his price analysis what may imprecisely be called 'changes on the side of money'. Not, of course, that Marshall was dealing with a barter economy. Money, and not simply a *numéraire*, is present in his stationary state. The sort of logical difficulties which here arise are such as Marshall tended to brush aside, valuing pure analysis simply instrumentally, and not for its logical perfection. It is laid down in the *Principles* that 'we may throughout this volume neglect possible changes in the purchasing power of money' (p. 62), but more precisely how the assumptions implicit in his stationary analysis are to be reconciled with the use of money, is not further worked out.

It may be legitimate to ask how far Marshall made absolutely clear to himself, and to his different sorts of readers, the full degree of abstraction involved in his tacit assumptions about money, though it

---

[1] See also *Industry and Trade*, p. 640, *Memorials*, p. 463, and the *Principles*, p. 524.

must be agreed that almost the very last words of the *Principles* warn the reader that 'in real life nearly every economic issue depends, more or less directly, on some complex actions and reactions of credit' not dealt with in the foregoing volume. In writing of the Ricardian assumption of competitive conditions, Marshall explained that 'the progress of events has brought into prominence many considerations, which might reasonably be neglected for the practical purposes of business at that time, but which the modern student is bound to examine with some care'. We shall not attempt to decide here how far a parallel argument provides, or fails to provide, an adequate defence (if such a defence is necessary) for Marshall's assumptions regarding money, uncertainty, and the level of employment in his *Principles*, whether read as 'Vol. I' or as 'an Introductory Volume'.

Of Marshall's more detailed contributions to the theory of money Keynes wrote in 1924: 'There is no part of Economics where Marshall's originality and priority of thought are more marked than here, or where his superiority of insight and knowledge over his contemporaries was greater.' Keynes summarized these contributions under seven headings:

(1) The exposition of the Quantity Theory of Money as a part of the General Theory of Value: (2) The distinction between the 'real' rate of interest and the 'money' rate of interest, and the relevance of this to the credit cycle when the value of money is fluctuating: (3) the causal train by which, in modern credit systems, an additional supply of money influences prices, and the part played by the rate of discount: (4) the enunciation of the 'Purchasing Power Parity' Theory as determining the rate of exchange between countries with mutually inconvertible currencies: (5) the 'chain' method of compiling index numbers: (6) the proposal of paper currency for the circulation based on gold-and-silver symmetallism as the standard: (7) the proposal of an official Tabular Standard for optional use in the case of long contracts. (*Memorials*, pp. 27–33.)

8. *The Principles of Economic and Industrial Policy*

The strong practical reforming purpose which was the initial impulse to, and always closely behind, Marshall's writings, dated from his university vacations in the middle sixties when 'I visited the poorest quarters of several cities and walked through one street after another, looking at the faces of the poorest people. Next, I resolved to make as thorough a study as I could of Political Economy.' (*Memorials*, p. 10.) As he later told a Royal Commission: 'I have devoted myself for the last 25 years to the problem of poverty; and very little of my work has been devoted to any inquiry which does not bear upon that.' (*Memorials*, p. 70.) The problem, as Marshall early formulated it for himself, was: 'How to get rid of such evils in society as arise from a lack of material wealth?' (*Memorials*, p. 16.) Not, of course, because Marshall was a materialist, but because a man who is destitute of material wealth, 'cannot be, if we may say so, what God intended him to be'. Or because, as Robert Blatchford put it, 'a man cannot be a Christian on a pound a week'.

Thirty years after this starting-point, having followed out what is, at all levels of thought, a fairly normal course of intellectual development, Marshall is asking (it is true of a bishop): 'Why should the economist be ashamed to admit that the more he studies "the mystery of evil" on its economic side, the more he is convinced that the key to the mystery is not in human hands?' He counsels, 'patience for the ills of others as well as for our own'. Though there are 'little ways' which seem wholly good, 'why should I be ashamed to say that I know of no simple remedy?' (*Memorials*, p. 387.) He held also that 'impatient insincerity is an evil only less great than moral torpor', and can do just as much harm. (*Principles*, p. 722.)

Marshall's main contribution to the pure analysis of the principles of economic policy lies in his brief comments on the doctrine of maximum satisfaction: that is, on the doctrine that the position of equilibrium of demand and supply resulting from free exchange is one of 'maximum satisfaction'. (*Principles*, pp. 470–6.) His emphasis on the ambiguity of this concept of maximum satisfaction was much needed at the time. He lays down two qualifications to the proposition. The first is that the doctrine assumes 'that all differences in wealth between the different parties concerned can be neglected', an assumption which invalidates any considerable practical significance claimed for the generalization. On the significance and merits of his second qualification it is much more difficult to decide:

> We have to admit that the manner in which a man spends his income is a matter of direct economic concern to the community. For insofar as he spends it on things which obey the law of diminishing return, he makes those things more difficult to be obtained by his neighbours, and thus lowers the real purchasing power of their incomes; while insofar as he spends it on things which obey the law of increasing return, he makes those things more easy of attainment to others and thus increases the real purchasing power of their incomes. (pp. 474–5.)

Marshall does not work this out in detail or by examples. Certainly there may be divergencies between private and social product such as Sidgwick had begun to reveal (showing the likelihood of 'under'- investment in afforestation, lighthouses, &c.) but decreasing or increasing returns due to higher or lower factor-prices necessary to draw units of factors from elsewhere, represent transfers irrelevant from the point of view of the social product. Subsequent controversies showed how open Marshall's hints were to misinterpretation.[1]

As Marshall was so extremely cautious and reserved in his statements of positive doctrines not immediately relevant to policy, how much more cautious, more acutely aware of all the possible complications and repercussions, and more adverse to generalization, was he bound to be in statements about the effects of policies, which, though they might be formulated, and strictly intended, as purely neutral and positive, were almost certain to lend themselves fairly directly to normative political interpretations and misinterpretations. It is clear that Marshall did not look for much guidance on general or particular economic policy in the elaboration of abstract social maximization formulae, but relied primarily on a detailed study of each case, illumined by a wide survey of the historical and contemporary facts, and by a trained cultivated judgement of human beings.

It is in *Industry and Trade*, at the end of a long survey of the contemporary industrial world, that he formulates with all that 'diffidence' which he claims to be 'the first duty of every student', his broad conclusions about the economic policies for his age. As he writes in his preface:

> The present volume is in the main occupied with the influences which still make for sectional and class selfishness: with the limited tendencies of self-interest to direct each individual's action on those lines, in which it will be most beneficial to others; and with the still surviving tendencies of associated action by capitalists and other businessmen, as well as by employees, to regulate output, and action generally, by a desire for sectional rather than national advantage. The hopes and fears of humanity in these matters underlie a great part of Book III, to which Books I and II are introductory. (*Industry and Trade*, p. viii.)

Industry and Trade represents Marshall's form of 'welfare' economics.

---

[1] Cf. Samuelson, *Foundations of Economic Analysis*, pp. 206–8; and the articles by A. Young, 'Pigou's *Wealth and Welfare*', *Quarterly Journal of Economics*, 1913, pp. 672 ff.; F. H. Knight, 'Fallacies in the Interpretation of Social Cost', *Quarterly Journal of Economics*, 1923; and D. H. Robertson, 'Those Boxes', *Economic Journal*, 1924, pp. 16 ff.

The main themes of *Industry and Trade* are, on the one hand, the trend to large-scale units which does much to shape the problems for contemporary economic policy; and, on the other hand, the precariousness of Britain's special economic position, as well as the general fallible nature of human beings and governments, which together set such limitations on possible solutions. After a survey in Book I of 'Some Origins of Present Problems', Book II on 'Dominant Tendencies of Business Organisation' deals with 'the growth of massive production and the ever-increasing size of the representative business unit in almost every branch of industry and trade'. (p. 178.) Marshall concludes on this subject:

> So far as the 'productive' side of business is concerned, it may be concluded that—though the volume of output required for maximum efficiency in proportion to capital is increasing in almost every industry—yet, at any given time and in any given condition of industrial technique, there is likely to be a point, beyond which any further increase in size gives little further increase in economy and efficiency. And this is well; for small businesses are on the whole the best educators of the initiative and versatility which are the chief sources of industrial progress. But this conclusion does not extend to the 'marketing' side of business; for we shall find that, on that side, the advantages of large capitals in competition with capitals of smaller size are constantly increasing almost everywhere. (p. 249.)

Marshall, like Jevons in his *Coal Question*, was keenly aware of the unique historical conjuncture which had made Britain the workshop of the world in the nineteenth century, and of the dangers to her leadership and prosperity that the twentieth century might be bringing. There is a 'Wake up England' note in some of his warnings and exhortations: Britain was behind Germany in scientific and industrial education, 'a chief cause of decline in their industrial leadership' which 'English businessmen were slow to recognise' (p. 95): 'It is specially incumbent on Britain to strive against that stiffness of the joints that is almost inevitable in each old industry, and in the general relations of industries and trades in each old country.' (p. 103.) His final message is:

> The predominance of constructive over destructive forms both of competition and of combination is even more important to Britain than to other countries: for her responsibilities in the world are far greater relatively to her natural resources than are those of any other land. Because she has achieved so much relatively to her resources, she is bound to foster her acquired sources of strength with exceptional vigilance and energy.
> She needs to obtain vast quantities of food and materials from countries,

that have relatively large natural wealth, by exporting to them commodities made by such excellent appliances that her working classes will be able to obtain the larger necessaries and comforts of life—even after allowance for expensive transport—at the cost of no great amount of labour of her own. If her industries follow America's lead in largeness of supply of plant to each worker: and if the short-sighted selfishness which has developed the evil practice of stinting output (whether by trade unions or by employers' associations on the cartel model) be abandoned, then she may prosper: but she may rapidly fall from her high place if she becomes slack in any respect. (p. 655.)

On the human problem Marshall was constantly expressing optimism about all sections of the population: 'The average level of human nature in the Western world has risen rapidly during the last 50 years.' 'The working classes have become better educated, less addicted to coarse enjoyments, and more appreciative of the quiet of a many roomed house with a garden'. 'The number of intelligent and upright directors increases.' But all this surprising optimism was blended with a tough streak of caution, and even pessimism, with regard to most of the current policies of reform, and with a steady insistence on the need to keep harnessed 'the strongest and not merely the highest, forces of human nature'.

Marshall supported measures for the control of monopoly, but he emphasized that there was an over-simplification in regarding all monopoly policies as evil, and that it is often extremely difficult, when it comes down to practical statistical investigation, to sort out the beneficial from the evil effects. Publicity can do much, but American experience showed that mere legislative enactments are of little use by themselves, and 'that investigations in regard to anti-social policy of trusts and cartels can be efficiently made only by a strong staff of men who give their whole time to the work'. (p. 543.)

Marshall's closing discussion of nationalization and State regulation is overwhelmingly negative and, for him, unusually free from qualification. It must, of course, be emphasized that his views relate to the conditions of 1919 or even long before, and that he was always very careful to leave open questions of what might be possible and desirable in the future. Pigou has argued (*Socialism versus Capitalism*, p. 87) that if Marshall had been alive in the 1930's he might have somewhat modified his verdict. The possibility cannot be denied, but the only verdict we have is a very decisive one: 'Much enthusiasm, but very little solid argument, has been prominent in pleas for nationalisation.' (p. 669.)

A. Marshall

... The industries in which government departments and local authorities have succeeded are few in number, but important. They are mainly concerned with 'things that sell themselves'; that is, things which are in large demand, and more or less standardised by natural causes. The chief of them are connected with facilities for transport, and the distribution (by aid of way-leaves) of water, light and power: they all meet elementary needs; call for little or no adaptation to changing habits, or varying tastes; and make use of plant the central ideas of which have been worked out by private enterprise and gradually become common property. . . . It may be noticed in passing that mining does not seem to belong to this class. (p. 668.)

(A majority of the Sankey Commission was already by 1919 reporting in favour of the nationalization of British coal-mines.) As regards the morale and self-respect of the worker: 'The postman is not made free by escaping from the control of an employer, who may be sympathetic; and coming under that of officials, who must obey orders, and have no power to indulge their sympathies.' (p. 658.)

Finally, socialist plans 'take little or no account of the super-human ability required on the part of those persons in whom the chief functions of "the State" are to be concentrated. . . . No doubt the state, like man himself, is to be born anew in the new age; but no definite provision is made for this rebirth; and meanwhile the intimate dependence of progress on the right taking of risks, seems to be ignored.' (p. 651.)

5
P. H. Wicksteed

1. *Early Influences: Wicksteed and the Socialist Movement*

OF Ruskin's influence on what in the 1870's might have been (though does not seem to have been) called 'the New Economics', Sir Ernest Barker has written:

> He taught that it is not the getting but the spending of wealth that matters; that the end of the State is not the clearing of the way in order that the economic man may have free scope in production, but an adjustment of conditions such that the whole man may have room for the use of his tools for the building of the life beautiful. Such teaching has influenced the doctrines of pure economics. It has helped to turn economists since the days of Jevons from the theory of production to the theory of consumption.[1]

There is little or no evidence that Ruskin's or similar teachings directly, or even indirectly, influenced Jevons himself. But they clearly had much influence on Jevons's one great disciple, and self-styled fellow-revolutionary, Philip Wicksteed (and also much more strongly on J. A. Hobson).

After studying classics and theology at University College, London, and Manchester New College, Wicksteed followed his father as a Unitarian minister. He was caught and held, though not irresistibly, by the ideas of Comte in the late sixties, and a close-up view for several years of north-country industrialism when minister in a small town near Manchester led him to the social problem. His friendship with Arnold Toynbee, and the Henry George campaign of 1879, brought him nearer to economics, and like a number of nineteenth-century economists he remained theoretically in favour of land nationalization. It seems to have been about 1882 that he met with Jevons's *Theory of Political Economy*. Anyhow, two years later he was one of the first economists to attack the Marxist theory of value from the marginal utility standpoint (and one of the very few English economists who have felt moved to do that, though Wieser, Böhm-Bawerk, and Pareto all made use of the new theory for that purpose). A not over-serious counterblast came from Bernard Shaw, who, however, as a result of the controversy admitted his conversion by

[1] *Political Thought from Spencer to Today*, p. 195.

Wicksteed, and, as he said, 'put myself in Wicksteed's hands, and became a convinced Jevonian' (at any rate for the next forty or fifty years till the Marxist revival of the late 1920's).

Wicksteed, like Sidgwick at almost exactly the same time, was strongly impressed by the contemporary tide of socialist legislation and aspiration. 'All agree', he said in 1885, 'that an era of socialistic legislation is upon us; the belief has laid hold of men, whether for weal or woe, that intolerable social hardship and wrong are the issue of our present civilisation, and that society, by its corporate and collective action, must, and can in large measure, make the crooked straight.' (*Our Prayers and Our Politics*, p. 10.)

In a sympathetic but pointedly critical review of Fabian Essays (*The Inquirer*, 16.8.1890), Wicksteed had expressed the hope that the ideas and aims of the Fabians and of 'such orthodox economists as Marshall, Foxwell, and Sidgwick' were coming very close together:

A wonderful change has come over us within the last years. Perhaps we are little nearer attaching any definite meaning to socialistic phrases than we were; but yet the moral indignation which till recently accompanied our intellectual irritation is yielding to a kind of vague sympathy. We preface our exposure of the 'transparent fallacies' of socialism by professing ourselves heartily at one with its aspirations and aims.

There was evidence 'that new methods are securing a growing harmony amongst those who have hitherto stood in opposing camps; and that socialists of the "Fabian" stamp must be recognised as fellow-workers by economists of the new school'.

Wicksteed noted with approval the Fabians' 'distinct and definitive abandonment of the system of Karl Marx'. But he complained of the vagueness of their constructive ideas about the industrial and economic organization of the socialist economy. Nevertheless, though he was 'far from hailing Fabian Essays as anything like a solution of the problem of our industrial civilisation', he expressed the hope that the Fabians and the 'orthodox' economists might work together with the same aims. These hopes however were promptly scotched by a letter from Bernard Shaw in the next issue of *The Inquirer*, which, though of doubtful accuracy in some of its claims, showed perhaps more realism than Wicksteed:

I may say that I see no prospect of any sort of rapprochement between the Socialists and the professors of political economy. There is not a single point in my analysis of the existing private property system which would not be accepted as perfectly orthodox at Cambridge, or any other University, if its practical application was omitted. Any person may agree with the Socialists, as far as economic theory is concerned, and yet hold that the present system is worth what it costs. If that is the professional view—and, on the whole, I am afraid it is—all the economics in the world will not make effective Social Democrats of these gentlemen, who have as good a right to their political opinions as we have to our own.

The attitude Wicksteed came to take up was very similar to that of Sidgwick in its deep but gentle scepticism, combined with much sympathy, rather warmer in Wicksteed's case, with socialist ideals. 'I am sometimes supposed', he said, 'to be a Socialist by my friends who are not Socialists, and I am generally not considered one by my friends who are.'[1] Wicksteed started with no extravagant expectations about human perfectibility, and with a realistic grasp of the well-attested fact that man does not live by bread alone, not even when equipped with free (or subsidized) false teeth with which to eat it:

> The practical struggles of the Labour Movement are necessarily concerned with the material conditions and the material reward of Labour. . . . But the great danger of the Labour Movement lies in the belief that the evils of life may be removed by the readjustment of social and industrial machinery, and that when this readjustment has been effected we shall all find life a May Day dance in the midst of peace and plenty. (*What the Labour Church Stands for*, 1892.)

Wicksteed's scepticism was also rooted in a very profound appreciation of the motive power of self-interest and of the spontaneous social organization its free development created, which he charged socialists with failing to understand:

> What a miraculous engine this existing system is. . . . No one has planned it. No creature ever planned for the supply of the wants of London day by day. It accomplishes itself spontaneously. My point is that the present system performs miracles but does not perform miracles enough, and does not perform them satisfactorily. Let us see how we can supplement it, how we can cultivate it, and how we can enlighten it. I think that, when we get a fundamental conception of how it does it itself, we shall not want to undertake the gigantic task of doing it all afresh by deliberate planning and schemes. (*The Inquirer*, 28.11.1908.)

Wicksteed did not contribute much directly to welfare economics or the analysis of economic policy. He saw the greatest service he could contribute to the cause of social reform as that of spreading an understanding 'of what the existing forces do', and of the economic motive

---

[1] 'The Social Ideals and Economic Doctrine of Socialism', *The Inquirer*, 28.11.1908.

with which reformers 'if they are wise . . . will constantly seek alliance in all their reforms', and which is 'a power ever active . . . a power which we cannot destroy or will to sleep, but which in a certain measure we can control or direct'. (*Common Sense* &c., vol. i, pp. 210–11.)

'A delight in abstract theory, close touch with concrete things, strong commonsense, and an overmastering moral sympathy, where these meet in a single mind the man is a born economist.' That was Foxwell's estimate of Wicksteed. But if Wicksteed was a born econo- mist he was able to make his major contribution to the subject (or write what he himself would certainly have regarded as his most important economic work), because, like Sidgwick, he was a good many other things besides. His contributions were of two kinds: (1) a great textbook exposition of marginal analysis; (2) two important pieces of technical analysis, which both followed closely from his general view of marginal economics; these were his analyses of the supply curve, and of the co-ordination of the laws of distribution.

2. *The Marginal Principle and the Common Sense of Political Economy*

We cannot attempt here to follow the details of Wicksteed's per- sonal philosophical synthesis of Aristotle, Aquinas, Dante, Comte, and Jevons, and to see how it all cohered. But we can notice how much his exposition of the marginal principle, and his constant insistence that 'the laws of economics were the laws of life', owed to Comte and Aristotle.

In holding that one cannot separate off for study, and hope to under- stand, one part of the life of the individual or of society in isolation from the whole of that life, Wicksteed was obviously following Comte, from whom the motto on the title-page of *Common Sense* is taken: 'L'analyse économique proprement dite ne me semble pas devoir finalement être conçue ni cultivée, soit dogmatiquement, soit historique- ment, à part de l'ensemble de l'analyse sociologique, soit statique, soit dynamique.'

Wicksteed continually insisted that the marginal principle could not be understood in all its generality and pervasiveness if it was not applied to every sort of resource-allocation. The entire life, whether of an individual or of the community, was a constant problem in the alloca- tion of the talents and span of years granted to men. To drive home the universality of the marginal principle, and of the complementary opportunity cost principle, Wicksteed employed an inexhaustible range of examples. He pressed the application of these principles up to the highest levels, attacking everywhere in economics, politics, and morals 'the cant of the absolute in a world in which all things are relative'. His analysis amounted to a refinement of Aristotle's doctrine of virtue as a mean into the doctrine that virtue lies in a nicely adjusted margin, or that virtue requires a conscientious balancing, as precisely as possible, of one's duties at the margin:

Virtue, wisdom, sagacity, prudence, success, imply different schemes of values, but they all submit to the law formulated by Aristotle with reference to virtue, and analysed by modern writers with reference to business, for they all consist in combining factors κατ᾽ ὀρθὸν λόγον, *in the right proportion*, as fixed by that distribution of resources which establishes the equilibrium of their differential significances in securing the object contemplated, whether that object be tranquillity of mind, the indulgence of an overmastering passion or affection, the command of things and services in the circle of exchange, or a combination of all these, or of any other conceivable factors of life. (*Common Sense*, &c., vol. ii, p. 776.)

The principle of the market—that the largest profit goes to him who best meets his neighbour's wants at the lowest cost to himself—works itself out in much higher senses than are commonly perceived, not simply within 'the circle of exchange'. The truly happy and satisfied man is bound to be the sincere intelligent altruist who knows best how to serve other people at no cost to himself, and even at a positive gain in pleasure. For such a man's services the market can never dry up.

That man is happy indeed who finds that in expressing some part of his nature he is providing for all his natural wants; or that in rendering services to friends in which he delights he is putting himself in command of all the services he himself needs for the accomplishment of his own purposes. A perfect coincidence of this nature is the dream of modern Utopias; but my present subject is only the economic side of the shield. (vol. ii, p. 773.)

Wicksteed's economic works are unique in their passages of homely but exalted *Lebensweisheit*, expressed in *Common Sense* in many passing wayside sermons: for instance, those on the meaning of character (p. 123): on the universal duty of economizing (p. 124): on the contradiction inherent in a Utopia where all work is enjoyed (p. 200): on the problem of finding one's personal niche in life (p. 198): on the confusion in the maxim 'Duty before all things' (p. 409): all so very remote from economic analysis as usually conceived, and perhaps connected with the neglect of Wicksteed's textbook.

Jevons's hedonist tendencies were, of course, not much followed by his enthusiastic disciple. In the *Alphabet of Economic Science* (1888), a brief pioneering textbook which included one of the first uses of the adjective 'marginal', Wicksteed took some of the preliminary steps in the critical analysis of the utility concept, which was to lead on, in some versions of economic theory, to its complete extrusion, though he was then still ready to consider the theoretical possibility of an accurate measurement of satisfaction. (p. 15.) A first and obvious step was to insist on the complete ethical neutrality of 'utility', stripping it of the sense of practical usefulness which it had had for example for Adam Smith, who was therefore inclined to deny the 'utility' of diamonds. Secondly, Wicksteed suggested in the *Alphabet* that the utility of a good is not a function simply of the quantity possessed of that good alone, but of all other goods; which leaves 'utility' seemingly much more elusive than it is in the simpler more direct conception of the relations between utility and particular goods and particular consumer's tastes. The more drastic steps towards eliminating or emasculating the utility concept were to be taken by Fisher and Pareto, before Wicksteed, without avoiding the term completely, based his *Common Sense* mainly on relative scales of preference and the rather indefinite and colourless term 'significance'. This more indefinite concept of the fundamental individual maximand led Wicksteed to a much more generalized—and though he perhaps did not realize it—a more formal and abstract conception of economics: 'There is no occasion to define the economic motive, or the psychology of the economic man, for economics studies a type of relation, not a type of motive.' (p. 780.)

The market or 'the economic relation' was also, for Wicksteed, like the concept of utility, something neutral. The market was a piece of social machinery, like the State, capable of being exploited for the most unjust purposes, but also for perfectly legitimate and beneficial ones. There was not necessarily any taint of sordid materialism about the economic relation, on the other hand: 'It is idle to assume that ethically desirable results will necessarily be produced by an ethically indifferent instrument and it is as foolish to make the economic relation an idol as it is to make it a bogey.' (vol. i, p. 184.)

Turning to the dynamics of Wicksteed's system, one would not expect to find him optimistically investing the concept of equilibrium with any special, or teleological, significance. Like most works of its period *The Common Sense of Political Economy* consists of a skeleton of comparatively precise and rigorously worked out static maximization formulae (as we would prefer to call what Wicksteed called the 'laws of the market'), clothed and made life-like by a dynamic apparatus of aperçus, and assumptions, along with some analyses of short-period developments from particular initial situations, and an extensive reliance, implicit or explicit, that in some rather indefinite 'long run' the economic system in general and in particular was self-adjusting, with supply and demand marrying and living happily ever after in equilibrium.

Expectations had an important part in Wicksteed's market analysis, and, like Jevons, he emphasized, here and there, the vital importance of uncertainty, and the speculative element in all economic activity. (vol. i, p. 113.) He pointed out that equilibrium meant the fulfilment of expectations and disequilibrium their disappointment owing to miscalculation or unforeseeable surprises. (vol. i, pp. 88–93.) He could not resist enunciating: 'In an exchange community . . . there is a perpetual tendency to establish an equilibrium.' (vol. i, p. 143.) But he does not try to force any conclusions for policy from this most ambiguous of ambiguities. He emphasizes, rather, the difficulties of the path to equilibrium, and that divergencies from this straight and narrow path react on the equilibrium price itself, and in turn alter the 'equilibrium' point to which the market is 'tending'. (vol. i, p. 226.) His claim, however, that 'although the consequences of mistakes may change the equilibrating price there always exists ideally such a price at any given moment if it can but be discovered' (vol. i, p. 227) seems again to be a somewhat doubtful reassurance.

Wicksteed's most interesting contributions to dynamics lie in his analysis of comparatively simple short-period cases, such as the daily village fruit-market, and of the speculative element in the transactions. His chapters on interest ('the market in advances follows the law of other markets') and on money and banking, do not seem to have the same sustained quality as the remainder of the work, nor to be closely integrated with it. He delivers an attack on 'the quantity law', and gives also an outline of a cash-balance approach to the theory of money (vol. ii, pp. 600–1) which, however, he unfortunately did not link up with his dynamic fruit-market analysis.

Nearly four pages out of the many hundreds of *Common Sense* are devoted to 'the connected problems of unemployment, depression, and commercial crises, which are admittedly among the most baffling in the whole field of applied economic science'. Wicksteed does mention by way of remedy that: 'It seems ideally conceivable that the

State should undertake public works, that must be executed some time, in the slack periods when they can be executed at least expense, and will at the same time, have a tendency to counteract a serious evil.' (vol. ii, p. 640.)

3. (a) *The Supply Curve;* (b) *The Co-ordination of the Laws of Distribution*

(a) Wicksteed's criticism of the supply curve and the 'Marshallian cross' is developed in *Common Sense*, but finds its most incisive expression in his paper on 'The Scope and Method of Political Economy in the Light of the Marginal Principle' (1914). He begins by asserting of the supply curve, with some terminological dogmatism: 'I say it boldly and baldly there is no such thing.' (One cannot help being reminded, by this way of putting it, of other definitional edicts of non-existence pronounced at various times on 'real cost', 'hoarding', 'the general price level', 'differences between savings and investment, etc.') However, much of the 'boldness and baldness' disappears when a line or two farther down Wicksteed explains: 'What is usually called the supply curve is in reality the demand curve of those who possess the commodity. . . . The separating out of this portion of the demand curve and reversing it in the diagram is a process which has its meaning and its legitimate function, as we shall see in a moment, but is wholly irrelevant to the determination of the price.' (*Common Sense*, vol. ii, p. 785.)

Wicksteed elsewhere demonstrates that for the determination of the price of a fixed stock of goods in a market, what has to be known is simply the quantity in the market and the relative scales, or demand curves, of all the participants. Which of the participants have brought the stock to market, or own any of it, and so are 'suppliers', is more or less a legal or sociological detail. In any case, in rapidly changing and uncertain conditions the same individual may be one moment 'supplying' and the next 'demanding'.

Wicksteed's most illuminating example is a characteristically homely short-period one of a peasant woman selling damsons, which brings out clearly the omnipresent speculative element and the seller's reserve demand for her own consumption and for jam-making:

A housewife who has just gathered her own damsons and goes to a closely adjacent market with the intention of buying more, and proceeding to a jam boiling on a lordly scale, may find the prices so unexpectedly high as to induce her hastily to send home for her stock and sell the whole of it, perceiving that, at such a price, there are many available substitutes for the damsons which would come cheaper for her own winter use.

But we have seen that the stall-keepers may refuse to sell at a certain price for other reasons than that the goods in question would be worth this reserved price to themselves for their own uses and purposes. They refuse early in the morning to sell at prices which would get rid of their whole stock in a few hours or minutes because they expect a constant flow of potential customers throughout the day. At the moment, then, they have a reserve price, not on their own account, to meet their personal wants, but in anticipation of the wants of others. At the moment these anticipations determine the place which the commodity takes on their own relative scales just as much as if they wanted it for their own use, and if this speculative holding of stocks ceased, the price would tumble down. (*Common Sense*, vol. i, p. 234.)

Wicksteed's analysis and diagrams of the supply curve, or 'commodity preference', have recently found a valuable application in the treatment of the demand and supply of money, liquidity preference, and interest.[1]

It was part of Wicksteed's economic credo to apply this analysis of the pricing of a fixed stock to general cases of continuous production, passing back the assumption of fixed stocks of resources to apply ultimately to the economic universe as a whole. This enables him to consider, in the Austrian manner, the treatment of cost of production as a separate element in determining market transactions in addition to demand, as ultimately misleading and unnecessary:

Again we have an alias merely. Cost of production is merely the form in which the desiredness a thing possesses for someone else presents itself to me. When we take the collective curve of demand for any factor of production we see again that it is entirely composed of demands, and my adjustment of my own demands to the conditions imposed by the demands of others is of exactly the same nature whether I am buying cabbages or factors for the production of steel plates. (vol. ii, p. 788.)

This is Wicksteed's statement of that ultimate assumption as to the fixity of the supply of all resources which distinguishes the analysis of himself, the Austrian school, and J. B. Clark, from that of Marshall and the English classics:[2]

The supply of one market then, so far as it is capable of regulation by the

[1] See G. F. Thirlby, *South African Journal of Economics*, vol. vii, 1939, and *Economic Journal*, 1948, p. 331. Also, E. Schneider, *Zur Liquiditätstheorie des Zinses*, Weltwirtschaftliches Archiv, 1949, p. 123.

[2] Cf. L. C. Robbins, 'On a Certain Ambiguity in the Conception of Stationary Equilibrium', *Economic Journal*, 1930, pp. 194–214.

action of man, constitutes a demand upon some other market. As we go higher and higher upstream towards the ultimate sources from which all human wants are satisfied, and examine them in less and less differentiated forms, we shall find that the market in them embraces, and directly or indirectly balances, an ever-wider range of the tastes and desires of the community. But the law of the market never changes. The price is always determined by estimates of the quantity of the commodity available and estimates of the relative scales of the community. Nothing can affect the market price of anything which does not affect one of these factors. (vol. i, pp. 261–2.)

(*b*) *The Co-ordination of the Laws of Distribution.* It has been convenient to leave till last Wicksteed's most specialized contribution to economic analysis, although he made it in 1894, comparatively early in his career as an economist.

In the early nineties, twenty years after the birth of the marginal utility theory of value, the marginal productivity analysis of distribution was for the first time being systematically formulated by a number of different economists almost simultaneously. J. B. Clark, Marshall, Edgeworth, Wicksell, and Walras, not to mention such less well-known writers as Stuart Wood and Arthur Berry, all within a few years produced the main essentials of marginal productivity analysis. Wicksteed's *Essay* stands out among these writings.

It was part of Wicksteed's economic philosophy that marginal analysis provided a single universal key to the economic cosmos applicable to all allocation problems of households or firms, whether of consumption goods or factors of production. Classical distribution theory, on the other hand, had consisted of separate explanations for the incomes of each of the three main social classes, based more on the particular characteristics of the factor they owned.[1] From the point of view of marginal analysis, as Wicksteed understood it, it was as irrelevant and arbitrary to classify factors of production into the three main groups, each with their special characteristics, as it would have been in the pure analysis of 'value', or consumer's behaviour, to group consumption goods under three arbitrary heads, say, of food, clothing, and entertainment. As an enthusiastic furtherer of what he regarded as the Jevonian revolution, Wicksteed sought to press to its logical conclusion the co-ordination of distribution analysis through the omni-

---

[1] This generalization hardly applies to Cairnes's treatment (*v. above* Ch. I, sect. 3) in his *Leading Principles*. Cairnes treats the 'laws of value' as solving also the problems of *relative* wages and profits, which follow the same laws that govern the exchange value of commodities. But on to this analysis of relative distribution Cairnes sought to add an analysis of average absolute wages, profits, &c.

relevant marginal principle, regardless of the established concepts and time-honoured terminology of the classics, and to base the values of all goods and services, whether for production or consumption, ultimately on consumer's utility. He begins his *Essay*:

In investigating the laws of distribution it has been usual to take each of the great factors of production such as Land, Capital and Labour, severally, to enquire into the special circumstances under which that factor co-operates in production, the special considerations which act upon the persons that have control of it, and the special nature of the service that it renders, and from all these considerations to deduce a special law regulating the share of the product that will fall in distribution to that particular factor.

Now as long as this method is pursued it seems impossible to co-ordinate the laws of distribution and ascertain whether or not the shares which the theory assigns to the several factors cover the product and are covered by it. For in order that this may be possible it seems essential that all the laws should be expressed in common terms. . . .

The modern investigations into the theory of value have already given us the lead we require. Indeed the law of exchange value is itself the law of distribution of the general resources of society. . . . And the exchange value of each commodity or service, if purchasable, is determined by the effect upon the total satisfaction of the community which the addition or the withdrawal of a small increment of it would have, *all the other variables remaining constant.*

The basis for a co-ordinated explanation of distribution to the factors of production must be the service rendered by those factors or by units of them, and the task of such a co-ordinated explanation is to show that when all the factors have been rewarded on that basis the total product is exactly exhausted without a residual.

Wicksteed attacks the problem by examining the classical residual theory of rent and shows that this can be construed as a marginal productivity theory of the doses of capital and labour, and that a marginal productivity theory of the return to land can be obtained simply by applying the doses in reverse, that is by applying units of land to a fixed quantity of labour and capital, leaving interest and wages as the residual.

The significant measure of 'product' for marginal productivity analysis is clearly not in physical terms, or in terms of social utility, but in revenue terms (the 'commercial' product). For Wicksteed's crucial 'adding-up' or 'exhaustion-of-product' theorem to be valid, the revenue product, or the price of the commodity, must remain constant. And this is the case under perfect competition, the assumption on which the main body of economic analysis rested.

Wicksteed, however, in a sense over-ran himself or the analysis of his day, and later, in the face of the not-very-well-conceived criticism of Edgeworth and Pareto, quite unnecessarily withdrew the central proposition of his Essay. To demonstrate fully the sense in which 'perfectly competitive' conditions (by definition, of course) precisely limit the payments of factors to their 'marginal products' required a more advanced analysis of the role and reward of the entrepreneur, and of the cost conditions of firms as distinct from industries, than was available to Wicksteed in 1894. But this hardly detracts from the achievement of his *Essay*, which, until Professor Robbins's new edition of his works in the 1930's, like his great textbook, failed to receive the appreciation from English economists which it is now recognized as deserving.[1]

[1] See the detailed discussion by G. J. Stigler, *Production and Distribution Theories*, Ch. XII, p. 320, 'Euler's Theorem and the Marginal Productivity Theory'.

6
F. Y. Edgeworth

1. *Edgeworth on Theory and Practice*

U NLIKE his great contemporaries Edgeworth never attempted a comprehensive treatise. It might seem on a first impression that his interest in economic theory was far more detached and in-tellectual than that of Marshall, Sidgwick, Wicksteed, and even Jevons, and that it had not the same strong practical and ethical interest and intent. Edgeworth's devotion to pure analysis certainly had its aesthetic side, but it would, of course, be a complete misunderstanding to inter-pret his comparative concentration on, and keen taste for, theoretical refinements and 'curiosa' as a kind of ninetyish intellectual aestheticism. In his *Autobiography* Mill speaks of the 'great practical good sense of the Edgeworth kind'. This had by no means entirely disappeared in F. Y. Edgeworth, the last of the family, in spite of all his oddities.

Edgeworth had optimistically started with what seem today rather extravagant hopes of what mathematical economic theory might con-tribute to the framing of the right economic policy. With the fading of these early utilitarian visions, a mature, restrained, but profound and persistently expressed caution, like that of Sidgwick's, set in. This caution derived from his insight into the history and logical structure of economic theory. He repeatedly inculcated 'the Socratic lesson of modesty taught by Cournot and Jevons', and in particular the former's dictum that those who are most concerned for the precision of their prin-ciples will be most sensible of the limits of their application (and there-fore ultimately the least unpractical) in their treatment of real questions.

In his inaugural lecture Edgeworth warned:

It is only at the heights that contemplation 'reigns and revels'. The descent to particulars is broken and treacherous; requiring caution, patience, and attention to each step. Those who without regarding what is immediately before them have looked away to general views have slipped.... It is possible to combine an enthusiastic admiration of theory with the coldest hesitations in practice. (*Papers*, vol. i, p. 8.)

Edgeworth was always far more concerned to instil caution and reserve than to stake out claims. Instead of emphasizing the great start, and greater certainty, that the nature of their subject matter, and the use of introspection, gave to economists, as contrasted with other scientists (in particular natural scientists), he urged that: 'In the race of the sciences we are, as it were, handicapped by having to start at a considerable distance behind the position of mere nescience. An effort is required to remove prejudices worse than ignorance; a great part of the career of our science has consisted in surmounting preliminary fallacies'. (*Papers*, vol. i, p. 5.)

The great danger in the application of economic theory was the danger of overlooking something:

No remedy can be prescribed except to cultivate open-mindedness and candour and above all sympathy, the absence of which has aggravated the most serious mistakes which have been committed in political economy. I refer particularly to errors relating to the remuneration of the wage-earning classes ... [through not entering] more fully into the life and conditions, views and wants of the wage-earner. . . . When we have done our best to correct our practical judgments, there will still be, as Mill says, 'almost always room for a modest doubt as to our practical conclusions'. This modesty and this doubt are particularly appropriate in the academic teacher, who, expected to know something about all branches of his subject, cannot be expected to have examined many of them closely at first hand. (*Papers*, vol. i, p. 9.)

If then Edgeworth remained mainly on what he called 'the heights', it was not merely from a temperamental preference for those regions as such. It was because he had come to be more keenly impressed than most, from his study of the history and logic of the subject, by the disastrous intellectual spills, to which those seem to be exposed, who embark over-confidently on the treacherous descent from their theoretical altitudes to the market place, the political pamphlet, and *The Times*. His detached scepticism was thus closely connected with 'the great practical good sense of the Edgeworth kind'. As it seemed to Edgeworth, the economist's equipment was a pruning-hook for the cutting away of false theories and speculations (of which there were an abundance both in his own garden and outside it), and 'in the vineyard of science to perform the part of a pruning-hook is an honourable function'. It is not honourable or practical to pretend that equipped with a pruning-hook one is fitted to take on the functions of a bulldozer.

2. *Mathematical Psychics: On the Content and Form of Economic Theory*

After taking 'Greats' at Oxford (1869) Edgeworth explored a wide range of subjects before coming to political economy. He was called to the Bar. He lectured (as befitted a nephew of Maria Edgeworth and a cousin of Beddoes) on English Language and Literature, at Bedford College, London. He came to economic theory via, or in, an attempt to 'extricate', as he put it, 'a clear mathematical conception of exact utilitarianism', that is, in order to try to formulate the utilitarian ideals quantitatively, which was the object of his early essay *New and Old Methods of Ethics* (1877), a work of which Keynes said: 'Edgeworth's peculiarities of style, his brilliance of phrasing, his obscurity of connection, his inconclusiveness of aim, his restlessness of direction, his courtesy, his caution, his shrewdness, his wit, his subtlety, his learning, his reserve—all are there full-grown'.

In *Mathematical Psychics* (1881) Edgeworth sought to extend the analysis a stage further by applying it to economic life. But the first theme of the 150 pages of this unique volume—the theme is returned to in one of the seven appendices included—is that of the applicability, legitimacy, and advantages of the mathematical formulation of economic theory as contrasted with what Edgeworth refers to elsewhere as 'the zig-zag windings of the flowery path of literature'. Today when it is more the advantages and legitimacy of 'the flowery path' which seem sometimes more in need of defence and emphasis, it is difficult to appreciate fully the importance and originality of Jevons's and Edgeworth's campaigns in the mathematical cause and to remember the obscurantism which they had to overcome. Like Pareto later, Edgeworth saw one of the main advantages of mathematical methods in the terse expression of relations of interdependence and mutual determination, a notion that the leaders of the Austrian school in particular, with their thorough-going rejection of mathematical methods, found it difficult to receive.

Edgeworth goes on to distinguish between economics and the economical calculus, on the one hand, and politics and ethics, or the utilitarian calculus on the other: 'Economics investigates the arrangements between agents each tending to his own maximum utility; and Politics and (Utilitarian) Ethics investigate the arrangements which conduce to the maximum sum total of utility'. (p. 6.) 'The central conception is *Greatest Happiness*, the greatest possible sum total of pleasure summed through all time and over all sentience.' (*Mathematical Psychics*, p. vii.)

In the economical calculus, therefore, the unit, 'utility', has only two dimensions, intensity and time. No inter-personal comparisons are required. For the utilitarian or moral calculus a third dimension is needed. It is necessary 'to compare the happiness of one person with the happiness of another, and generally the happiness of groups of different members and different average happiness'. (p. 7.) 'Such comparison', Edgeworth insists, 'can no longer be shirked if there is to be any systematic morality at all. . . . You cannot spend sixpence utilitarianly without having considered whether your action tends to increase the comfort of a limited number, or numbers with limited comfort'. (p. 8.) Edgeworth summons the economist to formulate and apply a three-dimensional utility, and proposes to solve the problem of this third dimension by the simple Benthamite rule that 'each is to count for one and one only'.

The 'number' and 'time' dimensions of utility can therefore be fairly simply dealt with. One is 'an affair of census', and the other of 'clockwork'. But there still remains the dimension of 'intensity'. This does, indeed, present 'peculiar difficulties':

> *Atoms of pleasure* are not easy to distinguish and discern; more continuous than sand, more discrete than liquid; as it were nuclei of the just-perceivable, embedded in circumambient semi-consciousness. . . . We cannot *count* the golden sands of life; we cannot *number* the 'innumerable smile' of seas of love, but we seem to be capable of observing that there is here a greater, there a less, multitude of pleasure-units, mass of happiness; and that is enough. (p. 8.)

If brilliance of phrasing and luxuriance of metaphor could have established the comparability of utility personally and interpersonally, this would have been achieved for all time in 1881.

In arguing that the economist had to apply the utilitarian calculus and its three-dimensional utility to all problems of work and wealth, Edgeworth was setting him a very wide task. Later on in *Mathematical Psychics*, Edgeworth challenged the ἀγεωμέτρητος (the non- or anti-mathematical economist) to face an examination paper, consisting of seven questions on 'Some Problems to be Solved without Mathematics', which he evidently regarded it as possible and obligatory for the economist—with Mathematics—to attempt to answer. Several of the questions come fully within what would be considered the normal range of the economist. But one of them, for example, was as follows:

2. When Fanny Kemble visited her husband's slave plantations, she found that the same (equal) tasks were imposed on the men and women, the women accordingly, in consequence of their weakness, suffering much more fatigue. Supposing the husband to insist on a certain quantity of work being done, and to leave the *distribution* of the burden to the philanthropist, what

would be the most beneficent arrangement—that the men should have the same *fatigue*, or not only *more task*, but *more fatigue*? (p. 95.)

Further Edgeworth believed that where the issue of wage-bargaining was 'indeterminate' the economist, as such, could, and should, with the aid of his three-dimensional utilitarian calculus, arbitrate, and that there was one objective utilitarian settlement which the economist could and should discover and define:

> The whole creation groans and yearns, desiderating a principle of arbitration, an end of strifes. . . . Now, it is a circumstance of momentous interest—visible to common sense when pointed out by mathematics—that *one* of the in general indefinitely numerous *settlements* between contractors is the utilitarian arrangement of the articles of contract, the contract tending to the greatest possible total utility of the contractors. In this direction, it may be conjectured, is to be sought the required principle. (pp. 51 and 53.)

It does not help very much to say that what Edgeworth was proposing was 'unscientific' or 'illegitimate'. No one can legislate in this region. One can only say that such statements as we have quoted are intolerably ambiguous, that there are no clearly stated means of ever testing them, and that it seems that any meaning that might reasonably be attached to them would, as far as one ever could test it, be very trivial. We cannot attempt here to boil away the steaming metaphysical fluids in Edgeworth's saucepan and weigh up, or 'extricate', the possibly unimpressive and uninteresting crystal of attestable fact that one may guess is all that would eventually be discoverable. We must be content to record, as Samuelson has expressively put it, that 'to a man like Edgeworth steeped as he was in the utilitarian tradition utility, nay social utility, was as real as his morning jam'. (*Foundations of Economic Analysis*, p. 206.)

Anyhow, Edgeworth seems largely to have abandoned the pursuit of these early visions, though now and then revealing an attachment to the utilitarian phrases and formulae, in particular to the inter-personal comparison of utility, in opposition to what he called 'Jevons' solipsism'. In his obituary biography (1926) Keynes described the development of Edgeworth's thought on this subject, in a passage perhaps significant also for Keynes's own intellectual history:

> But it implied in Edgeworth an unwillingness to revise or take up again the more speculative studies of his youth. The same thing was true of his work in Economics. He was disinclined, in company with most other economists of the Classical School, to reconsider how far the initial assumptions of the

Marginal Theory stand or fall with the Utilitarian Ethics and the Utilitarian Psychology, out of which they sprang and which were sincerely accepted, in a way no one accepts them now, by the founders of the subject. Mill, Jevons, the Marshall of the '70s, and the Edgeworth of the late '70s and the early '80s, *believed* the Utilitarian Psychology and laid the foundations of the subject in this belief. The later Marshall and the later Edgeworth and many of the younger generation have not fully believed; but we still trust the super-structure without exploring too thoroughly the soundness of the original foundations.[1]

If not many today can follow Edgeworth's early conception of what might be the content of theoretical political economy, all should appreciate his clear grasp of the form or structure of its abstract theorems. As a Benthamite, Edgeworth held that 'the principal inquiries in Social Science may be viewed as maximum problems'. He saw economic problems as maximum allocation problems similar in form to the problem of distributing 'a given quantity of fuel so as to obtain the greatest possible quantity of available energy, among a given set of engines which differ in efficiency'. His analogies, in fact, tend to be taken from the physical sciences.

Edgeworth saw, also, that a determinate maximization problem can, strictly, only be formulated for Robinson Crusoes or for individuals acting under 'perfectly competitive' conditions. He saw, that is, how closely dependent micro-economic maximization theorems are on the 'perfect competition' postulate. He even went so far as to argue that in a régime of general monopoly (and, presumably, of oligopoly) 'abstract economists would be deprived of their occupation, the investigation of the conditions which determine value. There would survive only the empirical school, flourishing in a chaos congenial to their mentality'. (*Papers*, vol. i, pp. 138–9.) This is Edgeworth's version of Mill's dictum that 'only through the principle of competition has political economy any pretension to the character of a science'.[2] It can at least be agreed that those whose mentality finds uncongenial

---

[1] *Essays in Biography*, p. 282. The echoes of this passage in the opening of the Preface to the 'General Theory' ten years later will be noticed: that is, the contrast between the 'initial assumptions' or 'premises', and the 'Superstructure' of the theories of the 'Classical School', and the doubts about the former.

[2] The same fundamental point has been made in a modern context by J. R. Hicks: 'Under monopoly the stability conditions become indeterminate; and the basis on which economic laws can be constructed is therefore shorn away. . . . It is, I believe, only pos-sible to save anything from this wreck—and it must be remembered that the threatened wreckage is that of the greater part of general equilibrium theory—if we can assume that the markets confronting most of the firms with which we shall be dealing do not differ very greatly from perfectly competitive markets'. (*Value and Capital*, 2nd ed., pp. 83–84.)

the complexity, variety, and even 'chaos', of the real economic world, had better leave it alone altogether than try to overtidy it, or over-simplify it, in order to make it fit some neat *a-priori* theory or geo-metrical diagram. Edgeworth appears to be arguing that the field of occupation of 'abstract economists' is restricted to that of individual maximizing-allocation problems, and that outside this narrow com-pass economic phenomena are not susceptible to the analysis of the abstract economist. It is not possible to say how widely held such a view of the nature and limitations of economic analysis was in Edge-worth's time, though overt traces of it remained as late as the 1930's.

Further, Edgeworth appreciated and developed, though only un-fortunately in a few *obiter dicta*, the nature of the distinction between static and dynamic analysis (as contrasted with the analysis of stationary or changing conditions), and he saw the importance of this distinction for the concept of equilibrium. It was the failure to draw it clearly which made for so much of the dangerous ambiguity of contemporary equilibrium theories, and rendered them so liable to misinterpretation. Edgeworth's perception is shown in his criticism of the rather obscure and noisy dynamics of Walras, where the path to equilibrium in a market is described as emerging from a process of *tâtonnements*, and the 'crying' of prices by the individuals in the market, until somehow the equilibrium price emerges. Edgeworth commented: 'He describes *a* way rather than *the* way by which economic equilibrium is reached. *For we have no general dynamical theory determining the path of the economic system from any point assigned at random to a position of equilibrium. We know only the statical properties of the position'.* (Our italics.) (*Papers*, vol. ii, p. 311.)

Again: 'What the author professes to demonstrate is the course which the higgling of the market takes—the path, as it were, by which the economic system works down to equilibrium. Now, as Jevons points out, the equations of exchange are of a statical, not a dynamical, character. They define a position of equilibrium, but they afford no information as to the path by which that point is reached.' (One need only add that they also, of course, afford no information as to whether that point ever is or will be reached.) However: 'Particular paths may be indicated by way of illustration, "to fix the ideas" as mathematicians say'. (*Papers*, vol. ii, p. 39.)

How much unjustifiable advice has been given based on an arbitra-rily assumed 'equilibrium' self-adjusting dynamics it is not possible or necessary to try to guess. But however large or small one's estimate, it could have been avoided if Edgeworth's pioneering warnings and distinctions had been followed up. In the light of these warnings and distinctions it would not appear that he could have attached any wide significance to his own dynamic model of 'recontracting'.

3. *Some Further Analytical Contributions*

In this section we shall try to point out one or two of the more central of Edgeworth's many and various contributions to pure analysis. In addition to the subjects touched upon here, Edgeworth wrote on the Theory of International Trade, Railway Rates, Taxation, and Index Numbers, but not on Industrial Fluctuations or Crises.

(*a*) *Indifference and Contract Curves*: embedded in the ever-remarkable pages of *Mathematical Psychics* is the first account of the indifference curve: in name, presumably suggested by Jevons's 'law of indifference', while the type of diagram in which it appeared may have been suggested by Marshall's privately printed diagrammatic studies of the Pure Theory of Domestic Values and of Foreign Trade.

Edgeworth was addressing himself to the analysis of contract, and was concerned to show that in the case of barter between two individuals of one commodity for another, the exchange rate is indeterminate. It was in the course of this same analysis that Edgeworth's contract curve appeared, the curve which traces out the possible points of settlement between the two parties. As contrasted with the procedures of Jevons and Walras, Edgeworth introduced an assumption of great ultimate consequence in the theory of consumer's behaviour, that the individual's utility is not a function of one commodity only, but of both (or all) the commodities involved. It is noteworthy that the most thoroughly 'utilitarian' work in the literature of economic theory initiated the assumptions, concepts, and technique, which led to the extrusion of the utility concept—from the point of view, at any rate, of many economists. On the new postulate, 'utility' is related to the consumer's entire consumption or *Versorgungslage*, and becomes at once much more shadowy and elusive than it had been when related to particular single goods and the particular tastes for them.

Edgeworth's original indifference curves (or iso-utility curves as W. E. Johnson called them), were drawn upside down as compared with their present familiar form (in which they were first drawn by Fisher, or Auspitz and Lieben). The price-lines radiated from the origin and the curves showed how much of one commodity the consumer would give up in return for one unit more of the other commodity, his total utility remaining the same. The curves were (normally) convex to the 'sacrifice' (negative) axis and concave to the 'receiving' (positive) axis, instead of concave to both axes as in the now common diagram.

(*b*) Edgeworth's paper on the Pure Theory of Monopoly (1897) is mainly concerned with problems of taxation, but the second section contains his discussion of duopoly, concerned to prove 'that in the case of two or more monopolists dealing with competitive groups, economic equilibrium is indeterminate'. Edgeworth propounds an 'oscillating' solution with the price 'dancing down' from the monopoly to the competitive level under the influence of competition, and then 'jumping back' to the monopoly level, as one seller (on Edgeworth's assumptions) finds himself in a simple monopoly position—a conceivable process but surely slightly far-fetched as a 'solution' to the problem of duopoly. We shall discuss it further in our chapter on theories of the firm and of markets (*see below*, Ch. 19, sect. 2).

(*c*) Edgeworth's paper on Distribution (1904) is mainly a critical commentary on his wide international readings in the theory of the subject. It represents the explanation of the distribution problem which generally came to prevail among orthodox economists, that is, mainly and fundamentally a 'marginal productivity' formula (which Edgeworth himself was among the first to elaborate in 1889) with some qualifications regarding the place of profit, some attachment to the classical rent concept and terminology, and (as with Marshall) some scepticism about the content and significance of the whole theory.

Edgeworth opens with a distinguished definition: 'Distribution is the species of Exchange by which produce is divided between the parties who have contributed to its production.' On the main principles of wages and rent he follows Marshall. The worker balances the pain or disutility from labour against the wage. The fact that its total quantity is fixed to society significantly differentiates land from capital, though Edgeworth stresses more than Marshall the inextricable 'capital' element in the form of improvements in all cultivated land. On the subject of capital Edgeworth adopted some of the terminology and concepts of Böhm-Bawerk, 'the Austrian leader', as to 'stages of production' and 'roundabout methods'. But he does not agree that 'increases in capital' necessarily 'lengthen the period of production'.

Edgeworth vigorously attacks Walras's, and later Clark's, doctrine that in static equilibrium the entrepreneur makes neither profit nor loss. But he bases his criticism on terminological common-sense rather than on an analysis or grasp of static assumptions. The doctrine of zero profits 'is violently contrary to usage', . . . it is 'a strange use of language to describe a man who is making a large income and striving to make it larger as "making neither gain nor loss".' (*Papers*, vol. i, p. 25.) Elsewhere, however, after some hesitation, Edgeworth came tentatively to accept the view that in equilibrium what the entrepreneur receives may be regarded as the (marginal productivity) wages of management.

On the general practical conclusions to be derived Edgeworth is typically cautious:

> The preceding hints and metaphors and warnings may assist the student to obtain a general idea of the process by which distribution of the national income is effected. An outline of theory so abstract is not to be despised as useless. It satisfies a legitimate curiosity. It is part of a liberal education. It is comparable in these respects with an elementary knowledge of astronomy. Such knowledge will not be of much use in navigation. And yet it has a certain bearing on real life. The diffusion of just notions about astronomy has rendered it impossible for astrologers any longer to practise on the credulity of mankind. (*Papers*, vol. i, p. 50.)

Edgeworth is clear that the phrase 'perfect competition' can give little help in the practical problem of distribution:

> Thus the coincidence of perfect competition with ideal justice is by no means evident to the impartial spectator: much less is it likely to be accepted by the majority of those concerned, whose views must be taken into account by those who would form a theory that has some relation to the facts. . . . We are now considering how the matter appears to the many, what régime they can be got to accept. It seems not to be competition pure and simple.
>
> Are we, then, to abandon the guidance of competition, and follow a higher, an ethical standard? . . . Can any one seriously pretend that the dictates of a moral sense are clear and decisive in such a matter?
>
> Let it be remembered also that the path of justice is not only dark, but dangerous. Striving to secure the rights of labour, you are very likely to hurt the interests of labour. The action of trade unions by lowering interest and harassing employers may result, as pointed out by Professor Marshall, in checking the accumulation of capital and the supply of business power. The increase in personal capital may indeed compensate for this check, but also it may not. Greater efficiency does not follow higher wages as the night the day. . . .
>
> Between two guides, of which neither can be followed implicitly, let us

walk warily. On the one hand, let us not aim at impossible ideals. But, on the other hand, let us not deserve the criticism which the advocates of trade unionism have with too much truth directed against 'the verdict of the economists' respecting trade unions. Let us not be as trenchant in act as we have been in thought. Let us be cautious in applying our abstract theory to flesh and blood. (*Papers*, vol. i, pp. 53–55.)

7

J. A. Hobson

1. *Edgeworth and 'The Physiology of Industry'*

IN 1890, a few months before succeeding to the Chair of Political Economy at Oxford, and almost simultaneously to the editorial chair of the new Royal Economic Society's *Economic Journal*, Edgeworth reviewed briefly, in the journal *Education*, 'The Physiology of Industry' by A. F. Mummery and J. A. Hobson: the former a famous mountaineer who never wrote anything further on economics, and the latter, till recently a 'classics' schoolmaster, who was then opening a new line of work as a University Extension Lecturer in Economics, and who was to be the author over the next fifty years of a very long list of books.

These champions of paradox [Edgeworth began], have chosen a very difficult battleground on which to encounter a very formidable adversary. They attack Mill's position that saving enriches and spending impoverishes the community along with the individual. . . . It is with literary as with ordinary justice, according to the old adage. One man may with impunity try to remove what seemed a secure possession of science, whilst another cannot safely look over the hedges and boundaries which received opinion fixes. The attempt to unsettle consecrated tenets is not very hopeful, unless the public, whose attention is solicited, have some security against waste of their time and trouble. It may fairly be required of very paradoxical writers that they should either evince undoubted speculative genius or extraordinarily wide learning.

The review continues in this strain.

Shortly after the publication of this book, and of Edgeworth's review, Hobson lost two Extension Lecturing posts, one in London and one in Oxford. 'This was due', Hobson tells us, 'to the intervention of an Economics Professor who had read my book and considered it as equivalent in rationality to an attempt to prove the flatness of the earth.' The identity of this professor is now of no moment, as is also the question of whether the London and Oxford professor's review in *Education* (the semi-official journal of the adult education movement) had anything to do with Hobson's dismissals.

Nearly fifty years after the review of *The Physiology of Industry*, the first of Edgeworth's successors in the Royal Economic Society's editorial chair claimed that the publication of the book 'marks, in a sense, an epoch in economic thought'. (Keynes, *General Theory*, p. 365.) Later a further successor found Hobson's subsequent economic work to show 'a fine grasp of what is valuable and enduring in the body of orthodox economics', and to be 'moderate reasonable and full of wisdom'. (R. F. Harrod, Introduction to Hobson's *Science of Wealth*, p. viii.)

Whatever the moral to be found in this episode in the history of ideas, it is only right to emphasize what Keynes said of Edgeworth (1926): 'His tolerance was all-embracing, and he combined a respect for established reputation which might have been thought excessive if there had not been a flavour of mockery in it, with a natural inclination to encourage the youthful and unknown'. (*Essays in Biography*, p. 290.)

The only point to add is that it seems less likely that there will be, in the future, the same opportunity for such a revision of expert opinion as occurred in the case of *The Physiology of Industry*. Hobson was able, in spite of his dismissals, to proceed to his long but persistent career as an economic heretic and eventually, at about the time of his death, receive the recognition of the 'orthodox', partly, or even perhaps largely, because (like the Webbs) he was the possessor of a private income. Those intellectual leaders devoted to 'received opinions' and 'consecrated tenets' which, as Edgeworth said, it is not 'safe' to look beyond, may be able to derive some (possibly much-needed) consolation from current taxation policies (behind which incidentally Hobson as much as any one was the intellectual inspiration), in that they make economically most improbable the occurrence of any future J. A. Hobsons. If, for better or for worse, there are going to be in the future, as seems on the whole unlikely, economic heretics of J. A. Hobson's stature, persistence, and prolixity, they will have to make their way, and find their jobs, within the 'received' system. It would surely be generally agreed that they will not be unfortunate if they and their notions meet with as much wide intellectual tolerance as Edgeworth commanded, even if, for once, he failed to employ it.

2. Hobson's Under-consumption Theory

A very clear outline of the main theme of *The Physiology of Industry* is given in the Preface:

We are thus brought to the conclusion that the basis on which all economic teaching since Adam Smith has stood, viz. that the quantity annually produced is determined by the aggregates of Natural Agents, Capital, and Labour available, is erroneous, and that, on the contrary, the quantity produced while it can never exceed the limits imposed by these aggregates, may be, and actually is, reduced far below this maximum by the check that undue saving and the consequent accumulation of over-supply exerts on production.

According to Keynes: 'This puts one half of the matter, as it seems to me, with absolute precision'. (*General Theory* &c., p. 368.) In any case the passage is historically very precise. It was the long and authoritative domination of Smith's (and also Turgot's) analysis of saving and investment, which historically (but not with any logical inevitability) came in with *The Wealth of Nations*, that made the message of *The Physiology* seem so very paradoxical to Edgeworth. To Petty, Barbon, Mandeville, Boisguillebert, Berkeley, Steuart, Quesnay, Lauderdale, and Malthus, the central idea of Mummery and Hobson would not have seemed to contain anything 'paradoxical'. What is indeed a paradoxical weakness of Mummery and Hobson's exposition is that they do not sufficiently clearly break, at any rate verbally, with Smith's concept of saving and investing and the doctrines of 'Say's Law' that follow from it, though all their conclusions run in the opposite direction. For example, Edgeworth described their doctrine as being that 'saving does not reduce the aggregate consumed but merely varies the consumers', and though this does not appear to be a quotation, it is a fair paraphrase of, or a fair deduction from, what at several points they seem to be saying. And, of course, this can easily be shown to upset the under-consumptionist thesis. The ambiguities in their analysis of saving and investment led them back to statements dangerously compatible with the usual interpretations of the proposition known as 'Say's Law'. For example, further on they inquire: 'Could a community save all it could produce with the exception of necessaries of life? If saving be taken merely to mean "not consuming", it is obvious that this is possible. But saving means something more than this. It signifies not only abstention from consumption, but application as a means of further production'. This is in close accord with Adam Smith's doctrine, according to which the process of saving *is* (or is, somehow, inevitably, or always, accompanied by) the process of investment. Mummery and Hobson's over-saving theory is really an over-investment theory, or a theory of the investment of excessive saving.

Their over-saving and over-investment theory was not based so much on a belief in secular stagnation, as on the notion that there is some technically fixed limit to the amount of capital employable, or that 'in a given condition of the productive arts, each labourer can only efficiently cooperate with a certain maximum amount of capital; if there could be brought into existence more forms of capital than sufficed to furnish the maximum for every labourer, the surplus must be waste' (p. 128). Erroneous though this notion seems to be, it might have been, and quite probably was, taken from the eminently respectable *Leading Principles* of J. E. Cairnes (see 1874 ed., p. 200). Furthermore, Mummery and Hobson thoroughly agreed with Cairnes, as contrasted with J. S. Mill, for example, in failing to recognize the significant distinctions, in respect of the processes of saving and investment, between a barter and a monetary economy: 'It must, however, never be forgotten that this money system is only an elaborated barter system. Products still exchange for products, though the exchange is not direct, but consists of products for money and money for products. Money while it obscures, in no wise changes the facts of barter'. (p. 189.)

These faults may indeed seem 'paradoxical' if one appreciates the central message of the book, but they do not much impair its merit in raising pointedly questions which for seventeenth-, eighteenth-, and twentieth-century economists have been among the central agenda of economics, but which when Hobson and Mummery were writing had for many decades, in England at any rate, been unduly neglected, or regarded as finally settled by the 'consecrated tenets' of orthodoxy.

In addition to the insight and originality of its central message there are in *The Physiology* a number of valuable pieces of analysis: for example, of the upswing of consumption and incomes which makes possible a higher rate of saving and investment (pp. 125–6); the early formulation of one of the basic macro-economic equations (Production — Saving = Consumption) (p. vii); the analysis of the war boom of 1870 and the subsequent depression; and finally the lesson, so expensively inculcated by Adolf Hitler half a century later, of how a war economy removes deficiencies of effective demand:

If, however, a nation or a community will not consent to consume all it can produce (allowing for due caution and reservations) in the ordinary ways of expenditure, the congestion brought about must vent itself in some extraordinary way, or the community suffers incessantly from the functional diseases which such congestion brings. It is, of course, obvious that if the community, instead of expending its surplus accumulations in the endeavour to cut its members' throats, consented to increase its consumption of luxuries, or applied the surplus funds to the improvement of the condition of the working classes or the sanitation of its great towns, all the contingent economic advantages of a war would be reaped, and the direct advantage of increased consumption of luxuries, of an improved condition of labourers, or of sanitary towns would be obtained. (p. 163.)

We do not quote these, today, surely rather platitudinous observations for their own sake, but in order to try to face the imaginative problem of how and why this could have seemed 'very paradoxical' to Edgeworth. Sixty years previously, in 1831, it had been the doctrine expounded by 'the new economists' (i.e. James Mill, Say, and Ricardo), of 'the impossibility of general over-production', which had still seemed to Chalmers a 'modern paradox'. But the 'modern paradox' had now become a 'consecrated tenet' which it was 'very paradoxical' to call in question, and, in fact, more than one's job was worth.

In *The Physiology of Industry*, in which Mummery was apparently the leading partner, there is virtually no mention of what eventually came to be an essential element in Hobson's underconsumption analysis, that is, the unequal distribution of income, which formed the connecting link with his 'surplus' analysis. This was introduced in his valuable pioneer study of *The Problem of the Unemployed* (1st ed. 1896). From Hobson's many subsequent formulations we may mention briefly that in *The Industrial System* (2nd ed. 1910, ch. III on Spending and Saving and ch. XVIII on Unemployment).

Hobson's analysis and definitions of saving and investing remain as weak links in his argument: 'Spending means buying consumption goods; saving means buying production goods. . . . In primitive industrial societies, or undisturbed conditions of more advanced societies, much refusal to spend takes the form of hoarding money. . . . In modern industrial societies, however, hoarding is abnormal'. (*The Industrial System*, p. 50.) He adds subsequently a reference to Johannsen's analysis of 'impair' savings, which was just what his own theory needed as a supplement, but he does not follow it up further beyond arguing that 'excessive' savings do not necessarily accumulate in depression, but may be absorbed in purchasing existing capital assets from those with falling incomes.

The chapter on unemployment contains a number of original and suggestive pieces of analysis. For example, that of the relation between the level of income and the level of consumption (p. 295); that of the irresponsiveness of the saving of the rich to a falling rate of interest

(p. 296); that of how, as income falls, the proportion of saving may fall and so gradually bring to an end excessive saving and depression (p. 303). Finally there is an analysis of the reflationary effects of public works policies (pp. 309–11). Here Hobson argues that the, then already growing, numbers of advocates of public works as a remedy for un-employment, must logically accept his hypothesis of underconsumption and over-saving as the chief cause of cyclical unemployment, the only alternative being to hold what twenty years later came to be known as the 'Treasury view', that public works will simply transfer employment to the public sector from private industry with no net gain in employment. Hobson discusses primarily the financing of public works out of current taxation, but refers approvingly to the proposals of the Minority Report of the Poor Law Commission that public works be financed by borrowing. He explains how, if financed by taxation,

the real issue depends upon the pace of the application of spending-power. If the taxpayer would have paid away his money in 'demand' as quickly as the State would have paid it in relief works, no increase in volume of employment is produced by taxing him. If, on the other hand, the effect of taxing him is to apply the money in demand for labour *more quickly* than it would have been applied, the aggregate of employment within a given period is increased by this acceleration of demand. The entire economic case for state relief insurance seems to turn upon the question of the acceleration or retardation of demand. Now, assuming that my hypothesis, that the largest proportion of saving proceeds from the upper portions of high incomes not required to satisfy any keen or constant pressure of need, be correct, the normal effect of taxing or rating such incomes for unemployed relief will be to accelerate the application of such income in demand for labour. (p. 310.)

3. *The Concept of Economic Surplus*

Hobson had considerable grounds for complaining of the neglect or misunderstanding of his work by more orthodox economists, except perhaps in the United States. But his own counter-criticisms, though they often contained extremely important truths, were often inclined to be somewhat undiscriminating. For example, it was certainly possible, and indeed necessary to emphasize the restricted significance of the marginal productivity analysis of distribution, and to criticize the reading into it by J. B. Clark of quite unjustifiable moral and political lessons. But much of Hobson's wholesale condemnation of what he called 'Marginalism', and marginal productivity analysis, exceeded the justifiable limits (see, for example, *The Industrial System*, pp. 122 ff.).

Another angle from which Hobson kept up a steady barrage against 'orthodoxy', or what he took to be 'orthodoxy', was that from which his mentor Ruskin had assailed classical political economy. He complained that the specialist economist does not adequately consider the whole social effects of economic measures, but simply their 'production' and 'distribution' effects in the narrower economic sense. Therefore, so Hobson argued, those for whom he writes, or whom he advises, may well be seriously misled as to the importance or validity of his conclusions. 'It is for this reason', Hobson says, 'that a mere economist is always disabled from giving practical advice in any course of conduct'. There is much force in this line of criticism, but the question at issue is to a considerable extent one of tactics, or of the choice of one's intellectual *métier*, about which it is very unsuitable to try to dogmatize. Marshall, for example, also rejected the separate discussion of economic effects from political and ethical effects, in his Memorandum on Fiscal Policy. (*Official Papers*, p. 367.) Hobson's conception of a comprehensive ethical 'welfare' economics which could and would lay down the right policy, and his rejection, on the other hand, of 'positive' economics, seems to derive from that inability or unwillingness, so common in some types of social reformer (both liberal and socialist), to keep absolutely cut, dried, and separated, their wishes about the social world on the one side, from the facts of the social world on the other.

Inevitably it was the social-economic problem of distribution to which Hobson turned. Rejecting the marginal productivity analysis, Hobson at the same time worked in the nineties for some time at a co-ordinated explanation of distribution not very far diverging in some respects from the orthodox theory.[1] His book *The Economics of Distribution* (delivered as lectures at the London School of Economics in 1897), marks the farthest point he reached on this path.

Hobson's point of departure was the generalization of the rent concept as applicable not simply to income from land but from all factors, an idea then emphasized by the exponents of marginal productivity analysis. The Fabians, and notably Bernard Shaw, had already seen the possibilities of this idea for a socialist analysis of distribution and redistribution alternative to the Marxist exploitation analysis. As Shaw had said in his Fabian Essay: 'Economic rent, arising as it does from variations of fertility or advantages of situation, must always be held as common or social wealth, and used, as the revenues raised by taxa-

[1] See his paper 'The Law of the Three Rents', *Quarterly Journal of Economics*, 1891.

tion are now used, for public purposes, among which socialism would make national insurance and the provision of capital matters of the first importance.' (*Fabian Essays*, 1889, p. 25.) In his attack on the landlords Henry George had simply shown himself a true disciple of Ricardo and James Mill, but now, with a generalized 'rent' concept, any form of higher income deriving from property, or educational or social advantages, could be subjected to a parallel attack. Hobson's 'surplus' analysis is an attempt to develop from this basis, rather more cautiously and discriminatingly than Bernard Shaw, a social reformist account of distribution, and of the possibilities of redistribution.

Hobson's analysis of distribution has something in common with that of the classical economists and suffers from a similar defect in its use of the concept of minimum 'subsistence' rewards. The national product of land, labour, and capital, may, according to Hobson, be divided into three parts: (1) what is barely necessary to maintain the efficiency, energy, and willingness to work of the existing factors in their existing state; (2) a provision for increasing these factors and/or their effectiveness, such as is necessary for economic growth; (3) an 'unproductive surplus' which is contributing nothing to maintain the industrial system or promote its growth. Hobson subsequently adds that a strong and progressive State is essential to economic stability and progress, and must therefore be regarded as a co-operating agent with its own claims to maintenance and growth. (*The Industrial System*, pp. 81–82.) If an industrial system produced just enough for the 'subsistence' minimum of its factors the problem of distribution would be much simplified. Either it would have to distribute its produce in the one single way which would barely ensure the maintenance of its productivity, or the system would decline and all factors sooner or later would suffer. The problem of distribution arises where the industrial system turns out a product that more than suffices for bare 'maintenance'. There is a struggle for the surplus, and it is in the social interest that as much as possible goes to promote economic growth, at any rate rather than that anything be lost through maldistribution in unproductive, or positively destructive, channels. (p. 78.)

Trade unions, and labour and social reform movements, represent attempts to get more of the surplus for labour, which, owing to its inherently weaker bargaining position, is forced down to a conventional 'maintenance' level, except when highly organized, or under 'boom' conditions (both of which, of course, since Hobson's day seem almost to have become more or less 'normal'). According to Hobson the competitive factor-market almost inevitably works against labour, and he subsequently went so far as to generalize that 'markets are intrinsically unfair modes of distribution'. (*Confessions of an Economic Heretic*, p. 168.)

Hobson himself recognized the conventional element in all conceptions of minimum standards, particularly the higher these minima became, and was later to be strongly influenced by Veblen's ideas on this subject. In fact, it is obviously quite impossible, in practice, to say of any individual's income whether derived from a wage, a salary, profit, interest, or rent, what part of it is going to bare maintenance, what is providing for growth, and what is 'unproductive surplus'. Moreover, all levels of income are to an inestimable extent freely devoted to 'surplus' expenditure (on yachts, tobacco, football pools, marriage feasts, and primitive festivals), before the needs of growth, or bare maintenance of efficiency, are met. This is especially the case if one takes into account Hobson's own emphasis on the errors of an excessively materialist interpretation of economic values. As a positive analysis of distribution under capitalism, Hobson's threefold classification provides only three rather empty and unfillable economic boxes.

Moreover, sudden increases in wealth which are liable to corrupt the individual, are similarly just as liable to corrupt cities and states:

> The organic conception of these social institutions obliges us to admit that their laws of growth impose certain limits upon their rate of taking on new functions and enlarging the activities of old functions, and therefore of applying public income in serviceable progress. A city or a state might easily become a reckless spendthrift if it took more 'surplus' than it could digest, as many a parasitic instance testifies in history. (p. 230.)

Of course this discussion relates to the English State of 1910. Hobson himself moved considerably leftwards (like the Webbs) after the First World War, especially with the onset of the world depression. His whole analysis gains considerably in significance if it is regarded as the right and duty of the State to redistribute income wholesale. The 'surplus' analysis then takes on some broad significance for the centralized macro-economic decisions about, for example, the level of investment for the economy as a whole, and in war economies about how much is to be left to 'maintain' the civilian sector, and how much can go to the war effort. The discussion of these collectivized decisions would seem to require, or to be assisted by, some broad classification, vague though it may be in detailed application, into 'maintenance', 'growth', and 'surplus'.

Hobson sought to apply his 'surplus' analysis in his discussion of the canons of taxation. But when he comes to apply his classification he admits how impossible it is to draw any clear defining lines:

It is evident that the greater part of the surplus is not thus clearly traceable and measurable, emerging as it does in a large and changing variety of forms amid the intricacies of industrial life. Wherever there accrues a permanent or temporary scarcity of some factor of production, a corresponding surplus income is created which passes to owners of this factor. But no particular register of these elements is possible; though most large incomes contain many of them, they are often indistinguishable even by their owners from the elements which are earned. It is tolerably clear that no taxing instrument for measuring directly these fluctuating 'surpluses' can be devised. (p. 239.)

Hobson's discussion of taxation in *The Industrial System*, though based on his surplus analysis, consists largely of warnings as to the difficulties and dangers of applying it. The minimum 'maintenance' incomes cannot be taxed, the tax is bound to be shifted (like the duty on corn in the analysis of the classical economists). 'Minimum profits and interest have the same power to throw off a tax as minimum wages, for even if the existing material capital will continue functioning at a rate below the minimum, no fresh capital or ability will enter such a trade.' Even the rough distinction drawn for income-tax purposes between earned and unearned income 'is open to serious criticism on the ground that it implies all 'interest' to be unearned without distinguishing between minimum and surplus rates. . . . The hypothesis that unearned surplus varies directly and closely with the size of income is probably not accurate, and is certainly incapable of verification (op. cit., pp. 239–40). Inheritance taxes run the same risk.

4. Hobson and the Economics of Democratic Socialism

Though he was too independent a thinker ever to become 'a good party man', J. A. Hobson's ideas became one of the most important single intellectual influences behind the economic programme of the British Labour party. He did not leave the Liberal party till the later stages of the First World War, and only joined the Labour party some time after it. Though he is said to have 'never felt quite at home in it', he is authoritatively described as being in the middle twenties 'the most respected intellectual influence in the Labour Movement', and also as one 'typical of the generation which made the difficult journey from Liberalism to Socialism'.[1]

[1] See H. N. Brailsford's lecture, 'The Lifework of J. A. Hobson', 1948.

Like the early Fabians Hobson was repelled by Marx's writings and ideas. The Fabians, or at any rate the Webbs, after some early questionings, devoted themselves to institutional studies and the detailed planning of socialist institutions, whereas Hobson provided much of the theoretical economic analysis for social democratic reform. The Fabians, it is true, announced through Bernard Shaw their rejection of the labour theory of value and their acceptance of Jevons's marginal utility theory. But they did not, of course, follow up the implications of this theory, or of marginal analysis, for the problem of the allocation of resources by a collectivist authority. At a theoretical level that required the 'general' equilibrium analysis which no English economist was following out sufficiently far, though Wicksteed was approaching it.

One slight sign of a practical implication being drawn from the marginal utility theory for the economic organization of a socialist community, was in Beatrice Webb's insistence on the role of consumers' co-operatives under socialism. The labour theory of value, Mrs. Webb argued, had led socialists to overlook consumers' demands and desires and 'all the processes by which the correspondence or union of a particular faculty with a particular desire is actually attained'. The trade unions would have the role of protecting producers, but the Co-operative Movement must be of equal power in protecting consumers: 'The proper relationship of Trade Unionism and co-operation (so I tell a conference of Trade Union officials and co-operators in 1892) is that of an ideal marriage, in which each partner respects the individuality and assists the work of the other, whilst both cordially join forces to secure their common end—the Co-operative State.' (*My Apprenticeship*, Pelican edition, vol. ii, p. 491.)

These two vast movements have of course since 1892 enjoyed in Britain a long and highly successful political liaison. But an 'ideal marriage' presumably implies some sort of ultimate union, and it can hardly be said that any practical techniques for unifying the trade unions and the consumers' co-operatives were worked out either by Mrs. Webb or by J. A. Hobson. Hobson followed the Fabians in laying great weight on nationalization. As his socialist biographer H. N. Brailsford somewhat revealingly says:

He sketched a surprisingly bold programme of nationalization. His long list of industries and services suited for nationalization, including steel as well as coal, transport, electricity, and banking, was based on tests which he did not always state in the same way. Sometimes he spoke of industries verging on monopoly. At other times he spoke of key industries, meaning presumably those vital for planning and, I suppose, for the control of the price structure. More often he designated the industries suited for nationalization as those which have reached the stage of standardization and routine. (p. 20.)

It was especially, also, with his under-consumption explanation of mass unemployment that Hobson long provided British social democracy with an important element in its intellectual equipment. The economic policies of the British Labour Government after 1945 in respect of 'full employment' and nationalization followed Hobson's ideas very closely, and these ideas may well go down as the most important single intellectual inspiration of that particular phase of British economic history and policy.

8

Political Economy in Germany

(c. 1870)

1. Introductory

ENGLISH classical political economy had been at certain key points closely allied with English Philosophic Radicalism, which in turn had been the main intellectual stimulus behind the great Liberal Reform movement which had attained its greatest triumphs in 1832 and 1846, and which continued to provide the dominant inspiration and the underlying principles for economic policy and legislation till well past the middle of the century. In Germany there had been no such single outstanding 'orthodox' body of opinion (outstanding at any rate outwardly, in its hold on the public mind, if not internally in uniting all the more distinguished economists). Nor, in Germany, had there been any triumphant movement of practical reform at the head of which any such school could have reached the extraordinary public influence of the English classical system (or of the widespread interpretation of that system). Nor was there in Germany a philosophical tradition providing comparatively agreed methodological principles or criteria for social and economic studies, like the tradition of Locke, Hume, Bentham, and J. S. Mill. The prevailing tradition in German philosophy had much more transcendental and comprehensive ambitions.

The mystical 'national socialist' economics of Adam Müller (1779–1829), the liberal nationalism of List (1789–1846), the State socialism of Rodbertus (1805–75), and later of Marxism, the liberal-conservative-cameralist tradition maintained by Hufeland (1760–1817), Rau (1792–1870), and Hermann (1795–1868), and a brand of extremist liberalism libellously known as 'Smithianism' or 'Manchesterism', all had their followers between whom there could be little common political or methodological ground. Each writer, or group, felt he had to begin for himself from the beginning (or even from before the beginning) and defend his method of approach, or *Richtung*, against rivals, with the result that the detailed discussion of particular problems according to generally accepted criteria, was very much obstructed. In addition there came the Historical Movement.

Here we wish simply to distinguish briefly two of the more important streams of economic thought running in Germany at the outset of our period in the sixties and seventies: (1) that of the Historical Movement and (2) (and by no means at many points diverging or clashing with the historical economists) the line of more theoretical writers, sometimes called the German Classical economists, among whom were Rau and Hermann mentioned above, Thünen (1783–1850), and Mangoldt (1824–68). (There was also, of course, separately and in addition, Gossen (1810–58), the most original of all, whose work had no influence until it was discovered two decades later by Jevons and others whom he had anticipated.)

2. *The Historical Movement*

The historical movement in Germany, with the powerful drive of Hegelian philosophy behind it, had been, in the second quarter of the nineteenth century, taking hold of more and more branches of the social and 'human' sciences. Jurisprudence and philology were the first to be reformed. The birth of German historical economics may be said to have taken place in 1843 when the encyclopaedic Roscher (1817–94) of Göttingen and Leipzig, published his programme in his *Grundriss zu Vorlesungen über die Staatswirtschaft nach geschichtlicher Methode*. He was followed later by Hildebrand (1812–78), and Knies of Heidelberg (1821–98).

The objectives of the movement were partly critical and partly positive. It was urged in criticism of English classical political economy, the value of which was not unappreciated by Roscher, that its conclusions were inapplicable to the contemporary political and industrial conditions of Germany and elsewhere, and that a system of political economy must be built up on a wider range of temporal and geographical facts, and must be as closely related as possible to the studies of other parts of the lives of nations. Much in these arguments, as a programme of objectives, remains thoroughly justifiable. More positively, and less justifiably, the historical programme saw the task of political economy in the discovery of the 'laws' and 'stages' of national economic development, as was particularly stressed by Hildebrand. It was also, of course, part of the historical conception of the 'social' sciences that these were fundamentally different, in some sense, in procedure and criteria, from the 'natural' sciences, as was particularly emphasized by Knies.

Neither Roscher nor Knies made any aggressive or revolutionary claims against other methods of approach. The pattern and balance of their works is not strikingly different from those of Rau or Hermann, or even from those of Adam Smith, J. S. Mill, and Marshall. On many points in the analysis of value and distribution they were very close to, and contributed something to, the work of Hermann, and Mangoldt and later even Carl Menger. One subject on which the German historical economists contributed some notable surveys, in a later period (1880–1910) when comparatively very little work was being attempted on it by English theoretical economists, was that of economic crises and cycles. Roscher himself, and later Nasse, Wagner, and finally Spiethoff, not to mention the followers of Marx and Rodbertus, all contributed to a body of work which compares very favourably with English and American writings during these three decades.

At the outset of our period in the later sixties and early seventies a new development of historical economics was led by Gustav Schmoller (1838–1917). In 1872 this new movement found a political rallying point in the *Verein für Sozialpolitik*, which stood for a 'paternal' policy of social reform. We shall return to Schmoller in a subsequent chapter.

3. German Theoretical Economics

The 'classical' school of German theoretical economists derived in part from Adam Smith, and in part from the French eighteenth-century 'utility' theorists, notably Condillac. Ricardian doctrines were at most points rejected, and the school maintained some of those fundamental truths about value, price, and distribution which tended to be neglected or obscured in the English classical system. Though, to a limited extent, the German 'classics' moved with the current of liberal ideas, they were also much influenced by the cameralist tradition, which gave their work a strongly realistic bent, with much analysis of detailed measures of State policy and taxation, and which led them to emphasize the important economic duties and leadership that the State must undertake. The titles of their journals, books, and chairs (of *Staatswirtschaft, Staatswissenschaft, Kameralwissenschaft, Verwaltungswissenschaft* and *Polizeiwissenschaft*) show their emphasis and approach, and the close association of the studies of political economy and of law in Germany.

In their analysis of value, production, and distribution one or two of the German 'classics' were, on many questions, several decades ahead of their English contemporaries. Stressing the relation of utility and consumers' demand to value led them in their account of distribution to stress the common influence of ultimate consumers' demand on the value of all the agents of production. This is much nearer the approach of marginal productivity analysis than the emphasis of the English classics on the separate characteristics of the services and rewards of three main factors, or the social classes owning them. It was from this point of view that Hermann attacked the Wages Fund doctrine with the arguments which were eventually to destroy it, nearly forty years before Mill's retraction. Similarly the rent concept was generalized and held to be common to all factors or their rewards, and not simply to be peculiarly applicable to land. In fact, Hermann included land in his definition of capital. We cannot here enter into Thünen's analysis of production and marginal productivity, but the specially refined analysis of entrepreneurs' profits in Hermann, Thünen, and Mangoldt deserves to be mentioned, as this subject also is bound up with the subsequent development of the marginal productivity doctrine.

4. *Mangoldt*

Mangoldt's analysis of profits and of the different constituent elements in the entrepreneur's income, with his stress on the uniqueness of profit as a form of income, is known from F. H. Knight's discussion in his *Risk, Uncertainty and Profit*. Edgeworth, with his wide knowledge of economic literature in many languages, considered Mangoldt's work on the theory of international trade the outstanding contribution in its field (1894), and recognized also that Mangoldt 'may claim to be one of the independent discoverers of the mathematical theory of demand and supply', along with Cournot, Dupuit, and Gossen (none of whom were known to Mangoldt). We wish here to discuss some of the contributions of Mangoldt's *Grundriss der Volkswirtschaftslehre* (1863), and to give some indication of the very high level to which Mangoldt, the final culminating representative of the German classical theorists, brought economic theory in several of its most important branches.

Mangoldt turned to the study and teaching of economics after twice resigning government posts in the reactionary years of the early fifties, because of political disagreement with his employers. His work on profits (*Die Lehre vom Unternehmergewinn*, 1855) was his *Habilitationsschrift* at Göttingen. His *Grundriss*, or *Outline*, is a very compressed but very comprehensive book, designed as a text for further discussion and elucidation in class, rather than to present a fully elaborated exposition. With its geometrical diagrams, and its derivations from the English classics on the one hand, and from Hermann, Thünen, and the German historical economists on the other, it might be a distant infant cousin of Marshall's *Principles*.

In his opening discussion of value Mangoldt points out that this depends on the urgency and extent of the needs which a good is able to satisfy, and that the value of a single good depends on the proportion this represents of the total stock available (p. 2). He begins his chapter on exchange with a Marshallian 'cross' diagram of intersecting supply and demand curves (p. 47), sets out what amounts to Jevons's law of indifference for competitive markets, and adds that in such markets the prices of goods of different quality will be proportional to their costs of production. He then turns to the demand curve, which will, in general, slope downwards, as 'the use-value (*Nutzwert*) of each unit, will always be smaller, the more one adds' (p. 48). This implies that a rise in price will lead to a decline in demand until 'the point is reached where the utility is balanced by the price'. On the diagram of the demand curve 'the distance' (of any point on the demand curve) 'from the quantity axis represents the utility of the last unit of the quantity demanded'. Mangoldt points out that fear of a further rise may lead to a rise in price being followed, contrary to the general rule, by an increase in demand. (p. 49.)

Turning to the supply side, Mangoldt draws and explains various differently shaped supply curves: a horizontal straight line represents constant costs; a horizontal straight line, rising abruptly vertically at a certain point, is the case of constant costs up to the limit of a certain rigidly fixed supply. Finally, a rather flat U-shaped curve, falling over a certain output owing to economies of large scale, and then subsequently rising, is explained (p. 50). Though not mathematically defined, the concept of elasticity of supply (*Ausdehnbarkeit*) corresponding to Mill's 'extensibility' is introduced. Finally, Mangoldt explains that with rising costs the lower limit for the market price will be given by 'the costs of the last unit, or the highest necessary production costs'. (p. 53.)

In his analysis of production and distribution Mangoldt combines the classical 'real' cost notion and the Malthusian doctrine of population and wages, with a marginal productivity analysis of the rewards to each factor. Rent, however, is treated not as the specific return to land but as an element which may enter into 'all separate types of income, profits and wages, as well as interest'. (p. 142.)

The level of wages will be determined by 'the prospective net return of the least productive, that is presumably the last, labour to be applied'. Mangoldt held, however, that according to the Malthusian doctrine of population this would be forced down to subsistence level (p. 129) (which Marshall held to apply to the greater part of the world).

Similarly for interest:

According to the law that similar goods in the same market at the same time must exchange at the same price, the least productive unit of capital must determine the price for the services of the others. We therefore arrive at the proposition . . . that the net yield of the last unit of capital applied determines the level (or *den relativen Schwerpunkt*—Mangoldt's term for the equilibrium maximizing level) of net interest.

Mangoldt's *Grundriss* also contains much advanced monetary analysis of interest, of the demand and supply of the precious metals, and of hoarding and the desire for liquidity. He devoted two sections to interest, one to 'Divergencies between Actual Average Interest Rates and the Equilibrium Rate', and the other on 'Interest and the Value of Money'. The former clearly outlines much of what was to be Wicksell's doctrine of natural and market rates, and gives an interpretation of cyclical fluctuations as a cycle of divergencies between natural and market rates of interest. Mangoldt brings out more clearly, on the whole, than Wicksell, the dependence of the natural rate on the *expected* marginal efficiency of capital and gives a distinct place in his outline model both to changing expectations and to innovations:

The average of actual interest rates diverges from the equilibrium rate (*von dem relativen Schwerpunkte*), being sometimes above and sometimes below the rate indicated by the yield of the last unit of capital applied. This is to be explained by the lack of agreement between the actual facts and the ruling opinions as to the prospects for the employment of capital. . . . The occurrence of mistaken views about the economic prospects for employing capital seem to be due above all to the speed with which the conditions of economic life alter. . . .

[Once speculation gets under way] . . . all capital is believed to be profitably employable, and while the continued increase in capital ought to lead to a fall in the rate of interest a demand has been created which prevents this. Gradually accumulation ceases to correspond with the continued demand, and the failure of the rate of interest to fall is followed by a positive rise. This is the turning point. This rise uncovers the mistaken calculations on which many undertakings have been based, and shows that the actual stipulated rate of interest, however low it may have *seemed*, *should* have been regarded as too high. But this conclusion is strongly resisted. The difficulties are treated as transient, and an attempt is made to surmount them by borrowing still more capital. The rate of interest is now driven well above its natural level. Meanwhile the distrust of creditors is aroused, and loans are not renewed but called in. Finally comes a general liquidation, and the capital which had been borrowed and lent at too high rates of interest, is lost, either by the creditors or the debtors. At this point opinion about lending is exactly the reverse of what it was previously. The capitalists are thinking only of a safe haven for the funds they have recovered, rather than of high interest rates, and in their panic even leave considerable funds lying 'dead' for the time being, rather than take any risk. The entrepreneurs, for their part, are excessively timid about the use of capital and the interest to be paid. In these circumstances the actual rate will for some time fall below the natural rate. Only gradually, when on the one side the fear of any speculative expansion of business activity disappears, and on the other the profitability of lending is considered equally with security, only then will the actual rate gradually approach the equilibrium rate, and often will not only reach it but again begin to diverge on the other side, so that the whole movement we have described begins over again. (p. 120.)

Mangoldt had built this analysis out of his marginal productivity doctrine and his studies in the early 'psychological' and over-investment theories of the trade cycle (including notably James Wilson, the first editor of *The Economist* whom he quotes elsewhere on the importance of the proportions between fixed and circulating capital).[1] He was also indebted to Roscher's sensible and comprehensive discussion of crises and of 'Say's Law'. Unlike many of the writers of the 'over-investment' school of thought, Mangoldt, following Rau and Roscher, was critical of 'Say's Law', pointing out that though in a two-commodity barter world 'general overproduction' of both commodities would be logically impossible, as would a 'general' excess of demand over supply, 'on the other hand it is quite conceivable that an oversupply of all other goods may periodically occur in terms of one particular good, especially in terms of that good which is being used as the general means of exchange, that is, of commodities in relation to money'. (p. 68.)

Mangoldt died at the age of 44 after a career as an economist lasting about fifteen years, and the further books he might have left must, like Jevons's *Principles*, be counted among the great unwritten works of economics. Marshall included his immediate predecessors Hermann

---

[1] *Volkswirtschaftslehre*, p. 190. This was an unfinished work more introductory (though lengthier), and more readable than the *Grundriss*, with none of its mathematics or diagrams, which had apparently made the earlier work unpopular.

and Thünen ('the great unrecognized') among four supreme examples of great 'classical' authors (the other two were Petty and Jevons), and he considered that 'the most important economic work that has been done on the Continent in this century (19th) is that of Germany'. (*Principles*, 2nd ed., p. 66.) The work of Mangoldt represents a culminating point in German theoretical economics but it received little or no recognition either from Marshall or from the Austrian School. But, of course, both Menger (in his first book) and Wieser recognize their indebtedness to their German predecessors. According to Wieser:

It may be said that, in great part, the German school long ago formulated the conceptions, leaving for us only the task of filling them out by adequate observation. In this it has laid up a treasure from which all succeeding economic effort may draw indefinitely. . . . The new value theory is in truth the fulfilment of what German theory had long demanded. (*Natural Value*, p. xxxiv.)

We must now turn to the founder of the Austrian School, and we shall find him in his first great work—the foundation stone of that school— paying a similarly generous tribute to his German predecessors. In his second work, as we shall see, he came to view German political economy in a very different light.

9

Carl Menger

1. Menger's 'Principles': Essays on Money and the Theory of Capital

WE come now to the second of the three economists who independently expounded the marginal utility theory of value in the early seventies. Unlike Jevons (but like Marshall), Carl Menger was also the founder of one of those curious, and in some ways often rather questionable intellectual-psychological phenomena, a great 'School'. His first two great pupils, Wieser and Böhm-Bawerk, became as famous economists as himself, and were followed in their turn by many descendants. On many important subjects the original triumvirate of the Austrian School, as well as its later members, held very divergent views, even, or particularly, about some of those subjects on which their writings have been especially celebrated. If there is more reason for speaking of an 'Austrian' School than an 'English' School (including all the writers discussed in Chs. 2–6), it is not because the considerable common ground in methods of approach and in political and philosophical presuppositions extended much farther in the one case than in the other, but rather because the Austrians were all pupils, directly or indirectly, of Carl Menger and his book the *Grundsätze*, and were all connected with the same university.

Little seems to be recorded about Menger's early interests and studies. It was apparently his task in the *Ministerratspräsidium* (or, approximately, 'Cabinet Offices'), which he joined shortly after graduating, to write surveys of market conditions, and this rather empirical stimulus acted on his own developing ideas about the theory of value. However, the foreword and extensive footnotes in his first and supreme work the *Grundsätze* (1871), give clear indications of the main influences on his thought. The book is dedicated 'with respectful esteem' to Wilhelm Roscher the founder of German historical economics. Menger is 'especially pleased' to note, in his foreword, that 'German political economy, by its latest developments, has really to a large extent made its own that part of the field which is concerned with the most general theories of the science', and that the reform he is attempting is based 'almost entirely' on the previous work of German writers. He hopes that his work may be regarded as 'a friendly greeting from an Austrian fellow-worker, and a slight return for what Austria owes Germany in learned men and distinguished writings'. (Op. cit., p. xlviii.)

Going back to the eighteenth century, Condillac and Adam Smith are the authors Menger cites most frequently. Auguste Walras's concept of *rareté* is also mentioned. But the English classics, notably Ricardo and the Mills are not influential. The nineteenth-century economists often referred to are Hermann, Rau, Roscher, Hildebrand, Knies, Schaeffle,[1] and on a few occasions, Schmoller. From these sources Menger would have started with a 'utility' approach to value, and, unlike Jevons, with no firmly established or orthodox labour and cost-of-production theory to 'revolt' against. He would have derived also an approach to distribution that would have encouraged a unified 'productivity' treatment, rather than the separate threefold 'class', and mainly 'macro-economic', treatment of Ricardo, the influence of which was still noticeable on Jevons and Marshall. Menger refers but once to Mangoldt's *Grundriss*, and does not seem to have recognized either the valuable contributions of the book itself or the extensive discussion of Thünen's work which it contains. Gossen, Cournot, and Dupuit had no influence on the *Grundsätze*, and Mangoldt and Thünen not the influence they might have had.

The opening three chapters of the book present, in contrast it must be said to Jevons's *Theory*, a superbly solid, finished, and carefully worked out argument, which, bearing in mind its marked degree of originality, must be placed with the supreme achievements of theoretical economics. At no point is there any attempt at mathematical formulation, the nearest approach to which being a number of purely illustrative numerical tables of valuations and reserve prices. Even brief convenient technical terms are eschewed. Nor is there anything of Marshall's wealth of illustration from modern industrial history, nor even of Wicksteed's homely parables from the everyday activities of the housewife. The analysis proceeds in a stark elemental 'ur'-world. Deep in the primeval forest (*'Urwald'*, p. 82), or on some distant island rock (p. 100), patriarchal Crusoe-like figures gravely allocate tree-

---

[1] Menger rightly gives special recognition to Schaeffle, and in particular his paper of 1862 'Die ethische Seite der nationalökonomischen Lehre vom Werte' (see *Gesammelte Aufsätze*, vol. i). Here Schaeffle contrasted 'usefulness' with 'use-value' in a good—the latter depending on the difficulty of obtaining it. Already by 1874 Schaeffle had made a penetrating critique of socialist economies based on the point that the labour theory of value provided no criterion for the economic guidance of production, for which the concept of use-value was indispensable. (*v. below* Ch. 18, sect. 3.)

trunks, measures of corn, or beakers of water, between alternative uses, or ponder the problem of whether to exchange a horse for a cow, all with the object of maximizing their *Bedürfnisbefriedigung* ('need-satisfaction'). Historical illustrations have to keep their distance, few getting much nearer in time or space than Tacitus, Ancient Mexico, or seventeenth-century Indonesia (p. 199). This considerable degree of abstraction and remoteness is common to most of the main work of Menger, Wieser, and Böhm-Bawerk. It is the more noteworthy because all three played a leading part at one stage or another in framing practical policies, the two latter as Ministers.

The opening chapter of the *Grundsätze* is on the Theory of Goods. From the start the valuation of production goods and services (or in Menger's terminology 'goods of a higher order') is treated in the same way as the valuation of final consumption goods which satisfy needs directly, and from which production goods ultimately derive their value. Complementarity between goods is first mainly illustrated in relation to production goods: for example, the services of cotton spinners are valueless without the complementary raw cotton. This strong emphasis on the complementarity of production goods is traceable in many subsequent writings of the Austrian School. A picture is thus built up of the structure of production as an immense combination of complementary production goods and services, each one of which is largely dependent for its value on the availability of all its other complementary goods and services at earlier and later stages in the process. Economic progress means that men adopt longer and more indirect processes of production, and thereby plan far ahead into the future in their economic activities (p. 33). Similarly, consumers' goods depend on one another for their values, and it is emphasized that it is not single goods by themselves, but totalities of interdependent goods of different kinds that are significant (pp. 30–31).

All economic activity is based on our foresight as to our future needs (*Bedarf*), and economic goods are those the needs for which are greater in quantity than the available supply. Since, therefore, some needs for them will have to go unsatisfied, the needs for economic goods have to be arranged in order if, with the available means, they are to be satisfied to the best advantage (p. 51). Between economic goods it is necessary to choose. Economic goods and private property, as Auguste Walras had pointed out, both ·derive from scarcity. It follows that production goods ('of a higher order') are only economic goods, if the final consumption goods ('of the first order') which they serve to produce are scarce economic goods. Non-economic goods may be 'useful' but not 'valuable'.

The third chapter on value is the keystone of Menger's work. Differences in the values of goods depend on differences in the needs they satisfy, and differences in the significance of needs occur not only between different sorts of needs, but between greater or lesser satisfactions of the same sort of need. The first units of food are worth life itself, but successive units gradually lose significance. Menger produces his well-known table to illustrate his argument (op. cit., p. 93):

I	II	III	IV	V	VI	VII	VIII	IX	X
10	9	8	7	6	5	4	3	2	1
9	8	7	6	5	4	3	2	1	0
8	7	6		(Tobacco)					&c.
7	6								
6									
&c.									
(Food)									

These numbers seem to have a purely illustrative significance, and to be in any case no more than ordinal. Menger is simply concerned to point out how needs may be arranged in order and does not even formulate a principle of diminishing marginal utility. He does not explain how his tables work when account is taken of the intricate complementarity relationships between goods, which he had earlier emphasized. On the whole, in spite of his early emphasis on complementarity, Menger's analysis seems to be based more on the assumption made by Jevons, Walras, and Marshall, that the utility of a good is a function of the quantity of that good only, than on the more general assumption introduced by Edgeworth in his *Mathematical Psychics* (1881). More broadly, though Menger did not try to fill out his analysis of the consumer with a hedonist content, it is not easy to say just what, and how much content he did ascribe to it.

The most important part of a man's economic activity is this constant weighing up and choosing of which needs shall be met and which not. As later with production goods, Menger defines the value of consumption goods in terms of the 'loss' principle: that is, what determines the value of a good is the satisfaction that would not be obtained if the good was not available: 'The value of a unit (*Teilquantität*) of the available stock of a good is for any individual equal to the significance of the least important want-satisfaction yielded by any unit of the total quantity of a good' (p. 99). The allocation formula for the consumer is not stated with any very full generality or precision, but a lengthy footnote concludes (p. 98): 'The most important of the needs of all different sorts which are not satisfied are of equal significance for each sort, so that all needs are actually satisfied up to the same degree.'

Menger then turns aside, as the three leading Austrian economists frequently did, to chastise labour and cost-of-production theories of value. In a passage reminiscent of Jevons's 'bygones are forever by-gones', Menger notes that

No-one asks about the historical origin of a good in estimating its value, but takes account of the services which it is going to yield. . . . Certainly, comparing the value of a good with the value of the means of production used in producing it, may tell one how far the past act of production was economic or worthwhile; but the goods used in its production have no necessary or direct influence on the value of a product. (p. 120.)

Menger went too far in dismissing the role of cost of production, and indeed attempts no analysis of the cost side, or of the principle of diminishing returns as Mangoldt had done. This subject was to be taken up by Wieser. But what came to be called the principle of imputation (*Zurechnung*) is clearly stated by Menger when he empha-sizes (p. 124) that the value of consumption goods cannot be determined from the value of production goods, but, on the contrary, it is the values of production goods that are always determined by the prospective values of the consumption goods they serve to produce.

In a section on the productivity of capital several of the ideas later to be developed by Böhm-Bawerk are sketched out, though some were withdrawn by Menger from his second edition: the increased use of production goods in more lucrative processes of production involves also longer processes; and the under-estimation of future wants is also appealed to. The function of the entrepreneur is to use his knowledge of the economic situation to calculate costs and choose the most economic method of production. Menger criticizes Mangoldt for emphasizing risk-bearing as the essential function of the entrepreneur.

He contends (p. 140) that there is generally a very wide field for varying the combinations in which complementary production goods are employed, and that chemically fixed proportions are not the rule, an *aperçu* which is the necessary starting-point for a marginal pro-ductivity analysis of distribution. As with consumption goods, the value of a unit of a factor depends on the difference to final satisfaction its absence would result in, via the effect on the product. Units of land, labour, and capital, or units of their services, are all to be valued on this common principle. Pieces of land have no such special place among economic goods as the analysis of the English classics had given them. Further, the cost-of-production theory as applied to the services of labour is not merely practically absurdly far-fetched, but in any case theoretically irrelevant.

We are more than half-way through the book before we pass from value to exchange, and from this point the thoroughness, finish, and interest of the analysis fall off somewhat. Rightly contradicting Adam Smith, Menger points out (p. 158) that it is through no sheer inclination to 'truck barter and exchange' that men enter the market, and that the possibility of exchange depends on the coincidence of each party possessing a good that he values less than one possessed by the other party. Under isolated barter the exchange rate is shown to be indeterminate. In discussing competitive and monopoly markets the significant distinction is drawn between the two lines of policy, or 'action-parameters', open to the monopolist, quantity and price. But with no diagrams and no analysis of costs the argument cannot proceed very far.

In a chapter on the Theory of Merchandise (*Waare*) there is some description of marketing and transport conditions. But the main point of the chapter is to lead up to the final subject of money. His concept of the 'marketability' or 'saleability' (*Absatzfähigkeit*) of goods introduces an analysis of 'liquidity', and it is the most *absatzfähig* or 'liquid' good that will come to be adopted as money. (p. 252.)

In his chapter on Money, and in his later article on the subject, Menger shows the clearest signs of the influence of the German historical movement. Most of the references are to ancient history, and there is considerable etymological discussion of the origin of the various names of coins (pp. 254 and 262). The different goods used as money at various periods of history are discussed. Above all, Menger is concerned to emphasize that it is the economic interests of individuals which lead to the emergence of money, without any formal agreement, legislative compulsion, or even any concern for the general public interest (pp. 253 and 259). Money is one of the spontaneous, unconscious, unplanned social discoveries, which are not inventions of the State or products of a legislative act, as Knapp was to emphasize.

Menger's encyclopedia article on Money develops further the argument of the final chapter of the *Grundsätze*. There is much historical discussion of terminological and legal issues. 'Stages' and 'laws' of economic development, corresponding with different monetary systems, are discussed. (*Works*, vol. iv, pp. 12 and 29.) The 'state' theory of money and the view that the status of legal tender is essential for 'money' are vigorously opposed. It is the sections on the 'internal' and 'external' factors affecting the value of money (*innere und äussere Tauschwert*), and the final section on the demands for money or the quantity needed, that are of most interest for modern analysis. Stability of the 'internal' factors affecting the value of money (that is stability of the 'factors on the side of money') seems to correspond with that elusive post-Wicksellian concept of 'neutral' money. Menger seems rather optimistically confident that theoretically and practically a stable measure of the 'internal' value of money (or of the changes in its value arising 'on the side of money') is attainable.

On the subject of the demand for money Menger describes the 'transactions' and 'precautionary' motives for holding money and the reasons for, and cost of, liquidity: 'Economic units of the same type and size often have very different holdings of cash, according as to whether their managers consider necessary a greater or lesser degree of security against disturbances in economic activity, and are ready to make the necessary sacrifice of interest' (p. 108). Menger criticizes an over-simplified concept of velocity of circulation. When business is more active what happens is not that units of money circulate more rapidly but that inactive precautionary stocks are drawn into the active circulation (pp. 110–11). These hints come right at the end of the essay. No formal or precise quantity equation is presented.

We cannot attempt to discuss here Menger's considerable practical contributions to contemporary problems of the Austro-Hungarian currency, his main contributions to applied economics. But mention might be made of a passage in an address by Menger on the revaluation of the currency, where he discusses the merits of a more inflationary favouring of the debtors, as contrasted with a more deflationary favouring of creditors. Menger held that as things were in Austria-Hungary it was the small men, who could not themselves get credit, who lent to the rich. Any revaluation that favoured the debtors would be strongly regressive and Menger favoured on the whole the deflationary side, like subsequent Austrian economists.

Menger's essay on Capital (1888) is mainly critical, implicitly but not explicitly, of Böhm-Bawerk, whose first work had then recently appeared. It is much concerned with terminological distinctions and clarifications, in a field where such analysis has always been particularly necessary. He attacks the notion of land and labour as being 'original' factors as contrasted with capital, or 'the produced means of production', holding that this distinction cannot be drawn in practice, and in any case is economically irrelevant. He argues that economists should follow what he considers to be the practical everyday monetary concept of capital and interest. (*Works*, vol. iii, pp. 37 and 44.)

2. The '*Methodological Studies*' and Later Essays

Two years after the publication of the *Grundsätze* Menger obtained a professorial post at Vienna, and at about the same time his two greatest disciples were discovering his work and building much of their own upon it. Menger's first work seems, therefore, to have received considerably more prompt and concrete recognition in its immediate surroundings than did that of Walras, or Jevons's *Theory*. The second of Menger's two books, his *Studies in the Methods of the Social Sciences and of Political Economy in Particular* appeared in 1883. It is a work very different from the detached, precise, carefully constructed, and thoroughly documented *Grundsätze*. In some respects powerful and profound, it ranges very widely, in its four books and nine appendices, over the manifold problems of what economists and social scientists are doing and how they are doing it, as contrasted with what they ought to be doing and how they ought to be doing it.

The main purpose of the book and such unity as it possesses, lies in the challenging attack on the German historical economists which is opened in the Introduction: 'Misleading methodological principles' (p. xix) are being followed by German economists, which have reduced their subject to a 'pernicious' condition (*Verderblichkeit*): 'The main objectives of the study are being lost sight of because trivial tasks are being given an exaggerated or even decisive importance' (p. xii): 'A senseless phraseology about fundamental problems' is being repeated (p. xx). It is Menger's intention 'to bring the study of political economy in Germany back to a consciousness of its true paths'. (p. xxi.)

It might well be asked what had happened in the twelve years since Menger's generous tributes in his first book to German economists in general, and to Wilhelm Roscher in particular, as well as to the latest German developments of the subject. The contrast between the prefaces to Menger's two books could not be greater. It is true that in 1872 the *Verein für Sozialpolitik* had been formed by a number of historical economists in Germany who were inclined towards social reform, but the significance of this body was political rather than methodological. Gustav Schmoller had also come more to the front as leader of a new school of historical economics, which, however, by no means a majority of German economists agreed with. For example, Schmoller's senior colleague at Berlin, Adolf Wagner, later inclined more towards Menger's point of view than Schmoller's, though neither Wagner nor any of the great classical German contributors to economic theory—Hermann, Thünen, and Mangoldt—relied on abstraction and deduction to the extent that Menger and his Austrian disciples did. As regards German political economy, at any rate, Menger was as much an innovator at one extreme as was Schmoller at the other. In any case, Menger does not concentrate on the more recent German writings. He takes as the representative exponent of the historical method Karl Knies, of the older historical school, much of whose work had been published long before, and he says explicitly, though very questionably, that all the more recent doctrines of Schmoller and others are given 'at least in outline' by Knies (p. 230). Menger also opens his pamphlet on *The Errors of the Historical School* (1884) by claiming that these 'were clearly apparent on the first foundation of the school nearly five decades previously'—that is by Roscher in 1843. Certainly a critical study of the historical method would have been most timely and was indeed most necessary. There was much to fasten on, particularly the whole notion of laws of historical development—a notion of the older historical school of which the younger, led by Schmoller, was most critical. But such a work would have had to have shown at least some comprehension of what the historical writers were contributing both critically and constructively.[1]

The first parts of the book are concerned with Menger's attempt to make a rigid separation between historical and statistical economics on the one hand, and theoretical economics on the other, and with his conception of the 'exact' laws of the latter and the assumptions on which they rest. Menger distinguishes (p. 3) between two main classes of sciences or of scientific knowledge. 'Individual', historical or statistical

---

[1] Perhaps at this point Marshall's verdict on the German historical school is worth recalling: 'The work of a few members of this school is tainted by exaggeration, and even by a narrow contempt for the reasonings of the Ricardian school, the drift and purpose of which they have themselves failed to understand: and this has led to much bitter and dreary controversy. But with scarcely an exception, the leaders of the school have been free from this narrowness. It would be difficult to overrate the value of the work which they and their fellow workers in other countries have done in tracing and explaining the history of economic habits and institutions. It is one of the great achievements of our age; and an important addition to the real wealth of the world. It has done more than almost anything else to broaden our ideas, to increase our knowledge of ourselves, and to help us to understand the central plan, as it were, of the Divine government of the world.' (*Principles*, 2nd ed., p. 68, 8th ed., p. 768.)

knowledge, and 'general' theoretical knowledge. To this he adds, subsequently, a third category of practical sciences or arts. The methods of these three separate disciplines are quite distinct and they must be kept strictly apart. There is no sense in speaking of '*the* method of political economy comprehending economic theory and economic policy'. (p. 21.) Menger repeatedly insisted on this strict separation of theory from history and statistics. In his pamphlet in which he replies to Schmoller's criticism, Menger objected strongly to Schmoller holding that economic history and statistics were 'the descriptive parts of political economy' since 'they are actually not parts of political economy at all but auxiliary disciplines'. (*Die Irrtümer des Historismus*, pp. 27 and 37.) Schmoller's view 'is comparable with that of a carter who wants to be considered as the architect because he has carried some loads of stones and sand to the building site'. (*Die Irrtümer*, p. 46.)

The exact laws of theoretical economics depend on assumptions of pure self-interest, and infallibility or omniscience (*Allwissenheit*), and freedom of movement. (*Untersuchungen*, pp. 72–75.) To point out, as Schmoller was alleged to have done, that such abstraction is unrealistic in that altruism and mistakes are common in the real world is to misunderstand the procedure of all sciences. Menger does not argue, as was later done, that the assumptions can easily be extended, though thereby made more empty, to include altruistic actions. He argues that chemistry, for example, makes use of such concepts as 'pure oxygen' and 'pure hydrogen', which like 'pure self-interest' are never to be found in the real world. (p. 76.)

It is doubtful whether the misunderstandings were all on the side of Schmoller. It might well have been inquired whether it does not make a fundamental difference that practically pure chemical substances can actually be isolated, tested, and observed in a laboratory, in a way in which pure self-interest and omniscience cannot be extracted, observed, and measured separately from the rest of human qualities.

Menger strongly rejected the notion of mutual determination and interdependence so emphasized by Marshall, Edgeworth, Walras, and Pareto:

That the parts of a whole and the whole itself can be at once the cause and effect of one another (i.e. that there is mutual determination) which is a point of view that has gained ground, ... is an idea so obscure and inadequate to our laws of thought that we can hardly be wrong in taking it as a sign that our age still lacks in many respects a profound understanding both of natural organisms and of social phenomena. (p. 144.)

148 Carl Menger

Various later members of the Austrian School were to follow this line of thought, as also Menger's small regard for the mathematical method. For example, Menger criticized severely the clear and precise abstraction of Auspitz and Lieben's mathematical analysis, and in a letter to Walras he insisted that what the economist is after is not only relationships between quantities (*Grössenverhältnisse*) but the essence (*das Wesen*) of economic phenomena: 'How can we attain' he asks Walras, 'to a knowledge of this essence, for example, the essence of value, the essence of land rent, the essence of entrepreneurs' profit, the essence of the division of labour, the essence of bi-metallism &c. by mathematics?'[1]

In spite of the rather metaphysical ring of his observations on the mathematical method, Menger makes much use throughout of comparisons (rather than contrasts) between the natural and the social sciences, and he was concerned to emphasize the common elements in the methods of the natural and social sciences. In his introduction to the *Grundsätze* Menger had explained his work as follows:

> We were concerned to study how the most complex economic phenomena developed in accordance with laws from their simplest elements. . . . That is, to follow that method of investigation which has come to prevail in the natural sciences, and has led to such great results, and which therefore has misleadingly been called the method of the natural sciences, whereas it is common to all empirical sciences and should more properly be called the empirical method. (*Grundsätze*, p. xlv.)[2]

His view of the practical application of economic science to practice was highly 'technocratic': 'The practical science of economics "masters" economic life in the same way as technology "masters" nature, and surgery and therapy the human body. . . . It is their task to teach us the principles and procedures by which the state and subordinate bodies analogous to it can suitably intervene in economic life.' (*Works*, vol. iii, p. 216.)

In some later essays Menger seems to be withdrawing somewhat from the more extreme arguments and phraseology he had adopted in 1883–4, but his final position is not easy to discern—one can seldom expect very clear communiqués from those engaged in a rearguard action. In a very appreciative review of a *Handbook of Political Economy* by a representative group of German economists, mostly influenced

---

[1] In a letter of 1884. *v*. W. Jaffé, *Journal of Political Economy*, 1935, p. 200.
[2] Cf. the interesting article by J. Dobretsberger, 'Zur Methodenlehre Carl Mengers und der Österreichischen Schule', *Zeitschrift für Nationalökonomie*, 1949, pp. 78 ff.

by, but not regular adherents of, the historical school, he again com-
plains that a sharp separation (*Trennung*) between economic history
and statistics on the one side, and economic theory on the other, is not
recognized, 'or that a recognition in principle is made, but in such a
way as in fact to be withdrawn' (vol. iii, p. 118). The German economists mistakenly regard as an advance the combination of the theoretical
and practical rather than their separation, whereas 'the efforts of all of
us should be directed' to pushing farther the separation of the two.
(p. 120.)

Menger certainly achieved his separation or *Trennung* in one respect.
German and Austrian economists were for a generation split to some
extent into extreme exponents of the historical viewpoint and extreme
exponents of pure theory, with no sort of co-operation, quite the
reverse, between the two. He did not succeed very far, however, in
lessening the influence or diminishing the extremism of the school of
Schmoller. His tactics probably worked rather in the reverse direction.
When one reads his last pronouncements on this subject in his obituary
of Roscher (1894), it is certainly tempting to inquire why the *Studies
in Method* took the form they did. Here he again recognizes Roscher's
great services as the founder of the historical school, reacting justifiably
against 'the abstract unempirical schematism of some of the followers
of Adam Smith'. Menger explains (*Works*, vol. iii, p. 280):

> The issue between the Austrian school and a part of the historical econo-
> mists of Germany was not at all one of method in the real sense of the word.
> If the historical German economists appeared often in scientific works as the
> representatives of the inductive method, and the Austrians of the deductive
> method, this does not really express their relative positions. Neither empirical
> studies as contrasted with abstract reasoning, nor induction as contrasted
> with deduction, characterize truly these schools. Both recognize in experience
> the necessary foundation for studying the real world and its laws; both, I
> presume, recognize in induction and deduction, means of knowledge which
> mutually support and supplement one another. What still remains as a con-
> trast not fully reconciled, is something much more important; it relates to the
> aims of their studies and to the system of tasks which science has to solve.

It would therefore seem that Menger was concerned with problems
of methodological *norms* rather than with 'positive' methodological
analysis or elucidation, that is, with trying to lay down what economists *ought* to aim at or study, and how they ought to study it, and with
fixing the value of history and statistics as being simply 'auxiliary'.

The *Methodenstreit* which Menger's *Studies* of 1883 introduced, did

not give rise to much positive methodological analysis, the problems
of which lie rather in how empirical, analytical, and 'practical' propositions combine and apply to one another. For such analysis it may well
be vitally significant to distinguish in respect of individual propositions
between their analytical or empirical significance. But this is quite
different from trying to classify whole sciences, or parts of them, into
separate watertight compartments. The episode has, however, a
certain sombre instructive value as an extreme example of the consequences of intolerant normative methodologizing: of trying to lay
down what people ought to aim at and be interested in, of what is
'auxiliary' and what is 'primary', instead of being content with detailed
positive analysis and the elucidation of particular propositions, their
ambiguities and inexplicit assumptions, which is hardly a field in the
social sciences where there is any shortage of material. Whether or not
it is in the province of the economist as such to lay down for the citizen
and politician what ought to be the aims of economic policy, it is even
much more doubtful whether he should try to lay down what other
adult students ought to be aiming at or ought to be interesting themselves in. In fact the *Methodenstreit*, opened in such a challenging
manner by Menger's *Studies*, was, as Schumpeter has described it, a
struggle for '*Luftraum oder Herrschaft*' ('breathing-space or mastery').
Neither of these rather Teutonically conceived desiderata has much to
do with the search for truth or the eradication of error. In fact, of course,
they usually beckon in precisely the opposite direction.

Menger's *Studies on Method* contain a number of interesting minor
themes. There is his doctrine of 'methodological individualism', where
he argues that all analysis must start from the individual, and not with
'aggregate' and 'collective' concepts which are meaningless until
reduced to the individual 'atoms' of which they are made up. It is not
always easy to distinguish in this doctrine of 'methodological individualism' how far simply a logico-scientific principle is being stated,
and how far a political judgement is being pronounced. Certainly in
some later Austrian writers the principle of 'methodological individualism' seems to be connected with the doctrine that socialism is in
some sense economically 'impossible', that the individualist competitive economy must be taken as the only possible norm.

There is also Menger's conception, derived from Burke, of the
importance and, on the whole, beneficence of spontaneous, 'un-
reflected', social phenomena, the result of no formally agreed plan or
legislation, like language, the State itself, competition, or money.

Certainly many things individual and social, have clearly been better done 'unconsciously' than when deliberately thought out and planned. Sudden accessions of self-consciousness are notoriously apt to produce crises in individual lives, and presumably also in societies. Since Menger's day there has been an immense further growth in what may be called 'social self-consciousness', with the spread of urbanization, literacy, popular means of communication, and (usually on a somewhat higher level) social and economic statistics, which have together produced that state of 'fanaticised consciousness' that characterizes the modern world. Among the most profound transformers of the socially unconscious into the socially conscious are, of course, the economists and social scientists. Perhaps this was particularly the case with writers like Booth and Rowntree in England who made one part of society conscious of how another part was living. Particularly in the field of monetary policy and institutions, which was one of Menger's main examples of a beneficent 'unconscious' creation, the collapse of a 'closed' traditional attitude has inevitably resulted—for better or for worse—from the advance of monetary analysis. For society, as for an individual, a heightening of self-consciousness is obviously an irreversible step, at least in a democratic society with free distribution of increased social knowledge. There is no going back to a blissful unselfconscious childhood either for society or the individual, and each has to learn to bear the burden easily, not to throw it off, which cannot be done except through madness or self-destruction.

In view of the immense and irreversible growth of social self-consciousness since his time Menger's distinction is of profound interest and importance. But he hardly gets beyond the initial distinction, and a general emphasis on the importance and beneficence of the spontaneous and unselfconscious. One can only wish that his views were available on what has happened since and what is happening now.

Menger's one essay touching directly on the political application of economic doctrines is that defending the classical economists against the criticisms of the social-reformist members of the German *Verein für Sozialpolitik*, such as Brentano. He defends the English classics against charges of dogmatic opposition to State intervention and callous disregard of the interests of the masses, and points out that they supported State activity in many directions, including tariffs. The true descendants of classical political economy are held to be not Cobden, Bright, and Bastiat, but John Stuart Mill with his liberal socialism. Menger's liberalism is shown in his emphasis on individual thrift and energy directed towards the individual's private advancement as the main stimulus to an improved standard for all, and in his warning that socialistic reformers never banish self-interest from the world, but fix it in national and class appetites far more dangerous and unpleasant. (vol. iii, pp. 232–3.)

Like the earlier editions of Marshall's *Principles*, Menger's *Grundsätze* has 'Part I' on its title-page. It was presenting '*General Principles*', to be followed by three further parts covering distribution money and credit, production and commerce, and economic policy. But unlike Marshall he never completed anything in publishable form of these later parts, though working at them for many decades. The loss is immeasurable, and the time and energy spent on the *Studies on Methodology* all the more regrettable.

10

F. von Wieser

1. *Wieser's Approach to Economics*

FRIEDRICH WIESER'S two early contributions to economic theory, his books *On the Origin and Laws of Value* (1884), and *Natural Value* (1889), both bear strong family resemblances to Menger's *Grundsätze*. There is the same abstraction from the facts of contemporary economic conditions and industrial organization, and the same preference for 'Crusoe', back-to-nature illustrations. Except for the simplest arithmetical examples, all mathematical or diagrammatic methods are avoided, as are statistical references or estimates. There is the same tendency to an 'essentialist' formulation of theoretical problems, that is, in terms of the 'nature' or 'essence' of value or costs, rather than in terms of consumers' or producers' actions. On the other hand, all Wieser's writings bear a highly individual stamp, and his ideas seem to have been worked out without reference or obligations to others, except for his initial point of departure, Menger's *Grundsätze*. He was sceptical of Menger's methodological investigations and polemics, and thought that Menger had erred in returning to the individualism of the classical economists (*Gesammelte Abhandlungen*, p. 124). The main difference in his approach, however, is that he regarded his early works on economic analysis as somewhat in the nature of preliminaries for his later historical and sociological studies. Meanwhile he contributed several essays in applied economics, and developed his 'income' theory of money in various papers (collected in *Gesammelte Abhandlungen*). In his *Social Economics* (or *Theory of Social Value*, 1913), his crowning achievement in economics, he combined economic analysis with an historical and sociological analysis of the development of modern economic society. In his final work, *The Law of Power*, he leaves economic theory behind, like Pareto, for a survey and analysis of political and social history.

Wieser came to economics via history and law. His early enthusiasm for history was given a new direction by Herbert Spencer's *Introduction to Sociology*, in which Spencer pours scorn on the 'great man' theory of history, and argues that serious history must concern itself with the great movements of the anonymous masses, a point of view strengthened, for Wieser, by his reading of *War and Peace*. His ambition at this point was to write 'anonymous history', of which economic relationships seemed the most important part, and to explain economic relationships it was necessary to have a theory of value. The theory of value of the English classics seemed to lead to inconsistencies, and the Marxian socialists simply carried to their logical conclusion the ideas 'which the classics themselves had not the courage to think through to the end' (*Gesammelte Abhandlungen*, p. 116). In this intellectual dilemma Menger's *Grundsätze* came as a revelation to Wieser when he first read the book in 1872.

Wieser's early views on the historical role of the anonymous masses, views which he was to change very considerably later, find expression in his methodological essays and are even connected by a curious argument with the emphasis he lays on the fundamental differences between the natural and the social sciences. He argues that 'the natural sciences result from the achievements of great and famous men . . . the beginnings of the sciences of man have been quietly created by the anonymous masses' (*Gesammelte Abhandlungen*, p. 9). Wieser includes economic theory with 'pure philosophy and psychology and the applied branches of morals and aesthetics', which are entirely different in basis and procedure from the natural sciences. In the natural sciences,

no one who claims to study them will believe that by examining the generally adopted language and concepts of everyday life he has contributed anything whatsoever to an understanding of the essence of things. But the opposite is the case with the sciences of man: In many cases the reader will in spite of the closest attention be unable to decide what his author really aims at investigating, whether the empirical condition of a phenomenon, or the concept connected with the name of the phenomenon. (p. 2.)

For Wieser this is not an unfortunate, if frequent, ambiguity but a norm:

The definitions of concepts which one sets out are almost always meant to serve both purposes at once, that of determining the essence of things and defining terms or concepts. (p. 2.)

The accusation of anti-empirical scholasticism which might be brought against this procedure, Wieser considers is both to some extent justified, and to some extent beside the point. For the social sciences differ from the natural sciences, which seek to discover the unknown, in that 'in those sciences to which theoretical economics belongs, man seeks to understand himself . . . and what he himself has experienced and done, and only to a small extent try to bring to light something he has not experienced or not already discovered'. This gives the social scientist a great start or advantage over the natural scientist:

> We can observe natural phenomena only from outside but ourselves from within. . . . This psychological method chooses the most advantageous position for observation. It finds for us in common experience all the most important facts of economy. . . . It finds that certain acts take place in our consciousness with a feeling of necessity. What a huge advantage for the natural scientist if the organic and inorganic world clearly informed him of its laws, and why should we neglect such assistance? (p. 17.)

In a later version Wieser wrote:

> For all actions which are accompanied by a consciousness of necessity, economic theory need never strive to establish a law in a long series of inductions. In these cases we, each of us, hear the law pronounced by an unmistakeable inner voice. (*Social Economics*, p. 8.)

The notion of the laws of the economic world being clearly revealed to the economist by a process of introspection or reflection, much easier and more certain than anything available to the natural scientist, goes back via the Physiocrats to Cartesian rationalism: 'Cogito, ergo the laws of the economic world are revealed to me.' Wieser gives his own twist to the doctrine with his notion of the inherent wisdom in popular language and concepts (rather than the ambiguities and paradoxes which are so often to be found).

Let us simply note how very different this sounds from the warnings of Sidgwick, Jevons, or Edgeworth, and potentially how much more confidence (and even possibly dogmatism) about its results it may engender. Wieser's own standards of caution, detachment, and responsibility were, of course, exemplary. But that is often not the case with those who listen to 'inner voices', and are struck by the certainty and infallibility of what they hear. It is one thing to emphasize the role, in all sciences, of introspection and *Gedankenexperimente* in suggesting hypotheses to be tested out. It is quite another thing to put introspection on the same level, or even on a higher level, than empirical observation by insisting on the certainty and infallibility of inner voices, the promptings of which seem to require no ordinary inductive testing in respect of other individuals, about whom, by definition, introspection can tell one nothing.

2. Cost and Imputation

Wieser's first essay on economics was a seminar paper entitled 'On the Relation of Cost to Value' (1876). Menger had not entered very far into this problem, though he had left important pointers to its solution. Among Wieser's best-known contributions, outlined in this early essay, is his formulation and analysis of the alternative cost concept, that is, that the costs of goods are what is foregone, or what might have been produced by the same resources. The alternative cost concept is not necessarily simply a definition of the term 'cost'. It is a corollary of the fundamental postulate of maximizing behaviour, and enjoys all the elusiveness of content belonging to that comprehensive generalization. The alternative cost analysis is most conveniently presentable on the assumption of fixed total stocks of resources, and permits of various rather elegant, if, of course, probably fairly empty, elaborations of the standard allocation formulae for household, firm, or society. To the extent that this alternative cost analysis has rested on this assumption of fixed stocks of resources, it may perhaps have had a part, though this is not a fault in the analysis itself, in fostering the assumption, tacit or explicit, of a fixed level of employment of resources, which is bound to be somewhat obstructive in the analysis of economic fluctuations.

Proceeding from this concept of cost, Wieser went on to build up his theory of distribution, or 'imputation' (*Zurechnung*) of shares to the different factors of production, which he compares to the procedure of a judge imputing the responsibility for a crime among the different parties to it. He starts by criticizing Menger's 'loss' principle, according to which the value of a unit of a factor is measured by what would be lost of the product by the withdrawal of this unit. He substitutes the principle of the 'productive contribution', or what is gained by the factor's retention, which, of course, assuming continuous variability, comes to the same thing. All through Wieser's discussion he fails to mark off, and take separately, the cases of fixed and variable proportions of the factors. His emphasis on fixed proportions is no doubt connected with the great emphasis on the complementarity of production goods and services, which had been laid by Menger, and which has been followed by subsequent Austrian writers. But Menger also clearly described the case of variable proportions, which is the necessary basis for a marginal productivity analysis, and the case to which marginal productivity analysis is applicable. The avoidance of even the simplest mathematical formulation seems undoubtedly to have been a great handicap to the Austrians against formulating the marginal productivity theory in a clear and precise manner.

Though Wieser's general treatment of imputation suffers severely from this lack of clarity, his discussion of the rewards to particular factors contains many sound points. The rent concept is generalized into a 'universal law of differential imputation', applicable to labour and capital as well as land. On the subject of wages, Wieser is mainly concerned to attack the labour theory of value (a constant preoccupation of his) as well as the Malthusian 'subsistence' theory. On profits Wieser does not follow up the analysis of Thünen and Mangoldt.

It is, of course, Böhm-Bawerk's theory of capital that has come to be known as 'the Austrian' theory. But Wieser, also, developed a considerable analysis of capital, differing markedly from Böhm-Bawerk's, and having much more in common with that of Walras, and also Clark and Fetter. He makes no use of the concept of the period of production, and is critical of, though does not dismiss, the element of the undervaluation of future wants in the explanation of interest. He sees sufficient proof of the productivity of capital, and the payment of interest, simply in its general employment, like labour and land.

3. *Social Economics*

We shall try to present some of the main points of Wieser's social economics and economic sociology under three heads: (*a*) his analysis of economic calculation and of the role of the State in an exchange economy, a mixed economy, and a socialist economy, (*b*) his critical sociology of capitalism, (*c*) his outline of a 'middle way', or mixed economy.

(*a*) Wieser's treatment of the problem of economic calculation in different forms of society along, perhaps, with Sax's work on public finance, represents the nearest Austrian equivalent to English 'welfare economics', and to Pareto's and Barone's formulae for the optimum allocation of a society's economic resources. But it is neither a systematic review of cases like the former, nor an elaboration of pure and precise theoretical formulae like the latter. It is rather a comparison of different types of economic system or economic order, differing in property relationships and in the way in which economic decisions are taken.

Economic problems arise out of the fact that the world is neither a paradise nor a prison: in a paradise all goods would be free, and in a prison all would be allocated in fixed unalterable rations to be taken or left. The private household in seeking the optimum solution of its economic or allocation problem tries to maximize utility, the exchange economy maximizes exchange values, and the State maximizes (or ought to try to maximize) social utility, or what Wieser calls 'natural values' (*v. Natural Value*, p. 55). The aim of the private enterpreneur to maximize exchange values will conflict with the aim of the State, though Wieser does not follow up precisely how this comes about, or examine cases.

It is because of the common form and characteristics of maximizing allocation formulae, whatever the maximizing units or authorities, and whatever the form of economy, that Wieser insists on the similarity of the 'laws' of a socialist and a capitalist economy. He omits to add that the social 'maximands', whatever they may be, and the processes by which the attainment of these social maximands is sought, in fact the whole aim and content of economic life, will be different in the two economies. There is obviously much difficulty in Wieser's concept of 'natural value' or social utility, the maximand of the socialist economy. Particularly, as he comes to insist on a thoroughly neutral or even empty concept of utility (or rather *Nutzen* which is in any case a rather more colourless term): 'The economic principle of maximizing utility, in the form in which it occurs in theoretical economics, is to be separated from hedonist philosophising. There is no doubt that it is reconcilable with ascetic views. . . . The principle makes no attempt to lay down the ends of existence or how they should be chosen.' (*Social Economics*, p. 33.) On the other hand Wieser considers that, through the principle of diminishing utility, progressive taxation finds 'a firm theoretical basis in the concept and laws of economic value'. (p. 433.)

In the exchange economy the exchange values of goods and services will be precisely calculable, and the controllers of a socialist economy, if they were carrying out their task 'rationally', would have to aim at accounting for and economizing goods and services (including not only the services of labour, but of land and machines), according to precisely the same formulae. The labour theory of value would provide no aid in the solution of such allocation problems, either in a socialist, or in any other economy.

However, though comparatively exact calculations can be made for exchange values in an exchange economy—(Wieser seems to abstract from uncertainty and speculation)—the 'natural' or social values which the state aims at maximizing are not calculable, and are bound to be vague and controverted. The more precisely calculable exchange values cannot be taken as criteria for social policy. (*Natural Value*, p. 231.)

Wieser emphasizes the function of free markets in an exchange economy in making possible economic calculation and a 'rational' allocation of resources. But he is also quite clear that many of the most important decisions in allocating social resources cannot possibly be based on the sort of calculations which may be possible for an entrepreneur in a fairly stable market, and that, in any case, these market calculations have no special social validity. He clearly has in mind the social considerations of distributive fairness, education, defence, and so on, which are bound to dominate so much of any society's allocation of resources:

It is the exact calculation *and* the incalculable but actually observed influences that, *together*, make up the full value of goods. The theorist must admit so much, however hard it is for him, when he considers how greatly economic theory loses by it in the exact conception of its formulae and precepts. How simple and how easy to apply any advice whenever only calculable quantities are concerned;—whatever, calculated by exchange value, yields a profit is economically permissible; everything else is forbidden! And how misty and obscure all theoretical solutions become when they put absolute laws aside, and are obliged to appeal to concrete existing circumstances to decide for them! In the end it is to politics we must leave the task of deciding. . . . However much the pride of theory may suffer in recognizing this, it is a fact not to be gainsaid. (*Natural Value*, p. 231.)

(*b*) *Competitive Capitalism*: Almost nowhere does Wieser attempt any contribution to analytical dynamics, except for a few passing assumptions of the stereotyped self-equilibrating mechanism ('Finally the disturbance will be overcome and an equilibrium re-established', *Social Economics*, p. 107,[1] or, 'Until with the establishment of a new price, the market once more recovers its equilibrium and supply and effective demand coincide', p. 194). But he certainly does not attribute any optimistic teleological significance to the workings of the free market. On the whole he sees competition as a dangerous rather than a beneficent force, and suggests that it is conventional notions of 'fairness' which fortunately prevent continual competitive price warfare:

Were every individual here to follow his private interests only, then a

[1] I have used the translation by C. A. Malloch of *Natural Value* (1893 edition), and that by A. F. Hinrichs of *Social Economics* (1927 edition), the latter with slight amendments.

struggle for the most profitable price would break up into any number of
single combats, where the stronger would too often find opportunities of
mercilessly exploiting the weaker. . . . [But] the exploitation of the individual
case is not countenanced; men endeavour to ascertain the just, the common
price; the mass of individuals falls voluntarily into line, following the call of
those 'natural controls', which step by step have come to dominate in human
affairs. Experience has gradually driven home its lesson, that the common
price will work out best for the benefit of all (*Social Economics*, p. 185.)

There is probably much realism in this notion of the stabilizing influence
of convention on price fixing, but it is not easily reconciled with the
assumptions of the usual analysis. It is also to 'excessive competition'
that Wieser attributes economic crises in one of his few references to
the subject. As new investment opportunities open up, the rush to
exploit them results in 'excessive production', and 'over-' or 'excessive
competition' (pp. 209–10). (In a single passing reference he orthodoxly
claims that 'an old doctrine asserts correctly that general overproduction is inconceivable'. (p. 285.))

Wieser holds that the English classical economists 'had no correct
idea of the dangers which accompany competition on a large scale.
Their later followers, looking at the new world around them should
have known better; but in their pedantry they clung to their dogmas
careless of the breadth and depth of the cleft which separated them
from actuality.' (p. 209.) Formerly one was justified in saying that the
competitive struggle performed a service of personal selection. But
today it is the power of vast aggregates of capital which decides the
outcome of competition 'Now, however, the revolutions of trade,
brought about by the irresistible advance of large-scale capitalism, are
mass phenomena. . . . The displaced masses of unemployed cannot
easily, and certainly not quickly, find employment under approximately equal conditions; meanwhile these workers are abandoned to
abject poverty, and, more lamentable still, their best powers may be
scrapped forever.' (p. 210.) In his rejection of the classical defence of
competition, Wieser was much nearer to the members of the German
historical school, and of the *Verein für Sozialpolitik*, than to Carl
Menger: 'The classical theorists thought the doctrine of non-inter-
vention applied for all succeeding periods. This is now rejected. . . .
The recognition of the state's protective duty is the most important
theoretical result of modern economic policy. German economists may
take pride in having established it and broken the spell of the classical
dogmas.' (*Social Economics*, pp. 409–10.)

Wieser was also critical of any unqualified opposition to monopoly. The nature of capitalism had, in any case, completely changed: 'The modern trend to production on a large-scale has called into being numerous novel intermediate monopoloid forms, which today are far more important than either of the pure forms. The classical formula, unconditional approval of competition and the absolute repudiation of anti-social monopoly, can no longer do justice to the institutions of today.' (p. 217.) Wieser was deeply impressed by what he considered 'the present trend to enterprises of vast size' (p. 216), both by the dangers to freedom, and by their creative possibilities: 'Today, at any rate, it must be insisted that the effect of the personal selection of leaders, usually ascribed to competition, is most strikingly illustrated by the trusts. The trusts are creations of men of extraordinary abilities in practical business pursuits, men who possess the insight, the knowledge, the energies, required to plan and organize the giant enterprises of modern commerce and industry.' (p. 227.) From his early romantic Tolstoyan notion of the role of the anonymous masses, Wieser had come to emphasize, like Pareto and Schumpeter, the role in economic as in political history of the élite leadership.

It was on the social rather than the economic weaknesses of competitive capitalism that Wieser concentrated. First, there was the inequality in the distribution of wealth. Secondly, there was the conglomeration in huge new urban industrial areas of workers short-sightedly attracted by the higher money wages, but threatened with the 'degeneration' he considered urban industrialism to bring, and the new and still obscure forces it was fostering: 'All through the Middle Ages and down to the beginnings of modern times, our ancestors were threatened with barbarian aggression. Modern civilisation has grown so strong that it no longer fears this outside invasion, but the people are haunted by the fear that there may spring from its midst a new barbarism which may some day overpower them.' (p. 383.) Indeed, possibly at the very moment Wieser was writing in Vienna, Adolf Hitler (not to mention Bukharin) was lurking in preparation for his subsequent career. Wieser approvingly quoted Wilhelm Foerster: 'Intellectually and morally modern society is unequally matched against the enormous material forces which it has unchained through its science and technology.'

Thirdly, the existing order had not solved the problem of the right relation between employer and employed, and the worker and his work. Wieser saw little immediate—though some long-run—hope in

162 *F. von Wieser*

systems of profit-sharing or partnership, and made a special study of producers' co-operatives. He saw trade unions as the inevitable and justifiable weapon of workers in the existing economic order, and regarded marginal productivity as in practice establishing an upper limit but no lower limit to wages. Trade unions could at least force the entrepreneurs to agree to the competitive price for labour (p. 378):

The freedom of personal contract, however, is not that supreme blessing that the liberal school sought to portray. With the existing weak position of the labouring class, class-consciousness, resting upon cooperative solidarity, is to be valued more highly than individual liberty based on private interest. Only the former is strong enough to represent with good effect the interests of the masses. Thrown upon his own resources, the individual is nearly powerless. In view of the helplessness of the individual, the slogan of the liberal school, '*Laissez-faire, laissez-passer*', becomes almost a mockery. Those who truly wish for freedom must not begrudge it to the working class, though they may be fully aware that in its own class interests it is inclined to encroach on the individual interests of some of its members too freely. (p. 379, see also p. 405.)

(c) *The Mixed Economy*: In spite of these grave weaknesses in the existing order, in spite of what he seemingly regarded as the inevitability of 'the march to socialism' in all countries including the United States, and of what he referred to as 'the socialistic state of the future' (p. 408), Wieser seems to have favoured a mixed economy relying mainly on the competitive spirit for its motive force: 'No economic order, without suffering very great disadvantages, may dispense with the use, in one way or another, of the supreme power of competition.' (p. 211.)

Only a competitive decentralized system provides the necessary adaptability and incentive. With extensive division of labour the different individual tasks

will be executed far more effectively by thousands and millions of human beings, seeing with thousands and millions of eyes, exerting as many wills: they will be balanced, one against the other, far more accurately than if all these actions, like some complex mechanism, had to be guided and directed by a superior control. A central power of this sort could never be informed of the countless possibilities, to be met with in every individual case. . . . The private constitution of the economy is what is needed to enlist the tremendous force of self-interest in the service economic life—the force which, in case of impending war, submits without demur to the command of one leader. (p. 396.)

Socialist ideals may seem to give an easy and obvious answer to the problems of distribution. But that is only one half of the matter, which must be weighed against the other half, the effects on production. Moreover the abuse of economic power is not necessarily inherent in an exchange economy, 'nor will, on the other hand, the dissolution of the exchange economy free society from the possibilities of economic despotism. Even the socialistic state of the future will need leadership; will, by leadership, create power; and, as the outgrowth of power there will again be despotism, . . . whenever the masses are not sufficiently strong to offer resistance to the prevailing leaders.' (p. 408.)

Wieser hardly examines cases but only briefly offers general directions in which the balance of free enterprise and State control can be corrected. He discusses the taxation of rural and urban rents and of the profits of speculation and company promotion (p. 413), social insurance, some middle way in industrial organization between complete socialization and 'the despotism of the all-powerful entrepreneur', and possible measures for the control of monopoly. He accepted List's case for tariff protection to develop a nation's productive powers.

Wieser's last book *Das Gesetz der Macht* ('The Law of Power') was completed just before his death, and he regarded his whole life-work as leading up to it. He had meanwhile served as Minister of Commerce in one of the last cabinets of the Austro-Hungarian Empire towards the end of the First World War. In this book Wieser develops on a much larger political and historical canvas the main sociological themes of his *Social Economics*: the dangers and the creative possibilities of the growing 'bigness' of modern political and economic organizations: the problems of leaders and led: that the liberal revolution of the nineteenth century had been simply the revolution of the bourgeoisie: 'Just as the bourgeois political philosophers demanded fundamental civil rights for the bourgeoisie, so the political philosophers of the proletariat demand fundamental economic rights. Without these economic rights the abstract principle of 'equal rights for all in practice amounts to complete inequality'.

Except for some not very systematic chapters in J. S. Mill's *Principles*, English political economists have not been much concerned with the sociological background of their economic analysis. English economists have, like Marshall, mainly combined their economics with, and applied it to, a more detailed background of industrial history and organization, and to the practical possibilities of contemporary government policy. They have not so much applied it to, or combined it with, an historical analysis of the sociological and political framework of capitalism, as have some continental economists. Presumably, the existence of the English Channel, and the background of a more assured social stability, had much to do with this difference. But recent history has, of course, somewhat altered the position, and for those who want it, the works of Pareto, Wieser, and Schumpeter, on economic sociology, do possess a certain lively, if controversial, relevance to, and awareness of, the social revolutions of our time, which is somewhat missing, for example, in the writings of Marshall and Keynes.

E. Böhm-Bawerk

1. The Nature of Böhm-Bawerk's Work

THE extensive writings of Böhm-Bawerk, the exact contemporary and brother-in-law of Wieser, have been more widely known and discussed than any other works of the Austrian School. On the subjects of value and distribution he added little that was of essential importance to the doctrines of Menger and Wieser, and we shall pass over fairly briefly this part of his work. Nevertheless, he formulated the Viennese doctrines with a lucidity and persuasiveness not previously achieved, and the translations of his writings made 'the Austrian leader', as Edgeworth called him, the best known representative of his school in England and the United States. In addition, in his great work on capital and interest, he developed, with an unparalleled weight of argumentation, a theme he made peculiarly his own. In fact his theory of capital is often referred to as 'the Austrian Theory', though Menger and Wieser profoundly disagreed with it in their own valuable writings on the subject.

In his work on methodology, and on value and distribution, or 'imputation', many of the Austrian family traits are discernible. His criticism of the historical school is much more moderate and tolerant than is Menger's but it is firm. He avoids, like Menger and Wieser, all mathematical formulation, and his work is stamped by a thoroughgoing rejection of the concept of 'mutual determination', all-pervasive in Walras and Marshall. This often lends to his exposition a confident monocausal simplicity, apt, however, to lapse into a rather one-sided dogmatism, for example in his pertinacious insistence that marginal utility is the sole 'ultimate standard of value'. There is a tendency also to dogmatism in terminology, and as to what are, or are not, legitimate simplifying assumptions. Though prepared for many sorts of extremely abstract assumptions he is never ready to agree to those of continuity and divisibility in economic quantities, so useful for a precise formulation of marginal analysis. On the subject of utility he rejects hedonistic interpretations, though occasional phrases of his point clearly in that direction, and he holds that utility is measurable and to some extent comparable inter-personally.

In his theory of distribution he professedly follows Menger, but misses the essential principle of the variability of the proportions of the factors, and gives an analysis based mainly on different cases of fixed proportions and employing the somewhat awkward concept of the *Schlußstück*, the last factor to join a productive combination (which is the 'last' is apparently arbitrary) which is in a position to bargain down the rewards to the other factors in the combination, to the advantage of its own share. His monocausal principles and his avoidance even of the simplest mathematical assistance make impossible a satisfactory formulation.

In examining Böhm-Bawerk's theories of capital and interest it should be remembered that he never rounded off his great work with the completeness and consistency he would have liked. His life fell into three main phases. The first lasted till 1889, by when his theory of value and the first editions of the two parts of his work on capital and interest had been written. But, as he explained to his distinguished disciple Wicksell, Böhm-Bawerk never properly revised or finished off the first edition of his work, and for fifteen years had no opportunity of preparing a second edition.[1] For in 1889, immediately on the appearance of the first edition of the *Positive Theory*, Böhm-Bawerk began a period of fifteen years' service in the Austrian Government, in the course of which he was three times Minister of Finance, and carried through an important reform of the income tax. For the third phase, and last ten years, of his life (1904–14), he returned to academic work as Professor at Vienna, and started on a thorough revision of his book. But he proceeded not by removing weaknesses or inconsistencies from the existing edition but by engaging in extensive controversies with the numerous critics it had attracted, notably with J. B. Clark, Fisher, and Schumpeter, which were summarized and extended in a third volume of fourteen *Critical Excursions* (*Exkursen*).

Böhm-Bawerk was an indefatigable but not pugnacious controversialist, more it seems from a conscientious sense of duty to his critics and to the truth as he saw it, than for any other reason. Every critic had to receive his full due, not in some oblique footnote, but in a full length 'excursion' where he could be informed plainly, but politely, as to just where he had gone astray. Marshall referred to what he called

---

[1] See Wicksell's last essay, 'Zur Zinstheorie', in *Die Wirtschaftstheorie der Gegenwart* edited by H. Mayer, vol. iii, p. 199, and the quotation and translation therefrom by G. J. Stigler, *Production and Distribution Theories*, p. 194. All our references to Böhm-Bawerk's *Kapital und Kapitalzins* are to the fourth German edition.

Böhm-Bawerk's 'rather rough method of thumping' (*Memorials*, p. 416), but Böhm-Bawerk could take 'thumps' with urbanity as well as give them, and it is only fair to cite also the judgement of Schumpeter: 'One cannot be a good controversialist without being a good, and above all an honourable man. On this point, than which there are in life few more exacting tests of character and qualities, and in connection with which the most unaimiable traits are all too often apt to reveal themselves where one least expects them, Böhm-Bawerk is a shining example beyond all praise.' (*Zeitschrift für Volkswirtschaft*, 1914, p. 454.)

It is obvious to look for parallels between Böhm-Bawerk's massive work on Capital and Interest, and Marx's book on Capital, both eventually comprising three volumes in all, the first of which were published within twenty years of one another. There are a number of superficial, and unfortunately mainly rather unpalatable, resemblances. There is the same prolixity, the same inclination to terminological pedantry, the same Teutonic insistence on the virtues of 'profundity' ('Professor Marshall' has a '*nicht genug tiefe Erfassung des Problemes*'). There is the same 'essentialist' philosophizing, and the same tendency to push towards, or even well over into, the confines of metaphysics. There is the same attempt to illuminate contemporary problems by models of a primitive pre-capitalist 'Ur'-world. But there is no history and no sociology in Böhm-Bawerk, and though he was long a Cabinet Minister nothing resembling Marx's masterly use of blue-books. Böhm-Bawerk agreed at one point that his problem of interest could be interpreted as amounting to the Marxian problem of surplus value. (*Positive Theorie*, 4th ed., p. 378.) But a 'capitalist' economy has a completely different meaning for the two authors. For Böhm-Bawerk the capitalist economy is not an historical phase of economic society, with a particular property system and class structure. A 'capitalistic' economy is one that uses indirect 'roundabout' methods of production, other than the hand-to-mouth method of employing simply the two 'original' factors land and labour. 'Capitalist' production can and does occur in any form of society or economy, and presumably most socialist societies will be trying to make themselves more 'capitalist' (or 'capitalistic') in this sense.

Böhm-Bawerk deals with an isolated social economy, and monetary problems, crises, or fluctuations, are hardly mentioned. Competition is generally prevalent, and few problems of monopoly are discussed. All savings in a period seem to be invested in that period, and full employment equilibrium is generally attained. As Haberler has stated,[1]

[1] *Quarterly Journal of Economics*, 1950, p. 361.

the analysis is essentially static or 'comparatively' static, though it may be difficult to generalize precisely about so voluminous a book, which is not always fully self-consistent. The main *quaesitum* of the *Positive Theory* seems to be to propound a static formula for the rate of interest, and to interpret with great thoroughness the factors in or behind the formula, which in the concluding chapter are displayed in a comparative static analysis. The problems Böhm-Bawerk raised undoubtedly called especially for dynamic treatment, of which here and there he gives indications. But the extensive discussion of the element of time is not concerned with analysing the course of economic actions *through* time (that is, with 'dynamic' analysis), but with arriving at a static 'maximizing' formula for allocating resources between different methods of production, which for technical reasons take different periods of time. Even if that elusive technical generalization which Böhm-Bawerk sought after, which would connect the 'productivity' of, and the time taken by, different methods of production could be satisfactorily formulated; even if the baffling problem of measuring the time taken by different production periods could be regarded as solved (a possibility which probably most readers would reject), Böhm-Bawerk's formula would remain a 'static' marginal productivity formula, though, of course, immensely elaborated in certain directions.

If one is to run with patience the somewhat exacting race that Böhm-Bawerk's three volumes on capital and interest set before one, it is particularly desirable to keep in mind a general outline of the course, and its main contours and detours. Further, as in many discussions of the theory of capital, it is particularly important to be clear all the time as to what sort of answer is being given to what sort of question, empirical or definitional, 'static' or 'dynamic', technological or economic, 'micro'- or 'macro'-economic.

2. *Capital and Interest: and Some Later Essays*

The first volume of Böhm-Bawerk's great work is a 550-page *History and Criticism of Interest Theories*, in which the views of more than 150 authors from Aristotle onwards are discussed. Here we shall only mention briefly his treatment of one or two particular authors, and something of the method of criticism. Generally, a specialist writer, with his own particular doctrine to 'sell', will not make a satisfactory historian of previous doctrines.

The authors to whom Böhm-Bawerk pays most tribute are John Rae, Thünen, with his marginal productivity analysis of interest, and

Carl Menger. Jevons, who had recently emphasized the time dimension of different methods of production, in the analysis he had built up on his own as a lonely young man in Australia, is referred to as a *geistvoller Eklektiker* ('an intelligent eclectic'). The chapter on John Rae, and his work the *New Principles* (1834) is perhaps the most interesting in the book. Rae had spent much of his life as a schoolmaster and medical officer in the remoter parts of Canada, the United States, and the Pacific islands and his work was comparatively unknown, except from some high praise by Mill, and from quotation, without always perhaps sufficient acknowledgement, in Hearn's *Plutology*. Rae had discussed the role of invention in relation to the formation of capital and economic progress, and also the under-estimation of future wants, and the period of consumption of durable goods (which Böhm-Bawerk was to call the *Wartezeit*—period of waiting). In discussing Rae's doctrines Böhm-Bawerk gives a brief preview of his own answer to the problem of interest:

> I hold it to be completely correct that a root cause of interest lies in a different estimate of present and future goods, and that this different estimate, as Rae argues, based on grounds of a purely psychological nature, plays a very important part. But I also hold that these grounds certainly do not give an exhaustive explanation of the actual phenomena of interest, as both Rae and Jevons well realised. The facts of experience leave no doubt that the existence and level of the rate of interest are not based simply on psychological considerations as to the shortness and uncertainty of human life, and of the capacity for enjoyment, or on the greater attractions of the present, but that the technical facts of production also play a part. These facts of experience lead us to the idea, already well-known, of the independent productivity of capital. The difficulty—as I believe the main and most acute difficulty—of the whole problem of interest, is to set out the ways and means by which these heterogeneous grounds, partly objective and technical, partly highly subjective and psychological, work together to produce the rate of interest as we know it. . . . For myself, I attempt to show that the technical facts of production, which I describe as the greater technical productivity of time-consuming methods of production, provide a partial ground for the higher valuation of present goods, the possession of which permits the use of those more productive time-consuming methods. From this point of view the technical and psychological facts are coordinated from the start, and their effects work together to produce the common result of present goods being valued more highly than future goods. This result provides the explanatory link between the partial grounds which produce it, and the rate of interest which emerges as a further consequence from it. (*Geschichte*, 4th ed., pp. 301–2.)

From this account one might have expected that elsewhere Böhm-Bawerk might have shown more appreciation of the notion of mutual determination. His criticism of other theories, classified as 'productivity', 'abstinence', 'exploitation', and the 'services of capital' theories, is usually to the effect that they are not sufficiently profound, or that they do not get to the essence of the problem. He holds that there is some 'riddle' (p. 60) or 'secret', the 'key word' for solving which has not been discovered. (p. 168.) He finally formulates the problem as follows: 'The problem of interest is that of studying and explaining the causes which direct a part of the stream of goods from the annual national production, into the hands of the capitalists. It is therefore, without doubt, a problem of the distribution of goods. (p. 444.) But Böhm-Bawerk does not regard it simply as a 'micro-economic' distribution problem of the buying and selling of a class of factors by individuals, but as a problem of an entire category of income, as analysed in the English classical account of distribution between the three 'classes' of society.

The *Positive Theory* opens with a long examination of the 'Concept and Essence of Capital', in which Böhm-Bawerk criticizes the many differing definitions of this much-controverted term. He wants to establish 'terminological discipline', and finds Marshall's attitude 'somewhat resigned', that 'economists remain therefore free to choose their standard definition of capital with a view to their own convenience'. His own concept of capital is that it consists, in by far its most important form, of 'intermediate products' or 'produced means of production'. This concept is refined further by his distinction between 'social' and 'private' capital, or 'produced means of production'. Machines, raw materials, stocks of finished consumption goods in the hands of traders, factories, but not schools &c., are 'social' capital, and all these, with the addition of the means of subsistence of workers and durable consumption goods (provided they are not consumed by their owners, but hired out to others), are 'private' capital.

This concept of capital follows directly from Böhm-Bawerk's doctrine of the two 'original' factors. Nature and labour are the only two fundamental factors of production, capital being simply 'intermediate' and not of itself 'productive', its function being to make it possible to transcend 'direct' hand-to-mouth production by 'indirect' roundabout methods. These indirect methods have the advantage of being more productive, though in given technological conditions their productiveness will be in decreasing proportion to the increase in 'roundaboutness'. But they have the disadvantage of demanding generally a greater sacrifice of time (though there may be exceptional cases where a more indirect method may be both more productive and 'quicker'). (p. 112.)

In his second book of the *Positive Theory* on 'Capital as an Instrument of Production', we are at the heart of the Böhm-Bawerkian matter. He subsequently makes it clear that it is only 'cleverly chosen' lengthenings of the method of production that are more productive. Of course, for every one 'longer' method that is more productive, there are an infinite number, which no one would ever dream of using, that are less productive. But there always exist at any moment these more productive longer methods available for the 'clever chooser' who possesses present goods.

As soon as one begins to discuss 'longer' and 'shorter' methods of production the problem arises of how to measure the temporal length of a method of production. Böhm-Bawerk's answer is that the period of production is measured by an average of the lengths of time between the application of the different inputs going to produce a good, and the final completion of the good. It is unnecessary today to emphasize how unsatisfactory this definition is, except possibly for highly over-simplified and unrealistic cases. Generally, particular inputs cannot be linked with particular outputs, and the problem of 'weighting' the average of the lengths of time between all the different inputs and the final output is more or less insoluble. Moreover, corresponding with the period of production is the period of consumption (or *Wartezeit*) of durable goods, and there is no particular relation between the length of the two 'periods' in respect of any particular good. An essential element of Böhm-Bawerk's analysis of the relation between the time taken by, and the productivity of, different methods of production is that every lengthening of the period of production requires 'more capital', and that every increase in the amount of capital must 'lengthen the period of production'.

Stripped of what is purely definitional, and somewhat arbitrarily so, and also of all doubtful technological generalizations, what remains in Böhm-Bawerk's analysis? That there are different methods of production, of different degrees of productivity: and that different methods would take different lengths of time, if one could agree on some method of measurement, but any such method of measurement would be arbitrary and without much economic significance. However, though Böhm-Bawerk did not answer the problem he posed, and though it is very doubtful whether he posed a meaningful problem, his discussion of the elusive relation between 'time' and 'productivity', ultimately perhaps completely elusive, may be said to have been a challenge that at one stage or another had to be met and disposed of.

Böhm-Bawerk closes this part of his work with a section on the formation of capital, or saving and investment. For the formation of capital the negative element of saving must be joined by the positive element of investing, or employing intermediate products. (p. 139.) Not only does Böhm-Bawerk distinguish the two processes in this way, but he corrected Adam Smith's long dominant dictum that 'parsimony and not industry is the immediate cause of the increase of capital'. 'To be correct', Böhm-Bawerk emphasizes, 'this must be precisely reversed. The direct cause for the existence of capital goods is production, the indirect cause is the previous saving.' However, after this promising emphasis Böhm-Bawerk reverts to the Smithian concept of the invariable (or inevitable) linking of saving and investment. He examines what happens in a free market economy when aggregate saving increases. Previously the entire national income (equal to the product of 10 million man-years) has been consumed. Now only the product of $7\frac{1}{2}$ million is consumed and that of $2\frac{1}{2}$ million is saved:

> If for a time the old disposition of production was continued by the entrepreneurs and 10 million worth of consumption goods put on the market, then the over-supply would result in a lowering of prices, and the pressure of losses would cause the entrepreneurs to adjust their production to the changed conditions of demand. They would now ensure that in one year only the product of $7\frac{1}{2}$ million man-years would be put on the market ... and the remaining $2\frac{1}{2}$ million, superfluous for the annual supply of consumption goods, can and will be devoted to increasing capital. It *will* be so employed because an economically educated people does not hoard but applies what is saved: by buying shares, depositing it in a bank or savings bank, lending etc. In these ways it is directed into productive credits, increases the purchasing power of producers for productive purposes, and so is the cause of an increased demand for means of production or intermediate products, which in the last analysis causes the directors of firms to invest the available productive factors in producing the required intermediate products. We therefore see, in fact, a precise connection between saving and capital formation. ... If individuals save, the changed demand forces employers by the impulse on prices to change their dispositions of the productive forces: less are devoted in the year to current satisfaction, and the quantity is increased of those devoted to intermediate products. (pp. 149–50.)

Without any particular warning as to any degree of abstraction involved, Böhm-Bawerk, as we shall see again later, was dealing with the case where all savings in a period are invested and there is full employment.

At this point, at the end of his Book II, Böhm-Bawerk asks what determines whether people save and produce intermediate products? The answer is in their valuations of different goods. Böhm-Bawerk then breaks off abruptly from problems of capital, for his lengthy third book on value and utility. We have already indicated very briefly something of Böhm-Bawerk's views on utility, value, and imputation. The order of subjects in the *Positive Theory*, that is, Capital, Value, Interest, certainly seems something of a 'roundabout method'. Whether it is a 'cleverly chosen' one, it is perhaps legitimate to question.

The subject of the final Book IV is that fitting together of the 'objective-technical', and 'subjective-psychological' explanations which, as we have seen, Böhm-Bawerk regarded as the main problem of interest. The 'objective-technical' grounds work on the side of the demand for capital, and the 'subjective-psychological' on the supply side of saving. But before proceeding to his analysis of the determination of the rate of interest in the market, Böhm-Bawerk seems to be trying to establish independently the necessity of a positive rate of interest. Wicksell argued that: 'Böhm-Bawerk's real error . . . is that at this point in his exposition he seeks to solve the problem of the *existence* of interest—as distinct from its actual rate—without referring to the market for capital and labour.' (*Lectures*, vol. i, p. 171.) Whether or not this is justly describable as his 'real' error, it is surely mainly one of exposition, and not necessarily fundamental.

The problem of interest is interpreted by Böhm-Bawerk as the problem of the relative values of present goods and future goods of the same kind and quantity. His explanation is summarized in his three 'grounds' for the general superiority of present over future goods.

(1) The first ground is described as the different relative needs for goods and the supply of them in present and future. (*Positive Theory*, p. 328.) For example, there will be those undergoing some present crisis in their affairs, and those also who look forward to a higher income in the future. To the objection (made, for example, by Wieser) that these valuations will be offset by those of other people with an opposite time-preference, Böhm-Bawerk replies that those who wish to have more future goods can simply store their present goods. As all goods have their cost of storage this is not a very satisfactory answer.

(2) The second ground is the general irrational under-estimate of future wants, partly a weakness of will, partly a tendency to wrong estimates, and partly an extravagant *carpe diem* regard for the uncertainties of the future. Böhm-Bawerk definitely treats this as a systematic irrationality, again a generalization that Wieser contested.

(3) Böhm-Bawerk's much-controverted third ground is based on his generalization about the greater productivity of roundabout time-consuming methods of production, causing the 'technical superiority' of present over future goods. The fisherman who has, or can, obtain a stock of 'present' fish is able to subsist while making a net which will enable him to catch many more 'future' fish when he has completed the net. Böhm-Bawerk insisted to the end against Fisher and others, that this should be called an entirely 'independent' ground. But of itself it seems to be a purely technological generalization, which can only obtain economic significance by working through the first ground and explaining a general subjective preference for present over future goods. Doubtless the concept of 'time preference' needed more elucidation by all parties to the lengthy debate over this third 'ground'.

The fixing of the rate of interest under the influence of these three grounds is worked out almost entirely 'macro-economically', for aggregate markets. Böhm-Bawerk first takes the general labour market. Here on the one side are the propertyless workers demanding present goods, and offering their services in return. On the other side are the capitalists in possession of present goods and demanding future goods, or more precisely the services of the workers which will produce future goods after an interval of time and in accordance with the degree of technical superiority of roundabout methods.

The labour market may be regarded as the most important component of the general market for the means of subsistence, or the principal source of demand on the subsistence fund of society. Böhm-Bawerk, in the first instance, abstracts from the demands of landowners, capitalists, and consumption-borrowers for subsistence goods. The function of this subsistence fund is to maintain the members of society over the average social period of production (the average of all the individual average periods of production of all the different goods). The function of the rate of interest is to set a limit to the length of the average social period of production, which, if no interest had to be paid, would be lengthened indefinitely. The supply of present subsistence goods is limited by the national wealth, and the rate of interest has to limit the length of the social period of production to this fund. The *agio* on present goods, or their higher valuation as compared with future goods, must correspond with the rate of interest. There is one paragraph at this point which suggests the application of these Böhm-Bawerkian concepts to the particular form of the 'capital shortage' explanation of crises adopted by later members of the Austrian School. If the rate of interest is too low:

> An excessive expansion will be undertaken so that the subsistence fund of society will be exhausted before the fruits of the longer production methods are available or ripe for consumption. The result is losses and shortages, and only as a result of the 'scarcity' prices will the misdirected productive forces be called back to provide as required for present needs. This can only be accompanied by severe disturbances, costs, and losses. (p. 405.)

Böhm-Bawerk turns at this point to the socialists. He argues that sometimes in the general labour market there is a possibility of monopolistic exploitation of the propertyless workers' needs for present goods, without which their labour cannot be applied except in the most sterile hand-to-mouth methods of production. But:

> Though the sellers (of present goods, i.e. the capitalists) may be few, they have all the more present goods to be employed fruitfully. If they are all to find their labour, the capitalists must, in competition, reduce the prices they demand from high to more moderate levels, which will make impossible the exploitation of the propertyless. Happily this sort of case is the rule in the real world. Only occasionally does something limit the competition of the capitalists' (p. 429),

—a generalization to which Adam Smith, for one, would hardly have subscribed. (In his later discussion, in his essay on 'Power and Economic Law', Böhm-Bawerk appeared to go very far towards reversing this generalization.)

Böhm-Bawerk agrees that private saving is not the only means by which capital can be increased, and further that Rodbertus and Lassalle are justified in denying the 'heroism' of the 'abstinence' by the rich. But, on the other hand, 'in the socialist state, just as in the present society, the owners of the present goods will earn interest on them from the workers who by their work are creating a future product'. (p. 435.)

Böhm-Bawerk deals with the formation of the market rate of interest, first for a simplified case where the workers' demand for present subsistence goods is the sole demand (landowners', capitalists', and consumption borrowers' demands being, for simplicity, excluded).

The entire supply and demand for present goods meets in a single 'giant' market covering the whole economy. He assumes, also, that all branches of production have the same productivity and yield the same increase in productivity if the methods of production are 'lengthened'. For this aggregate 'macro-economic' model, full employment of labour, and full investment of present goods, are assumed as inevitable: 'It is always *possible* to buy the whole labour supply with the existing stock of wealth (or subsistence), and there are strongly effective forces ensuring that this possibility is always realised.' (p. 448.) The workers would rather sell their labour cheap than not at all, and will always underbid one another for work if unemployed. The capitalists will always find it profitable to advance their capital to the workers rather than leave it inactive. Consequently: 'A period of production must be chosen just long enough to require the whole disposable subsistence fund for paying the entire available labour force, and no longer. The wage-level must be such that there is no idle capital to bid up wages and no idle labour seeking employment to bid them down.' (p. 453.) There may be various such wage-rates giving full employment (a point which Böhm-Bawerk neglects), but only one will be compatible with the capitalists' selection of the most profitable method of production—a condition of equilibrium. Assuming these equilibrium conditions, 'the level of interest is determined by the additional yield of the last permissible lengthening of the productive process'. (p. 457.) As Böhm-Bawerk recognizes, this is an adaptation or elaboration of Thünen's marginal productivity analysis.

The equilibrium rate of interest, therefore, varies (1) with the size of the subsistence fund (inversely), (2) with the number of workers (the more workers to be employed the higher the rate of interest), and (3) technological conditions (the more productive are the available lengthenings of the production process, the higher the rate of interest). (p. 464.) Böhm-Bawerk here provides a comparative static analysis, taking a given change in each of these three factors.

The dropping by Böhm-Bawerk of his simplifying assumptions makes little essential difference to the shape of his conclusions. Irrationalities and slowness in adaptation may prevent the equalization of returns to more roundabout methods from each line of production. Böhm-Bawerk does not believe that any precise or persistent calculation of investment yields does, or can, take place in a private enterprise economy, owing to the baffling uncertainties involved. Consequently saving and investment decisions are strongly under the influence of habit. (pp. 478–9.) He points out the similarities of his analysis with that of the classical wages fund doctrine. But he claims that his concept of the subsistence fund is far more precise, and that he has introduced the vital element of the length of the social period of production.

There is no doubt that a 'micro-economic' marginal productivity analysis of interest and wages *could* easily be presented, *mutatis mutandis*, in Böhm-Bawerk's terminology. But the significance of marginal productivity analysis applied to labour and capital, *as a whole, in aggregate markets*, is extremely doubtful. There is not much point in trying to argue that Böhm-Bawerk's model with its assumption of equilibrium full-employment is 'illegitimate'. It is simply remote from the dynamic problems of a modern monetary economy, and Böhm-Bawerk does not sufficiently emphasize his high level of abstraction, and the very special nature of the assumptions he is making. On the contrary, his final chapter is entitled 'The Capital Market in its Full Development'. Even if the insurmountable difficulties of his fundamental concept of the period of production are disregarded, his 'macro-economic', static, and comparative-static analysis remains highly abstract. This would not be a fair point for criticism if Böhm-Bawerk had clearly indicated to his readers (and to himself) the full importance of the elements from which he was abstracting. Translating the 'macro-economic' formulation into 'micro-economic' terms, and leaving out the period of production concept, one is left with a marginal productivity analysis of interest, filled out at great length by a number of interesting, but often highly questionable, 'grounds' or explanations.

In one of his last and finest writings, his essay on 'Power and Economic Law', Böhm-Bawerk carried much farther his long-run analysis of the relations between general wages and interest. He was concerned with the problem of how far trade unions had the power to raise wages above whatever level was fixed by 'economic law'. As contrasted with the *Positive Theory*, the assumption of generally perfect competition in the labour market is not made in this essay, nor is its realism upheld. The most important question analysed turns on whether a wage-rate can be held in the long run which, though it does not bring a positive loss to entrepreneurs on their investments, reduces the interest on their capital below the 'natural' level. (*Gesammelte Schriften*, p. 277.) The analysis again is in general 'macro-economic' terms, but its clarity is, as before, impaired by an occasional reference to 'micro-economic' conditions and the analysis of production plans of the individual firm. As the discussion also involves guessing at the shape of such very elusive concepts as the long-run supply curve of savings and business enterprise, it cannot, and wisely does not, come to any very clear-cut conclusions. Böhm-Bawerk does not try to insist that trade unions cannot raise wages, but argues that they certainly can in the short run, and that *possibly* by raising efficiency the higher wages can be held in the long run. He simply argues that very often the apparent success of unions in raising money wages is illusory because of consequential price increases, or that the gains are at the expense of other workers outside the unions. He argues, further, that unemployment is a likely consequence, though this may only prove 'frictional' because the unemployed workers will usually sooner or later bid down the wage-rate. He concludes, simply, by refusing to assent to the general proposition that trade unions can in the long run increase the share of labour at the expense of the share of capital, and that such success in raising wages as they had had in recent decades was made possible by the rapid technological progress then going forward. He is dealing with a society with a considerable trade union movement, but great inequalities in the distribution of wealth, and where the function of saving is performed largely or entirely by the rich, a set of conditions which the last half-century has, as a matter of historical fact, shown to be itself of doubtful stability in the long run.

We may mention, in conclusion, Böhm-Bawerk's essay on Marx: 'Karl Marx and the Close of his System', written as an essay in honour of Karl Knies in 1896. It is a criticism of the labour theory of value in the light of marginal utility analysis, written with all Böhm-Bawerk's pertinacity and urbanity. It does not discuss Marx's theory of crises, and demonstrates the limited significance simply of an intellectual refutation of the Marxian theory of value. Böhm-Bawerk concludes:

The Marxian system has a past and a present, but no abiding future. Of all sorts of scientific systems those which, like the Marxian system, are based on a hollow dialectic, are most surely doomed. A clever dialectic may make a temporary impression on the human mind, but cannot make a lasting one. In the long run facts and the secure linking of causes and effects win the day. In the domain of natural science such a work as Marx's would even now be impossible. In the very young social sciences it was able to attain influence, great influence, and it will probably only lose it very slowly, and that because it has its most powerful support not in the convinced intellect of its disciples, but in their hearts, their wishes and their desires. . . . Socialism will certainly not be overthrown with the Marxian system—neither practical nor theoretic Socialism. As there was a Socialism before Marx, so there will be one after him. . . . Marx, however, will maintain a permanent place in the history of the social sciences for the same reasons and with the same mixture of positive and negative merits as his prototype Hegel. Both of them were philosophical geniuses. Both of them, each in his own domain, had an enormous influence upon the thought and feeling of whole generations, one might almost say even upon the spirit of the age. The specific theoretical work of each was a most ingeniously conceived structure, built up by a magical power of combination, of numerous storeys of thought, held together by a marvellous mental grasp, but—a house of cards (as translated by A. M. Macdonald, pp. 218–21).

Perhaps it is of interest to ponder how much—(though certainly not all)—of this verdict, might justly and not uncharitably be applied to Böhm-Bawerk's own massive works.

12

Further Developments in Historical and Mathematical Economics in Germany and Austria (*c.* 1900)

1. *Schmoller and his School*

THE younger historical school, or the school of Schmoller (1838–1917), who after service as a government statistician was then Professor at Strasbourg, began to come to the front in Germany about 1870. It had two leading themes: the first, a devotion to current problems of social reform by State action; the second, a much more cautious 'monographic' application of the historical method, avoiding the ambitious attempts at comprehensive laws, and generalizations about 'stages of development', of the earlier historical economists.

There had in Germany been a similar movement of thought in the 1850's and 1860's to that in Britain in the '60's, which saw in the progress and application of science the key to the solution of most or all of man's problems, including social problems. As the philosopher Rudolf Eucken put it: 'In the '50s and '60s the attitude to the world of the speculative philosopher is superseded by that of the natural scientist, with the result that the main objective is no longer the 'inner' culture of the individual through art and literature, but the advancement of society, economically, politically, and socially.'[1] Soon after, the unprecedentedly rapid industrial development in Germany then under way, and the inequalities it brought, as well as the foundation of the Empire, were bound to result in increased attention to the role of the State in economic and social life. The idea that economists should place themselves and their works more immediately in the service of State measures for social and economic reform, found expression in the formation of the *Verein für Sozialpolitik* ('Union for Social Policy'), in 1872. The *Verein* had the support of the older historical economists, Roscher, Hildebrand, and Knies, and included a variety of political beliefs among its members. Among the leaders were conservative-socialist followers of Rodbertus like Adolf Wagner (see

[1] *v.* W. Eucken, 'Wissenschaft im Stile Schmollers', *Weltwirtschaftliches Archiv.* 1940, p. 470.

his *Rede über die Soziale Frage*, 1872) and adherents of the German 'Cameralist' tradition. The members of the *Verein* were not, as such, associated with any particular political party. Nor, of course, did they necessarily agree at all closely with Schmoller on methodological problems. The members of the *Verein* simply agreed in rejecting the more extreme liberalist and socialist policies as being 'Utopian' 'rationalist' over-simplifications. They became known as the 'academic socialists' or 'socialists of the chair' (*Kathedersozialisten*), but it should be emphasized that the brand of liberalism they were opposing, and to which they applied the counter-slogan of 'Manchesterism', was hardly that of Adam Smith or Ricardo, and certainly not that of John Stuart Mill. It followed rather the line of the professors who held that the imposition of an income-tax was the next step to communism, and of the 'liberal' Prussian nationalist Treitschke, who was opposed to any mitigation of economic inequalities as sentimental attempts to deny to the strong the rewards of their superior prowess as compared with the weak.[1] In a spirited reply to Treitschke, in 1874, Schmoller defended himself and the *Verein* against Treitschke's attack on them as 'patrons of socialism'. The *Verein* stood rather for the piecemeal study and preparation of practical immediate measures of reform in relation to hours and conditions of work, social insurance, factory legislation, and the like. It should also be remembered that it was leading members of the *Verein*, such as Schaeffle and Nasse, who were pioneers of what has become the main liberal criticism of socialist economics (*v. below* Ch. 18, sect. 3). The attitude of Schmoller himself was that of a forward-looking but loyal official of the German Empire, a strong supporter, on principle, of the monarchy (he even looked forward to a monarchy in the U.S.A.) because he saw in it a bulwark against the exclusive domination of any single class.

The second main theme of Schmoller related to the historical method. He rejected, like the older historical economists, the English classical conception of the science of political economy, as formulated, for example, by Senior, as a pre-eminently deductive study, 'not avid of facts', concentrating on logical deductions from a very small number of fundamental postulates. He sought to develop, as part of political economy, the study of economic institutions, economic classes, the nature of economic progress, and the wide field of economic sociology generally, rather than to treat these subjects as belonging to a 'given' background. For this purpose he drew extensively, but by no means

[1] *v.* Schmoller, *Über einige Grundfragen de Sozialpolitik u.s.w.*, 2nd ed., 1904, pp. 14 ff.

exclusively, on history, while recognizing that statistics and social psychology were to be other main sources of the necessary material. But Schmoller throughout emphasized his scepticism as to the 'historicism' of Roscher and Hildebrand, their notions of historical laws, and of laws and 'stages' of economic and social development, though he was, of course, not completely untouched by the ideas of Hegel, Comte, and Darwin, and shared with Marshall a solid belief in human progress, more difficult to maintain today. But he steadily resisted the more extravagant manifestations of Hegelian 'historicist' influence:

> By cloaking propositions as 'laws', one gives them an appearance of necessity which they do not possess, or one gives too high an importance to comparatively insignificant truths, thereby misleading those who apply them. . . . One may attempt to set out some general formula of economic progress, or even of human progress in general. But one is then in the realm of the philosophy of history, of teleology, prophecy, hopes and forebodings. The broader the basis of knowledge on which such attempts are based, the greater value they will have. Bold syntheses of this kind will always be necessary for the purposes of practical action, and it need not be held against the genuine prophets of the day when they believe they have found 'a law of development'. Herbert Spencer and the theorists of social development Mill and Comte, have attempted such formulae, as have the socialists and the 'Manchester' liberals. This sort of thing will, however, always remain far removed from what the natural scientist calls laws. Nor can they be described as empirical laws. What have been prematurely described as laws of history were either in many cases very doubtful generalisations, or simple age-old psychological truths, by which it was believed that whole series of historical events could be explained. It is more justifiable to doubt whether today we can and ought to speak of historical laws. (*Grundfragen der Sozialpolitik*, 2nd ed., pp. 351 and 356.)

Just as Schmoller rejected *a-priori* Utopian plans of wholesale social reorganization, socialist or liberalist, so he turned away from what he regarded as premature historical generalizations, and the attempt to promulgate laws of historical development. Just as he favoured the detailed study of piecemeal measures of social reform, so he directed his and his students' work to detailed monographs on particular subjects. Schumpeter describes the lessons Schmoller taught as:

> First, the avoidance of comprehensive phrase-making, secondly, a contempt for the general recipe and panacea, thirdly, the need for basing each judgement on a detailed knowledge of the facts of the individual case, fourthly, the need for a sense of responsibility corresponding to that required in a man of action, with a complete understanding of the concrete conditions

of political action. . . . He inculcated a balanced understanding of all the interests and functions at work at any moment, and that cool appraisal necessary for a quantitative judgement on social conflicts. (Schmoller's *Jahrbuch*, 1926, p. 352. 'Gustav Schmoller und die Probleme von heute.')

As Schumpeter goes on to point out, Schmoller had, in principle, no special preference for historical as against any other kind of empirical material: 'He himself in fact worked primarily with historical material since to master a single type of material, it is necessary to specialise in its methods and peculiar difficulties. That is the only way to achieve anything. But he did not work exclusively on historical material, and his pupils, for example Spiethoff, not even primarily.' (p. 355.) It is quite impossible to justify the charge, either from his precepts or his practice, that Schmoller held that economics should be an exclusively historical study.

It is almost equally difficult to justify from the record the charge that Schmoller stood for a naive unqualified empiricism, which sought to exclude all theoretical analysis. He repeatedly emphasized the inextricable interconnexions between observation and analysis, as in his oft-quoted analogy of how two legs are needed for walking:

All observation isolates a single occurrence from the chaos of phenomena in order to study it by itself. Observation rests always on abstraction; it analyses a part. The smaller and more isolated this is, the easier the observation. . . . The relative simplicity of the elementary phenomena of nature very much facilitates the observations of the natural scientist. The natural scientist even has it in his power to alter at will the surroundings and the causes at work, that is, he can experiment and look at the object from all sides. Not only is this seldom possible, or only with difficulty, in respect of economic phenomena, but even in their simplest form these are much more complicated, dependent on very different causes, and influenced by a series of cooperating conditions. If we take a rise in the price of wheat, or in wages, a change in the exchange rate, or a trade crisis, an advance in the division of labour, almost every such event is made up of the feelings, motives, and actions of certain groups of men, as well as of the massive facts of nature (e.g. a harvest), or of technology (e.g. new machinery), and is influenced by morals and institutions the origins of which are widely separated. . . . The observation of economic facts is always a difficult operation, the more easily upset by mistakes, the larger, the more extensive, and the more complicated, the individual phenomenon. (*Grundfragen*, p. 299.)

In his chapter in his main work the *Grundriss* (*Outline*), dealing with Value and Price he followed—it is true not with much refined expertize— the orthodox analysis, in particular that of Böhm-Bawerk, and he recognized that Jevons and the Austrian School with their new theory of value had 'grasped with more empirical precision some of the psychological phenomena of value and markets, and had analysed practical economic life at certain points more correctly'. (*Grundriss*, 1919 ed., p. 121.) But for Schmoller the theory of value and price, and what may today be called micro-economic maximization analysis generally, was simply 'one corner in a great mansion'. Nevertheless, he held that:

> What has been achieved is just as much the result of deductive as of inductive reasoning. Anyone who is thoroughly clear about the two procedures will never maintain that there are sciences explanatory of the real world which rest simply on one of them. (*Grundriss*, p. 110.)

The relative emphasis on observation and analysis, fundamentally inseparable, would vary with the particular problem, and more generally from period to period:

> The Cameralist and Mercantilist economists devoted themselves primarily to the painstaking, but often highly superficial collection of facts . . . ending in a sort of 'polyhistory' devoid of ideas. The 'natural' theory of political economy brought a solution. It represented an interim attempt to master the material theoretically. For a generation, observation and description took second place. But regarding things as more simple than they were, they believed that the key had been found in the general nature of man, which led more directly and effortlessly to valuable knowledge than tedious, time-consuming, empirical methods. The reaction to this one-sidedness came in our epoch. (*Grundfragen*, p. 304.)

Schmoller believed that, as they advanced, sciences generally became more deductive, a generalization which may well have much truth in it, but which seems to require at least some explanation.

Schmoller's main work, his encyclopaedic two-volume *Outline* (*Grundriss*) was first published in 1900, and is, as Schumpeter describes it, a vast 'mosaic'. The main order of subjects it goes through include in Volume I: Land, Population, and Technology: The Social Order and the Economy: The State and the Economy: The Division of Labour: Property: Classes: The Firm or Entrepreneur. And in Volume II: Markets and Exchange: Competition: Money: Value and Price: Capital and Credit: Banking: Labour Conditions, Contracts and Wages: Social Insurance: Trade Unions: The Distribution of Income: Economic Crises: Class Conflicts: The Economic Relations between States: Economic Progress.

Each theme is treated historically, statistically, analytically (to too slight an extent perhaps), and, in addition, practical precepts are usually added. We would note especially the discussion of the trade cycle and of fluctuations in the economy as a whole. This was the starting-point of Schmoller's assistant Spiethoff. Most books of 'Principles' at this time were not giving this subject much mention or else were treating it as 'a last chapter', which was often not reached.

Schumpeter went so far as to compare Schmoller with Marshall:

> The comparison with Marshall is obvious. Though because of their surroundings and training they turned to different tasks, they belong to the same world. Marshall's procedure also may be summarised as 'facts and inferences'. He, too, though a man of science and a teacher of positive achievement, derived his impulse subjectively from his social sympathies, and saw the significance of his work in its service to society. Both say, though with different emphasis, the same thing. . . . The social attitude of each of them had a very strong national note. For Schmoller the Hohenzollern state was not simply an object of study, nor was England's position for Marshall. This is obvious in the former case. But it is just the same in the latter. (p. 387.[1])

The discredit into which Schmoller's work subsequently fell, in Germany and elsewhere, went farther than was deserved. Partly, it was due to Schmoller's almost official association with the Hohenzollern Empire, the separation of his economic contribution from which apparently required too high a degree of discrimination after the First World War. His work certainly did not provide a firm line for the future development of political economy in Germany, if Schmoller can be blamed for that. His own practice—though not so much his precept—undoubtedly under-emphasized the role of analysis, and the standard of empirical caution he preached is impracticably austere, however admirable the discipline and restraint by which it was said to be motivated. Spiethoff's work on the trade cycle was surely one invaluable offshoot, and to a considerable extent a theoretical one. But Sombart, Schmoller's successor at Berlin, who started as a Marxist and ended as an anti-Marxian nationalist, devoted himself to a vast historical study of capitalism and its stages of development. (*v.* his *Der moderne Kapitalismus.*) It is grossly misleading to class Sombart and Schmoller together as followers of the same historical method.

The reaction against one of the main tenets of Schmoller and the earlier members of the *Verein für Sozialpolitik*, as well as against the

---

[1] Schumpeter maintained his high praise of Schmoller's work in much later writings and goes out of his way to make favourable comments in his *Business Cycles*, vol. i, pp. 228–9.

political-academic sermons of the liberal nationalist Treitschke, was led by Max Weber (1864–1920). In his influential essays 'On the Objectivity of Sociological and Social-political Knowledge' (1904), and on 'The Meaning of the "Neutrality" (*Wertfreiheit*) of Sociological and Economic Sciences' (1917), Weber was concerned to show how no definite ends for economic policy could emerge from a purely positive study, and in any case to insist that it was the moral duty of the academic teacher, as such, not to use his chair for preaching his own particular ethical and political ideas, however convinced of their rightness he might be. This is especially the theme of his memorable address to his students on 'Science as a Profession' (or 'Calling'—*Wissenschaft als Beruf*).

Weber's other main contribution to methodology lay in his concept of 'ideal types', intended to bridge the gulf between 'generalized' theoretical analysis and the historical study of particular phenomena. As Walter Eucken has pointed out, quite apart from the fact that Weber can hardly be described as the originator of this concept (a misunderstanding for which Weber himself was, of course, not responsible), he does not make clear the distinction between 'ideal' 'pure' types (like Thünen's isolated state, or a Robinson Crusoe economy), which are not constructed as pictures of the actual world or anything in it, and, on the other hand, the 'real' types as used by historical economists like Sombart with the object of capturing, or portraying in summary, a particular stage or cross-section of economic history (for example, Sombart's various 'stages' of capitalism). The former represent legitimate abstractions for purposes of analysis, the latter tend to lend themselves to 'historicist' over-simplifications.[1] Weber's methodological essays, particularly those emphasizing the objectivity of the social sciences, had a wide influence on economists, but his main work on sociology and economic history lies on, or over, the boundaries of economics, even on the widest interpretation, and, great thinker though he was, we can only briefly introduce him on the margin of this review. We shall refer in a subsequent chapter to his notable contribution to the subject of economic accounting in a socialist system.

2. *Launhardt; Auspitz and Lieben; Schumpeter's First Major Work*

(*a*) *W. Launhardt* (1832–1918) might be regarded as the main successor in Germany of Thünen and Mangoldt, and like them as a pioneer

---

[1] On Weber's theory of types see W. Eucken, *The Foundations of Economics*, pp. 347–8.

of mathematical analysis. His main interests seem to have been in engineering and railways, and he was for a long time Director of the Technical High School at Hanover. He belongs, therefore, with Dupuit, Lardner, and Ellet, all pioneers of mathematical analysis and anticipators, or nearly so, of the marginal concept, who developed this line of thought in an attempt to answer the new problems of the pricing policies of railways and public utilities. Launhardt's work follows primarily that of Walras and Jevons. He knew of Gossen's and Cournot's work, but the former's book was still unobtainable when he wrote (1885). When he at last got a copy of Cournot's *Recherches* from the library of a well-known German university, it was to find that in nearly fifty years it had never been opened. (Apparently economists had been too busy following the battles of Menger and Schmoller even to cut the pages of the *Recherches*.)

Among the features of Launhardt's book (*Mathematische Begründung der Volkswirtschaftslehre*, 1885) are an excellent analysis of capital and interest, based on a distinction between 'single-use' and durable goods which follows Walras closely, and an analysis of the application, and the supply curve, of labour, following, but much more thorough than, Jevons's chapter on the Theory of Labour.

However, Launhardt's most interesting contribution today seems to lie in his remarks on the subject of the pure theory of welfare economics. It is true that he began by trying to show that there is a sense in which exchange, when equilibrium is reached, yields a maximum of total utility for all the exchanging parties together, a very doubtful proposition for which he was criticized by Wicksell.[1] But Wicksell does not go on to mention (and perhaps Launhardt's not apparently consistent formulation of his arguments is to blame) that Launhardt only produced this proposition in order immediately to proceed to attack the conclusion from it that there is some harmony of interests promoting a maximum of utility under free competition which the State should therefore leave alone, a conclusion for which Launhardt, in his turn, criticizes Walras. Launhardt goes on to argue:

> The truth that with exchange at equilibrium prices the two parties obtain an equal gain, is only proved for the case where the utility equations for each are approximately of the form we have assumed. . . . When we showed that with exchange at equilibrium prices the sum of the gains of the two parties is a maximum, and that from the point of view of the general optimum,

---

[1] Wicksell, *Lectures*, vol. i, p. 81. See also Samuelson, *Foundations of Economic Analysis*, p. 205.

exchange at equilibrium prices is the most favourable, such exchange is by no means necessarily the most profitable for either party individually. (*Begründung*, pp. 31–32.)

Launhardt goes on to argue that if exchange takes place at a price more favourable to the poorer party than the equilibrium price, not only will the gain for the poor man be greater, but there will be a greater total gain, and concludes that the 'principles of *laissez-faire* laid down by "Manchesterism" simply mean handing over the weaker to the mercies of the stronger'. (pp. 38–43.)

Later in the book, after an extensive mathematical exposition of the—since Thünen—mainly 'German' subject of the theory of location, Launhardt pronounces in favour of marginal cost pricing for railways, and therefore, as he argues, for their national ownership, as a precondition for the necessary subsidies out of taxation: 'From the economic point of view it is most advantageous if freight is only charged in accordance with running costs (*Betriebskosten*). This proposition holds whatever the form of the demand equation. This proves most emphatically that railways are a concern which should never be left to private enterprise.' (p. 203.) He adds that of course the policy of subsidizing out of general taxes may have overriding fiscal disadvantages, by necessitating an unduly severe level of taxation. But only the State will be able to fix freight rates at the most beneficial level, taking into account general taxation policy.

At the same time as his '*Mathematical Basis*' Launhardt published a small book on Money (*Das Wesen des Geldes und die Währungsfrage*, 1885). His main theoretical point is his emphasis on, and analysis of, the concept of velocity of circulation. But he makes some use also of the 'income' approach to the theory of money when he describes how the general level of prices of goods depends on the total of annual incomes, made up of interest, wages, rent, and profits, which in the process of the circular flow go to make up the prices of goods, since the total annual production of consumers' goods, with the producers' goods used up annually, is purchased by the total of annual incomes. (pp. 36 ff.) With regard to both his 'income' approach to the theory of money, and in his analysis of marginal cost pricing, Launhardt may well have stimulated Wicksell, who seems to have studied his work closely, if often critically.

(*b*) *Auspitz and Lieben.* Rudolf Auspitz (1837–1906) and Richard Lieben (1842–1919) were two practical Austrian men of affairs, the former a sugar magnate and Member of Parliament, the latter a banker, whose work on the pure analysis of price makes them in some ways comparable with Ricardo, financier, M.P., and pioneer pure theorist. Their *Investigations on the Theory of Price* (1889) is a massive and difficult work, the technique of which is much more complicated than that subsequently developed for solving the same problems. But no work in our period, not even Marshall's or Pareto's, contains a greater number of precise and original contributions to the pure analysis of the individual consumer and firm, and to the clarification of the main assumptions on which this analysis has since been seen to rest.

Auspitz and Lieben start with a period ('a year') in which all prices are assumed to be in equilibrium and unchanging, and then abstract the price of a single divisible good for study, all other prices, tastes, and technology remaining unchanged, with all individual units having perfect knowledge and regarding all prices as given and unalterable by their own actions, and finally with the value of money to the individual assumed to be constant. (pp. 3–5.) This was certainly the fullest and most precise statement of the assumptions of price analysis and of partial equilibrium theory which had been made at that time. But for this clear and advanced procedure of abstraction Auspitz and Lieben were severely criticized by the head of the Austrian School, Carl Menger.[1]

After a long introductory analysis of their curves of total utility and cost, individual and market, and of the significance of their shape and continuity, Auspitz and Lieben turn to the analysis of the individual consumer. They begin by underlining their assumption that all other prices remain constant, as does the utility of money to the individual, however much the price of the particular good under examination alters, though they admit that this assumption may violate reality at some points. They clearly describe the case of a commodity which is important, perhaps indispensable, to the poor:

Such people may believe that at lower prices they would consume much more, but in fact, with a much reduced price, the resulting savings, and the alteration in the individual's valuation of money consequent thereon, may

[1] *v.* O. Weinberger on Auspitz and Lieben, *Zeitschrift für die gesamte Staatswissenschaften*, 1931, p. 457, and also on Menger, *Schweizerische Zeitschrift für Volkswirtschaft und Statistik*, 1948, p. 175. Menger accused Auspitz and Lieben of following 'not the analytical method but the method of Suppositions' (*Suppositionsmethode*), and of putting forward 'untenable theories' based on 'illegitimate and contradictory assumptions'. Menger's comments certainly do not make any easier the understanding of his own 'exact method'.

have such an effect that the quantity of the good with which they are fully satisfied, is smaller than before; because, like better-off people generally, they resort to better qualities of food and drink. (pp. 182–3.)

In an appendix Auspitz and Lieben take the case of variations in the value of money to the individual. This they analyse by means of a three-dimensional figure giving a 'satisfaction-surface' along which run 'curves of constant satisfaction' (*Kurven konstanter Befriedigung*): 'Each such curve tells us by its ordinates how the expenditure or the price must change if satisfaction is to remain constant, while the quantity of the good alters.' (p. 495.) In their introduction Auspitz and Lieben had referred very fully to their various predecessors to whose work they were indebted (including Thünen, Gossen, Mangoldt, Cournot, Dupuit, Walras, Jevons, and the three leading Austrians). They make no mention of Edgeworth or his *Mathematical Psychics*, to some of the inventions of which their own 'satisfaction-surfaces' and 'constant-satisfaction curves' bear a very close resemblance, and they may therefore be considered as independent discoverers of the indifference curve analysis. Their work certainly influenced, probably considerably, both Irving Fisher and Pareto. Like Edgeworth their aim was in no way to dispense with or exclude the utility concept. Edgeworth had been concerned with the analysis of the exchange of two commodities, the marginal utility of one depending on the quantity held of both commodities. Auspitz and Lieben were concerned with analysing the consumer's plan in respect of one commodity, taking into account the effect of changes in its price which alter the value of money to him. Auspitz and Lieben also give a full and clear exposition of competing and complementary relationships between goods, being the first, apparently, to define complementarity with precision, and also, after Dupuit, consumers' rent or surplus.

The section on the individual producer suffers from the difficulties in exposition already mentioned, but the analysis of the holder of stocks contains many interesting 'dynamic' suggestions. It is essentially an analysis of speculation, since they find no distinction can be drawn in practice between speculative and non-speculative holding of, buying for, or selling from stocks. The case of the consumer stock-holder is illustrated from male and female decisions about the size and variety of their wardrobes. The case of the firm's stocks and its decisions about its structure of assets is extensively analysed, and, as one would expect from the qualifications of the authors, the complexity and variety of the decisions facing the entrepreneur are fully faced. The roles of custom and of expectation about the future are emphasized, and the entrepreneur is not treated as though he were facing a simple problem of whether or not he is to maximize his profits.

In an appendix the consequences are studied of an increase in the quantity of money on the stocks thereof that individuals hold, and it is argued that the primary effect will be a fall in the rate of interest, and then a subsequent rise in prices. (pp. 548–51.)

The last section of Auspitz and Lieben's book studies 'The Influence of the Individual Unit on Price'. After a discussion of pure monopolies and state monopolies there is a study of an intermediate case under the title 'Monopolistic Price Determination under Free Competition'. (pp. 388 ff.) The case is that of a leading firm, larger or more efficient than the rest, adding its supply to the market, which by offering its own output at a lower price will force down the price of all the rest of the supply. Though the complexity of their 'total' diagrams prevents their arriving in so many words (or in so few words) at the precise modern formula of the equality of marginal cost and marginal revenue, they clearly lay down that the costs of the last unit must cover the return from it. (p. 405.)

(c) *Schumpeter's early works.* We may add here a very brief reference to the first works of a master of both the mathematical and the historical method, who knew the value of and the right place for both, J. A. Schumpeter (1883–1950). His *Das Wesen und der Hauptinhalt der theoretischen Nationalökonomie* ('The Essence and Main Content of Theoretical Economics') appeared in 1908 when he was 25, and the first edition of his *Theory of Economic Development* four years later. We shall not attempt in this volume to do anything like even relative justice to Schumpeter's work. We have the excuse that his crowning volumes on *Business Cycles* (1938) appeared some time after the close of our period, while a further major work on the history of economic analysis is still unpublished (1951). The full magnitude of his achievements and influence will be the theme of historians of a later period.

Schumpeter opened the foreword of his first book with the proverb 'Tout comprendre c'est tout pardonner'. The author of the most constructive appreciations written of such totally different economists as Walras, Böhm-Bawerk, and Schmoller throughout his writings lived up to this high philosophical motto to a unique degree. He was a pupil in Vienna of Böhm-Bawerk, but found Walras and Wieser to be the authors 'to whom he stood nearest'. His own theoretical analysis he built mainly on Walras, while the analysis of the historical and socio-logical background with which he co-ordinated his theoretical system and filled it out, has various points of likeness with that of Wieser, both in the general way in which economic sociology and analysis are combined and mutually illumined, and on some particular points, for example his emphasis on the role of the creative *élite* of innovating leaders as contrasted with the routine-following majority. (Whatever the exact relation between Wieser's and Schumpeter's ideas may have been, the latter had published some of the essential themes of his economic sociology before the appearance of the *Theory of Social Economy* in which Wieser first fully deployed his ideas on this subject.) J. B. Clark's analysis of the static state and of his five elements of dynamics must also have been an early stimulus to Schumpeter's ideas.

Schumpeter's *Wesen und Hauptinhalt* gives a very comprehensive interpretation and restatement of theoretical economics, aimed at reconciling different formulations of the basic concepts and proposi-tions (particularly the Walrasian and the Austrian formulations), and at meeting historical criticisms of marginal theory by marking off clearly and strictly the positive content of its propositions, and the justifiable conclusions that can be drawn from them, from the political and ethical prejudices with which they have so often, implicitly or explicitly, been interwoven and confused. Schumpeter emphasizes, for example, that the positive analysis of the equilibrium position must be completely freed from its associations with the doctrine of the maximum satisfaction from the free play of competition, and, further, that positive marginal productivity analysis must be separated com-pletely from attempts to justify the distribution of income in a com-petitive society. In regard to both these particular propositions Schumpeter's message has now long been widely accepted, but the keeping separate analytically of positive and normative propositions, and the exposure of that sort of 'double-think' which seeks to draw normative political conclusions from a positive analysis, and tries to buttress political preferences and policies with the prestige of a neutral 'scientific' analysis, this is a perennial task necessary often with every new major development in the subject.

The system of theory which Schumpeter was examining was almost exclusively that of individual 'micro-economic' maximization analysis. He defends 'methodological individualism', or micro-economic studies, as an indispensable procedure which yields many useful answers. But he again emphasizes that there is no logical connexion whatever between methodological individualism and political individualism. He rejects such concepts as 'national income', or 'the national capital' &c., which were being studied by some of the German economists (e.g. Wagner) as unnecessary, and 'full of obscurities and difficulties'. (p. 97.)

Schumpeter makes clear that the system of analysis he is expounding and interpreting is exclusively 'static' or 'comparative static', and that its practical relevance is very slight. Though by comparative statics, or the 'method of variations', as Schumpeter calls it, answers of highly limited significance can be given to certain problems of the effects of tariffs and taxes, he emphasizes the dangers of reading some true 'dynamic' interpretation into a purely comparative static analysis. The most challenging theme in the book is the insistence that interest, like profit, and unlike wages and rent, is a 'dynamic' income, and that the problems of interest cannot be answered within a static analysis. Just as there is neither profit nor loss to the entrepreneur in a static equilibrium system, so there is no net interest to the capitalist, an argument which was the subject of much subsequent controversy. The issues are, of course, principally conceptual and terminological, but it is clear that a mere static maximization theory seems to contribute even less to the explanation of the real problems of interest than it does to those of wages and rent, in view of the greater role of uncertainty in long-term investments.

In that it is concerned mainly with interpretation and evaluation Schumpeter's *Wesen und Hauptinhalt* was a methodological book, but in an exactly opposite manner from that of the participants in the *Methodenstreit.* He, above all, avoided laying down normative generalizations about what are the 'right' methods and what are the 'important' problems and what merely 'auxiliary', and he kept always to the detailed positive analysis and elucidation of particular propositions. Schumpeter is said to have come to dislike his first work, which is a not uncommon thing to come to do. Possibly he saw it as an over-optimistic attempt at a methodological book to end methodological books, which had so long been in excessive supply in Germany and Austria. But it seems today that the progress of economics in those countries could, in very many directions, only have been aided over the next quarter of a century if this book had wielded more influence than it did.

In his much better-known *Theory of Economic Development,* first published three years later (1911), Schumpeter passed from the critical elucidation of static analysis, to the construction of his own dynamic theory of development. Schumpeter starts by applying the familiar concepts of static analysis to what he describes as 'the circular flow of economic life': that is, where economic life runs on in channels essentially the same year after year, the only changes, if any, being very small and continuous, where the same goods are produced every year in the same way, and where for every supply there awaits somewhere in the economic system a corresponding demand, and for every demand a corresponding supply,—the economic life of a settled and fully adjusted routine. There supervenes on this 'circular flow', as a dominant feature of the actual capitalist world, the processes of economic development, 'entirely foreign to what may be observed in the circular flow or in the tendency towards equilibrium. It is spontaneous and discontinuous change in the channels of the flow, disturbance of equilibrium, which for ever alters and displaces the equilibrium state previously existing. . . . Add successively as many mail coaches as you please, you will never get a railway thereby.' (*Theory of Economic Development*, p. 64.)[1]

'Development' is essentially the carrying out of new combinations and covers five cases:

(1) The introduction of a new good . . ., (2) The introduction of a new method of production, that is, one not yet tested by experience in the branch of manufacture concerned, which need by no means be founded upon a discovery scientifically new, and can also exist in a new way of handling a commodity commercially, (3) the opening of a new market . . ., (4) the conquest of a new source of supply of raw materials or half-manufactured goods . . ., and (5) the carrying out of the new organisation of any industry, like the creation of a monopoly position . . . or the breaking up of a monopoly position. (p. 66.)

The activities of entrepreneurs, and also credit, credit institutions, and interest rates would hardly exist, in the routine circular flow of economic life, and belong essentially to 'development'. The function of credit is to enable the entrepreneur to withdraw the producers' goods which he needs for his innovations from their previous employments. The banker, too, is essentially a phenomenon of development though only when no central authority directs the social process. He makes possible the carrying out of new combinations, authorizes people, in the name of society as it were, to form them.

The entrepreneur provides the economic leadership or economic élite of society: 'Carrying out a new plan and acting according to a

[1] We are quoting from the English translation by Redvers Opie published in 1934.

customary one are things as different as making a road and walking along it', according to Schumpeter—a remark reminiscent of Marshall's epigram that running established routine public utilities bears the same relation to economic enterprise in the genuine sense, that printing a new edition of Shakespeare's plays has to the original writing of those plays.

Schumpeter's account of the business cycle is fused with his theory of economic development. His first statement of it is in a long article in 1910 (*Zeitschrift für Volkswirtschaft*, pp. 271 ff.). He sees the problem as that of explaining why economic development does not go forward regularly and smoothly, but occurs spasmodically in wave-like movements. Economic processes fall into three classes, those of the static (stationary) economy, those of development, and those which render development disturbed and irregular (op. cit., p. 288). This third class of processes may often be traceable to 'accidental' and non-economic factors. In fact all booms and crises have much that is individual about them. What is essentially and economically common to all is simply that they represent an upset of the regular advancing process of economic development and that they have occurred in a fairly regular wave-like movement.

The basic explanation of this wave-like movement is that innovations come in clusters, because when one leader has overcome the technical, legal, and financial difficulties barring a new path, this new profitable path is then open to a rush of 'routine' followers, and in fact nearly all booms have been associated with one particular new industrial development. The equilibrium of the whole economy is then upset and the economic horizon is unknown and incalculable. Hence static analysis based on the assumption that entrepreneurs have a full and correct knowledge of the economic situation, which will broadly hold in a stationary economy, becomes inapplicable: 'If we ascribe perfect foresight and a perfect calculation of all reactions to the economic plans of entrepreneurs, an essential part of the situation would escape our attention. Most entrepreneurs, if these assumptions corresponded with the facts, would not act at all.' (p. 310.) The explanation of economic development must involve the explanation of errors and miscalculations. The reorganization of the economy made necessary by the new burst of development inevitably involves many individual readjustments and a destruction of old values or losses in the resulting disequilibrium: 'The essence of these losses consists in the fact that economic subjects are forced to revise their systems of values, or, rather the revisions result from these losses: the valuations of the dynamic (innovating) economic individuals cannot be maintained—the realised returns differ from the expected.' (p. 314.) The depression is essentially a readjustment to a new situation during which everyone has to wait and discover the new relevant facts for their economic calculations. Some readjustment and loss is constructively necessary, but this is to be distinguished from the secondary depression, which may bring much further 'unnecessary' loss before the economy has gradually groped towards its new equilibrium.

This was the main outline of Schumpeter's first statement of his theory of economic development and business cycles, to be built up in subsequent decades into his massive work published in 1938. Schumpeter's system is unique among modern economic theories. Though, of course, fundamentally different in its motivation, since it aims simply at understanding the social world, rather than at rationalizing political appetites and programmes, it is to be compared with the Marxian system in the way in which it comprehends an economic interpretation of the history of capitalism, or of modern economic history, with a sociological analysis of economic leadership and *élites*. We shall refer again to Schumpeter's contribution to the subject of the trade cycle (Ch. 23 below) and to his theories of profit and money (Chs. 20 and 21), but we repeat that his work cannot be treated here in anything approaching its full magnitude.[1]

[1] See R. V. Clemence and F. S. Doody, *The Schumpeterian System*, 1950, also the distinguished symposium in the *Review of Economic Statistics*, May 1951.

13

L. Walras

1. *Léon Walras and French Political Economy*

IN earlier chapters, before coming to the leading English, German, and Austrian economists, we tried to describe something of the background of ideas and problems from which they started. The ferment of the seventies and the crumbling of the classical doctrines in England, the historical movement in Germany, and the rise of the Austrian marginal utility school, transcended the intellectual biographies and writings of single economists. We cannot attempt any such introduction, on anything like a similar scale, in the case of the French, Italian, Swedish, and American economists discussed in the following chapters. In any case, these countries, however outstanding one or two of the individual economists they produced, were hardly the scene at this period of any movements in economic thought of the same general significance as those taking place in England, Germany, and Austria. However, a few words must be devoted to the condition of political economy in France (and in a later chapter in America) which was the background to the work of Léon Walras (and to that of Clark, Veblen, and Fisher).

J. B. Say is the last of the great nineteenth-century French theoretical economists whose ideas had any appreciable influence in their own country before the close of the century. Those recognized today as the worthy descendants in the nineteenth century of the great French economists of the eighteenth century, were, in their own lifetimes, almost completely disregarded by the dominant 'orthodox' school of economic thought. This is certainly true of Auguste Walras, Cournot, Dupuit, and Léon Walras. In fact only one of these—Léon Walras— would have been described primarily as an economist by his contemporaries. Auguste Walras was a legal scholar and educational official, Cournot a mathematician, philosopher, and inspector of schools, and Dupuit an engineer. The best work on economic theory in nineteenth-century France, before Léon Walras, was done mainly by non-economists. The lack of recognition of these four great men is all the more striking because they can today easily be seen to lie in a direct line of intellectual descent from their great French predecessors,

Condillac and J. B. Say. Cournot and Léon Walras sinned by advocating and using mathematical methods,[1] and Auguste and Léon Walras by failing to accept uncritically the *laissez-faire* dogmas of what the latter described as 'la petite église de Frédéric Bastiat . . . qui a mutilé la science et paralysé tout développement véritablement progressif'. There were, of course, one or two other notable economists outside the dominant school, such as Laveleye, the Belgian historical economist, and Clément Juglar, the great pioneer of the statistical and historical analysis of the trade cycle, who received more recognition. But we have here a sombre example of how much a closed semi-official self-recruiting academy, stimulated by a measure of political dogmatism, is able to achieve. 'La France', wrote Léon Walras in 1901, 'est une Chine où les mandarins se tiennent et se soutiennent les uns les autres. . . . Les situations à ambitionner . . . étaient accaparées par l'école orthodoxe, c'est-à-dire par cette école qui en vertu d'arguments variés, souvent contradictoires, et toujours mauvais, nous donne le régime social actuel comme un nec plus ultra susceptible de suffire à l'humanité jusqu'à la consommation des siècles.

We come now, regrettably late, to .the third of the theoretical pioneers of 1871, Léon Walras, who has only comparatively recently come to receive the full recognition due to one who for pure theoretical constructiveness is unsurpassed among the economists of all time. However, if Walras constructed a much grander, more precise, and much more comprehensive theoretical system than Jevons or Menger, he had to hand, in the writings well known to him of his fellow countrymen, much more (than Jevons at any rate) which was immediately suitable on which to build. Since Galiani and Condillac a century previously, the nature and importance of the relation of utility to value had received much more explicit recognition in French political economy than it had in the writings of the English classics. The fundamental economic idea of scarcity had been expounded especially by Condillac and Auguste Walras. The idea of a general equilibrium in which all values in the economic system mutually determine one another, had been briefly but clearly outlined by Turgot, and, in a remarkable paragraph, by Cournot, the pioneer of 'partial' analysis. The

---

[1] Professor Leroy-Beaulieu on mathematical economics: 'L'école dite mathématique n'a aucun fondement scientifique ni aucune application pratique; c'est un pur jeu d'esprit, un ensemble de fictions en dehors de toute réalité et contraire à toute réalité. Cet exercice d'esprit ressemble à la recherche des martingales à la roulette de Monaco.' Quoted by E. Antonelli, *Principes d'Économie Pure*, p. 5: a book which gives an excellent summary of Walras's *Éléments*.

central role of the entrepreneur in the economic system, as Léon Walras was to see it, as the intermediary linking the general market for products in which he sells, with the general market for services in which he buys, had been described by J. B. Say. Finally, in the mathematical formulation of his theories Walras had the example of Cournot, who had been his father's classmate and whose neglected *Recherches* (1838) Léon Walras had read at the age of 19 or 20.

To refer to these previous presentations of a number of his central ideas hardly detracts from Walras's constructive achievement in bringing them together in a comprehensive explanatory picture of the whole economic cosmos, comparable with the great picture, a century earlier, of Adam Smith. Moreover, Walras's achievement was carried through after many years of difficulties and discouragements, greater even than those which had faced Jevons. To the end of his life he was a prophet unhonoured in his own country, and to his patriotic chagrin, he was never invited to teach there.

Born at Évreux, between Rouen and Paris, Léon Walras was, like J. S. Mill and J. M. Keynes, the son of an economist, and intellectually and temperamentally was to a quite exceptional extent the son of his father, and very devoted to him and to his ideas.[1] His education was mainly in the natural sciences, but as a young man he seems to have thought of turning to literature and actually published a romantic novel at the age of 24. It was his father who converted him to social science, and Walras has left a characteristically glowing account of the moment of this almost religious conversion:

The decisive hour of my whole life occurred one beautiful summer evening

[1] There is surely no parallel in political economy for the intellectual relationship between father and son, which held between Auguste and Léon Walras. The son followed out with the closest loyalty both the spirit and most of the technical details and definitions of his father's work. Auguste Walras was led to his analysis of value by his studies of the nature of property, and he traced the origin both of private property and of economic value to scarcity. He pointed out that utility was a necessary but not a sufficient condition for economic value, and argued that cost-of-production theories simply put off the explanation of value by one stage, and then fail to explain the values of production goods and services. In his two works (1831, *De La Nature de la Richesse, et de l'Origine de la Valeur*, and 1849, *Théorie de la Richesse Sociale*), his economic analysis is blended with much legal and political philosophizing, as to some extent in Léon Walras's works on economic policy. His reasoning led him to support the public ownership of all land. His work as an educational inspector left him little time for his economic ideas and writings, and he seems usually to have been out of favour with his ministerial superiors. He was considered to be 'un esprit plutôt dangereux et d'idées subversives' (quoted from G. Pirou, *Les Théories d'Équilibre Économique—L. Walras et V. Pareto*, p. 39, who gives a very full account of Auguste Walras's theory of value). See also M. Leroy, *Auguste Walras, sa vie et son œuvre, Paris, 1923.*

in 1858, when while we were walking in the valley of the Gave du Pau my father asserted energetically that two great tasks remained for the century to accomplish: to complete the creation of historical science, and to begin to create a social science. He hardly suspected how far Renan was to satisfy him on the first point. But it was the second which had occupied his whole life and which touched him much more profoundly. He insisted on it with a conviction which he passed on to me, and it was before the gate of a farm called 'Les Roseaux' that I promised him to give up literature and art criticism and devote myself entirely to the continuation of his work.

Walràs later said that it was to his father that he owed 'the economic definitions which are the basis of my system, and to Cournot the mathematical language which is most apt for formulating this system'. His father had traced the origin of property and value alike to 'scarcity' (*rareté*), and his analysis of scarcity as a combination of utility and limitation in supply influenced Carl Menger's work. Léon Walras retained the term *rareté* but redefined it as *l'intensité du dernier besoin satisfait*. From his father too he took over, with some adaptation, the concept of the *numéraire* or unit of account, and also, without alteration, the distinction between capital resources and the services yielded by them, which was at the basis of his analysis of production and distribution.

Though, after 1858, Walras had his ambition and even the plan of his life-work clear before him, he had twelve very hard years until he could settle down to it. He failed to make his way as a journalist, and the articles he sent to the *Journal des Économistes* were refused. For ten years he occupied posts as a minor official on the railways, and in a bank which collapsed. Even subsequently when his writings on pure theory were gaining him a reputation in England, Walras still received no recognition from the dominant academic circles of his own country.

Though now deservedly renowned as one of the greatest of all contributors to pure analysis, Walras was above all a passionate social reformer. Though he was a thorough-going disciple of neither, there are obvious traces of some of the leading ideas of both Comte and St. Simon in Walras's writings on the principles of policy. But J. S. Mill's highly unreconciled combination of socialistic aspirations and individualist maxims seems to have been at least an equally important influence. Walras was certainly, in the older sense of the term, a 'socialist', that is one who believed in the large-scale rational reform of society, rather than in the beneficence of its 'natural', traditional, and spontaneous harmonies. His first writings on *L'Économie politique et la justice* (1860), and *L'Idéal social* (1867), were essays in the philosophy of social reform, hardly likely to advance him to the semi-official academic posts of the Second Empire, as also was a drastic proposal for a single tax, similar to Henry George's doctrine of nearly 20 years later. Providentially, however, Walras had made and impressed an influential friend in the municipality of Lausanne, Louis Rachonnet, and when a chair of political economy was founded there in 1870, he was, at the age of 36, at last enabled to settle down to his life-work. He set out for his new post at Lausanne in the middle of the Franco-Prussian war, expecting to be recalled for military service at any moment. The opening passages of his inaugural lecture at Lausanne are not much less admirable for what may seem a certain strain of rationalist over-optimism: 'Meanwhile, whatever the future may have in store for us, let us settle down to work as if nothing might interrupt us. . . . I with a firm resolve to inculcate in you a knowledge and love of the principles of economics and of social ethics, which principles may guarantee the increase of wealth and the triumph of justice in a world that we now view with horror, a world today abandoned to the mercy of iniquitous ambitions.'

Walras held the chair at Lausanne till 1893 when owing to ill health and overwork he made way for Pareto. Many of his later writings were devoted to the same ardent reformist themes of his youth, and included the essay he unsuccessfully entered for the Nobel Peace Prize on *La paix par la justice sociale et le libre échange* (1907).

2. *Walras's Pure Economics*

Walras's comprehensive analysis of general equilibrium is built up by a step-by-step process of decreasing abstraction. He starts from the case of two-party two-commodity barter of given stocks of goods, and gradually elaborates his model to that of a multi-commodity, productive, capital- and money-using economic system. Throughout, Walras is concerned almost exclusively with what he takes as the general case, that of competition, as exemplified in an organized market or bourse: 'The world can be regarded as a vast general market made up of different special markets, where the wealth of society is bought and sold. Our task is to discover the laws according to which these purchases and sales tend to take place. For that purpose we suppose always a perfectly organized competitive market, just as in pure

mechanics we suppose machines to work without friction.' (p. 45.)[1]
This concentration on the case of free competition was necessary for
Walras's purpose, but for the realistic 'partial' analysis of the firm and
markets there are obvious advantages in the procedure of Cournot,
who began with his study of monopoly and oligopoly, going on to
perfect competition as the limiting case.

(a) *Two-commodity Exchange.* Walras starts from the case of the
barter of two commodities by two parties, each of whom has no desire
for the commodity possessed by himself but wants the one possessed
by the other party. Assuming that the whole stock of each commodity
is to be exchanged without remainder, Walras derives the demand
curve for each commodity from the supply curve of the other. He
then goes behind the demand curve and analyses the equilibrium of the
consumer, or the conditions for the maximization of his satisfaction.
For equilibrium in exchange each of the two parties must be maximizing his satisfaction, which requires that the ratio of the marginal
utilities (*raretés*) from each of the two goods must for each party be
equal to the ratio of their prices.

For Walras, as for Jevons, Marshall, and apparently Menger, the
utility of a good is a function only of the quantity of that good. Otherwise (apart from his unfortunate doctrine of maximum social satisfaction), Walras is non-committal about the utility concept and would
probably not have opposed its whittling away or extrusion. Already
in 1861 his father had raised the difficulty of its immeasurability (*v.*
Économie Appliquée, p. 467). In any case, the discovery of marginal
utility (*l'intensité du dernier besoin satisfait*) is, unlike for Jevons and
Menger, a very minor part of Walras's theoretical achievement, and
one may venture to guess that, under the pressure of criticism, he
would have been prepared to reformulate his system without the utility
concept, as was his mentor Cournot before him, and his followers
Pareto and Cassel after him.

(b) *Multi-commodity Exchange.* Walras then proceeds to extend his
analysis to cases of three or more commodities. With m commodities
there will be $m(m-1)$ prices (of each good in terms of all the others),
and $m(m-1)/2$ 'partial' markets in which one sort of good is exchanged
for another sort. For equilibrium it is clear that the ratios of exchange,

---

[1] All page references in this section except where otherwise stated are to the final
(1926) edition of the *Éléments d'économie pure*. The dates of Walras's main works are as
follows: 1874-7 *Éléments*, First Edition (in instalments) (2nd ed. 1889, 3rd, 1896,
Final, 1926); 1886 *Théorie de la Monnaie*; 1896 *Études d'économie sociale* (collected
papers); 1898 *Études d'économie politique appliquée* (collected papers).

or the prices of the two commodities in terms of each other, must be equal to the ratios of their prices in terms of any third good. Otherwise 'arbitrage' operations will take place until this is so. Therefore, in equilibrium, the $m(m-1)$ prices are determined by the $(m-1)$ prices (in terms of one good) of all the other goods (except that one in which prices are being reckoned). This good, in terms of which it is convenient to express all prices, is called the *numéraire*. It is to be regarded simply as a unit of account and not as a means of exchange, and as subject to no demand other than that which exists for it because of its ordinary properties as a commodity. Of course, theoretically it makes no difference which good is taken as *numéraire*. In terms, then, of a *numéraire* we have a set of relative exchange values which will be proportional to the marginal utilities of each of the exchanging parties.

(c) *The Theory of Production.* Up to now Walras has been concerned simply with the exchange of given stocks of goods. The next step is the analysis of the equilibrium conditions of the production of goods. His analysis is based on an elaborate classification of resources, and on two important distinctions, (1) between durable resources and the series of immediately consumed services which they yield; and (2) between durable resources (capital) and single-use resources (revenues). 'Capital' consists of all durable resources which yield a stream of services or revenues. The value of any piece of capital depends on the values of the services it yields, which are, therefore, the primary concept. If a potentially durable good is used so as only to yield a single service (for example, if a fruit-tree is cut down for fuel), then it counts as revenue. Stocks of food and raw materials are clearly, in this scheme, included not under 'capital' but under 'revenue' (Leçon 17).

Capital goods and services are grouped according to the usual three-fold classification into land, labour, and material capital ('capitaux fonciers, capitaux personnels, et capitaux mobiliers'). Each of these may yield either productive services (those of a factory site, an engineer, or a machine) or consumption services (those of a sports ground, an actor, or a radiogram), thus making six types of capital resources. Subsequently, as we shall see, Walras adds seven more types of capital or revenue resources, making thirteen in all in his complete classification (Leçon 18).

This elaborate work of classification leads up to a much more illuminating matter, that is to Walras's comprehensive picture of the productive system of a free enterprise economy, and of the circular flow of payments through it (Leçons 18–19). At the centre of the system are the entrepreneurs buying the three classes of productive services from their owners, the public, and selling consumers' goods back to the public. Analytically the entrepreneurs are completely separable from the ownership of resources, and are pure co-ordinators, or intermediary buyers and sellers. The public, on the other hand, will be buying consumers' goods from, and selling their three classes of services to, the entrepreneurs. There are thus two general markets in the economy, in which the entrepreneurs and the public meet:

> Thanks to the intervention of money the two markets, for services and for products, are perfectly distinct in reality, just as they are for scientific purposes. On each of them purchases and sales take place in accordance with the mechanism by which prices rise and fall. . . . However, although distinct in this way, the two markets are none the less closely linked with one another. For it is with the money that they have received on the first market for their productive services that the owners of resources (in land, labour, or capital) proceed as consumers to the second market to buy products. And it is with the money which they have received for their products, on the second market, that the entrepreneurs as producers purchase productive services on the first market.
>
> The condition for the equilibrium of production, contained implicitly in the equilibrium of exchange is now easy to define. It is, first, that the effective supply of productive services is equal to the effective demand, with the current price in the market for services stationary. Again, the effective supply of products must be equal to the effective demand, with the current price in the market for products stationary. Finally the revenue from the sale of products must be equal to the cost of the services by which they are produced. The first two conditions relate to the equilibrium of exchange, and the third to the equilibrium of production. . . . Thus with equilibrium in production the entrepreneurs make neither profit nor loss. They subsist not as entrepreneurs but as owners of resources (in land, labour, or material capital) employed in their own or other enterprises. (pp. 193–5.)

This idea of a zero-profit 'norm' has since become widely accepted in static analysis, and a similar concept is even employed in Keynes's *Treatise on Money*. But at the time it evoked some not very well-directed mockery from Edgeworth.

Walras opens his analysis of the equilibrium conditions of production (Leçons 20–21) by emphasizing that productive services have a direct utility for their owners, who may either use them directly for their own consumption, or sell them to entrepreneurs. The maximizing individual has, therefore, first to allocate the services he commands between his own private uses and selling them to entrepreneurs; and then, secondly, to allocate those he sells between different entrepreneurs competing for them. He will equalize the return from the last unit in all alternative uses, private and market. Walras immensely simplified his analysis of the equilibrium of utilities and costs for individuals, as well as that of the allocation of their outlay by entrepreneurs as between different services, by assuming fixed technical 'coefficients' (*coefficients de fabrication*), which lay down the technically given fixed proportions in which factors have to be combined to produce a good. He justified this procedure purely as a simplifying assumption, and did not supply an analysis of what determines these 'coefficients' until the third edition (1896) of his book (under the stimulus, it seems, of Wicksteed's *Essay on the Coordination of the Laws of Distribution*).

Under the assumption of fixed technical coefficients the earnings of factors are explained by the principle that for non-specialized services actual earnings must at least be equal to those obtainable in alternative uses. For specialized factors earnings are determined by the value of their product. This analysis, of course, leaves out the more detailed problems facing maximizing entrepreneurs which arise from the variability of the proportions in which factors can be combined, and which require a formula for the minimum cost combination of factors. Towards the end of the last edition (Leçon 36) a marginal productivity analysis is incorporated in a section on the Conditions and Consequences of Economic Progress, the assumption of variability being treated as belonging specially in this context. It has been argued that Walras assumed fixed technical coefficients in his theory of production because 'it would have been logically incongruous to assume anything else at that stage of the argument, for, until the theory of capital accumulation is reached, the technical coefficients in the theory of production cannot be considered as variable since this variation involves variations in the quantities of the capital goods which give rise to them'.[1] This may explain Walras's train of thought, but may not be acceptable as a full justification of it.

(*d*) *The Significance of General Equilibrium.* Although abstraction is still being made from capitalization, interest, and money, the analysis of the conditions for the equilibrium of production complete the central part of Walras's picture of general economic equilibrium. Unfortunately at this point Walras tried to fasten on two extensions to his static

[1] W. Jaffé, 'Léon Walras' Theory of Capital Accumulation', *Studies in Mathematical Economics and Econometrics, in Memory of H. Schultz*, edited by Lange, McIntyre, and Yntema, p. 38.

analysis of general equilibrium, both aimed at lending it considerably greater and more immediate significance than it really possessed. He tried to enliven his statics, first with a dynamic appendage, and secondly with a general conclusion for economic policy. Neither of these were *in pari materia* with his main analysis, and for neither is there much to be said on its own account.

First, Walras was not content simply to describe the static point of general equilibrium, but sought to lay down the path by which this point will actually be reached in the market by the mechanism of free competition. This is the purpose of the brief dynamic fantasia of the *tâtonnements* (approximations, or trials and errors) by which the equilibrium position is, or would be, actually attained—either '*ab ovo*' as Walras puts it, or starting from any disequilibrium position. This process had previously been described in expounding 'the law for the establishment of the prices of goods', and is later embodied in the exposition of 'the law for the establishment of the prices of services'. (*v.* pp. 129 and 214–15.) Apparently, when a market opens, prices will be 'cried' initially *au hasard*. Gradually as the answers to these 'cries', or other discoveries, reveal to the participants the facts of demand and supply, the equilibrium price marrying supply and demand emerges. It is not really made clear by Walras whether or no any exchanges take place at disequilibrium prices. If they did, the whole subsequent path and equilibrium position might be affected. Though he might have shown much more appreciation of Walras's achievement as a whole, Edgeworth's criticism of this almost incidental dynamic addition is justified:

What the author professes to demonstrate is the course which the higgling of the market takes—the path, as it were, by which the economic system works down to equilibrium. Now, as Jevons points out, the equations of exchange are of a statical, not a dynamical, character. They define a position of equilibrium, but they afford no information as to the path by which that point is reached. Professor Walras's laboured lessons indicate *a* way, not *the* way of descent to equilibrium. (See Edgeworth, papers, vol. ii, p. 311, and G. J. Stigler, *Production and Distribution Theories*, p. 245.)

A second and even more unfortunate extension to his equilibrium analysis that Walras makes is his doctrine of maximum satisfaction. (Leçon 22.) However, though his statement of the doctrine is certainly highly misleading, as well as either trivial or false, Walras does not base any considerable claims about policy upon it. His doctrine, as stated, simply relates to the conditions of production. (p. 231.) He at once warns against the drawing of *laissez faire* conclusions, and against the doctrines of 'those economists who, not content with exaggerating *laissez faire laissez passer* in relation to industry, apply it quite illegitimately with regard to property'. (p. 234.) Walras's comprehensive contributions to the analysis of policy and the role of the State in his two volumes on applied and social economics are not seriously impaired by this blemish in his pure economics, which incidentally provoked Wicksell's very sensible discussion of the maximum satisfaction doctrine. (*Lectures*, vol. i, pp. 72 ff.)

Finally, there is a criticism of theoretical and mathematical significance: that the demonstration of the equality of the number of equations and unknowns in the general equilibrium problem, did not show that any unique positive solution can be obtained. The necessary assumptions for such a solution, though they may be taken as implicit in Walras's analysis, were only long afterwards made explicit.[1] Theoretically this may seem an important oversight, but it hardly impairs either the essential idea which Walras's *Élements* conveys of the unity and interdependence of the economic cosmos, or the significance of his analysis for studying the allocation problems of different forms of society or economic order.

(*e*) *Capitalization*. The supply, demand, and prices of services have now been analysed, but not those of the capital resources which yield the services. In respect of these, transactions take place in a third general market alongside that for products and that for productive services. Walras's theory of capitalization deals with fixed capital. As we shall see, his analysis of working capital is included with his analysis of money and cash balances. The way in which Walras grafted his theory of capitalization on to his static equilibrium system gave rise to some difficulties. Particularly is this the case with his introduction of the assumption of a progressive society, with net saving, and adding to its capital equipment. But (as was shown by Barone) the difficulties and ambiguities in Walras's analysis are much more easily removable than his critics (for example, Wicksell) at first supposed.

The price of capital goods depends on the price of their services or revenues. Two elements must be deducted from the gross revenue to obtain the net revenue of a capital good, the first being a depreciation allowance and the second an insurance premium. The annual charge

[1] A. Wald, 'Über die eindeutige Lösbarkeit der neuen Produktionsgleichungen', *Ergebnisse eines mathematischen Colloquiums*, vi (1933–4), and 'Über einige Gleichungssysteme der mathematischen Ökonomie', *Zeitschrift für Nationalökonomie*, 1936, pp. 637 ff.

for each of these may be expressed as a proportion of the price of the capital good. If P is the price of the capital good, p its gross revenue, μ and ν the fractions of P to be deducted for amortization and insurance, then the net revenue $= p—(\mu+\nu)P$. The rate of net revenue is then the ratio of the net revenue to the capital value $= \dfrac{p—(\mu+\nu)P}{P}$

In equilibrium in a competitive economy the rate of net revenue on all types of capital resources must be the same and equal to the market rate of interest for credit, and on this rate will depend how individuals allocate their incomes between consumption and capitalization.

Walras is here concerned with a progressive society where incomes exceed consumption including, or plus, an allowance for amortization and insurance, that is, where there is net saving exchanging against new additions to capital resources. The problem for such a society is then to allocate its savings between different types of capital resources so as to equalize the rate of net revenue from each. The introduction of the assumption of a progressive economy is an unnecessary complication. It would have been much easier for his system as a whole if it had been confined to the case of a stationary economy with the rate of interest fixed through the reinvestment of the depreciation allowances necessary for maintaining the constant stock of capital.

Walras's analysis of capitalization sets out neat and comprehensive formulae for 'maximizing' savers and investors, and for the rate of interest on fixed capital. But it is not filled out with any considerable realistic explanation of the factors determining the demand for investment and the supply of savings. In these respects it is the opposite of, and the complement to, Böhm-Bawerk's treatment.

(*f*) *The Theory of Circulation and Money.* The final stage in the Walrasian scheme is to introduce the six 'revenue' items in the thirteenfold classification of resources set out in his theory of production. Six of the capital items had been durable capital resources either in land, labour, or material capital, and yielding services either for production or for consumption. Seventhly, there is, as a separate item, new material capital awaiting sale by its producers, and therefore not yet yielding revenues. There remain for incorporation and analysis: (8) stocks of consumers' goods held by consumers, (9) stocks of raw materials held by producers, (10) new 'revenue' goods, either consumption goods or raw materials awaiting sale with their producers, and (11), (12), and (13) money in circulation with consumers, money in circulation with producers, and money savings. (11) and (12) being

money spent on consumption goods and productive services respectively, and (13) the excess of income over consumption lent by
'capitalists'.

Walras now assumes that because of intervals between payments
and receipts in money, and between the delivery and consumption of
goods, consumers and producers will want to hold certain circulating
funds (*fonds de roulements*) part in goods and part in money (as distinct
from *numéraire*) and the holding of such circulating funds, either in
their real or their monetary form, will have a certain marginal utility
to the individual. In deciding how much money to hold the individual
consumer or producer will consider its 'real' purchasing power or the
command it gives over real resources. As Walras put it in his *Theory
of Money* (*Économie politique appliquée*, p. 95): 'The need for money
is nothing else than the need for the goods to be purchased with this
money. It is the need for holding a stock. The satisfaction from this is
obtained at the price of interest, and this is why the effective demand
for money is a decreasing function of the rate of interest.' The total
quantity of liquid balances that society wishes to hold Walras calls the
encaisse désirée. The price of the service which the holding of money
affords will rise or fall according as to whether this total *encaisse désirée*
is greater or smaller than the existing quantity of money. Of course,
the marginal utilities obtained by individuals from this service must be
in the same proportion to the price as with all other goods and services.
When a good is adopted as money both the price of the good, and the
price of the services of a stock of the good (as either money or working
capital) must, in equilibrium, be the same both in its monetary and in
its non-monetary commercial use, the good moving to and fro from
one use to the other until this equilibrium is reached.

Walras's 'cash-balance' theory of money is both valuable in itself
and remarkable in the way it is integrated into his general equilibrium
system. That this has not been more widely recognized is partly due
to the fact that the treatment of money in the final edition of the
Éléments by no means contains all Walras's best ideas on, or exposition
of, the subject, which are scattered about in earlier editions of the
Éléments, later altered, and in his essay on the *Theory of Money* (1886).
Among Walras's other specific contributions to monetary analysis are
his early formulation of the equation of exchange in the manner later
developed by Newcomb and Fisher, and his analysis of the process of
'forced saving'. At one time, in the discussion of that elusive concept
'neutral money' it was argued on one side that Walras's general

equilibrium analysis relates, and must relate, to a barter economy, and that Walras to some extent realized this by adding his treatment of money after the main part of his equilibrium analysis of exchange and production. There does not seem to be any good foundation for this view. Walras was following out a logical step-by-step process of decreasing abstraction, and his final step in introducing money is one of the most impressive both for its own interest, and for what it contributes to the significance of the general equilibrium system of analysis as a whole.[1]

3. *Walras's Theories of Applied and Social Economics*

According to Walras's conception of the subject, and according to the plan of his life-work, which he held to from first to last without ever rounding off, the whole of economics was divided into three parts, covered in the three courses of lectures he gave at Lausanne. First there was pure economics, to explain the workings of the economic system by means of a hypothetical competitive model; and then the analysis of economic policies divided according to policies affecting production, and those affecting distribution. Walras never completed any systematic treatise on either of these two divisions of economic policy, but he collected together essays and papers of various dates and lengths into two volumes in accordance with his original plan. These were entitled *Études d'économie sociale* (*Théorie de la répartition de la richesse sociale*), and *Études d'économie politique appliquée* (*Théorie de la production de la richesse sociale*), the latter of which includes his essay on the *Theory of Money* (1886). The most important writings in these two volumes date mostly either from the early part of his career, or from the years of his retirement, the main central phase of which was principally devoted to his pure economics. Walras's doctrines, unlike Pareto's, changed very little during his career, though shifts in terminology, and the gaps, ambiguities, and repetitions, inevitable in collections of papers from three or four decades of work, make difficult a clear-cut presentation.[2]

In Walras's scheme of the subject, pure economics dealt with the abstract analysis of a fully competitive economy, a hypothetical but broadly realistic model. He saw the relations between pure and applied theory as follows:

---

[1] On Walras's theory of money v. A. W. Marget, *Journal of Political Economy*, 1931, pp. 569–600, and ibid., 1935, pp. 145–80. Also O. Lange, *Economica*, 1938, pp. 20–23, and P. Samuelson, *Foundations of Economic Analysis*, p. 118.

[2] On Walras's writings on economic policy see the exhaustive study by M. Boson, *Léon Walras, fondateur de la politique économique scientifique*, Paris and Lausanne, 1951.

Pure theory is the guiding light for applied theory. When we understand thoroughly—what till now we understand so imperfectly—the mechanism of freely competitive exchange, production, and capitalisation, we shall know exactly how far it is automatic and self-regulating, and how far it needs to be supplemented and controlled. . . . When we have traced out the plan of a normal organisation of production and distribution, we shall see clearly where the actual organisation is satisfactory and where it is defective and must be modified. Then our children or grandchildren in the twentieth century will be able to refuse to be cast about, as we have been in the nineteenth century, between a smug conservatism which finds everything excellent and admirable, including the monopolies of the mines, railways, and banks, and the taxes on consumption, and, on the other hand, a muddled progressivism out to turn everything upside down. ('Appliquée', p. 68.)

As a rationalist reformer, faithful to the ideas of 1789, Walras seems to have regarded his doctrines on policy as following with logical directness and necessity from his pure analysis: 'La science doit être la lumière de la pratique.'

Walras started from his firm insistence that generally competitive conditions produced a maximum of utility for society. The attempt at a rigorous proof of this proposition had been the subject of his first essay in mathematical analysis in 1860, and he stuck to this formula to the end. But the extent of the qualifications and presuppositions which he found this proposition to rest on in his analysis of policies, seems to deprive it of much of the significance he ascribed to it in his pure economics as in some way a normal or general case. 'Freedom secures *within certain limits* the maximum of utility' he wrote in the *Éléments* (p. 232, our italics): 'The disturbing causes which hinder the reaching of this maximum, of whatever kind, must as far as possible be removed.' It was the task of *applied* economics to specify and prescribe for these hindrances, that is, 'to point out the cases where the social interest permits of economic enterprises being left to the individual, and on the other hand the cases which demand that initiative shall rest with, or be organised and regulated by the state'. As a much wider task than this, *social* economics has to examine the principles of distribution and the property-framework of society.

Walras summarized his principles of distributional justice in the slogan 'Equality of conditions, inequality of positions'. This is explained as follows:

Two things have to be distinguished here: the *general social conditions* and the *particular personal positions*. As to the *positions*, individualism is right and communism is wrong. It is contrary to order that the community should fix individuals' positions, and it is contrary to justice that the community should profit from the position an individual has created. As to the *conditions*, communism is right and individualism is wrong. It is contrary to order that the individual and not the state should fix social conditions and it is contrary to justice that the individual should turn to his exclusive profit the social conditions established by the state. Liberty for the individual and authority for the state, or equality of conditions and inequality of positions, that is the principle of our revolution and the fundamental constitutional formula for social science. . . . The task of our epoch is to bring into equilibrium the rights of the individual and those of the state. (*Économie sociale*, pp. 200–1.)

There is certainly present in Walras's writings, as is frequently the case with rationalist reformers, a certain fundamental disinclination to distinguish between his positive and his normative doctrines, and the sorts of validity they can respectively claim. Walras thought he had found the equilibrium between individual and state in the principle that incomes from, and property in, labour and personal abilities should go to the individual, while land and rents should be owned by or should accrue to the State. Here he claimed that he followed, besides of course, his father, James and J. S. Mill, and also Gossen. As a contribution to a policy of land nationalization Walras, like Gossen, worked out an elaborate analysis of the 'Mathematical Theory of the Price of Land and of its Purchase by the State'.

Let us turn to Walras's applied economics. Though he crowned competitive conditions with a somewhat nebulous optimal halo, Walras went, in extensive detail, into the measures by which these conditions had to be maintained, organized, canalized, supplemented, and replaced by State intervention. He several times emphasized the magnitude and extent of the State's economic duties both on the side of production and that of distribution: 'To set up and maintain free competition is a legislative task of very great complexity for the state to perform' (App., p. 476); and applied economics 'has to prescribe the careful detailed organization of a vast and complicated mechanism' (App., p. 277). Here are the main headings under which Walras called for state intervention:

(1) The State must be responsible for monetary policy and institutions and for ensuring monetary stability, for which Walras had very detailed prescriptions rather similar to those of Irving Fisher for a 'compensated dollar'. Walras (like Wicksell) regarded monetary reform as 'the most urgent of all social and

economic reforms'. But he did not in the then state of knowledge regard it as useful for the State to attempt to remedy crises or cycles, a problem to which he never devoted much study. (App., pp. 476–7.)

(2) It is a condition of effective free competition that the individual must be able to estimate rightly the utilities of goods and services and their quality. Walras specifically mentions advertising as perhaps calling for control, but under this heading he had in mind mainly the basic communal services of security, justice, education, &c., which meet public needs not adequately estimated by individuals. (App., pp. 198–9.)

(3) Effective competition presupposes that entrepreneurs can move freely and in sufficient numbers into those activities which are making a profit, and turn away from those making a loss. In respect of natural monopolies, public utility services, and (as J. S. Mill had urged) in any industry where increasing returns make competition self-destructive, there may be a case for State control or operation. Walras advocated the public control of railways and freight charges though not necessarily direct public operation. (App., pp. 200 ff. and p. 268.)

(4) Walras proposed to restrict speculative activities on stock exchanges or bourses to licensed professionals, holding that the free activities of masses of small, ignorant, non-professional speculators is damaging both to their own and the public interests. (App., pp. 436–7.)

(5) Walras believed that free competition in the labour market resulted in undesirably lengthy hours of work, which should therefore be subject to official limitation, and that many of the problems of labour legislation required international agreement. (App., pp. 275–6.)

Generally, Walras saw the relations between State intervention and private enterprise as a field for a 'great experiment':

The individual is to undertake the production of goods and services not of communal significance, which are susceptible to unlimited competition. Perhaps some of these fields of individual enterprise are destined to become monopolies as a result of technical, commercial, or other forms of progress. Perhaps all of them are. Nothing should stand in the way of a great experiment under the most testing conditions between individual initiative and the initiative or intervention of the state. It may be that the former will predominate where more activity and a more progressive spirit is necessary, and the latter where there should be more regularity and regard for tradition. Why cherish prejudices on this subject? If an absolute solution was necessary it would not be one exclusively of individualism. Strictly speaking, all enterprise *could* be collectivised, while it could not possibly all be left to individual enterprise. Collectivist production is possible, and would not necessarily conflict either with liberty, equality, order, or justice. It is simply a question of social advantage. One thing is certain, even under collectivism where the state was the sole entrepreneur ,and a fortiori before this condition is reached, the price of labour and personal services, like the rent of lands and the profit on capital, must be determined in the market for services by raising the price where demand exceeds supply and lowering it where supply exceeds demand, just as with the prices of products on the markets for products, and in fact in accordance with the prices of products. (App., pp. 272–3.)

Walras seems to have envisaged a liberal-socialist system combining central responsibility with extensive use of the price-mechanism. As well as supplying the theoretical basis, with his general equilibrium analysis, Walras pointed the way to those blueprints of a socialized price-mechanism of which Barone, a disciple of the Lausanne school, was to give a more detailed outline in his essay on the *Ministry of Production in a Collectivist State* (1908). (Barone, however, unlike Walras was not at all favourable to socialism and was concerned simply to demonstrate a theoretical possibility.)

Walras emphatically distinguished his 'liberal', 'synthetic', or 'scientific' socialism, as he variously called it, from Marxian socialism which, with its labour theory of value, prescribed no principles for the guidance of production:

Marxism still has to tell us how under its system an equilibrium of demand and supply for each product is brought about. . . . How is the state to set about its task in complete ignorance of the quantities of what should be produced? Certainly economists have not demonstrated scientifically the principles of free competition. Fortunately for them free competition organises production more or less well. In going into ecstasies over the admirable manner in which it does this they regard their task as accomplished. But socialism must proceed differently. It must distinguish itself from 'economism' above all in its knowledge of political economy, and it must explain why and how this or that principle will lead to and maintain equilibrium of the demand and supply for services and products. In doing this it will advance from the literary to the scientific stage. This is what Marx's collectivism fails to do. Even more lamentably than 'economism' which presents as working well a system which works badly, Marxism presents as working well a system which will not work at all. (*Économie sociale*, pp. 229–33.)

Walras was, of course, sufficiently firmly rooted in nineteenth-century progressive ideals to presuppose certain elementary freedoms. It was, above all, a free market for labour which Walras held to distinguish his form of collectivism from 'communism'.[1]

Walras was an enthusiastic supporter of consumers' and producers' co-operatives the great role of which he saw as 'not to abolish capital but to make everybody capitalists, their moral role, no less important, being to initiate democracy in the processes of production, to open up the path to business management, and to be a genuine school for the politically active'. (App., p. 285.)

Walras believed that with the abolition of monopolies and of private incomes from land, the amassing of excessively large fortunes would cease, but in so far as inequalities remained they should be tolerated. A very strong strain of individualism runs through his doctrines: 'If the individual wants liberty he must accept responsibility', Walras held, and he was strongly opposed to comprehensive schemes of state insurance. But he rejected any sweeping or unconstructive hostility to State intervention: 'We are not prepared to agree with the prejudice which allots every virtue to the individual and every defect to the state. . . . The state has its role just as the individual has his.' (App., p. 228.)

Walras's writings on policy show much of the rationalist reformer's high optimism and even over-confidence in the significance and automatic usefulness for practical policies of the mathematical formulae of the book. His statement of the doctrine of the maximum satisfaction from free competition, as given in his pure economics, was highly misleading. He is undoubtedly to some extent the ancestor of those completely abstract maximizing and 'optimizing' formulae, which have their analytical interest, but which are merely confusing when claimed by liberals or socialists as displaying some sort of realistic outcome of the institutional framework which they personally favour. Nevertheless, Walras himself avoided extremism and all-or-nothing simplifications, acknowledged how much must be left open for experiment, and presented an outline and classification of the main problems and cases of policy facing the economist. Even though they were never systematically completed, Walras's two volumes on policy are a great attempt, like Sidgwick's Book III, at a systematic review of economic policies.

[1] Walras's paper 'Théorie de la Propriété' (*Économie sociale*, pp. 205–39) gives the best statement of his views on this problem.

14

V. Pareto

1. *Introductory*

THE second occupant of the Chair at Lausanne was, in all respects
other than his cultivation for twenty years of the pure mathematical theory of general economic equilibrium, a completely
different intellectual personality from his predecessor. Walras belonged
to the type of rationalistic optimistic French radical reformer, and
from his first approach to the subject, which followed closely in the
footsteps of his father, his conception of the functions of pure and
applied economics hardly altered. He went to and stayed at Lausanne,
because, to his disappointment, he was not offered a post in France.
Pareto, on the other hand, was an angrily pessimistic self-exiled Italian
nobleman whose intellectual life, the creative phase of which began
remarkably late, was for the most part a lonely and lengthy personal
pilgrimage in revolt against the political ideas of his father and the
parliamentary régime (or 'pluto-democracy' as he called it), of his
country.

Pareto started as an ardent economic liberal, campaigning for free
trade, receiving congratulatory letters from Gladstone, and propagating
the kind of ardent Cobdenite sentiments which he would later have
treated with the deepest contempt. Economic ultra-liberalism, though
influentially represented in Italy, notably by Ferrara (1810–1900), had
not been nearly as exclusively dominant as it had been in France. The
ideas of the German historical school received much Italian support
after 1870, though Italian historical economists were in turn attacked
as 'Germanists' and 'socialists'. However, out of this Italian version of
the *Methodenstreit* a good deal of sensible theoretical and methodological eclecticism seems to have survived, as in the work of Pantaleoni,
for example.[1] But the young Pareto became a bitter opponent of the

---

[1] M. Pantaleoni (1857–1924), as a great teacher, drew both Pareto and the General-
Staff Colonel Barone to the study of economics. His earlier works included a study of the
incidence of taxes, and a calculation of the Italian national income (1884). His 'Pure
Economics' (1889) is a leading statement of marginal utility theory. Pantaleoni had drawn
in his studies both on German writings and on those of the Austrian school. As an
independent thinker he considered 'schools' to be 'obnoxious syndicates of fools'. He
was at various times active in banking and politics and was a supporter of d'Annunzio

economic *étatisme* indulged in by all the Italian parties in the last quarter of the nineteenth century, and was particularly incensed by the nationalization of the Italian railways in the early eighties. He attributed these policies to the vogue for German ideas, to the worship of Bismarckian methods, and to the influence of the academic (*Katheder*) socialists: 'One of the worst possible governments is a parliamentary dictatorship in possession of centralised control. . . . Each time the state absorbs the whole economic life of the nation the same phenomena of corruption and political disorganisation are to be observed. That is one reason, among many others, why Socialism is to be condemned.' His articles on L'Italie Économique (*Revue des Deux Mondes*, 1891) from which we have just quoted, anticipate remarkably closely the main themes to be associated half a century later with the phrase 'the Road to Serfdom'.

However, the most important and creative phases of Pareto's intellectual development were only to begin some years after, when he was in his later forties. In very bad odour with all parties in his own country, Pareto withdrew (1892–3) to a professorial chair abroad and the cultivation of 'neutral' and 'scientific' economic analysis, which in turn he was to abandon (*c.* 1912) for the construction of an immense system of political sociology, one of the main currents in which is an embittered scorn for the kind of naïve reformist caricature of liberalism from which he had started three or four decades previously. The comparatively advanced age at which Pareto took up systematically his great work in economic and social science is as remarkable as the fundamental intellectual elasticity he proceeded to show.

Pareto was born in Paris, the son of a Genoese nobleman exiled because of his activities on behalf of Mazzini. When his family returned to Italy, Pareto studied engineering, the natural sciences, and mathematics at Turin, and made himself also an extremely learned classical scholar, as the footnotes to his *Cours* and his *Trattato* testify. In due course he became an important industrial manager, holding a leading post in the Italian railways. Then came his political campaigning against the régime, on behalf of a kind of economic ultra-liberalism. Pareto entered, therefore, on the study of economics with a remarkable breadth of equipment: considerable mathematical as well as technological knowledge, a direct experience of industrial management, and some acquaintance with active politics and its frustrations. His interests

and of Fascism, being described as 'a reactionary anarchist'. (See the interesting laudatory note by P. Sraffa, *Economic Journal*, 1924, pp. 64 ff.)

in pure economics were stimulated and assisted by Pantaleoni and he was naturally attracted to Walras's writings by their use of mathematics. He had in any case planned to exile himself to Switzerland or England and his acquaintance with Walras led to his being offered the succession at Lausanne. Pareto had only specialized in economic studies for a very few years when (aged 45) he became a full professor in 1893. For twenty years he concentrated mainly on pure economics, though in his powerful critique of socialist doctrines (*Les Systèmes socialistes*, 1902), and in the methodological chapters of the *Cours* and the *Manuel*, the foundations of his sociological work were being prepared. His *Trattato di sociologia generale* (translated as 'The Mind and Society') was completed in the last decade of his life (1916). In his last few months Pareto was made a senator by the new Mussolini régime, but Pareto was no more a fascist than he was a socialist or a liberal, probably much less so. Above all, and to a rare degree, the mature Pareto was an independent. In one of the last of his many political newspaper articles he warned the new fascist government against five things: warlike adventures, restricting the freedom of the press and opinion, punitive taxation of the rich and of the peasants, alliances with the Church, and any infringement of the most absolute freedom of teaching in the universities.[1]

2. *The Cours and the Manuel*

Neither of Pareto's two books on economics comes near to being a well-finished well-balanced whole. The arrangement of the *Cours* seems to be almost completely haphazard, while in the *Manuel* the main analysis (Ch. 3–6) of the General Equilibrium of Tastes and Obstacles, is sandwiched between the first quarter devoted to a long introduction to the method of the social sciences, and a concluding series of lively but uneven and disconnected chapters on population, money, and applied economics. In both books a wealth of concepts and hypotheses is introduced, often almost as by-products, many of which are never fully worked out. The *Cours* and the *Manuel* are the interim reports of a gigantic intellect, moving impatiently on to ever-wider problems, and frequently leaving it to the reader to work out the full significance of the pregnant, concise, but often terminologically untidy hints so profusely scattered in its wake. Unfortunately, Pareto's

---

[1] *v*. G. H. Bousquet, *V. Pareto, sa vie et son œuvre*, 1928, p. 193. See also the work by J. Burnham, *The Machiavellians* in which Pareto is studied alongside Mosca, Michels, and Sorel.

impatience also resulted in some of Walras's best ideas being passed over or dismissed into an obscurity from which it was a long time before they were rescued (e.g. Walras's theory of money and interest).

The analytical economics of the *Cours* (1896) is comprised in two widely separated chapters (vol. i, p. 1 and vol. ii, p. 73), and represents the fruits of Pareto's first period of study. Some of the problems and solutions Pareto was to make his own are already suggested, but his theoretical treatment hardly moves beyond a masterly grasp and exploitation of the works of Walras, Edgeworth, Auspitz and Lieben, and Fisher. Of the wide range of applied problems examined, all with a wealth of international statistical evidence and illustration, we may briefly mention two: one is his Curve of Distribution, and the second his chapter on Crises.

1. As a result of immense statistical researches Pareto showed that for a wide range of countries in the latter part of the nineteenth century the distribution of income followed a closely similar pattern. In the *Cours*, though he does not appear to have used the word 'law' for his discovery, he did suggest that some strongly anti-socialist conclusions could be drawn from it as to the possibilities and effects of redistributing incomes more equally. (vol. ii, p. 328.) But these suggestions were severely modified in the *Manuel* (1909), and he denied that any general law as to the way in which the inequality of incomes could be diminished was derivable. (*Manuel*, p. 391.) Of course, this is so, and, of course, any such statistics are quite certain to come in for political misinterpretation from one direction or another. Nevertheless such limited, tentatively asserted regularities must surely be one of the main instruments, however fragile, for any realistic analysis of a given economic system. What is important about 'Pareto's law', as it has been rather misleadingly called, are not the detailed statistical criticisms to which it was subjected, nor the interpretations or misinterpretations of Pareto and others, but that it represents an extraordinary pioneer example of econometric investigation, which has since then hardly ever been followed up.

2. Pareto's brief chapter on Crises is one of the comparatively few treatments of the subject by one of the leading analytical economists between 1880 and 1910. He describes the problem as one of the aggregate dynamics of the system as a whole, or of the rhythmic movements of aggregates. As was to be increasingly emphasized by various authors after the turn of the century, the problem to be solved, according to Pareto, was not simply one of 'accidental' crises: 'A crisis must

not be regarded as an accident breaking in on a normal state of things. On the contrary it is the wave-like movement which is normal, with prosperity turning into depression and depression leading back to prosperity.' (*Cours*, vol. ii, p. 278.) Pareto emphasizes the psychological fluctuations of optimism and pessimism and seeks to relate them to the 'real' processes. The significance of saving and investment is seen but hardly explored. Pareto was, however, one of the few economists to make use of the immense pioneer monetary-statistical studies of Juglar. He concludes by asking whether it would be beneficial completely to suppress fluctuations, if it were possible, and whether a rhythmic movement is not one of the conditions of economic progress. (*Cours*, vol. ii, p. 297.) After a few pages of posing and probing the problems for a life-work, Pareto breaks off. But this chapter and that on the Curve of Distribution, show what a formidable econometrician Pareto might have been had he not turned to the pure analysis of value and later to sociology.

Let us now turn to the principal subjects of Pareto's theoretical analysis as developed mainly in the *Manuel*:

The Pure Theory of Consumers' Behaviour: It has been suggested that Pareto's analysis of consumers' behaviour is his outstanding contribution to pure economics. This is hardly the case, though it remains a conspicuous example of his frequent and vigorous attempts to insist on what he called 'logico-experimental' methods in the social sciences, and to apply such scientific criteria by rejecting all concepts and propositions which did not meet them. In the *Cours* there is little or nothing on the subject of the consumer which gets beyond the pioneer ideas of Edgeworth, Auspitz and Lieben, and Fisher, except for the term 'ophelimity'. 'Ophelimity' is simply a neutralized version of 'utility' expressing an attempt to empty out all suggestions of utilitarian or hedonist ethics from the analysis of value. 'Ophelimity' simply means 'what makes a good desirable to the consumer', whether it is really going to do him any 'good' or not. This terminological novelty is hardly in itself of much significance, and never secured wide adoption, but it does mark a certain stage in the conscious emptying out of content from the utility concept, preparatory to the proposal for its complete abandonment.

Even in the *Manuel* Pareto does not advance this subject much beyond the point reached in Irving Fisher's pioneer *Investigations*, of 1892. He starts from Edgeworth's suggestion in *Mathematical Psychics* that a general analysis of value must cover the cases of com-

plementary and rival goods, and not be confined to where the utility or
ophelimity of a good simply depends on the quantity of that good
alone available to the individual. Indeed, throughout the *Manuel*, the
achievement of the widest generality is the main objective of Pareto's
pure analysis. In his definition of complementarity and rivalry he continues to use the notion of ophelimity (in fact he continues to use it
freely throughout). With two rival goods A and B, the 'elementary
ophelimity' (or marginal utility) of good A diminishes as the quantity
of B increases, and if the two goods are complementary it increases.
Pareto does not even avoid the term 'pleasure' and his fundamental
assumption, as he formulates it, is that the individual 'knows whether
the pleasure he procures from a certain combination of goods (i) is
equal to that from another combination, or (ii) is greater or less'.
(*Manuel*, p. 264.) He assumes further that the individual can arrange
these pleasures in an order, or number them with purely ordinal
indices. In the mathematical appendix Pareto emphasizes that 'the
whole theory of economic equilibrium is independent of the notions
of utility, value in use, or ophelimity. . . . A complete treatise of pure
economics could be written without such concepts, and one day it
may be convenient to write it.' (*Manuel*, p. 543.) Pareto's implication
seems to be that though such a treatise could be written, he did not
think it worth attempting at that stage.

Pareto also develops the distinction between income and substitution effects: 'In passing from a certain combination of goods A, B,
C, . . . to another A^1, B^1, and C^1, we may divide the operation into
two: first we preserve intact the proportions of the combination and
increase (or decrease) all the quantities in the same proportion;
secondly, we change the proportions and so arrive definitively at the
combination A^1, B^1 &c.' (*Manuel*, p. 283.)

The Theory of Production is one of the most original parts of Pareto's
analysis and also one of the most difficult to follow in detail. He
regarded it, with its apparatus of production and profit-indifference
curves, as superseding by its much fuller generality the 'erroneous'
marginal productivity analysis, just as his consumer analysis superseded
a marginal utility theory limited by the assumption that the utility of a
good was a function of the quantity of that one good only. He criticized
the usual marginal productivity analysis as being dependent on the
assumption of variable technical coefficients, which was questionable
in a theory aiming at full generality, and as neglecting 'limitational'
factors (i.e. factors the quantity of which employed bears a technically

fixed relation to the quantity of product, e.g. cocoa to chocolate and iron ore to pig-iron). A fully generalized analysis must include both cases, that of fixed and that of variable proportions: 'Certain authors assume that all the coefficients of production are constant, others assume them to be variable. These two ways of considering the phenomenon are equally erroneous: these coefficients are partly constant or almost constant, and partly variable.' (*Manuel*, p. 636.)[1]

Monopoly and Oligopoly : Walras had confined his pure economics, by definition, to the analysis of 'a hypothetical régime of free competition'. Pareto rejected this restriction and aiming again at a wider generality, made a number of highly important and fundamental distinctions and *aperçus* about the analysis of monopoly, product differentiation, and oligopoly, without achieving anything like a finished theory satisfactorily integrated into his general equilibrium theory. In fact, it emerges that his general equilibrium analysis must relate to a fully competitive economy, in which, however, certain completely isolated enclaves of pure monopoly may be admissible.

Pareto's most important and fundamental distinction here is that between Type I and Type II phenomena. Type I phenomena occur where the individual unit 'accepts the prices of the market without trying to modify them directly, though it contributes, without knowing or wishing it, to modifying them indirectly. . . . The firm can, on the contrary, have the aim of modifying directly the market prices for the sake of profit', then we have Type II phenomena. (*Manuel*, p. 288.) Type III phenomena are described as those of monopolies trying to influence prices in the public interest. The three types correspond to a competitive firm, a private monopolist, and a socialized monopoly. The aim of maximum profit is common to Types I and II. Type I behaviour is that of a quantity-adjusting maximizer acknowledging the limitations of a competitive market, and simply deciding the quantity he will sell or buy at a given price. With Type II, or 'monopolistic' behaviour, the individual unit fixes its own price on the basis of a conjectured price-sales function.

This distinction had also been indicated by Auspitz and Lieben, but Pareto saw its importance and developed it more explicitly. In concentrating, as this distinction does, on the plans of the individual unit,

---

[1] For criticism of Pareto on this point *v*. Stigler, *Production and Distribution Theories*, p. 364. For a favourable exposition, of Pareto's views *v*. Schultz, 'Marginal Productivity and the General Pricing Process, *Journal of Political Economy*, 1929, pp. 505–51. See also J. R. Hicks, 'Marginal Productivity and the Principle of Variation', *Economica*, 1923, pp. 86 ff.

and in analysing what the individual takes as given in drawing up his plans and what he reckons himself able to influence, it makes possible a much more significant and fundamental classification of market relations, than if this is drawn up simply in accordance with whether, objectively, there are large or small numbers, or a single individual, in the market. Here again Pareto was opening up a path to be more generally followed several decades later. Pareto did not, however, achieve any systematic analysis outside the two limiting cases of competition and monopoly. He recognized the fact of product differentiation (*Manuel*, p. 602) as consisting in 'accessory circumstances, in credit, and certain attentions given to customers which may differentiate goods otherwise identical'. But he treated these differences, however slight, as completely shutting off the markets of the different 'monopolists' leaving a pure monopoly case with closed entry.

Pareto is also quite clear in dismissing all oligopoly from the purview of pure economic analysis (as, by implication had Marshall): 'It is pointless to ask of pure economics what will happen if two individuals having the power to exercise a monopoly by the sale of one and the same good find themselves confronting one another.... We must turn to the observation of the facts.... Still less must it be imagined that the observation of the facts will lead to a unique solution. On the contrary there are an infinity' (either in terms of warfare or of combination). (pp. 601–2.)

However, it may be added that along with much of fundamental interest for future analysis to build on, Pareto's rather untidy treatment of markets in the *Manuel* includes a number of odd and unhelpful conceptions like his 'incomplete competition', where marginal costs are rising (*Manuel*, pp. 185 ff.), and his very unrealistic duopoly model.[1]

Statics and Dynamics: Pareto at one stage divided 'the study of pure economics' into three parts: 'a static part—a dynamic part which studies successive equilibria—and a dynamic part which studies the movement of economic phenomena.' (*Manuel*, p. 147.) But his work is not presented under these three headings, nor is it easy to tell precisely what is to be understood under each of the three. As Schumpeter suggests, the study of successive equilibria seems simply to amount to comparative statics, while the third part is an unsatisfactory amalgam of analytical and evolutionary-historical dynamics.[2] Pareto's general

---

[1] On the subject of the foregoing paragraphs see R. Triffin, *Monopolistic Competition and General Equilibrium Theory*, especially pp. 52 ff.

[2] See Schumpeter's centenary article, *Quarterly Journal of Economics*, May 1949.

equilibrium is of course static throughout. As with later writers on imperfect and monopolistic competition, there is hardly even a hint of the distinction between objective and subjective, or *ex-ante* and *ex-post*, sales and cost curves.

One fairly well-known but purely incidental contribution to analytical dynamics is his *courbes de poursuites*. (*Cours*, vol. i, p. 18, and *Manuel*, p. 289.) These are usually illustrated by the analogy of a dog pursuing his master by a roundabout curve rather than by a straight line. Also incidental are Pareto's references to unstable equilibrium, and 'continual vibrations'. Pareto seems to have regarded problems of economic dynamics as too closely inter-connected with their social framework for any purely economic analysis to be able to yield significant conclusions. For his dynamics Pareto went over to political and sociological analysis. Neither Pareto (nor Wieser) could take the existing economic order in Europe as given to the extent that Marshall, slightly their senior, could virtually take as given the existing order of free enterprise and competitive individualism in Britain.

3. *Pareto's Welfare Economics and his Analysis of Socialism*

Though politically disillusioned, Pareto came to economics an apparently firm believer in the main tenets of *laissez-faire* liberalism, that is, in the unconditional benefits of free trade, and in the doctrine of the maximum social satisfaction from free competition. In the *Cours*, Pareto states the 'maximum satisfaction' doctrine rather similarly to, though perhaps in rather more ambiguous terms than Walras. With a 'persuasive' pseudo-neutrality he writes:

Observe that the theory does not give us any precepts either in favour of or against free competition. It simply indicates what the equilibrium is which is established under this régime. We shall also study other régimes. Now if any one believes that it is a good thing to obtain the maximum of ophelimity he knows in what direction he must act. If he believes that it is an evil he knows what route he must avoid. Science confines itself and must confine itself to giving these indications. (vol. i, p. 28.)

Nevertheless, Pareto, like Walras, disassociates himself from the optimistic dogmas of Bastiat: 'To be fair, it should be added that the socialists, including K. Marx, at least attempt an outline demonstration of their doctrines with the aid of facts, while the optimistic school is more often content with dogmatic assertion.' (vol. i, p. 416.)

In the *Manuel* the study of the issue goes much deeper, and the pseudo-neutrality is replaced by a much more genuinely detached analysis. The very able and critical review article on the *Cours* by Bortkiewicz entitled 'The Marginal Utility Doctrine as the basis of an Ultra-Liberal Economic Policy',[1] probably helped Pareto along his road. Pareto starts from a more precise and subtle definition of 'maximum ophelimity':

> There are, as we have seen, two problems to be resolved in obtaining the maximum of well-being for a collectivity. Given certain rules of distribution, we can investigate what positions, following these rules, will give the greatest possible well-being to the individuals of the collectivity. Let us consider any particular position and suppose that a very small move is made compatible with the relations involved. If, in doing this, the well-being of all the individuals is increased, it is evident that the new position is more advantageous for each one of them; vice versa it is less so if the well-being of all the individuals is diminished. The well-being of some may remain the same without these conclusions being affected. But if, on the other hand, this small move increases the well-being of certain individuals, and diminishes that of others, it can no longer be said that it is advantageous to the community as a whole to make such a move. We are, therefore, led to define as a position of maximum ophelimity one where it is impossible to make a small change of any sort such that the ophelimities of all the individuals, except those that remain constant, are either all increased or all diminished. (pp. 617–18.)

What Pareto fails to emphasize in the *Manuel* is that this definition does not define a single position but covers an entire range of positions. He notes simply that the problem of optimum distribution is one of social ethics, which involves comparing the ophelimities of different individuals. A competitive economy solves these according to its own rules within its given historical and social framework. A collectivist economy has to make its own conscious decision according to its principles of social ethics. (pp. 362–3.)

In a subsequent article, and in his treatise on sociology, Pareto returned once more to the problem of defining social maxima, and he again very much improved his analysis, though, as throughout most of his work, a certain untidiness in his use of terms remains. He makes it clear that there are 'an infinite number of points at which maxima of individual ophelimities are attained' (*The Mind and Society*, para. 2128), and he distinguishes two types of 'points' P and Q: 'The points of the type P are such that we cannot deviate from them to the benefit or detriment of all the members of the community—we can deviate from them only to the benefit of some individuals and the detriment of others' (para. 2128 n.). These points P may be said to represent 'maxima of utility *for* a community', as contrasted with 'the maximum utility *of* the community':

Let us take a community made up of just two persons, A and B. We can move from a point p, adding 5 to A's ophelimity and taking 2 from the ophelimity of B, and so reaching a point s; or adding 2 to A's ophelimity and taking 1 from B's, so that a point t is reached. We cannot know at which of the two points, s, t, the ophelimity *of* the community will be greater or less until we know just how the ophelimities of A and of B are to be compared; and precisely because they cannot be compared, since they are heterogeneous quantities, no maximum ophelimity *of* the community exists; whereas a maximum ophelimity *for* the community can exist, since it is determined independently of any comparison between the ophelimities of different individuals. (para. 2130.)

Nevertheless, interpersonal comparisons of utility are not absolutely 'meaningless' or 'illegitimate':

We are to conclude from that not that problems simultaneously considering a number of heterogeneous utilities cannot be solved, but that in order to discuss them some hypothesis which will render them commensurate has to be assumed. (para. 2137.) . . . Let us imagine a community so situated that a strict choice has to be made between a very wealthy community with large inequalities in income among its members and a poor community with approximately equal incomes. A policy of maximum utility *of* the community may lead to the first state, a policy of maximum utility *for* the community to the second. We say '*may*' because results will depend upon the coefficients that are used in making the heterogeneous utilities of the various social classes homogeneous. The admirer of the 'superman' will assign a coefficient of approximately zero to the utility of the lower classes, and get a point of equilibrium very close to a state where large inequalities prevail. The lover of equality will assign a high coefficient to the utility of the lower classes and get a point of equilibrium very close to the equalitarian condition. There is no criterion save sentiment for choosing between the one and the other. (para. 2135.)

Pareto had clearly travelled a long way from the naïve liberalistic generalizations of his Free Trade campaigns, strong traces of which still remain in his *Cours*. In fact, in spite of a certain superficial untidiness, his treatment of the pure analysis of the social maximum was to remain far in advance of all others for at least three or four decades to come.

Let us pass now to Pareto's comparisons of individualist and socialist economies. Theoretically, both a competitive and a collectivist economy can, with a given distribution of income, reach a position of maximum ophelimity (a position that only exists in the formulae of pure analysis in any case). But there is a slightly less unrealistic reason which makes this theoretical attainment much more difficult for the competitive economy than for the collectivist. This reason is that in a competitive economy it is difficult or practically impossible for a private firm to use price-discrimination or two-part tariffs in cases where there are fixed costs. To sell the optimum output a private firm must make its customers first pay the fixed costs (*dépenses générales*), and then subsequently sell at cost price, the fixed costs having been deducted. Except in special cases one cannot see how this could be done. The socialist state on the other hand could cover fixed costs by a tax on the consumers and then sell at cost price. It could therefore follow the line of complete transformation [i.e. optimum output]. (*Manuel*, pp. 363–4.)

In the conditions of a competitive economy, where there are fixed costs 'it is impossible to obtain maximum ophelimity with uniform prices'. (*Manuel*, p. 623.) Under Pareto's 'Type I' conditions, that is under competition, the optimum position is not reached 'where prices must remain uniform although there are fixed costs, for in this case consumers can act strictly in accordance with Type I (i.e. can prevent discrimination); but producers cannot realise together both the conditions for Type I action: that is, equality of cost of production and revenue, not only for the total output, but also for the last unit produced at the equilibrium point'. (*Manuel*, p. 648.) Pareto points out that it is a particularly bad way of controlling the privately owned Italian railways to make them pay to the State a charge fixed according to the gross or net product (just as Wicksell had earlier condemned the high profit-making of the Prussian railways).

In the *Manuel* Pareto is very brief in pointing out that from such purely theoretical analysis one can derive no decisive criterion for choosing between a society based on private property and a socialist organization. (*Manuel*, p. 364.) Perhaps he thought such a warning ought hardly to be necessary, but in view of the considerable history both previously and subsequently of attempts to prove the superiority of one system or the other by means of pure economic theorizing, a much more emphatic disclaimer might have been suitable. 'The problem' he simply noted 'could only be resolved by taking account of other sorts of phenomena'.

Many of these 'other sorts of phenomena' Pareto had examined in his lengthy and masterly work on socialist systems, in which, incidentally he was as severe in his examination of the Utopian liberalist dogmas of Bastiat and his followers, as in his criticism of socialist doctrines. He held that in most of liberalist political economy there was no attempt to state with any precision what was to be covered by the individualist minimum of State action, the over-simplifications of which like those of the other Utopians, the socialists, concealed the fact that society is continually faced with one difficult detailed choice after another. Pareto never attempted a systematic review of cases and principles such as Walras had outlined (though only in part completed). But in spite of their different philosophies they both came to the same, perhaps obvious, conclusion, in favour of a mixed economy guided by experience in seeking the dividing line between state action and competitive individualism, and they both were opposed to any attempt to prove that the theoretical optimum was in some sense *a priori* more impossible for a collectivist system than it was for a private enterprise economy. Pareto, who though neither a 'liberal' nor a 'socialist' was, on the whole, as an economist (but not as a political philosopher), less of a 'socialist' and more of a 'liberal' than Walras, particularly emphasized the problem for the socialist economy of selecting its enterprises and who was to manage them:

> The effects of economic competition are well-known. If it is to be suppressed another instrument of selection must replace it, or an immediate decay of the economic organisation of society will set in. . . . The socialists are knocking at an open door when they insist on the advantages for society of avoiding the costs of free competition. These undoubtedly exist. But the question is quite a different one. We have to know whether the new mechanism will be more advantageous for society or less, than that which it replaces. (*Les Systèmes*, &c., Tome II, pp. 416 ff.)

On the side of distribution the formula 'To each according to his need' could only, in practice, mean 'To each according to the decisions of the central authority', as such central bureaucratic decisions were the only alternative mechanism for deciding needs if the market mechanism was scrapped.

Pareto's critique of Marxism, by far the most penetrating and profound of its day, and perhaps also of any subsequent day, cannot be followed out here. We may note that it was far from being limited, like Böhm-Bawerk's, to an examination of the Marxian theory of value, but dealt with Marx's whole system, distinguishing particularly between (1) the actual words of Marx, (2) the esoteric interpretations, and (3) the popular *mystique*. He above all ridiculed the Utopian Marxistic myth that when just one more huge class-war had been fought out, 'a classless society', free of all class-struggles, would establish itself, with the State gradually 'withering away'.

As contrasted with his attitude to most socialist doctrines and dogmas, Pareto in a number of passages revealed a respectful interest in the British Trade Union movement, which he then saw to represent an empiricism free of destructive Utopianism. In the *Cours*, Pareto had pointed out (vol. ii, pp. 135 ff.) how on a realistic 'dynamic' analysis there were several possible ways in which trade unions could genuinely raise wages particularly in a rapidly progressing economy. They could also gradually alter the equilibrium position of the distribution of income by modifying the expectations of both sides of industry: 'English workers in their Trade Unions would never resign themselves to living like the unhappy peasants of the Neapolitan provinces, held down by their masters in a condition worse than that of animals' (vol. ii, p. 137). He praised what he then described as the 'new English *élite*' for managing its own affairs and 'not being guided by politicians'.

But socialist movements had their role if society was to progress:

Every impartial observer must recognize that if socialism has not been able to do any good by the measures it has directly inspired, it has been, at least indirectly, an essential element in the progress of our societies, independently of the logical value its theories intrinsically possess. *It is of little importance, from a certain point of view, if its theories are false if the sentiments they inspire are useful.* The socialist religion has served to give to the proletarians the energy and strength necessary for defending their rights, and in addition has raised them morally. In this task, if we except the English trade unions, it has scarcely had any serious rivals. As for the ancient religions, socialism has stimulated their zeal on behalf of the popular classes. At the present time *socialism appears to be the form of religion* best adapted to the workers in heavy industry. Whenever the latter is established the socialist religion appears, and recruits its adherents in proportion to the development of industry. Socialism facilitates the organisation of *the élites rising from the lower classes*, and in our epoch it is one of the best instruments in the education of these classes. (*Les Systèmes*, &c., Tome I, p. 64.)

In the foregoing paragraph, in the phrases we have italicized, occur the two basic conceptions around which the bulk of Pareto's vast sociological analysis was built up, at which we can simply take a momentary glimpse in passing. First, there is his extensive account of the 'non-logical' actions of individuals, groups, and nations. These cannot be explained by the 'false theories', slogans, and creeds with which the political religious-believer seeks to justify himself, the scientific falsity or logical nonsensicality of such 'ideologies' being almost entirely an irrelevance. It is rather their effectiveness as political myths which must be explained, through their appeal to something deeper than surface rationality. Secondly, there is Pareto's theory of the role and circulation of *élites*, implying that it is always a minority that really governs but that these minorities can never perpetuate themselves: 'History is the graveyard of aristocracies'.

The roots of both of Pareto's great intellectual labours may be traced to the ardent political experiences and frustrations he went through between, approximately, the ages of 25 and 45. His pure economic analysis, primarily and psychologically, may be said to start as an attempt to re-examine and restate, with ever-increasing detachment, the naïve liberalistic free trade economism in which he had invested as a young man. His sociology starts as an attempt to discover how far, or how little, the sort of 'rational' arguments good or bad, which he thought he had expounded on behalf of his free-trade views, can, by themselves, succeed in politics, and from what other sources they need to be, or actually get, reinforced or supplanted. But though there may be this subjective unity for Pareto, relating his entire work, objectively there are wide gaps between his pure economic analysis of individual and social maximization, and his mainly political sociology. They seem to be on different planes, hardly related to or illuminating one another. In between these two planes he made a number of remarkable isolated contributions to the intermediate fields of applied economics and economic sociology, but these are not co-ordinated in any system or in any one volume. There are, for example, his econometric studies of crises and of the distribution of incomes (*Cours*); his practical criticisms of socialist economics (*Les Systèmes socialistes* and *Manuel*); his theory of population (*Cours* and *Manuel*); his sociology of inflation and of the 'S''s and 'R''s (speculators and rentiers), and of protection and pressure groups (in the *Trattato*). Today, now that his main great discoveries in pure analysis have at last been caught up with, it is possible to regard his essays in applied econometrics and in economic sociology, uncoordinated though they are, as the most interesting signposts Pareto left for the future progress of economics.

15

K. Wicksell and G. Cassel

1. *Wicksell on Value and Capital*

IT was only 'in the middle of the journey' at the age of 35, after the very lengthy studies of a Swedish graduate in philosophy and mathematics, that Wicksell came to devote himself, as a specialist, to the subject to which he was to make such distinguished contributions. Enthusiasm for social reform, and anxiety, in particular, about the population problem, drew him to political economy. Never a social democrat, he considered the insights of Malthus more important than those of Marx, he always remained a friend of the working-class movement and an outspoken radical reformer, so outspoken that at the age of 57 he served a term of imprisonment for offending orthodox religious sentiments in one of his public speeches. Wicksell's first studies in political economy were made in J. S. Mill's *Principles*, and he continued to draw on the English classics, especially on Ricardo, in his book on *Interest and Prices*. As a mathematician he based his theory of value on Walras, but he regarded Böhm-Bawerk's theory of capital as having an important part in his synthesis.

Unlike those of his fellow mathematician Marshall, Wicksell's works, except perhaps those concerned with population and public finance, remained at a fairly high level of theoretical abstraction. According to Professor Ohlin he came to regret this at the end of his career:

> As an economist Wicksell lacked one important quality that of being able to get into contact with what is generally called practical economics. From this point of view I think that his Austrian training was unfortunate. . . . At a dinner for his seventieth birthday (1921) it was pathetic to hear him express in his speech his envy of those who now started economic studies with all the advantages of having at their disposal a growing mass of factual material about what was actually happening. Himself an economist who had learned from all schools of economic thought except the German historical school, his advice turned out to be: Study history, study the development of economic life. (*Economic Journal*, 1926, p. 503.)[1]

[1] For criticism, by a fellow Swede, of Wicksell's utilitarian and hedonist preconcep-

Wicksell presented his ideas on value, capital, and distribution in his first important publication at the age of 42 (his essay on *Value, Capital, and Rent*, 1893). He extended his work on these subjects without major alteration in Volume I of his *Lectures on Political Economy on the Basis of the Marginal Principle*. His clear outline of the marginal productivity principle in the introduction to his first essay is especially noteworthy, and in the *Lectures* he built it up into the most satisfactory account of the marginal productivity doctrine then given, with its rider the adding-up theorem, along with the necessary underlying assumptions (see *Lectures*, vol. i, pp. 124–33).

In his treatment of markets Wicksell concentrated nearly all his analysis on the extreme cases of monopoly and free competition, but he notes that 'the sharp distinction between monopoly prices and competitive prices which we (in common with other economists) have drawn here scarcely ever exists in reality'. (*Lectures*, vol. i, p. 96.) Wicksell also made an influential contribution to the discussion of oligopoly, championing Cournot's reasoning and criticizing the assumption of Bertrand and Edgeworth 'that each monopolist aims at the maximum net profit on condition that the other does not change his price—an assumption which seems to me quite unjustifiable where they both produce the same commodity'. Wicksell also emphasized that the study of monopoly 'is peculiarly liable to be disturbed by great differences between theory and practice'. (pp. 95–7.)[1]

We wish to refer particularly to Wicksell's remarks on the doctrine of maximum satisfaction, which seems to have specially interested him, and to which he several times briefly returned. In the Introduction to *Value, Capital, and Rent*, after noting that Gossen had rejected the doctrine that free competition produced the maximum social advantage, Wicksell concentrated his criticism on Walras's proposition that given a uniform price, free competition affords the maximum satisfaction to each of two exchanging parties. In his section in the *Lectures*, on 'The Gain from Free Exchange' (vol. i, pp. 72–83), Wicksell develops this subject further:

If we assume that the rich man carries his consumption so far that the marginal utility, the utility of the last unit, is little or nothing to him, whilst

tions, see G. Myrdal, *Das politische Element in der nationalökonomischen Doktrinbildung*, pp. 28–33. For an account of his writings on social reform and population, mainly in Swedish, see C. G. Uhr, *American Economic Review*, 1951, pp. 829 ff., who gives a very comprehensive review of all Wicksell's work.

[1] See also one of Wicksell's last articles, on A. L. Bowley's 'Mathematical Groundwork of Economics', translated into German in the *Archiv für Sozialwissenschaft*, 1927, pp. 252 ff.

on the other hand, the poor man must discontinue his consumption of practically all commodities at a point at which they possess for him a high marginal utility, then it is not difficult to imagine . . . that an exchange between a rich man and a poor man may lead to a much greater total utility for both together—and therefore for society as a whole—if it is effected at a suitable price fixed by society, than if everything is left to the haphazard working of free competition. And what is here true on a small scale is just as true on a large scale. Thus, for example, the fixing by society, or by a union of workers, of a minimum wage or a maximum working day would, within certain limits (which may sometimes be very narrow), be of distinct advantage to the workers and consequently to the most numerous class of society. (p. 77.)

Later Wicksell criticizes Cassel's emphasis on the economic superiority of free competition and on the importance of the free choice of consumption goods under free-market capitalism:

He [Cassel] emphasises as often as possible its economic superiority and if he can do nothing else he praises 'the free choice of consumption goods' which it provides in contrast with, for example, a similar socialist state. . . . Actually the lower classes in present day society do not in the least possess free choice in consumption; as far as means of subsistence proper are concerned, they are allotted all the cheapest brands, and their remaining consumption is similarly organised. A compulsory rationing of the most important commodities, as in wartime, would certainly give them greater freedom in their 'choice of consumption goods'. (*Lectures*, vol. i, p. 227.)

While on the subject of 'welfare' analysis, mention should be made of Wicksell's remarkably clear and precise presentation of the case for marginal cost pricing (see *Finanztheoretische Untersuchungen*, 1896, pp. 125–38). Public ownership will often make possible a marginal cost pricing-policy which would not be possible for a private firm. Wicksell also points out that the taxation levied by the State to meet the fixed costs can, if it is considered distributively desirable, be levied on those who mainly make use of the service and not simply on income-tax payers. Wicksell condemns the big profits of the Prussian State railways as indicating a quite uneconomic pricing policy from the point of view of the general interest.[1]

What has sometimes been regarded as one of Wicksell's major services was his analysis of 'capitalistic' production based on the work of Böhm-Bawerk. Wicksell rejected Walras's very complete, though

---

[1] See J. M. Buchanan, *Southern Economic Journal*, 1951, No. 2, p. 173. This argument of Wicksell's may well have been suggested by Launhardt's treatment of the same point.

of course static, maximization formula for the rate of interest, on the rather ambiguous ground that

the time element in production was never properly appreciated by Walras and his school. The idea of a *period* of production or of capital investment does not, as we have said, exist in the Walras–Pareto theory; in it capital and interest rank equally with land and rent; in other words, it remains a theory of production under essentially non-capitalistic conditions, even though the existence of durable, but apparently indestructible instruments, is taken into account. (*Lectures*, vol. i, p. 171.)

Certainly Walras's formula was a static formula, so ultimately was Böhm-Bawerk's, but Wicksell considered that the concept of the period of production had an essential explanatory role. He made many detailed criticisms and precisions amounting virtually to an independent reconstruction of Böhm-Bawerk's theory, but the fatal indefiniteness or indefinability at the core of that theory remains in Wicksell's version. That being so, Wicksell's theoretical ingenuity and constructiveness in this direction must be regarded as largely wasted, though by making the theory clearer he helped to exhaust its possibilities and reveal it as a blind alley.

Wicksell had introduced in his essay on *Value, Capital, and Rent*, Böhm-Bawerk's period of production concept; but three years later he replaced this (as being 'rather vague and in no case capable of precise definition'[1]) by the concept of 'the period of investment', that is: 'The time which elapses between the investment of a unit of capital through purchase of labour and its replacement through the sale of finished objects of consumption is called the circulation or investment period of the unit of capital in question.' As G. J. Stigler has commented: 'The new concept is just as vulnerable as the old one—since they stand in fixed relationship to one another. The period of investment, like the period of production, cannot be defined unless one assumes that capital goods can be separated from other "factors" (land and labour), and unless the latter work separately in capital creation.' (*Production and Distribution Theories*, p. 278.)

Linked with his theory of capital is Wicksell's analysis of the problem of aggregate relative shares (*Lectures*, vol. i, pp. 133–44), where his close interest in Ricardian problems is clearly apparent (as also in his study of the reasons for a long-term fall in rates of interest, which we shall mention in the next section). Wicksell's study of aggregate relative shares is directly inspired by Ricardo's chapter 'On Machinery'.

[1] See Wicksell's *Finanztheoretische Untersuchungen*, 1896, p. 30.

He argued that 'the theory of marginal productivity will enable us, I believe, to put it on a firmer foundation'. But it seems rather doubtful how much firmer and more realistically significant the marginal productivity theory can render the analysis of this macro-economic distributional problem. Wicksell concludes that 'it is scarcely possible to discover a simple and intelligible criterion which will indicate whether a change in the technique of production is in itself likely to raise or to lower wages'. (p. 143.)

2. *Interest and Prices*

Wicksell's *Interest and Prices* (1898) is by far the fullest and most penetrating account of his path-breaking doctrines on this subject, though he restated them more briefly and simply in the second volume of his *Lectures*. At various times he modified some of the details, and his views seem to have been shifting in minor respects down to his death, but the fundamental nature of his doctrines remained unchanged. His treatment was stimulated on the one hand by Ricardo's suggestions as to the relation between the quantity of money and the rate of interest,[1] and on the other by Tooke's criticisms of the quantity theory. Wicksell only came to know later of the work of Henry Thornton. He referred much to the more recent German writings, for example those of Wagner[2] and Nasse, though often in strong criticism,

[1] Wicksell's central notion is contained in the following sentences from Ricardo's chapter on 'Currency and Banks' in his *Principles*: 'The applications to the bank for money, then, depend on the comparison between the rate of profits that may be made by the employment of it and the rate at which they are willing to lend it. If they charge less than the market [sic] rate of interest, there is no amount of money which they might not lend; if they charge more than that rate, none but spendthrifts and prodigals would be found to borrow of them.' Ricardo writes of the 'market' rate of interest where Wicksell would write of the 'natural' rate of interest.

[2] Adolf Wagner, though much influenced by Tooke and the Banking School, kept alive the ideas of Thornton and Ricardo about the rate of interest, until they were taken up again by Marshall and Wicksell. See his *Beiträge zur Lehre von den Banken* (1857) for such passages as the following (p. 277): 'Let us assume that because of the increased need for capital the rate of discount would ordinarily have risen but that it is kept unnaturally low. . . . In that case the inclination to ask for credit would be greater than if the rate of discount were at its higher, and natural level; for the low rate would not then be in the right relation to the expected profit which could be made by the use of the loan. The consequence of the low rate is, therefore, that an excessive speculation develops, which later has to be followed by a sudden rise in the rate which then works twice as drastically.' Wagner here gives much of the essence of what came to be known as the Austrian monetary overinvestment analysis of crises. There are further statements of the same ideas on pp. 237–9. See also A. W. Marget, *Theory of Prices*, vol. i, pp. 192–3. Wagner does not use the term 'natural' rate of interest, but calls 'artificial' a rate of interest that is 'not correctly related to the disposable capital'. (p. 237.)

and he makes a single reference to Mangoldt who had stated in outline the central message of Wicksell's doctrine and applied it very briefly to the explanation of the trade cycle. It should be emphasized that Wicksell himself was not directly concerned in *Interest and Prices* with the trade cycle and did not regard his monetary doctrines, as they stood, as a contribution to that problem.

One of the difficulties of Wicksell's exposition in his *Interest and Prices* is that he is exploring along a number of different paths more or less simultaneously. The paths constantly intersect but they are at any rate analytically separable and are each of the greatest importance. We may distinguish three such paths (of course there were others). First, Wicksell was seeking to construct a theory of money, not to overthrow or replace the quantity theory but to supplement its somewhat meagre content and conclusions. Here in particular he starts from what we may call the Ricardo–Tooke problem. Secondly, in so doing he was trying to link up the theory of money with the theory of value and price, or, more accurately, the analysis of relative prices with the analysis of the absolute level of money prices—perhaps the most fundamentally significant of the three paths he was exploring, though he hardly gets beyond suggestions. Thirdly, stimulated by the monetary controversies towards the end of the Great Depression, which centred round the international gold standard and bimetallism, Wicksell was trying to arrive at and justify a principle of monetary policy. Though Wicksell did not sort out his discussion in this comparatively tidy way we shall try to present his doctrines under these three headings.

1. Wicksell first states his central doctrine as an answer to the Ricardo–Tooke problem. Ricardo, arguing from the basis of the quantity theory, had concluded that 'an excess of money will ... show itself in two ways, partly through a rise in all prices, partly through a fall in the rate of interest', which seems to suggest fairly clearly the association of falling interest rates and rising prices. Tooke, however, starting from his statistics, had pointed out that rising prices usually coincide with high and rising interest rates, and vice-versa. Wicksell largely accepted Ricardo's reasoning, as far as it went, and Tooke's facts (but not Tooke's explanations). Wicksell's solution—which, as we have seen, is discoverable in Thornton, Ricardo himself, Wagner, and Mangoldt—was as follows:

> The rate of interest charged for loans can clearly never be either high or low in itself, but only in relation to the return which can, or is expected to be obtained by the man who has possession of money. It is not a high or low

rate of interest in the absolute sense which must be regarded as influencing the demand for raw materials, labour, and land or other productive resources, and so indirectly as determining the movement of prices. The causative factor is the current rate of interest on loans as compared with what I shall be calling the natural rate of interest on capital. This natural rate is roughly the same thing as the real interest of actual business. A more accurate, though rather abstract, criterion is obtained by thinking of it as the rate which would be determined by supply and demand if real capital were lent in kind without the intervention of money. . . . [This] is clearly in complete accord with the observed fact that rising prices have seldom been associated with low or falling rates of interest, that far more often they are associated with high or rising rates of interest, and that falling prices accompany falling interest rates. (*Interest and Prices*, pp. xxv and xxviii.)

We may note here Wicksell's introduction of expectations simply as a qualification regarded apparently as not essentially modifying his formula. Later we shall mention the difficulties in his assumption that the rate of interest which is equal to the marginal productivity of capital is also that which would equate the supply and demand for real capital in a barter economy.

As to the quantity theory, Wicksell's conclusions were that it provided a starting point but not much more:

The theory provides a real explanation of its subject matter, and in a manner that is logically incontestable; but only on assumptions that unfortunately have little relation to practice. . . . It assumes that everybody maintains, or at least strives to maintain, his balance at an average level that is constant (relatively to the extent of his business or his payments). Or, what really comes to the same thing, that the *velocity of circulation* of money is, as it were, a fixed, inflexible magnitude, fluctuating about a constant average level; whereas in practice it expands and contracts quite automatically and at the same time is capable, particularly as a result of economic progress, of almost any desired increase, while in theory its elasticity is unlimited. . . . Meanwhile it is far easier to criticise the quantity theory than to replace it by a better and more correct one. (pp. 41–43.)

In the course of examining Tooke's criticisms of the quantity theory, which were mainly negative, and very varying in value and significance, Wicksell came upon Tooke's thirteenth proposition on the quantity theory, which he quotes as follows:

That it is the quantity of money, constituting the revenues of the different orders of the state, under the head of rents, profits, salaries, and wages, destined for current expenditure, that alone forms the limiting principle of the aggregate of money prices. . . . As the cost of production is the limiting principle of supply, so the aggregate of money incomes devoted to expenditure for consumption is the determining and limiting principle of demand.

An economist such as Cairnes, for example, following the logic of 'Say's Law' would probably have denied that there can be any basis for explaining the level of general prices on this principle of 'aggregate demand', simply because aggregate demand must always be equal to aggregate supply. But Wicksell comments: 'It is my belief that this observation of Tooke's, or more precisely its first half, does really provide a starting point from which a theory of the value of money and of prices can be developed.' (p. 45.)

This starting-point is sometimes described as that of the 'income approach' to the theory of money, and it leads fairly directly to the central macro-economic concept of aggregate demand, and then to the analysis of aggregate income and output as divided into their consumption and savings-investment components.[1] Wicksell did not formulate precise 'fundamental equations' of this kind. But the path he opened up led straight in that direction and away from 'Say's Law', though his references to the law are only gently critical.

2. The central doctrine of Wicksell, relating the money-market rate of interest with the 'natural' marginal productivity of capital, at once brings together the theory of value and price, and the theory of money. This was a second main path which Wicksell was exploring.

Cannan has said of Ricardo that he kept 'his theories of the value of currency so to speak in a different side of his head from that occupied by his general theory of value',[2] and some such schizophrenia was later attributed, at one stage, by Keynes to 'classical' economists. But it is not altogether accurate to say that the dominant explanations of value and price were separate and different from the explanations of money prices and the value of money. In the later classical authors the cost-of-production explanation had been applied both to the values of goods and services and to the value of money, and the neo-classical marginal utility analysis had been extended in the same way to apply both to the values of goods and services *and* to the value of money, by Marshall, Menger, and Walras. The gap which remained unbridged, the fundamental significance of which had not, before Wicksell, been sufficiently or correctly assessed, is better described as that between the explanation of exchange values and relative prices, and the explanation of the absolute levels of average money prices. This distinction too,

---

[1] *v. below* Ch. 21, sects. 2 and 3.   [2] *Review of Economic Theory*, p. 182.

had been clearly brought out by Cairnes, but his adherence to 'Say's Law', in its strictest sense, prevented him from appreciating its significance correctly.

Wicksell had no difficulty in showing the very slight significance of the cost-of-production theory of money. He did not criticize in detail the theories of Marshall and Walras, but showed (*Interest and Prices*, Chapter III) that they did not bridge this gap between the explanation of relative prices and money prices. The static equilibrium analysis of relative exchange values left the missing multiplicative factor for arriving at absolute money prices to be explained separately by the quantity theory. The micro-economic maximizing formula for the individual's holding of cash balances could only be of limited significance in explaining general inflationary and deflationary movements and at least needed some considerable supplementing.

That Wicksell did not move further along this second path was due to his keeping too closely to the procedure of the static analysis of relative values, concentrating on the equilibrium concept and conditions.[1] A more deliberate step towards a general dynamic treatment was taken by Wicksell's Swedish successors. As Professor Ohlin put it in his Introduction to *Interest and Prices*:

> The general theory of pricing and distribution is, after all, static in character, and its concepts are not likely to lend themselves to the more dynamic analysis of, say, problems of inflation. Rather than build monetary theory on this static analysis, it would seem more natural to pursue the monetary analysis of the actual determinants of the various rates of interest in a dynamic world and then, in the light of such analysis, to revise the theory of distribution. Work along this line seems to me the natural consequence of the ... innovation of Wicksell's. It would bring monetary theory into harmony with price theory by making the latter more dynamic and would probably give up not only concepts like the natural rate of interest but the whole idea of a monetary equilibrium and thus also the concept of a normal rate of interest defined in equilibrium terms. (*Interest and Prices*, p. xv.)

But this is anticipating by nearly thirty years. Wicksell's first step was to link the theory of money and the theory of value by relating (i) the 'normal' market rate which would equate the supply and demand for savings, with (ii) the 'natural' rate representing the 'real' marginal productivity of capital, which would, he held, in turn coincide with (iii) the rate which kept the price level constant.

[1] Myrdal goes so far as to say that Wicksell 'always thought in quasi-stationary terms' (*Monetary Equilibrium*, p. 131 n.).

3. This brings us to the third of the paths which Wicksell was following up, leading, he hoped, to a principle, or objective, for monetary policy. Here he had behind him the controversies over the organization of an international gold standard and over bimetallism of the last two decades of the nineteenth century.

Carl Menger had taken money as one of the great examples of a spontaneous social phenomenon, arising 'unconsciously' without deliberate planning or decisions of state, in answer simply to individual economic interests. Wicksell, on the other hand, regarded money and monetary institutions as providing the greatest possibilities in the economic world for replacing a traditional spontaneity by conscious control: 'It is the part of man to be master, not slave, of nature, and not least in a sphere of such extraordinary significance as that of monetary influences.' (*Interest and Prices*, p. 4.) . . . 'In all other economic spheres other circumstances, such as technique, natural conditions, individual or social differences, play a role which science can only imperfectly survey and control. But, with regard to money, everything is determined by human beings themselves, i.e. the statesmen and (so far as they are consulted) the economists.' (*Lectures*, vol. ii, p. 3.) This distinction between 'natural conditions' and 'human institutions' is not illegitimate, but the general reformist assumption that 'everything that is determined by human beings' as contrasted with 'natural conditions' can be 'surveyed and controlled', more than imperfectly, is at best an unconfirmed working hypothesis.

Wicksell started from the assumption, like most of his contemporaries, that, by and large, a stable price-level should be the prime objective of monetary policy. According to Myrdal, 'he accepted the comfortable formula of a constant price-level more by sentiment and as a result of a normative, *a priori* intuition'. (*Monetary Equilibrium*, p. 128.) Anyhow, one of Wicksell's main concerns was to explore what this objective required of banking policy. Though the original stimulus behind it was probably practical, this led him to some of his most complicated and controversial abstract analysis, one or two salient points in which we may now consider under this third heading.

Let us take, first, Wicksell's identification of the interest-rate which was equal to the marginal productivity of capital, and which equated the supply and demand of savings, with that rate which maintained a constant price-level. This identification was contested in the objection made by Wicksell's colleague Davidson[1] that with technical progress

[1] See Myrdal, op. cit., p. 129. On Davidson's work see B. Thomas, *Economic Journal*,

and increasing productive efficiency, the equilibrium condition required a fall in the price-level in proportion to the increase in efficiency. Wicksell apparently conceded some importance to this objection but never finally answered it.

Combined with Wicksell's central doctrine of monetary equilibrium was his doctrine of the cumulative 'unstable' consequences of disequilibrium. The equilibrium of the general level of money prices, as contrasted with that of particular relative prices, was essentially unstable:

> The movement and equilibrium of actual money prices represent a fundamentally different phenomenon, above all in a fully developed credit system, from those of *relative* prices. The latter might perhaps be compared with a mechanical system which satisfies the conditions of *stable* equilibrium, for instance a pendulum. Every movement away from the position of equilibrium sets forces into operation—on a scale that increases with the extent of the movement—which tend to restore the system to its original position, and actually succeed in doing so, though some oscillations may intervene. The analogous picture for *money* prices would rather be some easily movable object, such as a cylinder, which rests on a horizontal plane in so-called *neutral* equilibrium. The plane is somewhat rough and a certain force is required to set the price-cylinder in motion and keep it in motion. But so long as this force—the raising or lowering of the rate of interest— remains in operation, the cylinder continues to move in the same direction. . . . The motion is an accelerated one up to a certain point, and it continues for a time even when the force has ceased to operate. Once the cylinder has come to rest, there is no tendency for it to be restored to its original position. (*Interest and Prices*, p. 101.)

If the natural rate for some reason was above the market rate an expansion of investment would be started and soon be carried on more rapidly, gathering its own momentum through the elastic expectations and temporarily self-justifying optimism of entrepreneurs. It should be pointed out that in seeking to establish this doctrine Wicksell almost at times turned it into an empty definition. He is clear that the 'natural' rate of interest is not something that can ever conceivably be discovered by the banks, except by watching the movements of general prices. If, in some sweeping but vague sense, 'other things are equal', and the general level of prices is constant, then the bankers can deduce that the market rate of interest equals the natural rate:

> We had arrived at the conclusion that, so long as the situation in the

1935, pp. 36 ff. and *Monetary Policy and Crises* (1936) by the same author, especially Chapter III.

market remains unaltered, any permanent fall, no matter how small, in the rate of interest maintained by the credit institutions will cause the general level of prices to rise to an unlimited extent in a continuous and more or less uniform manner. . . . These statements sound extremely bold, and indeed paradoxical. But it has to be remembered that the rate of interest referred to as the 'previous' or the 'normal' rate, away from which our deviations are imagined to originate, does not always remain the same and cannot be thought of as so much per cent. It merely means that rate which, having regard to the situation in the market, would be necessary for the maintenance of a constant level of prices. (*Interest and Prices*, p. 100.)

This would seem almost to amount to saying that if the market rate is not at that level which maintains a constant level of prices the price-level will not remain constant, but will rise (so long as the market rate is below the natural rate) or fall (so long as the market rate is above the natural rate), the whole argument resting on the assumption of particular expectations on the part of entrepreneurs. However, Wicksell's introduction of these cumulative unstable *processes* into the centre of economic analysis was a major challenge to the adequacy of the simple self-adjusting dynamics of the stationary and quasi-stationary 'normal' equilibrium models. But Wicksell to a lesser extent than Marshall, freed his analysis from static and stationary limitations, and a systematic dynamic analysis of aggregate processes, and of the expectations on which they depend, was left for his successors in Sweden to develop.

In the *Lectures* Wicksell explicitly makes it clear that he is starting from an assumption of full-employment conditions: 'As a first approximation we are entitled to assume that all production forces are already fully employed.' (p. 195.) At one point in *Interest and Prices* he even claims that a *general* expansion of production is impossible has been 'demonstrated by the figures of unemployment at different periods recently collected in various countries. The average number of unoccupied workers is relatively small, about 1 per cent.' (*Interest and Prices*, p. 143.) Wicksell says nothing more precise about the origin of these figures but his taking as normal an unemployment level of 1 per cent. was a notable difference in the data of his analysis from that of economists thirty years later, when his work came to receive the wider attention it deserved.

As a pioneer explorer of what was almost a new continent of theoretical economics, Wicksell never regarded his doctrines on interest and prices as providing a precise map, or anything like a well-rounded definitive analysis. Nor, as we said above, did he regard his work as having any direct significance for the explanation of the trade cycle. In the brief note on this subject included in his *Lectures*, Wicksell expressed his agreement with Spiethoff's theory:

My view closely agrees with that of Professor Spiethoff. Its main feature is that it ascribes trade cycles to *real* causes independent of movements in commodity price, so that the latter become of only secondary importance, although in real life they nevertheless play an important and even a dominating part in the development of crises. . . . The principal and sufficient cause of cyclical fluctuations should rather be sought in the fact that in its very nature technical or commercial advance cannot maintain the same even progress as does, in our days, the increase in needs—especially owing to the organic phenomenon of increase of population—but is sometimes precipitate, and sometimes delayed. (*Lectures*, vol. ii, pp. 209–11.)

Wicksell was acutely conscious of how much remained to be clarified in the analysis of savings, investment, and the rate of interest, as may be seen from his section on 'Capital Accumulation' at the end of Vol. I of the *Lectures*. Here he starts by noting that 'a rational theory of saving' has never been worked out, and that 'among the many influences affecting the accumulation of capital, the rate of interest is undoubtedly one—although even its influence is uncertain and ambiguous'. (p. 208.) Wicksell then addresses himself to the problem of why 'the long prophesied ideal of economists in which interest will have fallen to a minimum is tardy in its realisation'. (p. 211.) Here Wicksell turns again to one of the main problems of the English classics. Though risks, wars, &c. are important, it is above all technical and colonial development, and an increasing population, that is keeping up the rate of interest. Nevertheless, in the long run the rate of interest will fall:

It is clear that these cases are only exceptions to the rule. The unprecedented growth of population recently witnessed in Europe (1900), and still more in certain extra-European countries will certainly, sooner or later—probably in the course of the present century—prepare the way for much slower progress and possibly for completely stationary conditions. Then interest will also fall, and the capitalist will have to be content with quite a small share in the product. (p. 214.)

On this subject Wicksell concludes with an account of the saving-investment process:

Real productive saving therefore always assumes the form of *real capital*. In the normal course of business this process is clearly visible. The commodities which a person foregoes by saving, and by restricting or postponing his consumption . . . he places directly (or by means of money, credit or credit-institutions) at the disposal of an entrepreneur who converts them gradually, as the savings are effected, into more or less fixed capital goods, i.e. real capital. At the close of a boom, paper credit often seems to make up, in part (though actually it does not), for the shortage of real capital—and still more in a period of depression when investment in fixed capital hardly pays, but savings continue, though perhaps at a slower pace. The process of capital accumulation is here not a little enigmatic. It *must* continue in some real form, since there is no other; but in what? Further investigation of this question is highly desirable and would probably throw much light on the field which is still the darkest in the whole province of Economics, namely the theory of the trade cycle (and of crises). (pp. 217–18.)

Here Wicksell is working towards that question of 'What happens to savings during depressions?', on his answer to which the neglected genius Johannsen was to base his theory of crises.

The fate of Wicksell's *Interest and Prices* was, in England and America, not so very different from those of the great pioneer works of marginal analysis in the nineteenth century by Cournot and Gossen. Although he derived to a large extent from English classical sources, Wicksell's work aroused almost no interest among English or American economists for some thirty years until about 1930. Until then Wicksell was a prophet honoured only, or mainly, in his own country and in Germany and Austria, where Spiethoff, Mises, and Schumpeter, and in Italy where M. Fanno, saw something of importance for problems of the trade cycle in his analysis of interest and money, an importance which Wicksell himself did not emphasize. When widespread attention did come to be paid to *Interest and Prices*, such a variety of fertile and fundamental ideas could be found therein, either clearly stated or implicitly suggested, that economists of fundamentally diverging lines of thought could all find inspiration in its pages and claim their own writings to be its true descendents. The Swedish 'dynamic' theorists, the followers of Keynes, and also of Mises, all agreed, surely for rather different reasons, in paying tribute to Wicksell. His 'income' approach to the theory of money, and his concepts of aggregate income and output, pointed on to much of modern macro-economic analysis (anathema to others of Wicksell's admirers). His idea of 'cumulative processes', or his introduction of it into the centre of economic analysis—(the idea itself was fairly common)—suggested the need for a dynamic analysis of processes to replace the normal self-equilibrating dynamics of neo-classical theory. At the same time, there remained in Wicksell's writings a sufficient attachment to stationary or quasi-stationary analysis to encourage those who were aiming at trying to fit major economic fluctuations onto a neo-classical self-equilibrating model, starting from that most ambiguous of assumptions 'a tendency to equilibrium', which would be realized if money were 'neutral'. Few books can have contained such a wealth of fundamental ideas calling for further elucidation and development, and though probably even now there would be no complete or even close agreement as to which were the best of Wicksell's ideas, or the line of development to which they pointed, it is safe to write down *Interest and Prices* as one of the two or three outstanding theoretical works of our period.

3. G. Cassel on the Theory of Price and the Theory of Interest

If it was only at the end of the period with which this book deals that Wicksell's work became at all widely known in Britain and America, the writings of Gustav Cassel, on the other hand, Wicksell's Swedish colleague, or rather rival, had almost all along been available in English, and their author was recognized as an international authority both for his comprehensive treatise on the *Theory of Social Economy*, and for many more or less topical writings on monetary problems after 1914, and on the quantity theory and the purchasing-power parity theory. Since 1930 there has been a considerable reversal in the see-saw of opinion and it has been some of Cassel's works rather than Wicksell's which may have been in danger of undue neglect. To a considerable extent this change is due to faults in Cassel's method of presentation. Rather scathing and dogmatic in his criticism of widely accepted theories, Cassel seemed to be too eager to 'differentiate his own product', and, so it is also alleged, did not sufficiently recognize his indebtedness to other authors, especially to Walras. (In this connexion it should be pointed out that Cassel begins his first important essay by describing it as in part an attempt to present Walras's theories in a tidier and more lucid form.) Nevertheless, though they may not quite be ranked with Wicksell's *Interest and Prices*, Cassel's critical articles on utility theory, his *Nature and Necessity of Interest* (1903), and his contribution to the problem of the trade cycle (in Book IV in his *Theory of Social Economy*, 1918) remain as very important services to the understanding of these subjects.

Like Wicksell, Cassel was over thirty before he devoted himself to economics, and his first important papers presenting the essentials of his system of price theory appeared in 1899 and 1901. We shall briefly examine here these early papers, and also his book on interest. His contributions to the trade cycle will be discussed in a later chapter dealing with that subject. (See Ch. 23, sect. 5.)

Cassel's *Outline of the Theory of Price*[1] has its place in that criticism of the concept of utility which transformed the marginal utility theory of value into the pure logic of choice between scarce means—the transformation of which Fisher and Pareto were the best-known pioneers. But Cassel did not develop or adopt the indifference curve technique. He argued that the marginal utility theory of value was based on the concept of units of utility which no one could define or measure, although marginal utility theorists mostly seemed to assume some sort of measurability, and that this concept and procedure should be entirely dropped and replaced by a theory of price starting from empirically ascertainable demand functions (such as Cournot had started from), which would be obtained by hypothetically questioning consumers in the market. (p. 406.) The explanation of prices was the primary task of the economist and the pseudo-psychological elaboration of the marginal utility theory, insofar as it sought to penetrate behind the facts of market behaviour, contributed nothing of explanatory content.

Cassel added to this main argument a great deal of rather undiscriminating criticism of the marginal utility analysis, to the effect that it rested on invalid assumptions as to the complete divisibility of goods, and of continuity in the utility function. This line of criticism had been followed by other opponents of 'marginalism' and Wicksell, in a rather acrimonious discussion, had no difficulty in answering these supplementary points, but he did not answer Cassel's main contention on the measurability of utility, which, on the whole, seems to have been borne out by the subsequent history of the subject.

Cassel also directs some heavy though imprecise fire on the doctrine of maximum social satisfaction, attacking, in particular, Pareto's earlier formulation in the *Cours* that 'the equations of maximum satisfaction being part of the system determining equilibrium, each party obtains the maximum of opheliminity', under free competition:

The attempt is made with such general formulae to persuade oneself that the conclusion contains something more than the premisses, and finally it suc-

[1] *Grundriss einer elementaren Preislehre, Zeitschrift für die gesamten Staatswissenschaften*, 1899, p. 395.

ceeds in vesting a mathematical formula with an optimal penumbra of a kind unpleasantly similar to the doctrines of the 'harmony' economists, the sole basis for which being, however, that the individual, even in the most unfavourable circumstances, tries to allocate his means to the best advantage. (p. 431.)

All that can be said is that in competitive equilibrium there can be no increase in total satisfaction by voluntary purchases and sales at the existing prices, an extremely thin and even trivial conclusion.

Cassel also directed his criticism against the marginal productivity analysis of distribution. He conceded that this analysis provided a formula for the maximizing problem of the individual entrepreneur purchasing factors of production, but he claimed, not very lucidly, that this only provided 'partial laws', which did not explain the general inter-connexions in the social process of price formation. He claimed that it was necessary for such an analysis to be based, as his was, on the assumption of fixed coefficients throughout (following Walras and Wieser). Cassel's analysis certainly led him to concentrate on the social problems of allocating resources as a whole to the best advantage, and on the social function of the price mechanism. Cassel in his first paper argued, as against Wieser, that a socialist economy could not solve this allocation problem:

'Imputation' in Wieser's sense presupposes as a practical necessity a system of private property, and a fully developed system of exchange. It is the great fundamental defect of the Communist state that *it can never evaluate rightly the different factors of production, and therefore can never be in a position to direct production in the right way.* To overlook this is to fail completely to understand the activity of the business man. The idea that the productive contribution of different factors can be rightly accounted for is a fiction which only takes on a definite meaning through the processes of price formation, for the prices of the factors of production express simply what the market imputes to them. (p. 456.)

These ideas were, of course, to be developed much further by Mises. But Cassel did not take up any extremist position on this subject. He wrote soon after: 'We know that free competition is in many cases impossible, and that the classical assumption of free competition throughout the entire economic society is an illusion. The modern school of social reformers has given economic policy a much broader scope and has taken a great many different social forces into its services.' (*The Nature and Necessity of Interest*, 1903, p. 76.)

Four years after this first paper Cassel published his *Nature and*

Necessity of Interest. He begins with a survey of previous doctrines on the subject much briefer and more understanding than Böhm-Bawerk's. He emphasizes, as contrasted with Böhm-Bawerk, that 'economic investigations in the last two or three centuries have thrown light upon almost every side of the problem; and to construct a theory there hardly remains more than to present, as a consistent and systematic whole, what is already known as a multitude of scattered observations'. (p. v.) His essay is all the more valuable because it is constantly illustrated by realistic examples. His analysis rests on assumptions common to many of the writings of that time, but these assumptions are at any rate explicitly stated. Employment is full, an all-pervading stable self-adjusting mechanism works throughout the system, and all savings generally get invested.[1]

Cassel starts from Walras's distinction between single-use and durable goods, the services of the latter only being obtainable by, or after, 'waiting'. This term 'waiting' had first been employed to replace the much-ridiculed term 'abstinence', by the American economist Macvane (*Quarterly Journal of Economics*, 1887), and was being adopted, of course, by Marshall. Some might consider it to suffer, like 'abstinence', from the same objectionable overtones approbatory of the rentier class, but Cassel rightly insists: 'We are not, so far, concerned with the question whether anything should be paid for this waiting. The only thing here insisted upon is that waiting is necessary, partly on the ground that the consumption of durable goods takes time, and partly on the ground that production takes time.' (p. 88.)

The 'waiting' entailed by the use of capital, 'is a quantity of two dimensions, measured by the product of a certain sum of money multiplied by a certain time' (p. 90), and it must be regarded as a separate factor of production, not produced by more elementary factors, 'a human exertion of quite a separate and particular character'.

The demand for waiting arises from the demand for more durable goods. Cassel argued firmly that increasing population, higher standards of living, and technical progress, would maintain the scarcity

---

[1](a) 'It is also to be understood that the economy of the society in question is so directed that there is no surplus of articles unsold nor of productive services which cannot find employment.' (p. 75.)

(b) 'No price can be altered without the equilibrium being disturbed and forces counteracting the alteration of the price being brought into play. This is, however, obvious enough.' (p. 80.)

(c) 'In modern society however, the person who saves money generally *invests* it.' (p. 132.)

of waiting and prevent the rate of interest falling below 3 or 4 per cent. He recognizes that inventions do occur which diminish the quantity of durable goods required for production (e.g. 'the Marconi system of telegraphy'), but concludes that

the scope for such progress is not, and indeed cannot be very extensive, whereas that for the use of more expensive instruments is limited only by the price to be paid for the waiting required. . . . One may say that there is always—lying in stock as it were—any amount of technical possibilities in the way of substituting the use of capital for other factors of production. Every fall in the rate of interest will result in the setting free of a part of these possibilities and the conversion of them into actualities; and thereby a further fall will be prevented. (p. 123.)

Turning to the causes governing the supply of waiting, Cassel first mentions the capacity for saving, that is the level of income, as governing the supply, and quotes J. S. Mill to that effect. He then turns to one of the most original arguments in the book explaining why the rate of interest cannot (in a free market economy) fall below a certain critical level of about 2 to 3 per cent. Above this critical level Cassel agrees that there are no very strong grounds for supposing that reductions in the rate of interest will result in a fall in saving. He points out that much saving done by those with huge incomes is for no other reasons than power, prestige, and accumulation for its own sake, and that a fall in the rate of interest will hardly affect these big sources of 'waiting'.

Cassel takes the case of 'the great class of accumulators who aim at acquiring a capital large enough to enable them to live on the interest'. For this class

there must be some reasonable proportion between sacrifice and end, between the annual savings and the future income they are intended to assure. . . . We may conclude therefore that most people are not prepared to save annually a larger sum than that which they intend to provide for themselves as future annual income (pp. 145–6). . . . Let us suppose, then, that a person has decided to provide for himself a future income of £1,000 but that he is not prepared, under any circumstances, to set aside more than this same sum of £1,000 a year. If the rate of interest is 6%, he may easily attain his end by accumulating a capital which affords the desired income. Such a capital need not be more than $16\frac{2}{3}$ times as large as his annual savings. But if the rate falls the task will be more and more difficult. At 3% he must accumulate $33\frac{1}{3}$ times as much as his annual savings; at $1\frac{1}{2}$ per cent, $66\frac{2}{3}$ times as much. We now see where the difficulty arises. The *shortness of the active period of human life* must, sooner or later, if the rate of interest is supposed steadily to fall, absolutely prohibit any attempt to accumulate capital sufficient to yield an income equal to the sum annually saved or even anything like it. . . . With a rate of interest of something like 1½%, all forces would combine in weakening considerably the desire of accumulation in the very classes which now contribute the largest part of the total supply of waiting. . . . If the rate went down to 2% it would be possible to draw double the income in the form of an annuity for 35 years, which period would cover the remainder of life for most adults. . . . There is, in fact, an intimate connection between the average length of human life and the rate of interest. (pp. 145–52.)

Cassel's analysis relates, of course, to the income distribution and institutional background of 1903, but it retains some relevance and importance for the problem of the supply of voluntary savings in Western countries in subsequent decades.

16

J. B. Clark and Thorstein Veblen

1. *Introductory: Political Economy in America*

IN the closing decade of the nineteenth century two theoretical works of first-rate importance were published in the United States: J. B. Clark's *Distribution of Wealth* (1899) and Irving Fisher's *Mathematical Investigations in the Theory of Value and Price* (1892). In diametric contrast with Clark's book were the writings of his one-time pupil Thorstein Veblen, which began to appear during the nineties. Fisher, on the other hand, in his works on money, interest, and income was to a considerable extent building on the ideas of Simon Newcomb, as presented in Book IV, *On the Societary Circulation*, in Newcomb's *Principles of Political Economy*. These are the four American economists—Clark, Veblen, Newcomb, and Fisher—whose works we shall be discussing in this chapter and the next. A number of other books of not quite the same key importance, from before or after the turn of the century, can only be mentioned in passing: for example, those of Walker, Taussig (*Wages and Capital*, 1896), Patten, Carver (*Distribution of Wealth*, 1904), Davenport (*Value and Distribution*, 1908), Fetter, and H. L. Moore. Some of the contributions of these writers on special subjects will be discussed in Parts II and III, as will Wesley Mitchell's work on *Business Cycles*, F. H. Knight's on *Risk, Uncertainty and Profit*, and the much less well-known doctrines of effective demand and under-consumption of F. B. Hawley and U. H. Crocker.

The earlier history of political economy in the United States has been given considerable attention by American economists, and it was the subject, also, of an interesting essay by Cliffe Leslie (1880).[1] Beyond a tendency to take over 'ready-made' the systems of J. S. Mill and Bastiat, Leslie noted four special characteristics of American political economy in his day: a thorough-going rejection of Malthusian

---

[1] See the two essays of E. R. A. Seligman: 'Economics in the United States' in *Essays in Economics*, p. 122, and 'The Early Teaching of Economics in the United States', in *Economic Essays in Honor of J. B. Clark* (edited by J. H. Hollander, p. 283); also J. Schumpeter, '*Die neuere Wirtschaftstheorie in den Vereinigten Staaten*', Schmoller's *Jahrbuch*, 1910; Wesley Mitchell, *Lectures on Types of Economic Theory*, vol. ii; J. Dorfman, *The Economic Mind in American Civilization*; A. G. Gruchy, *Modern Economic Thought, the American Contribution* (on the 'Institutionalists').

doctrines, a close association between the teaching of political economy and of theology, a distaste for the severely deductive pursuit of the subject, and a wide acceptance of Protectionism in orthodox teaching. These earlier peculiarities do not retain much significance in our period. For our purposes we may take the American contribution to modern economics as dating from the early 1880's, when the writings of F. A. Walker ('the American Hermann'),[1] particularly his attack on the Wages-Fund theory and his analysis of profit, were helping to clear the ground for much that was to come; when Henry George's peculiar development of Ricardian doctrine was adding to the general ferment on the subject of distribution, which existed in the interim between the abandonment of classical doctrines and the rise of marginal productivity analysis; when, also, a number of American economists, having returned from studies in Germany (e.g. J. B. Clark, Ely, Hadley, Taussig, and Seligman), were raising the pursuit of the subject on to a higher level in their own country; and when, finally, the American Economic Association was founded in 1885. As was mainly the case in England at the same period, it was the subject of distribution that was the main centre of interest in the eighties and nineties.

Partly stimulated by German ideas, and partly independently, there was then in America a widespread but rather vaguely formulated re-action against the narrow versions of economic theory and policy associated with 'orthodox' classical political economy, a reaction parti-cularly apparent in J. B. Clark's *Philosophy of Wealth* (1885). The influence of the German *Verein für Sozialpolitik* is very clear in the statement of principles of the new American Economic Association, for example in such propositions as these:

1. We regard the State as an agency whose positive assistance is one of the indispensable conditions of human progress.
2. We believe that political economy as a science is still in an early stage of development, while we appreciate the work of former economists, we look not so much to speculation as to the historical and statistical study of actual conditions of economic life for the satisfactory ac-complishment of that development.

In fact there can have been little, if any, substantial and lasting unity

---

[1] General Francis Amasa Walker (1840–97), son of the economist Amasa Walker, and author, notably, of *The Wages Question* (1876), which contained an important attack on the Wages-Fund doctrine, and an analysis of the role of the entrepreneur. As super-intendent of the censuses of 1870 and 1880 Walker had an important part in building up United States official statistics. For his contributions to the theories of profit and of economic crises see Chs. 20 and 22 below.

on such principles. In the new century there was to break out another
major version, in American contexts, of the perennial conflict between
a comparatively compact 'orthodox' body of doctrine, mainly deductive in method and liberalist in policy, and, on the other hand, a
critical 'revolt', historically, sociologically, and socialistically inclined.
Of the former of these approaches, J. B. Clark's work is undoubtedly
the leading example. After the earlier criticisms of Ely and Patten it
was Veblen who became the outstanding leader of the other side, the
'rebels', seconded by J. R. Commons who concentrated particularly
on labour problems and the legal framework of the economic order.

2. *J. B. Clark: From the Philosophy of Wealth to the Distribution of Wealth*

The Philosophy of Wealth: There can be few, if any, parallels to the
degree of fundamental contrast between J. B. Clark's first book the
Philosophy of Wealth (1885), published at the age of 38, and his outstanding work of fourteen years later the *Distribution of Wealth*. The
Philosophy of Wealth consists of a series of rather loosely connected
essays expressive of an economic philosophy in which are apparent
the influences of New England moral earnestness, Ruskin's teachings,
and the ideas of the German historical economists, in particular Knies,
under whom Clark had studied at Heidelberg. The *Philosophy of
Wealth* has in it the strain of Ruskinian protest evident in J. A.
Hobson's writings and to some extent in those of Wicksteed, its main
critical theme being an attack on what is described as 'Ricardianism'.

In the first place, Clark argued, 'the traditional system was obviously
defective in its premises'. In starting from the concept of the economic
man this system was based on a fundamental falsification: 'The better
elements of human nature were a forgotten factor in certain economic
calculations. . . . A degraded conception of human nature vitiated the
theory of the distribution of wealth.' (Preface.) And these errors were
not merely superficial: 'Inaccuracies in the science which result from
inadequate conceptions of man are not to be rectified, as has been
asserted, by a proper allowance for "disturbing forces".' (p. 33.)

This insistence that economic theorizing must start from 'a correct
conception of human nature', or from 'correct psychological premisses', was to become a theme, lengthily debated by subsequent
American economists, both theoretical and institutional, who sought,
somewhat vaguely, to call in the new conclusions of psychology to

redress the balance, or to fill the void, resulting from the discredit into which the economic man, on the one hand, and hedonism on the other, had fallen.

According to Clark, the second false assumption of 'Ricardian' theory was that of competition, and it is his remarks on this subject in the *Philosophy of Wealth* that are in sharpest contrast with his later doctrines:

> Competition is no longer adequate to account for the phenomena of social industry. . . . Competition of the individualistic type is rapidly passing out of existence (p. 147). . . . Individual competition the great regulator of the former era, has, in important fields, practically disappeared. It ought to disappear; it was in its latter days, incapable of working justice. The alternative regulator is moral force, and this is already in action (p. 148). . . . The present state of industrial society is transitional and chaotic.

It is especially in the labour market that competition has been superseded. Here Clark is almost Marxian in his analysis if not his conclusions:

> The solidarity of labour on the one hand, and of capital on the other, is the great economic fact of the present day; and this growing solidarity is carrying us rapidly towards a condition in which all the labourers in a particular trade, and all the capitalists in that trade, acting, in each case, as one man, will engage in a blind struggle which, without arbitration, can only be decided by the crudest force and endurance. . . . It is Ricardianism, the competitive system duly 'let alone', the natural action of self-interest in men, that has brought us face to face with this condition. (p. 68.)

Ricardianism 'prepares the soil for revolutionary seed'.

Clark's hopes for improvement rested on arbitration, profit-sharing, and co-operation (of producers rather than consumers). Though sympathetic with Christian socialism Clark believes that 'it can come no sooner, stay no longer, and can rise, in quality, no higher than intelligence and virtue among the people'. (p. 199.) Of socialism he concludes: 'Men will not want it in the millennium, and they cannot have it earlier.'

So far the contrast with Clark's later and better-known doctrines in the *Distribution of Wealth* could hardly be greater. But the optimistic starting-point of the later work, that is, that morally sound laws of distribution are active and discernible in an individualist society, can also be traced in the *Philosophy of Wealth*. Economic laws can be emptied of what is called 'golden-calf worship', and 'if it is humanly possible to thus settle the questions at the basis of the law of wages, no scientific work can be more immediately and widely beneficent'. (p. 109.) Clark asserts, moreover, that fixed laws of distribution do hold, 'which society is not at liberty to violate'. But these are hardly the beginnings of a marginal productivity doctrine, nor does Clark explain the relation between the 'fixed laws' on the one hand, and the need for the reform of competitive capitalism, on the other.

It has been claimed for Clark, on the basis of his essay on the theory of value in the *Philosophy of Wealth*, that, with his concept of 'effective specific utility', he was an independent discoverer of the marginal utility theory of value, but his analysis is not comparable in detail and precision with that of Jevons, Menger, and Walras (whose work he did not know when he wrote his own essay in about 1880).

The Distribution of Wealth: Clark's massive work the *Distribution of Wealth* was built up out of a number of earlier articles containing his analysis of capital (*Capital and its Earnings*, Publications of the American Economic Association, 1888), his marginal productivity theory (*The Possibility of a Scientific Law of Wages*, ibid., 1889), and his generalization of the Ricardian rent analysis ('Distribution as Determined by a Law of Rent', *Quarterly Journal of Economics*, vol. v, 1890-1).

The central doctrine of the book, partly ethical and partly methodological, is set out at the start and kept constantly at hand throughout the subsequent positive analysis with which it is combined. Clark saw his achievement as that of justifying the distribution of income under 'static' conditions as being in accordance with the rights of property 'ordinarily regarded', since under such conditions each man gets what he produces. Clark does not try to justify property rights, but only the 'natural' laws of distribution as being in accordance with them as ordinarily understood. The initial distribution of property is not included in the problem. Clark regarded as hinging on this thesis (that under static conditions each man gets what he produces) no less than 'the right of society to exist in its present form, and the probability that it will continue so to exist'. (p. 3.)

If this thesis is proved then 'Property is protected at the point of its origin, if actual wages are the whole product of labor, if interest is the product of capital, and if profit is the product of a coordinating act'. If this thesis is disproved then the existing social order must be based on 'institutional robbery—a legally established violation of the principle on which property is supposed to rest'. (p. 9.) Clark seems certainly to misplace somewhat the centre of gravity of socialist criticism of the existing order by not taking account of the existing initial distribution of property.

In expounding the methodological procedure by which he sets out to establish his thesis, Clark, in contrast with his views in the *Philosophy of Wealth*, now criticizes Ricardo not for an excess, but for a deficiency of abstraction. Ricardo only 'unconsciously and imperfectly' separated static from dynamic forces. This separation must now be made completely clear-cut. The 'natural' or 'normal' laws of the static state can then be discovered, and these laws, though not holding precisely at all times in the real world, do reveal the more important forces at work in it. Natural, normal, or static values 'are the values about which rates are forever fluctuating in the shops of commercial cities. You will also have a régime of natural wages and interest; and these are the standards about which the rates of pay for labour and capital are always hovering in actual mills, fields, mines, etc.' (p. 29.) Although the static state requires a 'heroic' application of the isolating method, nevertheless: 'All the forces that would work in the unchanging world are not only working in the changeful one, but are even the dominant forces in it.' (p. 30.) . . . 'They are the more powerful of the two sets of forces that there operate.'

The static laws abstract from (or 'sweep remorselessly from the field') the five main types of dynamic change, four of which are that population, capital, technology, and consumers' wants are increasing or improving, and the fifth is that 'the forms of industrial establishment are changing: the less efficient shops, etc. are passing from the field, and the more efficient are surviving'. This fifth type of dynamic change, with its optimistic assumption that in some significant sense the fittest always survive the economic struggle, is different in kind from his other four types of 'dynamic' change, but is typical of Clark's later 'social Darwinist' economic philosophy.

Economic statics are an exercise in deduction based primarily on the postulate of the well-informed maximizing individual (a postulate not searchingly examined by Clark). Economic dynamics will be more historical and inductive. It

will, in its entirety, incorporate into itself historical economics. The changes that are going on in the world will in future be studied inductively, as well as deductively; and it is the inductive part of the work that falls to the historical economist. In the long run, it is this part that will need to absorb the most scientific labor. The static laws of economics ought consequently to be known at an early date. Dynamic laws will not be known so early; but whenever they shall be scientifically established, there will remain to be done the work of measuring the effects of particular influences that act on society. *How great*, for example, is the effect of a mechanical invention or of the settlement of a new country on the rate of wages? Such a question, if it can be answered at all, will demand a far more difficult kind of research than does the question whether migrations and inventions naturally raise wages or lower them. (p. 74.)

This passage is very reminiscent of Marshall's dictum that the nineteenth century had built up a 'qualitative' analysis, but that 'quantitative' analysis stood over for the twentieth century. But whether or not Marshall's 'stationary state' analysis helps towards more realistic conclusions than Clark's apparently more rigidly abstract 'static' analysis, Marshall would probably not have held so definitively, that in completing the qualitative 'static' analysis 'the dominant forces' in the real world had been accounted for.

Two other characteristics of the static state and its natural laws may be noted: it appears to be a state (1) of full employment, and (2) of maximum satisfaction for society:

(1) Labor, as a whole, always has under normal conditions, an outlook for employment where its product will set the standard of its pay. An industrial society can, in some way, absorb any amount of labor. If capital is freely transferable in form, labor becomes freely transferable and able to count on an indefinitely elastic field of employment. (p. 115.)
(2) Competition is the activity that causes prices to be, in the customary sense of the term, natural. . . . One effect of it is, however, to insure to the public the utmost that the existing power of man can give in the way of efficient service. (p. 77.)

We have examined Clark's static analysis at some length because it is the most deliberate, lucid, and rigorous statement in its time of common static assumptions in any literary exposition of the theory of distribution. This analysis is combined with the most forthright and outspoken attempt to read some vitally significant content into the marginal productivity theory comparable with the older interpretation (or misinterpretation) of the classical 'iron' laws of distribution.

From Clark's extremely exhaustive treatment of marginal productivity analysis we shall simply extract a few leading points:

1. The law of diminishing returns becomes a generalized universal law applicable not simply in agriculture but in any case where successive units of a variable factor are applied to a fixed quantity of another factor. (pp. 49–50.)

2. The Ricardian rent doctrine is correspondingly generalized, with doses and patient reversed, a point common to much of the distribution analysis of the nineties (e.g. in Hobson and Wicksteed). (pp. 191–2.)

3. The proportions in which factors are combined are taken as variable, and 'capital' (as contrasted with particular capital goods) is perfectly fluid and adaptable to the conditions of labour supply. (pp. 159–60.)

4. The wage given by marginal productivity does not involve any exploitation of the 'intra-marginal' workers as had seemed to be suggested in Thünen's analysis. As successive workers are employed with a fixed total quantity of equipment, the average equipment that each works with declines. The apparently higher productivity of the 'intra-marginal' workers is due not to the workers themselves, who are assumed to be homogeneous, but to the larger amount of equipment per head that the 'intra-marginal' workers would be working with. (pp. 319–33.)

5. Static assumptions imply the elimination of profit (as in Walrasian equilibrium) and the division of the whole product between factors in accordance with the marginal productivity law, entrepreneurs being paid according to the marginal productivity of their purely supervisory services. 'Profit' emerges simply from the frictions of dynamic change as a dynamic surplus, which attracts new entrepreneurs into activity from the ranks of the passive capitalists, so that profit is forced down again to the 'normal' zero level. As Professor Knight was to show, it was not change as such, but incalculable uncertainty that should be recognized as the source of profit in this sense.

In addition to its main contribution to the subject of marginal productivity analysis Clark's *Distribution of Wealth* contains his account of capital and capital goods, the main rival on this subject to the contemporary theory of Böhm-Bawerk. Clark starts from a distinction between 'pure' capital, and 'actual capital goods' (which are conceived by Clark to include all production goods but not durable consumption goods and not services). Pure capital is the permanent fund of wealth, represented by the actual transitory impermanent capital goods (including land in all its forms) in existence at any moment: 'The point of sharpest contrast between capital and most capital goods is indeed the permanence of the one, as compared with the perishability of the other. . . . Again, capital is perfectly mobile; but capital goods are far from being so.' (p. 118.) Capital *goods* are fixed in form and wear out, *capital* is permanent and can always be renewed in new forms: 'We may think of capital as a sum of productive wealth, invested in material things which are perpetually shifting,—which come and go continually,—although the fund abides.' (p. 119.) Capital as a sum of productive wealth is permanent because the capital goods (*sc.* if 'cleverly chosen') provide for their own maintenance and renewal, without further 'abstinence'. Clark often seems to abstract from the possibility that the owners of capital goods may choose to consume the sinking funds they yield, instead of using them for maintenance and replacement, and that the capital fund might thus be depleted and 'impermanent'. Clark makes some concessions to Böhm-Bawerk's concept of the 'period of production', but it is an advantage of his own treatment that this concept is not at all essential to it.[1]

Whatever the virtues may be, for some purposes, of Clark's definitions and analysis of capital, he does not explain them with sufficient precision and concreteness, and there are some grounds for Böhm-Bawerk's reference to Clark's 'mythology of capital'. The lengthy controversy about 'capital' between Clark and Böhm-Bawerk was to a considerable extent repeated a quarter of a century later by Professors Knight and Hayek. It is not easy to extricate from this controversy any issues other than terminological or conceptual differences. Nor is it easy to judge of the significance of the differences over terminological and conceptual 'tools' when there is little attempt to indicate the particular concrete problems in the solution of which these 'tools' are being designed to assist.

In his *Distribution of Wealth*, Clark had announced a later volume on *Economic Dynamics or the Laws of Industrial Progress*. This plan was partially fulfilled in his *Essentials of Economic Theory* (1907). The book in its later chapters makes some examination of those five forms of dynamic change present in the actual economic world. But it illustrates the immensity of the difficulty facing economists in the first

---

[1] In his essay on 'Clark's Reformulation of the Capital Concept' (in *Economic Essays in Honor of J. B. Clark*, edited by J. H. Hollander), Fetter has traced the sources of Clark's capital concept partly to the much earlier American writers who in the vast new continent were naturally not impressed with the distinction between 'land' and 'capital' based on the ultimately fixed and limited quantity of the former, so obvious in insular Britain. But a more direct source of Clark's ideas was his teacher at Heidelberg, Karl Knies, and before him Hermann, who did not mark off land from capital in his distribution analysis.

Fetter also points out that Clark's monograph on *Capital and its Earnings* (1888) though it 'wears the mien of pure theory', bears 'on almost every page reflections of the contemporary single-tax discussion'. In fact, just as Fabian socialists used the generalizing of the rent concept, so commonly argued in the nineties, to generalize Henry George's (and many liberal economists') attacks on property in land, so J. B. Clark was using the rent generalization to defend 'the capital that vests itself in land' against discriminatory confiscation.

quarter of the new century (and frequently referred to by them), of getting significantly beyond purely or mainly static or 'stationary' analysis and conclusions. Clark held that the main 'dynamic' changes, though calling for immense detailed studies, did not in fact bring the world, or at any rate the modern Western world, far away from its static norm: 'Taking on the theoretically static form would not strikingly alter its actual shape. The actual form of a highly dynamic society hovers relatively near to its static mode though it never conforms to it.' (p. 195.) 'Normality' rules the world. Dynamic changes tend to neutralize one another around the static equilibrium norm. The modern American industrial society (1907) conformed 'more closely to a normal form than do the more conservative societies of Europe and far more closely than do the sluggish societies of Asia'. (p. 197.) Static standards apply, apparently, to what Clark called 'the economic center' (i.e. western Europe, North America, Japan, and 'the more fully settled parts of Australia'): 'Apply the test of the static state to the economic center, and it will give a generally true result; but it will give a false one if it be applied to the world as a whole. The merely static adjustment of the world would take more centuries than we care to reckon.' Perhaps these statements indicate something of the differences between the economic world of 1950 and that of 1900.

In his discussion of dynamic influences Clark finds no place for the trade cycle or aggregate fluctuations.[1] The one great practical problem of the actual dynamic world which prevents the emergence of static harmony is that of monopoly. In his preface to the *Essentials* (p. viii) Clark holds that 'the actual tendencies of the economic system are against it'. Nevertheless:

There is in many quarters an impression that monopoly will dominate the economic life of the twentieth century as competition has dominated that of the nineteenth. If the impression is true, farewell to the progress which in the past century has been so rapid and inspiring. . . . No description could exaggerate the evil which is in store for a society given hopelessly over to a régime of private monopoly. Under this comprehensive name we shall group the most important of the agencies which not merely resist, but positively vitiate, the action of natural economic law. (p. 375.)

[1] Clark did, however, show some interest in the ideas of Johannsen, and reviewed his *Neglected Point in Connection with Crises*, in the *Bankers Magazine*, 1909, p. 256. He also wrote an introduction to a translation of Rodbertus's called *Overproduction and Crises*, where he adheres to the Smithian conception of saving and investment, referring to 'the unquestionable fact that saving is in reality demanding and getting productive instruments as a part of an income'. (p. 15.)

There is certainly a very large field for State action in fighting monopoly, though Clark does not set out to define its frontiers in detail: 'Great indeed is the contrast between the present condition and one in which the government had little to do but let industry alone. . . . If we should try to do nothing and persist too long in the attempt, we might find ourselves in the end forced to do everything.' (p. 384.) If the choice is between governmental production and private production under a monopoly, 'we are at liberty to select the latter only if potential competition shall be made to be a satisfactory regulator of the action of the great corporation'. (p. 383.) The State, for example, 'may own coal mines and either operate them or control the mode of operating them, for the purpose of curbing the exactions of monopolistic owners and securing a continuous supply of fuel. . . . The selling of coal by the state may help to keep independent manufacturing alive, and carrying by the State may do so in a more marked way.' (p. 386.) However, Clark was opposed to State *ownership* if State *regulation* was possible, but he did not in the *Essentials* go at length into the immense practical difficulties of regulating monopoly.[1]

In conclusion we may inquire, or speculate, as to how it was that Clark came in his *Distribution of Wealth* to build a great system of thought on a procedure and assumptions so similar to those which he had so strongly attacked in his first book: that is, a deductive system based on the assumptions of the enlightened maximizing individual acting in generally competitive conditions. Perhaps he believed that the mere disclaimer of all materialist or hedonist assumptions was sufficient to protect the system of thought he was helping to build up against the attacks that he himself had earlier launched against 'Ricardianism'. But it does seem that at least part of the explanation must lie in that fatal attractiveness, when first elaborated, of a rather elegant and comprehensive deductive structure, like the general static marginal productivity analysis of distribution, in the building of which, in the nineties, Clark became a leader. One cannot help being reminded of Gossen, forty years before, comparing the discovery of marginal utility analysis with the work of Copernicus, and believing that a new moral and social science, leading on to a new and higher order of human society, would arise on the basis of 'marginal utility'. For along with a certain intellectual attractiveness which they found in marginal utility and marginal productivity analysis respectively, Gossen and

---

[1] His book *The Problem of Monopoly*, 1904, a reprint of six lectures, is comprehensive but not very detailed or penetrating in its recommendations.

Clark both tended to read into their deductive structures a much greater and more realistic content than their basic postulates, on examination, will justify.

3. *Thorstein Veblen*

Thorstein Veblen had been a pupil of J. B. Clark at Carleton College, Minnesota, at the end of the seventies, and some of his critical ideas may well have been stimulated by the earlier teachings of Clark as represented in the *Philosophy of Wealth*. But no wider contrast can be imagined than that between the system of thought of Clark's *Distribution of Wealth*, and the critical ideas of Veblen. These two are a pair as nicely representative of two extreme poles, or 'ideal types', of economic thinking as can be found in the history of the subject, much more widely and diametrically opposed or apart than Malthus and Ricardo, or perhaps even than Schmoller and Menger. It is impossible to do justice to so peculiarly original and encyclopaedic a writer as Veblen in the second half of a chapter. But Veblen and Clark (though they never engaged in any lengthy controversy), belong together, and as representative extremes almost depend upon one another, and perhaps, therefore, historically deserve to be enclosed together in the same chapter. Happily, and to the great credit of both (and perticularly, perhaps, to that of Clark), they retained to the end the highest respect for one another and a genuine friendship, while J. B. Clark's son, J. M. Clark, showed how the contrasting influences of his father and Veblen could be fruitfully combined. We shall here attempt to mention only Veblen's critical essays on the methods and 'preconceptions' of orthodox economics, and to outline one or two of his main socio-economic ideas as portrayed in the *Theory of Business Enterprise* (1904), probably his most important economic work, which contains his contribution, notable in its day, to the subject of business cycles, to be discussed in a later chapter (23).

After leaving Carleton College, Veblen took his doctorate at Yale (1884) with a dissertation on Kant. Then he spent seven years at home without an academic post, in which time, doubtless, his inclinations for the role of the detached satirical observer were strengthened and developed. Veblen's manner is all his own, marked especially by an air of quizzically detached 'scientific' neutrality, hardly concealing, in fact rather heightening, the effect of the blistering criticisms he is intending. An ingenious phrase-maker he sometimes seems to be the victim of his own peculiar phraseology. Above all, as Wesley Mitchell has said, Veblen was 'a born tease', and often, so it appears, a highly successful one.[1]

The title of one of his lengthiest essays is *The Preconceptions of Economic Science* (1898) and it is at 'preconceptions' that Veblen is trying to get, throughout his criticism of economic theories. This three-part essay is in some ways comparable with Bagehot's essay of twenty years previously on the postulates of classical political economy; except that the 'preconceptions' that Veblen is seeking to expose and examine are something deeper and vaguer than the postulates questioned by Bagehot.

Going back to the classical economists Veblen emphasizes the influence in their theories of what he calls 'natural law' teleology, and he argues that traces still survive to flavour the neo-classical marginal theories (in particular J. B. Clark's theory of distribution which Veblen takes as the most explicit species of a large genus):

The ultimate laws and principles which they [the classical economists and their interpreters] formulated were laws of the normal or the natural, according to a preconception regarding the ends to which, in the nature of things, all things tend. In effect, this preconception imputes to things a tendency to work out what the instructed common sense of the time accepts as the adequate or worthy end of human effort. (*The Place of Science in Modern Civilisation*, p. 65.)

. . . With later writers especially, this terminology is no doubt to be commonly taken as a convenient use of metaphor, in which the concept of normality and propensity to an end has reached an extreme attenuation. But it is precisely in this use of figurative terms for the formulation of theory that the classical normality still lives its attenuated life in modern economics. (p. 66.)

. . . With this normalised scheme as a guide, the permutations of a given segment of the apparatus are worked out according to the values assigned the several items and features comprised in the calculation; and a ceremonially consistent formula is constructed to cover that much of the industrial field. This is the deductive method. . . . The outcome of the method, at

---

[1] Here is Veblen commenting on 'normal' equilibrium economics: 'If we are getting restless under the taxonomy of a monocotyledonous wage doctrine and a cryptogamic theory of interest, with involute, loculicidal, tomentous and moniliform variants, what is the cytoplasm, centrosome, or karyokinetic process to which we may turn, and in which we may find surcease from the metaphysics of normality and controlling principles? What are we going to do about it? The question is rather, What are we doing about it?' *The Place of Science in Modern Civilisation*, p. 70 (reprinted from the *Quarterly Journal of Economics*, vol. xii, July 1898). Presumably this is intended as a parody of a kind of academic 'Cherokee' (to use Keynes's term), but it is not easy to say with certainty, for it is a parody of which Veblen's own prose is often suggestive.

its best, is a body of logically consistent propositions concerning the normal relations of things—a system of economic taxonomy. (p. 67.)

Veblen attacks marginal utility analysis for adopting a conception of man as an automatic maximizer of pleasure, with given tastes. It is quite true that, even at the time Veblen was writing (1898), the hedonist content was being emptied out of economic theory, so that from a later point of view the accusation of hedonism does not find the centre of the target. But Veblen could very well have asked what remained when the hedonist content was removed from the theories he was examining, beyond a 'taxonomic' maximizing calculus of automatic activities in a model 'world' from which all uncertainty was removed.

Veblen charged neo-classical theory, and in particular J. B. Clark's version of it, with being incapable of explaining processes of growth and change, and cumulative sequences. Nor did Marshall's treatment of economic growth satisfy him: 'Any sympathetic reader of Professor Marshall's great work . . . comes away with a sense of swift and smooth movement and interaction of parts; but it is the movement of a consummately conceived and self-balanced mechanism, not that of a cumulatively unfolding process or an institutional adaptation to cumulatively unfolding exigencies.' (p. 173.)

His criticism of the assumption of given individual tastes, and his analysis of 'snob' values and conspicuous consumption in his *Theory of the Leisure Class* (1898) is one of his best-known and most typical achievements. More broadly, he objected to the whole scheme of assumedly self-equilibrating dynamics:

The growth of culture is a cumulative sequence of habituation, and the ways and means of it are the habitual response of human nature to exigencies that vary incontinently, cumulatively, but with something of a consistent sequence in the cumulative variations that go forward; incontinently, because each new move creates a new situation which induces a further new variation in the habitual manner of response; cumulatively, because each new situation is a variation of what has gone before it and embodies as causal factors all that has been effected by what went before; consistently, because the underlying traits of human nature (propensities, aptitudes, and what not) . . . remain substantially unchanged. (*The Place of Science in Modern Civilisation*, p. 242.)

'Propensities, aptitudes, and what not'—it is not unfair to pick on this looseness of expression—these are the socio-economic *institutions* which Veblen considered it his task to discover and account for. He defined institutions as 'widespread social habits' or 'widely prevalent habits of thought', and he considered that these rather indefinite entities were more important and interesting objects of study, than rationalist calculi. He summarized his intellectual tastes as follows:

To any modern scientist interested in economic phenomena, the chain of cause and effect in which any given phase of human culture is involved, as well as the cumulative changes wrought in the fabric of human conduct itself by the habitual activity of mankind, are matters of more engrossing and more abiding interest than the method of inference by which an individual is presumed invariably to balance pleasure and pain under given conditions that are presumed to be normal and invariable. (p. 240.)

Veblen's most solid statement of his more narrowly economic ideas is in his early book the *Theory of Business Enterprise* (1904). The book opens with the distinction between 'the machine process' (making goods), and 'business enterprise' (making money). These are the two supreme and characteristic institutions of the economic organization of modern society, and 'to a greater extent than any other phase of culture, modern Christendom takes its complexion from its economic organisation'. A very large part of Veblen's socio-economic theories derives from this distinction between the machine process and business enterprise, and from his analysis of the tensions between the two. Business enterprise controls the productive process ('industry is carried on for the sake of business, and not conversely') and business enterprise of necessity aims at monopolistic practices restrictive of machine production. Veblen had inevitably been much impressed by the large movement towards trustification in the last two or three years of the nineteenth century, and the revelations of the U.S. Industrial Commission shortly after.

Veblen's theory of crises and chronic depression, and his technocratic theories of an industrial system controlled by engineers, also start from this same distinction between the machine process and business enterprise, which has a great deal of work to do in Veblen's writings. His analysis is at these points very close to the Marxian picture of the concentration of capitalist industry, and chronic capitalist crisis, springing from the tension between the technique of production (making goods) and the social order (making money). In later works he seems to have laid still more emphasis on the separation of technological knowledge from the financial ownership and control of industry.

One of Veblen's first essays was on the *Theory of Socialism* (1892) and in that essay and in the closing chapters of the *Theory of Business*

Enterprise he gives a remarkably prescient analysis of the forces dis-
rupting the system of competitive individualism and making for some
form of socialism. He agrees 'that the system of industrial competition,
based on private property, has brought about, or has at least co-existed
with, the most rapid advance in average wealth and industrial efficiency
that the world has ever seen'. (*The Place of Science in Modern Civilisation*, p. 391.) It is palpable nonsense now to say that this system makes
the poor *absolutely* poorer: 'But it does tend to make them relatively
poorer, in their own eyes, as measured in terms of comparative economic importance, and, curious as it may seem at first sight, that is what
seems to count. It is not the abjectly poor that are oftenest heard pro-
testing.' The system of competitive individualist industrialism has
produced a spirit of 'economic emulation' that no other system has
ever known and—as Schumpeter was later to predict on somewhat
similar grounds—it will be destroyed by its own offspring:

> By increasing the freedom of movement of the individual and widening
> the environment to which the individual is exposed—increasing the number
> of persons before whose eyes each one carries on his life, and, *pari passu*,
> decreasing the chances which such persons have of awarding their esteem
> on any other basis than that of immediate appearances, it has increased the
> relative efficiency of the economic means of winning respect through a show
> of expenditure for personal comforts. . . . Inasmuch as the aim of emula-
> tion is not any absolute degree of comfort or of excellence, no advance in
> the average well-being of the community can end the struggle or lessen
> the strain. A general amelioration cannot quiet the unrest whose source is the
> craving of everybody to compare favorably with his neighbor. . . . The
> inference seems to be that, human nature being what it is, there can be no
> peace from this—it must be admitted—ignoble form of emulation, or from
> the discontent that goes with it, this side of the abolition of private property.
> Whether a larger measure of peace is in store for us after that event shall
> have come to pass, is of course not a matter to be counted on, nor is the
> question immediately to the point. (pp. 396–8.)

Veblen criticized the Marxian prophecy of the inevitable advent of
socialism, and he tried to set out the main alternative possibilities:

> It may be that the working classes will go forward along the line of the
> socialistic ideals and enforce a *new deal*, in which there shall be no economic
> class discrepancies, no international animosity, no dynastic politics. But then
> it may also, so far as can be foreseen, equally well happen that the working
> class, with the rest of the community in Germany, England, or America, will
> be led by the habit of loyalty and by their sportsmanlike propensities to lend
> themselves enthusiastically to the game of dynastic politics, which alone

their sportsmanlike rulers consider worth while. It is quite impossible . . . to foretell whether the 'proletariat' will go on to establish the socialistic revolution or turn aside again and sink their force in the broad sands of patriotism (p. 442, italics supplied).

Equally remarkable, as coming out of America at the beginning of this century, is Veblen's vision of the possibility of a new form of reactionary régime (*Theory of Business Enterprise*, p. 373):

In the nature of the case the cultural growth dominated by the machine industry is of a sceptical, matter-of-fact complexion, materialistic, unmoral, unpatriotic, undevout. . . . The spread of materialistic, matter-of-fact preconceptions takes place at a cumulatively accelerating rate, except insofar as some other cultural factor, alien to the machine discipline, comes in to inhibit its spread and keep its disintegrating influence within bounds.

Therefore a régime to establish and maintain its hold, whether it is one dominated by business interests (or any other) might seek it in

a militant, coercive home administration and something in the way of an imperial court life—a dynastic fountain of honor and a courtly bureau of ceremonial amenities. Such an ideal is not simply a moralist's day-dream; it is a sound business proposition, in that it lies on the line of policy along which the business interests are moving in their own behalf. If national (that is to say dynastic) ambitions and warlike aims, achievements, spectacles, and discipline be given a larger place in the community's life, together with the concomitant coercive police surveillance, then there is a fair hope that the disintegrating trend of the machine discipline may be corrected. (p. 399.)

Veblen's legacy was a sceptical attitude of mind and a ferment of bright ideas, some more accurate and profound than others: not a compact system of definitions to elaborate further, or a firm scheme of analysis of a well-defined subject, on which to build. Though the rather amorphous school of thought known as 'Institutionalism' acknowledged Veblen as its leader, its members mostly followed out very different subjects and methods. For example, Wesley Mitchell's patient, precise, and cautious quantitative analysis was almost the exact opposite of Veblen's lively manipulation of ideas. Furthermore, many of the younger 'Institutionalists', in direct contrast with Veblen's scepticism, devoted much of their work to problems and techniques of economic and social 'control'. But Veblen's work came to lead and typify a native American 'leftist' approach to economic problems, and to 'orthodox' economic teaching, which in spite of his own air of fatalism, gave him after his death an intellectual position *vis-à-vis* the earlier phase of Roosevelt's New Deal, somewhat similar to that of

J. A. Hobson *vis-à-vis* the British Labour policies of 1945–50. His work was so extremely American in its subjects and background that its great vogue in its own country was mainly matched by an almost complete neglect in Britain. (No book of Veblen's was reviewed in the *Economic Journal* until the ninth impression of the *Theory of the Leisure Class* in 1925.) But the time may be at hand when, for various reasons, Veblen's work may be seen to have a wider interest and importance than has been realized.

17

Simon Newcomb and Irving Fisher

1. *Newcomb and 'The Societary Circulation'*

NEWCOMB'S *Principles* (1885), although little known outside the United States, was a textbook with a number of outstanding features, one part, especially, of which deserves a place in the history of economic thought of our period. Newcomb is authoritatively stated to have been one of the foremost astronomers of his time and one would have to go back perhaps to the seventeenth century to find a distinguished natural scientist doing such a useful service to political economy as is rendered in his *Principles*.[1]

One of the noteworthy sections of Newcomb's book is the opening one on the 'Logical Basis and Method of Economic Science'. Whether or no the opening chapter of a textbook of principles is the best place for a disquisition on scientific method as applied to economics, Newcomb's treatment in its clarity, precision, and balance, must still be among the best that has been given. In writing his outline of scientific method Newcomb was unquestionably able, and entitled, to apply the often persuasively misused adjective 'scientific' with reasonable precision and authority. Though describing the processes and criteria common to all 'science' reasonably so-called, Newcomb fully recognized all the differences in application in the 'social' sciences, studying human actions governed by will and choice, as contrasted with the 'natural' sciences.

In the ensuing chapters there are a number of noteworthy contributions on particular topics. Newcomb had been among the very first writers to give a cordial recognition to Jevons's new theory of value and his claims for the mathematical method. On the rate of interest, as regulated by the supply and demand of 'loanable funds', Newcomb makes a number of points, important in subsequent treatments of the subject, explaining the effects of changes in the value of money on debtors and creditors: e.g. that the price of holding banknotes and coins

---

[1] Keynes considered Newcomb's *Principles* to be 'one of those original works which a fresh scientific mind, not perverted by having read too much of the orthodox stuff, is able to produce from time to time in a half-formed subject like Economics'. (*Treatise on Money*, vol. i, p. 233.)

is the interest forgone: and that, as subsequently worked out in more detail by Cassel, the rate of interest historically

has rarely fallen below that which would yield a young man, in the course of his average life, a profit equal to the principal invested. The expectation of life for a man of 20 may be put at 40 years. If he has gained a certain capital it will, without any investment, last him his average life, if he consumes $2\frac{1}{2}\%$ of it per annum. Hence, so far as he is individually concerned, he has no motive for saving unless he can gain the rate of interest. Now this is about the minimum rate yet known. (p. 309.)

With economic progress the rate will tend to fall to this level: 'As a country increases in wealth, the rate of interest tends to fall . . . nature continually offers less and less as the resources of a country are developed.' (p. 309.)

The specially valuable part of Newcomb's *Principles* is his Book IV on 'The Societary Circulation', or on 'the exchanges within a social organism considered in their totality'. Newcomb opens this book by drawing absolutely lucidly and consequentially the fundamental distinction between a 'fund' and a 'flow'—a contribution of vital importance. The two fundamental flows are the flow of currency, or the monetary circulation, and the flow of goods, or the industrial circulation. These two opposite 'circulations' make up the societary circulation.

Newcomb then proceeds to build up the equation of exchange VR = KP (Volume of Currency × Average Rapidity = Total Transactions × Price). Newcomb clearly indicates the psychological factors behind 'R' (Rapidity):

Every cause which leads him to doubt what is the most satisfactory disposition to make of his money interferes with his expenditure, and leads him to keep his money longer than he otherwise would. The general rule will be that before he receives his money he forms more or less definite conclusions as to what he will do with it. If anything happens to disappoint the expectations on which those conclusions are based, he is likely to keep his money longer than he otherwise would. . . . In periods of uncertainty, investors of money, that is, purchasers of capital, become apprehensive, and their money lies on their hands longer than it would otherwise have done. (pp. 340–1.)

Newcomb then relates his equation of exchange to demand and income, distinguishing between *market demand* as the hypothetical quantity of a commodity 'which a community would purchase in a year at a price fixed in dollars', and the *actual demand* or the *quantity sold* which is the quantity which as a matter of history, the community really does purchase: 'We see, then, that there are two distinct ways of measuring demand between which we must carefully distinguish. Both are perfectly legitimate, and may be useful if we do not confound them.' (p. 350.) This vital distinction, between what were later called *ex-ante* and *ex-post* concepts, had been recently emphasized by Cairnes, but the failure to appreciate it was to cause much confusion, both in the theory of the firm and in the theory of money and of the trade cycle, for half a century or more after 1885.

The concept of individual income is then analysed and the uses of income are distinguished, that is, spending on consumption, capital investment, or, thirdly, stopping the flow of currency by sending it abroad, melting it into jewels, or depositing it in a bank which does not loan it out. Newcomb analyses the effect of 'hoarding' to be un-employment in the short run and a fall in prices, but his further analysis rests on perhaps rather facile assumptions as to the power of self-adjust-ment in the economy, and he concludes that if only prices were flexible enough a broad adjustment of the flow of currency (aggregate demand) and the flow of goods (aggregate supply) can and will come about.

However superseded one may choose to regard the terminology or concepts of the equation of exchange, the fact remains that an impor-tant part of the foundations of modern macro-economic and monetary analysis can be found systematically set out in Newcomb's Book IV on 'The Societary Circulation', probably as much as can be found together in any other single group of chapters of its time.

2. *Fisher on Value and Prices*

Irving Fisher started as a student and teacher of mathematics, widely interested in the natural sciences as well as in economics. It was as a teacher of mathematics that he wrote his doctor's dissertation *Mathe-matical Investigations in the Theory of Value and Prices* (1892), one of the outstanding theoretical works of our period. A very large part of the modern micro-economic analysis of the consumer appears for the first time in this essay. Fisher started with the works of Jevons and Walras, and more especially to his purpose with that of Auspitz and Lieben. He only knew of Edgeworth's *Mathematical Psychics* after he had completed the main part of his work and, in any case, Edgeworth's indifference curves are drawn in a different form from Fisher's, which is now the generally adopted form. Fisher was, however, presumably much assisted in his discoveries by Auspitz and Lieben's 'curves of constant satisfaction' and 'satisfaction-surfaces', and along with the much wider recognition due to Fisher must go a tribute to the two Austrian business men.

'The very foundations of the subject require new analysis and definition', Fisher began. In particular he sought to clarify the fundamental concept of 'utility' and to repel the intrusions of utilitarian and hedonist psychologizing:

I have always felt that utility must be capable of a definition which shall connect it with its positive or objective commodity relations. A physicist would certainly err who defined the unit of force as the minimum sensibile of muscular sensation. . . . This foisting of Psychology on Economics seems to me inappropriate and vicious. . . . To fix the idea of utility the economist should go no further than is serviceable in explaining economics facts. It is not his province to build a theory of psychology. (pp. vi, vii, and 11.)

Part I of Fisher's Essay is entitled 'Utility of Each Commodity assumed to be Dependent only on the Quantity of that Commodity'— the assumption of Jevons, Marshall, Walras, and, apparently, of Menger. Fisher proceeds to show how, on this assumption, the concept he is continuing to call 'utility' may be measured. Of course this 'utility', of which he is seeking to demonstrate the measurability (in 'utils'), is not the 'utility' steeped in hedonist psychologizing as then still widely employed, but something which Fisher elsewhere urged might better be described as 'desiredness'. What useful role this alternative measurable concept, and the demonstration of its measurability, had to play, is a separate question, and something of a side issue from the point of view of the development of modern micro-economic technique and analysis.

Part II of Fisher's *Investigations* is entitled 'Utility of One Commodity a Function of the Quantities of all Commodities', and starts by examining the 'two ways in which the quantity of one commodity can affect the utility of others'. (p. 64.) To summarize this part would be simple to summarize many of the main concepts and techniques of the modern theory of the consumer: complementary and substitute relations between commodities and precisely how these affect the shape of indifference curves: price lines and the significance of the points of tangency of price lines to indifference curves: income and substitution effects: and inferior goods.

On the place of the concept of utility and the significance of its measurability, Fisher concludes (p. 86) that 'in order to study prices and distribution it is not necessary to give any meaning to the ratio of two men's utilities', though this might be of service in 'ethical investigations': 'When it is done the comparison will doubtless be by objective standards. If persons alike in most respects show to each other their satisfaction by similar gestures, language, facial expressions, and general conduct we speak of their satisfaction as very much the same. What, however, this may mean in the "noumenal world" is a mystery.' (p. 87.)

Fisher insists that

these inquiries, however, do not belong here. Let us instead of adding to the meaning of utility do the very opposite and strip it of all attributes unessential to our purpose of determining objective prices and distribution. . . . Thus if we seek only the causation of the *objective facts of prices and commodity distribution* four attributes of utility as a quantity are entirely unessential, (1) that one man's utility can be compared to another's, (2) that for the same individual the marginal utilities at one consumption-combination can be compared with those at another, or at one time with another, (3) even if they could, total utility and gain might not be integratable, (4) even if they were, there would be no need of determining the constants of integration. (pp. 87–89.)

About the question of whether anything essential, and if so what, is left of the concept of utility after this stripping process, Fisher does not inquire further. Nor, as we have seen, was he dogmatic about the use of the term 'utility'. But clearly the 'Utility-arianism' of (above all) Edgeworth (but to a lesser extent also of Jevons and Marshall) was now a slightly deflated tyre on which to try to 'shunt the car of economics'. Fisher's essay may be taken as marking the beginning of the passing of the hedonist content from the theory of value. Among Fisher's American contemporaries the consequences of the resulting vacuum were lengthily debated. Fetter, for example, sought unsuccessfully to fill the vacuum with a content drawn from a brand of 'instinct' psychology then more up to date than hedonism. Davenport's solution was to abandon the problems of the psychology of valuation altogether, and concentrate on the analysis of price—the path that was to lead to the concept of economic theory as the logic of choice. Veblen considered generalizations of the former kind to be invalid, and the analysis of the latter to be fairly empty, and sought to trace the institutional framework shaping economic behaviour.

In this first essay and in later works, Fisher carried on an American counterpart of the crusade for the mathematical method in economic analysis, to which Jevons and Edgeworth had devoted themselves in

Britain, and of which today it is not easy to appreciate the great originality and importance. Their, for that time, severely mathematical exposition as well as, no doubt, their forbidding mechanical illustrations of cisterns and levers was fatal to the influence of Fisher's *Investigations*, which for several decades received very little attention.

3. Fisher on Income, Capital, and Interest

We cannot here attempt to do justice to Irving Fisher's immensely wide range of writings, interests, and activities, to his mechanical inventions, his business achievements, his crusades against alcohol and tobacco and in favour of the League of Nations and stable money. His *Investigations on Value and Prices* is historically his most important work. But his *Nature of Capital and Income* (1906) and his writings on the theory of interest (*Appreciation and Interest*, 1896, and the *Theory of Interest*, 1907, revised as the *Rate of Interest*, 1930) represent his most solid and recognized achievements. His *Purchasing Power of Money* (1911) will be briefly mentioned in other chapters (21 and 23).

Fisher's book *The Nature of Capital and Income* 'forms a sort of philosophy of economic accounting, and, it is hoped, may supply a link long missing between the ideas and usages underlying practical business transactions and the theories of abstract economics'. (p. vii.) He complained that 'there seems to be no systematic study of capital accounts in any work on political economy'. (p. 67.) His work consists of the preparation and analysis of a convenient and self-consistent set of economic accounting concepts. Though its practical analysis and applications are nearly all micro-economic, applied, that is, to the accounts of individual firms or households, it does also contribute pioneer macro-economic ideas on the subject of national income analysis and social accounting. (pp. 113 ff.) Another fundamental contribution of the book lies in the attention it devotes to the concepts of capital values and income. The distinction between 'stock' and 'flow' concepts (taken over from Newcomb) inevitably led on to, and pointed to the need for, a dynamic 'dated' analysis, with a more systematic attention to the expectations on which all capitalizations are based.

Fisher's first work in this field had been his essay on *Appreciation and Interest* (1896), which in some important respects bears comparison with Wicksell's *Interest and Prices* of two years later. Both books, though mainly devoted to highly abstract analysis, had as their practical background the debates on the principles of monetary policy and monetary standards of the eighties and nineties. Fisher's statement of the problem as to 'the connexion between monetary depreciation and the rate of interest', is very similar to Wicksell's, but Fisher saw the problem more narrowly as one of justice between debtor and creditor rather than as covering the whole subject of monetary policy.

Both books tried to sort out the relation between different levels of interest rates and the levels of prices and business activity, and culminated in an answer to what may be called the Ricardo-Tooke conundrum of why the rate of interest had often been low during times of falling prices and high during times of rising prices. Wicksell's answer had been to point out that 'the rate of interest charged for loans can clearly never be high or low in itself, but only in relation to the return which can, or is expected to, be obtained by the man who has possession of money'. (*Interest and Prices*, p. xxv.)

Fisher's answer was different but not incompatible, and it likewise emphasized the cumulative character of general price movements: 'We can now understand why a high rate of interest need not retard trade nor a low rate stimulate it. These facts have puzzled many writers. . . . All these writers mistook a high or low nominal interest for high or low real interest.' (pp. 67–69.) The 'nominal' rate of interest is the actual market rate, and the 'real' rate is the nominal rate corrected for changes in the value of money. When an upward movement of prices begins business profits will rise:

Borrowers can now afford to pay a higher 'money interest'. If, however, only a few persons see this, the interest will not be fully adjusted and borrowers will realise an extra margin of profit after deducting interest charges. This raises an expectation of a similar profit in the future and this expectation, acting on the demand for loans, will raise the rate of interest. If the rise is still inadequate the process is repeated. . . . When a fall of prices begins, the reverse effects appear. . . . Since at the beginning of an upward price movement the rate of interest is too low, and at the beginning of a downward movement it is too high, we can understand not only that the averages for the whole period are imperfectly adjusted but that the delay in the adjustment leaves a relatively low interest at the beginning of an ascent of prices and a relatively high interest at the beginning of a descent. This would explain, in part at least, the association of high and low prices with high and low interest. . . . What has been said bears directly on the theory of credit cycles. In the view here presented periods of speculation and depression are the result of *inequality* of foresight. If all persons under-estimated a rise of price in the same degree, the non-adjustment of interest would merely produce a transfer of wealth from lender to borrower. It would not influence the volume of loans. . . . Under such circumstances the rate of interest would be below the normal, but as no-one knows it, no borrower borrows more and no lender lends less because of it. In the actual world, however, foresight is very unequally distributed. . . . While *imperfection* of foresight transfers wealth from creditor to debtor or the reverse, *inequality* of foresight produces over-investment during rising prices and relative stagnation during falling prices. In the former case society is trapped into devoting too much wealth to productive uses and in long production processes while in the contrary case under-investment is the rule. (pp. 75–78.)

Marshall's brief but penetrating discussion of this point, in his evidence to the Gold and Silver Commission, is referred to by Fisher. More theoretically, Fisher shows that a rate of interest, like a price, is relative to the standard in which it is expressed. If debts are contracted optionally in either of two standards, gold and wheat, and one of them is expected to change relative to the other, the rate of interest will not, of course, be the same in both standards. If the gold rate of interest is 8 per cent., then if wheat depreciates 4 per cent. in terms of gold, the wheat rate of interest will be 12½ per cent., the formula being that the rate of interest in the (relatively) depreciating standard is equal to the sum of three terms, i.e. the rate of interest in the appreciating standard, the rate of appreciation itself, and the product of these two elements:

The rate of interest is as Professor Böhm-Bawerk shows, an agio on present goods exchanged for future goods of the same kind. It is a simple corollary of this theorem, though Professor Böhm-Bawerk does not express it, that this agio may be in theory and must be in practice a different agio for each separate kind of goods. . . . These rates are mutually connected and our task has been merely to state the law of that connexion. We have not attempted the bolder task of explaining the rates themselves. (p. 92.)

'The explanation of the rates of interest themselves' (rather than simply of the inter-connexions between different commodity rates) was the subject of Fisher's work on the *Rate of Interest* (1907) later revised as the *Theory of Interest* (1930). Fisher builds up his explanation from his concept of income developed in his book on *The Nature of Capital and Income*. Interest is the link between expected future income values and the present capital values based on them: 'The value of the orchard depends upon the value of its crops; and in this dependence lurks implicitly the rate of interest itself. The statement that "capital produces income" is true only in the physical sense; it is not true in the value sense. . . . On the contrary income-value produces capital-value.' (*Rate of Interest*, p. 13.)

Fisher then develops his theory by means of three approximations:

1. The first deals with the case of consumption loans, or conditions where 'every man is initially endowed with a fixed and certain income-stream which, by borrowing and lending, can be freely bought and sold and thereby redistributed in time'. This abstraction allows an unimpeded view of the workings of time-preference.

2. In the second approximation income streams are not fixed, though all possible variations can be definitely foreseen. The owner of any capital property is not restricted to a single use to which he may put it, but has open to his choice several different uses, each of which may yield a different income stream. Here Fisher introduces his concept of 'the (marginal) rate of return on sacrifice'. This 'comes close to being "a natural rate of interest", by means of it we are enabled to admit into our theory the elements of truth contained in some of the claims of the productivity theories, the cost theories, and Böhm-Bawerk's theory of the technique of production'. (p. 159.)

By 'sacrifice' is meant 'a comparative loss from one's income stream at first, caused by substituting one use of capital for another', and by 'return' is meant the comparative gain which later accrues by reason of this same substitution.

3. The third approximation is to introduce risk and uncertainty: the individual now has a choice of any one of a number of uncertain income-streams with the result that 'instead of a single rate of interest representing the rate of exchange between this year and next year, we now find a great variety of rates according to the risk involved'. (p. 207.)

Fisher's treatment of 'productivity' and his criticism of Böhm-Bawerk's third ground for interest, that is the technical superiority of present over future goods, led to much lengthy logomachy including a long critical 'excursion' from the Austrian leader in defence of the significance of his third ground. From the other side, Fisher was criticized for his concessions to the productivity theory by Fetter, an exclusivist exponent of the time-preference theory of interest. Nearly a quarter of a century later (1930) Fisher published a masterly revision and restatement in his *Theory of Interest*, 'As Determined by Impatience to Spend Income and Opportunity to Invest It', which was dedicated to the memory of John Rae and Böhm-Bawerk. This systematic analysis left very little if anything to be said (even by disputants on the theory of interest) on the subject of time-preference and productivity, and their inter-relations. As compared with the 1907 edition, the term 'impatience' replaced 'time preference', and the 'rate of return over cost' was substituted for the 'rate of return on sacrifice'. The concept of the 'rate of return over cost' has in turn been re-designated 'the (marginal) efficiency of capital', or the 'internal rate of interest'.[1]

---

[1] *v.* E. Schneider, *Pricing and Equilibrium*, Ch. II, sect. 6.

Part II

FROM 'STATIC' TO 'DYNAMIC' ANALYSIS

THE method of presentation in this part is different from that adopted in Part I. In this part we attempt to set out the most important works in our period in each of four main branches of economic thought. In each branch the contributions by the economists discussed in Part I are very briefly recapitulated, and then we continue with the more representative and important works in the following two or three decades down to about 1929. To a considerable extent the story is one of the logical development or exploitation of a central idea or group of ideas, and we try to concentrate on the logical skeleton of this body of doctrine rather than to document with any completeness the vast literature with which the skeleton was covered.

One fundamental theme in this logical development was the gradually increasing importance of the distinction between static and dynamic analysis resulting from the increasing precision and narrowness of the definition of 'statics'. This theme is not illustrated in the next chapter on Welfare Economics, the abstract analysis of which has always been almost exclusively static. But it emerges clearly at a number of points in the subsequent chapters on the problems of firms, of profit uncertainty and expectations, and of interest, investment and money.

18

'Welfare' Economics and the Economics
of Socialism

1. *The Name and Nature of 'Welfare' Economics*

THE term 'welfare economics' has come into very common, though rather indefinite, use in recent decades. It seems to fill a useful terminological need and probably has a sufficiently agreed coverage, despite the fact that neither the term nor the concept of 'welfare' (or 'economic welfare') has ever had any at all precise or widely accepted place or function in economics. 'Welfare economics' (as contrasted with 'price economics') seems to be commonly used to cover the general analysis of economic policy, or of certain general economic effects or criteria of economic policies, whatever part the term or concept 'welfare' has to play therein. It is not necessary here to try to sort out this terminological issue, or to give to 'welfare economics' any sharper definition than it currently possesses. In the very broad sense of its having been related pretty directly to policy, or to the principles, objectives, and criteria of policy, economics and political economy was in its origin, and has for the greater part of its history, been 'welfare' economics. Except for isolated works like Cantillon's *Essay*, it was only with the later classical economists that a positive 'price' economics began to grow up, regularly and distinctly separate from the analysis of the causes of the wealth of nations. But here, too, the vulgar interpretation (for which the classical economists themselves cannot be acquitted of every trace of responsibility) regarded this 'positive' analysis as directly justifying and establishing a normative principle or maxim of policy, which later came to be known as the *laissez-faire* maxim. So that by 1870 political economy had come to be widely regarded, as Cairnes bitterly complained, 'as a scientific development of laissez faire'. (This fact may be further confirmed from the observations of such leaders as Gladstone, Lowe, Newmarch, and Leslie Stephen, quoted in Ch. 1, sect. 1.)

In the last quarter of the nineteenth century economists were therefore faced with two major tasks with regard to their doctrines on economic policy. The first was to achieve a much wider recognition for the distinction between 'normative' maxims and neutral 'positive' analysis, and to build up a positive economics not so mixed up as classical political economy had been (in important sections of the public mind at any rate) with particular political maxims and principles. And the second task was to meet the social questionings of the time by re-examining in a much more detached, systematic, and detailed way than previously, the role of the State in economic life, or, as Jevons put it, to construct 'a new branch of political and statistical science which shall carefully investigate the limits to the laissez-faire principle to show where we want greater freedom and where less'.

We may distinguish three analytically different lines of develop-ment taken by this new branch of political economy which Jevons had called for (that is, three branches of 'welfare' economics or of the analysis of economic policy). Some writers (e.g. Walras) contributed something to all three, but most of the leading works fall mainly into one of these three divisions: (1) First, there were empirical case-by-case reviews of economic policies; (2) Secondly, there was the analysis of the doctrine of maximum satisfaction under competitive conditions, at increasingly high levels of abstraction and precision; (3) Thirdly, growing out of the second, but to some extent separate, there was the criticism of socialist economics and of the possible workings of a collectivist economy as compared with an individualist and competi-tive economy.

1. The case-by-case review of economic policy, or of some depart-ment of it, was made against a background of the broadly competitive and individualist economy of the day, in order to examine where, in particular cases, the State might intervene to regulate, replace, or supplement the workings of the market. Jevons and Sidgwick made considerable progress along this line, setting out from competitive conditions, without understanding these in any very rigorous sense, and not so much because these conditions were held to afford a 'maximum' or 'optimum' of some kind, but because, in the then com-mon and loose sense of the concept of 'competition', it broadly com-prised the main part of the existing economic system. Marshall's *Industry and Trade* might also be put in this class. It had as its theme 'the limited tendencies of self-interest to direct each individual's action on those lines in which it will be most beneficial to others' (p. viii), and it consisted of a case-by-case review of monopolistic practices and of State control of industry and public utilities.

The discussion of the special problem of the pricing policies of public undertakings by Launhardt, Wicksell, and Pareto, might also be mentioned under this heading, though these were also closely associated with the more abstract analysis of the social maximum.

2. Secondly, there was this much more abstract analysis and criticism of the doctrine of maximum satisfaction from competitive conditions. When Marshall briefly discussed and criticized this doctrine in his *Principles*, he only referred to Bastiat and mentioned no English expositor of the doctrine. Indeed, Marshall only devoted a handful of pages to this subject, however suggestive his analysis may have been to subsequent theoretical economists.

Although the notion of 'maximum happiness' or 'satisfaction' as an objective or criterion of policy derives above all from Bentham, the economic doctrine of maximum satisfaction did not, throughout the nineteenth century, receive any considerable attention in English political economy. In his supreme expression of Benthamite hedonism, in *Mathematical Psychics*, Edgeworth summons economists to the search for nothing less than 'the greatest possible sum total of pleasure summed through all time and over all sentience'. But he did not stay long in the quest of this holy grail, nor even in *Mathematical Psychics* did he seek to locate his ideal in any particular economic order or arrangement of society, competitive or otherwise, or attempt much further detailed examination of the 'maximum satisfaction' doctrines, and the criticisms thereof, by Walras, Pareto, and others.

The general predilection for the free market solution in nineteenth-century Britain was not based on any very close or narrow economic reasoning as to 'optima' and 'maxima', however widespread the vulgar notion may have been that the *laissez-faire* maxim had some definitive scientific halo about it. Of course, there were several branches of economic analysis in which the competitive market was associated with some sort of maximum of production and exchange, as in Adam Smith's analysis of the division of labour and the extent of the market, and of the social allocation of resources brought about by competition, and particularly in the free trade conclusions derived from the classical analysis of international trade. But generally, the more narrowly economic reasoning on behalf of the competitive market consisted of nothing more complex and penetrating than the simple principle that where there was free exchange there could be no robbery, but rather there must be some advantage to both parties. The general case for free competition, and against State intervention, was based much rather on frankly ethical, political, or pseudo-Darwinian social-biological principles.

It is only with the formulation of the marginal utility theory of value, with its maximizing formula for the individual consumer, that the doctrine of 'maximum satisfaction' begins to emerge in a really closely reasoned form. The marginal utility analysis had, of course, at once come in for political exploitation from left and right. On the left, the principle of diminishing utility was used to prove the desirability of an equal distribution of income, an idea that had been suggested by Bentham and followed up by his socialistic former secretary William Thompson. On the other side, the marginal utility analysis, when built up into Walras's theory of general equilibrium, made possible an apparently much more rigorous attempt to prove that the free competitive system led to a maximum of social satisfaction; or, as Bortkiewicz put it in the title of a critical article, there emerged 'The Marginal Utility Theory as the Basis of an ultra-Liberal Economic Policy'. The development and examination of this doctrine had to be based on the Walrasian general equilibrium analysis, never much exploited by Jevons, Sidgwick, Marshall, or Pigou.

3. Just as socialist economics had obtained a much fuller exposition in various German writings, mainly by German Social Democrats, than was available at that time in English, so the first main criticisms of the mechanism of a collectivist economic system were the work of German economists, in fact of some of those associated with the *Verein für Sozialpolitik*. But the problems of a socialist economy came in for much more precise treatment later, on the basis of Walras's analysis of general equilibrium. Walras, Pareto, and finally Barone all contributed to this criticism. Later still there came the examination of socialist economics by Mises and Max Weber which, however, probably owed little to Walras's analysis, and followed rather the lines of the German writers. The experience of war economies, and of the post-war collectivist régimes in central Europe were a lively stimulus to this school of thought.

We turn now to Pigou's *Economics of Welfare*, the major work on 'welfare' economics in our period. This book is, for the greater part, a case-by-case review on the lines of Sidgwick's, but it also had as one of its starting-points Marshall's criticism of the abstract doctrine of maximum satisfaction.

2. *Pigou's Economics of Welfare*

Much of Pigou's early writing was devoted to applied economic problems of direct practical and even topical interest, such as, for example, *The Riddle of the Tariff* and *The Principles and Methods of Industrial Peace*. Emphasizing that 'fruit' rather than 'light' should be the primary and direct object of the economist's pursuit, Pigou quoted approvingly Comte's dictum that 'the only position for which the intellect is primarily adapted is to be the servant of the social sympathies'.[1] On succeeding Marshall in the Cambridge chair in 1908 Pigou explained in his inaugural lecture:

> I shall be glad if a man comes to Economics because he has been interested by Professor Edgeworth's Mathematical Psychics or Dr. Fisher's Appreciation and Interest: just as I shall be glad if he comes to it because he is looking forward to business and wishes to learn something of the broader aspects of his future career; but I shall be far more glad if he comes because he has walked through the slums of London and is stirred to make some effort to help his fellow men. Wonder, Carlyle said, is the beginning of philosophy: social enthusiasm, one might add, is the beginning of economic science. (*v. Economic Science in Relation to Practice*.)

Pigou's *Economics of Welfare* (1st ed., 1920) grew out of his *Wealth and Welfare* (1912) which is stated in its preface to have grown out of the study of the causes of unemployment. These causes were found to be 'so closely interwoven with the general body of economic activity that an isolated treatment of them is scarcely practicable'. The fourth and final part of *Wealth and Welfare*, on the subject of the 'Variability of the National Dividend', was devoted to economic fluctuations and irregularity of employment. But after the second edition of the *Economics of Welfare* (1924) this part was dropped and dealt with in a separate monograph. So that, somewhat paradoxically, the problem of unemployment out of which the work originally grew came, by the assumptions of the analysis adopted, to disappear, except incidentally,

---

[1] Thirty years later, by 1939, the bottom seemed to have fallen out of the 'fruit' market: 'The ambition, I have claimed elsewhere, of most economists is to help in some degree, directly or indirectly, towards social betterment. Our study, we should like to think, of the principles of interaction among economic events provides for statesmen data, upon which, along with data of other kinds, they, philosopher kings, build up policies directed to the common good. How different from this dream is the actuality! . . . The hope that an advance in economic knowledge will appreciably affect actual happenings is, I fear, a slender one. It is not likely that there will be a market for our produce. None the less, by a sort of reflex activity, we cultivate our garden. For we also follow, not thought, but an impulse—the impulse to inquire—which, futile though it may prove, is at least not ignoble.' (*Economic Journal*, 1939, pp. 220-1.)

We seem to be confronted, on an individual long-period scale, by one of those 'fluctuations of optimism and pessimism' which Pigou himself invoked in the study of the trade cycle.

and it is expressly stated in respect, at any rate of Part II of the *Economics of Welfare* on 'The Size of the National Dividend': 'Throughout this discussion, except when the contrary is expressly stated, the fact that some resources are generally unemployed against the will of the owners is ignored.' (*Economics of Welfare*, 3rd ed., 1929, p. 129.)

The *Economics of Welfare* is built round the concept of the economic welfare of the community and the size and distribution of its national dividend, and is the leading modern example of the approach to economics adopted in the *Wealth of Nations*, and described more recently as the 'National Income' approach. Pigou considered the concept of the National Dividend (along with the treatment of 'time'), to be the central contribution of Marshall's *Principles*, and that: 'The dividend constitutes the kernel of economic theory because—along with those moral and other aspects of practical problems which Professor Marshall would be the last to neglect—it is the centre of sound philanthropic endeavour.' (*Economic Journal*, 1907, p. 535.) But the book, though deriving a certain unity from its central concept the national dividend, falls into two fairly distinct sections, analytical and applied. The first and analytical section contains the opening analysis of 'welfare', 'economic welfare', and 'the national dividend', and the important contribution to the theory of index numbers contained in the chapters on changes in the national dividend and their measurement. The opening chapters of Part II, on the size of the national dividend and the distribution of resources among different uses, are also almost purely analytical, covering the definitions of marginal private and marginal social net product, and the very general theoretical cases where these diverge, and where, therefore, the free play of self-interest will probably not result in the optimum distribution of resources socially. These very general cases include imperfect mobility and divisibility of resources, and increasing and decreasing costs.

Of course, the dividing line in the book cannot be made clear-cut, but it might be said to come in about the middle of Part II. After a highly abstract analysis of the general cases of 'increasing and decreasing supply price' in Chapter XI, Chapters XII and XIII give a description of the problems of State regulation of competitive prices and of supplies, based on British experience in the 1914–18 War. Nearly all the remaining two-thirds of the book are concerned with a series of particular studies of the main problems of economic policy arising in Britain in the first quarter of the twentieth century: the control of monopoly, co-operation, the public operation of industry, industrial peace, conciliation and arbitration, hours of labour, methods of wage payment, employment exchanges, interference to raise wages, minimum wages, sliding scales, rationing, subsidies, the redistribution of income, and a national minimum standard of real income, all problems which either for themselves, or for the analytical methods with which they are approached or attacked, are of perennial significance. But the connecting unifying principle between the examinations of all these particular policies, that they all have their effects on the size and/or distribution of the national dividend, only binds together the whole in the very loosest way. The discussion of each selected policy could, of course, be taken separately and extracted from this loose-leaf compendium—just as all the problems of the variability of the national dividend, and also of public finance, in due course dropped out for separate monographic treatment.

Let us now trace out briefly the analytical framework built up in the first phase of the book. Though economics should be regarded as a 'fruit-bearing' rather than a 'light-bringing' science, it must be 'a positive science of what is and tends to be, not a normative science of what ought to be'. (p. 5.)[1] The goal aimed at 'is to make easy practical measures to promote welfare'. In *Wealth and Welfare*, it was stated that 'welfare means the same thing as good', but this proposition was dropped from the *Economics of Welfare*, where it was explained that welfare 'is a thing of very wide range. There is no need here to enter upon a general discussion of its content. It will be sufficient to lay down more or less dogmatically two propositions; first, that the elements of welfare are states of consciousness and, perhaps, their relations; secondly that welfare can be brought under the category of greater and less.' (p. 10.)

'Welfare', however, has so many causes and origins that it is necessary to limit the study of how to promote it to where 'there is present something measurable, on which analytical machinery can get a firm grip. The one obvious instrument of measurement available in social life is money. Hence, the range of our inquiry becomes restricted to that part of social welfare that can be brought directly or indirectly into relation with the measuring-rod of money. This part of welfare may be called economic welfare.' (p. 11.)

But 'the possibility of being brought directly or indirectly into relation with the measuring-rod of money', in the well-known Marshallian phrase, does not provide any precise criterion or hard and fast boundary

[1] All page references are to the 3rd (1929) edition of the *Economics of Welfare*.

line between 'welfare' and 'economic welfare'. Nor can any rigid inferences be drawn from effects on economic welfare to effects on total welfare. However, there may be 'an unverified probability that qualitative conclusions about the effect of an economic cause upon economic welfare will hold good also of the effect on total welfare', and Pigou even goes so far as to hold that 'the burden of proof lies upon those who hold that the presumption should be over-ruled', probably a quite excessively bold claim. (p. 20.)

Economic welfare consists broadly of 'that group of satisfactions or dissatisfactions which can be brought into relation with a money measure'. (p. 23.) These satisfactions can be held to be measured by the money demand price offered for them, these prices measuring both the desire and the satisfaction felt when the desired thing is obtained. The assumption of this equivalence between desires and satisfactions seems to amount to the assumption of correct foresight on the part of the consumer. (There is, however, one important exception to the equivalence arising from the 'irrational' under-estimation of future wants.)

At this point the fundamental concept of 'the national dividend' is introduced and its relation with 'economic welfare' is explained:

Generally speaking, economic causes act upon the economic welfare of any country, not directly, but through the making and using of that objective counterpart of economic welfare which economists call the national dividend or national income. . . . The two concepts, economic welfare and the national dividend, are thus coordinate, in such wise that any description of the content of one of them implies a corresponding description of the content of the other. (p. 31.)

Since the national dividend is as elastic a concept as economic welfare, any attempt to define precisely what is or is not to be included will inevitably be arbitrary at the edges.

However, to describe the national dividend as 'the objective counterpart' of economic welfare (it is later said to be 'intimately connected' with it, p. 54), is not, of course, to say that the amount of economic welfare enjoyed by a community varies simply with the size of the national dividend. Another dimension of economic welfare is the distribution of the national dividend (and yet another, presumably, its variability, or distribution through time). Without hesitation Pigou lays it down as

evident that any transference of income from a relatively rich man to a relatively poor man of similar temperament, since it enables more intense wants to be satisfied at the expense of less intense wants, must increase the aggregate sum of satisfaction. The old 'law of diminishing utility' thus leads securely to the proposition: Any cause which increases the absolute share of real income in the hands of the poor, provided that it does not lead to a contraction in the size of the national dividend from any point of view, will, in general, increase economic welfare. (p. 91.)

Having now reached 'the objective counterpart of economic welfare,' that is, the national dividend in its size and distribution, we may glance back for a moment at the ups and downs of Benthamite philosophizing and Marshallian moralizing over which we have been led. The introduction of the terms 'welfare' and 'economic welfare' into the centre of economic analysis was something of a terminological novelty, with presumably some new implications not possessed by such older terms as 'happiness', 'satisfaction', 'utility', 'social utility', 'ophelimity', and so on. But it is not easy to say precisely how 'economic welfare' should be differentiated from its predecessors except that it seems to carry about a rather more persuasive and morally uplifting aroma, which none the less is not apparently held to disqualify it from a central place in 'a positive science of what is and tends to be, not a normative science of what ought to be'. Nor need we enter here into the problems of distinguishing one sort of welfare ('the elements of which are states of consciousness') from other sorts of welfare, or from 'total welfare', or into whether one can conceive of 'states of consciousness' arising from 'purely economic' causes.

The apparatus of 'welfare', 'economic welfare', and 'the national dividend', represents an attempt to define some supreme criterion or objective of economic policy, some comprehensive social maximand, so that the problems of economic policy can be formulated precisely and even mathematically (like those of positive micro-economic analysis) as maximizing problems, or so that actual policies can be compared with an ideal maximum or optimum. This national maximand is a less obviously imprecise, and more narrowly economic, successor of Bentham's 'greatest happiness' principle, and is invested with all the normative-positive ambiguity with which much of utilitarian philosophizing is so ubiquitously shot through: people both somehow are and somehow ought to be maximizers of something-or-other. The national dividend is not simply a positive statistical concept, but, as we have seen, 'the centre of sound philanthropic endeavour'. Nobody today would hold that the phrase 'the greatest happiness of the greatest number' can be of very much service as a criterion for choosing between policies. But in its day it had a great liberating effect as against taboos and vested interests. As Macgregor has put it, this seemingly empty phrase was 'an invitation to a continuous review of economic policy'. 'The maximum economic welfare or national dividend' was an invitation to a much more precise and detailed review—though as some sort of ultimate criterion no more satisfactory than 'greatest happiness'. And, of course, in the name of 'the maximum of economic welfare', much invaluable positive analysis can be carried out. Ultimately, however, the help obtainable from formulating problems of policy as maximizing problems seems apt to be limited.

It is sufficient here to point out that the ability to appreciate fully the wealth of analysis and great range of practical conclusions in the *Economics of Welfare*, does not in any way depend on the degree of soundness and significance one is capable of attaching to the amalgam of Benthamite concepts, Comteist social enthusiasm, Marshallian moral uplift, and G. E. Moore definitions, which we have just attempted to summarize. What is achieved in the *Economics of Welfare* is a vast loose-leaf review of different measures of economic policy, and an assessment of their principle economic 'effects', that is, their effects on the size and distribution of incomes and the national dividend. The significance and validity of each detailed piece of analysis of the production and distribution effects of the various policies discussed, would stand unimpaired by the total omission of 'welfare' and 'economic welfare' from the book (or unimpaired, at least, for those who do not approach economic analysis with extravagant expectations as to the 'fruit' it can bring them).

There follows an extremely penetrating discussion of the definition and measurement of the national dividend and of changes in it. Marshall's concept of the national dividend as the flow of goods and services produced during the year is adopted in contrast with Fisher's concept of the flow of services received by ultimate consumers. There then arises the (index-number) problem of how the national dividends of different periods, consisting of physically dissimilar sets of goods, to be consumed by people with tastes differing from period to period, can be compared. The upshot of the discussion is only to lay down broad indications, and not to define precisely a social maximand, the effect on the maximization of which should be the criterion for all economic policies.[1] This indefiniteness is not, of course, a confession

---

[1] See P. A. Samuelson in *Oxford Economic Papers*, Jan. 1950 and Pigou's reply in the subsequent issue.

of weakness, but a recognition of complexity, and of the practical inadequacy or inapplicability of any narrow formula. The background of the whole treatment is the British economy of 1920 still largely competitive in the older broader sense: 'The general form of our questions will be: What effect on economic welfare as a whole is produced by such and such a cause operating on the economic circumstances of 1920?' (p. 36.) The social framework is one where the 'adjustment of institutions to the end of directing self-interest into beneficial channels has been carried out in considerable detail'. (p. 131.) But many imperfections and many obstacles to the most efficient use of social resources remain, though 'the free play of self-interest, so far as it is not hampered by ignorance, tends, in the absence of costs of movement, so to distribute resources among different uses and places as to render rates of return everywhere equal'. (p. 144.) But only when marginal private and marginal social net products are identical will this free play result in equality in the values of marginal social net products, and therefore make the national dividend a maximum.

The central problem of economic policy in an effectively competitive economy is, therefore, to eliminate divergencies between marginal private and marginal social products. This amounts to a more precise economic formulation of the basic Benthamite principle of legislation.

But there are considerable difficulties in the concept of a 'marginal social net product', which must be noticed before we pass on to the main cases of divergencies between private and social products. Here is the account of the concept: 'The marginal social net product is the total net product of physical things or objective services due to the marginal increment of resources in any given use or place, no matter to whom any part of this product may accrue.' For example, there may be costs thrown upon other people not directly concerned 'through say uncompensated damage done to surrounding woods by sparks from railway engines . . .'. (p. 136.)

Again an increase in the quantity of resources employed by one firm in an industry may give rise to external economies in the industry as a whole and so lessen the real costs involved in the production by other firms of a given output. . . . For some purposes it is desirable to count in also indirect effects induced in people's tastes and in their capacity to derive satisfaction from their purchases and possessions. Our principal objective, however, is the national dividend and changes in it. . . . Therefore psychical consequences are excluded, and the marginal social net product of any given volume of resources is taken, except when special notice to the contrary is given, to consist of physical elements and objective services only. The marginal private net product is that part of the total net product of physical things or objective services due to the marginal increment of resources in any given use or place which accrues to the person responsible for investing resources there. In some conditions this is equal to, in some it is greater than, in others it is less than the marginal social net product. (pp. 136–7.)

A 'marginal social net product' is thus made up of a marginal private net product plus a possibly very large number of positive or negative items accruing to other members of society than the investor of the resources. If the social product is to have as precise a content as the private product the additional items must be such as have a recognized market price. Even then interpersonal comparisons of utilities would seem to be involved. But, in any case, many of the additional items making up a social product will, practically speaking, involve no precisely known market prices even though they might, somewhat arbitrarily, be assigned a money value (e.g. the 'uncompensated' sparks from railway engines, and the ubiquitous smoke nuisance).

Three principal groups of divergencies are set out, arising out of the fact that under simple competition 'in some occupations, a part of the product of a unit of resources consists of something, which, instead of being sold by the investor, is transferred, without gain or loss to him, for the benefit or damage of other people'. (p. 176.)

1. The first arises from the separation between tenancy and ownership of certain durable instruments of production, in particular of farm land. Tenants, not being sufficiently compensated for maintenance and improvements, do not invest as much as would be socially beneficial, but take as much out of the land as possible. This is not a divergence which arises if rents are being fixed by effective competitive pricing (however difficult it might be in practice to get competition to operate in this market).

2. In the second class of divergence between social and private net product 'the essence of the matter is that one person A, in the course of rendering some service, for which payment is made, to a second person B, incidentally also renders services or disservices to other persons C, D, and E, of such a sort that technical considerations prevent payment being exacted from the benefited parties or compensation being enforced on behalf of the injured parties'. (p. 185.) Sidgwick's case of the well-placed lighthouse is the first example, also afforestation, smoke prevention, scientific research, and on the negative side, the 'illth' resulting from congested industrial cities.

3. Professor Pigou's third case of divergence seems to have had its origin in Marshall's proposal, first broached in his *Pure Theory of Domestic Values*, that the Government theoretically should so arrange taxes and bounties as to cause each individual 'to augment his consumption of those commodities, an increase in the total demand for which will lower the price at which they can be produced'. This proposition was not worked out with precision by Marshall, and as first stated by Pigou in *Wealth and Welfare* came in for destructive criticism. However, in the final re-statement by Pigou it was agreed that the doctrine does not apply where variations in cost are due to changes in factor prices, which simply represent 'transfers'.[1] It is difficult to find examples of what precisely remains under this heading as amended, and it was agreed by Pigou that the results in this third case are results in pure theory providing 'empty' boxes which after several decades still show no signs of being filled up.

The concept of 'marginal social net product' is the most important single element in the analytical apparatus of the *Economics of Welfare*. In very few cases, however, is it practically possible to give any precise money values to many or most of the other items, positive or negative, which differentiate 'social' from 'private' product. It is significant that when he comes to the clearest cases of divergence, those under heading (2), Pigou deliberately disregards the criterion of measurability in money terms:

> If we were to be pedantically loyal to the definition of the national dividend given in Chapter III of Part I, it would be necessary to distinguish further between industries in which the uncompensated benefit or burden respectively is and is not one that can be readily brought into relation with the measuring rod of money. This distinction, however, would be of formal rather than of real importance, and would obscure rather than illuminate the main issues. (p. 185.)

This is surely to put the concept of marginal social net product in a rather doubtful position. Any economic action has a vast range of heterogeneous 'products' or rather 'effects'. First and most direct, in a private enterprise economy, there is the private pecuniary net 'product'. Then there will be other 'social products' which can without excessive arbitrariness be 'brought into relation with the measuring rod of money'. Then, again, there will be more or less 'economic'

[1] Cf. A. Young, 'Pigou's Wealth and Welfare', *Quarterly Journal of Economics*, 1913, pp. 672–86; F. H. Knight, 'Fallacies in the Interpretation of Social Cost, ibid. 1923; D. H. Robertson, 'Those Empty Boxes', *Economic Journal*, 1924, pp. 16–31.

products which cannot be so brought with any considerable precision, gradually shading into sociological, psychological and political 'products'. Any summation even of the more strictly economic 'products' into the single 'social product' of an economic act is bound to be more or less arbitrary, but would have nothing 'illegitimate' about it if the result emerging from this use of 'the measuring-rod of money' was significant for a particular purpose. But under the one relevant heading where a wide range of clear practical examples is given, the introduction of 'the measuring rod of money' (and the calculation by this measuring rod of a 'social net product') is held to 'obscure rather than illuminate the main issues'. It is presumably most 'illuminating' simple to set out the various separate effects (or 'products'), admitting that they are best treated as incommensurable by the economist as such.

The concept of the marginal social net product does force attention upon, and help to disentangle, the 'indirect' effects of individual economic actions, the prime purpose of much of economic analysis. But when the economist has tabulated fully all these 'effects' and quantified those that are susceptible to some form of practically significant quantification, any sort of summation process, even of the narrowly 'economic' effects on production and distribution, will always remain of somewhat questionable significance, and even such significance as it possesses will often fade when the other practically unquantifiable effects are brought into the account. We may again cite Marshall's words in the preface to his *Memorandum on Fiscal Policy*: 'The indirect are often much more important than the direct effects; in some of them the economic element predominates, and in others the ethical and political. It is impossible to discuss fiscal policy without reference to all these elements.' (*Official Papers*, p. 367.)

We must break off our discussion of the *Economics of Welfare* at this point. We have had to concentrate on what appears as the main theoretical apparatus of the book (and also the main interest of the author), and have omitted its review of particular policies. Whether or not any theoretical unity which may be ascribed to it is largely illusory, the book certainly attains to a unified significance of another kind: that is, as a review of the policies of the enlightened social-liberal economic thought of its period.

3. *Some German Criticisms of Socialist Economics*

We have seen, in the opening chapters of Part I, that apart from an

essay or two of Wicksteed and Sidgwick, no very systematic critique
of socialist economics was made by English economists in the seventies
and eighties. The most obvious reason for this was that there was, in
English, no coherent account of socialist economic organization and
principles for economists to examine. In Germany the position was
rather different. The writings of Marx, Lassalle, and the Social Democrats provided much more on which economists' criticism could fasten.
Anyhow, German liberal-social-reformist writers such as Schaeffle,
Brentano, and Nasse, associated with the *Verein für Sozialpolitik*, and
sympathetic to the historical school, developed in the seventies a
criticism of socialist economics which anticipated most of the central
arguments subsequently deployed by liberal economists, emphasizing
especially the inadequacy of the labour theory of value for the direction
of production in a centralized collectivist economy.

Perhaps the most interesting of this group is Schaeffle, who on the
one hand vehemently emphasized the dangers to freedom of choice in
goods and jobs which would follow the abandonment of the competitive market system, but who, on the other hand, like Sidgwick and
Wicksteed, foresaw, for better or for worse, an epoch of socialist
legislation. He therefore tentatively sketched out a scheme for a
liberal-socialist economy with a centralized authority, plentifully supplied with statistical intelligence, and manipulating a system of taxes
and subsidies, which would retain the freedom and stimuli of the competitive market. Schaeffle's idea was essentially that later developed by
Barone, Lange, and others, but without the precise mathematical formulation and the background of Walrasian and Paretian analysis.

Of Schaeffle's voluminous writings over a long period the most
valuable for our purpose is his booklet *Die Quintessenz des Sozialismus*.[1]
He there describes the problem of a socialist economic authority:

How would the requirements for the different kinds of goods be ascertained
under the closed and unified system of production of the socialists? . . . In
the present liberal economy there is complete freedom of individual tastes,
limited only by competition between buyers. . . . This freedom to decide
one's own needs is surely the fundamental basis of all freedom. (pp. 39–40.)
. . . We emphasise that if socialism removed the freedom of individual tastes
it would have to be regarded as the mortal enemy of freedom of every kind,
and of all material and spiritual well-being. . . . If the freedom of the individual,
in his own household arrangements, was threatened, then socialism would be

---

[1] The first edition appeared in 1874. We have translated from the 1878 edition, giving
page references to the English translation (introduced by Bernard Bosanquet, 1892).

unacceptable whatever else it promised and could actually perform. The liberal order, for all its faults, would be ten times superior and more favourable to culture. (p. 45.) . . . We must point out that, as at present formulated, socialism still does not indicate how such an immense collective body of labour and capital would be organised so as to bring all its units into useful activity. . . . In particular the socialist theory of value, so long as it only takes account of social costs in determining values—(and disregards use-values which are constantly changing according to place and time)—will be completely incapable of solving the problem of collectivist production, which socialism imposes, on any really sound economic principle. So long as socialism has not something quite different and more positive to offer on this problem it is hopeless. (pp. 55–56.)

What are the criteria according to which labour is to be distributed throughout the broad field of production? Will it consent to be moved around, resettled, and retrained by economic bureaucrats? . . . Without introducing use-values—that is without fixing values in a manner analogous to, or similar to, the existing market—it is inconceivable that any directing authority of a unified productive system could fit the needs for labour and goods to the stocks of these available, and so maintain that economic equilibrium of labour and consumption, which is now maintained from day to day, even if with considerable disturbances, by market prices which take account of changes in use-values. It is clear that three things depend on the correctness of one's theory of exchange value: (1) the possibility of keeping in equilibrium and directing such a huge working, producing, and consuming body; (2) the provision of the necessary individual freedom of jobs and consumption; and finally, (3) the stimulus to each individual to use economically his labour and goods. Whether it would be possible to organise a fiscal scheme for a social determination of exchange-values . . . we shall not discuss here. The question has never previously been raised and is not yet ripe for discussion. But we state without qualification that the first and decisive preliminary task must be that of accounting for use-values in the determination of the exchange-values (or social values) of labour and goods. In other words: if socialism does not preserve all the good aspects of the liberal freedom of labour and of consumption, whatever its additional and undeniable advantages may be, it has no prospects and no claim to be carried out. . . . Any advantages will turn into their opposites in a mechanically organised system of forced labour, if freedom of individual movement is not fully preserved. It is remarkable, and even comforting, that everything that could make socialism a practical discussable proposition depends on its maintaining or intensifying the economic virtues of a liberal economy. (pp. 90–95.)

(The virtues which Schaeffle granted to socialism were a more equalitarian form of labour discipline and control, prevention of overwork and protection of women and children, prevention of exploitation, abolition of social parasites, and the prevention of corruption and inordinate luxury.)

Elsewhere Schaeffle discussed his scheme for a liberal-socialist economy (*Bau und Leben des sozialen Körpers*, 1881, vol. iii, pp. 469 ff.), and held that socialism would not necessarily mean that 'production had to be organised in an absolute, authoritative and centalised way— that is destroying all freedom and levelling out and dictating all tastes, jobs, and rewards, by a single authority according to some plan or other'. Schaeffle then outlined very faintly a scheme by which the State would act as an intermediary between individual firms and consumers in the market for goods, and between firms and the owners of factors of production in the market for factors. But whatever may be thought of his embryo scheme he continued to make it perfectly clear that: 'If it was true that the social control of production was incompatible with the freedom of the household and of the individual then socialism would be impracticable. If every one had their needs laid down by a central authority then such a state in which production was socialistically controlled would represent the apogee of slavery and boredom.' (p. 479.)

Two other economists, Brentano and Nasse, may be mentioned, both like Schaeffle connected with the *Verein für Sozialpolitik* and the historical school. They both dismissed Schaeffle's liberal-socialist notions with some contempt, and strongly emphasized the incompatibility of socialist planning with the freedom of tastes and jobs. Brentano argued:

So long as there is individualism in consumption then mistakes will be unavoidable by those who have so to guide production that the goods produced have an actual use-value corresponding to the costs of production. Goods will often be produced for which there is no corresponding effective need, and these errors of calculation will occur just as much under 'a planned direction of production' as they would under free private enterprise. Indeed, if human nature did not undergo a radical change, these errors in calculation under a planned direction of production, would be far more frequent. For however large the number of officials one may conceive a country to be covered with, whose sole duty it would be to ascertain quantitatively and qualitatively the different requirements at different places, these 'consumers' councils' will never have the same interest in directing production in accordance with consumers' tastes as would the free private entrepreneur whose whole economic existence depends on fulfilling his function correctly. . . . [Short of the perfection of the human race] there is only one possibility by which a planned direction of production could be conducted better than the direction of production through the interests of private entrepreneurs; that is that all individual choice in consumption ceases. If, as in a prison, it is precisely laid down what everyone is to consume, then only a counting of heads is necessary in order to regulate production according to needs. (*Jahrbuch für Gesetzgebung*, 1878, p. 119.)

Erwin Nasse was still more emphatic, and made the issue of economic planning and freedom a very simple one. He was particularly concerned in his article with the role of the State in preventing economic crises (*Jahrbuch für Gesetzgebung*, 1879, p. 164: see also below Ch. 22, sect. 5):

A planned direction of production *without* free choice of goods and jobs would not be inconceivable, but would bring with it a destruction of culture and everything that makes life worth living. To combine a planned direction of all economic activity *with* free choice of goods and jobs is a problem which can only be compared with that of the squaring of the circle. For if everyone is allowed to decide freely the direction and nature of his economic activities and his consumption, then the direction of the economy as a whole is abandoned. The only possibility would be the collection, daily, weekly, monthly, quarterly and annually of statistics of free individual needs, and the adjustment of the direction of production to meet the needs ascertained in this way by a fiscal policy, in that by higher or lower rewards to the different economic services, production was so directed as to correspond with consumption. But in two respects this would set a task far beyond the limits of human intelligence both in ascertaining tastes and in adjusting taxes. The field would be wide open for mistakes and crises in production. When Schaeffle argues that a system of organised collective production could obtain statistics of requirements as easily as is done now by demand in the market, then it must be replied that the problem is not one of obtaining current statistics, but of estimates of future needs. . . . It has to be assumed with Fourier and other French socialists that animals and men in the socialist community would take on quite a different and more perfect nature, if one is to believe that an army of socialist officials would be able to estimate future requirements without making vast mistakes, when big changes in consumption and production are taking place. . . . Of course, there are particular branches of economic activity which because of their regularity could well be directed by experienced and conscientious officials.

In the writings of some of the later critics of socialist economics, which have followed very much the ideas we have just presented, great emphasis is sometimes laid—for one reason or another—on the German ancestry of socialist doctrines. It does not seem to have been similarly emphasized that, correspondingly, some of the main liberal criticisms of socialist economics were also first formulated by German economists sympathetic to the historical school and the *Verein für Sozialpolitik*, long before they were exploited elsewhere.

4. *Barone, Mises, and Max Weber on Socialist Economics*

What may be taken as the modern starting-point of the doctrine of maximum satisfaction is the conclusion Walras drew in his *Pure Economics* that free competition procured the maximum utility of goods and services. But if Walras thought there was a sense in which competition yielded a 'maximum', he planned to devote two volumes to examining the ways and means, on the side of production and on the side of distribution, by which competition would have to be regulated, modified, supplemented, or replaced, if this maximum or optimum was to be attained. Pareto, on the other hand, worked rather on the definition and pure analysis of this maximand, than on the institutional qualifications. He seems to have believed, when he first came to economics, that free competition maximized 'ophelimity' (even then a rather colourless neutralized maximand). But later he went on to show that what competitive equilibrium attained was hardly describable as the maximization of a maximand at all, but consisted rather in the realization of a range of opportunities comprising all positions where it was impossible to move any one party to a higher ophelimity index without moving some other party to a lower one.

In his article of 1908 on 'The Ministry of Production in a Collectivist State',[1] Pareto's Italian disciple Enrico Barone carried farther the analysis of this competitive 'maximum' concept. Barone begins by removing three implications that the competitive 'maximum' does *not* possess: (1) To say that free competition maximizes a 'sum of products' is 'an incorrect expression and unscientific concept' which in any case leaves leisure out of the account. If people were satisfied with less leisure this 'sum of products' might be increased: (2) nor is it significant to say that competition leads to a 'maximum' simply because, within the limits of their budget, individuals have a free choice between consumption goods and services and saving. Individuals might have a free choice under quite a different economic régime or different initial conditions: (3) the 'maximum' of free competition does not imply that each individual obtains a higher position on his scale of choice than he might have under a different régime. The privileged in an alternative

[1] A translation is included as an appendix to *Collectivist Economic Planning*, edited by F. A. Hayek, pp. 245 ff.—to which our page references relate.

régime might obviously come off better than they had under competition.

Free competition implies two fundamental conditions, (1) minimum costs of production, and (2) equality of prices and costs of production. These two conditions imply, in their turn, a 'maximum' simply in the sense that any alteration could not bring a benefit to each and all. If some benefited their gain would be less than the loss of those who suffered, for there would be 'a destruction of wealth'. (p. 257.) Even this tenuous conclusion of Barone's is perhaps an overstatement or an over-description. In particular, this concept of 'the destruction of wealth' by monopoly is perhaps not fully satisfactory as it stands.

After a very succinct and precise summary of the conditions of general equilibrium under competitive individualism, Barone turns to a collectivist régime. The institutional background is only very faintly touched in. A Ministry of Production is in ultimate control of the economy. It is a by-no-means omniscient body, but one equipped with an unprecedentedly extensive and accurate statistical and intelligence service, and it is operating in comparatively stable conditions. Capital and land are collectively owned but there is free choice of consumption goods and of jobs. The Ministry, inheriting certain prices and wages from the previous régime, would proceed by trial and error raising them or lowering them until in respect of all commodities the two essential conditions were everywhere fulfilled: (1) prices equal costs of production, (2) costs of production are at a minimum.

The Ministry starts with 'a certain formula of distribution which has been established by the community, and with private ownership of labour or freedom of jobs, all other resources being collectively owned'. (p. 266.) Its main distributional task is to parcel out the product of the collectively owned resources. Unless the services of these resources have been priced as they would have been if privately owned under competition, and *a fortiori*, if, in accordance with the pure labour theory of value, they are priced at zero, waste of resources will occur. Barone follows Wicksell and Pareto in making the point, rather briefly, that multiple prices may be socially advantageous where there are decreasing costs, and that it is an advantage of a socialist régime that it can arrange to discriminate more easily than private enterprise. (p. 283.)

Barone is simply concerned to establish a theoretical possibility, while bringing out clearly the magnitude of the practical task the Ministry would face: 'a tremendous—a gigantic work (work therefore taken from the productive services): but not an *impossibility*.' (p. 287.)

He emphasizes that the same fundamental conditions must be fulfilled by a collectivist economy, which has the aim of maximizing the welfare of its members, as are fulfilled by a perfectly competitive economy. But this is hardly saying much, or anything, more than that, formally, a maximum is a maximum, whatever the character of the maximizing body and the institutional setting. While undoubtedly Barone's article is an outstanding performance in pure analysis, its practical significance either as a proof of the 'possibility' of a socialist economy, or as a demonstration of its immense difficulties, is, of course, very slight indeed. The concept of a whole economy, individualist or collectivist, attaining and maintaining an economic 'optimum' or 'maximum' position (while the formulation and analysis of this position may have some theoretical interest) becomes grotesquely Utopian if it is employed, on one side or on the other, as some sort of economic criterion in the perennial debate between socialism and individualism. (Though Barone has since been regarded as 'rendering a service to socialist doctrine' by his article, this does not seem to have been his intention. Such indications as he gives seem to show that he was an anti-socialist.)

We have seen how Cassel, in the course of his first statement of his Walrasian general-equilibrium price theory, drew the conclusion (which Walras himself had never drawn) that a socialist economy could have no way of 'evaluating rightly the different factors of production'. It, therefore, could not cope with the problem of allocating the resources of society to the best advantage, the perfect solution to which problem being then often regarded as given by the self-equilibrating competitive pricing system. In the turbulent years at the end of the First World War, during the period of war communism in Russia, before the N.E.P., and with several shorter-lived socialist experiments recently in operation, the time was at hand for further examination, critical or constructive, of the practical and theoretical problems of socialist economics. In 1920, against this background in central and eastern Europe, L. Mises of the Austrian School, in the first of many writings on a theme he made peculiarly his own, took up the line of criticism of socialist economics suggested by Cassel, and followed out earlier by Schaeffle, Brentano, and Nasse. Mises's thesis was that socialism made rational economic calculation impossible, or that 'rational economic activity is impossible in a socialist commonwealth'[1]—a seemingly

---

[1] Collectivist Economic Planning, edited by Hayek, p. 130. Mises described the relation between liberalism and economic science as follows: 'Liberalism is the application of the doctrines of science to the social life of men, to Politics. . . . Knowledge of Political

challenging generalization (which, however, can soon be seen to contain much ambiguity). Mises not merely argued this thesis but added the claim that it was conclusively demonstrated by the full authority of economic science. This was certainly to restore with a vengeance the nineteenth-century alliance between political economy and a certain rationalistic form of liberalist individualism.

At exactly the same time (1920), Max Weber was advancing an analysis similar at some points, but quite different, indeed in some respects diametrically opposed, in its general attitude and conclusions, to the thesis of Mises. In his sections in his *Theory of Economic Organisation* on 'The Formal and Substantive Rationality of a Money Economy', and on 'Market Economies and Planned Economies', Weber agrees that 'monetary calculations' ensure, and are necessary for, a certain purely formal rationality in economic activity, but points out that this *formal* rationality may, and usually will, conflict with a *substantive* rationality in the direction of economic activity:

Where complete market freedom is given, the highest degree of formal rationality in capital accounting is absolutely indifferent to all the substantive considerations involved. But it is precisely the existence of these substantive factors underlying monetary calculations which determine a fundamental limitation on its rationality. This rationality is of a purely formal character. No matter what the standards of value by which they are measured, the requirements of formal and of substantive rationality are always in principle in conflict, no matter how numerous the individual cases in which they may coincide empirically. It is true that they may be made to coincide theoretically in all cases, but only under assumptions which are wholly unrealistic. (*Theory of Social and Economic Organisation*, p. 195.)

Weber also held that it may be quite false to contrast the freedom of choice in a market economy with the restrictions of this freedom in a planned economy.

When, in a planned economy, the prospect of individual income is used as a means of stimulating self-interest the type and direction of the action

Economy leads necessarily to liberalism. . . . Liberalism and Political Economy were victorious together. No other politico-economic ideology can in any way be reconciled with the science of catallactics. One cannot understand Liberalism without Political Economy. For Liberalism is applied Political Economy, it is state and social policy on a scientific basis. . . . Science has succeeded in showing that every social construction which could be conceived as a substitute for the capitalist social order is in itself contradictory and senseless and could not work out in the way its advocates explained. . . . Anyone recommending a third type of social order, of regulated private property can only deny altogether the possibility of scientific knowledge in the field of economics.' (See *Liberalismus*, 1927, pp. 3, 78, and 170; and *Kritik des Interventionismus*, 1929, pp. 23–24.)

thus rewarded is heteronomously determined. It is possible for the same thing to be true of a market economy, though in a formally voluntary way. This is particularly true where the unequal distribution of wealth, and particularly of capital goods, forces the low-income group to comply with the authority of others in order to obtain any return at all for the utilities they can offer on the market. It may be subjected to the authority of a wealthy householder or to that of the owners of capital interested in maximizing the profit from it, or of their agents. In a purely capitalistic organization of production, this is the fate of the entire working class. (p. 197.)

Finally Weber warned:

Honesty requires that all parties should admit that, while some of the factors are known, many of those which would be important are only very partially understood. In the present discussion, it is not possible to enter into the details of the problem in such a way as to arrive at concretely conclusive results. (p. 200.)[1]

Down to 1929 this debate over the nature and essential workings of 'planned' and 'market' economies was mainly confined to German and Austrian economists. Its importation into Britain and America came after the end of our period. Then, unfortunately, unlike the views of Mises, Max Weber's analysis of the problem—brief as it is—received little attention, as also did Pareto's masterly treatment of socialist problems in Les Systèmes Socialistes and Schaeffle's much earlier analysis in his Quintessence of Socialism.

[1] The quotations from Weber's Theory of Social and Economic Organisation, are from the translation by Henderson and Talcott Parsons, edited by the latter, London, 1947.

19

Consumers, Firms, and Markets

1. From the Marginal Utility Theory of Value to the Pure Theory of Consumers' Behaviour

FOUR main stages can be distinguished through which the theory of value, and the theory of consumers' behaviour, passed between Jevons (1871) on the one hand, and Slutsky (1915), Hicks, and Allen (1934) on the other.[1] The first stage was that of Jevons's original formulation, in which the marginal utility of a good was treated as a function of the quantity of that good only, the procedure of Walras, and also of Marshall. Then, secondly, in 1881 came Edgeworth's introduction of complementarity relations between goods and his treatment of utility as a function of the quantities of both or all goods. Auspitz and Lieben first defined complementarity precisely, using a similar technique of analysis, apparently independently, eight years after Edgeworth. Though Edgeworth hardly intended it, 'utility', on this treatment, at once becomes a much more shadowy and elusive concept, and also an immeasurable one. Thirdly, between 1892 and 1900, Fisher and Pareto set about extruding 'utility' from the theory of value as being unmeasurable, if account was taken of complementarity relationships, and, in any case, superfluous. The indifference curve analysis, of which, paradoxically, the 'utility-arian' Edgeworth was the pioneer, was built up by Fisher and Pareto for the purposes of a non-utility analysis of consumers' behaviour. Neither Fisher nor Pareto carried through the extrusion completely rigorously, complementarity and the law of diminishing utility not being precisely re-defined in non-utility terms. This was left to the fourth and final stage undertaken by Slutsky in a little-known article in 1915, and by Hicks and Allen in 1934.

It may be noticed that the connexion between the emasculation and eventual extrusion of the utility concept, and the development of the indifference curve technique is an historical one and not a logically necessary one. On the one hand, Edgeworth and Auspitz and Lieben, the originators of indifference curves, had maintained a thoroughly

[1] v. H. Stackelberg, 'Die Entwicklungsstufen der Werttheorie', *Schweizerische Zeitschrift für Volkswirtschaft u. Statistik*, 1947. Also G. J. Stigler's two-part article in the *Journal of Political Economy*, 1950, 'The Development of Utility Theory'.

virile notion of utility, and, on the other, the extrusion of utility was argued and carried out by economists who made no use of indifference curves. As we have seen, Wicksteed carried the attack quite a long way, and Cassel (*c.* 1899) all the way, basing his analysis (like Cournot long before) on the hypothetically recorded facts of the 'revealed' behaviour of market demanders. Barone, too, was quite explicit in rejecting 'utility' while not requiring the aid of the indifference curve.[1] Simultaneously, in America, Davenport proceeded in the same direction. His aim was 'to rid the science of doctrines that do not belong in it, e.g., labor-time, labor-pain, utility, and marginal utility determinants or measures of value; real costs', &c. (*Value and Distribution*, 1908, p. ix). This, in particular, had been the aim of his concept of costs as 'opportunities foregone' (also put forward almost simultaneously by D. I. Green).[2] Fetter, on the other hand, sought—unsuccessfully it would seem—to retain some content in the theory, by filling the void left by the default of hedonism by drawing on some more up-to-date psychological knowledge of human wants and behaviour.

The Austrian School had on the whole—though there are a number of hedonist phrases in Böhm-Bawerk—insisted on a utility concept free of hedonist and utilitarian taints, but on the other hand were critical of Pareto's and Cassel's attack on utility.[3] A concept of utility (or *Nutzen*) was retained of somewhat uncertain content. On the other hand, an attempt was made to advance from a static to a dynamic treatment of consumers' behaviour, notably by H. Mayer, who reformulated in dynamic terms the law of diminishing marginal utility as the law of the periodical recurrence of wants. ('Untersuchung zu dem Grundgesetz

---

[1] See Barone's article on the 'Ministry of Production in a Collectivist State' (translated in *Collectivist Economic Planning*, edited by Hayek), p. 246: 'I propose to prove also, that to define the economic equilibrium,—be it in a régime of free competition, in one of monopoly, or in the collectivist state,—there is no need to have recourse to the concepts of *utility*, or the *final degree of utility*, and the like; and neither is it necessary to have recourse to Pareto's concept of the *Indifference Curve*, although it represents a notable step in freeing the Mathematical School from all that seems metaphysical. The old and simple ideas of demand, supply, and cost of production suffice not only to construct into a system of equations the most important inter-relations of economic quantities, but also to treat the various dynamic questions which relate to the greater or smaller welfare of individuals and of the community.'

[2] Green was, by a few months, the first to publish the concept. See his article 'Pain Cost and Opportunity Cost', in the *Quarterly Journal of Economics*, Jan. 1894, and Davenport's article in the *Journal of Political Economy*, Sept. 1894.

[3] On Böhm-Bawerk's and Wieser's treatment of utility Davenport commented: 'One wonders why, if all this hedonism is, in fact, so inessential, one finds so much of it.' (*Value and Distribution*, p. 307.) Possibly the answer lay in a certain realization that once the hedonism went, not much content remained in the analysis of the consumer.

der wirtschaftlichen Wertrechnung', *Zeitschrift für Volkswirtschaft*, 1922.)

An important contribution to indifference curve analysis was that of W. E. Johnson, the Cambridge logician, in his article 'The Pure Theory of Utility Curves' (*Economic Journal*, 1913). Building, apparently, entirely on Edgeworth's *Mathematical Psychics*, without reference to Fisher and Pareto, he turned Edgeworth's indifference curves upside down, thus dealing with cases in which two quantities both contribute positively to the resultant utility, instead of, as in Edgeworth's analysis of exchange, one positively (the good received), and one negatively (the good given up). He called them 'iso-utility' curves, but appears to have been the first English economist to draw these indifference curves with their price lines in their present shape. Johnson saw the irrelevance, for the problems then under discussion, of the measurability or non-measurability of utility, and described, without precisely defining, the concept of the marginal rate of substitution:[1] 'This impossibility of measurement does not affect any economic problem. Neither does economics need to know the marginal (rate of) utility of a commodity. What is needed is a representation of the ratio of one marginal utility to another. In fact, this ratio is precisely represented by the *slope* at any point of the utility curve.' (p. 490.)

This article seems to have met with little or no interest, as was also the case with Slutsky's *Sulla teoria del bilancio del consummatore* in the Italian *Giornale degli Economisti* two years later (1915).[2] Slutsky completed the extrusion of utility from the analysis of consumers' behaviour, and made use of the fundamental distinction between the substitution and income effects of a change in prices, the substitution effect, with real income constant, consisting in a shift along the same indifference curve, and the income effect being equivalent to a change in real income, or in all prices simultaneously, and consisting in a shift to a higher or lower indifference curve. Slutsky also introduced the concept of the compensating variation in money income necessary to offset a particular price change and maintain the original indifference level. But this highly abstract contribution from Russia had no influence until its main conclusions were independently rediscovered by Hicks and Allen ('A Reconsideration of the Theory of Value', *Economica*, 1934). It was not until later in the 1930's that the preference

---

[1] This passage has been cited by G. J. Stigler, op. cit., p. 385.
[2] On Slutsky's article *v.* R. G. D. Allen in *Review of Economic Studies*, 1936, and in *Econometrica*, 1950.

analysis of the consumer, and the technique of indifference curves and isoquants developed by Pareto and Fisher, began to be widely adopted in Britain and America, A. L. Bowley's *Mathematical Groundwork of Economics* (1924) having given the lead.[1]

Meanwhile, throughout all this period, Marshall's demand analysis held its ground, possessed of a seemingly elemental, but perhaps deceptive simplicity, and based on the concept of utility as a function of the quantity of one good only, as had been employed by Jevons, Walras, and, on the whole, Carl Menger. As Marshall claimed: Edgeworth's innovation (in *Mathematical Psychics*) 'has great attractions to the mathematician; but it seems less adapted to express the everyday facts of economic life than that of regarding, as Jevons did, the marginal utilities of apples as functions of x simply' (x = the quantity of apples). (*Principles*, p. 845.) Certainly there seems to be something attractively graphic and graspable about each individual consumer getting his 'utility' from each individual good, which is lost in the account of an indefinite 'household' choosing between baskets of miscellaneous goods. But it is very doubtful what definite content was left in Marshall's concept of utility. In his earlier years Marshall seems to have read a great deal of hedonism into the marginal utility theory of value, but to have become markedly cautious about this by about 1895. As Guillebaud has pointed out:

> Particularly in his First Edition, Marshall used very freely the contrasting words 'pleasure' and 'pain'. . . . By the Third Edition (1895), however, Marshall was becoming sensitive to contemporary criticisms of utilitarian phraseology, and he went through the various pages in which he had used the words 'pleasure' and 'pain' deleting 'pain' and substituting in most (though not in all) cases, for 'pleasure' the word 'satisfaction' or 'benefit' or 'gratification'. Thus the total utility of a commodity to a person was defined as 'the total benefit or satisfaction yielded to him by it'; and utility as 'benefit-giving power'. (*Economic Journal*, 1942, p. 342.)

How far this careful terminological operation altered Marshall's marginal utility theory of value, or what precise content was left in it, were not problems about which Marshall would have considered any pedantic precision to be worth while, since it was intended purely as an instrumental preliminary to statistical studies of demand.

Two more features of Marshall's demand analysis may be noted: as

[1] In 1931 H. L. Schultz wrote of the indifference curve approach that it 'is rarely if ever referred to in American texts on economics'. (*Journal of Political Economy*, 1931, p. 77.)

contrasted with Jevons and the Austrian school Marshall lays much emphasis on the real (and not simply formal or theoretical) inter-dependence of 'wants and activities', rather than on ultimate consumers' tastes as the given sovereign starting-point for economic analysis.[1] He also gave some recognition to the desire for distinction (quoting Senior's statement that this was 'the most powerful of human passions', *Principles*, p. 87). But as with the case of inferior goods he felt justified in leaving it out of his normal model, and including it under the assumption of 'other things remaining equal'.[2] Apart, of course, from Veblen's essays there are very few other references to this element in demand behaviour among the better-known writings of our period.

2. Firms and Markets: Imperfect Competition and Oligopoly

For some time after 1871 the main development of marginal analysis was applied to the consumer and his problems, and why he 'valued' goods and services. There were three main sources from before that time out of which a new analysis was to be constructed of the producing unit, and of the industries and markets in which such units operated. These were Cournot's *Recherches* (1838), the works of Thünen and Mangoldt (the latter comparatively neglected), and, thirdly, parts of the English classics' analysis of supply and demand, and of the entrepreneur, or farmer, applying factors or 'doses' of them up to the margin. Jevons has little on the firm. But Marshall, of course overwhelmingly the most constructive on this subject, drew on all these three sources, and added in his unrivalled realistic and historical knowledge. Walras's assumptions of perfect competition (maintained virtually throughout) and of fixed technical 'coefficients', limited his contribution to the analysis of firms and markets, and in that particular respect he is behind Cournot whose analysis was concerned with three different market situations. Pareto's contributions to the theory of firms and markets were not rounded off, and of very varying value, but his distinction between types of market behaviour, competitive quantity-adjusting (Type I), and oligopolistic or monopolistic (Type

[1] See Talcott Parsons, *Quarterly Journal of Economics*, 1931–2, pp. 101 and 316.
[2] See A. C. Pigou's article, *Economic Journal*, 1903, p. 60, for a defence of Marshall's treatment and a further discussion of the cases where 'the utility of A to I is a function not only of the quantity of different commodities that he possesses but also of the quantity that other people possess'; and earlier, H. Cunynghame, ibid. 1892, p. 37.

II), is an important distinction leading to modern analyses of 'strategies', and is one of the points on which he was probably indebted to Auspitz and Lieben. The Austrian School, with the exception of Auspitz and Lieben, did not concern themselves much with the analysis of markets and firms, except in respect of their general principle of imputation.

The consumer can be, and is, generally assumed to be buying competitively, though an aspect of 'monopsony' was dealt with in the discussion of bilateral barter. For the analysis of the firm, problems of different forms of market become unescapable. Cournot had dealt with three forms, monopoly (with and without costs), duopoly, and competition, which he had conceived as an extreme limiting case and defined with some precision as such. Walras seemed, at least at some points, to regard competition as generally realistic and representative of the economic world. Marshall also confined his pure analysis in the *Principles* to 'competition' with a single chapter on monopoly. But, as we have seen, he emphasized in *Industry and Trade* the 'interpermeation' and 'interlacing' of monopoly price policy with competitive price policy, and that monopoly and competition 'in practice shade into one another by imperceptible degrees'. He did not explore *in abstraction* the intermediate region, perhaps believing that competition was the only case susceptible to abstract analysis where 'determinacy' reigns. But his concept of competition is loose enough to include imperfections, and is simply meant to be marked off from monopoly, duopoly, and oligopoly.

It was obviously not the case that the vast 'intermediate zone' between competition and monopoly was somehow overlooked through some blind spot or defect of vision. The 'intermediate zone' was only opened up as the earlier, and (apart from Cournot's) more imprecise 'everyday' concept of competition (which included much of what is now technically regarded as monopolistic competition), came to be replaced by the much more rigorous, and mathematically and geometrically defined, 'perfect' competition. Only then did it begin to appear what an extremity of perfection 'perfect' competition involved, how ubiquitous and 'normal' 'imperfection' was, and how much in the real world could only be explained by elements of 'imperfection'.

There is no doubt that the imprecise and ambiguous concept of 'competition', regarded at times as a picture of reality, at times as an optimum or norm, and at times as an heuristic analytical device like Robinson Crusoe, did leave room for much misinterpretation and permitted quite unjustified conclusions for policy. A noteworthy complaint on these lines was that of H. L. Moore (who seems to have been particularly concerned with J. B. Clark's unjustifiably optimistic conclusions about distribution under static competitive conditions, to which the real world was always 'approximating', and in which labour 'gets what it produces'). In his notable article 'Paradoxes of Competition' (*Quarterly Journal of Economics*, 1906), Moore complained of the 'bewildering vagueness of a fundamental term', that of 'competition', and asked:

> In what respect is the idea of competition changed when the modifiers 'perfect', 'unlimited', 'indefinite', 'free', 'pure', are added? If by these additions there is a change in the term, then, in cases in which the state of industry admits only of competition what is the nature of the limitation of the applicability of propositions deduced under the hypothesis of perfect competition? The almost invariable answer to this last question is that the imperfection of competition is simply a form of friction, producing, for the most part, a negligible variation from the standards that prevail in a régime of perfect competition. (p. 211.)

Moore went on to present with some precision the conditions of perfect competition, emphasizing the requirement of large numbers of competitors, and that 'the term competition undergoes a change of meaning according as competition is between many or a few competitors', and consequently 'marginal productivity changes its meaning according as to whether there are few or many competitors'.

He pointed out, following Cournot and Marshall, the impossibility of increasing returns under conditions of competitive equilibrium, and emphasized, with a dig presumably at J. B. Clark, that 'great harm is done when, in approaching the problems of actual industry,—which, to a large extent, is in a state intermediate between perfect monopoly and perfect competition,—the economist flings the inquirer into the vague with the assurance that static standards will tend to prevail.' (p. 215.)

Meanwhile Schumpeter followed Edgeworth's analysis of monopoly (1897) in noting the theoretical significance of 'competition among the few':

> In the case, also, of limited competition, that is when there are more than one, but only a few, independent controllers of an article, the position is even worse from the theoretical point of view, than in the case of monopoly. This is a completely new point for most economists. Even the mathematicians, above all the great pioneer Cournot, failed to see this. Nothing is more common than that 'free competition' is spoken of when only two sellers are in the field. (*Wesen and Hauptinhalt*, u.s.w., 1908, p. 269.)

Schumpeter insisted on the condition of large numbers for 'free' competition, and concluded: 'The result we have reached is somewhat surprising: not only does free competition never anywhere exist, it cannot possibly in the theoretical sense ever exist at all.' This was certainly to press home to the full the concept of free competition as the theoretically extreme limiting case.

A later well-known work of realistic analysis which constituted a challenge to a revision of the existing pure analysis of firms and markets was J. M. Clark's *Economics of Overhead Costs* (1923). The book emphasized that in the contemporary American economic world the majority of markets lay in the intermediate zone between 'theoretical' competition and 'theoretical' monopoly: 'Theoretical competition virtually assumes that a very small cut in prices will secure a very large increase in business for the concern which makes it. . . . Theoretical monopoly assumes that if the concern cuts prices its business can increase only in the ratio of the increase in total demand created by the reduction of prices. . . . The type of industry we are considering is intermediate between these two limiting cases.' (p. 441.)

Generalizing about markets Professor Clark noted:

A market is a connected system of purchases and sales of goods of identical kind, or so similar that the demand for each one is very closely dependent upon the prices of all the others. This system is so tied together that differentials in prices are limited but not eliminated. Prices may differ from place to place, subject to the costs of transportation and the trouble and cost of investigating the facts and of making a shipment and sale. They may vary from dealer to dealer, subject to the customers' inertia and 'goodwill'. They may differ from brand to brand, subject to the buyers' willingness to take other brands as substitutes. All these limitations require time to take effect, and act progressively rather than instantaneously. And these differentials are not imperfections in the competitive market, but are essential to its 'normal' operation, affording the producer who cuts prices his opportunity to profit by his move without having his gains instantly taken away by the action of his competitors. In a sense the typical large-scale manufacturer sells, not in one market but in a connected series of markets, so related that given the price in one place, the other prices cannot be deduced from the natural laws of competition, though one can set down the limits between which such prices must lie, if competition is actively at work. . . . Competition is necessarily a thing of self-imposed restraints, governed by the folk ways of the business community. . . . Competition is a varied and elastic thing. (pp. 459–61.)

Moreover, Clark's work, with its discussion of the calculation of overhead costs and its regard for the effect of cyclical fluctuations on the firm's plans, made for a clearer emphasis on the role of expectations about the future in the firm's planning and actions. The calculations which determined the firm's plans and actions are in terms of *ex-ante* estimates:

A knowledge of what has actually happened is the necessary basis for all intelligent judgment. However, this will not of itself tell the manager what his costs will be next week or next month if he follows a given policy, and for many purposes he needs to be able to prophesy in this fashion. This the accounts, taken by themselves, will not enable him to do. However, the accounts themselves involve some prophecy. Depreciation is essentially a prophetic item. (p. 222.)

Clearly a major operation was due to prune, rearrange, and tidy up the terminology and postulates of 'competition', and the 'perfection' or 'imperfection' thereof. In his powerful article on 'The Laws of Returns under Competitive Conditions' (*Economic Journal*, 1926), P. Sraffa repeated some of H. L. Moore's complaints and questions and pointed to what was to some extent the analytical answer.[1] Sraffa, like Moore and J. M. Clark, complained that the existing treatment of markets dealt simply with two extreme cases, while the cases of the real world 'will be found scattered along the intermediate zone', and that 'many of the obstacles which break up that unity of the market which is the essential condition of competition are not of the nature of "frictions", but are themselves active forces which produce permanent and even cumulative effects'. (p. 542.)

The central theoretical antinomy of the irreconcilability of competitive equilibrium with increasing returns to the firm had been suggested by Cournot. Marshall had propounded a practical working solution of this analytical antinomy in terms of economies external to the firm (but internal to the industry). Sraffa objected to this attempted reconciliation as insufficient to bear the weight of the facts of the industrial world. This class of external economies was comparatively too small, while falling costs to the firm were obviously too important. The explanation of equilibrium must lie in market imperfections. Sraffa went on:

Business men, who regard themselves as being subject to competitive

[1] Sraffa's article was the starting-point for a long series of articles in the *Economic Journal* on the interpretation and reconstruction of Marshall's analysis. See articles by A. C. Pigou (1927 and 1928), Shove (1928), Schumpeter (1928), Robbins (1928), Young (1928), and the Symposium by Sraffa, Robertson, and Shove (1930).

conditions, would consider absurd the assertion that the limit to their production is to be found in the internal conditions of production in their firm, which do not permit of the production of a greater quantity without an increase in cost. The chief obstacle against which they have to contend when they want gradually to increase their production does not lie in the cost of production—which, indeed, generally favours them in that direction—but in the difficulty of selling the larger quantity of goods without reducing the price, or without having to face increased marketing expenses . . . that is, the absence of indifference on the part of buyers of goods as between the different producers. (pp. 543–4.)

These 'imperfections' will render 'a stable equilibrium possible even when the supply curve for the products of each individual firm is descending'.

Sraffa was therefore concerned with a reformulation of the analysis of 'atomistic' competition 'among the many', which would be able to retain a stable 'determinate' equilibrium solution as its quaesitum, while taking account of the range of realistic phenomena comprised in market imperfections, instead of dismissing them as 'frictions'. He was not concerned with the problem of competition where sellers are few and sufficiently large to affect one another's policies. We must now turn to developments in this other subject.

As we have seen, 'the intermediate zone' had from the start (that is, from Cournot) not been left completely uncultivated. It had been represented by the theoretical discussions of duopoly, which though in a sense 'intermediate', was itself something of an extreme case, or even what Edgeworth called a 'curiosum'. Cournot had presented his duopoly 'solution' as though it was *in pari materia* with his pure competitive and monopoly 'solutions'. Of course his case was based on very special assumptions, not completely and explicitly stated, to the effect that the price was always the same for the two duopolists, the 'commodity' was homogeneous, and that each seller decided his own supply on the assumption that his rival's supply was independent of his own (the first seller's) actions. In 1883 the French mathematician Bertrand, in an article in the *Journal des Savants*, called attention to Cournot's work, but sought to refute it by reasoning from different, though again highly questionable and highly incomplete assumptions.[1]

[1] Bertrand's comments appeared in a joint review of Walras's *Théorie Mathématique de la Richesse Sociale* (1883) and Cournot's *Recherches* (then 45 years old). The main aim of the review is to criticize the application of mathematics in economics, and on this subject Bertrand's remarks today appear somewhat obscurantist. His comments on Cournot's duopoly solution and his own positive suggestions are extremely brief, less

Bertrand's comments suggested the 'solution' in terms of price competition on the assumption that each duopolist takes his rival's price as given and unchanging. Neither Cournot nor Bertrand took account of the duopolists' expectations as to the reactions of their rivals resulting from their own policies.

The introduction of this factor into the problem was suggested by Edgeworth in his paper on the 'Theory of Monopoly' (1897, see *Collected Papers*, vol. i, p. 137). He recognized that each duopolist has to base his policy on an estimate of his rival's expected reaction: 'It is thus that a chess-player when making his move takes account of the move which his adversary will probably make.' As he had just stated, following J. S. Mill, that only the competitive case was accessible to the theoretical economist and that the realm of monopoly (or duopoly) would have to be left to the empirical school 'floundering in a chaos congenial to their mentality', it is not quite clear what validity or significance he attached to his oscillating solution of duopoly with the price 'dancing down' to the competitive level, and then 'jumping' back to the monopoly level ('and so perpetual motion is set up', op. cit., p. 121). But it was, at any rate, a 'dynamic' answer in terms of a process of action and reaction, and not a static 'solution' describing an equilibrium point. Edgeworth recognized the 'serious objections' applicable to Cournot's 'transition from the case of pure monopoly to that of perfect competition by the introduction of first one and then more competitors'. He found these objections valid not merely against Cournot's particular 'solution' to the duopoly problem 'but rather because he has missed the general theorem: that the solution is indeterminate where the number of competitors is small'. (*Economic Journal*, 1898, p. 113.)

At about the same time as Edgeworth's contribution, Irving Fisher, in an article introducing his edition of Cournot (*Quarterly Journal of Economics*, 1898, p. 126), pointed out the lack of realism in Cournot's (and Bertrand's) assumptions, and emphasized the many different possible developments of a duopoly situation, according to the different expectations each duopolist might have of his rival's moves. Like Edgeworth he introduced the analogy of games and economic behaviour:

As a matter of fact, no business man assumes either that his rival's output or price will remain constant any more than a chess player assumes that his

than half a page in all, and they form a very slight foundation indeed for Bertrand's reputation as a modern pioneer of duopoly analysis, the main credit on this subject surely being due to Edgeworth.

opponent will not interfere with his effort to capture a knight. On the contrary, his whole thought is to forecast what move the rival will make in response to one of his own. . . . The whole study is a 'dynamic' one, and far more complex than Cournot makes it out to be.

Later, Pigou describing the case as one of 'Monopolistic Competition' (*Wealth and Welfare*, 1912, pp. 192 ff.), also emphasized that the supply of each duopolist 'depends on his judgement of the policy which the other will pursue, and his judgement may be anything, according to the mood of each and his expectation of success from a policy of bluff. As in a game of chess, each player's move is related to his reading of the psychology of his opponent and his guess as to that opponent's reply.' Finally, A. L. Bowley based his treatment on the assumption that the output of each producer 'depends on what each producer thinks the other is likely to do'. (*Mathematical Groundwork of Economics*, p. 38.)

In the 1920's the debate over the problem of duopoly swung back in favour of Cournot's general approach as against Bertrand's, the return to Cournot being led by Wicksell. But it had become clearer that, as Chamberlin concluded, 'duopoly is not one problem but several' ('Duopoly, Value where Sellers are Few', *Quarterly Journal of Economics*, Nov. 1929, p. 91). In fact, it was a not easily limitable number of problems.

By 1929 the analysis of firms and markets was attempting in two different directions to break out of the two limiting cases of pure competition and pure monopoly into which it got pressed when these two concepts came to be rigorously defined, and when they had then been shown to exclude many, or most, of the important problems of the real world. There seems often to have been present an optimistic belief that in both directions static maximization analysis (in which it was not always clear whether *ex-ante* schedules of supply and demand or *ex-post* 'actual' quantities were under discussion) would continue gradually to produce more realistic and applicable results. One direction was leading to a reformulation of the 'atomistic' competitive analysis of conditions of competition among the many, taking account of imperfections. This involved enforcing more precision on Marshall's loose concept of 'competitive' conditions and on the assumptions underlying such conditions, without essentially extending the range of phenomena which his analysis covered. The other direction led to a more systematic review of oligopolistic conditions, inevitably, however, somewhat lacking in significant generality, as Marshall had hinted it was bound to be (*v. Principles*, p. 459), and consisting eventually, and inevitably, largely of a classification and analysis of sometimes rather arbitrarily selected cases.

It has been suggested that the increasing attention to problems of monopoly and imperfect competition, and the new analyses of these subjects forthcoming in the early 1930's, somehow reflected the increasing importance of monopoly, oligopoly, and market imperfections in modern industry. There does not seem to be much truth in this generalization. For one thing, no one could have been more seriously impressed with the problem of monopoly than Marshall and J. B. Clark already had been at the turn of the century. The new analyses seem rather to have been due much more to more rigorous academic standards of logical and terminological tidiness and precision, than to any close confrontation with newly emerging problems in the real world of industry and trade. The rigorous definition of perfect competition, a logical and analytical achievement, cleared and defined for new analysis—or for a new application of the older monopoly analysis—the field of 'imperfect' competition on the one hand, and of 'competition among the few' on the other.

3. *Marginal Productivity and Distribution*

We have dealt briefly with one-half of the firm's calculations and decisions, those about how much to sell and what price to sell at in different market situations. The other half, as to the decisions about what factors to buy and what price to pay for them, was answered by the marginal productivity analysis of production and distribution. Before the formulation of this theory there had been a considerable interim period of nearly a quarter of a century following the breakdown of the distribution analysis of the English classics. This interim had coincided, to a large extent, with the beginnings of the rise of the modern labour and socialist movements. The belief in the possibilities of the deliberate redistribution of income, on the one hand, and of such a modification of the conditions of ownership and earnings, on the other hand, as would make for much greater economic equality, gained a hold it was never to lose.

The marginal productivity theory, which received its full elaboration in the nineties, never recaptured the magisterial authority in assigning incomes, including, of course, wages, their normal 'natural' limits, which had been exercised by the dominant and widely held interpretations of the older classical doctrines. Marginal productivity analysis was, however, sometimes rather doubtfully invoked for the explanation of unemployment. The theory had been completed by Marshall (who included an even greater array than usual of reservations and qualifications) and by Edgeworth, Wicksell, Wicksteed, Walras, and J. B. Clark.

Over the greater part of our period, alongside the continued refinement in formulation, and the attenuation in content, of the marginal productivity doctrine, went an ambition, with some economists, to make it fulfil something of the function of the older and more rigid versions of the classical doctrines of wages. Perhaps it was not sufficiently clear, to what very different, and much more strictly limited questions the marginal productivity analysis was a kind of answer, as compared with the Ricardian analysis of relative aggregate shares combined with a somewhat wavering application of the Malthusian principle. On the one hand, Wicksell tried to apply the marginal productivity analysis to the Ricardian problem of relative shares, and Böhm-Bawerk tried to reformulate the wages-fund concept with its aid, while Marshall, obviously sceptical of the limited content of the marginal productivity analysis, went on to a cautious restatement of the Malthusian doctrine of wages. On the other hand, the more thorough-going and exclusive exponents of marginal productivity, such as Wicksteed and Clark, abandoned these very difficult classical problems, and concentrated on the full generalization of the marginal productivity formula, and thereby marked it off sharply from the classical analysis.

Generalizing the marginal productivity formula meant generalizing (1) the classical rent concept, (2) the diminishing returns concept, and (3) liquidating much of the significance of the old threefold classification of factors of production, and of the distinction between 'price-determining' and 'price-determined' incomes. It is interesting to note how the generalizing of the rent concept immediately came in for political exploitation by both sides. On the left, by J. A. Hobson and the Fabians, it was used for a general attack on higher incomes whatever their source. On the other side, J. B. Clark used the generalized rent concept to defend the incomes of those who had invested in land, rather than in industrial capital or education, from discriminating attack.

The generalization of the concept of diminishing returns implied raising it from its special classical application to agriculture to a general principle of proportions, applicable to all factors.[1] This implied, further, the dissolving of the classical threefold classification of factors (particularly insisted upon by Wicksteed and Davenport)—a classification which had served for the analysis of the relative shares of the three social-economic classes, but which had little significance for the maximization or minimization problems of the individual entrepreneur.

In respect of the internal coherence of the marginal productivity theory itself there remained for subsequent elucidation simply a number of points of formulation required by the more rigorous analysis of competitive conditions and the laws of returns, and some disagreements over the assumption of the variability of the proportions in which factors could be combined.[2] Externally, however, there remained much scope for debate and 'grumble' about the content and significance of the theory. Nevertheless, 'marginal productivity' may be said to have remained the orthodox doctrine of distribution in the sense defined by D. H. Robertson: 'The proposition that of all the single statements that can be made about wages, the statement that 'wages tend to measure the marginal productivity of labour' is at once the most illuminating analytically and the most important practically for the consideration of wage policy.' ('Wage Grumbles', 1931, reprinted in *Readings in Income Distribution*, pp. 221 ff.)

The unassailable 'grumble-proof' core of the marginal productivity analysis lay in the maximization formula for the individual producing unit in a factor market, the total turnover of which involved a very small proportion of the national income. The various forms of 'wage grumbles', or 'marginal productivity grumbles', arose mainly from trying to read into the marginal productivity analysis, either in expounding it, or in 'grumbling' at it, more than this basic minimum.

We have seen how J. B. Clark at one stage expounded the marginal productivity theory as containing not merely a generally valid positive

---

[1] See H. J. Davenport, *Value and Distribution*, 1908, Ch. 23. He applied the principle of diminishing returns to 'the entrepreneur as the fixed quantity' in the firm. See also F. Y. Edgeworth's paper on the Laws of Return (*Papers*, vol. i, pp. 61 ff.), which carefully distinguished the often confused marginal and average formulations of the law of diminishing returns.

[2] For a survey of, and answer to, criticisms of the principle of variation, *v.* W. L. Valk, *The Principles of Wages*, and D. H. Robertson, op. cit. See also Schultz, 'Marginal Productivity and the Pricing Process', *Journal of Political Economy*, 1928; Hicks, 'Marginal Productivity and the Principle of Variation', *Economica*, 1932; Schultz, 'Marginal Productivity and the Lausanne School', *Economica*, 1932; and Georgescu-Roegen, 'Fixed Coefficients of Production and Marginal Productivity Theory', *Review of Economic Studies*, vol. iii, p. 40.

truth about actual distribution, but a normative principle of distributive justice. However, most of the orthodox expositions were concerned to defend it by emptying out and limiting its content in the manner of Böhm-Bawerk in his well-known essay on *Power and Economic Law* (1914).[1] He argued that there could be no conflict in explanation between the action of the economic laws of distribution on the one side, and the facts of the institutional power of trade unions, employers' associations, and governments on the other. The factor of institutional power worked through, not against, economic laws, with which its effects were perfectly compatible. The facts of economic power determined the assumptions about institutions and markets on which the laws hinged. Similarly, as D. H. Robertson later put it: 'There is therefore nothing *necessarily* inconsistent between the orthodox theory and the observed fact that wages are nowadays often fixed by outside authority, or as the outcome of a process of collective bargaining in which the factors of bluff and strategic strength play a large part.' But, of course, the fewer possibilities that are inconsistent with the theory, or the less it rules out, the less content and interest it can have. If everything uncontradictory is compatible with them, and anything uncontradictory or conceivable may happen without infringing them, the 'laws of distribution' do not forbid anything, and cease to be laws of empirical science. It may be asked how much there was left worth defending when all the content had been withdrawn, which had to be withdrawn if these laws of distribution were to be thoroughly defensible in the way their expounders desired.

As Robertson showed, the marginal productivity analysis can be formulated to take care of the various 'dynamic' objections or 'grumbles' to the effect that a self-justifying wage-policy over a period of time can force up or force down the initial equilibrium wage to a new higher or lower equilibrium level by its repercussions on the efficiency or bargaining position of the worker, either by stimulating entrepreneurs, or by depressing the health and morale of exploited workers.[2]

[1] Another masterly essay on the same theme is J. Schumpeter's 'Das Grundprinzip der Verteilungstheorie', *Archiv für Sozialwissenschaft u. Sozialpolitik*, 1917, pp. 1 ff. Schumpeter here combats Tugan-Baranovsky's revisionist-Marxist essay, 'Die Soziale Theorie der Verteilung' (1913) and argues that institutional 'power' can be given the same role in the framework of a marginal productivity analysis as it has in the Marxian analysis.

[2] Various doctrines of this kind were in the 1920's presented as conflicting with orthodox marginal productivity analysis: see, for example, J. W. F. Rowe, *Wages in Theory and Practice*; M. H. Dobb, *Wages* (1928), Chs. IV and V, and 'A Sceptical View of the Theory of Wages', *Economic Journal*, Dec. 1929. These criticisms are reviewed in Robertson's essay on 'Wage Grumbles' cited above.

There was, however, one important point where the orthodox doctrine did seem to leave a flank exposed, and not completely to withdraw its content in time. The Wages Fund doctrine, which it eventually replaced, had been a macro-economic analysis of the limits of average aggregate wages. It is extremely doubtful whether the marginal productivity analysis should be ascribed any significance for the determination of wages 'as a whole', at least without the addition of some further very thoroughly analysed assumptions, which are not easy to discover in an explicit form in the writings of our period. It seems that Marshall's reservations about the marginal productivity doctrine were connected with this particular limitation. But in the analysis of Böhm-Bawerk, for example, marginal productivity analysis had been applied to a single 'giant' market for the whole labour force of society. As Robertson later put it, in expounding the theory, 'it has always been emphasised that to the individual employer it is the wage-rate that is normally the fixed thing, and the number employed that is the variable. ... It has perhaps been less emphasised, because until recently it has been less important, that the same may be true if we are considering the field of employment for labour as a whole.' (p. 222.) There is no question of the applicability of marginal productivity analysis to the problem of the amount of employment a particular firm or small industry will give, the total wage bill of which is a negligible percentage of the whole national income. But the analysis tended to be applied also to the problem of general unemployment, for example to the British unemployment problem of the late 1920's. Beveridge was probably expressing by no means only his own point of view when he wrote: 'If and in so far as unemployment is now resulting because, through fall of prices, real wages have risen and become rigid at a point above the productivity of the marginal labourer, the remedy must be sought in restoring the equilibrium thus disturbed. It cannot be found elsewhere.' (*Unemployment*, 1930, p. 416.) The argument appears to be applied to *general* wages and employment, not to those in some particular small industry. We are not, of course, concerned with the problem of whether or no a reduction of wages throughout British industry would or would not have reduced unemployment in Britain in 1929. We are simply calling attention to the way in which at the end of our period, as earlier, the 'micro-economic' marginal productivity analysis, without any more complex assumptions being worked out or stated, was being directly applied to problems of general wages and aggregate unemployment.

20
Profit, Uncertainty, and 'Expectations'

1. *Profit and Uncertainty*

IN the previous chapter we have noticed two points where criticism began to focus on the postulates on which the analysis of the firm was based. First, as the implications of a rigorous definition of 'perfect' competition began to become more apparent, they became more and more clearly irreconcilable with the empirical fact of decreasing costs to large-scale enterprise. Here the reconciling element was in due course found largely to consist in the ignorance and uncertainty of the real world, that is in the ignorance either of consumers (making for market imperfections), or of firms (necessitating an inevitably fixed entrepreneurial factor which limited their size). Secondly, the analysis of the firm's actions under conditions of oligopoly was seen to require assumptions as to its inevitably imperfectly prescient expectations about the reactions of rivals. A more general and penetrating examination of the relation of uncertainty and ignorance to the postulates of economic analysis was also developing out of the theory of profit. This was not a subject to which English analysis made a great contribution. The main work in the nineteenth century was by Germans (Thünen and Mangoldt), and later, towards the end of the nineteenth and the beginning of the twentieth century, by Americans.

One of Francis Walker's (1840–97) main services was to separate profit, as the reward for a specifically entrepreneurial ability and activity, which he held to be the real motive force in the modern economy, from the rent of land and from interest. But his distribution theory as a whole, coming between the complete decay of the classical analysis and the construction of the marginal productivity theorems, has been said to amount simply to the statement that each factor in turn gets what is left over when the others have been paid. The analysis of profits took on a new significance with the completion of the marginal productivity analysis. This was notably the case with J. B. Clark's version, with its comparatively clear-cut presentation of the postulates of the static state, from which his five main types of dynamic change were excluded, and where marginal productivity analysis was shown to account precisely for the whole product, with no residue for 'profit'. Profit then becomes a 'dynamic' surplus, dependent on friction and change, which are absent from the static state, where 'the power of accurately foreseeing the future' is, as far as is necessary, universal, 'where there are no discrepancies between the anticipated and the actual result of economic activity'. (A. H. Willett, quoted by F. H. Knight, *Risk, Uncertainty and Profit*, p. 39.) Schumpeter's analysis of profit as the reward for 'innovation' in methods of production or in products, and therefore non-existent in the stationary 'circular-flow' economy, has much the same significance as Clark's. (*v. Theory of Economic Development*, pp. 128 ff.) Contrasted with Clark's analysis was the 'risk' theory of profit contributed by that original and penetrating thinker, the Philadelphian business-man, F. B. Hawley:[1] 'This surplus of consumer's cost over entrepreneur's cost, universally regarded as profit, and from the nature of the case, an unpredetermined residue, is the inducement for the assumption by the entrepreneur, or enterprise, of all the risks.' Profit is the reward for 'risks wisely selected'.

The difference between Clark and Hawley was not wide. They agreed on profit being, in a sense, residual, but Clark distinguished between the reward for risk which went to the 'capitalist', and 'pure profit' as the outcome of 'dynamic' change. The missing piece required to complete the picture was inserted by F. H. Knight in his *Risk, Uncertainty and Profit* (1921), who in defining precisely what this piece was, and in fitting it into its place, shed a great deal of much-needed light on the assumptions underlying much of economic analysis.

Knight started by emphasizing that

in economics a distrust of general principles, fatal as it is to clear thinking, will be inevitable so long as the postulates of theory are so nebulous and shifting. They can hardly be made sufficiently explicit.... We shall endeavour to search out and placard the unrealities of the postulates of theoretical economics, not for the purpose of discrediting the doctrine, but with a view to making clear its theoretical limitations (p. 11).... [The aim is] to bring out the content of the assumptions or hypotheses of the historic body of economic thought, referred to by the classical writers as 'natural price' theory. By this is meant, not the assumptions definitely in the minds of the classical economists, but the assumptions necessary to define the conditions of perfect competition, at which the classical thought was aimed, and which are significant as forming the limiting tendency of actual economic processes. . . .

[1] F. B. Hawley (1843–1929) was the author of two valuable books: *Capital and Population*, 1882, and *Enterprise and the Productive Process*, 1907. The earlier book is discussed below in Ch. 22, sect. 2.

The key to the whole tangle will be found to lie in the notion of risk or uncertainty and the ambiguities concealed therein. . . . Uncertainty must be taken in a sense radically distinct from the familiar notion of Risk, from which it has never been properly separated. (pp. 18–19.)

Finally uncertainty emerges as 'the most important underlying difference between the conditions which theory is compelled to assume and those which exist in fact'. (p. 51.)

Professor Knight's analysis, which is in the main describable as stationary or quasi-stationary dynamics, relates to 'a society in action' (p. 81), which so rapidly and perfectly adjusts itself as to be constantly in or very near to 'equilibrium', in the sense that there is general, and therefore compatible, maximization, and universal fulfilment of plans by each individual unit.

Though the people in this model are supposed to be 'normal human beings', and a 'random sample of the population' of the industrial nations (p. 76), they are completely 'rational', free, independent individuals, not subject to 'habits preferences or aversions', enjoying unrestricted and costless intercommunication, and exchanging a wide variety of commodities divisible into an indefinite number of units. (pp. 78–79.) In the first instance they are living in a model world where 'all given factors and conditions remain absolutely unchanged', and of which they therefore soon acquire 'perfect knowledge': 'Under static conditions every person would soon find out, if he did not already know, everything in his situation and surroundings which affected his conduct.' (p. 79.) The assumptions of this model were to be regarded as 'idealizations or purifications of tendencies which hold good more or less in reality'.

Having constructed this model, and put it through some of its necessarily rather stylized paces, Knight in Part III ('Imperfect Competition through Risk and Uncertainty') returns to the assumption of omniscience: 'Chief among the simplifications of reality pre-requisite to the achievement of perfect competition is, as has been emphasised all along, the assumption of practical omniscience on the part of every member of the competitive system' (p. 197), whereas, in reality, 'the essence of the situation is action according to *opinion*, of greater or less foundation and value, neither entire ignorance nor complete and perfect information, but partial knowledge'. (p. 199.) With uncertainty absent there would be no entrepreneurial activity: 'It is doubtful whether intelligence itself would exist in such a situation; in a world so built that perfect knowledge was theoretically possible, it seems likely that all organic readjustments would become mechanical, all organisms automata.' (p. 268.)

Professor Knight's wide attribution of the postulate of omniscience to much of economic thought has been questioned, but we cannot attempt to pass judgement here on how far he was justified, historically, in implying that his model 'brought out the content of the assumptions or hypotheses of the historic body of economic thought referred to by the classical writers as "natural price" theory'. As we have seen, Knight did not say that the postulate of omniscience was 'definitely in the minds of the classical economists', but was 'necessary to define the conditions of perfect competition at which the classical thought was aimed'. Questionings are bound to be possible of any attempt to attribute wholesale such a far-reaching postulate, to a not very compact and homogeneous body of thinkers, as being not consciously held, but logically implied in their thought. In face of such a *reductio ad extremum*, some of the classical and neo-classical economists might well have preferred to withdraw. Knight himself is prepared to sacrifice a certain amount of precision by withdrawing his analysis to an *approximately* 'static' state, with a certain minimum of uncertainty and ignorance. (pp. 266–7.)[1]

However, when the postulates of classical political economy had been under keen examination in the controversies of the 1870's, the assumption of full knowledge had been pointed out by Cliffe Leslie in his long-forgotten essay on *The Known and the Unknown in the Economic World*:

> The orthodox, a priori, or deductive system thus postulates much more than a general desire of wealth. It postulates, also, such full knowledge of the gains in different employments and such facilities of choice and change of employment that any special attacks can be evaded or shifted ... the fundamental error of the *a priori* system (is that of) confounding the unknown with the known in the economic world. (*Essays*, 2nd ed., 1888, pp. 229–30.)

[1] Knight's attribution of this assumption of omniscience to the classical economists was to be followed, from a very different point of view, and for very different purposes, by Keynes 15 years later: 'I accuse the classical economic theory of being itself one of these pretty, polite techniques which tries to deal with the present by abstracting from the fact that we know very little about the future. . . . The orthodox theory assumes that we have a knowledge of the future of a kind quite different from that which we actually possess. This false realisation follows the lines of the Benthamite calculus. The hypothesis of a calculable future leads to a wrong interpretation of the principles of behaviour which the need for action compels us to adopt, and to an underestimation of the concealed factors of utter doubt, precariousness, hope, and fear.' (*v. The New Economics*, edited by Seymour Harris, pp. 186 and 192.)

Carl Menger, also, explicitly stated that omniscience was among the general assumptions of economic analysis as he understood it. (*Studies in Method*, p. 72.) As we have seen, Marshall also agreed that a 'theoretically perfect long period will be found to involve the supposition of a stationary state of industry in which the requirements of a future age can be anticipated an indefinite time beforehand. Some such assumption is indeed unconsciously implied in many popular renderings of Ricardo's theory of value.' (*Principles*, p. 379.)

2. *Expectations*

'The fact that all economic activity is governed by expectations has been [according to R. G. Hawtrey] universally taken for granted from the beginning of the science.'[1] 'Taken for granted' is a two-edged phrase. It might imply either 'fully appreciated' or 'completely overlooked', or it might mean that expectations have often been assumed to be perfect and were therefore dismissed from the problem. In this section we shall try to summarize briefly the evidence as to how far increasingly explicit emphasis on the expectations on which the plans and actions of economic individuals are based, may have contributed to a fundamental and new clarification of economic analysis. It should be added that the term 'expectations', though it seems suggestive of a rather narrowly calculating rationality, should often be interpreted to cover also vague barely formulated 'hunches', habits, and quirks of mind and action, and susceptibilities to mass-suggestiveness and herd pressures.

Certainly any attempt to explain human actions must inevitably involve some reference, implicit or explicit, as to the expectations about future situations or contingencies which the actions are taken to meet or to accompany. Certainly, also, a long series of examples could be cited where, to explain particular actions or special cases, the nature of the expectations of the individuals engaged has been explicitly explored or invoked. W. T. Thornton, Fleeming Jenkin, and Cairnes, in discussions of supply and demand, and Jevons and Wicksteed at a number of points, all clearly refer to expectations. Auspitz and Lieben, and Davenport, also deserve mention on this subject. We have previously referred to Marshall's repeated discussions of entrepreneurs' expectations, and his emphasis that, if precisely stated, the assumptions of the

[1] *Economic Journal*, 1937, p. 439. Quoted by Marget, *Theory of Prices*, vol. ii, p. 150.

stationary state involve the correct anticipation of the future. In Menger's *Grundsätze*, and at many points in Böhm-Bawerk's writings, it is frequently emphasized how all economic activity is based on planning for the future, a fact summarized with characteristic terminological terseness in the phrase 'das in-die-Zukunft-gerichtet-sein der Wirtschaft' ('The into-the-future-directedness of economic life'). But Menger also explicitly stated that theoretical economics depended on the assumption of omniscience (*Allwissenheit*), that is, that expectations were always prefectly correct, an assumption which more or less dismisses them from further investigation. This remained the approach of later members of the Austrian School who did, nevertheless, attempt a dynamic study of the consumer. They sought to introduce the element of time (*das Zeitmoment*) into the study of economic behaviour, while retaining the assumption of infallible expectations. For example: 'For economic theory only the expected not the realised utility is relevant. But as a result of economic experience the two will hardly essentially diverge from one another.' (Rosenstein Rodan, on 'Grenznützen', *Handwörterbuch der Staatswissenschaften*, 4th ed., 1927.)

The explicit introduction of changing and not necessarily infallible expectations was made particularly in the analysis of concepts in which the time dimension was more or less inescapable, and which especially required a dynamic 'dated' analysis, for example, those of income, capital, and interest, as analysed in the early works of Irving Fisher (*Appreciation and Interest*, 1896, and the *Nature of Capital and Income*, 1906). Changing and fallible expectations were obviously introduced very early in the explanation of particular phases of the trade cycle (for example, by Sismondi, John Mills, Overstone, and Bagehot). Schumpeter's early exposition of his theory of fluctuations had described the rupture of equilibrium conditions in the crisis and depression as the unfulfilment or disappointment of expectations (1910).[1] A particularly full and explicit analysis of fluctuations in expectations and how they come about is given in Pigou's chapter on 'Errors in Business Forecasts' (Ch. 7, Part IV of *Wealth and Welfare*, 1912).

These latter examples, however, and no doubt many more could be produced, relate mainly to explanations of particular problems, especially those of investment and of cyclical fluctuations, and were not worked into the central theorems of micro-economic maximization analysis, and the self-adjusting dynamics of prices and distribution. Here ignorance and uncertainty were more often treated as a 'friction'

---

[1] *Zeitschrift für Volkswirtschaft*, 1910, pp. 271 ff. See also Ch. 12, sect. 2.

from which it was permissible to abstract, and any distinction between expected and realized values was frequently entirely ignored.

An important step was, however, being taken in the second half of the 1920's, mainly by Scandinavian writers. What these writers set out to achieve was not simply a scattering of the adjective 'expected' amid an otherwise static discussion, but a type of analysis which began to explain systematically the course of particular economic processes and of particular central variables through time (or successive periods of time), in terms of the changing and fallible expectations and plans of individuals and their reactions to the over-fulfilment or under-fulfilment of those expectations and plans. It may be, as Schumpeter has said, that to introduce expectations as an explanation of economic activities is, of itself, simply 'filling in a blank space by another blank space'. It does not necessarily amount to much more than that, but it does define more clearly the nature of the blank space, and what it is that has to be discovered to fill it in. The explicit introduction of expectations and of the *ex-ante* and *ex-post* concepts obviously help to clarify the distinction between static and dynamic analysis, and do away with many fundamental ambiguities.[1]

Myrdal in his *Price Formation and Economic Change* (1927) was concerned, in particular, with the effect of uncertainty on the investment plans of the firm, showing how the notion of the capital value of an asset rests on the anticipation of imperfectly foreseen future receipts and interest rates through the life-time of the asset.[2] Lindahl developed a macro-dynamic 'sequence' analysis of successive equilibria and of cumulative processes. (*Methods of Monetary Policy*, 1929, and *The Place of Capital in the Theory of Price*, 1929.)[3] Though both Myrdal and Lindahl made major studies of the problems which Wicksell's *Interest and Prices* had opened up, the dynamic treatment they developed, and Myrdal's distinction between expected or *ex-ante* values and realized or *ex-post* values, owed little or nothing directly to Wicksell, for whom expectations—as for many of his contemporaries—were hardly a formulated problem. The pioneer work in distinguishing and defining clearly the significance of static and dynamic analysis (foreshadowed in Edgeworth's distinction between the study of the equilibrium *point*

---

[1] As is well known, the distinction between *ex-ante* and *ex-post* concepts is due to G. Myrdal. But H. J. Davenport (*Value and Distribution*, 1908, pp. 332–3) had contrasted 'the forward-looking attitude to exchange' with 'the *ex-post* concept'.

[2] For an account of the earlier works of Lindahl and Myrdal see Brinley Thomas, *Monetary Policy and Crises*, Ch. III, and H. Dickson, *Weltwirtschaftliches Archiv*, 1952, pp. 54 ff.   [3] Translated in *Studies in the Theory of Money and Capital*, 1939.

and the study of the *path* to or from equilibrium), was that of R. Frisch's essay on 'Statics and Dynamics in Economic Theory' (1929).[1]

Let us summarize by tracing the gradually more explicit introduction of a more rigorous form of dynamic analysis in the different branches of economic theory:

1. In 'welfare' theory, dynamic analysis was hardly introduced at all.

2. In the theory of the consumer, it is perhaps latent in Pigou's distinction between 'desires and satisfactions' (*Economics of Welfare*, Ch. 2). It is far more explicitly introduced by some of the later members of the Austrian school, for example, H. Mayer and P. Rosenstein-Rodan. In fact, Mayer's insistence on a 'causal-genetic analysis' is, when trimmed of its metaphysics, an insistence on the need for dynamic analysis.[2] But on the whole the analysis of consumers' behaviour does not provide the most obvious and significant field for the development of any form of 'dynamics'.

3. In much of the theory of the firm very little advance was made towards a dynamic analysis. In fact, the fundamental distinction between subjective expected quantities and objective realized quantities was for long largely disregarded—(far more than it had been by Marshall). As R. Triffin has pointed out:

> The whole analysis of monopolistic competition, however, whether it be that of Chamberlin, Robinson, Stackelberg, or Pareto, is conducted as if this subjective sales curve were merely the exact reflection of an objective sales curve, embodying the actual reactions of the market. In this way, the distinction between a subjective and an objective definition of demand becomes irrelevant; no matter what the definition used at the start, the same sales curve is interpreted as representing identically both the expectations of the seller and the happenings on the market. . . . It must be recognised that the usual statement of equilibrium conditions is valid only when the entrepreneurs succeed in gauging correctly the shape of their sales curves. If such is not the case, then mistakes may very well introduce dis-equilibrium into a situation which would, otherwise, have been in equilibrium. (*Monopolistic Competition and General Equilibrium Theory*, 1940, pp. 63 and 66.)

But in the theory of oligopoly the expectations of the firm about its rivals' conduct came more and more explicitly to be emphasized as an

---

[1] See *Review of Economic Studies*, vol. iii for a shortened translation of the original article in the 'Nationaløkonomisk Tidskrift', 1929.

[2] See his long critical article, mainly directed at mathematical versions of equilibrium analysis: 'Der Erkenntniswert der funktionellen Preistheorien', in *Wirtschaftstheorie der Gegenwart*, Bd. II.

essential ingredient of the problem, and the solution soon came to be sought in the description of the processes of manœuvre rather than in analysing a point of equilibrium (e.g. already by Edgeworth and Fisher).

4. It was especially in the treatment of overhead costs (for example, in J. M. Clark's work on the subject), and in the analysis of profit and investment policies that dynamic treatment and concepts received most development. The reason for this is fairly clear. As D. H. Robertson wrote:

> While the marginal utility to them of *consumptive* goods is a thing about which most people are capable of forming fairly accurate and stable judgements, their estimate of the marginal utility of *construction* goods is by no means so likely to be constant. For this estimate depends on the expected future marginal productivity of those goods; and since both this productivity itself is liable to variation, and also any forecast of it is at best a matter of guess-work, there is clearly room for considerable variation in the estimates formed of the marginal utility of construction goods. (*Study of Industrial Fluctuations*, 1915, p. 157.)

Here, obviously, an analysis based on the assumption of a perfect correspondence between expected and realized quantities can hardly claim much significance even as a 'first approximation'.

5. It was even more in the theories of interest, money, and aggregate fluctuations, that the development of dynamic analysis received most impetus, and for which it had most significance. Here, for example, Irvine Fisher's writings on interest and income, and a whole host of writers on the psychological aspects of crises and the trade cycle can be cited.

21

Interest, Money, and Macro-economic Analysis

1. *Theories of Interest*

THIS chapter is a very brief and schematic treatment of a vast and immensely complicated subject. Though we make some attempt to deal in outline with the history of monetary theories and problems to the extent to which these were an intimate part of the main body of economic theory, there are many less central monetary topics which we completely omit: for example, bimetallism, the State theory of money, many legal, terminological, and even metaphysical debates about the nature of money and the classification of different sorts of money, controversies over the functions of banks and the creation of deposits, theories of index numbers and of the foreign exchanges, and many other topics. The picture which we are trying to reproduce is the more complicated because much of the most important work on monetary theory and problems has not taken the form of independent treatises on money; there are few really leading works of this kind. Monetary theory has developed, on the one hand, from the exploration of the monetary aspects of 'normal' equilibrium analysis and from the extension of that analysis to the theory of money; and, on the other hand, and often quite separately, from the monetary analysis of crises, cycles, and fluctuations. The theory of money (and to some extent also the theory of interest) lay, in our period at any rate, in a no-man's-land intermediate between the two main, and none too clearly co-ordinated, branches of economic theory, the 'normal' equilibrium analysis of relative values, and the analysis of fluctuations in economic aggregates.

There is, however, one mainly non-monetary topic which we shall rapidly dispose of. There were few or no highly important developments in the non-monetary theory of interest down to 1929, apart from the works of Walras, Clark, Böhm-Bawerk, Cassel, and Fisher, which we have already discussed. Not that there was any shortage of lengthy controversies. Clark, Schumpeter, and Fisher all had some strenuous debates with Böhm-Bawerk, and in America Fetter engaged in a number of controversies. At some points these debates led to some slight re-conciling modifications (as exemplified in Fisher's *Theory of Interest,* 1930). In other cases they petered out inconclusively, sometimes only to flare up again over closely similar issues two or three decades later.[1]

Fetter's theory of interest, which we have not previously men-tioned, laid extreme, or even exclusive, emphasis on 'time-preference' or 'time-valuation'. Fetter started from the prices of durable goods as the primary expression of 'time valuation', or of 'acts of choice of goods with reference to time'. The rate of interest is thus expressed through present prices. Fetter summed up his theory as follows:

> This, then, is the essence of the capitalization theory of interest as nearly as we can put it in a proposition: the rate of interest (contractual) is the reflection, in a market price on money loans, of a rate of capitalization involved in the prices of the goods in the community. The price of durable agents is a capitalization which involves a discount of their future uses; and this is logically prior to the rate of contract interest. The logical order of explanation is from numberless separate acts of choice of goods *with reference to time,* to the value (and prices) of durable goods embodying future incomes, and finally to the market rate of interest. This interest theory was new in its *order of development* from elementary choice; in the *priority it assigns to capitalization* above contract interest; in its *unified psychological explanation* of all phenomena of the surplus that emerges when under-valued expected incomes approach maturity.[2]

Fetter was critical of Fisher's term 'impatience' and insisted on 'time preference' or 'time valuation' as the comprehensively explana-tory concept. He also criticized all productivity theories as involving a confusion between physical productivity and value productivity, and held that in the course of their reasoning there is a shift from the one idea to the other. The 'productivity' of capital exists solely because one can today get at present prices goods whose services in the future are going to be worth more than the present price of these goods. This fact depends on time-preference and wholly suffices to explain the pay-ment of interest.

We may describe the various theories of Böhm-Bawerk, Clark,

---

[1] Böhm-Bawerk's contributions to these debates are to be found in Vol. III of the 4th edition of *Kapital und Kapitalzins.* His lengthy criticism of Schumpeter's view of interest as an exclusively 'dynamic' phenomenon (with Schumpeter's reply and Böhm-Bawerk's rejoinder) is in *Zeitschrift für Volkswirtschaft,* 1913.

[2] See Fetter's article in the *American Economic Review,* March 1914, p. 77. For a good discussion of Fetter's theory of interest see Wesley Mitchell, *Lecture Notes on Types of Economic Theory,* vol. ii, Ch. XXI.

Cassel, Fisher, and Fetter, as well as those incorporated in most of the main books of principles, as relating to the non-monetary aspects of interest. That is not, of course, to suggest that their authors were necessarily concerned, explicitly or implicitly, with a model of a non-monetary economy. It is difficult to generalize, but it does seem that the assumptions about monetary policies and processes on which the 'normal' self-equilibrating stationary and quasi-stationary models rested, were often far from fully and clearly elaborated, and that these models were, in fact, necessarily somewhat limited and unrealistic in their significance. It seems, further, that they were directed rather to explaining the equilibrium rates of exchange between goods, rather than their absolute money prices. Nevertheless, these models were of money-using economies, though the 'complex action and reaction of credit' on which, as Marshall put it in the closing sentences of his *Principles*, 'nearly every economic issue depends', were generally omitted. We may note briefly three limitations, which applied generally to the 'normal' self-equilibrating models, but which were particularly relevant to these theories of interest:

First, as 'first approximations' these theories of interest, apart from Wicksell's, were not concerned to analyse and distinguish in any depth the monetary and banking processes involved in saving and investing in the contemporary credit economy. In fact, several of the leading exponents of the theory of interest seemed to abstract from 'hoarding' after the manner of 'Say's Law': 'An economically educated people does not hoard but applies what is saved', wrote Böhm-Bawerk: 'The key to the solution lies in recognising the unquestionable fact that saving is in reality demanding and getting productive instruments as part of an income', held J. B. Clark. Passages in Marshall's early writings could be quoted to much the same effect (e.g. on page 34 of the *Pure Theory of Domestic Values*). So, for that matter, wrote J. A. Hobson that 'saving means buying productive goods with income'. (*Industrial System*, 2nd ed., p. 50.)

Secondly, a self-adjusting mechanism by which all savings got invested, and all labour got employed, also seems to have been widely assumed in neo-classical accounts of the theory of interest. (We have already quoted Böhm-Bawerk and Cassel explicitly to this effect in earlier chapters. (Ch. 11, sect. 2 and Ch. 15, sect. 3.)

Thirdly, neo-classical theories of interest, more even than the rest of neo-classical economic theory, were often very seriously handicapped by the absence of a clear and explicit distinction between *ex-ante* schedules of the demand and supply of savings, 'waiting', &c., and the *ex-post* realized quantities.

2. *Different Approaches to the Theory of Money*

In this section we are distinguishing, for the purposes of our review, three different sorts of approach to the theory of money.[1] By some economists these different approaches were regarded and stated as being by no means incompatible, and elements of one approach were combined with elements from another. In other cases, one approach was held (often unjustifiably as it seems) to exclude and invalidate the others. Of course, within each of the three categories, there were many refinements and differences of emphasis which we shall mainly disregard.

1. The first of the approaches which we shall discuss is the 'cash balance' or 'liquidity' approach, naturally developed by the main founders of micro-economic marginal analysis, notably Walras, Menger, and Marshall. It started from the choices and decisions of the individual and analysed his demand for a cash-holding of a particular size, in the same way as marginal-utility and -productivity analysis examined the household's demand for consumption goods and the firm's demand for factors. A maximizing formula can be arrived at in respect of the individual's cash-holding and the rate of interest. The most elaborate example of this approach and the most subtly integrated with the rest of his general equilibrium analysis was, as we have seen, given by Walras.

Carl Menger, in particular, in accordance with his principle of methodological individualism, insisted that the theory of money must start from the individual's demand for cash (see *Works*, vol. iv, p. 112). L. Mises in his comprehensive *Theory of Money and Credit* (1st ed., 1912) was the main successor of Menger on the subject of monetary theory, and argued vigorously for the same kind of approach: 'The price of money, like other prices, is determined in the last resort by the subjective valuations of buyers and sellers' (English ed., p. 108). The task of the theory of money is to develop 'a complete theory of the value of money on the basis of the subjective theory of value and its peculiar doctrine of marginal utility'. (p. 114.)[2]

---

[1] In this section, and in the following one on the 'income' approach to the theory of money, I am deeply indebted to A. W. Marget's monumental work on the *Theory of Prices*, 2 vols., 1938–40. Cf. also A. H. Hansen's *Monetary Theory and Fiscal Policy*, Ch. VI.

[2] Mises goes on to explain his fundamentally 'micro-economic' approach—that of

The best-known example of this broad line of approach is the Cambridge quantity equation. Keynes's composite quotations of the words of Marshall best sum up the doctrine:

'In every state of society there is some fraction of their income which people find it worth while to keep in the form of currency; it may be a fifth, or a tenth, or a twentieth. A large command of resources in the form of currency renders their business easy and smooth, and puts them at an advantage in bargaining; but on the other hand it locks up in a barren form resources that might yield an income of gratification if invested, say, in extra furniture; or a money income, if invested in extra machinery or cattle.' A man fixes the appropriate fraction 'after balancing one against another the advantages of a further ready command and the disadvantages of putting more of his resources into a form in which they yield him no direct income or other benefit'. 'Let us suppose that the inhabitants of a country, taken one with another (and including therefore all varieties of character and of occupation), find it just worth their while to keep by them on the average ready purchasing power to the extent of a tenth part of their annual income, together with a fiftieth part of their property; then the aggregate value of the currency of the country will tend to be equal to the sum of these amounts.' (*v. Money, Credit, and Commerce*, I. iv. 3, and Keynes, *Treatise on Money*, vol. i, p. 230.)

This analysis was developed and expressed algebraically by A. C. Pigou ('On the Exchange Value of Legal Tender Money', *Quarterly Journal of Economics*, Nov. 1917, reprinted in *Essays in Applied Economics*, p. 177), who also enlarged the Marshallian quantity equation, ($P = KR/M$), to cover the case where cash is held partly in legal tender, notes and coins, and partly in bank deposits.

Pigou claimed that this equation is preferable to Irving Fisher's, based on velocity of circulation, because 'it brings us at once into relation with volition—an ultimate cause of demand—rather than with

Menger's 'methodological individualism'—as follows: 'For a long time it was believed that the demand for money was a quantity determined by objective factors and independent of subjective considerations. It was thought that the demand for money in an economic community was determined, on the one hand by the total quantity of commodities that had to be paid for during a given period, and on the other hand by the velocity of circulation of the money. There is an error in the very starting point of this way of regarding the matter, which was first successfully attacked by Menger. It is inadmissible to begin with the demand for money of the community. The individualist economic community as such, which is the only sort of community in which there is a demand for money, is not an economic agent. It demands money only in so far as its individual members demand money. The demand for money of the economic community is nothing but the sum of the demands for money of the individual economic agents composing it.' (pp. 131–2.)

334 *Interest, Money, and Macro-economic Analysis*

something that seems at first sight accidental, arbitrary and more or less in the air'. (*Essays*, p. 178.)[1]

Keynes in his *Tract on Monetary Reform* (1924, Ch. 3, para. 1) followed this same approach in his 'Real Balances' equation based on 'the idea that what a holder of money requires is a quantity of real balances which bears the appropriate relationship to the quantity of real transactions upon which he employs his balances'. By 1930, however, in his *Treatise on Money*, Keynes had become dissatisfied with this sort of analysis: 'Formerly I was attracted by this line of approach. But it now seems to me . . . that we cannot get any real insight into the price-making process without bringing in the rate of interest and the distinctions between incomes and profits and between savings and investment.' (*Treatise*, vol. i, p. 229.)

This whole cash-balance approach to the theory of money is preeminently that of the micro-economic marginal analysis of individual maximizing behaviour. It extended the marginal utility theory of value, and the analysis of the supply and demand for a single commodity, to explain the value of money, just as the labour and cost of production theories of value had previously been extended to the case of money. This kind of formula did not, of course, necessarily remain purely micro-economic. The desired cash-holdings of all individuals were aggregated into what Walras called the *encaisse désirée* of the community or the public. But this approach remained closely subject to the limitations of individual maximization analysis, and though containing a contribution of permanent importance in its analysis of the individual's demand for 'liquidity', it was apt to lapse into a rather empty formalism, and required to be exploited and filled out by an analysis departing from a different fundamental formula than that of the maximizing individual.

2. The second approach, particularly common over a considerable period in textbooks, but not much the subject of advanced developments, was that expressed by Irving Fisher's formula $MV = PT$, developed from Newcomb's $VR = KP$.[2] Although individual valuations were recognized to be operating behind these symbols, parti-

---

[1] For another distinguished example of this approach see E. Cannan, 'The Application of the Theoretical Apparatus of Supply and Demand to Currency', *Economic Journal*, 1921, p. 453. Compare also D. H. Robertson, *Money*, 1928 ed., p. 29: 'The value of money is primarily determined by exactly the same two factors as determine the value of any other thing, namely, the conditions of demand for it; and the quantity of it available.'

[2] See I. Fisher, *The Purchasing Power of Money*, 1911. For a defence of Fisher's analysis see A. W. Marget, *Theory of Prices*, vol. ii, pp. 99 ff.

cularly behind Fisher's V (Newcomb's R), this approach was much more explicitly in aggregate terms, or 'macro-economic'. Newcomb's concept of the 'societary circulation' suggests a revival of the mercantilist and physiocratic concepts of the circulation of payments. Unlike the cash-balance approach, the Fisher version of the quantity theory separated the theory of value from the theory of money (and *money prices*), and put them much more distinctly into two separate compartments, than did the cash-balance approach. The theory of value was a theory of the purely relative values of goods, and the theory of money, departing from an equation of exchange, studied the multiplicative factor which transformed the relative values of goods into actual absolute money prices.

The equation of exchange is about the most comprehensively mechanical of all aggregative formulae, the whole of monetary analysis, it has been said, being contained in Fisher's V. It represented for some time during the neo-classical period the most widely invoked piece of macro-economic analysis. As a 'first approximation' it was perhaps more useful and less misleading than some other 'first approximations'.

3. *The 'Income' Approach to the Theory of Money*

The third approach to the theory of money which we are here discussing, that is the 'income' approach, is not so compact and recognizable as the other two, and, considering also its great importance, both needs and deserves rather longer treatment and a separate section. The 'income' approach began to emerge in the works of a number of widely different authors, and traces of its influence may be found on many other economists who did not pursue it exclusively or mainly. But in our period it never achieved any explicit predominance.

We quoted Keynes in his *Treatise on Money* (1930) as expressing dissatisfaction with the cash-balance and quantity theory approach. Elsewhere in the *Treatise* he described the income approach:

I propose, therefore, to break away from the traditional method of setting out from the total quantity of money irrespective of the purposes on which it is employed, and to start instead . . . with the flow of the community's earnings or money income, and with its two-fold division (i) into the parts which have been *earned* by the production of consumption goods and of investment goods respectively, and (ii) into the parts which are *expended* on consumption goods and on savings respectively. (*Treatise*, vol. i, p. 134.)

Whether or not the break with what he calls 'the traditional method' was as sharp as Keynes seemed to wish to imply, this 'income' approach had been followed by a considerable, if rather heterogeneous, line of economists. There is at least a suggestion of it in Cantillon, Sir James Stewart, and many 'Mercantilists'. But it might best be described as starting from Tooke's 13th thesis on the quantity theory:

It is the quantity of money, constituting the revenues of the different orders of the state, under the head of rents, profits, salaries and wages, destined for current expenditure, that alone forms the limiting principle of the aggregate of money prices [the only prices that can properly come under the designation of General Prices]. As the cost of production is the limiting principle of supply, so the aggregate of money incomes devoted to expenditure for consumption is the determining and limiting principle of demand. (*History of Prices*, vol. vi, pp. 635–7.)

It was this proposition that Wicksell picked out and quoted (omitting the passage we have put in square brackets) in his *Interest and Prices* (p. 44). Wicksell was not satisfied with the marginal utility and cash-balance approach of his fellow neo-classical economists (ibid., p. 18), and it is an important part of his achievement to have seized upon this suggestion of Tooke's and to have sensed its possibilities. Wicksell emphasized that it 'does really provide a starting point from which a theory of the value of money and of prices can be developed'. It is emphasis on the 'aggregate of money incomes', and on how this aggregate is expended or held, which marks the 'income' approach. The concept of 'the aggregate of money incomes' leads on immediately, particularly in Wicksell's *Interest and Prices*, to the concept of 'the money demand for all kinds of goods' (ibid., p. 96), (i.e. 'aggregate effective demand'), and led Wicksell to approach the theory of money from the standpoint that 'any theory of money worthy of the name must be able to show how and why the monetary or pecuniary demand for goods exceeds or falls short of the supply of goods in given conditions'. (*Lectures*, vol. ii, p. 160.) Furthermore, the 'income' approach, as developed by its most outstanding neo-classical exponent, leads on to an analysis of the uses of aggregate income in terms of consumption, investment, and saving, to the analysis of the *processes* of monetary saving and investment, and to the monetary analysis of the rate of interest, though these subjects soon take us beyond the theory of money in any precise or narrow sense, and into the theory of fluctuations and cycles in aggregate economic activity.

Wicksell's successors in Sweden in the first instance followed up his theory of interest, rather than this quotation from Tooke and his consequent suggestion about the theory of money. However, Lindahl's analysis was certainly on the lines of the income approach, whether or not the main influence had come from Wicksell.[1] Meanwhile a number of writers in German, before and after Wicksell, had been suggesting similar ideas about the theory of money, if not always in such a generally fertile and stimulating way. Wicksell had perhaps been assisted in his discovery of the significance of Tooke's suggestion by some passages in Launhardt's work (*Das Wesen des Geldes*, 1885) which he (Wicksell) refers to immediately after his discussion of the significance of the 'income' approach. Launhardt writes, for example:

The economy does not proceed to some once-and-for-all balance, but is involved in a permanent process in which consumers' goods are continually being produced, and titles to consumers' goods continually being earned. In this continuous process we have to consider a time-period of a particular length . . . preferably a year. We can then see that in this period, the total annual production of consumption goods and the annual quantity of production goods used up, is purchased by the total annual income. . . . The total annual income consists of the total of interest on capital, and the total of wages and of profits. . . . The annual income of all individuals strictly determines . . . the level of prices of all goods, and therefore the level of profits, rents, interest-rates, and wages, out of which again the total annual income of all individuals is made up. (pp. 36 and 42.)

Later, Adolf Wagner, to some extent Spiethoff, and especially the 'outsider' Johannsen, followed out the line of the 'income' approach. In Johannsen's work, as we shall see in a following chapter, the income approach led on to his analysis of 'Impair Savings', and of 'the Multiplying Principle', and to his theory of trade depression as due to a deficiency of effective demand. In fact, the concept of 'effective demand', implicit in all under-consumption theories, necessarily contains much of the income approach to the theory of money (as was exemplified also, for example in the writings of Foster and Catchings, the American under-consumptionists of the nineteen-twenties).[2]

A famous exponent of an 'income' theory of money was F. Wieser in his essay on 'The Value of Money and its Changes' (1909). But this

---

[1] See especially Lindahl, *Studies in the Theory of Money and Capital*, p. 142, and A. W. Marget, *Theory of Prices*, vol. i, p. 328.

[2] See A. Wagner, *Sozialökonomische Theorie des Geldes und Geldwesens*, 1909, pp. 159 ff.; A. Spiethoff, in *Festgaben für A. Wagner*, pp. 249 ff., especially p. 259; also O. v. Zwiedineck-Südenhorst, *Einkommen als Geldwertbestimmungsgrund*, *Schmollers Jahrbuch*, 1909. Of the works of Foster and Catchings see 'Money', 1923.

essay is too much of a philosophical and historical disquisition on the concept of 'the value of money', and does not lead on to the concepts and questions of 'the money demand for all goods and services', and how this exceeds or falls short of supply, explored by Wicksell.

Wieser's essay was, however, followed by a long paper of Schumpeter's on 'The Social Product and the Unit of Account' (*Archiv für Sozialwissenschaft*, 1917, p. 627) which deserves a lengthier mention, and is of importance not simply as an example, to some extent, of the 'income' approach, but as incorporating much of the most interesting monetary analysis of its time (e.g. of 'forced saving', of the monetary over-investment theory of the trade cycle, of the analysis of different forms of inflation, and of the equilibrium between 'market' and 'natural' rates of interest).

Schumpeter prefaces his essay by listing the principal contemporary writers on the theory of money from which his own work sets out, the most important being Menger, Wieser, Wicksell, Fanno, Walras, Marshall, Keynes (*Indian Currency and Finance*), Fisher, and Mises. Schumpeter himself starts from the circular flow of production and consumption in a static 'Walrasian' economy. Here there is a flow of real goods and services, 'the social product' or Marshall's 'national dividend', and in the opposite direction there is a flow of monetary payments between the households (buying consumption goods and services, and selling production goods and services) and entrepreneurs (selling consumption goods and services and buying production goods and services). Money incomes are here acquired by households in the market for production goods and services, and are spent on the market for consumption goods and services. The fundamental proposition about the monetary circulation is that: 'In conditions of stationary equilibrium the sum of the prices of all consumption goods must be equal to the sum of the prices of all production goods, and both must be equal to the total of all money incomes.' (p. 635.) ('Money income' here means the monetary value of consumption, and does not include savings or taxes, but does include consumption loans.)

Money is therefore essentially a claim to goods. Schumpeter then proceeds to criticize the variant of the cash-balance approach which seeks to explain the value of money on the lines of the marginal utility theory of value, in the same way as the value of any other good or service. He claims it to be circular reasoning, 'if one explains the purchasing power of money as a special case of the general phenomenon of exchange-value, and at the same time regards the money prices of goods as the results of exchange between money and goods. That would amount to the assertion that one obtains goods for money because money has exchange value, while it only has exchange value because one obtains goods for it.' (p. 647.) The application of the marginal utility theory of value to the value of money, or to the value of output as a whole, in the same way as it is applied to the theory of the value of any particular good or service, was always strongly opposed by Schumpeter.

What Schumpeter sets out as the fundamental equation of his 'income' theory of money is as follows:

$$E = MU = p_1 m_1 + p_2 m_2 \ldots + p_n m_n,$$

where E is the total of all money incomes, M the quantity of money in circulation, U the average velocity of circulation, and m and p the quantities and prices of particular goods and services. Schumpeter emphasizes the complete identity of this equation with the Fisher equation, and notes that 'those who in analysing the value of money substitute a concept of aggregate income for that of the quantity of money, are usually, in all innocence, repeating the fundamental idea of the quantity theory which they believe themselves to be superseding'. The quantity theory is 'a hydra', each of the many times its head has been cut off it has promptly grown another one.

Schumpeter then examines the monetary processes involved in capitalist economic progress, and the fluctuations with which this is bound up. An essential part of the capitalist mechanism is 'forced saving' and the reduction of real incomes which results from an expansion of bank-money and the consequent rise in prices: 'This is the method of bringing about economic development specifically belonging to capitalism.' (p. 707.) Here Schumpeter gives one of the first clear outlines of the monetary over-investment theory of crises. Assuming that the expansion of bank-credit goes to producers, the resulting shift in prices will favour an increased output of production goods and will be against that of consumption goods. An investment boom of the cumulative kind analysed by Wicksell and Fisher will result. The money-market rate of interest will be below the 'natural' rate. But when, in the end, the banks have to cease the expansion of credit the boom is punctured. Schumpeter here introduces Wicksell's doctrine that if the 'real' or 'natural' rate of interest, or the return on capital, is equal to the money-market rate the price-level will remain stable, but that any divergence between the two will lead to an unlimited cumulative movement. (pp. 711–12.) But unlike later versions of the Austrian

340 Interest, Money, and Macro-economic Analysis

monetary over-investment theory, Schumpeter held that 'forced saving' could finance permanently valuable investment.

A final important example of the use of the 'income' approach may be found in R. G. Hawtrey's writings, in particular in Chapter II of his first book, *Good and Bad Trade* (1913): 'The total effective demand', Hawtrey begins, 'for all finished commodities in any community is simply the aggregate of all money incomes. The same aggregate represents also the total cost of production of all finished commodities.' (p. 6.) Hawtrey then proceeds to ask: 'Given that such and such commodities are being produced and consumed per unit of time, how will their respective prices and how will their total money value compare with the total stock of money in the hands of the community at a given time?' This leads to his analysis of consumers' and traders' balances. Hawtrey carried this approach farther in his chapter on consumers' income and consumers' outlay in his *Currency and Credit* (Chapter IV), where the compatibility of a 'cash-balance' approach with an 'income' approach is well exemplified.[1]

The 'income' approach, as soon as it gets beyond one or two, in themselves rather thin generalizations, or 'fundamental equations', about aggregate income and its consumption and investment components, passes beyond the vague undefinable frontiers of the theory of money into the problems of fluctuations in aggregate income and output, and of crises and cycles—especially in Johannsen and Hawtrey, and, if not in Wicksell's own writings at any rate in the significance others later saw in them. In particular, the analysis of savings and investment contained in the 'income' approach was developed also in the various 'over-investment', 'over-saving', and 'under-consumption' explanations of the trade cycle (for example, by Hobson and Johannsen on the one hand, and Tugan-Baranovsky and Spiethoff on the other hand).

4. The Sources of Modern Macro-Economics

The neo-classical economics of our period, and particularly of the earlier part of it, was fairly predominantly (though much more implicitly than explicitly) concerned with the analysis of the plans and activities of individual consumers, owners of factors, and producers.

[1] A. Aftalion also developed the 'income' theory: see his essay 'Die Einkommenstheorie des Geldes und ihre Bestätigung durch die gegenwärtigen Phänomene', in *Wirtschaftstheorie der Gegenwart* (edited by H. Mayer), vol. ii, p. 376, and his two-part article in the *Revue d'Economie Politique*, 1925.

This meant that the theories of interest and money were primarily in terms of the households' and firms' maximizing plans for their savings, investments, and cash-balances in relation to the rate of interest. The macro-economic elements in the English classical system, that is the analysis of distribution between the three economic classes, and the historical-dynamic analysis of 'the tendency of profits to a minimum', almost entirely disappeared. Neo-classical attempts to develop a macro-economic theory of distribution based on marginal productivity (for example, the attempt of Böhm-Bawerk) were fundamentally of doubtful soundness, and were not pursued very far or worked out with precision.

But however predominant micro-economic analysis became, especially in the nineties, a number of scattered elements of macro-economic analysis are discernible, in which static and dynamic treatment were combined in a very different way from that in which the static analysis of maximizing values was combined with its complementary 'normal' self-equilibrating dynamics. In regard to the macro-economic problems of the variability of aggregate quantities ('income', 'output', 'investment', 'consumption' &c.) a static treatment combined with an assumed self-adjusting dynamics was obviously more inadequate than in the case of the normal self-adjusting micro-economic models. Simply to assume a long-run mechanism of self-adjustment was to come near to assuming out of existence the very problems of large-scale fluctuations which had to be analysed. Moreover, unstable and cumulative processes, psychological and monetary, were from the start recognized as having a part so important in aggregate fluctuations that it could hardly be abstracted from, as was possible to a large extent in respect of such processes in micro-economic analysis. Differences between expected and realized quantities, or errors in forecasting, were obviously a central element of the problems. Futhermore, it was in respect of the main macro-economic concepts that Newcomb and Fisher early emphasized the important distinction between 'stock' and 'flow' concepts, a distinction which points the way to a dynamic 'dated' analysis. In another sense of 'dynamic', the main type of aggregate fluctuations calling for study, those of the trade cycle, were very early recognized as being connected with the *growth* of capitalist economies. From the start, therefore, macro-economic analysis was bound in one way or another to be to a greater extent in dynamic terms, and its static formulae to be of much more definitely subordinate significance, than in the case of micro-economic 'equilibrium' analysis. Let us conclude this chapter and this part of the book by drawing together under the following five headings the main sources of modern macro-economics, including the concepts from which it started and the problems it sought to deal with.

1. First, there is in Walras, Böhm-Bawerk, and Schumpeter, the idea, and the beginning of an analysis, of 'the circular flow' of payments through the economy, or of the economic circulation or *Kreislauf.* The descendant of one of the leading conceptions of the Physiocrats, this is by itself simply a general notion rather than an analysis, but it is one which forms a starting point for much of macro-economics.

2. A second fundamental concept is Marshall's 'National Dividend', 'the aggregate net product of, and the sole source of payment for, all the agents of production within the country'. The main employment and development of this concept was, of course, in Pigou's study of welfare and the national dividend. This started in *Wealth and Welfare* (1912) as a study of the causes of unemployment (see Preface) and an important part of the book was then devoted to 'The Variability of the National Dividend'. In the later editions of the *Economics of Welfare* this subject dropped out and was left for separate monographic treatment, and throughout most of the book in its later form 'the fact that some resources are generally unemployed against the will of the owners is ignored' (3rd. ed., p. 129). This limitation inevitably excluded much of the subject of the variability of economic aggregates (i.e. the main problems of macro-economics) and the *Economics of Welfare*, in spite of its fundamental concept of the national dividend, is probably more suitably described as largely a normative development of micro-economic analysis.

3. Thirdly, there was Simon Newcomb's concept of the 'Societary Circulation', closely similar to the idea discussed under heading (1) above. It crystallized into the Fisher equation of exchange. This provided a macro-static formula as a starting-point, but it did not, on the whole, turn out to be a starting-point from which a realistic and practically useful dynamic analysis could be developed, perhaps because it submerged unduly the individual 'volitional' element.

4. Fourthly, we come to an approach which led on much farther, which we have just described as the 'income' approach to the theory of money. From this proceeded the concepts of aggregate effective demand and supply and their analysis into their components, aggregate consumption, investment, and saving. This approach is obviously at many points closely connected with the analysis of crises and cycles.

In many cases an economist's monetary analysis along the lines of the income approach can hardly be distinguished from his analysis of problems of the trade cycle (e.g. especially in Johannsen and Hawtrey).

5. Fifthly, there is the analysis of the trade cycle and of depressions as the leading realistic case of aggregate fluctuations, and therefore the leading contributor to a general macro-economic theory of the variability of economic aggregates. Towards the end of our period in Britain, the post-war problem of chronic unemployment to a considerable extent replaced the trade cycle in this role. The subjects of this fifth heading are discussed in the next part of the book.

Part III

THE ECONOMICS OF INSTABILITY AND DISTURBANCE

22

Crises and Cycles (I): Before *c.* 1900

1. *Introduction*

IN the four chapters of Part II we were able to take up a branch of economic theory as it had been left by the writers we discussed in Part I, and we could then try to carry on with some of the more important parts of the story through the ensuing two or three decades. In this chapter and the next we cannot proceed in this way. Apart from some of Jevons's *Investigations*, and, of course, the work of J. A. Hobson, there were very few contributions of first-rate importance on crises and cycles from the twenty or so leading writers discussed in Part I. Wicksell treats the subject very briefly in his *Lectures*. His *Interest and Prices* is primarily intended as a study of monetary theory rather than of crises or cycles. Marshall and Pareto devoted to this subject only a comparatively minor chapter in one of their earlier works (with the addition, perhaps, on Marshall's part, of some miscellaneous essays and papers). Menger, Wieser, Böhm-Bawerk, Walras, Edgeworth, Sidgwick, Wicksteed, and J. B. Clark wrote either fragmentarily or not at all on the subject of this chapter. In particular, it is note-worthy how comparatively little was first published on this problem in English between 1880 and 1910, as compared with the decades of the sixties and seventies preceding this period, and the years following it after 1910. Micro-economic 'maximizing' analysis and its complementary self-equilibrating dynamics seem to have been regarded as the primary task.

Consecutive and systematic discussion first really begins in our period at about the turn of the century, with the works of Tugan-Baranovsky, Spiethoff, Aftalion, and Schumpeter, followed somewhat later, in the Anglo-Saxon world, by those of Mitchell, Pigou,

Hawtrey, and Robertson near the beginning of the First World War. Only then does the subject begin to be taken up and regularly discussed at the academic level, with Britain and the United States—at any rate at the outset—some way behind Germany.

Before 1900 there had been various important isolated works and many *ad hoc* topical discussions. Valuable ideas, the main elements of subsequent fuller explanations, are presented amid a mass of partial, biassed, 'cranky', or scape-goat-hunting effusions. Writing of the literature of the 1878 crisis Jevons said (*Investigations*, p. 221):

> It is curious to notice the variety of the explanations offered by commercial writers concerning the course of the present state of trade. Foreign competition, beer drinking, over-production, trades-unionism, war, peace, want of gold, superabundance of silver, Lord Beaconsfield, Sir Stafford Northcote, their extravagant expenditure, the Government policy, the Glasgow bank directors, Mr. Edison and the electric light, are a few of the happy and consistent suggestions continually made to explain the present disastrous collapse of industry and credit.

(Sun-spots, it has been remarked, should be added to this list.)[1]

All we can attempt here is to trace out some of the main valuable and subsequently important ideas of before 1900, and give an account of one or two of their more representative treatments. We shall begin with a reference to the classical controversies over the possibility or impossibility of 'general over-production', in particular contrasting J. S. Mill's statements on this problem with his later analysis of the consequences of 'the tendency of profits to a minimum'. We discuss Mill's views at this length mainly because of the dominating influence (of some aspects) of them at the outset of our period, but also because two very interesting statements of under-consumptionist doctrines by the little-known Americans, Hawley and Crocker, took their starting-point from Mill's *Principles*. We shall then group the different explanations of crises under three very broad and rough headings: (1) under-consumption and effective demand theories (in sect. 3); (2) over-consumption, over-investment, and disproportionate investment theories (in sect. 4); and (3) psychological and credit theories and the explanations of cumulative movements (in sect. 5). To these we add a very brief discussion of ideas about the periodicity and inevitability of

[1] *v. Economic Crises*, by E. D. Jones (1900), p. 14. This little book has a useful bibliography, as has also another American book of the same period, T. E. Burton, *Financial Crises*, 1903. E. Bergmann's *Geschichte der nationalökonomischen Krisentheorien*, 1895, is still an indispensable work, being the only attempt at a systematic account of nineteenth century and earlier theories.

crises (sect. 6). Of course, wide and conflicting differences of emphasis are possible within each of these broad headings. Furthermore, although in some versions each of these main types of explanation is presented as excluding any elements from other types, a number of the most distinguished writers combined elements from several or all of the main groups of ideas.

2. *J. S. Mill and the Doctrine of 'The Impossibility of General Overproduction'*

The fundamental notion that economic activity in an exchange economy is in response to an effective or 'effectual' demand, and that a deficiency thereof may reduce the level of activity and national wealth below what it advantageously might be, may be traced back at least as far as the seventeenth century. It was one of those simple massive ideas, like the productive benefits of the division of labour, or the general beneficence of free competition at home and free trade abroad, which were presented and contended not on the plane of any close or refined analysis of the modern sort, but on that of a broad enlightened common sense. Petty's, Barbon's, and Sir Dudley North's remarks on the subject are well known, and so is Mandeville's satirical eulogy of luxury in his *Fable of the Bees* (1705). But the same line of thought continues right through the eighteenth century in such leading English authors as Berkeley (*The Querist*, 1735), Steuart (*Enquiry into the Principles of Political Economy*, 1767), and finally in Lauderdale (1804) and Spence, in the opening years of the nineteenth century. In France, Boisguillebert, the first great French economic theorist, strongly emphasized the same ideas (see *Détail de la France*, 1696), and he was followed by Melon (*Essai Politique sur le Commerce*, 1734) and Quesnay (*Maximes Générales*, 1758, and *Du Commerce*, 1766). In Germany, Joseph von Sonnenfels (*Abhandlung von der Teuerung in Hauptstädten*, u.s.w. 1769), and several of the German cameralists followed the same line. Nor were these ideas confined simply to economic writings in any narrow sense. Mandeville's defence of luxury spending was fully appreciated and propagated by such outstanding figures as Dr. Johnson, Voltaire, and Montesquieu. It is noticeable that this list of leading writers contains both forerunners of economic liberalism like Mandeville, as well as such *étatiste* economists as Steuart and Quesnay, and at the same time both advocates of the beneficence of luxury spending, as well as critics of luxury (like Berkeley).

All these writers were 'under-consumptionists', at least in the weak sense of regarding a general deficiency of demand, or 'general over-production' (or under-consumption) as being at least a distinct possibility worthy of examination. Many of them were 'under-consumptionists' in the stronger sense of regarding deficiencies of effective demand as a regular and serious menace. If it is held that the term 'under-consumptionist' should be reserved for the explanations of nineteenth-century capitalist crises and depressions, then it may be pointed out that the doctrines of such seventeenth- and eighteenth-century economists as we have mentioned, led straight on to what was later called the 'under-consumptionist' theory of capitalist depression and of the trade cycle. As Bergmann points out:[1]

Any one imbued with the mercantilist idea that a powerful demand is the real driving force behind the economic mechanism, and that this force can only be created by a large consumption of goods—even by pernicious private luxury; or anyone adopting the Physiocratic theory that a particular relationship must be maintained between the expenditures and receipts of the different social classes, must then come to the conclusion that economic disasters are symptoms of the general fact that the balance of total production and total demand has been upset as a result of technical progress and the freedom of productive activity . . . and that the sole and indispensable cure is an increase in consumption.

The idea of deficiencies of effective demand was expressed in a number of different ways in eighteenth-century writings, especially, for example, in the many warnings against 'hoarding', and in the advocacy of a large and active monetary circulation. It is implicit also in the notion of 'the circulation of payments', and possible interruptions or disturbances therein, and in the common idea that one man's expenditure is another man's income. It found expression, too, in the doctrine that the more advanced and civilized nations held their position because they advanced more energetic claims or 'demands' on a high standard of living, than the more indolent, less 'demanding' and less civilized. It is present also in the frequent defences of the luxury expenditure of the eighteenth-century nobility as providing employment and income for the poor. In the nineteenth century, of course, when under-consumption had become in England a doctrine of the

---

[1] See his *Geschichte der nationalökonomischen Krisentheorien* (1895), p. 28. See also, P. Vialles, *La Consommation et les Crises économiques*, 1903, Ch. IV on 'Les Origines de la Théorie de la Sous-Consommation'; D. H. MacGregor, *Economic Thought and Policy*, 1949, Ch. IV on 'Effectual Demand and Employment'. For the predecessors and successors of Mandeville on the subject of luxury spending, see Kaye's Introduction to his edition of the *Fable of the Bees*.

opposition to competitive capitalism, it was used, on the left, to strengthen denunciations of the unequal distribution of wealth.

We cannot trace out here the remarkable story of how these common notions of eighteenth-century thinkers were in due course, in England at any rate, driven almost completely underground by Adam Smith's unconditional eulogy of the beneficence of saving, supplemented by his dictum that no one holds money for its own sake; by James Mill's dogmatic rigmarole about the impossibility of general over-production; by the 'theory of markets' which Say, after comparing its fundamental novelty with the discoveries of Galileo and Copernicus, then restates as a palpably insignificant tautology; by the influential support of Ricardo and his 'New Political Economy';[1] and by the general nineteenth-century evangelical prejudices against luxury and in favour of 'abstinence'. This story must surely represent the most successful and important campaign of intellectual aggression and terminological dogmatism in the history of economic thought. It may be summarized in the phrase: 'from paradox to paradox'; in 1831 Chalmers, who may be seen as the last of a line of thinkers in England going back to Sir William Petty, could still complain of what he called 'this modern paradox' of 'the new economists' that 'general over-production is impossible'. Sixty years later, the secretary of the Royal Economic Society condemns J. A. Hobson's attempt to question the doctrine of the impossibility of general over-production (or the unconditional beneficence of saving) as a 'very paradoxical' attempt 'to unsettle consecrated tenets'.

John Stuart Mill clearly has a central if complex role in this story, and as he was still overwhelmingly the dominant orthodox influence on the subject, in 1870, the gist of his writings must be examined. His ideas, in Britain at any rate, were left largely unquestioned for decades by leading thinkers, and were never searchingly examined except by a few little-known and unorthodox writers. His first work on the subject was his essay—written (*c.* 1829) at about the age of 22 or 23—'Of the Influence of Consumption upon Production' (in *Essays on Some Unsettled Questions*).

J. S. Mill began this essay by hailing the recent revolution in economic thought in the sort of terms which have become familiar in more recent years:

Before the appearance of those great writers whose discoveries have given

[1] See Checkland, 'The Propagation of Ricardian Economics in England', *Economica*, 1949, p. 40.

to political economy its present comparatively scientific character, the ideas universally entertained both by theorists and by practical men, on the causes of national wealth, were grounded upon certain general views, which almost all who have given any considerable attention to the subject now justly hold to be completely erroneous.

Among the mistakes which were most pernicious in their direct conse-quences, and tended in the greatest degree to prevent a just conception of the objects of the science, or of the test to be applied to the solution of the questions which it presents, was the immense importance attached to con-sumption. . . . An extensive demand, a brisk circulation, a great expenditure of money, and sometimes *totidem verbis* a large consumption, was conceived to be the great condition of prosperity. . . . In opposition to these palpable absurdities, it was triumphantly established by political economists, that consumption never needs encouragement. All which is produced is already consumed, either for the purpose of reproduction or of enjoyment. The person who saves his income is no less a consumer than he who spends it. He consumes it in a different way; it supplies food and clothing to be con-sumed, tools and materials to be used, by productive labourers. (*Essays on Some Unsettled Questions of Political Economy*, p. 47.)

At the end of the essay it appears that this 'triumphant' intellectual revolution is an event of the last thirty years. The idea 'that produce in general may, by increasing faster than the demand for it, reduce all producers to distress, . . . strange to say, was almost a received doctrine as lately as thirty years ago; and the merit of those who have exploded it is much greater than might be inferred from the extreme obvious-ness of its absurdity when it is stated in its native simplicity'. (p. 73.) In his *Principles*, Mill states explicitly who it is that deserves the credit for the new doctrine: 'It is but justice to two eminent names, to call attention to the fact, that the merit of having placed this most important point in its true light, belongs principally, on the Continent, to the judicious J. B. Say, and in this country to Mr. Mill' . . . who 'had set forth the correct doctrine with great force and clearness in an early pamphlet.' (*Commerce Defended*, 1808.)

So much for the youthful J. S. Mill's account of the history of 'the new economics', and how it had finally superseded (or 'exploded') a doctrine held by a great line of writers all through the seventeenth and eighteenth centuries. What subsequently is especially remarkable is that as soon as Mill comes to grips with the facts of general fluctua-tions he proceeds with great penetration and precision to expose this new doctrine for its trivial verbal character and its extremely unrealistic assumptions:

In the present state of the commercial world . . . general eagerness to buy
and general reluctance to buy, succeed one another in a manner more or less
marked at brief intervals. Except during short periods of transition, there is
almost always either great briskness of business or great stagnation; either
the principal producers of almost all the leading articles of industry have as
many orders as they can possibly execute, or the dealers in almost all commodities have their warehouses full of unsold goods.

In this last case, it is commonly said that there is a general superabundance;
and as those economists who have contested the possibility of general superabundance, would none of them deny the possibility or even frequent occurrence of the phenomenon which we have just noticed, it would seem incumbent
on them to show, that the expression to which they object is not applicable
to a state of things in which most or all commodities remain unsold, in the
same sense in which there is said to be a superabundance of any one commodity when it remains in the warehouses of dealers for want of a market.
This is really a question of naming, but an important one, as it seems to us
that much apparent difference of opinion has been produced by mere difference in the mode of describing the same facts, and that persons who at
bottom were perfectly agreed, have considered each other as guilty of gross
error, and sometimes even misrepresentation, on this subject. (pp. 68–69.)

Surely this is to make the new doctrine of 'the impossibility of
general over-production' look very much like a rather trivial verbal
rigmarole. Even James Mill might hardly have gone so far as to attempt
to decree a general terminological prohibition against describing 'a
general excess of commodities' which, according to his son, occupied
regularly nearly half the nation's economic life, as 'general over-
production'. Moreover, it hardly seems to be rising to the seriousness
of the subject to argue, as does J. S. Mill at some points, and his disciple
Henry Fawcett throughout his chapter on the subject, that there could
not be 'general over-production' until the poorest person on the earth's
surface had everything he desired.

J. S. Mill goes on to show very acutely how unrealistic were the
assumptions on which the validity of the new doctrine rested:

There can never it is said, be a want of buyers for all commodities; because whoever offers a commodity for sale, desires to obtain a commodity
in exchange for it, and is therefore a buyer by the mere fact of his being a
seller. The sellers and the buyers, for all commodities taken together, must,
by the metaphysical necessity of the case, be an exact equipoise to each other;
and if there be more sellers than buyers of one thing, there must be more
buyers than sellers for another.

This argument is evidently founded on the supposition of a state of barter, and, on that supposition, it is perfectly incontestable. When two persons perform an act of barter, each of them is at once a seller and a buyer. He cannot sell without buying. Unless he chooses to buy some other person's commodity, he does not sell his own.

If, however, we suppose that money is used, these propositions cease to be exactly true. . . . Although he who sells, really sells only to buy, he need not buy at the same moment when he sells; and he does not therefore necessarily add to the *immediate* demand for one commodity when he adds to the supply of another. The buying and selling being now separated, it may very well occur, that there may be, at some given time, a very general inclination to sell with as little delay as possible, accompanied with an equally general inclination to defer all purchases as long as possible. This is always actually the case in those periods which are described as periods of general excess. And no one, after sufficient explanation, will contest the possibility of general excess, in this sense of the word. (pp. 69–70.)

There is much that must be admired in this later passage. Nevertheless, a profound and confusing ambivalence runs through the essay as a whole, which is quite certainly very unfair to the eighteenth-century thinkers condemned in such sweeping terms and whose entire approach is dismissed from any consideration as a 'palpable absurdity'. What one wishes that Mill (and his followers for several decades subsequently) had done, is to have elucidated more carefully the distinction between those 'periods of general excess', the possibility of which 'no-one denies', and the periods of 'general over-production' when 'produce in general increases faster than the demand for it', which it is such a monstrous error even to conceive of, and the proof of the impossibility of which had apparently constituted such an amazing intellectual revolution.

In the *Principles* Mill's treatment is even more ambivalent than in the early essay. Above all, there is the additional discussion of 'the tendency of profits to a minimum' (not referred to in the essay) the reconciliation of which with the earlier denial of the possibility of general over-production is left completely to the reader. Secondly, the denial of the possibility of general over-production is still more dogmatically and terminologically stated, and the doctrines of Lauderdale, Malthus, Sismondi, and Chalmers, are dismissed as confused and erroneous without any attempt to examine their underlying ideas.

Mill again agrees that in fact in commercial crises 'there is really an excess of all commodities', which is a regular, though transient, phenomenon; but, on the other hand, 'it is a great error to suppose with Sismondi that a commercial crisis is the effect of a general excess of production'. He goes on to denounce the latter notion (but not of course the former) as being (all in one paragraph) 'a chimerical supposition', 'a confused idea', 'essentially self-contradictory', 'a fatal misconception', 'a fatal error', and 'a veil not suffering any one ray of light to penetrate'. Finally he makes a pronouncement (later faithfully quoted by Fawcett) affecting the whole shape and task of political economy:

> The point is fundamental; any difference of opinion on it involves radically different conceptions of political economy, especially in its practical aspect. On the one view, we have only to consider how a sufficient production may be combined with the best possible distribution; but on the other hand there is a third thing to be considered—how a market can be created for produce, or how production can be limited to the capabilities of the market.

And this *third thing* (or the problem of the equilibrium of aggregate effective demand and supply) was 'a chimerical supposition'. (*Principles*, Bk. III, Ch. XIV, para. 4.)

We must now briefly contrast this doctrine of 'the impossibility of general over-production' with Mill's analysis of 'the tendency of profits to a minimum'. The fullness of the contrast between the two may be briefly and clearly appreciated by confronting Book III, Chapter 14 (from which we have just quoted on 'General Over-production') with Book IV, Chapters 4 and 5 on 'The Tendency of Profits to a Minimum'. These two latter chapters in Book IV present a 'stagnation' thesis of the tendency of profits to fall with economic progress. Here Adam Smith is criticized—(although he suggested the idea of economic stagnation)—while Mill approvingly follows E. G. Wakefield.[1] Mill describes Wakefield's doctrine as stating that 'production is limited not solely by the quantity of capital and labour', but also by 'the extent of the field of employment' (Bk. IV, 4. 2) (i.e. there *are* limits to remunera-

---

[1] Wakefield's arguments occur in his *England and America* (1833). He argued: 'It does not follow that, because labour is employed by capital, capital always finds a field in which to employ labour. This is the non-sequitur taken for granted by Bentham, Ricardo, Mill, McCulloch and others. Adam Smith, on the contrary, saw that there were limits to the employment of capital, and therefore limits, besides the limit of capital, to the employment of labour: the limits namely of the field of production, and of the market in which to dispose of surplus produce.' (p. 252.) Wakefield claimed to have converted Bentham from the views about capital and colonization expressed in the *Manual of Political Economy*, to Wakefield's own views. It is true that Adam Smith suggests the stagnation theory (see the *Wealth of Nations*, Bk. II, Ch. 4), along with his famous eulogy of parsimony, so he is in some respects responsible for the ambivalence running through J. S. Mill's *Principles* on these subjects.

tive accumulation, which is just what had been argued against James Mill by Spence when Mill was making his revolutionary discoveries). Wakefield's mistake, J. S. Mill holds, is to consider that his doctrines ran counter 'to the principles of the best school of preceding political economists, instead of being, as they really are, corollaries from these principles; though corollaries which, perhaps would not always have been admitted by those political economists themselves'. (This last remark surely makes an interesting concession.)

In Mill's account of 'the tendency of profits to a minimum' the principal function of crises is to ward off the stationary state by the waste of capital and the unproductive consumption which they bring, while it is the constant 'tendency of profits to a minimum' which produces these crises. (*Principles*, IV. 4. 5.) But the upshot of Mill's analysis is that he completely undermines the relevance of his theoretical analysis of the impossibility of general over-production, as well as the established practical conclusions about the inevitable harmfulness of government expenditure on unproductive consumption: 'The theory of the effect of accumulation on profits, laid down in the preceding chapter, materially alters many of the practical conclusions which might otherwise be supposed to follow from the general principles of political economy, and which were, indeed, long admitted as true by the highest authorities on the subject.' (Here, it must be surmised, Mill is referring not to the unenlightened 'Mercantilists' and Physiocrats but to Adam Smith and his classical followers):

It must greatly abate, or rather altogether destroy, in countries where profits are low, the immense importance which used to be attached by political economists to the effects which an event or a measure of government might have in adding to or subtracting from the capital of the country. . . . In such a state of things as this, a sudden addition to the capital of the country, unaccompanied by any increase of productive power, would be but of transitory duration; since, by depressing profits and interest, it would either diminish by a corresponding amount the savings which would be made from income in the year or two following, or it would cause an equivalent amount to be sent abroad, or to be wasted in rash speculations. Neither, on the other hand, would a sudden abstraction of capital, unless of inordinate amount, have any real effect in impoverishing the country. After a few months or years, there would exist in the country just as much capital as if none had been taken away. The abstraction, by raising profits and interest would give a fresh stimulus to the accumulative principle which would speedily fill up the vacuum. . . . In the first place, then, this view of things greatly weakens, in a wealthy and industrious country, the force of the economical argument against the expenditure of public money for really valuable, even though industriously unproductive, purposes. If for any great object of justice or philanthropic policy, such as the industrial regeneration of Ireland, or a comprehensive measure of colonisation or of public education, it were proposed to raise a large sum by way of loan, politicians need not demur to the abstraction of so much capital, as tending to dry up the permanent sources of the country's wealth, and diminish the fund which supplies the subsistence of the labouring population. The utmost expense which could be requisite for any of these purposes, would not in all probability deprive one labourer of employment, or diminish the next year's production by one ell of cloth or one bushel of grain. In poor countries, the capital of the country requires the legislator's sedulous care; he is bound to be most cautious of encroaching upon it, and should favour to the utmost its accumulation at home and its introduction from abroad. But in rich, populous, and highly cultivated countries, it is not capital which is the deficient element, but fertile land; and what the legislator should desire and promote is not a greater aggregate saving but a greater return to savings.

Mill is here contrasting the economics of new undeveloped countries with those applicable to advanced industrialized societies such, apparently, as Britain in 1848. For the latter, Mill appears to cast doubt on Adam Smith's profoundly influential doctrine of the unconditional benefits of parsimony, which Mill himself had previously seemed to hail with such enthusiasm as destroying the erroneous view (of Malthus, Sismondi, and the 'Mercantilists') that capital might possibly accumulate too fast. Furthermore, Mill refutes, by implication, the dogma, propagated by Ricardo, which later came to be called the 'Treasury View', of a fixed capital fund and that employment on public works would simply be subtracted from employment in private industry.[1]

However, Mill's analysis of the tendency of profits to a minimum and its consequences never seems to have exercised any subsequent influence on later classical and neo-classical economics. It certainly had no influence sufficient to counter-balance his doctrines about the impossibility of general over-production, and the frequent, though not universal and explicit, assumption of 'Say's Law'. Cairnes, as we have seen in his *Leading Principles* (1874) is perhaps the most rigidly and

---

[1] Bergmann even goes so far as to argue that in this chapter Mill 'finally comes to agree with Malthus. . . . It is clear that in his explanation of crises Mill develops the ideas of the Malthusian theory of overproduction, which he himself had condemned. It is principally through Mill that the theory of Malthus has exercised an influence on political economy' (op. cit., p. 216). This last statement seems somewhat exaggerated. Nevertheless Mill's earlier dogmatic castigations of Malthus and eighteenth-century ideas become all the more obviously regrettable in the light of this later chapter in the *Principles*.

regularly faithful of all upholders of 'Say's Law'. Henry Fawcett, in his *Manual*, was rigidly opposed to any public works and accused 'all political economists who preceded James Mill and Ricardo' of the fundamental error of anticipating 'a general over-production of commodities as a possible, or even probable contingency', and he argued that it is probable that what was meant by 'general over-production' was that 'a greater quantity of all commodities may be produced than people really want', not merely a greater quantity than can be sold at remunerative prices (see *Manual*, 1st ed. 1863, 6th ed. 1883, p. 472).

Marshall, Fawcett's successor at Cambridge, gave only a fragmentary treatment of the subject, which, however, closely follows Mill's, on which it can hardly be said to attempt any advance. It is true that after having approvingly quoted Mill's dictum that 'all sellers are inevitably and by the meaning of the word buyers', Marshall added the qualification that 'though men have the power to purchase they may not choose to use it'. (*Principles*, p. 710.) But the essence of this qualification can be found in several places in Mill's own writings. And when Marshall adds that a remedy for problems of depression 'is not to be got by a study of consumption, as has been alleged by some hasty writers' (p. 712), he simply seems to be echoing in a milder and more oblique way (for the benefit of J. A. Hobson) Mill's rebukes of Lauderdale, Sismondi, and Malthus, whose views Marshall never discussed.

Jevons also, who was always ready to attack Mill's doctrines root and branch, never questioned his whole treatment of 'general over-production', crises, and 'the tendency of profits to a minimum'. In fact, as we have seen, he agreed with Mill that no meaning, other than 'an evidently absurd and self-contradictory' one, can be given to the concept of a general glut or general over-production, 'so that industry would be stopped, employment fail, and all but the rich would be starved by the superfluity of commodities'. (*Theory of Political Economy*, 4th ed., pp. 183 and 202–3.) That is all Jevons has to say on Mill's analysis.

Adam Smith's analysis of saving and investing, which had been the basis and starting-point for James Mill's and Say's doctrines continued to be generally upheld.[1] In fact no recognized English economist in

---

[1] Here are some representative examples from our period, several of which we have quoted already:

1. Böhm-Bawerk: 'An economically educated people does not hoard, but applies what is saved.' (*Kapital und Kapitalzins*, 4th ed., p. 149.)
2. J. B. Clark: 'The key to the solution lies in recognizing the unquestionable fact that

the nineteenth century considered Lauderdale's or Malthus's arguments worthy of any further examination. A penumbra of crankiness and 'paradox', as Edgeworth called it, was fastened on to all varieties of the under-consumption thesis, so that it became impossible to see through differences of terminology and deficiencies of logic to the very real and formidable problems that were being suggested. Of course, there were many excesses and misformulations on the part of the under-consumptionists, but there were at least as disastrous mistakes in other contrasting approaches which nevertheless retained an impeccable respectability.

There was a fleeting mention of the principle of the general effective demand for labour in Longe's attack on the wages fund. But this was nowhere followed up. Apart from some socialist writers, there were in Britain, after Malthus, very few apart from the comparatively little-known Chalmers, E. G. Wakefield, and R. S. Moffatt,[1] who questioned the orthodox formula about 'the impossibility of general over-production'. Finally, in 1889, J. A. Hobson began his long and persistent career as an economic heretic. We have already described the sort of reception which his ideas obtained.

3. *Under-consumption and Effective Demand Doctrines in Germany and the United States*

In Germany the status of under-consumption doctrines was completely different from what it was in Victorian England. Say's 'theory of markets' had at once come in for steady and sensible criticism by academic writers following Rau's discussion (1821) of the Say-Malthus controversy, in which he sided with the latter. There was also the influential under-consumption analysis of Rodbertus, and the theories of Marx gave some support to elements in the under-consumption case. Rodbertus's views, at any rate, won considerable academic respect.

We may take Wilhelm Roscher's discussion of 'general over-production' and 'Say's Law' as an early example of the sensible treatment of the problem, and of economic fluctuations in general, given by

saving is in reality demanding and getting productive instruments as part of an income.' (Introduction to *Over-Production and Crises*, by K. Rodbertus, p. 14.)

3. A. Marshall: 'It is a familiar economic axiom that a man purchases labour and commodities with that portion of his income which he saves just as much as he does with that which he is said to spend.' (*The Pure Theory of Domestic Values*, p. 34.)

4. G. Cassel: 'In modern society, however, the person who saves money generally invests it.' (*The Nature and Necessity of Interest*, p. 132.)

5. J. A. Hobson—(who it is paradoxical to find in this company): 'Saving means buying productive goods with income.' (*The Industrial System*, 2nd ed., p. 50.)

[1] Author of a massive and difficult work, *The Economy of Consumption*, 1878.

a number of German writers in the second half of the nineteenth century. His essay 'On the Theory of Crises' first appeared in 1849.[1]

Say's Law is, according to Roscher, irrelevant for all practical purposes, since it holds only for a barter and not for a monetary economy: 'Among other reasons, the mere introduction of money is quite sufficient to rule out Say's theory in the strict sense.' This is a proposition that was flatly denied by Cairnes, for example, who held fast to the implications of Say's Law when he argued that 'the essential character of exchange is not altered by the employment of a circulating medium'. (In their *Physiology of Industry*, Hobson and Mummery illogically followed Cairnes on this point.)

Roscher asks what would happen if all men suddenly became misers, and upholds Lauderdale's criticism of Adam Smith: 'As Lord Lauderdale has very rightly remarked, savings are only truly useful so long as they run parallel with a real demand for labour or a really increasing demand for goods and services. Here is one of the many distinctions between the case of private individuals and that of the nation as a whole which economists have all too frequently overlooked.' (p. 287.)

Roscher was not an under-consumptionist in believing that there was any inevitable or general tendency in the system towards under-consumption or under-investment. But he was too well versed in the great writers of the seventeenth and eighteenth centuries to swallow entire the 'new economics' of James Mill, Say, and Ricardo, and to exclude altogether from analysis the very possibility of deficiencies in effective demand. In the main, however, Roscher's discussion of economic crises belongs with those of the psychological and synthetic group along with Bagehot's, Marshall's, and F. A. Walker's, where we shall discuss it further. We have mentioned it here simply to show that an excessive respect for Say's theory of markets, whatever may have been the case with the more orthodox writers in England, was not adopted in Germany.

Though Adolf Wagner expressed his agreement with Say's analysis, several other German economists were very forthright in their criticisms. Lexis (in his article on Over-production) held 'these arguments to suffer from an excess of anaemic abstraction and a total neglect of the actual conditions of a monetary and capitalist system of production and exchange'. H. Herkner in his authoritative article on crises, wrote: 'It is today, difficult to understand how a theory, which was reduced by

[1] Roscher's essay 'Zur Lehre von den Absatzkrisen' was republished in his *Ansichten der Volkswirtschaft* (various editions).

its originator himself to the most insignificant of tautologies, nevertheless has been able to maintain such a highly respectable reputation among economists. Yet we find a whole series of people hailing this "theory of markets" as one of the most valuable items in the whole of economic theory.'[1]

In the United States, too, the orthodoxy of James Mill, Say, and Ricardo had not the same exclusive hold, and we come now to two noteworthy criticisms by American economists which started from J. S. Mill's treatment on the one hand of general over-production, and on the other of the tendency of profits to a minimum.

F. B. Hawley (1843–1929) was a Philadelphia business-man who took up the challenge in Mill's *Principles* in his book *Capital and Population* (1882). He later made a valuable contribution to the analysis of profit (v. above, Ch. 20, sect. 1).

Hawley claimed not so much to be refuting Mill, but, though apparently reaching opposite conclusions, to be more consequentially 'Millian' than Mill, starting rather from his 'stagnation' analysis of 'the tendency of profits to a minimum', than from his remarks on 'general over-production'. Hawley's main thesis is stated as follows:

In the absence of war, famine, and bad government, capital will constantly tend to outstrip population, will periodically succeed in so doing, and will be in excess, to the detriment of production, for a greater or less portion of the time. . . . *Taking Mill's definition of what constitutes the stationary state, viz. the decline of the rate of profit to the minimum, what is more evident than that such decline is the most important occurrence in every period of industrial stagnation* and that not only in such times is the stationary state as defined by him reached, but that the rate of profit then declines below the minimum and carries the community for a time into the retrogressive state in which a decrease of production takes place. That the state of civilized communities is still on the average progressive, is certainly no proof that the other states are not occasionally reached. A permanent stationary or retrogressive state cannot occur until all the fertile land of the globe is reclaimed, and then only in the absence of further improvements and inventions, and of a decrease of population, except, indeed, population increases as fast as or faster than, the reclamation of fertile land. *The condition of mankind in the stationary and retrogressive states, instead, however, of being a curious problem, the solution of which has a practical interest for future generations alone, is a topic of pressing importance.* (pp. 62–63: our italics.)

Basic to Hawley's discussion was the awkward but nevertheless

[1] See Lexis's article on 'Überproduktion' in *Handwörterbuch der Staatswissenschaften*, 1894, and Herkner's article on 'Krisen' in the same publication.

suggestive concept of 'dead stock', a kind of 'real' hoarding, or goods which were not consumed directly or employed in profitable investment. It was over-accumulation of 'dead stock' that resulted in crises, more being accumulated than is induced to flow into 'active stock' by new investment opportunities. At least, the concept represents an attempt to break out from the Smithian analysis of saving, and pointed to a third possibility for the use of income besides consuming or investing it.

The tendency to over-accumulation is due to society possessing 'an undue proportion of the accumulating class', and is generally apt to increase markedly when there are rapid increases in production. Hawley held that the tendency could only be removed, (1) by the creation of new wants, or an increase in existing wants, (2) by the opening up of new outlets for capital, or (3) by the readjustment of social relations in such manner that the inequality of individual fortunes is diminished.[1] He connected the rate of saving with the rate of change of income: 'A sudden increase of income will yield a larger percentage for investment than a gradual one of equal extent. The more gradual it is, the closer will the increased expenditure approximate to the increased income, and, if it be very gradual, may almost or quite equal it.' (p. 92.) In the upswing, which is generally aggravated by credit expansion, the comparatively few profit incomes are immensely increased, which brings about a sharp rise in the rate of saving, which, in turn, is not met promptly enough by a fall in the rate of interest.

Hawley saw, too, the consequences of his analysis for the free trade argument. But he ranges very widely without concentrating sufficiently, perhaps, on the clarity and precision of the central core of his analysis. His book is a powerful and original one, and that it did not attract the attention it deserved is all the more noteworthy in that it built directly on Mill's ideas without indulging in the kind of 'revolutionary' claims and terminology which is always suspect to the orthodox. It points to the valuable and fundamental problems and discussions, so long neglected, which might have been opened up if the varied approaches to be found in Mill's *Principles* had been examined in a reasonably critical spirit, and if Mill's aggressive and undiscriminating attacks on Malthus, Sismondi, and eighteenth-century writers generally, had not encouraged the thorough-going intellectual boycott of the whole line of thought they represented.

[1] See Hawley's article, 'The Ratio of Capital to Consumption', *National Quarterly Review*, July 1879.

Uriel H. Crocker (1832–1903), a Boston lawyer, took as his text Proverbs xi. 24: 'There is that scattereth, and yet increaseth; and there is that withholdeth more than is meet, but it tendeth to poverty.' In a number of pamphlets (1877–95) he complained that the facts of mass idleness and depression were not receiving their due attention from professors of political economy.[1] Crocker's criticisms of Mill are interesting and penetrating, and he specially takes up the point, so emphasized by Mill, that the issue of 'general over-production' is crucial for the whole scope and shape of political economy. If Mill is wrong, a whole new third dimension, at present overlooked, is added to the subject: Mill 'seems strangely to have overlooked the consideration that, even if it was impossible that production should run ahead of demand, it was still possible that the two being, as it were, tied together, production might be limited and held back by a lagging demand'. In addition to production and distribution there is really a third thing for economists to consider, namely 'how a market can be created for produce', and Mill's conception of political economy, namely, that its only province is 'to consider how a sufficient production may be combined with the best possible distribution', is, to use his own expression, 'radically different' from the true conception. . . . (*Hard Times*, p. 81.) 'The doctrine of the impossibility of general overproduction is one that lies at the basis of the whole of the accepted system of political economy; and if the doctrine is proved to be false, the greater part of that system will have to be reconstructed.' (*Overproduction and Commercial Distress*, p. 22.)

Crocker made the point, common to under-consumptionists, that although saving might always be a private virtue, it was by no means inevitably beneficent to society. He saw a rush of investment in some new field as an important source of instability. His crucial defect in formulation, like Hobson's, was in not carrying far enough his analysis of saving and investing. Though concerned to demolish the conclusions drawn from 'Say's Law', both Crocker, and later Hobson,

---

[1] Crocker's criticism of Mill appeared in a note in the *Quarterly Journal of Economics*, 1892, and rather paradoxically was answered on behalf of Millian orthodoxy by Thorstein Veblen, who later considerably revised his views. Among Crocker's other writings were two little books: *Excessive Saving a Cause of Commercial Distress: being a Series of Assaults upon Accepted Principles of Political Economy*, Boston, 1884, and *The Causes of Hard Times*, Boston, 1895. Crocker seems to have kept challenging the Harvard professors to refute his arguments, and once asked them for their answer to one of their own examination questions—surely a most unprofessional inquiry. The question, couched in the accepted Millian terminology ran: 'Suppose everybody resolved to consume productively only, what would be the result?' Apparently Crocker did not get a reply from Harvard.

accepted, at critical points in their argument, the idea of the automatic investment of savings, without supplying any concept of 'hoarding', as is suggested in Hawley's 'dead stock'.

Crocker mentioned the role of the unequal distribution of wealth in causing 'excessive' saving, but did not give it the key importance which Hobson later did. He foresaw for the twentieth century the danger of a revolution of the masses resulting from widespread unemployment, and claimed that 'a new light is thrown on the question of the policy of establishing public workshops, and of carrying on public improvements for the purpose of giving employment to the idle'. (*Hard Times*, p. 70.)

4. 'Over-consumption', 'Over-investment', and 'Disproportionate Investment' Theories

Our second broad group of explanations, or partial explanations, consists of those in terms of 'over-consumption', 'over-investment', 'capital shortage', and 'disproportionate' investment. Marx's analysis of the trade cycle included an important element of this kind, which was later to be developed by Tugan-Baranovsky and Spiethoff. One of the original exponents was James Wilson, the first editor of the *Economist*, who traced, in particular, the 1847 railway boom and crisis to disproportionate investment in fixed and working capital respectively. It is mentioned in a few suggestive phrases, but never followed up, by Jevons and Mangoldt, on the one hand, and by Cairnes on the other. F. A. Hayek has called attention to some later English and French economists who adopted especially the 'over-consumption' type of explanation.[1] The most influential and eloquent of these in England was Professor Bonamy Price (1807–88) for a long while occupant of the Drummond chair at Oxford. Price's writings date from the years following the onset of the 1873 depression.

According to Price, the cause of the depression 'is one and one only: overspending, overconsumption, destroying more wealth than is reproduced. . . . This is the real *fons mali*, the root of all the disorder and suffering.' (*Contemporary Review*, Apr. 1877, p. 787.) As a result of over-consumption 'there are few commodities, few goods to buy with. . . . Manufacturers and sellers cannot dispose of the commodities they have produced, because the usual purchasers have few or no goods wherewith to buy.' (*Contemporary Review*, May 1879, p. 270.) Any form of sudden and drastic 'over-consumption'—a bad harvest, war,

[1] *Prices and Production*, 2nd ed., pp. 101 ff.

excessive government expenditure—may start the trouble, but especially 'that particular brand of over-consumption which consists in excessive investments in fixed capital, generates effects which greatly exaggerate commercial disaster'.

Price works out an example of a landlord with an income of £50,000 who tries to put through in one year improvments in drainage to his land which cost £100,000, and so overstrains his resources that he has to break off the work unfinished, before it yields any of its services:[1]

A single individual may borrow, but a nation which puts itself in that position has no resources beyond itself, and must suffer. Railways and other fixed capital are to a people what draining is to the landlord—most powerful instruments for obtaining wealth; but they cannot be constructed without great destruction of wealth involved in making them. It is long before they come into action to replace what they have consumed; meanwhile food, clothing, iron, coals are gone. . . . There is no cause so common of financial crisis and commercial depressions as an excessive construction of fixed capital. . . . Amongst these offenders none are so mischievous as railways. (*Chapters on Practical Political Economy*, 2nd ed., 1882, pp. 118–20.)

However, over-investment in fixed capital is not the only mischievous form of 'over-consumption':

Men of the mood of mind of the unionist workmen are emphatically not savers. . . . What they extort from employers they consume unproductively— they destroy it in indulgences and only too often in drink. This engenders a very marked distinction between exceptional wages and exceptional profits. . . . A heavy holding in railway stocks is the ownership of an instrument which enriches not the shareholders only but the whole country, which calls into being a vast power of employing and rewarding labour. The mighty towns of England, the countless factories of her manufacturing regions are all savings out of profits. How feeble are the productive instruments to which wages can point as the fruit of the labourer's thrift! It cannot be doubted that enormous waste of wealth, of unproductive consumption, often of the worst kind, has been the result of the augmented wages of the working classes. (*Contemporary Review*, Apr. 1877, p. 795.)

There is also the 'overconsumption' of governments: 'Can any one feel surprised if trade languishes and suffering weighs down great industries, when soldiers are extinguishing the wealth wherewith to buy.'

[1] The analysis, though not so elegantly developed, is similar to that of Labordère in his parable of the one-man crisis in his article 'Autour de la Crise Américaine de 1907' (see p. 383 below). We need hardly mention that a distaste for some of Price's prejudices should not lead to an underestimate of his positive analysis.

Surveying the state of the nations in the second half of the seventies, there was one seemingly very paradoxical fact that called for a special explanatory effort by Bonamy Price as an exponent of the 'over-consumption' theory of depressions. France, through the ravages of war and defeat and the heavy indemnity she had paid, had obviously suffered from an 'over-consumption' far more drastic than victorious Germany, or neutral Britain or the United States. However, whereas Britain, the United States, and Germany were sunk in depression, France in the later seventies was lively and prosperous in comparison:

> Her industry is in full play, no sense of poverty weighs down the people. . . . To what was this most unlooked-for and most astonishing sight due? To the practice of one of the very greatest of economical virtues. She had saved. . . . The French people, with instinctive genius applied, with most painful effort, the one lesson which political economy pointed out for the cure. Without knowing political economy they practised what it prescribed. They could do this, because political economy is common sense. France saved. . . . Thus France has come forth from the commercial depression with a freshness and strength which have called forth the astonishment and the admiration of the world. (*Contemporary Review*, 1877, p. 792 and 1879, p. 280.)

Without yielding to anyone in admiration and astonishment at the prudence and virtue of *la belle France* at this critical juncture, one may today consider that the explanation of her comparative prosperity by the under-consumptionist Crocker, who took up Price on this point, was more accurate. Crocker's 'under-consumptionist' explanation was in terms of the expansive effects of the extra 'effective demand' represented by the indemnity France had to pay. (Sixty years before, after the Napoleonic wars, Malthus had correspondingly remarked that those countries which 'have suffered the most by the war have suffered the least by the peace'.)

The Oxford Professor far outdid even Adam Smith in his unqualified eulogy of saving: 'The man who saves, be he prince or peasant, is the benefactor of his country; for it is capital which bestows all necessaries and all comforts, which rescues populations from poverty, which sustains and increases their numbers. Nothing can be more fatal to the happiness of a people than to bring profit into discredit.' (*Chapters*, 2nd ed., p. 128.)

The influence of the sort of views which Price held could no doubt be traced on later economists, and in debates on economic policies at least until 1931. It would have been interesting if Edgeworth, who found J. A. Hobson's views on saving so 'very paradoxical', had got

round to analysing the views on the same subject ('in all their unmitigated authority') of his predecessor in the chair at Oxford.[1]

The 'over-consumption' analysis also had its exponents in France,
one of the best-known being the Cabinet Minister and liberal individualist Yves Guyot (1843–1928). Guyot emphasized more than Price,
and more in the manner of James Wilson, the disproportionate character of over-investment and the shortage of circulating capital:

> Fixed capital cannot be utilised if there is no available circulating capital.
> Ships and railways are useless if there are no commodities for them to con-
> vey; a factory cannot be worked unless there are consumers ready to buy
> its products. If the circulating capital has been so far exhausted as to take a
> long time replacing, fixed capital must meanwhile remain unproductive, and
> the crisis is so much the longer and more severe. . . . We see this going on
> in the United States. A crisis raged there for two or three years; by that
> time the capital consumed had been replaced and the crisis came to an end.
> (*Principles of Social Economy*, English translation, 1892, Bk. V, Ch. 3.)

Guyot regarded as the great blessing of depressions that they forced
governments, either willy-nilly, or in their efforts at cure, to cut down
heavily their expenditure. It was only by cutting down expenditure
both on consumption and on investment that crises could be cured, and
Guyot instanced the apparently exemplary action of New York State
in reducing its expenditure from £3½ million in 1874 to £1½ million
in 1878 because of the depression. (Op. cit., p. 249.)

5. *Psychological, Credit, and Synthetic Theories*

Our third group of explanations is much looser and far less concerned with a compact all-explanatory formula or solution. This type
of explanation is usually based on a more relaxed empirical acknowledgement that a multitude of things can go wrong, and bring depression, in a complex economic society. Such explanations lack that faint
strain of scapegoat-hunting which is apt sometimes to be detectable
in the seekers after thoroughgoing theoretical formulae fully and
exclusively explanatory of these great social disasters, tracking them

---

[1] Price served as an economic expert on a number of government commissions and
was paid the following extraordinary tribute by Gladstone himself (a study of whose
views on the nature and significance of economic theory would be of great interest both
epistemologically and historically): 'The only man—to his credit be it spoken—who has
had the resolution to apply, in all their unmitigated authority, the principles of abstract
political economy to the people and circumstances of Ireland, exactly as if he had been
proposing to legislate for the inhabitants of Saturn or Jupiter.' (See the article on Price in
the *Dictionary of National Biography*.)

down to the exclusive fault of the 'rentiers' or the trade unionists, the 'capitalists' or the 'socialists'.

It was increasingly clear that the most far-reaching economic errors were possible either through the psychological instability of human beings, particularly in the mass and when subject to competitive emulation, or because of the increasing 'real' complexity of the division of labour and 'roundaboutness' of production in an interdependent modern economic society. These sources of instability could be shown to be powerfully reinforced through the mechanism of credit. Consequently, comparatively slight initial causes could set off cumulative 'multiplying' or 'accelerating' upward and downward movements. Initial changes might be psychologically cumulative, or might multiply through the circulation of payments, or be aggravated or accelerated in the demand passed back from one group of industries to another. Out of these, at first rather loose, generalizations grew the precise modern formulae for the multiplier and the acceleration principle.

The errors of competing entrepreneurs had been used by Sismondi as a reinforcement of his under-consumption analysis earlier in the century. In our period it forms the main element in Roscher's balanced and comprehensive discussion of crises. He argues that the more highly developed is the division of labour the more difficult it will be to keep supply and demand balanced, so that any factor suddenly and markedly affecting production or consumption may start trouble: 'Important improvements in machinery will result in a rush to exploit them by competing manufacturers.' (*Ansichten*, p. 315.) An over-optimistic estimate of their possibilities will lead to excessive investment, while at the same time consumption (particularly of agricultural products in inelastic demand) may not increase with the same rapidity: 'When the incomes of one group of producers fall, the depression will not be limited simply to them, for they will have to buy less from others.' (p. 289.) The possibilities of a deflationary spiral are increased by the fact that in the course of fluctuations 'those who gain do not usually expand their consumption as rapidly as the losers are forced to contract *theirs*'. (p. 301.) Changes in the money and credit supply may also aggravate the instability. (p. 297.)

Roscher's discussion is one of the earliest of a number of balanced and comprehensive surveys by German economists, some emphasizing one factor more than another, most of them recognizing the possibility of deficiencies of effective demand, and in the main prepared to be restrained in their theorizing by the existing paucity of facts and figures. The contributions of Wagner, Nasse, Brentano, Lexis, Herkner, and others all belong in this category.[1] Tugan-Baranovsky and Spiethoff could hardly have got as far as they later did without the foundations and suggestions provided by the comprehensive surveys and criticisms of these writers.

Particularly noteworthy is the article of Nasse (*Jahrbuch für Gesetz-gebung*, 1879; already quoted above, Ch. 18, sect. 3). It emphasizes the psychological factors but also includes the explanation of booms as the outcome of the rush to exploit a new invention: 'Most advances in production yield an extraordinary profit when first exploited. . . . This extra profit is, however, a powerful stimulus to all other producers to make the improvement. If they follow rapidly in the new paths, perhaps they too may share in the extra profit.' (p. 151.) Nasse points out how particular booms have been associated with improvements, and bursts of investment, in particular industries (for example, steel, ship-building, and railways).

But Nasse not only gives a strong hint of the explanation forty years later developed by Schumpeter, but also of that of Aftalion. The original impetus in one branch of industry will lead to an increased demand for the products of others, and the different branches will mutually stimulate one another. As a rule, primarily those industries will be affected which are producing permanent capital equipment, and not goods for direct consumption. Increased productive activity needs especially, in order to take place at all, increased means of production, buildings, machines, and plant. A speculative demand will soon add immensely to the initial increase in demand, particularly in the case of goods the production of which takes a long time:

> Every rise in the prices of goods leads to speculation about a further rise. Many people buy only in order to sell later with a profit at the higher prices. *This is especially the case with goods that cannot be produced in increased*

[1] See A. Wagner's article 'Krisen' in Rentzsch's *Handwörterbuch der Volkswirt-schaftslehre*, 1870, a valuable work for its date, except that it defends Say and Ricardo on 'general overproduction' (an interesting reflection on the doctrine that Germany at this time was given over to rabidly anti-classical and anti-theoretical doctrines). L. J. Brentano's main contribution was to suggest a plan for the insurance of the wage-earning classes against crises, see his article in *Jahrbuch für Gesetzgebung*, 1878, quoted above in Ch. 18, sect. 3. H. Herkner's article on 'Krisen' in Conrad's *Handwörterbuch der Staatswissenschaft*, 1892, is described by Jones (1900) as 'the best single article upon the subject of crises' and it certainly gives a comprehensive review of the literature of the subject. Herkner's own theory follows the 'mal-distribution-of-income' variant of the under-consumption theory in the tradition of Lauderdale and Rodbertus. We have already quoted Herkner on 'Say's Law' in sect. 2 above. See also the article of Lexis on 'Handel' in Schönberg's '*Handbuch*', 2nd ed., 1886.

quantities within a short interval of time. With an increase in demand they open a field for speculation, while with goods the production of which can rapidly be increased speculation has no such field. . . . But in all branches of production there are hindrances in the way of a large increase of output. Factories and means of production must be enlarged, new workers obtained, before the expansion can take place. (p. 158: italics supplied.)

Much of Nasse's article is given up to discussing various possible measures of State intervention to prevent crises—socialist planning, protection, and monetary policy. About all of these he is strongly sceptical, particularly about the socialists' 'planned regulation of production', as we have seen in our section on criticisms of socialist economics.

In England an early exposition of the more emphatically psychological explanation was given by at least two members of a notable group of investigators belonging to the Manchester Statistical Society, namely W. Langton and John Mills. In his paper of 1867 Mills concluded that 'the malady of commercial crises is not in essence a matter of the purse but of the mind'. . . . 'Broadly defined, panic is the destruction in the mind of a bundle of beliefs.' (See Mills's paper on 'Credit Cycles and the Origins of Commercial Panics' in *Transactions of the Manchester Statistical Society*, 1867.)[1]

The most influential and distinguished English exponent of the broad approach we are discussing in this section was Walter Bagehot. It is perhaps suitable to begin with a characteristic sentence from his essay on Gibbon: 'Much has been written on panics and manias, much more than with the most outstretched intellect we would be able to follow or conceive; but one thing is certain, that at particular times a great many stupid people have a great deal of stupid money.' Of course, Bagehot's main exposition comes in Chapter VI of *Lombard Street* (1873) on 'Why Lombard Street is Often Very Dull and Sometimes Extremely Excited'. In this chapter Bagehot shows no signs of following up the 'disproportionate-investment' type of explanation developed a quarter of a century earlier by his father-in-law and predecessor in the editorial chair of the *Economist*, James Wilson.

In the complex modern exchange economy 'there is a partnership in industries. No single large industry can be depressed without injury to other industries. . . . Under a system in which everyone is dependent

---

[1] On Mills, Langton, and other Manchester investigators who wrote on the subject of crises in the 1850's and 1860's, and to whom Jevons was presumably much indebted, see T. S. Ashton, *Economic and Social Investigations in Manchester*, Ch. VI.

on the labour of everyone else, the loss of one spreads and *multiplies* through all, and spreads and multiplies the faster, the higher the previous perfection of the system of divided labour.' (*Lombard Street*, new ed., 1910, pp. 128–9.)

. . . The most common, and by far the most important, case where the depression in one trade causes depression in all others, is that of depressed agriculture. When the agriculture of the world is ill off, food is dear. And as the amount of absolute necessaries which a people consumes cannot be much diminished, the additional amount which has to be spent on them is so much subtracted from what used to be spent on other things. All the industries, A, B, C, D, up to Z, are somewhat affected by an augmentation in the price of corn . . ..every one by becoming poorer, makes every other poorer too. All trades are slack from diminished custom, and the consequence is a vast stagnant capital, much idle labour, and a greatly retarded production. (p. 130.)

Bonamy Price would have agreed that a bad harvest would cause depression (since it causes 'over-consumption') but would have traced the trouble rather to the fall in farmers' purchasing power through their having nothing to exchange.

According to Bagehot 'a great calamity to any great industry will tend to produce the same effect'. The cumulative processes will be immensely reinforced by the system of credit, 'the disposition of one man to trust another', which is 'singularly varying'. He goes on to outline a psychological or credit cycle:

In a year or two after a crisis credit usually improves, as the remembrance of the disasters which at the crisis impaired credit is becoming fainter and fainter. Provisions get back to their usual price, or some great industry makes, from some temporary cause, a quick step forward. . . . In so far as the apparent prosperity is caused by an unusual plentifulness of loanable capital and a consequent rise in prices, that prosperity is not only liable to reaction but *certain* to be exposed to reaction. (pp. 152–5.)

This is because the gathering momentum of the upswing cannot proceed indefinitely unchecked: 'The plentifulness of loanable capital causes a rise of prices; that rise of prices makes it necessary to have more loanable capital to carry on the same trade.' But the trade will not be the same but will have increased, the initial increase having 'secondary' and 'tertiary developments'. The general over-optimism will also certainly have led to extensive misdirection of resources, which will eventually be discovered with consequent disaster to the structure of psychology and credit.[1]

[1] See W. W. Rostow, *British Economy of the 19th Century*, Ch. VIII, on 'Bagehot and

Marshall's brief account of the cycle, first given in 1879 in his *'Elements'*, describes it as a credit cycle in terms similar to those of Bagehot, for whose works Marshall had a very high regard. Marshall never got round to revising or extending this early account at all significantly, except on the monetary side in his *Evidence to the Gold and Silver Commission* (1887).

Another account which seems to have owed something to Bagehot's chapter, but which penetrates farther at a number of points is that of Francis A. Walker.[1] Walker believed that considerable fluctuations in activity were 'inseparable from the modern organization of trade and industry', one main source of trouble being disproportionate production. He carried farther a very similar analysis to Bagehot's of 'the progressive aggravation and acceleration of economic mischief from industry to industry'. (*Political Economy*, p. 182.) Owing to a bad harvest, or some other exogenous reason,

the merchant feels the demand for his goods fall off abruptly. He fears there is more to come. He is determined not to be caught with a large stock on his hands, and in his orders to the manufacturer, he exaggerates the natural and proper effect of the change in the market. The manufacturer on his part, knows nothing directly of the actual falling off in demand. He only learns it as it comes to him heightened by the apprehensions of the merchant. In his turn he exaggerates the evil and reduces his production more than proportionally. . . . As he pays less wages, his workmen have less to spend for the products of other branches of industry. The merchants in these lines feeling the falling off in demand, exaggerate it in their orders to manufacturers. . . . These, in turn, apprehensive of worse to come, curtail their operations more than correspondingly, and so the movement proceeds, with increasing violence. (pp. 182–3.)

Walker is thus describing a multiplying or accelerating process similar in effect to that described by Roscher and Bagehot, but emphasizing the adjustment of stocks, rather than the length of time taken in production, as contrasted, on the other hand, with Nasse, and later Carver and Aftalion. Walker held that 'the actual time covered by the period of depression is sometimes much longer than can be accounted for by the mere loss and destruction of a panic', and he asked: 'May the movement to check production proceed until all industry is locked fast the Trade Cycle'. Rostow quotes some very interesting suggestions from Bagehot's articles in the *Economist* as to the equilibrium of savings and investment and its significance.

[1] We are quoting from his *Political Economy*, 3rd ed., 1888. Earlier, in his book *Money*, 1877, Walker had outlined views suggestive of the 'disproportionate investment' theory. On Walker see P. Barnett, *Business-Cycle Theory in the United States*, 1860–1900, Chicago, 1941.

in a vicious circle: no-one producing, because others will not consume, while no-one is able to consume the products of others because he himself has nothing with which to buy them?' Walker concluded that depressions might well last indefinitely were it not for the steady demand for the necessities of life which prevents the system running right down, until a gradual revival of confidence takes place.

'Monetary' explanations of crises and cycles did not obtain much articulate and generalized formulation after 1870 during the period with which this chapter is mainly concerned. There was some mention of the role of the rate of interest in some of the over-investment explanations, and the classical analysis of Thornton and Ricardo, though on the whole in eclipse, was suggested in Marshall's *Evidence to the Gold and Silver Commission* (1887), without being built up into a general analysis of cyclical fluctuations. There were, also, numerous discussions of particular defects in banking and money market organization, technique, and legislation, as affecting crises. But there was, of course, no clear-cut conceptual apparatus for the analysis of the generation and expenditure of incomes. Apart from this, H. D. McLeod's[1] ideas about the instability of credit, and the possibilities of credit creation and contraction by the banks to counter booms and slumps, were among the most important on the subject of the monetary analysis of fluctuations—ideas later to be followed up by Schumpeter, Hawtrey, and Hahn.

6. The Periodicity and Inevitability of Economic Crises

With the subject of the periodicity and inevitability of crises we come to a name which perhaps should have had the most prominent place in this chapter as that of the economist, more deserving than any other, of the title of 'Discoverer of the Trade Cycle'.

Clement Juglar (1819–1905) was a Parisian doctor who soon found the study of financial fluctuations both more interesting and more lucrative than his medical practice. Like Cantillon, Ricardo, and Keynes, Juglar amassed an immense fortune, which at any rate seems to provide some sort of tangible testimony for the serviceability of the financial barometer which he worked out for himself. In other respects Juglar could hardly have differed from Ricardo and Keynes more widely. He was statistical and historical, rather than primarily deductive in method, and a detached observer rather than politically *engagé*. His great work is his *Des crises commerciales et de leur retour périodique*

[1] *v. Lectures on Credit and Banking*, 1882.

en France, en Angleterre et aux États-Unis. The first edition, 1862, was a comparatively small book of some 250 pages, the second (1889) is almost three times as large, though it does not provide more than a massive expansion of the methods and ideas of the first. Juglar had first come to notice the existence of a regular pervasive cycle in economic affairs when studying the statistics of population, marriages, births, and deaths, which seemed to be markedly influenced by the fluctuations of prosperity and depression. He had discovered what later came to be called the 'pulse of the nation', or rather of the nations. Juglar criticized the writings of McCulloch, Newmarch, Tooke, and McLeod for not insisting on the periodic recurrence of commercial crises, but studying each one in isolation. As one would expect, his metaphors tend to be medical (just as Jevons's were meteorological): 'Crises', he held, 'like diseases, appear to be one of the conditions of societies dominated by commerce and industry.' Though they can be to some extent foreseen and mitigated they cannot be entirely suppressed in advanced economic societies. Bad harvests and war may aggravate the fluctuations, but the periodic wavelike movement is something separate, and an international phenomenon. There is a regular, rhythmical tendency for periods of prosperity to end with a crisis, and for periods of liquidation to prepare the way for a new prosperity.

Juglar concentrated on four series of financial statistics in addition to those for prices and interest rates, and set them out for each of the three leading countries. These were: (1) discountings and advances; (2) the metallic reserves; (3) the note circulation; and (4) deposits and current accounts. The movements of the first two indicated the special regularity of periods of crisis and prosperity. They showed that when bills and acceptances were rising, and the metallic reserve falling, inflation and crisis was near at hand. After the crisis the metallic reserve rose. It was the reduction in the reserve of coin in the banks which gave the signal for the explosion. Juglar then traces out statistically the history of crises from 1800 to 1860 in the three leading countries, following as far as possible the movements of the main financial statistics in each boom and slump, and comparing the causes of different crises.

In his much larger second edition, 27 years later, Juglar found that the trade cycle had repeated itself in the second half of the nineteenth century in the same manner as in the first half. It was an autonomous phenomenon aggravated by, but fundamentally independent of, 'outside' political and climatic events: 'The periods of prosperity, crisis, liquidation, although affected by the fortunate or unfortunate accidents in the life of peoples, are not the result of chance events, but arise out of the behaviour, the activities, and above all out of the saving habits of the population, and the way they employ the capital and credit available' (2nd ed., p. xix). Juglar concentrated on trying to discover and set out 'what happened in business cycles' in the nineteenth century, particularly on the financial side. He attempted only the most obvious of generalizations, for example about the movements of prices, and therefore expounded no compact explanatory formula about what determines what, which could become a centre of debate. Perhaps partly for this reason his work has never seemed to receive much attention from English and American economists, though he himself drew much from Tooke, Newmarch, Giffen, Overstone, and others. However, after the turn of the century, Tugan-Baranovsky, Spiethoff, and Schumpeter all owed something to Juglar's pioneer researches.

If, by the massive and definitive character of his pioneer work, Clement Juglar easily deserves pride of place in this section, the idea of the periodicity and inevitability of crises was, of course, being advanced by many other writers in the latter part of the nineteenth century. The idea of a seven-year cycle can, in fact, be traced back to Sir William Petty, exactly 200 years before the first edition of Juglar's book. The idea of a certain periodicity of crises is also to some extent contained in the classical analysis of the tendency of profits to a minimum, particularly, as we have seen, in J. S. Mill's treatment of crises as periodically warding off this tendency ('that such revulsions are almost periodical, is a consequence of the very tendency of profits we are considering'). That crises were inevitably recurring and inherent in the system, if not necessarily with precise periodicity, was naturally the view of Marxist and socialist investigators following out a line of analysis very similar to the classical theory of 'the tendency of profits to a minimum'.

The idea of a psychological cycle of optimism and pessimism was expounded particularly forcefully by Bagehot, but had been expressed earlier by Overstone in his epigrammatic account of the cycle: 'State of quiescence—next improvement—growing confidence—prosperity—excitement — over-trading — convulsions — pressure — stagnation —distress—ending again in quiescence.' (*Tracts and Other Publications on the Metallic and Paper Currency*, edited by McCulloch, 1858, p. 31.)

Especially worthy of mention on this subject are the papers of John

Mills and Langton already referred to.[1] From the history of the first half of the century Mills argued for a cycle of ten or twelve years divided into one year of crisis and three roughly three-year periods which he described as the post-panic period, the middle or revival period, and the speculative period. But perhaps the best-known theory of periodicity, if very controversial in its basis, was Jevons's sun-spot theory. Jevons's statistical research certainly helped to establish the notion of the periodicity of crisis, even if his attempt to link this up with a meteorological periodicity was not entirely successful or widely supported.

However, the complete transition from the study of crises to that of cycles may be considered as having really got under way at the turn of the century, when the works of Tugan-Baranovsky, Spiethoff, and Sombart laid emphasis on the inherent 'normality' rather than the 'abnormality' of crises and cycles in an evolving capitalist economy, and attempted to show much more precisely how each stage of the cycle grew out of the preceding one.

[1] *v.* p. 367 above.

23

Crises and Cycles (II): From *c.* 1900

1. *Introductory*

AFTER about 1900 a series of works, the first of which were by continental economists, led to a much more systematic and continuous study of the trade cycle. It was, too, the cycle as a whole, and the inter-connexions between its phases, rather than simply the crisis, which became increasingly the main object of study.

Several of the leading contributors to the study of the trade cycle were either highly critical of the equilibrium analysis of 'normal' value, price, and distribution, or, if they accepted this analysis, found little or no application for its concepts and procedure in studying the trade cycle. On the other hand, neo-classical economists seemed to look to some sort of eventual integration of 'normal' equilibrium with trade cycle analysis, the latter finding its place in that 'last chapter' of economic theory which Böhm-Bawerk had awarded it. Meanwhile before that last chapter was reached the 'normal' equilibrium physiology of the economic system was still given first place as compared with the 'abnormal' pathology of crises and cycles.[1]

As Wesley Mitchell put it: 'It was not the orthodox economists, however, who gave the problem of crises and depressions its place in economics, but sceptics who had profited by and then reacted against their teachings. From Adam Smith to Mill, and even to Alfred Marshall, the classical masters have paid but incidental attention to the rhythmical oscillations of trade in their systematic treatises. They have been concerned primarily to elucidate principles which hold "in the long run", or apply to the "normal state". To them crises and depressions have been of secondary interest—proper subjects for special study or

---

[1] The following statement may fairly be regarded as typical: 'Underlying all changes and perturbations in the economic system there is, in spite of superficial irregularities, a normal element determined by various special laws. Hence just as we have in medical branches of science not only normal anatomy and physiology, but also special branches going into a description of the organs and functions of the human body in a pathological condition, so it is in political economy, where there is a theory of perturbations or crises . . . which is a necessary complement of the theory of normal economic functions.' (L. Cossa, *Introduction to the Study of Political Economy*, translated L. Dyer, 1893, p. 47.) Of course, the primary study should be that of the 'normal', and the complementary that of the 'abnormal', provided one has a reasonable hunch as to what 'normality' is.

occasional reference but not among the central problems of economic theory.' (*Business Cycles*, 1927, p. 3.)

Though this generalization of Mitchell's may not be quite fair to some of the classical economists, it does apply fairly accurately to the 'neo-classical' period between 1880 and 1900 or 1910, covering, for example, in our period Marshall, Edgeworth, Wicksteed, Menger, Wieser, Böhm-Bawerk, Walras, Pareto, J. B. Clark, and a large number of less well-known names.

After 1900 there was an increasing tendency to treat the trade cycle not so much as the consequence of 'outside', or largely fortuitous, disturbances of a normally self-equilibrating process (e.g. by wars, crop failures, psychological weaknesses, or defects in financial organization) but to emphasize much more that it should be regarded as a normal inherent or 'endogenous' consequence of capitalist development and progress in its present phase. To this line of thought Tugan-Baranovsky, Sombart, Spiethoff, and Schumpeter, all ultimately following a Marxian line of thought, were the main contributors.

A main line of division running across the many various explanations of fluctuations continued to be that between those who asserted the possibility of 'general over-production' or under-consumption, against what, in England, became the dominant orthodoxy, and, on the other hand, the orthodox, who, accepting the formula of the Mills and J B. Say as to 'the impossibility of *general* over-production', sought to explain crises in terms of *disproportionate* production or investment, and under-saving. As we have seen, throughout much of the nineteenth century this highly terminological issue of whether 'general over-production' was impossible, possible, or a regular actual occurrence, had been running through many of the discussions of economic crises and fluctuations. The unorthodox exponents of the possibility and actual frequent occurrence of general over-production, whatever the defects in their logic, clung to the glaring facts of unemployed resources and to the paradox of poverty and unemployment, and deduced from this the simple conclusion that if resources were unemployed it could only be because there was a deficiency of effective demand for them ultimately traceable to under-consumption by final consumers. The upholders of the impossibility of general over-production seem usually to have started more theoretically, from the law of markets, though they may not have succeeded in holding to this abstraction throughout their analysis. But they had one well-attested fact which could be used to support the view that it was *dis-*

proportionate production rather than *general over-production* to which crises were due. This fact was that the fluctuations between boom and slump took place overwhelmingly in the capital goods industries (a fact which also impressed Spiethoff, for example, who of course completely rejected Say's Law of Markets). It followed that the disaster to these capital goods industries must come from a deficiency or a shortage of demand for the products of the capital goods industries, that is from a shortage of 'savings', which was equated by some exponents of this line of thought with an *excess* of consumption.

Perhaps the most fundamental conflict in the discussion of the trade cycle continued in the next decades to be this one between the 'under-consumptionists' of one kind or another, and the advocates of the 'under-saving' or 'excess consumption' thesis. But the antithesis was not always regarded as irreconcilable. Elements of both types of explanation had earlier been combined by Marx, and were again in our present period to some extent blended by Tugan-Baranovsky, Spiethoff, and Robertson. Around this central debate as to the role of consumption and saving were grouped those who emphasized, in different degrees, psychological factors and errors, defects in or the misuse of the monetary and credit system, and the special position of agriculture. The thorough-going under-consumption thesis of Hobson was fairly widely rejected, and continues simply as a distant and unharmonious accompaniment to the debates of the more orthodox.

This chapter is divided into four further sections in which chronology and subject-matter are made roughly but not precisely to fit together. The first section deals with a series of writers who concentrated on the central relations between consumption and investment, whose pioneer works in German and French appeared in the first decade of the century. In the second section comes a series of writers, who in the years just before the first world war, from various points of view, studied especially the money and credit mechanism. Thirdly comes a group of writers in English who sought, either with the aid of statistics or with that of analysis, to reconcile or combine conflicting points of view about the cycle and about the relations between consumption and investment. Fourthly, we deal very briefly with the writings of the middle and later twenties, when the subject again came to the forefront after the upheavals of the First World War. These post-war writings mainly consist of more comprehensive and precise restatements of their views by the pre-war pioneers, though much more attention is given in several cases to the monetary aspects of the problem. Throughout we have tried to keep reasonably close to the actual temporal-historical order of development, as well as to supply as much as possible of the actual words of the original authors, though this has been at a considerable cost to the tidiness and clarity of our survey.

2. The Instabilities of Capitalistic Production

(a) TUGAN-BARANOVSKY

A book which may deservedly be taken as opening a new phase in the study of crises and cycles is Tugan-Baranovsky's *Industrial Crises in England* (Russian edition 1894, German 1901, French 1913). This book was described by Spiethoff as the first scientific monograph on its subject which combined history, statistics, and analysis. Tugan-Baranovsky (1865–1919), who was Professor at St. Petersburg, and later, after 1917, for a short time a Minister in the Ukraine, was a socialist 'revisionist', strongly influenced by, though not uncritical of, Marx.[1] Among his predecessors he discussed the contributions of Say, Sismondi, Jevons, and Juglar, in the main highly critically. His own analysis to a large extent follows Marx's pattern, emphasizing strongly that crises are, to some extent, inherent in the capitalist system, though he contested the Marxian thesis of the inevitable breakdown.[2] He combined elements both of the 'disproportionate-investment' explanation, and, to some extent, of the 'under-consumption' and 'maldistribution of income' doctrine. But the latter theme is not developed at any length by Tugan-Baranovsky. The maldistribution of income under capitalism is introduced only in the last paragraph of the socialistic peroration of his theoretical chapter.

Tugan-Baranovsky's analysis is confined to a single chapter in the middle of his book (Ch. 3 of Part 2), the first part of which is devoted to English economic history, and the third to the social consequences in England of economic crises. Tugan-Baranovsky first examines the classical theory of markets, concluding that Say was forced so to qualify his original law as virtually to abandon it. He charges the under-consumptionist Sismondi with having implied that consumer demand

---

[1] In his authoritative study (*Business Cycles and National Income*, pp. 277 ff.) A. H. Hansen gives very high praise—from which no one would wish to detract—to the originality of Tugan-Baranovsky's work. But it is odd to find such a very full account which does not so much as mention once the name of Marx.

[2] See his article 'Der Zusammenbruch der Kapitalistischen Wirtschaftsordnung', *Archiv für Sozialwissenschaft*, 1904.

has to purchase the whole national output, and points out that there may be a decrease in aggregate consumption, without any rupture of aggregate equilibrium, if demand for investment replaces the demand for final consumption goods. What upsets the capitalist economy is not a deficiency of final consumption demand (or not that directly), but that a proportionate development of production is impossible under capitalism (ultimately because of, or partly because of, the unequal distribution of income).

It follows that Tugan-Baranovsky rejects Jevons's and Juglar's explanations and indeed all 'exogenous' explanations as inadequate: 'Wars, famines, the abuse or over-issue of credit cannot provoke an industrial crisis if the general economic situation does not assist them.' (French edition, 1913, p. 242.)

The basis of Tugan-Baranovsky's own theory is that the chaotic unorganized character of capitalistic production, combined with its constant drive to accumulate capital, resulting from the unequal distribution of income, creates a permanent tendency to the over-production of capital goods. This is aggravated by monetary factors. In a monetary economy 'partial over-production' can, and does, develop into 'general over-production'. Economic fluctuations consist primarily in fluctuations in the production of capital goods. The capitalist economy renews and expands its fixed equipment mainly in fits and starts (a point on which Tugan Baranovsky acknowledges his indebtedness to the German historical economist Nasse). Speculation in land also flares up during the boom. Though this occurs only to a small extent in England itself, English capital takes part in speculative excesses in other countries, for 'England is the heart of the capitalist world and consequently every event in the world economy has its repercussions in England'. (p. 255.)

Why does the extension of fixed capital not proceed regularly? 'Loanable' capital is accumulated at a fairly regular rate, out of profits during the boom and out of savings from fixed incomes during the slump. But (quoting Marx, vol. iii): 'An increase in loanable capital does not mean a real accumulation of capital or an extension of the productive process.' In the slump the steadily accumulated loanable capital mounts up. An upswing gets under way by the loanable capital 'forcing its way' into industrial investment at a low rate of interest. The unused savings accumulate like steam behind a piston. When at length they drive the piston forward they are exhausted in the process and the accumulation has to begin over again.

The upswing is cumulative. A 'now-or-never' spirit seizes the entrepreneurs who draw on the accumulated funds as fully as they dare. As the level of these funds falls the rate of interest rises, a sign of 'capital shortage', and the financial crisis breaks with the exhaustion of loanable capital. The industrial crisis follows subsequently with the falling off of investment resulting from an over-production of capital goods relative to the demand for them. Prosperity for society comes when it is creating its new fixed capital, but this does not happen in the right proportions. The rapid accumulation of capital which results in crises is possible 'because the greater part of the national income goes to the capitalist class, and the worker gets such a small part of the product of his labour'. (p. 279.)

Tugan-Baranovsky claimed that the 1907 crisis in America was a perfect example of over-investment in fixed capital combined with a shortage of loanable capital, and forecast a further such crisis for 1914, a forecast which looked like being fulfilled but for the war.

Tugan-Baranovsky contributed a much-developed restatement of the 'capital shortage' and disproportionate investment explanation of crises, as well as an attempt at a fully 'endogenous' theory, or explanatory outline, of the whole cycle. Above all, he put the process of investment in the centre of the picture. Of course there are ambiguities and hesitations in his central thesis not clearly resolved in this pioneer work. For example, in his notion of loanable capital accumulating through the depression, and also in his answer to the question why capital investment is so spasmodic.

In a final chapter on the General Character of Modern Unemployment, Tugan-Baranovsky expresses the conviction that crises in England are ceasing to be short and sharp as in the middle of the nineteenth century and are becoming far more prolonged: 'A comparison of the crises of today and those of 1850 to 1870 is not to the advantage of the new type.' (p. 462.) Various British authorities, such as Booth, Hobson, and Llewellyn Smith, are cited in support of this view (which was not shared by Marshall) that the unemployment problem was growing steadily more serious. Tugan-Baranovsky's conclusions are severely Marxian. Insurance schemes are ineffective palliatives. The problem of unemployment and of the industrial reserve army will only disappear with the supersession of the capitalist economic order.

(b) SPIETHOFF

The German edition of Tugan-Baranovsky's work was followed

shortly after in 1902 and 1903 by the first contributions of Arthur Spiethoff. Spiethoff had been an assistant of Schmoller, and had had much to do with the considerable, mainly historical, contribution to the subject of economic fluctuations in Schmoller's *Grundriss*. Werner Sombart of the same school, the historian of capitalism, was also contributing some noteworthy essays on the subject at this time, emphasizing that it was the cycle as a whole that must be explained, and that the crisis alone could not be understood except as part of this cyclical process. Sombart explained this process as an inherent tendency for disproportionate investment in industry as contrasted with agriculture, the over-investment being started off by an increased money supply due to gold discoveries.[1]

Spiethoff, like Tugan-Baranovsky, started from the analysis of Marx, the surveys of his German historical predecessors, the statistical discoveries of Juglar, and his own detailed study of the historical facts. He addressed himself first to the problem of 'general over-production' as contrasted with 'disproportionate production'. He dismisses, like Marx and Roscher, the argument known as 'Say's Law', as completely irrelevant for a monetary economy, and says of the theory of markets associated with James Mill and Say, that the whole analysis 'is much less a theory explaining crises than a theory seeking to prove their impossibility, in complete disregard of all the facts'. (Schmoller's *Jahrbuch*, 1903, p. 681.) Nevertheless, Spiethoff argues that although 'Say's Law' need not hold, the capitalist's search for profit will prevent him from keeping money lying idle. It is wrong, therefore, to look for the cause of over-production in some fundamental deficiency of aggregate demand inherent in the present social and economic order.

The upswing begins in some specially profitable branch of industry. There will be special reasons in each case, such as discoveries, and the opening of new overseas markets, resulting in a 'vacuum' of investment opportunities, some new and some left over from the previous depression, to be filled up to a certain point of saturation. (Ibid. 1902, p. 738.) In the first stage of the upswing existing plant is gradually brought into full use, then in the second phase new plant is built which absorbs capital without for some time resulting in a counter-balancing output of consumption goods. When the output of consumption goods does increase, prices ought to begin to fall, but are held up by a wrong pricing policy, often the result of cartels, which when it finally

[1] See his essay 'Versuch einer Systematik der Wirtschaftskrisen', *Archiv für Sozialwissenschaft*, 1904, p. 1.

collapses results in much more severe falls in prices and in depression. Spiethoff's description of the cycle is in terms rather of a cycle of investment outlets as contrasted with Tugan-Baranovsky's description in terms of a cycle of gradual accumulation and sudden exhaustion and shortage of savings.

In explaining the downward spiral of depression Spiethoff found a place for the unequal distribution of income:

> In the upswing . . . the distribution of national income does not influence total demand. In that a part of total income comes into the hands of people who do not wish to consume their share directly, but transform it in part into capital, nothing remains unused, since what is not directly consumed goes to 'reproductive consumption'. This does not hold in the depression, when the unequal distribution of income results in over-production. In that a part of the total income is saved, it is lost to consumption, for in the depression it is not immediately used reproductively, but massed in idle hoards. (1902, p. 743.)

Hence, while in order to maintain investment during the boom consumption might have to be restricted or cut, in the depression 'it is absolutely correct above all to maintain labour incomes and final consumption as far as possible'. (p. 747.)

Periods of over-production 'spring from the difficulty of foreseeing the activities of all the different branches of the national and world economy, and of forecasting future needs rightly; they are the natural accompaniment of a free private control of production and consumption guided mainly by prices and rates of profit'. (p. 749.) Maintaining the proportionality of production is thus impossible. Spiethoff follows Nasse in arguing that difficulty in foreseeing future needs correctly would remain under socialism, and if crises were to be avoided it could only be by the compulsory regimentation of consumption. (p. 755.) Like Wesley Mitchell later, he maintained that there are certain constant factors common to all economic crises. Nevertheless, whether the transition from upswing to downswing is a gentle one or an acute catastrophe, depends on 'variable' factors.

In his first article Spiethoff only outlined comparatively briefly the mechanism of 'capital shortage'. In a series of three articles in *Schmoller's Jahrbuch* for 1909 he examined this concept much more closely, emphasizing the complexities hidden behind such phrases as 'the capital market', and 'the rate of interest'. Spiethoff begins these articles by emphasizing that saving and investing in real terms are two, in the main, entirely separate activities, carried on by two separate sets of

individuals with no satisfactory co-ordinating mechanism. (p. 446.)
But the main theme of his analysis is that the shortage of capital in the
crisis was a 'real' shortage of particular capital goods which could not
be alleviated by monetary measures. It is 'real' shortages which lead
to a tightening of money and credit conditions. The tightening on the
money market gives the impression of an excess of goods which may
exist in certain lines, although it is acute shortages in *other* lines that
are at the root of the crisis. Similarly, the easier credit conditions at the
beginning of the upswing could lead nowhere unless there were unused stocks of goods available on which the whole possibility of an
expansion must be based:

What is the real state of affairs in respect of actual goods, which corresponds
to the 'shortage of capital' and 'over-production'? As we have shown, the
over-production is most marked in respect of instrumental goods and certain
durable consumption goods (houses, railways, etc.). These cannot be sold
because there is a shortage of free capital (*'Erwerbskapital'*), with which
alone they can be purchased. In respect of concrete goods this shortage of
capital corresponds to a shortage of the goods complementary with other
factors of production, with the labour necessary for working them, and with
the necessary consumption goods. The excess of goods of one kind, is simply
the obverse of a shortage of another kind. Capital shortage is a shortage of
goods . . . the trouble cannot be removed by any sort of credit or monetary
measures. (1909, p. 949.)

Spiethoff's analysis was so very much in 'real' terms that it seems to
have taken little account of banking policy which, within its limits,
may 'force' the saving of these labour supplies and consumption goods
by raising prices against consumers. He insisted on the *absolute*
shortage of certain complementary goods: 'The shortage is like that
of a missing glove, its partner by itself being valueless and superfluous. It is just the same with the goods that have been over-produced.
They are in excess because they are useless without the goods which
necessarily go with them. . . . Here again, one and the same situation
represents an excess from one point of view and a shortage from the
other.' (p. 1418.)

In a capitalist society the resulting losses and unemployment set off
a downward spiral. But

on the assumption of a socialist economy, when over-production occurs it
need not lead to a general depression (*Stockung*). Even when the authorities
do not succeed in maintaining a balance between all the goods produced,
this is no great misfortune. There will simply be a building up of stocks,

which will not be completely valueless, and at least in the future may again be usable. But even if this is not the case, and the over-produced goods represented a complete loss, this would be the sole consequences of the over-production. The rest of the economy would proceed undisturbed. (p. 1419.)

In an article in 1925 Spiethoff re-stated his theory much more systematically, setting out a model cycle filled out with a wealth of statistical and historical material. The role of invention and of monetary hoarding were given more importance but the central analysis was not essentially altered (see *Handwörterbuch der Staatswissenschaften*, 4th ed.).

Spiethoff's writings represent a methodologically admirable fusion of historical statistical and analytical investigation, each being used to their best mutual advantage, as they should in any empirical science. His insistence on the shortage of capital being so essentially a shortage of actual goods is, of course, open to criticism, and the emphasis of subsequent exponents of the theory, such as Cassel, was rather different. But the 'capital shortage' analysis was widely regarded as having been borne out by the crisis of 1907, as was argued in the paper of Marcel Labordère 'Autour de la Crise Américaine de 1907' who illustrated it with the parable of the one-man economic crisis, as had Bonamy Price thirty years before. This analysis seems even at one stage to have been held by Keynes in his paper to the London Political Economy Club (3 Dec. 1912) entitled 'How Far are Bankers Responsible for the Alternations of Boom and Depression?'.[1]

(c) VEBLEN

The next three authors we discuss, Veblen, Davenport, and Bouniatian were on the side of underconsumption rather than of undersaving, as the main explanation of crises, and laid their emphasis rather on excessive 'capitalisation' or on excessive investment, though emphasizing also psychological fluctuations and errors, as well as deficient consumption. Veblen and Bouniatian represent a type of explanation of which Sismondi had been the pioneer early in the nineteenth century.

Veblen's contribution to the trade cycle is in a lengthy chapter (curiously entitled 'The Theory of Modern Welfare') in his book *The Theory of Business Enterprise* (1904). It would in any case be a noteworthy contribution as being the only place in English or American

[1] *v.* Robertson, *A Study of Industrial Fluctuations*, p. 171 n., and appendix to new ed.

writings at that early date where one can find a mention of Tugan-Baranovsky's book, of Spiethoff's early articles, of Carver's pioneer note on the acceleration principle, and of J. A. Hobson's underconsumption theory.

Veblen held that fluctuations of prosperity and depression had, in the last decades of the nineteenth century, tended to turn into a chronic depression only fleetingly relieved by weaker and shorter-lived revivals. The root cause lay essentially in the modern 'business' organization of economic life, which is subject to severe fluctuations, 'because industry is managed on a business footing, in terms of price and for the sake of profits'. Fluctuations are in fact 'normal' to this organization, and are simply phases of a single normal process: 'The true or what may be called the normal, crises, depressions, and exaltations in the human world are not the result of accidents, such as the failure of a crop. They come in the regular course of business. The depression and exaltation are in a measure bound together.' (p. 183.)

As the economy emerges from a depression, a price rise in one industry may rapidly and cumulatively extend to a general upswing: 'In part by actual increase of demand and in part through a lively anticipation of an advanced demand, aggressive business enterprise extends its ventures and pushes up prices in remote lines of industry. This transmission of the favourable disturbance of business (substantially a psychological phenomenon) follows very promptly under modern conditions.' (p. 195.)

The cumulative upswing leads to the phenomenon much emphasized by Veblen of 'excessive capitalisation':

The expectation in either case leads the businessmen to bid high for equipment and supplies. Thereby the effective (market) capitalisation is increased to answer to the increased prospective earnings.... There results a discrepancy between the effective capitalisation during prosperity and the capitalisation as it stood before the prosperity set in, and the heightened capitalisation becomes the basis of an extensive ramification of credit. (p. 198.)

Veblen had emphasized earlier the instability of credit and the cumulative nature of a credit expansion in his chapter on The Use of Loan Credit:

Whenever the capable business manager sees an appreciable difference between the cost of a given credit extension and the gross increase of gains to be got by its use, he will seek to extend his credit. But under the régime of competitive business whatever is generally advantageous becomes a necessity for all competitors. . . . The extension of loans on collateral, such as stock and similar values involved in industrial business, has therefore in the nature of things a cumulative character. (pp. 96 and 106.)

A rise in costs and particularly a rise in wages, prejudicing prospective profits, is a major element in bringing the boom to an end. The decline in the profit-earning capacity of business reveals the unsoundness of the over-extended structure of credit. One liquidation leads to others and the downswing gathers momentum from a cutthroat competitive lowering of prices in the general struggle for survival. Competitive price-cutting, according to Veblen, tends to perpetuate depression and over-capitalization, and modern business increasingly resorts to monopoly in one form or another to protect its profits.

Although in his early days Veblen had appeared in the role of defender of John Stuart Mill against Crocker's under-consumptionist criticisms,[1] in his *Theory of Business Enterprise* he expresses a general, if rather imprecise, approval of the under-consumption explanation of depressions and of the doctrines of Malthus, Lauderdale, Chalmers, and Hobson, but he hardly adds anything to this subject himself.

(d) H. J. DAVENPORT

A brief mention may be made at this point of H. J. Davenport as an economist who was mainly concerned with the critical analysis and elaboration of the neo-classical theories of value and distribution, but who felt stirred to profound misgivings about the orthodox criticisms of under-consumption theories and who returned, rather diffidently, to these misgivings in most of his books. He never followed up his ideas very far, and his contribution hardly gets beyond the expression of uneasy questionings in his lengthy footnotes. But some of his points are worth recalling.

In his first main work Davenport had held that 'the problem of the unemployed is the most important practically and perhaps the most difficult theoretically of all the problems of economic science. Theory and fact here seem somehow out of harmony.' He recommended public works in time of depression. (*Outlines of Economic Theory*, 1896, p. 355.)

[1] *v.* His article 'The Overproduction Fallacy', *Quarterly Journal of Economics*, July 1892, p. 484.

Later, in *Value and Distribution* (1908) Davenport went back to the classical debate of Malthus and James Mill over 'the possibility of general over-production', which it had long been orthodox in England to regard as finally settled against Malthus. As Davenport put it: 'It is doubtless anathema to talk in economics of over-production.' (p. 227.) He then returns to his 'specific question—the social bearing of an unusually marked disposition on the part of producers and sellers to refuse to exchange present goods against present goods and to demand in exchange deferred rights of purchase—money cash, credits, or well-secured promises; it is clear enough that a generally lower price level must result'. (p. 231.)

In a further note, Davenport discussed the problem of 'the fallacy of saving' and held that 'Ruskin, Robertson [J. M.], Hobson, and Veblen seem to have done the best work here, not perhaps toward the solution of the problem, but to the development and definition of it'. (p. 529.) Reproducing this note in his *Economics of Enterprise* (1913) Davenport then went on to dispose of Say's Law, asking 'What if, for a while, the money intermediate is receiving a marked and extra-ordinary emphasis—is sought for substantively, rather than as inter-mediate—is held as provision against pressure of creditors or for the purpose of later speculative purchases?'

Davenport then discusses the possibility that 'savings will not capitalize into forms of intermediate social welfare' as a result of a 'restriction of the disposition to consume'. This brings him to the more radical under-consumptionist question: 'Is all saving well, even upon the assumption that all of it is saving which adds to the aggregate social equipment?' (p. 306.) In this case, again,

the expansion of product is, then, justified by and limited by the expansion of the disposition to consumption ... and it appears to be true that the very fact that, through developing technique and increasing equipment, a high per capita productivity obtains, with a large margin of average individual income over imperative individual need, explains how it may occur and does often occur that the volume of consumption varies, and that, through sharp restriction of consumption, industry is subjected to the periodic reverses. (*Economics of Enterprise*, p. 308.)

After considering the economic effects of charity, Davenport comes to the conclusion that 'this argument, if valid—which is doubtful enough—means much for the methods and times of the carrying for-ward of public work ... it should be fairly obvious that public improve-ments ought to be undertaken in times only of slack employment, and ought to be paid for in times of prosperity, rather than, as in present practice, carried on in prosperous times'. (p. 309.)

(e) M. BOUNIATIAN

Mentor Bouniatian's *Economic Crises and Over-Capitalisation* (*Wirtschaftskrisen und Überkapitalisation*, 1908) has much in common with Veblen's chapter. He starts by paying a tribute especially to Lauderdale, the critic of Adam Smith's theory of saving and investing, and to 'the brilliant book of Mummery and Hobson *The Physiology of Industry*'.[1]

In his first chapter Bouniatian introduces the subsequently common distinction between 'exogenous' and 'endogenous' factors in cyclical fluctuations, the former arising outside the economic system and the latter within it. (p. 3.) He specially emphasizes all those elements from which equilibrium analysis largely abstracts, but which are inherent in a rapidly changing competitive economy with extensive division of labour: the long temporal and geographical distances between ultimate consumers and ultimate producers, the resulting ignorance and uncertainty, speculation, fickle expectations, and mass psychology, all of which can lead to cumulative fluctuations, especially when reinforced by the modern credit organization.

A good harvest or an increase in foreign demand may start the upswing. Any initial rise in the price of some important good or group of goods will spread as a result of the rush to invest, and this price rise will concentrate purchasing power in the hands of the entrepreneur class, which will promote further investment. When the new capital goods begin to turn out a much increased supply of consumption goods, the maldistribution of income prevents consumption rising sufficiently to take this increased supply off the market. (p. 120.) Maldistribution of income and over-capitalization mutually generate one another. The 'shortage' at the crisis is therefore not one of capital goods but of general purchasing power. After the crisis some of the excess capital is left idle and will be 'consumed' or destroyed.[2]

---

[1] Bouniatian's later and larger work was *Les Crises économiques*, Paris, 1922.

[2] A partly similar explanation in terms of chronic over-capitalization, omitting the element of the maldistribution of income, was given by W. H. Beveridge (*Unemployment*, 1909, pp. 39 and 61): 'There is at times in the community a demand for more boots or ships or houses. The demand is felt and met not by one producer but by many, and not by many each providing a definite share in agreement with the rest, but by many each acting independently and dominated by the desire to do as much business as possible, i.e., to engross as large a share as possible of the market. Inevitably, therefore, all the producers

(*f*) AFTALION

Albert Aftalion, then Professor at Lille, first explained his central thesis about the trade cycle in a series of articles in the *Revue d'Écono-mie Politique* in 1908–9, under the title of 'La Réalité des Surproductions Générales'. His massive two-volume work published in 1913, added a great deal of statistical material without altering the fundamentals of his explanation. Based as it is on the Austrian principles of value and imputation, and on Böhm-Bawerk's analysis of capitalistic production, Aftalion's theory of the trade cycle might well be described as an 'Austrian' theory, though it is completely different from the theory which later received that title. Aftalion starts from the marginal utility theory of value and imputation and tries to put this analysis to practical use by tracing the fluctuations in the economic process directly to the final consumer. The two pillars of his analysis are: (1) the temporary saturation of final consumers' demand, in that a rapidly increasing output of consumption goods will lead to a fall in their marginal utility so that they will not be taken up at existing prices: and (2) the length of the modern roundabout 'capitalistic' methods of production, which aggravates the fluctuations in consumer demand by making for still greater 'accelerated' fluctuations in investment demand: 'The long duration of the process of production explains the duration of the boom and the excessive production of capital goods, and the over-capitalisation. The immense output of consumption goods produced with the aid of the newly completed capital goods explains the crisis, the duration of the subsequent depression, and the under-capitalisation which leads to a new upswing.' (*Revue d'Économie Politique* 1908, p. 704.)

In a pre-capitalistic economy, where production is almost instantaneous, the small entrepreneur is not severely affected by the fall in prices. His money costs of production fall at the same time as the selling-price of his products. But 'owing to the long duration of the capitalistic

together tend to overshoot the demand and to glut the market for a time. This is the result not of wild speculation nor of mis-calculation of the total demand; it must be a normal incident wherever competition has a place at all. . . . There can be no doubt again that in a competitive system of industry this excess in the means of production is commonly realised. In other words, such a system normally works with a reserve of capital as well as with a reserve of labour; the machinery in a trade is never or seldom all fully employed at the same time; a fraction of it would probably suffice to satisfy the whole existing demand. This is forcibly illustrated whenever complete combination among employers replaces competition. The normal accompaniment to the formation of a trust is the closing down of many of the factories acquired.'

process of production the entrepreneur has paid out long before in money the various elements in his costs at the *earlier* rates (for his raw materials, labour, etc.), when the fall in his selling price occurs'. (1909, p. 116.)

However lengthy and indirect the process of production may be, it is final consumers' demand and the prices of final consumers' goods which guide the whole system of production, for in accordance with the Austrian principle of imputation the values of consumers' goods are 'reflected back' to the investment goods with which they are produced: 'Since capital goods are only produced with a view to final consumption, and the final product, the demand for such goods, and their value, depend on the value of these final consumption goods. The high values of final consumption goods keep up the values of capital goods and the whole structure of high prices.' (1909, p. 105.)

But changes in the prices of consumption goods are not simply reflected back to the capital goods which produce them, but are aggravated or intensified because of the length of the capitalistic productive process: 'Until the work of investment is completed the final demand continues to be incompletely met. The high level of receipts and the profits from the existing capital stimulate over-production. . . . Quite a small excess or deficiency of consumption goods, with only moderate fluctuations in their value, can lead to a more than proportionate alteration in the demand for and value of instruments of production.' (1909, pp. 220–5.)

Aftalion illustrates his principle with his analogy from the heating of a room:

If because of the low temperature we revive and feed the fire, some time will elapse before the desired warmth is obtained. Because the cold persists and the thermometer continues to register it, we are led, unless guided by past experience, to heap more fuel upon the fire. A more than appropriate quantity of fuel is used which, when it is all alight, will produce a quite unbearable heat. In being guided by our present feelings of cold and the present readings of the thermometer, we grossly overheat the room, because of the time which necessarily elapses before all the fuel is ablaze and heating the room. . . . It is exactly the same with the economic system. (1909, p. 209.)

Aftalion's is therefore essentially a psychological or 'error' theory, though one of a specially reasoned kind. Though his use of the principle of diminishing marginal utility is of very doubtful soundness, his theory of the temporary 'gluttability' of consumers' wants (as Robertson later described it) can easily be supported by other reasoning.

Aftalion's main contribution is in his development of the acceleration principle by means of a kind of macro-economic cobweb theorem. The accelerator principle can be traced in a loose imprecise form in various nineteenth-century writings explaining how fluctuations in the demand for one group of products are 'propagated' to, or 'aggravated' in, the demand for the products of other industries (for example, in Nasse's and Walker's explanations discussed in the previous chapter). Previous to Aftalion an analysis coming very near to that of the acceleration principle had also been formulated by Carver in his brief 'Suggestion for a Theory of Industrial Depressions', in the *Quarterly Journal of Economics*, 1903 (pp. 497–500). It was Aftalion, however, who raised the acceleration principle into a main explanation both of fluctuations and their cyclical periodicity.[1]

(g) SCHUMPETER

We have already discussed Schumpeter's *Theory of Economic Development* in which his analysis of the trade cycle has a part. Here we shall only mention very briefly the main upshot of his analysis in respect of cyclical fluctuations. One of his principal general contributions to the theory of the trade cycle was to put it in this much wider setting of capitalist economic development. Schumpeter's analysis of why innovations come in 'clusters' and result in investment booms, was his most widely appreciated special contribution to the analysis of the trade cycle. His account of the upswing was easily reconcilable with that of Spiethoff, but his analysis of the upper turning point resembled rather that of Aftalion: the boom ends and depression begins when the products of the new investments begin to come on to the market. This, like the original innovating investment, happens in a roughly simultaneous cluster bringing about a fall in prices and the starting of the depression. (See also Ch. 12, sect. 2 above.)

3. *The Monetary Analysis of the Trade Cycle*

By this time (*c.* 1910) most of the central processes and relationships involving the action and inter-action of consumption, investment, and economic activity as a whole, had been clearly described though not with mathematical precision: the cycle of investment activity and of

---

[1] Later expositions of the acceleration principle were given by C. F. Bickerdike, 'A Non-Monetary Cause of Fluctuations in Employment', *Economic Journal*, Sept. 1914; and J. M. Clark, 'Business Acceleration and the Law of Demand', *Journal of Political Economy*, Mar. 1917. The latter introduced the term '*acceleration* principle'.

investment opportunity (Spiethoff); the shortage of savings and the shortage of 'real' capital goods (Tugan-Baranovsky and Spiethoff); the 'gluttability of wants' (Aftalion and the under-consumptionists); the maldistribution of income (Hobson and Bouniatian, &c.); the acceleration principle (Aftalion); the cumulative, unstable, 'multiplying' nature of upward and downward movements (Bagehot, Wicksell, Veblen, Spiethoff, and many others); the appearance of innovations in clusters or swarms (Nasse, Spiethoff, and Schumpeter); the psychological explanation (Mills, Bagehot, Marshall); and the agricultural explanation (Jevons), had all been clearly stated.

What the intellectual conjuncture now required was: (a) a much more thorough analysis of the monetary and credit processes involved in the trade cycle, in particular of saving, loanable funds, and investment in a modern credit economy; (b) much fuller historical and statistical material to test and assess the quantitative importance of the different explanations; and (c) a reconciling synthesis of these various often superficially conflicting elements—a task which would call for more intellectual tact and tolerance and hardly less originality than the previous work on the subject.

Of course it would also have been of great methodological interest and importance to have attempted to define the relevance for one another of this comparatively new body of generalizations about the fluctuations in the economy as a whole, and the closely knit scheme of formulae comprised in the theory of 'normal' equilibrium value, price, and distribution, and to have examined the postulates of the latter in the light of the former. But except for the isolated suggestions of Wicksell more than a decade previously there was little sign of any fundamental stirrings on this subject.

(a) JOHANNSEN

In this section we are concerned with (a) above, that is the monetary analysis of the trade cycle. First in our group of monetary writings we may take the book of a man who by some might be regarded as a 'crank', but who was certainly intensely and obstinately original, and whose work had little or no influence on any orthodox economist, except perhaps Adolf Wagner (who wrote an introduction to his book on the *Circulation of Money* (1903)), and much later, Keynes. N. Johannsen (1844–1928) was a German-American employed in business in New York, who published his books in two different languages, and also under two pen-names besides his own, because he feared, apparently, that his employers might disapprove of his devoting so much time and energy to monetary and trade cycle analysis. His first pamphlet on *Cheap Capital* had appeared in 1878, but his best-known work is *A Neglected Point in Connection with Crises*, which appeared in 1908, though all the main ideas it discusses, including the theory of 'Impair' Saving and the Multiplying Principle, had been set out in his earlier books on the Circulation of Money and on Depressions, both published in 1903 (*Der Kreislauf des Geldes*, and *Depressions-perioden und ihre einheitliche Ursache*). Johannsen may conveniently be fitted in at this point, though he stands apart from the main development of ideas. No economic work in our period is more brilliantly original than his.

Johannsen accepted much in current explanations of the crisis and concentrated on the problem of what happens in the subsequent depression and why this was often so prolonged. He looked for a solution in the answer to the question 'How are savings invested at times of depression?' He rejected the notion that savings, having been exhausted in the boom, pile up in the form of 'liquid capital' in the depression. He pointed out that in times of depression, with reduced incomes, there will be a reduced quantity of savings, but he did not regard this as giving a complete answer to his question. He was also prepared to recognize the role of 'hoarding'. But Johannsen considered that the real answer to his question was to be found in a harmful diversion of savings away from the investment necessary to offset them:

What is simply described as the process of saving consists in reality of two distinctly separate factors, on the one hand what is really the process of saving or withdrawing money, and on the other hand the process of investment by which new capital is constructed. . . . Many of our economists believe that as saving and investing go hand in hand, and even form to some extent a single process, and as the result of the combined activities is highly beneficial to the community, therefore the process of saving by itself must be regarded as in the public interest. . . . This assumption does not correspond with the facts. (*Der Kreislauf des Geldes*, 1903, p. 178.)

In its primary stage the saving process is always accompanied by an injurious tendency, inasmuch as the saver is constantly trying to buy less from the community in the line of goods or services than he sells to it and thus is disturbing the equilibrium of supply and demand. This equilibrium is restored only by the investment, it is understood that by means of the investment the demand for goods or services—i.e., for working forces—will reappear in the market. (*A Neglected Point*, p. 78.)

These savings become in fact 'impair savings'. The 'impair' form of saving—(as contrasted with the 'hoarding' form, and the 'capitalistic' form)—occurs

> where savings are invested not in the creation of new wealth but in the acquisition of property already existing; this, in connection with the impoverishment of the previous owners, and *the impoverishment being brought about by the very saving activity on the part of the savers.* This form of saving differs from the Hoarding Form inasmuch as the savings funds are not left idle for any length of time, but are seeking *and finding* investment. It differs from the Capitalistic Form inasmuch as it does not lead to the formation of new capital. It enriches the savers at the expense of the non-savers, making the latter lose as much property as the savers gain, but in addition making the community lose income to a much larger amount. (p. 87.)

Johannsen agrees that insofar as the distressed sellers keep up their standing of living from the proceeds of their forced sales there will be no curtailment of total demand for consumption and investment, though there may be lags in which a downward spiral may be started. Mr. Harrod has described as one of the main doctrines of Keynes's *Treatise on Money* (1930) the following: 'Thus if the savers buy securities this does not ensure that real capital outlay will be undertaken since the action will be counteracted by the sale of securities of an equivalent amount by businesses which are making losses.' (*Life of J. M. Keynes*, p. 408.) This is very close indeed to Johannsen's doctrine of impair saving.

Perhaps of even greater interest than his concept of impair saving is Johannsen's analysis of what he calls the 'Multiplying Principle' (which he works out mainly for downward movements) and of the reciprocal action of decreases in investment and consumption.[1] As soon as one class suffers a loss in income 'the multiplying principle' comes into play aggravating the initial effect. The class affected reduce their expenses, and the class they buy from in turn suffer a loss of earnings:

> To illustrate this matter by an example, let us single out ten working men forming part of Class C, and assume that when employed, their aggregate earnings amount to 5,000 dollars per annum. They spend that money in the purchase of commodities. When these commodities are produced anew, that money will become income for those who are engaged in reproducing them. Let us designate these producers (including the distributors), *so far as they*

---

[1] In his note on the Principle (*Depressions-perioden*, 1903, p. 87), Johannsen recognizes that it may work in an upward direction, but he is above all concerned with depressions.

are directly affected by the purchases of those ten men, as 'Class D'. When the members of Class D, in turn expend their earnings, that same money becomes income for Class E, and so on for Classes F, G, &c. the succession of income and expenditure forming practically an endless chain. Now cut off the income of those ten men in Class C, and the whole chain will be affected. The expenditures of Class C may be reduced from 5,000 dollars to 1,000 dollars thus diminishing the income of Class D by 4,000 dollars; which means a total loss of income of 9,000 dollars to the two classes combined. (p. 44.)

[A footnote here points out: 'the members of Class C surely do not reduce their expenditures to *nothing* for they do not exactly *starve* with their families and are not left without food and clothing and shelter, but will manage, by hook or crook, to obtain the most urgent necessaries of life.'] . . . 'The income of class E may decline to the extent of 2,000 or 3,000 dollars, which brings the total loss up to 11,000 or 12,000 dollars. This total will keep on swelling as the harmful effect spreads further. True, for each successive link of the chain the loss becomes smaller, being divided up, at the same time, among a greater number of individuals. Still, the losses are there and, whether light or heavy, they are felt by all the classes affected, and in their aggregate represent a much larger amount than the original loss of 5,000 dollars which befell Class C. Here we have an illustration of the modus operandi of the "Multiplying Principle".' (pp. 44–45.)

As might be expected, Johannsen was an exponent of the stagnation thesis. The 'boundless opportunities' for the expansion of productive capital do not exist (p. 65). But with a more even distribution of wealth, or in a new, growing country like the United States (1908), 'the propensity for saving' (p. 63) may usually be adequately offset by investment: 'The concentration of wealth in a few hands is not desirable, especially in old countries. It will unduly promote the saving process.' (*A Neglected Point*, p. 181.)

Johannsen made little or no reference to or criticism of other writers, but he was aware of the general place of his doctrines in the history of ideas:

> The mercantilist theory dominant in previous centuries was based on the principle that the more money created in a country the greater the prosperity of the people—a view which often led to extreme consequences and which was devastatingly criticized by Adam Smith. But since then the other extreme has been reached, and the attempt has been made to play down as much as possible the immense importance of this monetary factor in modern development. (*Der Kreislauf des Geldes*, 1903, p. 232.)

Johannsen never seems to have received—except earlier from Adolf Wagner—the constructive criticism that might have helped him to perfect and develop his ideas even further. J. B. Clark gave his book a thoughtful review. J. A. Hobson noted his analysis of 'impair' saving but did not follow up its possibilities for his own analysis. Wesley Mitchell also seems to have attributed some importance to Johannsen's analysis. Keynes's sole reference to Johannsen is in a footnote in his *Treatise on Money* (vol. ii, p. 100) where he held Johannsen's theory of impair savings 'to come very near to the truth'. Keynes then goes on:

But Mr. Johannsen regarded the failure of current savings to be embodied in capital expenditure as a more or less permanent condition in the modern world due to a saturation of the capital market, instead of as a result of a temporary but recurrent failure of the banking system to pass on the full amount of the savings to entrepreneurs, and overlooks the fact that a fall in the rate of interest would be the cure for the malady if it were what he diagnoses it to be.

Johannsen had already given his answer to this objection in 1903 (*Depressions-perioden*, p. 29): 'This argument is one of those which are not based on practical experience but which are derived solely from theories, without regard to whether these theories agree with actual conditions. In fact the activity of saving is very little affected by the level of the rate of interest.' As by 1936 Keynes might have been ready to agree more with Johannsen's answer of 1903 than with his own criticism of 1930, he should, perhaps, have made some amends by including Johannsen in the very curiously selected gallery of pioneers commemorated in Chapter 23 of his *General Theory*. We have already referred to Johannsen as a pioneer of the 'income' approach to the theory of money. (See Ch. 21, sect. 2 above.)[1]

(b) FISHER AND MISES

A few years later (1911–12) two more orthodox and widely recognized works somewhat briefly applied their analysis of money and credit to the explanation of the trade cycle. Irving Fisher's *Purchasing*

---

[1] Johannsen must stand in this book as easily the outstanding representative of a whole army of more or less inspired economic and monetary heretics and cranks, in which Gesell, Eisler, Soddy, Douglas, and many others were prominent at various times. Like Gesell, Johannsen had a plan for stamped money (see *Die Steuer der Zukunft*, 1913). An interesting comparison of Johannsen's and Keynes's ideas is made by Dr. H. W. Schnack in his dissertation *Der Wirtschaftskreislauf bei Johannsen und Keynes*, Kiel, 1951.

Power of Money and Mises's *Theory of Money and Credit* were both published in 1912.[1] Both writers made some reference to Wicksell's ideas.

As we saw above (Ch. 17, sect. 3), according to Fisher any initial price rise (set off for example by an increase in the amount of gold) will be cumulative, because the rate of interest (i.e. the market rate) will not be sufficiently raised to allow for the future fall in the value of money. Therefore, entrepreneurs will be encouraged to indulge in a cumulative investment boom. Eventually, the banks in self-protection will be forced to raise the rate of interest in face of the excessive demand, and after a financial and psychological crisis a corresponding downward cumulative movement will set in. Fisher concluded that of the causes of crises 'the monetary causes are the most important *when taken in connexion with the maladjustments in the rate of interest*'. The other factors often emphasized are mainly effects of this maladjustment: 'Over-consumption and over-investment are cases in point.' (*Purchasing Power of Money*, p. 66.)

In Mises's work of 1912 there is a notable, if very brief, application of Wicksell's theory of interest rates to the analysis of economic crises (see *Theory of Money and Credit*, pp. 357–66). We shall discuss this theory when dealing with some of the works of the monetary over-investment school of thought which became prominent some fifteen years later. As we shall see, Mises's theory was not a purely monetary explanation in the same sense as that of Irving Fisher. Schumpeter also was employing Wicksell's theory of interest to the monetary analysis of the trade cycle in his article on 'Das Sozialprodukt und die Rechenpfennige', 1917 (see above, Ch. 21, sect. 2), and Marco Fanno was another who was following Wicksell's line of thought at this time (in *Le banche e il mercato monetario*, 1913, see his 'Die reine Theorie des Geldmarktes', in *Beiträge zur Geldtheorie*, edited by Hayek, 1933).

(c) R. G. HAWTREY

A year or two later came the first of R. G. Hawtrey's statements of the extreme monetary explanation of the cycle (*Good and Bad Trade*, 1913). Hawtrey claimed that 'at one time economists were so anxious to guard themselves from the fallacy of identifying money and wealth that they slipped into an almost pedantic disregard of the influence of

---

[1] There is, of course, much of value and relevance for the analysis of business cycles in Fisher's earlier works on interest (see above, Ch. 17), but he must surely be classified with the monetary theorists of the cycle.

money in economic phenomena'. Hawtrey started with a statement of the 'income' approach to the theory of money, prices, and incomes in terms of aggregate demand and supply, on the lines suggested by Tooke's thirteenth proposition about the quantity theory—a starting-point which was to become common in later decades: 'The total effective demand for all commodities per unit of time is the aggregate of all money incomes. The total cost of production of all commodities per unit of time is the aggregate of all money incomes.' (p. 7.)

Hawtrey then goes on to show, in a way similar to Fisher, how the instability of credit and the failure of the banking authorities to adjust the 'real' rate of interest when the value of money is changing, leads to cumulative movements, first in a community without a banking system, and then taking into account credit, banking policies, and foreign trade. His analysis, as there presented, may be described as a blend of Fisher's and Wicksell's. (pp. 66–76.) Hawtrey concludes that 'whereas the influences arising out of the banking system are very important, those which arise from the conditions of production and consumption have but little bearing (except perhaps in the case of actual famine) upon the state of trade as a whole'. (p. 130.)

It is, above all, the class most sensitive to fluctuations in demand and supply that is also most sensitive to changes in the rate of interest. This is the class of dealers, both wholesale and retail, who, according to Hawtrey, occupy a key position in the economic system. Hawtrey agrees that a stagnation of trade may occur 'if the rate of depreciation of prices is actually greater than the natural rate of interest', and it is the *expected* rate of depreciation of prices that is relevant. But he held (1913) that such stagnation of trade is exceptional and that there will still be a way out—'a drastic reduction of money wages. If at any time this step is taken the spell will be broken.' (pp. 186–7.)

With the mechanism of credit so inherently and extremely unstable, any policy of stabilization sets very delicate and difficult tasks. But Hawtrey held that stabilizing the purchasing power of the monetary unit on the lines suggested by Fisher 'would somewhat reduce, per-haps would greatly reduce, the extent of the fluctuations'. He bluntly dismissed the counter-cyclical public works policy proposed in the *Minority Report of the Poor Law Commission* (1909): 'The writers of the *Minority Report* appear to have overlooked the fact that the govern-ment by the very fact of borrowing for this expenditure is withdrawing from the investment market savings which would otherwise be applied to the creation of capital.' (p. 260.)

4. *Constructive Synthesis: Statistical and Analytical*

As leading contributions, differing in emphasis, to the then (1912–15) much-needed work of constructive synthesis, we take the writings of Mitchell, Pigou, and Robertson. Along with Hawtrey's *Good and Bad Trade* their works may be described as the first major recognized, comprehensive, and specialist contributions to the analysis of the trade cycle *in English* since Jevons's and Bagehot's writings of thirty or forty years previously—(J. A. Hobson's works perhaps excepted). Mitchell sought to over-ride or reconcile the many theoretical conflicts by a massive 'descriptive analysis' of what happens in business cycles. Pigou and Robertson sought to do so by both statistical and theoretical analysis.

(*a*) WESLEY MITCHELL

Wesley Mitchell's volume on *Business Cycles* (1913) may be described as the first large and comprehensive monograph on its subject in the English language. As a student at Chicago (1892–99) Mitchell had come under the influence of Veblen, and his interest from his earliest work on the history of the Greenbacks (1903), had been in the realistic study of the processes of the actual fluctuating monetary economy, rather than in the theoretical study of 'normal' equilibrium values. To Mitchell, as to Veblen, what were 'normal' were processes of fluctuation and disturbance rather than a system of effective self-equilibration:

One who turns from reading economic theory to reading business history is forcibly impressed by the artificiality of all assumptions of a 'static' or even a 'normal' condition in economic affairs. For, despite all efforts to give technical meanings to these ambiguous terms, they suggest the idea of an unchanging order, or of an order which economic principles are always tending to re-establish after every aberration. But a review of business annals never discloses the existence of a 'static' or a 'normal' state in either of these senses. On the contrary, in the real world of businessmen, affairs are always undergoing a cumulative change, always passing through some phase of a business cycle into some other phase. . . . In fact, if not in theory, a state of change in business conditions is the only 'normal' state. (p. 86.)

Business cycles are phenomena of a monetary economy of which the quest for private profit is the main driving force: 'The whole discussion must center about the prospect of profits' (p. 450), and, the prospects or expectations of profits, and the resulting business decisions, are not the result of precise calculation, or of an automatic profit calculus, but of guesswork deeply influenced by the hopes and fears of the moment:

Practically all business problems involve elements which are not precisely known, but must be approximately estimated even for the present, and fore-cast still more roughly for the future. Probabilities take the place of certainties, both among the data upon which the reasoning proceeds and among the conclusions at which it arrives. This fact gives hopeful or despondent moods a large share in shaping business decisions. (p. 455.)

One is reminded here of Cliffe Leslie's essay on 'The Known and the Unknown in the Economic World'.

It is through the monetary and credit processes that 'the alternating waves of over-confidence and unreasoning timidity' work themselves out. Here Mitchell closely follows Veblen. But in his statistical and historical technique, and in his emphasis on the cycle as a whole rather than simply on the crisis as the object of study, and in his explanation of how recurrent phases of the cycle normally 'grow out of and into each other', Mitchell's intellectual forerunner was Juglar, though Mitchell does not make much reference to his work.

It must be recognized, Mitchell holds, that 'every business cycle, strictly speaking, is a unique series of events and has a unique explana-tion'. This inevitably sets limits to the possible significance of general theoretical explanations. Nevertheless, there are certain regular sequences which occur in every period of revival, prosperity, crisis, and depression, and Mitchell sees his task as the discovery and *descrip-tive analysis* of these regular sequences. Mitchell would have agreed that 'All cases are unique, and very similar to others', and that this indicates both the possibilities of, and the limits to, the systematic study of human problems.

In his opening chapter Mitchell gives a very rapid but conscientious summary of the many conflicting theories current in 1913. He makes it plain that though all these theories may have something to contribute, there is, in the existing knowledge of the facts, not very much to choose between them. He emphasizes 'how easy it is to make many dissimilar explanations of crises sound convincing when attention is confined to a restricted range of phenomena. Only by putting any theory to the practical test of accounting for actual business experience can its value be determined.' (p. 570.) Mitchell clearly did not see his task as that of adding another explanation to the existing long list, but rather as that of trying to discover much more fully and accurately 'what happens during business cycles'. His aim is the descriptive analysis of 'how depression breeds prosperity and how prosperity breeds depression' in alternating self-generating cumulative movements.

How do these alternating processes mutually generate one another? A revival of business after depression may often be stimulated by some specially propitious event—technical developments in a particular industry, extra demand for export or war purposes. But such extraneous 'accidents' generally do no more than hasten a revival already under way: 'The quiet processes of business recuperation during dull times are quite competent to develop into revival without the adventitious help of any "disturbing circumstance".' (p. 453.)

After a time, depression brings reductions in prime and supplementary costs in manufacturing, reductions in stocks held by merchants, the liquidation of debts, low rates of interest, and a banking position favouring an increase of loans. The more inefficient enterprises have been squeezed out, timidity is wearing off, improved techniques are awaiting adoption, and there is a growth in consumers' and producers' demand put off during the crisis but now no longer so easily delayed. After a depression has run its course for some time all these factors in the situation are sufficient to generate revival.

Just as depression gradually brings itself to an end by the lowering of costs and by the more favourable psychological and credit conditions it engenders, so correspondingly prosperity breeds depression by the eventual rise in costs and the stringent monetary and credit conditions which in due course must supervene:

Prosperity breeds an increase in the cost of doing business—an increase which threatens to diminish profits. The decline in supplementary costs per unit ceases; equipment of less than standard efficiency is brought back into use; the price of labour rises while the efficiency of labour falls; the cost of materials, supplies, and wares for resale advances faster than selling prices; discount rates go up at an especially rapid pace, and all the little wastes incidental to the conduct of business enterprises grow steadily larger. (p. 494.)

Why cannot prices continue to rise to protect profit margins from the rise in costs? In some industries this will be prevented by convention, or even government regulation. Elsewhere, the over-optimism of the boom will have led to over-production in some lines: 'The twist given by over-confidence to forecasts of future demand, always difficult to make with accuracy, thus leads in every period of prosperity to an overstocking of certain markets. . . .' (p. 498.) An actual or even a prospective decline of profits in a few important industries suffices to create financial difficulties of great seriousness for all industries. But where Mitchell would have put his main emphasis in explaining the upper turning-point is left rather uncertain.

Mitchell did not consider that under-consumption is important in bringing the boom to an end: 'Until the under-consumption theories have been shored up by more convincing evidence than has yet been adduced in their favour, therefore, the view must prevail that the difficulty of warding off encroachments upon profits by advancing costs comes to a head earlier in other lines of business than in those concerned with consumers' goods.' (p. 502.) It is investment expenditure, according to Mitchell, which is the key determinant throughout the cycle.

Mitchell's main contribution has often been regarded as the accumulation of a wealth of statistical material, and this is obviously partly true. But beneath the surface of his 'descriptive analysis' there is at least as much 'analysis' as there is 'description', or rather there is a masterly balance of the two (such as is also to be found in Spiethoff's work). As in the text of Marshall's *Principles*, the analysis is not expressed in pure and tight mathematical formulae but is integrated with the description, and so has often not been recognized for what it is. We have tried to give the outline of Mitchell's treatment and not, of course, the wealth of both statistical and theoretical content it possesses. Of the often neglected theoretical content of Mitchell's *Business Cycles* it has been claimed:

The business cycle theory . . . from Part III of Mitchell's 1913 volume contains practically every element that is significant in the business cycle theories that are currently prominent [1950]. Here are the multiplier process, the acceleration principle, the Pigovian cycles of optimism and pessimism, the Marshallian and Hawtreyan drain of cash from the banking system and the resultant tightening of the money market, a decline in the expected yield of new investment at the peak that is the counterpart of the Keynesian 'collapse of the marginal efficiency of capital' except that it is a continuous decline rather than a discontinuous 'collapse', the Keynesian changes in liquidity preference. Here, too, is an attempt at a reasoned explanation and integration of these phenomena.[1]

Whether or not this judgement inclines towards a generous hind-sighted interpretation, it certainly comes very much nearer the truth than does the view of Mitchell's work as a methodologically naïve mass of statistical raw material.

[1] See Milton Friedman, 'Wesley Mitchell as a Theorist', *Journal of Political Economy*, Dec. 1950, p. 487.

(b) A. C. PIGOU

Part IV of Pigou's *Wealth and Welfare* (1912) on the subject of the variability of the national dividend, though presented as an aspect of a much wider subject, includes a discussion of the causation and remedies of cyclical fluctuations. Pigou followed in the main the 'exogenous' monetary and 'psychological' type of explanation of Bagehot and Marshall, which he later built up into his comprehensive study of *Industrial Fluctuations* (1927). There is, in particular, a detailed analysis in *Wealth and Welfare* of 'The Variability of Error in Business Forecasts' (Ch. 7). The type of explanation which Pigou followed is hardly in itself a 'synthetic' one, but it is elastic and undogmatic enough easily to permit of synthesis with other explanations.

Irving Fisher's plan for stabilizing the general level of prices is considered likely to result in 'a very considerable net benefit'. A somewhat reserved support is given to the counter-cyclical public works policy of the Minority Report of the Poor Law Commission, some of its assumptions and statistics being questioned. But (as we shall see in the next chapter) in his inaugural lecture (1908) Pigou had given what is probably the first definite refutation of what came to be called 'the Treasury view' of the inefficacy of public works as a remedy for unemployment.

(c) D. H. ROBERTSON

D. H. Robertson's study of *Industrial Fluctuations* (1915) may be said to be the first monograph devoted to the subject by an English academic economist combining historical, statistical, and theoretical analysis. Methodologically it provides a synthesis of theoretical analysis with historical and statistical material, and it also contains a fairly sharply critical review of all the really important explanations and partial explanations of the trade cycle then in the field. Over-investment and capital shortage, deficiency of consumption demand, inventions, errors in investment, and crop fluctuations, are all given a place, either as working together or as alternative possibilities in the various phases of different cycles.

Robertson's over-investment analysis was similar to that of Spiethoff, but is combined with elements emphasized by Aftalion. The virtual impossibility of stable and correct forecasts by entrepreneurs of the marginal utility of capital goods, as contrasted with consumption goods, is emphasized, and it is the variations in these forecasts 'which furnish the key to the most important aspects of modern industrial fluctuations'.

(p. 157.) Special stress is laid on the rise in costs as a factor tending to bring the boom to an end. An actual 'real' shortage of consumable goods as described by Spiethoff (and illustrated by Bonamy Price's and Labordère's parable of the one-man crisis), is recognized as a possible ground for the breakdown of an investment boom, but is not held to be the only possible ground:

> The relapse in constructional industry is seen to be due to the existence or imminence of an over-production of instrumental as compared with consumable goods. Whether or not this over-production is indicated by an actual shortage of consumable goods which renders it impossible to maintain investment on the scale which has prevailed during the preceding years or months, or whether it is due to miscalculation or to the inevitable characteristics of modern large-scale production, its essential nature is the same, a failure to secure the best conceivable distribution through time of a community's consumption of consumable goods. (p. 187.)

Particularly detailed attention is given to the role of fluctuations in crop values in the trade cycle, a subject which had been much studied, but with highly ambiguous and diametrically conflicting conclusions as to the processes involved. (Part I, Chs. 5–7.)

The remedies discussed include 'a more centralized investment policy' and Fisher's plan for stabilizing the general price-level, which is approved with reservations, though it is emphasized that not all movements of the price-level are injurious. Wage reductions in the slump are considered to be of very doubtful aid:

> It must be remembered first that if the men are employed in constructional industry, the demand for their labour at such a time is likely to be inelastic, and the aggregate income of members therefore lessened, even though unemployment be avoided, by the acceptance of lower wages. . . . On the whole I cannot help feeling, that, in spite no doubt of errors of judgment, the trade unions have known their own business in this matter better than is always admitted. (p. 249.)

'Cordial support' is given to the public-works proposal of the Minority Report of the Poor Law Commission, and 'Mr. Hawtrey's attack upon the proposal scarcely deserves formal refutation'. (p. 253.) The final emphasis of the book is somewhat similar to Schumpeter's, being on the clash of progress and security in the existing economic order: 'What is meant' it is asked 'by the most desirable distribution of the community's income through time?' Under the existing order 'out of the welter of industrial dislocation the great permanent riches of the future are generated'. (p. 254.)

5. *Post-war Writings on the Trade Cycle (1918–29)*

We must deal very briefly with writings on the trade cycle in the decade following the First World War, and we shall begin to 'fade out' our treatment some time before 1929 and the spate of new contributions and controversies, which was beginning to gather momentum even before that year. There have been countless surveys of this later and vastly important stage of the subject, to which we simply wish to lead up and not to enter upon. From now on, of course, Haberler's *Prosperity and Depression* is the comprehensive and authoritative work.

The financial disasters of the war and the immediate post-war period had for some time put rather in the background the more 'normal' problems of cyclical fluctuations. When interest in the subject revived in the middle twenties, it was with a considerably heightened awareness, at any rate in some circles, of the possibilities of monetary management and manipulation. Though it may seem remarkable that the experiences of war finance and war economics did not influence all levels of opinion more deeply than they did, the greater attention to the possibilities of a deliberate monetary policy, evident in writings on trade cycle problems in the 1920's, seems to be traceable to the experience and education in monetary pathology gained in the years following 1914.

Most of the main contributions in these years took the form of revised and perfected versions of their theories by the pre-war pioneers, for example, Spiethoff's article of 1925,[1] Wesley Mitchell's *Business Cycles* (1927), and various restatements of his purely monetary theory by R. G. Hawtrey. Finally there was the *Industrial Fluctuations* (1927) of A. C. Pigou, the most complete and balanced single-volume survey of the entire problem. It is in no way to detract from the value of these works to say that as compared with their pre-war predecessors they did not bring any essentially new approach or explanation demanding further discussion here.

(*a*) CASSEL

Let us take first among post-war writings Cassel's lucid restatement of the over-investment theory, written as long previously as 1914 but first published in German in 1918 as Book IV of his *Theory of Social Economy*. Cassel made a number of modifications and improvements as compared with Spiethoff's earlier version of the over-investment

---

[1] On 'Krisen' in the *Handwörterbuch der Staatswissenschaften*, 4th ed.

analysis, and his work had some influence both on D. H. Robertson's *Banking Policy and the Price Level*, and on the subsequent Austrian monetary over-investment theory.

The cycle according to Cassel is essentially a cycle in the production of fixed capital in a growing economy. He emphasizes the regularly stimulating effects of technological progress, and he recognizes the principle of the acceleration of derived demand as making the capital goods industries much more sensitive to fluctuations in final consumers' demand than the consumption goods industries. The changing inter-relations between profits and wages are shown to have an important part in the cyclical process: at the beginning of the upswing the encroachment of profits on wages leads to over-investment which is subsequently upset by a reverse encroachment of wages on profits in the later stages of the boom.

In contrast with Spiethoff, Cassel argues that the stores of consumption goods and raw materials accumulated in the slump are not of any essential consequence for the subsequent boom. Nor does 'free' money-capital accumulate during the depression. There is simply available for the upswing an excess capacity of efficient fixed capital or durable instruments. (pp. 587–8.) Cassel emphasizes much more than Spiethoff the role of banking policy, the rate of interest, and 'forced saving' so that, in his analysis, a shortage of capital at the crisis is one of monetary savings and not of real goods:

A study of the influence of trade cycles upon the capital market must take into account still another factor, namely, the attitude of the banks. At the very outset of a trade revival they generally continue to supply means of payment at the earlier rate of interest, or, at all events, hesitate to raise the rate as quickly as the growing scarcity of capital-disposal would require. Consequently, the capital goods are capitalised at too low a rate of interest, i.e. their prices are pushed upward. Hence the production of capital goods appears to be particularly profitable, and the entrepreneurs make free use of the purchasing power which the banks put at their disposal so cheaply. This leads to a diversion of the community's purchasing power in the direction of capital goods. There ensues a corresponding change in production, so that the consumer's demand cannot be fully met. Thus this action of the banks has the same effect upon the distribution of the community's total purchasing power between capital goods and consumers' goods as an increase in the savings of the community. (p. 625.)

When eventually the banks raise the rate of interest an acute shortage will be revealed not so much of 'real' goods as of what Cassel calls

'capital-disposal' or of 'savings for purchasing the real capital produced': 'The primary cause of crises is a wrong estimate of the possibilities of obtaining, on the capital market of the future, the funds
necessary for completing an enterprise that has been begun.' (p. 651.)
It was this form of the 'shortage of savings' explanation that was
adopted and developed by Austrian writers led by L. Mises in the
following decade.

(b) HAHN AND ROBERTSON

A work which examined the processes of saving and investment and
which was of considerable importance in Germany after 1920, but
remained almost unknown in Britain and America, was L. A. Hahn's
Volkswirtschaftliche Theorie des Bankkredits (1st ed., 1920). Hahn
started from the dictum that 'capital formation is not the result of
saving but of the granting of credit'. (p. 120.) From this it follows that
with an expansion of credit there will be an expansion of production,
where, as Hahn assumes usually to be the case, unemployed resources
are available. Theoretically, 'a perpetual boom is by no means impossible or Utopian' (p. 159), if State action is applied to this end, particularly, Hahn suggests, by the government purchase and storage of
goods when private demand falls off. Booms, in fact, come to an end
because of an increase in saving out of larger incomes, for, in general,
people save more when their incomes increase. (p. 148.) Hahn invoked
Malthus's 'effective demand' analysis as an anticipation of his own
ideas, though the resemblance is probably not very close. It should be
added that Hahn later came to repudiate much of his earlier analysis,
or at any rate the conclusions for policy associated with it.

The outstanding example of the increased attention given after the
war to monetary aspects of crises and cycles, as compared with pre-
war theories, is D. H. Robertson's *Banking Policy and the Price Level*
which appeared in 1926. As the author has said, the first object of the
book was to restate the analysis of his *Industrial Fluctuations* and 'to
interweave with the mainly non-monetary argument of that work a
discussion of the relation between saving, credit creation and capital
growth'. (See Preface to new edition, 1949.) In particular, Robertson's
essay examined the significance of divergencies between saving and
investment. It also introduced a 'day-by-day' model of an inflationary
process which represented a pioneer essay in macro-dynamic analysis
of the kind that was being developed at about the same time by the
Swedish economists, notably Lindahl. The main conclusion for

policy of the book, as had been briefly suggested in the *Study of Industrial Fluctuations* a decade before, was that stability of the price-level, then widely accepted as the best objective for monetary policy, was not always compatible with stability of aggregate output, and was not necessarily economically desirable when rapid economic progress was under way.

(c) THE MONETARY OVER-INVESTMENT THEORY

The monetary over-investment theory of Mises and Hayek which became important towards the end of the 1920's, accepted in its main outline the over-investment analysis of Cassel. But Mises built on to that a monetary analysis based on Wicksell's account of the cumulative inflationary processes resulting from divergencies between the 'natural' and the 'market' rates of interest. Existing banking systems were chronically incapable of maintaining equality between the natural and the market rates of interest, and inevitably tended to produce inflationary investment booms by their over-generous credit policies inspired by 'an inflationary ideology'. The re-awakening of attention to Wicksell's work (foreshadowed, as we have noted, by Mises's reference in 1912) was one of the main contributions of this school of thought, though Spiethoff, Fanno, Fisher, and Schumpeter had also seen something of Wicksell's importance. Other additions by the Austrian theory were an infusion of Böhm-Bawerk's concept of the period and structure of production, and a severely deductive and even *a priori* methodology, which laid it down as 'a methodological rule that the analysis of the cyclical movement should never start on the assumption of existing unemployment'.[1]

The full elaboration of this theory belongs to the 1930's, and we must refer the reader to the well-known writings of F. A. Hayek and to the account in Haberler's *Prosperity and Depression* (Ch. 3, sect. A). We would simply emphasize that though it may be described as an 'over-investment' theory of the crisis, a special characteristic of this theory was that it gave an 'over-consumption' theory of the depression and its duration, reminiscent of the doctrines of Bonamy Price and Guyot half a century before. For the depression the conclusion was 'that the deflation was the necessary consequence of the boom. If once the boom has been allowed to develop and to give rise to mal-adjustment, the price has to be paid in the shape of a process of defla-

---

[1] See Haberler, *Prosperity and Depression*, 3rd ed., p. 63.

tion.' (*Prosperity and Depression*, 3rd ed., p. 59.) Nothing could be done to get out of a depression before 'its natural end'.

It should be noted that this austere conclusion was not always, or even usually, taken to follow from an 'over-investment' analysis. Spiethoff, in his first essay, favoured the maintenance of purchasing power during the depression, and D. H. Robertson had been among the first to give 'cordial support' to a public works policy in a slump. The Austrian monetary over-investment school was also strongly critical, more so even than D. H. Robertson, of attempts to stabilize the value of money. It was held that, with technical progress gradually lowering costs, a policy of stabilization would lead straight to inflationary over-investment and the inevitable depression. The American slump of 1929 was held to bear out this analysis.

We must break off our review at this critical point. Further advance in the study of economic fluctuations was only gradually making inevitable a re-examination of the fundamental postulates of the equilibrium analysis of normal values and prices, and of the significance of this analysis for an economic world were politico-economic disturbances and consequent State intervention were to become a new 'normality'. At the same time, in Britain particularly, the problem of cyclical fluctuations had now become to a considerable extent merged with and replaced by the inter-war problem of chronic unemployment, and we must now turn to the doctrines on this subject.

24

Economists and the Problem of Unemployment in Great Britain, 1885–1929

1. *Charity and Relief Works*: 1885–1909[1]

ACCORDING to the *Oxford English Dictionary*, the word 'unemployment' first began to come into common use in about 1895. As we have already noticed, in the index to Marshall's *Principles* under the neologism 'unemployment', one is referred to 'inconstancy of employment'. Differing opinions were held as to how far the emergence of an 'unemployment' problem was due to an actual increase in the numbers or percentages of 'unemployed' in the last two decades of the nineteenth century, or how far the problem was created rather by greater publicity, a more sensitive social conscience, and the misinterpretation of such incomplete statistics as were available. Marshall seems to have inclined to the latter view. But, in any case, economists did not regard the increasing prominence of the problem of unemployment as raising any fundamentally new economic questions, practical or theoretical. The trade cycle was receiving increased study, but down to 1900, and even later, very much as a special problem of abnormality, or 'pathology', to be tackled after the 'normal' laws had been discovered. We certainly do not wish with hindsighted wisdom to imply any judgement on those economists who around 1900 failed to see in unemployment a problem of fundamental practical and theoretical significance. There were still very few statistics from which significant and reliable conclusions could be drawn. (We have seen that in 1898 Wicksell believed that the statistical evidence from various countries pointed to a normal level of unemployment of

---

[1] We are confining ourselves to the insular history of this subject in Britain only, partly because it was out of the British writings and controversies alone that the ideas of Keynes's seem to have grown. At some stages, thought and practice in Sweden on the subject of unemployment and its causes and cures, seem to have been ahead of British ideas. There were also some highly important writings in America, notably the 1923 *Report of a Committee of the President's Conference on Unemployment*, with contributions by Wesley Mitchell.

1%.) Nevertheless, surely some tribute is due to those like Foxwell and Hobson who were early to proclaim the practical and theoretical importance of the problem.

Even down to about 1910 the problem of unemployment was treated primarily as one of charity and relief, hardly carrying a challenge to economic theory or policy. For example, the article on the subject in the 11th (1911) edition of the *Encyclopedia Britannica* begins as follows:

Unemployment: a modern term for the state of being unemployed among the working classes. The social question involved is intimately bound up with that of relief of the poor, and its earlier history is outlined in the article *Charity and Charities*. It is more particularly within the 20th century that the problem of unemployment has become specially insistent, not by reason of its greater intensity . . . but because the greater facilities for publicity, the growth of industrial democracy, the more scientific methods applied to the solution of economic questions, the larger humanitarian spirit of the times, all demand that remedies differing considerably from those of the past should at least be tried. In most civilised countries attempts have been made to solve this or that particular phase of the problem by improved methods. There is, however, always a great difficulty in knowing the extent of unemployment even in any one particular country.

But let us now go back 25 years to 1886, to a lecture of H. S. Foxwell's which surely belongs among the boldest contributions of our period to social and economic policy.[1] It was a lecture entitled 'Irregularity of Employment and Fluctuations of Prices'. Foxwell begins and ends by stating his 'conviction, continually increasing in strength, that uncertainty of employment is the root evil of the present industrial régime (p. 7). . . . It is my most rooted and settled conviction that, of all the many claims of labour, the most grave, the most pressing, and the most just, is the claim I have brought before you tonight, the claim for more regular employment.' (p. 96.)

Foxwell based his conviction on the fundamentally evil social effects of fluctuating and uncertain conditions of work: 'The fact is, that where human beings are concerned, where personal relations should be formed, and where moral forces are at work, a certain permanence of conditions seems to be essential', and he quotes William Cobbett on 'that fixedness which is so much the friend of rectitude in morals,

---

[1] One of Foxwell's first publications. On Foxwell (1849–1936) see Keynes's obituary article, *Economic Journal*, Dec. 1936. Foxwell never followed the subject further. The quality of his few writings makes his lapse into bibliophily a sad loss.

and which so powerfully conduces to prosperity, private and public'. (p. 11.) Foxwell holds that 'these considerations apply to all classes equally, rich and poor, weak and strong. But sudden change is peculiarly injurious to the weaker class.' He charges Ricardo and his school as follows: 'Ricardo and the economists of his school, more familiar with the money market than with industry, greatly underrated the difficulty which the weaker classes find in adapting themselves to sudden changes.' As Petty had said: 'Better to burn a thousand men's labours for a time, than to let those thousand men by non-employment, lose their faculty of labouring.'

A pioneer of the idea of 'social security', Foxwell continues: 'I cannot venture to say what would be the general opinion of the working class upon the point; but my own feeling would be that when a certain necessary limit had been reached, regularity of income was far more important than amount of income. Where employment is precarious, thrift and self-reliance are discouraged.' (p. 17.) He quotes the 'labour' writer Howell: 'If the science of political economy is to be of any practical value, its expounders ought to try and find some means whereby these frequent fluctuations can be avoided; instead of which they only teach men how to increase them, by declaring that wages must be dependent on the variations of "the market".' Foxwell felt that Howell 'was right, not only as to the injury caused by fluctuations, but when he charged economists as a body with having in some respects helped to increase it. Many of them, however, have done good service in this field, and one in particular,' i.e. Jevons.

Foxwell then goes on to an analysis of price fluctuations. In the main he follows Jevons, not referring to Juglar's massive works on the subject. He sets out the curve of general prices for a whole century:

> Let us think for a moment, as the eye sweeps over this great series of changes, what it really implies. There is something very impressive—to my mind almost awe-inspiring—about this strange curve. Its vast ground-swell, the greatest rhythm known to economic science, can only be exhibited on a scale of centuries. It forms the backbone of our commercial history. It marks redistributions of wealth such as no Acts of Parliament have ever ventured to decree. It is difficult to exaggerate, and impossible to realize the untold misery and innumerable changes of fortune caused by its terrible fluctuations. (p. 31.)

After discussing the unjust social effects of changes in the value of money, Foxwell concludes that a general stability of the price-level should be the aim of policy, but, unlike Marshall, he favoured a slightly rising level, rather than a slightly falling one. In industry he called for more organization and more publicity, that is, for more public control along these two lines:

Laissez-faire is already a thing of the past. It is true that, as a general political theory, this principle is somewhat out of fashion; but it has left us pernicious legacies from the time of its dominance. (p. 93.) . . . Not that I agree with those who hope to displace competition by some system of state or collective administration. . . . The force of competition is immensely powerful and at present indispensable. . . . Indeed if the power of the state organization by which it was replaced were even half as efficient, half as pervasive, it would be a grinding tyranny over the individual, the like of which has never yet been seen. . . . All the writings of the socialists put together, have done less towards the positive reconstruction of industry, than the single, modest but practical step taken by the English trade unionists. (pp. 72–74.)

Foxwell held that the abolition of the existing undue 'irregularity of employment' should be a major objective of economic policy, and to this end was ready for a comprehensive reorganization of industry and a profound change in the status of the worker: 'I say without hesitation that we ought not to rest content, till in one way or another we have succeeded in giving to the artisan and labourer as much social security as is commonly enjoyed by the salaried professional classes.' (p. 95.)

As the Great Depression continued, and the social conscience gradually became wider and wider awake, interest increased both in the study of cyclical fluctuations and in public organization for the relief of poverty. John Burns (*Nineteenth Century*, Dec. 1892) proclaimed that 'the unemployed question . . . will be for years to come the chief question for discussion'. Charles Booth made a statistical estimate as part of his study of poverty in east London, and this Conservative M.P. echoed Marx in his generalization: 'Our modern system of industry will not work without some unemployed margin.' He put the actual percentage of chronically 'superfluous' workers at this time in the East End of London at $11\frac{1}{4}\%$.

An important addition to firm knowledge of the subject came in 1895 with the *Third Report of the House of Commons Committee on Distress from Want of Employment*. H. Llewellyn Smith of the Labour Department of the Board of Trade gave some estimates of the magnitude of seasonal and cyclical unemployment, and distinguished the comparatively stable from the comparatively unstable industries, confirming that these latter were, on the whole, producers' goods industries, and in particular the engineering industry.

But there was still no accepted definition of 'unemployment', and little agreement on its magnitude. In the same year (1895) J. A. Hobson wrote in the *Contemporary Review* (pp. 415 ff.) on 'The Meaning and Measurement of "Unemployment" ' (the term still required inverted commas).[1] He began by complaining that

'Unemployment' is perhaps the most elusive term which confronts the student of modern industrial society. This elusiveness exposes the subject to grave abuses. Well-meaning but somewhat hasty social reformers stretch the term and bloat it out to gigantic proportions; professional economists and statisticians, provoked by this unwarranted exaggeration, are tempted to a corresponding excess of extenuation, and are almost driven to deny the reality of any unemployed question, over and above that of the mere temporary leakages and displacements due to the character of certain trades, and to the changes of industrial methods. (p. 415.)

Hobson quoted the Labour Department of the Board of Trade as unwilling to describe as 'unemployed' those idle for purely seasonal reasons: 'The bricklayers idle during frost are in no sense superfluous if the whole year be taken as a unit.' But the official view even suggested extending this definitional procedure to cyclical unemployment: 'In a period of contraction like the present there are many men who are out of work. They are industrially "superfluous" if so short a period as a year be taken as a unit; but over a period of seven years—which for shipbuilding appears to be about the period of the cycle—they are necessary, and were they lifted off the labour market in slack years there would not be enough men to execute the work when trade revived.' But it was finally agreed that it would be 'a strain of ordinary language' to refuse to these men the title of 'unemployed'. (pp. 418–19.)

Hobson advocated a comprehensive definition of 'unemployment' in accordance with what came to be ordinary modern usage, that is, to cover any form of involuntary idleness of the able-bodied. Although he emphasized that no close estimate was possible, he believed that, so defined, the problem was larger than was suggested by the current statistics based on trade union returns, and that by far the most important component of the problem was due to the partly cyclical and partly chronic deficiency of effective demand, as argued in his under-consumption theory. He held that this central problem was shirked by

[1] See also *The Problem of the Unemployed* (1st ed., 1896), one of Hobson's most valuable and original books.

those who 'analysed away' the causes of unemployment under a series of particular personal and frictional headings. The fundamental solution lay in preventing over-saving by a redistribution of income, with higher wages and probably shorter hours. 'Palliatives', such as relief works, were helpful so far as they aided this 'high consumption' policy.

At the same time as this current of opinion and inquiry was slowly gathering momentum, led by such men as Foxwell, Hobson, Booth, and Llewellyn Smith, a start was being made in dealing with the unemployed, outside the Poor Law. In 1886 Joseph Chamberlain of the Local Government Board had circularized local authorities urging them to provide relief work without taint of pauperism. This circular was repeated in 1892, and in 1905 a more systematic measure, the Unemployed Workmen's Act, was passed. But the policy was on too small a scale and was unsuccessful. Even in 1911 the *Encyclopedia Britannica* still held that 'municipal or state-organized relief works more properly fall under the description of charity (see *Charity and Charities*)'. This latter article (by C. S. Loch, secretary of the influential Charity Organization Society, and a member of the Royal Commission on the Poor Laws) was apprehensive even that the 1905 policy would lead the nation down the road to serfdom:

If the line of development that the act suggests were to be followed (as the renewed Labour agitation in 1908–1909 made probable) it must tend to create a class of 'unemployed', unskilled labourers of varying grades of industry who may become the dependent and state-supported proletariat of modern urban life. Thus, unless the administration be extremely rigorous, once more will a kind of serfdom be established, to be, as some would say, taken over hereafter by the socialist state.

2. *1909: The Royal Commission on the Poor Laws and Counter-cyclical Relief Works*

1909 was, of course, a most important date in the history of the British unemployment problem. The Royal Commission on the Poor Laws reported in that year and the Majority Report favoured the continuation and development of the existing policy of relief works. But the very influential Minority Report suggested a much more drastic and systematic counter-cyclical policy of public works and investment. The statistical details of the proposal were worked out by A. L. Bowley, the main point being as follows:

We think that there can be no doubt that, out of the 150 millions sterling annually expended by National and Local Authorities on works and services, it would be possible to earmark at least 4 millions a year, as not to be undertaken equally, year by year, as a matter of course; but to be undertaken, out of loan, on a 10 years programme, at unequal annual rates, to the extent even of 10 or 15 millions in a single year at those periods when the National Labour Exchange reported that the number of able-bodied applicants, for whom no places could be found anywhere within the United Kingdom, was rising above the normal level.

This is an advance in principle a long way beyond the 1905 policy of relief works. Four differences from the earlier policy were emphasized:

(a) The work concerned would be started before Unemployment became acute, say, when the percentage Unemployment Index reached 4 per cent.

(b) There would be no artificial demand made for labour, only an adjustment in time of the ordinary demand.

(c) The Unemployed, as a class, would not be attracted, for the demand would come through ordinary trade sources, and before there was any considerable dearth of employment.

(d) The wages paid would be measured only by the work done, being contracted out on the ordinary commercial basis.

In general the authors of the Minority Report (pre-eminently S. and B. Webb), were highly optimistic about the tractability of the unemployment problem as it then stood, and about the efficacy of the measures they proposed: 'It is now administratively possible, if it is sincerely wished to do so, to remedy most of the evils of Unemployment.' (Minority Report, vol. ii, p. 324.) Frictional, seasonal, and casual unemployment could be removed by the organization of the labour market, and cyclical unemployment by the policy of systematically planned public works.

In the same year as the Reports of the Poor Law Commission, *Unemployment, a Problem of Industry*, by W. H. Beveridge, was published. Though emphasizing the uncertainties in the existing statistics, Beveridge concluded as to the percentages of unemployed that 'the crest of each wave is at about 98; the depressions are anywhere between 89 and 94'. (p. 41.) He supported public works policies, but emphasized the practical and administrative difficulties, distinguishing between the different types or causes of unemployment then recognized (frictional, seasonal, cyclical &c.). Beveridge did not then hold that unemployment 'could be attributed to any general want of adjustment between the growth of the demand for labour and the growth of the supply'. (p. 11.) But he added the qualification: 'Because up-to-date industry has expanded, the inference is made that it is still expanding, and capable of expansion. Because this expansion in the past has taken place through alternations of good years and bad years, the inference is made of any particular period of depression that it is only a temporary phase and will give way to renewed prosperity. All this, however, is far from inevitable.' (p. 15.) When he summarized the problem as one of 'making reality correspond with the assumptions of economic theory' (p. 237) Beveridge perhaps wrote more profoundly than he knew, but he was presumably only referring to the raising of the mobility of labour, not to the adequacy of the aggregate effective demand for it.

At about this time increasing attention was being given to more theoretical economic analysis of remedies for unemployment. In his inaugural lecture as successor to Marshall at Cambridge in 1908, on the subject of 'Economic Science in Relation to Practice', A. C. Pigou took the concrete practical problem of unemployment to exhibit the nature and method of economic analysis. He gave what is perhaps the first modern refutation of what later came to be known as 'the Treasury view', that is, the doctrine that public works cannot increase aggregate employment but simply divert it from the private to the public sector (a 'view' probably first expressed in Parliament by Ricardo):

> One view, recently expressed in Parliament, runs thus: If you employ public monies in this way, you take funds, which would have been used by private persons in the employment of better workmen on tasks that are wanted, to use them in employing worse workmen on tasks that are not wanted. You, therefore, tend to impoverish the community without really lessening the aggregate mass of unemployment.

However, it is not true, Pigou continued,

> that the levying of rates and taxes for relief works would contract private industry by an amount *equal* to the expansion of public industry. It would, no doubt, contract it to *some* extent. But it is probable that only a part of the extra taxes people pay would be taken from funds they would otherwise have devoted at that time directly or indirectly to wage-payment. Hence, the true result of relief works and so on is not to leave the aggregate amount of unemployment in the country unaltered, but to diminish that amount. (pp. 27–28.)[1]

[1] See also Ch. XI of Pigou's *Unemployment* (Home University Library, 1913), where he counters the argument of the Transvaal Indigency Commission that when 'a Government gives work to the unemployed, it is simply transferring wage-giving from the

On the other hand, Pigou was subsequently critical of the statistics of the Minority Report's proposals, and argued that the efficacy of a public works policy depended on mobility in the labour market (*Wealth and Welfare*, 1912, p. 186). A few years later (1913) R. G. Hawtrey made his first statement of 'the Treasury view' that public works were no remedy for unemployment: 'The writers of the Minority Report appear to have overlooked the fact that the Government by the very fact of borrowing for this expenditure is withdrawing from the investment market savings which would otherwise be applied to the creation of capital. . . .' (*Good and Bad Trade*, 1913, p. 260.) This argument was in turn sharply countered by D. H. Robertson who gave 'cordial support' to the public works proposals of the Minority Report. (*Industrial Fluctuations*, 1915, p. 253.)

3. *1923–9: Keynes and Public Investment Policy*

The First World War put the whole problem of unemployment and its causes and cures in the background for nearly a decade. It seems remarkable that when discussion revived, in about 1923, the experience of war economics had seemingly had so little effect on the approach to the unemployment problem adopted by dominant sections of opinion. The analogy of war had, of course, been used long before by Mummery and Hobson in discussing the remediability of unemployment. Also, already by 1915 the facts of war economics had seemed to be suggesting a fundamental revision of ideas on monetary policy:

> One of the most formidable obstacles to currency reform—the alleged impossibility of persuading the well-to-do Briton to live without chinking golden sovereigns in his pockets—vanished in a week-end. The sacred machine of high finance has been shown to be at once infinitely vulnerable, and far more amenable than its hierophants supposed to conscious manipulation and control. . . . Though the event demanded far other measures, there was in the early days of the war a readiness to apply on an unprecedented scale the device of bringing a Government demand for structural work to bear upon a slack labour market. Above all, the co-existence of brisk trade and employment with a war expenditure of £3,000,000 a day has compelled clear thinking on the real nature of saving and investment in the most unlikely quarters. (D. H. Robertson, *A Study in Industrial Fluctuations*, 1915, p. xix.)

individual to itself. It is diminishing employment with one hand, while it increases it with the other. It takes work from people employed by private individuals, and gives it to people selected by the State.' For Ricardo, see *Works*, vol. v (ed. Sraffa), p. 32.

But by the early twenties many of these 'unlikely quarters' seem to have achieved a rapid reconversion to their pre-war 'normalcy' of unclear thinking, and to have sought to carry on with their pre-war intellectual equipment for at least another decade.

However, the fact that complete and authoritative monthly statements of the numbers unemployed were now being published added immensely to the public consciousness of the unemployment problem, and it gradually became clear that it was taking on a new scale and seriousness as compared with the pre-1914 decades. By 1923 a group of investigators aided by Pigou and Bowley, produced two studies entitled *The Third Winter of Unemployment*, and *Is Unemployment Inevitable?* At the same time a similar group in the Liberal party (including Keynes, H. D. Henderson, and D. H. Robertson) was also concentrating attention on the new and more serious form of chronic unemployment then beginning to emerge. We may follow something of the treatment the problem received in the middle and later years of the 1920's in Keynes's addresses to the annual Liberal Summer School, and in his and H. D. Henderson's articles in the weekly *Nation and Athenaeum*.

Keynes had first been arguing for a deliberate conscious policy of monetary management (in his *Tract on Monetary Reform*), but he took up the case for a deliberate State investment policy soon after. At the Liberal Summer School of 1923 Keynes took the subject of 'Currency Policy and Unemployment'. He then saw the problem as one of the price-level, or rather as 'a lack of confidence in the existing level of prices'. But he also saw unemployment as a major challenge to economic analysis and policy:

> The absurdity of labour being from time to time totally unemployed, in spite of everyone wanting more goods, can only be due to a muddle, which should be remediable if we could think and act clearly. The most serious charge which can be brought against the system of private enterprise in business and of capitalistic investment as it exists today, is that it has failed so far, to deal with this muddle. As time goes on things seem to get worse rather than better. (*Nation and Athenaeum*, 11.8.23.)

This is very much in the vein of Foxwell's lecture nearly forty years before, as also was D. H. Robertson's statement on the same occasion that 'the Liberal Party in particular should adopt once for all as the first plank in its social policy—the word "stabilization" '.

In 1924 Keynes moved forward an important step with an article entitled 'Does Unemployment Need a Drastic Remedy?' (ibid.,

Unemployment in Great Britain (1885–1929)   419

24.5.1924.) He proposed 'The Treasury should not shrink from promoting expenditure up to (say) £100 million a year on the construction of capital goods at home' (a sum which represented then about one-eighth of the annual budget): 'There is no place or time here for *laissez-faire*. Furthermore we must look for succour to the principle that *prosperity is cumulative.*' As an example of 'cumulative' prosperity Keynes cited the condition of France after five years strenuous rebuilding of devastated areas, an example of which Uriel Crocker and Mummery and Hobson would have approved. He saw a big new field for State economic activity. However, he held that 'a drastic reduction of wages in certain industries and a successful stand-up fight with the more powerful Trade Unions might reduce unemployment in the long run', but he regarded such a policy as quite unpractical and inequitable. (ibid., 7.6.1924.)

For a year or two attention was turned to other problems, the return to the Gold Standard and reparations difficulties. But in 1927 it was being laid down that: 'In its practical tendency today the general, undiscriminating preaching of economy is obscurantist and reactionary.' (ibid., unsigned editorial, 23.4.1927.) The *laissez-faire* inertia of the government in respect of the unemployment problem was also attacked: 'It is a common opinion that no large issues of any sort arise, that if the export industries are languishing, and seem likely to languish, and unemployment seems likely to grow—well, it is a profound misfortune, but there is really nothing to be done, nothing at all events which any Government can do.' (ibid., unsigned editorial, 30.7.1927.) The country should realize that it was faced with a fundamentally new problem:

What essentially is our unemployment problem? It is not a problem of a temporary depression of trade affecting all industries alike. It is a problem of a large quasi-permanent excess of the supply over the demand for labour in certain industries. ... This phenomenon is totally different from the sort of unemployment with which we were faced before the war—arising from the seasonal irregularities of certain trades, fluctuations of general business activity, and the like. And it calls accordingly for different treatment. (ibid., unsigned article, 26.11.1927.)

In his lecture on 'The End of *Laissez-faire*' (1926) Keynes gave as a main example for the economic agenda of governments the regulation of savings and investment: 'I believe that some co-ordinated act of intelligent judgement is required as to the scale on which it is desirable that the community as a whole should save, the scale on which these savings should go abroad in the form of foreign investments, and whether the present organization of the investment market distributes savings along the most nationally productive channels.'

By 1928 the *Nation and Athenaeum* was presenting an outline of a savings and investment analysis with which to support theoretically its practical policy proposals:

As public utilities come more and more under public control, it rests increasingly with the State to determine the volume of real investment, and the policy which the State pursues in this matter becomes a factor of the first importance in the general economic situation. If the volume of real investment falls short of the money savings of the community, this means that so much purchasing power is withdrawn from the demand for goods and services and is rendered sterile. The result is a deflationary tendency, marked inevitably by trade depression and increasing unemployment. [The State] . . . should aim at securing that the volume of real investment keeps pace with the savings of the community. The state of trade will supply the practical test of whether it should press forward or hang back. . . . The deflationary process involves so much loss and waste that it reduces the supply of savings almost as much as the demand for them. (ibid., unsigned article, 4.8.1928.)

This debate over a public works policy as a remedy for unemployment was carried on, to a large extent, at the level of party politics, though at a comparatively very high level of party politics. Discussion was focused on the Liberal party programme as expounded in its 'Yellow Book' *Britain's Industrial Future*. The implications which the case for public works policies might have for the central body of economic theory, and the postulates on which this was based, were hardly referred to. Unemployment and wages policy were discussed in the *Economic Journal* by Pigou and Clay, for example, who both lent some support to the case for public works, but who both also came to the conclusion that a general reduction in wages would lessen unemployment, a conclusion not then challenged by Keynes or any other leading economist except perhaps J. A. Hobson. On the other hand there was then no articulate body of opinion among British economists (with the exception of R. G. Hawtrey), who challenged in principle the case for public works. Fundamental opposition to public works as a remedy for unemployment came rather from 'spokesmen' of the Treasury, the City, and the Government. To a questionnaire from the International Labour Office in 1927 the British Government replied: 'The decision taken by the Government at the end of 1925 to restrict grants for relief schemes was based mainly on the view that, the supply of capital in this country being limited, it was undesirable to divert any appreciable proportion of the supply from normal trade channels.'[1] In his Budget speech of 1929 Winston Churchill made his frequently quoted statement: 'It is the orthodox Treasury dogma, steadfastly held, that whatever might be the political or social advantages, very little additional employment can, in fact, and as a general rule, be created by State borrowing and State expenditure.' Shortly after, a Treasury White Paper (Cmd. 3331, 1929) was published criticizing the Liberal party's public works policy for unemployment.

Keynes at once attacked this statement of the Treasury view: 'Not one of the leading economists of the country who has published his views, or with whose opinion I am otherwise familiar, would endorse the general character of their argument.' The Treasury experts were completely mistaken in believing in their own orthodoxy, and 'were not familiar with modern economic thought' (18.5.1929). Of course, some of those authorities who were opposed in practice to the public works policy agreed that it would absorb unemployed labour (the main theoretical, though not necessarily the main practical point at issue) and that it would at least temporarily stimulate home demand by increasing purchasing power. But they gave priority to other objectives bound up with international financial stability.[2]

R. G. Hawtrey, however, had continued to challenge the underlying principles of the case for public works, as he had in 1913 challenged the proposals of the Minority Report of the Poor Law Commission. He agreed that 'additional public expenditure can give additional employment, but only if it increases the rapidity of circulation of money'. He contended that

what has been shown is that expenditure on public works, if accompanied by a creation of credit, will give employment. But then the same reasoning shows that a creation of credit unaccompanied by any expenditure on public works could be equally effective in giving employment. The public works are merely a piece of ritual, convenient to people who want to be able to say that they are doing something, but otherwise irrelevant. To stimulate an expansion of credit is usually only too easy. . . . The original contention that the public works themselves give additional employment is radically fallacious. When employment is improved, this is the result of some reaction

[1] See the Report of the Macmillan Committee on Finance and Industry, 1931, p. 203.
[2] Cf. para. 14 of Addendum III by T. E. Gregory to the Report of the Macmillan Committee on Finance and Industry, 1931 (p. 229).

on credit, and the true remedy for unemployment is to be found in a direct regulation of credit on sound lines. (*Economica*, 1925, pp. 44 and 48.)

Another case fundamentally critical of public investment policies during the depression, based on the Austrian analysis of the trade cycle, was to be heard in the 1930's, but it was not widely audible in Britain in the years with which we are here concerned.

This, then, was the state of opinion in the fateful summer of 1929, when for eight years unemployment in Britain had only once fallen slightly below 10 per cent., and when the world was on the brink of the greatest economic cataclysm of modern times. A majority of economists in Britain supported the general case for public works to combat unemployment (e.g. Keynes, Henderson, Pigou, Robertson, Clay, &c.). Public works policies were opposed by Hawtrey and later by the supporters of the Austrian monetary theory of over-investment. At the same time a considerable body, probably a large majority, of economists held that general wage reductions would, in the then existing circumstances diminish unemployment (e.g. Pigou, Clay, Beveridge, and perhaps Keynes).

We may conclude by noting the three main phases through which the case for public works passed, between the later stages of the Great Depression (*c.* 1885), and the onset of the World Slump (1929):

In the first phase, public works had simply been a policy of charity relief by local authorities, without economic significance. In the second phase, the proposed policy of public works, as presented in the Minority Report of 1909, took on a more definite economic significance as deliberately planned to counter cyclical fluctuations. But it was a policy of timing and spacing out a given secular level of government expenditure, and did not envisage any rise in total government expenditure over a seven- or ten-year cycle. The third phase saw the emergence in the 1920's of a new problem of chronic unemployment. The State had now, according to Keynes and the Liberal party, to raise the chronically depressed level of home investment and employment and make itself responsible for maintaining an adequate level of investment by filling any gaps left by a deficiency of private investment.

Down to 1929, in the analysis of the problems of a public investment policy, it does not seem to have been suggested that anything in the basic postulates of the main body of economic theory was at stake. But the fourth phase, shortly to begin, was to be played out more on the plane of pure analysis and its postulates, rather than on that of the discussion of practical policy, and several of those authorities who had been in broad agreement on policy were to get into severe disagreement over the terminological apparatus and empirical generalizations out of which a theoretical justification for policy could be formulated, as well as over generalizations about the previous and recent history of economic thought. It has been said that the question of building roads was now transformed into the question of building incomes. But this new fourth phase lies outside this chapter and this book.

25

Conclusion

1. *Two Main Lines of Advance*

WE are not in this conclusion going to attempt to sum up the foregoing chapters in some clear-cut outline of tendencies, much less to venture upon comprehensive summarizing judgements on, or classifications of, the roughly two generations of economic writings which we have surveyed. Though we hope that this whole attempt at such a survey is not itself premature in time or over-comprehensive in scope, such a concluding summary almost certainly would not escape these faults. Possibly, when in due course we can see these writings in a clearer perspective, and when the whole history of this period of thought has been worked on further from different points of view, useful and valid verdicts and generalizations, and a much tidier history of it, may be possible. For the moment, on this subject, as on many others, it remains true that 'every dogma that is short and simple is false'. In any case, there is already available a wide range of short and simple doctrines in circulation, to which it is super-fluous to add, beginning with the generalization that 'it is all in Marshall' (or Menger, or Marx), and moving across to the view that modern economics begins in 1936.

We have attempted to portray the main advances in the two princi-pal departments of economic theory (and if the story is tortuous and complex so also is the path of intellectual advance). First, there was the development of the micro-economic analysis of normal value, price, production, and distribution. The firm core or basis of this was a series of static formulae analysing maximimum 'equilibrium' points. These formulae were filled out, or given a realistic flavouring, by the assump-tion of a self-adjusting mechanism based on often not very precise stationary or quasi-stationary postulates. The line of progress here was, while tightening up and making explicit the postulates of the static formulae, to recognize, and then to meet systematically the need for a rigorous 'dynamic' analysis of the paths of economic processes, which would replace the somewhat loosely assumed stationary dynamics of self-adjustment. Meanwhile the vastly increased precision and elaboration of the micro-economic static formulae in 1929, as compared with the corresponding formulations of 1870, comprised one of the main lines of advance in our period, partly at any rate because it pointed to the need for advances in other directions.

The second main line of advance was in the study of crises, and of cyclical and other fluctuations in economic aggregates. In the nineteenth century this study had been extremely discontinuous and uncoordinated, but from about 1900 to 1929 a large body of much more detailed theoretical, statistical, and historical work had grown up. The relation and the co-ordination between this second line of development and the first (the mainly static formulae of normal value and distribution) was either non-existent, or at least far from clearly and precisely formulated in its basis. The theory of money and credit became, to a large extent, an ambiguous intermediate ground between these two lines of advance, in part occupied from one side by the first, and in part from the other side by the second. When Wicksell (1898) sought to emphasize the contrast between the progress in the theory of relative prices and the neglect of the theory of money prices (however criticizable this way of putting it) he may be said to have been pointing to this lack of co-ordination, or clear relation, between the analysis of normal equilibrium relative values, and the analysis of aggregate fluctuations affecting all money values.

The leading contributors to the analysis of normal equilibrium and quasi-stationary values and prices, seem mostly to have regarded the problems of aggregate fluctuations as eventually finding their solution in what Böhm-Bawerk described as that 'last chapter' on the pathology of the economic system which would find its place when the normal physiology had been worked out. Or, as with Marshall and Menger, the problem of aggregate fluctuations was to find its place in a second or third volume of economic principles which in the end never got written. In fact, many of the pioneer contributors to this second line of advance were sceptical or ignorant of, or at any rate little interested in, the first line of advance, that of the normal analysis of equilibrium values (for example, Juglar, Bagehot, Tugan-Baranovsky, Spiethoff, Veblen, Hobson, Johannsen, and Mitchell). Moreover, many of those who showed elsewhere an appreciation of the theory of normal values and distribution sought to make little application of its concepts and results to problems of crises and fluctuations.

Without trying to comment on or interpret any further this phase of intellectual history, we wish finally to refer to a third general development, or line of advance, which affected all branches of economics, that is the growth of economic statistics between 1870 and 1929. We shall then comment on the relations between this third line of advance and the other two, and note very briefly the change, or lack of change, in views on the scope and method of economics.

2. *The Growth of Economic Statistics*

We have already made various incidental references to new additions to the statistics of various branches of economics, for example as to prices and unemployment. Let us now take a very rapid and general glance round the field.

In 1900 Sir Robert Giffen referred to the past century as 'the statistical century par excellence', and, with the optimism of the period, expressed the hope that 'the coming century, like the one which is passing away, will be characteristically a statistical century'. By 1950 the award of the statistical laurels to the nineteenth century seemed somewhat premature, while the hopes for the twentieth century seemed to have been much too modestly expressed. Looking through the economic reports of government commissions and committees in the last two decades of the nineteenth century, one is bound to be struck by the amount of time and energy which had to be devoted to groping for facts and figures which today would be firmly available from the start. Nevertheless, in 1900 the growth of economic statistics in the past century may well have seemed phenomenal. It was no longer possible, as it had been in the eighteenth century, for expert debates to rage over whether the population of the country over a decade or so had markedly increased, or markedly diminished. Since Jevons's time it had hardly been possible for disputes to exist about the main movements of the general level of prices. Towards the end of the century the expansion of the statistical work of the Board of Trade and its Labour Department added considerably to the statistics of prices and wages. 1886 was a particularly memorable year, from which the Board of Trade Journal, the Labour Department of the Board of Trade, and Sauerbeck's price index-number all date their origin. The United States Bureau of Labor had been organized by Carroll D. Wright two years before, and in 1886 he produced his First Report devoted to a massive review of the history, statistics, and theories of crises and fluctuations. But we shall only refer to American economic statistics to say that already by the 1870's and 1880's, when led by F. A. Walker, they seem to have been well in advance of their British counterparts.

Unemployment figures began to be much more systematically collected and analyzed in Britain in the nineties, though they were only to become really complete and reliable some thirty years later. The Census of Production of 1907 may be taken as to some extent the startingpoint for modern calculations of national income and output, though by 1929 the position of such calculations was still comparable with that of the general level of prices at the time of Jevons. The statistics which most profoundly and immediately affected social policies, and the assumptions on which the principles of economic policy were based, were those of Charles Booth in the eighties and nineties, and of Rowntree (1899), who revealed with unprecedented detail and precision the extent and nature of poverty in British cities. These were the statistics Carlyle had called for fifty years before. They spoke for themselves, as did later the monthly figures of unemployment.

3. *Conclusion*

This all-round growth of economic statistics was thus profoundly affecting the background of economists' work, and public opinion on economic problems. It might well be argued that while formulae, 'fundamental equations', hypothetical generalizations, 'tools' of thought, 'models', terminologies, and classifications, have come and gone, sometimes with a somewhat disconcerting rapidity, it was on the growth of economic statistics that most, or all, of the solid, permanent, unspectacular progress in economic knowledge was necessarily being founded (apart from that negative but invaluable form of progress which consists in keeping the death-rate of intellectual error slightly above its always high birth-rate). In addition, this growth in statistical knowledge had pervasive and imponderable effects on social selfconsciousness and 'sophistication'. What was the relation between this third line of development, the growth of economic statistics, and the other two lines of advance discussed in section 1 above?

1. The micro-economic analysis of normal equilibrium values did not issue many very pressing invitations to statistics 'to endorse the cheques drawn by speculation'. The utilitarian hopes of a quantified economic calculus, originally associated with the marginal utility theory of value and with the increased adoption of the mathematical method, had very soon faded. The definitions and concepts of the normal analysis of value, production, and distribution, did not lend themselves at all easily to being filled out by statistical investigations— though isolated work of this kind was attempted, for example by H. L.

Moore and H. Schultz.[1] In any case, the theories of consumers' and firms' behaviour had not a very extensive, agreed, and precise content for statistics to fill out, and some of the exponents of these theories even seemed generally critical of any attempts to fill them out. On the one hand, it was very difficult to get the material that was to go into these empty boxes, and on the other hand these boxes, or some of the more important of them, would not have held very much material even if it had been obtainable. In a celebrated controversy it was agreed that the boxes were then largely empty, and pending the arrival of many more Jevonses might long remain so, but it was held by Pigou that this emptiness provided no grounds for the disparagement or abandonment of the boxes. (See A. C. Pigou, *Economic Journal*, 1922, p. 465.)

2. The relation of the growth of statistical knowledge to our second main line of development (the study of crises and aggregate fluctuations) was potentially different and more lucrative, and there were some signs of its becoming so right at the end of our period in 1929. It is true that there were a number of well-known contributions on crises, cycles, and fluctuations in which not a single appeal to, or quotation of, any statistical data was attempted. But from the beginning of our period, in the works, notably, of Juglar and Jevons, massive attempts had been made to increase and use the statistical knowledge of crises and cycles. Within the practicable limits then confining isolated individual research, it was statistics of prices and of bank-rates and balances which were mainly collected and set out at first. It was then quite impracticable for an investigator to try to assemble significant figures of aggregate employment and income as a basis for theoretical analysis. It is sometimes asserted that investigators of aggregate fluctuations and cycles concentrated too much on the concepts and phenomena of prices and price-levels, and neglected those of income and employment. It is only fair to point out that such pioneers as Juglar, Jevons, and later Mitchell, not being concerned with some mainly deductive logical manipulation about 'employment' and 'income', sought to relate their approach to the statistics available, or to those practically collectable by individual research. But though they

---

[1] Wesley Mitchell (*American Economic Review*, 1925, p. 3) pointed out that H. L. Moore had had considerably to reformulate the theoretical concepts before seeking to fill them out quantitatively. Mitchell continued: 'There is slight prospect that quantitative analysis will ever be able to solve the problems which qualitative analysis has framed, in their present form. What we must expect is a recasting of the old problems into new forms amenable to statistical attack. In the course of this reformulation of its problems economic theory will change not merely its complexion but also its content.'

had been steadily growing since the nineties—notably since Llewellyn Smith (1895) had been able to estimate the extent of cyclical unemployment in different types of industries—full and reliable statistics of unemployment in Britain had, by 1929, only been available for comparatively a very few years. Meanwhile, statistics of national income and output, of which, in Britain, Flux, Bowley, and Stamp were the pioneers at this stage, represented little more than isolated estimates for particular years. But by 1929 such works as the Censuses of Production of 1924 and 1930, and the Censuses of Earnings by the Ministry of Labour relating to 1924 and 1928, were about to make possible some great advances in national income statistics in the near future.

To summarize, we may say that in 1929, although there was not much advance in, or prospect of, fruitful co-operation and co-ordination between the analysis of normal equilibrium values and the growing body of economic statistics, the gradual beginnings of a potentially vast advance, such as Jevons had aimed at sixty years previously, was just being made in the study of what he had called 'the science of the money market and of commercial fluctuations'. The econometric combination of mathematical analysis and statistical content which Jevons had called for in 1871 was on the eve of important advances (and the Econometric Society was in fact founded in 1930).

However, the growth of economic statistics had hardly, by 1929, affected the leading discussions of the scope and method of economics. In the 1920's, where such discussions were carried on at all, the same sorts of methodological battles were being waged (then mainly in America), as had been carried on half a century previously between the champions of the historical and theoretical methods. Though the growth in the precision and refinement of what Keynes called the 'super-structure' of the analysis of normal values, had been immense and impressive as compared with 1870, it cannot be said that any correspondingly precise attention had, by 1929, been successfully directed at the postulates on which this superstructure rested, or to its significance for problems of crises, fluctuations, employment, and money.

The inquiries of Bagehot, Toynbee, and Leslie, and the essays of such masters of scientific method as Jevons and Sidgwick, were scarcely followed up in subsequent decades. Such inquiries related to the topic of 'Scope and Method', a topic which, as we noticed earlier, it was 'not fashionable among us to think much about. . . . We thought we knew pretty well what sort of things we wanted to know about' (at Cambridge in 1910 at any rate). What apparently held for Cambridge economics in

1910 may fairly be applied to most of English economics in the later stages of what Pigou has called 'the Marshallian dictatorship'.

From Austria, some of the successors of Carl Menger were propagating a more exclusively deductive and *a priori* approach to the subject, closely combined with a Katheder-Liberalismus which advocated ultra-liberal and anti-socialist economic policies.[1] But the precise examination and explicit statement of its postulates can hardly be counted among the more striking achievements of this school of thought. Only in the United States was the position then rather different, but the American controversies over Institutionalism scarcely had any stimulating influence outside that country. Along with problems of scope and method the study of the history of economic thought was also somewhat in eclipse. This subject had been prominent among the many interests of Jevons. Marshall had lectured on it in the seventies, Edgeworth had considered it 'particularly important', and it had been a main pursuit of such authorities as Foxwell, Bonar, Higgs, and Cannan. By 1929, in Britain, these were beginning to leave the field. Nor, in some leading English-speaking circles, was there even any very keen interest in recent work in other languages, a very different attitude from that of Jevons, Marshall, and Edgeworth. Consequently, many of the best ideas of Walras, Pareto, Wicksell, and others remained disregarded for decades, until rediscovered in the 1930's. How far, and in what way, this neglect of the logic and history of the subject was connected with the unstable and even, as some would say, 'revolutionary' intellectual situation which developed subsequently, and how far the confidence of 1910 (and after) in its grasp of 'what things it wanted to know about'[2] may have been connected with the vehemence of the controversies over precisely this problem twenty-five years later—these are questions which we leave to historians of a subsequent period to examine.

Meanwhile, the fundamental motivating assumptions and beliefs of British economists remained essentially similar in outline to those which had moved Jevons and Marshall, though of course they were often rather attenuated in content and mostly less ardently, optimistically, and even religiously held. Instead of walking through the poorer quarters of great cities, as Jevons and Marshall had done, the modern economist simply had to look at (or at photographs of) the long queues of unemployed outside the labour exchanges. Here was a 'muddle',

---

[1] See L. Mises, *Grundprobleme der Nationalökonomie*, 1933.
[2] See the quotation from Prof. D. H. Robertson on p. 22 above.

as Keynes described it, which formed a challenge not fundamentally dissimilar to the general problem of poverty, which had moved the great economists half a century previously.

Moreover, in 1929 confidence in the almost inevitable beneficence of scientific progress, natural and social, was, if not so imperturbable as in its mid-Victorian heyday, still far less fundamentally shaken than it was soon to be by the political experiences of the next two decades. In the afterglow of Edwardian optimism in the 1920's it was still possible to dismiss from all serious consideration the possibility that scientific progress, natural and social, might be creating new problems or dangers, almost as, or even more, profound and unmanageable than those which it was solving. It may well eventually appear that a period in economic thought may more appropriately be regarded as closing not in 1929 but a decade or two later, when, internally in Britain at any rate, the problem of poverty in the sense in which it had moved Jevons and Marshall (and in which it had made economics for the latter 'the study which bore most obviously on moral problems'),[1] as well as the role of the State in economic life, had been considerably transformed; and when, also, the common naïve attitude to scientific progress had been considerably shaken up. A more comprehensive 'revolution' may become discernible, of which the intellectual events often described as 'the Keynesian revolution' were an important part, but only a part, of a considerably wider whole. Of all this, it is, of course, much too soon to judge, or even clearly to perceive. Meanwhile, we must break off at 1929, a year perhaps as fateful in world history as either 1914 or 1939:

> Thus far, with rough and all-unable pen,
> Our bending author hath pursued the story,
> In little room confining mighty men,
> Mangling by starts the full course of their glory.

[1] See N. Annan, *Leslie Stephen*, 1951, p. 243.

Suggestions for Reading

THIS list is intended simply as an introductory guide for those who have read very few, if any, of the works discussed in the foregoing chapters.

Firstly, two books may be mentioned which deal with many of the economists discussed in Part I above:

J. SCHUMPETER: *Ten Great Economists*, 1952.

G. J. STIGLER: *Production and Distribution Theories, the Formative Period*, 1941.

Chapter I: Political Economy in England after 1870

There are a number of essays from the controversies of this period which are still relevant and interesting:

J. E. CAIRNES: 'Political Economy and Laissez-Faire', in *Essays in Political Economy*, 1873.

W. BAGEHOT: 'The Postulates of Political Economy', in *Economic Studies*, various editions.

CLIFFE LESLIE: *Essays on Political Economy*, 1888 (especially 'On the Known and the Unknown in the Economic World').

W. S. JEVONS: *The Future of Political Economy* (reprinted in *The Principles of Economics*, ed. H. Higgs).

Chapter II: Jevons

The Letters and Journal (especially the earlier chapters).

'A Serious Fall in the Value of Gold', in *Investigations in Currency and Finance*, 1884.

Theory of Political Economy (especially the Preface to the 2nd (1879) ed., and Chapters I–IV and VII).

On Jevons:

J. M. KEYNES in *Essays in Biography* (2nd ed., 1951).

L. C. ROBBINS: 'The Place of Jevons in the History of Economic Thought', *The Manchester School*, 1936.

Chapter III: Sidgwick

Principles of Political Economy, especially the Introduction, and Book III, on 'The Art of Political Economy'.

Chapter IV: Marshall

Principles of Economics, 1920 (8th ed.).

Industry and Trade, 1919.

The Pure Theory of Foreign Trade and of Domestic Values (1879, reprinted by London School of Economics).

Essays in 'Memorials of Alfred Marshall' (ed. A. C. Pigou, especially 'The Present Position of Economics', 1885, and 'The Old Generation of Economists and the New', 1897.

On Marshall:

J. M. KEYNES, in *Essays in Biography*.

G. F. SHOVE: 'The Place of Marshall's Principles in the History of Economic Thought', *Economic Journal*, Dec. 1942.

J. VINER: 'Marshall's Economics, the Man and his Time', *American Economic Review*, 1941.

M. FRIEDMAN: 'The Marshallian Demand Curve', *Journal of Political Economy*, 1949.

Chapter V: Wicksteed

The Common Sense of Political Economy, and selected papers, 2 vols., edited with an introduction by L. C. Robbins: especially vol. i and the essay on 'The Scope and Method of Political Economy in the Light of the Marginal Principle' in vol. ii.

Chapter VI: Edgeworth

Mathematical Psychics (reprinted by London School of Economics: there is much that is highly rewarding in this little book even if one is quite unable continuously to follow the argument).

Papers on Political Economy, 3 vols. (especially 'The Scope and Method of Political Economy', 'The Theory of Monopoly', and 'The Theory of Distribution', all in vol. i).

On Edgeworth: KEYNES, in *Essays in Biography*.

Chapter VII: Hobson

The Industrial System, 1909.

The Science of Wealth, Home University Library, new edition introduced by R. F. Harrod.

On Hobson: P. T. HOMAN, in *Contemporary Economic Thought*, 1928.

Chapter VIII: German Political Economy

H. MANGOLDT: *Grundriss der Volkswirtschaftslehre*, 1863.

J. SCHUMPETER, in *Wirtschaftstheorie der Gegenwart*, ed. H. Mayer, 1928, vol. i.

Chapter IX: Menger

Principles of Economics (translated and edited by Dingwall and Hoselitz).

On Menger: F. A. HAYEK, Introduction to vol. i of Menger's works in 4 vols., reprinted by London School of Economics.

Chapter X: Wieser

Natural Value (translated by A. Malloch), 1893.
Readers of German should consult Wieser's *Gesammelte Abhandlungen*, including the introduction by F. A. Hayek, and also his first book *Ursprung des wirtschaftlichen Wertes*, u.s.w., 1884.

Chapter XI: Böhm-Bawerk

Positive Theory of Capital (translated by Smart), 1891.
Control or Economic Law, translated by J. R. Mez (from 'Macht oder Ökonomisches Gesetz', in *Gesammelte Schriften*). (The chapters on Böhm-Bawerk in Schumpeter's and Stigler's books mentioned above give particularly valuable contrasting treatments.)

Chapter XII: Historical and Mathematical Economics in Germany

G. SCHMOLLER: *Grundriss der Volkswirtschaftslehre*, 1900, vol. i, chapter iii.
On Schmoller: J. SCHUMPETER, in *Schmollers Jahrbuch*, 1926.
R. AUSPITZ and R. LIEBEN: *Theorie des Preises*, 1889 (large, difficult, but of great interest to specialists).
M. WEBER: *The Methodology of the Social Sciences* (essays translated and edited by Shils and Finch).
—— *Theory of Social and Economic Organisation* (translated and introduced by T. Parsons).
J. SCHUMPETER: *Theory of Economic Development* (translated by R. Opie).

Chapter XIII: L. Walras

Élements d'économie politique pure, 1926.
Économie politique appliquée (especially 'Théorie de la Monnaie', pp. 86 ff., and 'Esquisse d'une doctrine économique et sociale', pp. 449 ff.).
Économie sociale (Preface, pp. v ff.).
On Walras:
  E. ANTONELLI: *Principes d'économie pure*, 1914.
  W. JAFFÉ: 'Unpublished Papers and Letters of Léon Walras, *Journal of Political Economy*, 1935.
  A. W. MARGET: 'Léon Walras and the Cash-Balance Approach', ibid. 1931.
  —— 'The Monetary Aspects of the Walrasian System', ibid. 1935.
  J. R. HICKS's centenary article in *Econometrica*, 1934.
  G. PIROU: *Les Théories de l'équilibre économique de L. Walras et V. Pareto*, 1938.
  M. BOSON: *L. Walras, Fondateur de la politique économique scientifique*, 1951.
  F. OULÈS: *L'École de Lausanne, textes choisis de L. Walras et V. Pareto*, 1950.

Chapter XIV: Pareto

Cours d'économie politique (especially vol. i, chapter 1; vol. ii, livre ii, chapter 2; and vol. ii, livre iii, chapter 1), 1896.
Manuel d'économie politique (especially chapters iii–vi), 1909.
On Pareto:
G. H. Bousquet: *V. Pareto, sa vie et son œuvre*, 1928.
G. Pirou
F. Oulès } see previous chapter.
Schumpeter's essay in 'Ten Great Economists' is especially valuable.

Chapter XV: Wicksell and Cassel

K. Wicksell: *Interest and Prices* (translated by R. F. Kahn, introduction by B. Ohlin).
—— *Lectures on Political Economy*, 2 vols. (translated by E. Classen, introduction by L. Robbins).
On Wicksell: The two introductions to the above-mentioned, also:
C. G. Uhr: 'Knut Wicksell—A Centennial Evaluation', *American Economic Review*, Dec. 1951 (a comprehensive account).
G. Myrdal: *Monetary Equilibrium*, 1938 (an advanced critique of Wicksell's monetary theories).
G. Cassel: *The Theory of Social Economy* (translated by Barron, 1932), vol. i. (See also Chapter XXIII below.)

Chapter XVI: Clark and Veblen

J. B. Clark: *The Distribution of Wealth*, 1899.
On Clark: P. T. Homan, in *Contemporary Economic Thought*, 1928.
T. Veblen: *The Theory of Business Enterprise*, 1904.
—— *The Place of Science in Modern Civilisation* (critical essays, 1919).
On Veblen: P. T. Homan, op. cit.

Chapter XVII: Newcomb and Fisher

S. Newcomb: *Principles of Political Economy*, 1885, Book IV.
I. Fisher: *Mathematical Investigations in the Theory of Value and Price*, 1892, reprinted.
—— *The Theory of Interest*, 1930.

Chapter XVIII: Welfare Economics

In addition to the writings on the subject by Sidgwick, Marshall, Walras, Wicksell, and Pareto:
A. C. Pigou: *The Economics of Welfare*, 1920 and subsequent editions.
A. Schaeffle: *The Quintessence of Socialism* (introduction by B. Bosanquet), 1892.
E. Barone: *The Ministry of Production in a Socialist Economy*, 1908.

L. Mises: *Economic Calculation in a Socialist Commonwealth*, 1920.
(Both Barone's and Mises's essays are translated into English in
Collectivist Economic Planning, edited and introduced by F. A.
Hayek.)

P. Samuelson: *The Foundations of Economic Analysis*, 1947, chapter viii.

H. Myint: *Theories of Welfare Economics*, 1948.

Chapter XIX: Consumers, Firms, and Markets

In addition to the main books of *Principles* reviewed in Part I:

H. Stackelberg: *Die Entwicklungsstufen der Werttheorie, Schweizerische
Zeitschrift für Volkswirtschaft und Statistik*, 1947.

G. J. Stigler: 'The Development of Utility Theory' (2 parts), *Journal of
Political Economy*, 1950.

R. G. D. Allen and J. R. Hicks: 'A Reconsideration of the Theory of
Value', *Economica*, 1934.

—— 'Professor Slutsky's Theory of Consumer's Choice', *Review of Economic Studies*, 1936.

I. Fisher: 'Cournot and Mathematical Economics', *Quarterly Journal of
Economics*, 1898.

H. L. Moore: 'Paradoxes of Competition', ibid. 1906.

P. Sraffa: 'The Laws of Returns under Competitive Conditions', *Economic
Journal*, 1926.

E. Chamberlin: *Theory of Monopolistic Competition*, chapter iii (6th ed.,
1948).

H. Stackelberg: *Marktform und Gleichgewicht*, 1934, chapter v.

D. H. Robertson: *Wage Grumbles*, 1931 (reprinted in *Readings in Income
Distribution*, Blakiston).

Chapter XX: Profit Uncertainty and Expectations

F. H. Knight: *Risk, Uncertainty and Profit* (N.B. chapter ii on history of
profit theories).

Chapter XXI: Interest and Money

Interest: The writings on interest of Böhm-Bawerk, J. B. Clark, and Cassel
discussed in Part I, and in particular those of Irving Fisher and Wicksell.

Money: In addition to the writings on money of Walras, Menger, Marshall,
Wicksell, and Newcomb, discussed in Part I:

A. C. Pigou: *Essays in Applied Economics*, pp. 189 ff.: 'On the Exchange
Value of Legal Tender Money.'

L. Mises: *Theory of Money and Credit* (translated by H. E. Batson, introduced
by L. Robbins, 1934).

I. Fisher: *The Purchasing Power of Money*, 1911.

R. G. Hawtrey: *Currency and Credit*, various editions.

J. SCHUMPETER: 'Das Sozialprodukt und die Rechenpfennige', *Archiv für Sozialwissenschaft und Sozialpolitik*, 1917.

N. JOHANNSEN (J. J. O. Lahn): *Das Wesen des Geldes*, 1903.

A. W. MARGET: *Theory of Prices*, 1938 (especially vol. i, part 2, chapter 12, and vol. ii, part 1, chapter 1).

Chapter XXII: Crises and Cycles (down to c. 1900)

W. BAGEHOT: *Lombard Street*, many editions (especially chapter vi).

W. S. JEVONS: *Investigations in Currency and Finance*, 1884, pp. 194–244.

F. B. HAWLEY: *Capital and Population*, 1882.

B. PRICE: *Chapters on Practical Political Economy*, 1882, pp. 110 ff.

H. HERKNER: 'Krisen', in *Conrads Handwörterbuch der Staatswissenschaften*, Band iv, pp. 891 ff., 1892.

C. JUGLAR: *Des crises commerciales et de leur retour périodique en France, Angleterre, et aux États-Unis*, 2nd ed., 1889.

E. D. JONES: *Economic Crises*, 1900 (a short survey of the main theories with a useful bibliography).

E. BERGMANN: *Geschichte der Krisentheorien*, 1895 (still an outstandingly valuable work covering the nineteenth century and going well back into the eighteenth).

Chapter XXIII: Crises and Cycles (after c. 1900)

M. TUGAN-BARANOVSKY: *Les Crises industrielles en Angleterre*, 1913.

A. SPIETHOFF: articles in *Schmollers Jahrbuch*, 1902, 1903, and 1909, and on 'Krisen' in *Handwörterbuch der Staatswissenschaften*, 1925 edition.

A. AFTALION: *Les Crises périodiques de surproduction*, 1913.

N. JOHANNSEN: *A Neglected Point in Connection with Crises*, 1908.

J. SCHUMPETER: *Theory of Economic Development* (translated by R. Opie).

W. MITCHELL, *Business Cycles*, 1913 and 1927.

D. H. ROBERTSON: *A Study of Industrial Fluctuations*, 1915 and 1948.

G. CASSEL: *Theory of Social Economy*, vol. ii, book iv.

A. C. PIGOU: *Industrial Fluctuations*, 1927 and 1929.

A. H. HANSEN: *Business Cycles and National Income*, 1951 (Part III gives a historical survey).

—— *Business Cycle Theory, its Development and Present Status*, 1927.

G. HABERLER: *Prosperity and Depression* (for theories current in the 1930's).

Chapter XXIV: The Unemployment Problem in Britain

H. S. FOXWELL, *Irregularities of Employment and Fluctuations of Prices*, 1886.

J. A. HOBSON: *The Problem of the Unemployed*, 1896 and subsequent editions.

W. BEVERIDGE: *Unemployment, a Problem of Industry*, 1909 and 1930.

A. C. PIGOU: *Unemployment*, 1913.

J. M. KEYNES: *Essays in Persuasion*, 1931, Part II.

Table of

	Principles and Methodology	Welfare and Policy	Utility and the Consumer	Firm, Distribution, and Profit
1860	..	..	..	..
1861	..	..	..	..
1862	Jevons: *Paper on General Mathematical Theory of Political Economy*	..	Jevons: op. cit.	..
1863	Mangoldt: *Grundriss* Fawcett: *Manual*	..	..	..
1864	Hearn: *Plutology*	..	..	..
1865	..	..	..	..
1866	..	..	..	Longe: *Refutation of the Wages Fund Theory*
1867	Marx: *Das Kapital,* vol. i	..	..	..
1868	..	..	..	..
1869	..	..	..	Thornton: *On Labour*
1870	..	Cairnes: *Political Economy and Laissez-faire*	..	..
1871	Jevons: *Theory* Menger: *Grundsätze*	..	Jevons: op. cit. Menger: op. cit.	..
1872	..	..	..	..
1873	..	..	..	..
1874	Cairnes: *Leading Principles* Walras: *Élements*	Schaeffle: *Quintessence of Socialism*	Walras: op. cit.	..
1875	..	..	..	..
1876	..	..	..	Walker: *The Wages Question*
1877	Bagehot: *Postulates of Political Economy*	..	..	..
1878	..	..	..	..
1879	Marshall: *Economics of Industry*	George: *Progress and Poverty*	..	..

Dates

Interest and Money	Crises, Cycles, and Unemployment	Economic History and Statistics	Biographical and Miscellaneous
..	..	..	..
..	..	..	..
..	Juglar: *Crises Commerciales*	..	..
Jevons: *Serious Fall in Value of Gold*	..	..	..
..	..	..	..
..	..	..	..
..	..	Jevons: *Coal Question*	..
..	..	..	..
..	Mills: *Credit Cycles*	..	..
..	..	..	..
..	..	..	..
..	..	..	..
..	..	..	..
..	..	..	*Verein für Sozial-politik* founded
Bagehot: *Lombard St.*	Bagehot: op. cit.	..	Death of J. S. Mill Onset of Great Depression
..	..	..	..
Jevons: *Money*	..	..	..
..	..	..	Centenary of Wealth of Nations
..	..	..	..
..	Moffatt: *Economy of Consumption*	..	..
..	Marshall: op. cit.	..	..

	Principles and Methodology	Welfare and Policy	Utility and the Consumer	Firm, Distribution, and Profit
1879	Marshall: *Pure Theory of Foreign Trade and Domestic Values*	..	..	..
1880	..	..	..	..
1881	Edgeworth: *Mathematical Psychics*	..	Edgeworth: op. cit.	..
1882	..	Jevons: *State in Relation to Labour*	..	..
1883	Sidgwick: *Principles* Menger: *Untersuchungen* Walker: *Political Economy*	Sidgwick: op. cit.	..	Bertrand: *Mathematical Theory and Duopoly*
1884	Wieser: *Ursprung*	..	..	..
1885	Launhardt: *Mathematische Begründung* Newcomb: *Principles* Clark: *Philosophy of Wealth* Marx: *Capital,* vol. ii	Launhardt: op. cit.	..	..
1886	Böhm-Bawerk: *Grundzüge*	..	..	..
1887	..	..	..	..
1888	Wicksteed: *Alphabet*	..	Wicksteed: op. cit.	..
1889	Auspitz and Lieben: *Theorie des Preises* Wieser: *Natural Value*	Wieser: op. cit.	Auspitz and Lieben: op. cit.	Auspitz and Lieben: op.cit.
1890	Marshall: *Principles* Keynes: *Scope and Method*	Marshall: op. cit.	..	Marshall: op. cit.

Interest and Money	Crises, Cycles, and Unemployment	Economic History and Statistics	Biographical and Miscellaneous
..	Nasse: *Produktionskrisen u.s.w.*	..	..
..	..	..	..
..	..	..	..
..	Hawley: *Capital and Population*	Cunningham: *Growth of English Industry*	Death of Jevons
..	..	..	Fabian Society founded Death of Marx Keynes and Schumpeter born
Böhm-Bawerk: *Capital and Interest* Jevons: *Investigations in Currency and Finance*	..	Rogers: *Six Centuries of Work and Wages*	U.S. Buro of Labour founded
Newcomb: op. cit.	Foxwell: *Irregularity of Employment*	..	American Economic Association
Walras: *Théorie de la monnaie*	..	Sauerbeck's Price Index-number *Board of Trade Journal*	Labour Department of Board of Trade
Marshall: *Evidence on Gold and Silver*	Crocker: *Overproduction and Commercial Distress*	..	..
..	..	..	..
Böhm-Bawerk: *Positive Theory*	Mummery and Hobson: *Physiology of Industry* Juglar: *Les Crises commerciales,* 2nd ed.	Booth: *Life and Labour*	Fabian Essays
..	..	..	Royal Economic Society founded

	Principles and Methodology	Welfare and Policy	Utility and the Consumer	Firm, Distribution, and Profit
1891	..	..	..	..
1892	Fisher: *Mathematical Investigations*	..	Fisher: op. cit.	..
1893	Wicksell: *Wert, Kapital u. Rente*	..	..	Wicksell: op. cit.
1894	Marx: *Capital*, vol. iii	..	..	Wicksteed: *Co-ordination of the Laws of Distribution*
1895	..	..	..	..
1896	Pareto: *Cours*	Pareto: op. cit. Wicksell: *Finanztheoretische Untersuchungen*	Pareto: op. cit.	Taussig: *Wages and Capital*
1897	..	..	..	Edgeworth: *Theory of Monopoly*
1898	..	..	..	Cournot's *Investigations*, translated into English
1899	Cassel: *Preislehre* Clark: *Distribution of Wealth*	..	Cassel: op. cit.	Clark: *Distribution of Wealth*
1900	Schmoller: *Grundriss*	Pareto: *Les Systèmes socialistes*	..	..
1901	Wicksell: *Lectures*	..	..	Wicksell: op. cit.
1902	..	..	..	..
1903	..	..	..	..
1904	Weber: *The Objectivity of the Social Sciences*	..	..	Edgeworth: *Theory of Distribution*
1905	..	..	..	..
1906	..	..	..	Moore: *Paradoxes of Competition*
1907	Pareto: *Manuale* Marshall: *Principles*, 5th ed.	Pareto: op. cit.	Pareto: op. cit.	Pareto: op. cit.
1908	Davenport: *Value and Distribution*	Barone: *Ministry of Production*	Barone: op. cit.	..

Interest and Money	Crises, Cycles, and Unemployment	Economic History and Statistics	Biographical and Miscellaneous
..	..	..	..
..	..	..	..
..	..	..	..
	Tugan-Baranov-sky: *Les Crises industrielles* (*Russian ed.*)	Webb: *History of Trade Unionism* Cannan: *Theories of Production and Distribution*	..
..	Hobson: *The Unemployed*	..	London School of Economics founded
Fisher: *Appreciation and Interest*	Pareto: op. cit.	..	..
..	..	Webb: *Industrial Democracy*	..
Wicksell: *Interest and Prices*	..	..	..
Clark: op. cit.	..	Rowntree: *Poverty* Veblen: *Theory of Leisure Class*	..
..	..	..	..
..	..	..	..
..	Spiethoff: *Vorbemerkungen*	..	..
Johannsen: *Money* Cassel: *Nature and Necessity of Interest*	Johannsen: op. cit.	..	Cambridge Economics Tripos founded
..	Veblen: *Business Enterprise*	Weber: *Protestant Ethic and the Spirit of Capitalism*	..
..	..	..	..
Fisher: *Capital and Income* Wicksell: *Lectures,* vol. ii	..	..	..
Fisher: *Rate of Interest*	Labordère: *La Crise américaine*	British Census of Production	..
..	Johannsen: *A Neglected Point*	..	..

	Principles and Methodology	Welfare and Policy	Utility and the Consumer	Firm, Distribution, and Profit
1908	Schumpeter: *Wesen u. Hauptinhalt*	..	..	..
1909	Hobson:*Industrial System*	..	..	..
1910	Wicksteed: *Common Sense*	..	..	..
1911	Taussig:*Principles*	..	..	..
1912	Pigou: *Wealth and Welfare*	Pigou: op. cit.	..	..
1913	Davenport: *Economics of Enterprise*	..	Johnson: *Pure Theory of Utility Curves*	..
1914	Wieser: *Theorie des ges. Wertes* (Social Economics)	..	..	Böhm-Bawerk: *Power and Economic Law*
1915	..	..	Slutsky: *Equilibrium of the Consumer*	..
1916	..	..	..	..
1917	..	..	..	..
1918	Cassel: *Theory of Social Economy*	..	..	..
1919	Marshall: *Industry and Trade*	..	..	Marshall: op. cit.
1920	Pigou: *Economics of Welfare*	Pigou: op. cit. Mises: *Economic Calculation*	..	..

Interest and Money	Crises, Cycles, and Unemployment	Economic History and Statistics	Biographical and Miscellaneous
..	..	..	..
..	Hobson: op. cit. Aftalion: *Surproductions générales* Beveridge: *Unemployment*	Royal Commission on Poor Laws	...
..	..	..	Death of Walras
Mises: *Theory of Money* Fisher: *Purchasing Power of Money*	Pigou: op. cit. Schumpeter: *Theory of Economic Development*	..	..
Keynes: *Indian Currency*	Tugan-Baranovsky: *Les Crises industrielles* Hawtrey: *Good and Bad Trade* Mitchell: *Business Cycles* Aftalion: *Les Crises périodiques de surproduction*	..	..
..	..	..	Death of Böhm-Bawerk
..	Robertson: *Industrial Fluctuations*	..	..
Schumpeter: *Das Sozialprodukt und die Rechenpfennige*	..	..	..
..	Cassel: op. cit.	..	..
Hawtrey: *Currency and Credit*	..	Marshall: op. cit. Sombart: *Modern Capitalism* Keynes: *Economic Consequences of the Peace*	..
..	Hahn: *Bankkredit*	Bowley: *The Division of the Product of Industry*	..

	Principles and Methodology	*Welfare and Policy*	*Utility and the Consumer*	*Firm, Distribution, and Profit*
1921	..	Weber: *Economic Organisation*	..	Knight: *Risk, Uncertainty and Profit*
1922	..	..	..	..
1923	J. M. Clark: *Economics of Overhead Costs*	..	..	Clark: op. cit.
1924	Bowley: *Mathematical Groundwork*	..	Bowley: op. cit.	Bowley: op. cit.
1925	..	..	..	..
1926	..	Keynes: *End of Laissez faire*	..	Sraffa: *Laws of Returns*
1927	..	..	..	Myrdal: *Price Formation and Economic Change*
1928	..	..	..	..
1929	H. L. Moore: *Synthetic Economics*	..	..	..

Interest and Money	Crises, Cycles, and Unemployment	Economic History and Statistics	Biographical and Miscellaneous
..	..	Weber: op. cit.	Death of Menger
Marshall: *Money, Credit, and Commerce* Keynes: *Monetary Reform*	..	..	Death of Pareto
..	..	British Census of Production	Death of Marshall
..	Robertson: *Banking Policy* Spiethoff: 'Krisen'	..	..
..	..	..	Death of Edgeworth, Wieser, and Wicksell
..	Pigou: *Industrial Fluctuations*	Bowley and Stamp: *National Income* (1924)	..
..	Hayek: *Monetary Theory and the Trade Cycle*	..	..
..	Keynes and Henderson: *Can Lloyd George do it?*	..	..

Index of Names

Covering p. 1 to p. 431

(Page-numbers in heavy type indicate main references)

Index of Subjects